WAR AND INDEPENDENCE IN SPANISH AMERICA

D1571226

During the period from 1808 to 1826, the Spanish empire was convulsed by wars throughout its dominions in Iberia and the Americas. The conflicts began in Spain, where Napoleon's invasion triggered a war of national resistance. The collapse of the Spanish monarchy provoked challenges to the colonial regime in virtually all of Spain's American provinces, and demands for autonomy and independence led to political turbulence and violent confrontation on a transcontinental scale. During the two decades after 1808, Spanish America witnessed warfare on a scale not seen since the conquests three centuries earlier.

War and Independence in Spanish America provides a unified account of war in Spanish America during the period after the collapse of the Spanish government in 1808. Set in the context of Spain's responses to inter-power rivalry during the eighteenth century, the author traces the courses and consequences of war, combining a broad narrative of the development and distribution of armed conflict with analysis of its characteristics and patterns. He maps the main arenas of war, traces the major campaigns of crucial battles between rebels and royalists, and places the military conflicts in the context of international political change. Readers will come away with an understanding of how war and military mobilization undermined Spain's empire, why new patterns of violence affected Spanish American societies, and how military conflict and political violence acted as the catalysts for the formation of independent states.

Anthony McFarlane is Professor Emeritus of History at the University of Warwick, UK.

WAR AND INDEPENDENCE IN SPANISH AMERICA

Anthony McFarlane

NEW YORK AND LONDON

First published 2014
by Routledge
711 Third Avenue, New York, NY 10017

Simultaneously published in the UK
by Routledge
2 Park Square, Milton Park, Abingdon, Oxon OX14 4RN

Routledge is an imprint of the Taylor & Francis Group, an informa business

Library of Congress Cataloging-in-Publication Data

McFarlane, Anthony, 1946–
War and independence in Spanish America / Anthony McFarlane.
    pages cm
  Includes bibliographical references.
  1. Latin America—History—Wars of Independence, 1806–1830.   I. Title.
F1412.M44   2013
980'.02—dc23   2013014212

ISBN: 978-1-85728-782-0 (hbk)
ISBN: 978-1-85728-783-7 (pbk)
ISBN: 978-0-203-47030-5 (ebk)

Typeset in Bembo
by Apex CoVantage, LLC

Printed and bound in the United States of America by
Edwards Brothers Malloy, Inc.

CONTENTS

PREFACE

I would like to thank Professor Jeremy Black of Exeter University for first suggesting that I write a book on the Spanish American wars of independence. It has taken me much longer to complete it than I intended, and I have incurred many debts along the way. I am grateful, first, to the British Academy for a grant that allowed me, a decade ago, to undertake research in libraries and archives in Madrid and Seville, and to the University of Warwick for a sabbatical year to take advantage of the grant and start this project.

I would also like to thank those colleagues and friends who invited me to conferences and symposia dedicated to commemorating the bicentenary of Spanish American independence between 2007 and 2011. These were no doubt distractions from the task of writing this book, but they were both productive and pleasant. They allowed me to amplify my knowledge of independence by listening to other scholars working in this field, and gave me a chance to present some of the work that has gone into this book.

In addition to thanking the people who took part in these events, I am particularly grateful to those who organized them for their invitations and their hospitality. I'd like to record my thanks to Margarita Garrido, Mauricio Nieto, and Diana Bonnett of the Universidad de los Andes, Bogotá; Clément Thibaud and María Teresa Calderón at the Universidad Externado de Colombia, Bogotá; Adolfo Meisel and Haroldo Calvo Stevenson for their series of seminars on Cartagena; Enrique Ayala Mora of the Universidad Simón Bolívar in Quito; Manuel Chust Calero of the Universidat Jaume I at Castellón; Juan Marchena Fernández at the Universidad Pablo de Olavide in Seville; Juan Bosco de Amores Carredano of the Universidad del País Vasco at Vitoria; Annick Lempériere, Véronique Hebrard, and Genevieve Verdo at the Université Paris-Sorbonne; Pilar González Bernaldo and Zacarias Moutakias at the Université Paris-Diderot; Allan Kuethe of Texas Tech University and John Fisher of the University of Liverpool for invitations to give papers at the AHILA Conference in Leiden and the SLAS Conference in Bristol; Roberto Breña and Marco Palacios at the Colegio de Mexico; Gabriel Paquette at Trinity College, Cambridge; Jeremy Hobbs at The Americas Research Group of the Foreign and Commonwealth Office; Philip Davies at the British Library; Christopher Abel at University College London; Paolo Drinot and Deborah Toner at the Institute for the Study of the Americas, London University; and Francisco Eissa-Barroso at the University of Warwick. I must, of course, also acknowledge the debt owed to the many historians cited in this book. Without their contributions to research and analysis, it would have been impossible to attempt a synthesis of the kind found in these pages. If I have not always been able to do justice to their works, I hope that the endnotes and bibliography will show readers where they might pursue key narratives, issues, and arguments in greater depth and detail.

At the University of Warwick, the History Department provided an encouraging environment for teaching and research during my many years there. Among my colleagues, special thanks go to fellow historians of Latin America, Rebecca Earle, John King, and Guy Thomson. Above all, thanks to Angela for her patience over the years it took to write this book and for the spur to finish it. I dedicate the book to her, and to the memory of my mother, Alice McFarlane her.

Tony McFarlane,
Leamington Spa, March 2013

INTRODUCTION

This book is about the crisis and collapse of Spain's American empire during the years from 1808 to 1825 and its transformation into a set of independent states. This is, of course, a subject that has attracted a great deal of attention among historians during the two centuries since independence, for the obvious reason that it marked a major historical turning point. In Spain, the turn was towards decline: Spanish American independence quite simply shattered Spain's power. From an Atlantic empire of great historic and cultural influence, huge territorial extent, and vast resources, Spain became a ghost of its former self, overshadowed by the northern European powers that had been its rivals and relegated to the sidelines of a world redefined by new empires and nation states. Spanish America, on the other hand, entered a new phase of its history as a collection of modern independent states, all with written constitutions that gave their citizens equal rights before the law and representation in government.

Not surprisingly, these great changes have generated a large body of historical work devoted to explaining how and why Spanish America's republics replaced Spanish authority. Much of this work is organized by country and oriented towards explaining the origins of each of the new states, but it includes a good number of synthetic and interpretative studies of independence in Spanish America as a whole.[1] This book also aims at a synthesis, though of a different kind. Whereas existing accounts concentrate on the political and social dimensions of the conflict within the empire, I aim to reframe Spain's imperial crisis in two ways. In the first place, I set the collapse of the empire in the broad framework of international war and revolution in the Atlantic world from around the mid-eighteenth century until the end of the Napoleonic wars. Second, I seek to reexamine Spain's crisis and the emergence of independent states through the prism of warfare.

Starting from the premise that warfare can have important, sometimes trans-formative, effects on society and politics, my intention is to provide an integrated history of the wars that led to Spanish American independence by tracing their origins, development, and character during the two decades of crisis that stemmed from Napoleon's invasion of Spain in 1808. This is not simply a contribution to military history of the kinds that focus solely on campaigns and battles, the organization and operations of armies, or the strategies and tactics of their commanders.[2] My focus is wider, taking in the impact of international war on Spain's empire, the outbreak of internal warfare within the empire, the interactions of armed conflict and political struggle in Spanish America, and the implications of war for the Spanish monarchy and the independent states that came to replace it. And, unlike histories that concentrate on the political and social dimensions of independence, I place the phenomena of war in the foreground, worthy of attention in their own right rather than as mere props in dramas of political transformation.

Before proceeding, the reader might find it useful to survey in summarized form the main narratives and interpretations that have underpinned our understanding of Spanish American independence. A rapid sketch of the historiography reveals several major currents. The first, and for long the most powerful, is found in the national histories, or *historias patrias*, that emerged during and immediately after the struggles against Spain—namely, the history of the "revolution" and its leaders. Often written by men who had witnessed or participated in the struggles for independence, these histories were designed to justify and glorify the break with Spain, to cultivate loyalty to the new states, and to judge the value of past governments and leaders. This style of history of independence, first invented by participants in the struggle for power that displaced Spanish rule, was—as François-Xavier Guerra has pointed out—given powerful support later in the nineteenth century by liberals engaged in the struggle to establish their ideal of nation states founded on popular sovereignty and endowed with representative institutions).[3] To justify this goal, liberal historians argued that the cause of independence was resistance to Spanish "despotism" and its purpose the pursuit of national emancipation by peoples who had grown to political maturity.

The portrayal of independence in nationalist terms, as the struggle of oppressed peoples against colonial rule, has long since given way to the more complex explanations of independence. Like other histories of regions in the Atlantic world, more recent histories of Spanish American independence have linked politics to social and economic problems, and to class, race, and ethnicity. The most lucid and widely cited modern synthesis is by the British historian John Lynch.[4] Lynch sees the origins of independence in the efforts of the Bourbon dynasty to rebalance the Spanish monarchy during the eighteenth century, principally by tightening control over Spain's American territories. This was, Lynch argues, tantamount to a "second conquest" that was profoundly disturbing in America. Bourbon reforms provoked tensions and rivalries, which, interacting with Enlightenment critiques of the ancien régime and new visions of social progress, accentuated a creole consciousness of separate identity and nurtured liberal and separatist ambitions that surfaced during Spain's crisis of 1808–14. Once given tangible form in written constitutions and new systems of government, the anticolonial revolt proved impossible to expunge.

Another important element of the modern historiography has focused on the part that Spain played in the empire's downfall. Starting from the assumption that Spanish American independence was not inevitable, several historians have asked how Spain responded to rebellions in America and why it proved unable to cope with them. One approach was to look into Spain's attempts to implement military solutions to the problem of American rebellion. Here, Edmundo Heredia was the first to trace in detail the military reactions of Spanish governments, showing how these were framed, what they achieved, and why they failed.[5] A broader and more effective approach to the study of Spain's part in the imperial crisis came from Brian Hamnett in his study of revolution and counterrevolution in Mexico and Peru.[6] Hamnett's major contribution was to focus on the interactions between Spanish and Spanish American politics, giving as much weight to the effects of Spanish liberal politics on the viceregal regimes of New Spain and Peru as to the American revolutionary movements that opposed them.

While Hamnett shed new light on the ways in which metropolitan politics and policy affected Spanish rule in America, several books published a decade later further illuminated the part that Spain played in the loss of its empire. In an impressive trilogy encompassing Spain, Mexico, and Peru, Timothy Anna argued that independence owed as much to the breakdown of authority at the core of the monarchy, in Spain itself, as to the challenges from revolutionaries in Spanish America.[7] In his view, the major failure of Spanish politics and policy came during the years of Ferdinand VII's first restoration to the throne (1814–20) due to his inability to understand the American rebellions or to create a realistic and consistent policy for dealing with them. Michael Costeloe also emphasized Spain's inability to develop workable political solutions to American rebellion, an inability that he found embedded in Spanish attitudes and policies throughout both the interregnum and restoration, and which, he showed, owed much to the role of the Cádiz merchants in underpinning entrenched prejudices and unsustainable policies.[8] Jeremy Adelman's recent synthesis has further strengthened the case for seeing the disintegration of Spain's empire as a consequence of Spanish policies that made it impossible to rebuild the political coalitions and pacts on which colonial rule depended.[9]

Attention to the part that Spain's internal problems played in breaking the pact between Spanish Americans and the Spanish state is also found in the work of economic historians, such as Josep Fontana and more recently Carlos Marichal, who have analyzed the economic and financial problems that afflicted Bourbon Spain.[10] They demonstrate that these problems were greatly aggravated by the wars in the Peninsula and Spanish America: both required huge expenditures when the American revenues needed to pay for the military effort were in sharp decline. Spain's financial problems not only weakened the ability of the metropolitan government to reassert its authority by force, but, regional studies show, they contributed to undermining the legitimacy of Spanish rule in America, too. For, because Spain could only finance its military operations from American revenues, it imposed fiscal demands which alienated colonial subjects by forcing them to bear the brunt of heavy government spending in difficult times. Stephen Stoan's study of Morillo's reconquest of Venezuela and Rebecca Earle's book on the re-establishment and overthrow of Spanish government in New Granada during the same period both make important contributions to our understanding of the effects of Spanish policy in this respect, for they show how political and military repression tended to deplete rather than restore Spanish authority.[11] Patricia Marks's recent analysis of the Peruvian viceroys' difficulties in financing the defense of Peru further reinforces the view that Spanish policy, working through the mercantile defense of the colonial commercial system, did more to undermine than preserve the empire, even in its greatest South American stronghold.[12]

Seeing Spanish American independence in terms of a wider crisis of the Spanish monarchy has also transformed our views of the origins of independence, as interpretation has shifted towards seeing the imperial crisis as the product of an external shock rather than the outcome of internal pressures. American rebellion, it is argued, sprang not from long-standing grievances stirred by Bourbon regalism, but from the sudden and surprising decapitation of the Spanish monarchy caused by Napoleon's invasion of Spain and usurpation of its throne in 1807–8. As François-Xavier Guerra and Jaime Rodríguez, the leading exponents of this interpretation point out, the first instinct of Spanish Americans at the start of this crisis was one of loyalty to Spain, not its repudiation. Many of Spain's American subjects remained committed to defending the rights of the overthrown Bourbon king and sustaining historic links to Europe, while those who spurned the royal authorities, it is argued, were more often in search of autonomy within the empire than separation from it and wanted reform rather than revolution. Seen in this light, the movement toward independence was a consequence of crisis rather than its cause, a response to the breakdown of power at the center of a long-established, hegemonic political system rather than an intentional effort to overthrow it.[13]

François-Xavier Guerra found a useful analogy in the collapse of the Soviet Union, a historical experience close to the time in which he wrote his seminal book, *Modernidad e independencias*. After a long period of stable government from the Russian center, where a central executive commanded an array of dependent states that were formally integrated into one political, ideological, and economic system, the authority of the center collapsed when dispute among the ruling elites overturned the existing structures of government. The crisis of change at the center soon spread throughout the Soviet empire, and, despite efforts to salvage the old transnational structures within a loose federation, the Soviet Union fragmented into separate parts amid a nationalist upsurge from regions that now claimed to be sovereign nation states. The analogy with the fall of the Spanish monarchy is intriguing, for the decline of the Spanish monarchy also began with a collapse of authority at the center, followed by a dispute over how government should be organized in the absence of the previous sovereign power and who had the right to exercise sovereignty. The transformation at the center started a process of political change, which not only altered the system of government at the center but also had profound repercussions throughout the wider political entity of the Spanish monarchy: first, political crisis at the center destabilized government in Spain, provoked local struggles for power, generated aspirations for new forms of government, and led to the creation of new institutions; these changes in the constitution of the center in turn led to similar processes of destabilization, conflict, and reconstruction among Spain's overseas possessions, leading ultimately to the creation of independent states and the collapse of the old union—in Spain's case, an entity that had enjoyed an extraordinary three-centuries-long history.

This analogy is illustrative rather than exact, as there were important differences in the character of the two crises. Not least of these was the fact that the collapse of the Spanish monarchy was the result of foreign intervention and occupation, followed by a war in which Spain called on its overseas subjects for aid in the name of a single "Spanish Nation." Another major difference is that, while the political transformation of both began peacefully with the collapse of central power under external pressures rather than its violent overthrow from within, political change in the Spanish world involved the widespread, organized use of violence by rival claimants to power in internal wars over political ends. Between 1808 and 1825, Spain and many regions of the four viceroyalties of continental Spanish America were all affected by war, some occasionally, others persistently; some deeply, others more superficially. Thus, the principal question considered by this book concerns the nature and effects of these wars, and its principal aim is to show why and how wars in Spain and Spanish America contributed to the fragmentation and collapse of one of Europe's greatest overseas empires.

In this, the present study differs from the political histories of independence that concentrate on ideas, institutions, and interests. Such studies generally treat war as an epiphenomenon, and if they pay attention to military matters at all it is only to remark on those rare campaigns and battles that had a decisively destructive effect on the enemy's war-fighting capacity.[14] In my view, this tendency to underplay, even ignore, the military dimensions of independence is misleading, for without these wars there would have been no independent states, and the Spanish monarchy would not have collapsed as completely as it did. Moreover, as several historians have recently shown, the wars had important social repercussions, particularly in widening social participation in politics and giving peasants and plebeians the chance to fight for their own interests. In Mexico, Eric Van Young shows, civil war among the elites provided a new context for collective rural protest, and Peter Guardino argues, a mobilization of the lower classes that was to affect the character of the new states that emerged from Spanish rule.[15] The same was true of areas in southern New Granada and the central and southern highlands of Peru, where the leaders of Indian peasant communities aligned themselves with royalists according to their estimates of what best accorded with their long-term interests.[16] In New Granada and Venezuela, military organization also played a key part in forging new identities and institutions, through what Clément Thibaud calls the "republic in arms."[17] Equally important was the corrosive effect of war on one of America's most entrenched social institutions, for, as Peter Blanchard points out, the recruitment of slaves for war was an important conduit for changes leading to the abolition of slavery.[18]

My purpose here is, then, to assess the part played by war and military mobilization in reshaping colonial Spanish America during the opening decades of the nineteenth century. My main purpose is to trace the course of Spain's American wars, showing their contexts, similarities, and differences, and analyzing the part played by competing forces in both protecting and destroying Spanish rule in the Americas. I therefore address questions about how and why the wars originated and developed; who they involved and affected; and how and why they evolved—in different forms and at different speeds—into a force that eventually collapsed Spain's empire and replaced it with a series of independent states. I have organized the book chronologically in overlapping narratives of events and developments in the major regional theaters of war, as this seems the best way to show how revolution and counterrevolution interacted and how the forms of war varied by time and place. This takes us beyond the simple descriptions of armies and navies and campaigns and battles, which are recounted in the standard military histories of the period.[19] I seek, instead, to give the reader a sense of the contexts and dynamics of war in the Spanish world, the character and color of its regional variants, its relationship to international political change, and its role in the fall of Spain's empire.

I concentrate on the wars of independence themselves rather than their aftermath. The implications of the wars of independence for society and government in postindependence Latin America is a considerable subject in itself, with its own historiography, particularly on the *caudillos* who emerged from the wars and became leading political figures in the new republics.[20] However, by seeing the course, character, and impact of the wars more clearly, we might better appreciate the extent to which war contributed to shaping postindependence politics.

Notes

1. For recent reviews of the historiography, see Gabriel Paquette, "The Dissolution of the Spanish Atlantic Monarchy," *The Historical Journal* 52, no. 1 (2009): pp. 175–212; and Anthony McFarlane, "La caída de la monarquía española y la independencia hispanoamericana," in *Las independencias hispanoamericanas. Interpretaciones dos años después,* ed. Marco Palacios (Bogotá: Norma, 2010), pp. 31–60. For a recent brief synthesis, see John Charles Chasteen, *Americanos: Latin America's Struggle for Independence* (Oxford: Oxford University Press, 2008).
2. For definitions of military history, see Stephen Morillo and Michael T. Parkovic, *What Is Military History?* (Cambridge: Polity Press, 2006), pp. 3–5.
3. François-Xavier Guerra, "Lógicas y ritmos de las revoluciones hispánicas," in *Revoluciones hispánicas: Independencias americanas y liberalismo español,* ed. François-Xavier Guerra (Madrid: Editorial Complutense, 1995), p. 15.
4. John Lynch, *The Spanish American Revolutions, 1808–1826* (London: Wiedenfield & Nicolson, 1973).
5. Edmundo A. Heredia, *Planes españoles para reconquistar Hispanoamérica* (Buenos Aires: Universidad de Buenos Aires, 1974).
6. Brian Hamnett, *Revolución y contrarrevolución en México y el Perú: Liberalismo, realeza y separatismo, 1800-1824* (Mexico City: Fondo de Cultura Económica, 1978).
7. Timothy E. Anna, *The Fall of the Royal Government in Mexico City* (Lincoln: University of Nebraska, 1978); *The Fall of the Royal Government in Peru* (Lincoln: University of Nebraska, 1979); *Spain and the Loss of America* (Lincoln: University of Nebraska, 1983).
8. Michael Costeloe, *Response to Revolution: Imperial Spain and the Spanish America Revolutions, 1810–1840* (Cambridge: Cambridge University Press, 1986).

9. Jeremy Adelman, *Sovereignty and Revolution in the Iberian Atlantic* (Princeton: Princeton University Press, 2006).

10. Josep Fontana, *La quiebra de la monarquía absoluta, 1814–20* (Barcelona: Ariel, 1987). For a more complete and detailed analysis of Spain's financial problems in the years leading up to independence, see Carlos Marichal, *The Bankruptcy of Empire: Mexican Silver and the Wars between Spain, Britain and France, 1760–1810* (Cambridge: Cambridge University Press, 2007).

11. Stephen K. Stoan, *Pablo Morillo and Venezuela, 1815–1820* (Columbus: Ohio State University, 1974); Rebecca A. Earle, *Spain and the Independence of Colombia 1810–1825* (Exeter: University of Exeter, 2000).

12. Patricia Marks, *Deconstructing Legitimacy: Viceroys, Merchants, and the Military in Late Colonial Peru* (University Park: Pennsylvania State University Press, 2007).

13. The two leading exponents of this interpretation are François-Xavier Guerra, *Modernidad e independencias* (Madrid: Mapfre, 1992); and Jaime E. Rodríguez O., *The Independence of Spanish America* (Cambridge: Cambridge University Press, 1998).

14. An exception to this tendency to separate the military from the political is suggested by Jeremy Adelman, "The Rites of Statehood: Violence and Sovereignty in Spanish America, 1789-1821," *HAHR* 90, no.3, pp. 391-422. He proposes instead the need to study the development, character, and impact of political violence, and thus to understand "why politics became a matter of life and death." (p. 395)

15. Eric Van Young, *The Other Rebellion: Popular Violence, Ideology, and the Mexican Struggle for Independence, 1810–1821* (Stanford, CA: Stanford University Press, 2001); Peter F. Guardino, *Peasants, Politics, and the Formation of Mexico's National State: Guerrero, 1800–1857* (Stanford, CA: Stanford University Press, 1996).

16. Jairo Gutiérrez Ramos, *Los indios de Pasto contra la República (1809–1824)* (Bogotá: ICAH (Instituto Colombiano de Antropologia e Historia) 2007); Cecilia Méndez, *The Plebeian Republic: The Huanta Rebellion and the Making of the Peruvian State, 1820–1850* (Durham: Duke University Press, 2005).

17. Clément Thibaud, *Repúblicas en armas: Los ejércitos bolivarianos en la guerra de Independencia en Colombia y Venezuela* (Bogotá: Planeta, 2003).

18. Peter Blanchard, *Under the Flags of Freedom: Slave Soldiers and the Wars of Independence in Spanish South America* (Pittsburgh, PA: University of Pittsburgh, 2008).

19. Some general descriptive studies are Julio Albi, *Banderas olvidadas: El ejército realista en América* (Madrid: Ediciones de Cultura Hispánica, 1990); Jorge Semprún and Alfonso Bullón, *El ejército realista en la independencia americana* (Madrid: Mapfre 1992); José Cervera Pery, *La marina española en la emancipación de Hispanoamérica* (Madrid: Mapfre, 1992); Robert L. Scheina, *Latin America's Wars: The Age of the Caudillo, 1791–1899*, 2 vols. (Dulles, VA: Brassey's Inc., 2003), vol.1. For a strong English-language narrative of Bolívar's campaigns, see Richard Slatta and Jane Lucas de Grummond, *Simón Bolívar's Quest for Glory* (Texas: A & M University, 2003).

20. Three general works on the social and political impact of the wars in Latin American stand out: Tulio Halperín-Donghi, *The Aftermath of Revolution in Latin America* (New York: Harper and Row, 1973); John Lynch, *Caudillos in Spanish America, 1800–1850* (Oxford: Clarendon Press, 1992); and, for a broader theorization of the effects of war in nineteenth-century Latin America, see Miguel A. Centeno, *Blood and Debt: War and the Nation State in Latin America* (University Park: Pennsylvania State University Press, 2002). Two very useful case studies of caudillos in Peru are Charles Walker, *Smoldering Ashes: Cuzco and the Creation of Republican Peru, 1780–1840* (Durham: Duke University Press, 1999); and Natalia Sobrevilla Perea, *The Caudillo of the Andes: Andrés de Santa Cruz* (New York: Cambridge University Press, 2011).

PART I

War and the Crisis of the Spanish Monarchy

MAP 1. Spanish America

1

WAR IN THE SPANISH EMPIRE

In 1808, the peoples of the Spanish monarchy entered into a period of war and political convulsion that was without precedent in the history of the Spanish world. The great upheaval began within Spain itself, when Spaniards reacted against Napoleon's removal of the Bourbon King Ferdinand VII by fighting back against the French forces that occupied their country; it then spread across the Atlantic as Spanish Americans responded to the reverberations of the crisis in Spain. Thus, from 1810, Spain's war against France in the Iberian Peninsula was paralleled by the outbreak of wars of a different kind in Spanish America, where the crown's subjects fought among themselves to appropriate the authority of the displaced king.

The combination of these events was entirely novel, as were their outcomes. It is true that Spain had fought foreign armies on Spanish soil previously (as in the War of the Spanish Succession at the beginning of the eighteenth century and the War of the Convention at its end). The Spanish crown had also faced challenges to its authority from outlying kingdoms in its composite monarchy (from the Dutch, the Portuguese, and the Catalan rebellions of the seventeenth century to the large regional rebellions in the viceroyalties of New Granada and Peru in the late eighteenth century). But the combination of war and revolution that spread throughout the Spanish world after 1808 was a crisis of a different order, unique in both character and consequences. The removal of the legitimate king took away the touchstone of the monarchical system, which bound the Hispanic world together, causing it to fragment in many parts. Once broken, the great structure of monarchy was not readily repaired. For while some sought to bring it together again as a "Spanish nation," others sought to build it anew, creating separate states that sustained themselves. Thus, during the two decades after 1808, the Spanish monarchy was transformed from within, amid a complex process of political demolition and reconstruction, war and revolution.

The Bourbon Century

The great crisis was unexpected, but the political storm that caused it did not issue from cloudless skies. Spain's Bourbon kings were increasingly buffeted by external turbulence, arising from competition between the leading European powers, which, over the course of the eighteenth century, became more intense and globalized. This turbulence took on a new scale and ferocity during the French Revolutionary and Napoleonic wars of the late 1790s and early 1800s, but its origins go back to the early 1700s, when Philip of Anjou, grandson of Louis XIV, succeeded to the throne of the Spanish monarchy. By making possible the future merger of France and Spain under a single dynasty, his succession as Philip V of Spain provoked an international struggle that set the pattern for much of the warfare between the leading colonial powers over the course of the eighteenth century. On one side, France wanted access to American silver—whether through direct trade with Spanish America or indirectly through Spain; as Louis XIV observed, the main object of the war in the Indies was trade and the wealth it produced.[1] Britain and the Dutch, on the other hand, also wanted greater access to Spanish American markets and resources; indeed, Britain entertained hopes of creating a commercial hegemony over Spain comparable to that which it imposed on Portugal by the Methuen Treaty, with its privileged access to Brazilian trade.[2] Britain and the Dutch Republic thus joined a coalition with Austria, which claimed that the throne should go to a Habsburg, to oppose French annexation of Spain and, with it, the emergence of an immensely rich and powerful Franco-Spanish bloc at the heart of Europe.

The ensuing War of the Spanish Succession (1702–13) ended in compromise. The powers recognized Philip V on the understanding that he renounced his claim to the French throne and abjured any right to unite France and Spain; Britain secured important commercial concessions that gave access to Spanish American markets, and the Treaty of Utrecht (1713) restored stability to the international system around a new set of principles.[3] This did not, of course, forestall the renewal of war between the opposing blocs. On the contrary, Utrecht simply recognized that war was the mechanism for making the periodic adjustments needed to sustain a balance between powers of unequal strength, and it was followed by a century of increasingly intense competition between the leading European states.

After the Bourbon succession, the main priority for successive Spanish kings was to rebuild Spain's power and prestige after decades of Habsburg retreat and to confront the shift in international relations announced by the War of the Spanish Succession, particularly the emergence of Britain as a naval power.[4] Philip V initiated the revival of Spanish power with policies designed to establish a more unified and centralized state, with structures of government that would draw power to the king and away from his most powerful nobles.[5] Coupled with these reforms was a new emphasis on strengthening Spain's capacity to project military power. When Philip V inherited the throne, Spain's army was small and weak, and Spain's navy even more enfeebled.[6] By 1704, Philip V had embarked on military reforms that set the direction for his successors. He established a new army based on Spanish soil and replaced the outdated system of the *tercios* with the modern military system of regiments, battalions, and companies. This standing army was, according to some historians, the beginning of a "military monarchy" quite different from its predecessors. Senior military officers were appointed to leading administrative positions, notably as viceroys and captains-general in both Spain and Spanish America, and as this policy continued under successive Bourbon kings, it brought a militarization of the upper echelons of Bourbon government, with key posts increasingly allotted to senior army officers chosen for their proven merit rather than simply their social connections.[7]

Philip V's ministers also initiated administrative and economic reforms aimed at exerting closer control over the Americas. A Ministry of the Indies was created in 1714, followed by the establishment of the Viceroyalty of New Granada in 1719 (the first new viceroyalty created in more than 150 years); they also introduced new measures for strengthening Spain's economic relations with the colonies by reorganizing the transatlantic fleet system in 1720.[8] These reforms marked a new departure for the monarchy and set new directions for its policies, in line with a new conception of monarchy. Under the Habsburgs, the American territories had been regarded as kingdoms in a composite monarchy; the Bourbons, by contrast, aspired to turn them into subordinate colonies organized for the benefit of the metropolitan power in a unitary monarchy ruled from Madrid.

The other major new direction under Bourbon rule was the development of a foreign policy that tied Spain more tightly to France. The War of Succession was the first of a series of wars in which Spain fought on the side of France against Britain, in a pattern of conflict that was increasingly associated with competition for overseas trade and territory. Between 1700 and 1808, Spain engaged in nine international wars, eight of them against Britain. In the first half of the eighteenth century, these were concentrated in the Mediterranean and aimed at recovering Gibraltar and Minorca and annexing Italian territories for Bourbon princes. In the latter part of the century, most wars involved competition outside Europe and sprang from struggles over trade and territory in the Americas, where Spain and France tried to hold back British commercial encroachments and territorial expansion.

The War of Jenkins' Ear (1739–48) was the first round in these wars for empire, stemming from conflict over British violations of Spain's commercial monopoly in America and aggravated by British pretensions to take and hold territory, either by invasion or by encouraging Spain's American subjects to seize independence under British protection.[9] In the event, British warmongers achieved little of permanent value, and less than a decade later, a greater war for empire broke out when Anglo-French clashes in North America triggered the start of the Seven Years' War (1756–63).

The war was a turning point for the Bourbon monarchy. Spain suffered less than France, which lost Canada to the British, but Spain's loss of Havana and Manila, however temporary, delivered a tremendous shock to Spain's new king, Charles III. The capture of Havana in 1762 had, in the first place, revealed unexpected weakness in Spanish American defenses. But this wasn't all. By taking Canada from France and Florida from Spain, Britain had made itself the major colonial power in North America, and this, coupled with its bases in the Caribbean, greatly enhanced its capacity to threaten Spanish trade and territory in both North and South America. Defeat in the Seven Years' War thus provoked a swift reevaluation of Spanish strategy.[10] The question of American defenses now came to the forefront of Madrid's attention, and, in the wake of the Peace of Paris, Charles III and his ministers became increasingly committed to a strategy that focused on the Atlantic and America.

The Evolution of Imperial Strategy

Compared to Britain, Spain faced formidable strategic and logistical challenges in defending its empire. British American territories were concentrated in two relatively small geographical regions—the eastern seaboard of North America and the eastern Caribbean—both with good maritime connections to the metropolis. Spanish America, on the other hand, spread over a huge expanse of North and South America and included territories that looked to the Pacific as well as the Atlantic. Spanish America was, moreover, an assemblage of largely unconnected geopolitical entities, each of which had developed independently. New Spain, Cuba, and the other Spanish Caribbean islands, the Isthmus of Panama, Venezuela, New Granada, Peru, Chile, and Río de la Plata were all distinctive economic regions with very different combinations of human and material resources, governments that reported separately to Madrid, and marked differences in their ability to communicate with the center (communications with Peru and Chile, for example, were much slower than those with the Caribbean islands or Venezuela, which had ready access to the main Atlantic sea lanes). There was, then, no single colonial nucleus to defend but several, many of them very distant from the others.

In these circumstances, Spain had evolved a strategy for imperial defense that focused on key points in its far-flung territories.[11] The primary goal was to defend Spanish Atlantic commerce by fortifying the *entrepôts* for the great mercantile fleets at Havana, Cartagena, Portobelo, Panama, Lima, and Callao. Another crucial aim was to defend territory where there was pressure from foreign nations (notably in the Caribbean, where the French, English, and Dutch had established colonies on territories claimed by Spain). A third, more minor defensive concern was to guard frontier zones against hostile Indians (in northern Mexico, for example, or southern Chile, where there was also a risk that they might aid foreign invaders).

During the eighteenth century, this long-standing strategy was modified to take account of new threats created by international competition. Whereas the first Bourbons had set out to create a larger, more efficient navy and to send more Spanish soldiers to serve as garrison troops in the American *plazas fuertes* and as reinforcements in times of war, Charles III's ministers went a step further, with a wider strategy for America. At its core was a new approach to the American territories, which aimed to ensure that Spanish America provided more resources for its own governance and defense, while also enlarging the economic and fiscal base needed to underpin Spain's mercantile and naval power. While previous Bourbon policies often had an improvised air, Charles III's policies were more coherent. Between the mid-1760s and the late 1780s, a program of interconnected reform unfolded, aimed at economic development, closer administration, and defense in depth in the main regions of Spanish America. The fundamental strategic aim was, of course, to defend the integrity of Spain's American empire, and it found its military expression in a strategy designed for deterring and containing British attacks.[12]

Seen in broad perspective, Spanish strategy in the late eighteenth century revolved around two axes.[13] The first was to project power at sea. By building up its navy, Spain aimed to command British respect at sea and, by asserting naval strength, to guard the transatlantic trade that was so crucial to the Spanish economy and the royal treasury.[14] The second was to strengthen the crucial links in Spanish America's defensive chain. To this end, local committees were established and military experts sent to America with responsibility for drawing up detailed defense plans for key points.

These "plans for defense" followed a more or less uniform pattern. Starting with a description of the geography, population, and economic resources of the region, they set out a critical analysis of existing defenses, defined possible threats, reviewed them with reference to all relevant local factors, and recommended any measures needed to improve defenses in the light of such knowledge. Some of these plans, such as that drawn up by the military engineer Antonio de Arévalo for Cartagena de Indias, were embedded in analyses of the geography, economy, and society of the regions that they examined, and their application of contemporary military theory reflects a high degree of professionalism among Spanish officers. Such planning was, moreover, directed and overseen from the center by a new body: the Junta de Generales, established in March 1763, who set out benchmarks for military planners and judged their reports and recommendations. Plans were sent to the Ministry of the Indies, which passed them to the Junta for professional assessment; from there, further consultations might be undertaken before they were submitted for royal approval and if approved, orders given, for their implementation.[15] In principle, this allowed the Madrid government to build up an overall picture of defensive needs in America and provided a bureaucratic system for implementing recommendations. In practice, paper projects were blocked by obstructions in the bureaucratic maze and abandoned in the face of high costs. The new system did, however, at least bring some definite improvements in the fortifications and artillery defenses of key points at Havana, Veracruz, and Cartagena.[16]

Finally, the development of Bourbon defensive strategy was underpinned by a determination to build larger and better forces in America. After the Seven Years' War, Spanish ministers recognized that reinforcements from the Peninsula were not a sufficient prop for American defense and that a further form of military mobilization was needed to meet the demands of modern warfare. Charles III's ministers, therefore, turned to the creation of a new kind of army in the colonies. Their goal was to establish regional standing armies, together with new militia units trained for deployment in wartime emergencies. This started the most substantial process of military mobilization seen before the onset of the wars of independence a half-century later.

Military Reform after the Seven Years' War

The attempt to revitalize imperial defenses, prompted by the fall of Havana, entailed two important changes. The first involved reorganization of the regular forces deployed in the Americas; the second brought a large and rapid expansion of colonial militias and their training as support forces for the army in time of war. The starting point for reform was in Cuba, where, while investigating the reasons for the fall of Havana and charging leading officials with dereliction of duty, the government undertook a rapid reappraisal of the island's defenses. This not only meant providing immediate replacements for the regular army in Cuba, but Charles III also accepted the arguments of the Conde de Ricla, a senior Spanish army commander, that Cuban defenses would be viable only if local militias were made into an effective instrument of war.[17]

The ensuing changes to Cuba's military organization soon proceeded to other colonies. In 1764, the Junta de Generales in Spain extended these reforms into a more comprehensive project for rationalizing American defenses.[18] Their plan called, first, for enlargement of the regular army in America. This involved raising new infantry and cavalry regiments composed largely of local recruits around a core of Spanish soldiers while periodically renewing the latter by sending army units on rotation from Spain. The second, more innovative, element of reform was the extension of the Cuban model of disciplined militias to other areas of the empire.[19]

With this extension of military reform, the crown took a new direction in colonial defense policy. While professional military men preferred to strengthen American defenses by using regular soldiers, the crown could not meet the huge expense of a standing army in America. They had therefore opted for the creation—in line with practice in Spain itself—of large reserve forces, composed of men conscripted into "disciplined militias," which were armed at the expense of the colonial treasuries, obliged to submit to regular training by professional soldiers, and expected to mobilize as auxiliaries at times of war. In 1779, José de Gálvez, then minister for the Indies (1776–88), justified the reform on the principle that for Americans, like Spaniards, "the defense of the King's rights is united to the defense of their property, their families, their patria and their happiness."[20]

The method for choosing militiamen was also similar to that used in Spain. Municipal and other officials organized lotteries to select men from the 15 to 45 age group, including men of mixed race who might be organized into companies of their fellows. Those selected for service were organized into units and, under the command of militia officers and experienced regulars or ex-regulars, subjected to a routine of drilling and arms training at weekly intervals. To compensate for their new responsibility, the crown offered an important incentive: members of the disciplined militias were granted the *fuero militar*, or inclusion in the military jurisdiction that gave them the privilege of trial by military courts; they also enjoyed some tax exemptions, and during times of mobilization, they were paid for their services.

Greater reliance on local populations to provide armed forces did not alter Spain's fundamental doctrine of defense. It continued to rest on the tried and trusted combination of *plazas fuertes* and *fijos*—that is, fortified cities manned by garrison troops–bolstered in wartime by reinforcements from Peninsular regiments and auxiliary forces supplied by colonial militias. However, this reorganization of colonial armed forces was more than simply a tightening of military sinews in reaction to the shock of defeat; it was part of a larger, more ambitious project for imperial reform, informed by a new vision of empire. Under Charles III, Spanish government aimed at strengthening the monarchy by modernizing the society on which it was based and infusing new life into its economy. This meant challenging corporate structures and privileges, broadening channels for commerce, encouraging economic enterprise, and bringing the colonies into a more integrated, neo-mercantilist empire. The idea of the disciplined militias clearly reflected the new conception of empire; henceforth, colonials were given a key role in their own defense by being turned into an armed citizenry, ready to show loyalty to the Spanish monarchy by defending its territories in time of war.

The trajectory of military reform followed a broadly similar pattern in Spain's major colonies. The introduction and progress of military reform, like the reforms of colonial administration and commerce undertaken during the reign of Charles III, had some common characteristics in all four Spanish American viceroyalties.[21] The central aim was to enhance Spain's military strength by expanding military personnel and improving their readiness for war. This meant making the regular army larger and more efficient while also creating large and permanent reserve forces in the form of militia units. The emphasis was, in short, to raise the rate of military participation in colonial societies, or in a very broad sense, to "militarize" American communities by requiring that all eligible males were enrolled in militia units and trained in the use of arms.

The New "Army of America"

One outcome of reform was to change the scale and composition of regular forces. Although it is impossible to give precise figures for the number of regular soldiers stationed in the American garrisons, estimates based on contemporary records indicate an unmistakable upward trend in the Army of America, reflected in both numbers of men and expenditure. The number of regulars stood at around 6,000 in 1700; by 1750, it had doubled to about 12,000; by 1775, it had reached over 30,000, a level that was sustained into the 1780s.[22] This fivefold growth in numbers since the start of the century had its counterpart in costs; expenditure on the army grew from about 3 million pesos in 1700 to a peak of about 20 million pesos in 1790.[23] Expenditure was then cut back in the decades around the turn of the century, and by 1810, the numbers of regulars in the Army of America had fallen back to about 20,000–25,000 men.[24]

Spain's regular forces in America were very modest in comparison to Britain's. During the Seven Years' War, Britain had 32 battalions, or close to 30,000 men in America, an extraordinary concentration of troops that was larger than the British army deployed in Europe. Even when pruned back after the war, British forces were still substantial. In addition to several thousand troops defending the West Indies, Britain aimed at sustaining a standing army of 10,000 regulars in North America—most of them from Europe, with regular rotations of troops from Britain and an American component of only about 15%. When the American Revolution began in 1775–6, Britain increased this level to over 25,000 regulars.[25]

Spain, by contrast, deployed a similar number to defend a much larger area. Mexico alone had a territory and population larger than the 13 British colonies of the eastern seaboard put together but did not have a comparable army. And, as the following table shows, the regular forces in other large continental colonies were even smaller.

While Spain's regular forces in America grew modestly, they also came to depend disproportionately on American recruits. During the 1770s and early 1780s, Spain increased the number of regulars sent to the colonies through the rotation of Spanish regiments through American garrisons. But from 1786 onwards, garrison strengths had to be maintained by greater recruitment of Americans, which brought a pronounced "Americanization" of the regular army. Recent calculations suggest that while some 68% of soldiers were American in 1740–59, the proportion had grown to about 80% by 1780–1800. The officer corps still retained a relatively large proportion of Peninsular Spaniards, especially in the highest ranks, but it too

TABLE 1.1 Spain's Army in America (c.1800–10)

Region	Regular Army (approx)	Militias (approx)
Mexico	8,800	22,000
New Granada (incl. Panama and Quito)	3,600	7,740
Venezuela	2,000	13,136
Peru and Upper Peru	2,000	40,000
Río de la Plata	400	3,000
Chile	2,358	29,639
Cuba	3,591	8,076

These approximate figures are drawn from estimates found in the following sources: Archer, *Army in Bourbon Mexico*, pp. 110–11; Juan Ortiz Escamilla, *Guerra y gobierno. Los pueblos y la independencia de México* (Sevilla: Universidad de Sevilla et al., 1997), pp. 184–6; Kuethe, *Military Reform and Society in New Granada*, pp. 217–8; Thibaud, *Repúblicas en armas: Los ejércitos bolivarianos en la guerra de independencia en Colombia y Venezuela*, p. 31; Leon G. Campbell, *Military and Society in Colonial Peru*, pp. 216-7; John R. Fisher, *Bourbon Peru, 1750–1824* (Liverpool: Liverpool University Press, 2003), p. 35–6; Juan Beverina, *El Virreinato del Río de la Plata*, pp. 197–222, 263–32, 417; Albi, *Banderas Olvidadas*, pp. 52–3; Domínguez, *Insurrection or Loyalty*, p.76.

was affected by Americanization, as creoles pursued military commissions for the career and prestige that they could confer. In 1760, about 33% of army officers were creoles; by 1800, that proportion had almost doubled to 60%.[26] The maintenance of standing armies in the colonies thus came to depend increasingly on local recruitment, which gradually altered the social composition of Spain's regular forces.

Recruitment of Americans allowed expansion in the scale of regular forces but did not necessarily improve the quality of the professional army. Reports from New Spain suggest that recruits were mostly from the dregs of society, and the same was probably true in other areas, especially those like Buenos Aires, where the local labor market offered better wages.[27] The quality of leadership probably declined too. During the 1770s and 1780s, Spanish officers had visited America on military missions or on rotation with their regiments; the subsequent end of rotations from the Peninsula meant that many officers spent their entire careers in American postings where they were rarely exposed to war and where, their critics said, they lost their professional edge. The appointment of American officers did not balance this loss, as many were men whose families bought their commissions in order to reflect or improve the family's social standing.

The flaws in Spanish American regular forces stemmed from those in Spain's army as a whole. At the start of the nineteenth century, the Spanish army was, despite repeated efforts at reform, an institution that fell short of standards set by rival armies.[28] The sale of officer commissions provided the state with money to finance the army and allowed men from outside the nobility to enter the officer corps, but given that their chief purpose was to advance in social rank rather than achieve professional merit, such officers had no incentive to improve their military expertise.[29] Consequently, the entry of such candidates did not improve the quality of leadership, a fact made obvious by the army's dismal performance against the French in the War of the Convention in 1793–5. After the war, the army high command tried to appropriate the reforms that Guibert had brought to the French army but to no effect. In the war against Portugal in 1802, regiments were employing different maneuvers and orders for deployment in battle. Some used the old regulations of 1768, others used the tactics laid down in 1796, and others used the drills set out in 1798: indeed, "disorder had reached a point where there were barrack parades in which the soldiers of the same regiment loaded their muskets in different ways."[30] Manuel de Godoy tried another reform in 1802 via new military regulations, which emphasized improvement of the appointment, education, and training of the officer corps. This final Bourbon attempt at military modernization failed, however, and there are many signs that Spain's army was weaker at the end of the eighteenth century than at its start.[31]

The regulars continued, at the start of the nineteenth century, to be very thinly spread across the Americas. The main bases in the Greater Caribbean region, from Veracruz to Caracas, all saw their regular forces grow, while some new garrisons were established to defend vulnerable borderlands, such as Guayana and Texas, or installed in cities such as Montevideo, Bogotá, and Guayaquil, where ministers perceived threats of external attack or domestic rebellion. But additions at strategic points did not create a unified "Army of America." At the highest level of military command were the crown functionaries, whose political posts carried military responsibilities: viceroys and intendants acted as captains general, provincial governors as lieutenants general, and all forces within their jurisdictions, whether regulars or militias, were ultimately subject to their authority. The term "Army of America" is therefore something of a misnomer, as there was no single body of imperial forces that could be deployed anywhere in the empire, nor unity of command over colonial forces. Spain's American army was still—as it had always been—an agglomeration of static forces of varying strengths, under the commands of viceroys and governors, who held commanding military ranks as captains general and lieutenants general. The largest contingents were concentrated in cities of strategic military or political importance and in time of war were reinforced by units sent from the Peninsula. No colony had a field army ready for operations; regular troops were distributed between distant garrisons, and their commanders rarely deployed troops outside the garrisons and their hinterlands.

The Militias

The other major strand of military reform undertaken when Spain was seeking to strengthen its American defenses was the introduction of the "disciplined militias," created by Charles III. In theory, these new units were organized in standardized battalions and regiments, provided with arms and equipment, dressed in uniforms, and properly drilled, disciplined, and led by professional soldiers seconded from their regiments. They were, moreover, to be modern fighting units, designed to provide essential reserve forces in time of war, particularly at strategic coastal strongholds, such as Havana, Cartagena, Veracruz, and Lima. At the same time, the principle of militia service was introduced throughout colonial societies, with a view to creating "armies of the people" composed of subjects of the crown drawn from all social ranks, whose loyalty would be expressed in, and enhanced by, military service.[32]

The impact of this "civic militarism," measured in terms of a "military participation ratio" varied widely. It seems to have been strongest in two relatively small colonies. Chile, where defense on the Indian frontier and vigilance against foreign incursions involved relatively large contingents of regulars and substantial militia numbers, had the highest ratio at 36 men per 1,000 people. Cuba, where anxieties about external attack and slave uprising were constant, also had a high rate at about 32 men per 1,000 people.[33] In New Spain, Peru, New Granada, and Río de la Plata, by contrast, rates of military participation were notably lower. This was partly because populations included substantial numbers of Indian peasants, who were mostly excluded from militia service, and partly because militias were active in coastal regions that were exposed to external attack and neglected in internal regions that faced no such threat. In coastal areas close to military strongholds and garrisons, military service appears to have been more popular than elsewhere. This was very likely because military service offered *pardos* (people of mixed African and European descent, also known as mulattos) and *morenos* (free blacks) a chance to assert a special dignity within urban communities and to improve their social standing. Creoles were also often attracted to the militias for similar reasons; commissions as militia officers—and commanding other men—were ways of expressing personal standing and improving status in the wider local community.

This integrative effect of the militias in tying men more closely into the social and political structures of their local societies was, however, matched by a possibly contrary effect—namely, the tendency for an "Americanization" of the colonial military to feed feelings of distinctive identity among Americans in ways that made them less loyal to Spain. Certainly this was a fear periodically voiced by contemporary observers, especially military men, who feared that armed Americans might be less dependable subjects of the crown and might even turn their arms against the authorities.[34]

Historians of the military in Bourbon Spanish America have tended to echo such contemporary critiques, accepting that the enlargement of the military sphere had disruptive effects on colonial societies. The clearest instance in which the militia reform may have rebounded against the state was through the extension of military corporate privileges—especially the fuero militar, or military jurisdiction—to larger numbers of men (and sometimes even their families) in time of mobilization. This, it is said, nurtured a new military elite that was not only damaging to the Spanish state because its corporate privileges allowed militiamen to avoid civil law but also implanted a tradition of military autonomy that was to disrupt civic life long after independence.[35]

Another aspect of colonial militarization that may have infringed on traditional hierarchies was the recruitment of men from the *castas*, or people of color, regarded as social inferiors by reason of birth. Among whites, officer commissions in the militias could provide those outside the great landed families with a way of displaying claims to honor and prestige; some merchants were so keen to show off their status that they wore military regalia when attending customers in their shops.[36] Among the lower classes, particularly for the free pardos and morenos, service in the militias also offered access to a relatively prestigious occupation, which brought self-respect, recognition of social worth, and even social advancement. The achievement of officerships in militia companies certainly provided some individuals with a step up the social ladder, enabling them to claim the honor and prerogatives accorded to whites.[37] For communities in which the tradition of pardo and moreno militia service was particularly strong, such as those on Mexico's Gulf coast, the connection to the military also yielded another benefit: it provided an identity for the community, and because the fuero militar allowed avoidance of some taxes and the ordinary jurisdiction of civil law, it gave an important sense of autonomy to groups who were normally subject to negative discrimination in a justice system administered by whites.[38]

In this sense, black and pardo militarization did not necessarily raise unmanageable expectations of social mobility nor subvert the rankings of the *sociedad de castas*.

There were misgivings among whites, of course. In Venezuela, for example, whites complained that militia reform offered privileges previously denied to pardos, and in 1796, the Caracas *cabildo* (city council) complained specifically about the arrogance of the pardo militias. This was, however, probably more closely related to anxieties about the implications of black and mulatto rebellion in the contemporary Haitian Revolution than to any immediate danger from the pardo militias, which were small and largely officered by whites.[39] In Cartagena de Indias, pardo militiamen also occupied a key position in local defenses and enjoyed a position of relative power during the late eighteenth century without posing any threat to political stability. On the contrary, the authorities recognized the importance of their loyalty and treated them with due respect.[40] Close study of the free-colored militias in late eighteenth-century New Spain also suggests that pardo militarization had ambiguous implications. It is difficult to find evidence that service in New Spain's militias disrupted the social hierarchy by offering significant improvements to life chances among pardos, such as enabling them to secure better jobs or make more advantageous marriages. Indeed, it is more likely that free coloreds joined the militias in order to improve their status among free-colored peers rather than to assert their equality with whites.[41] In this sense, the extension of military privileges may have hardened caste differences rather than dissolving them, reinforcing rather than weakening the status quo. Certainly, there were no obvious signs that loyalty to the crown among military and militias diminished during the years that immediately followed the military reforms.

It would be misleading, then, to conclude that government-sponsored militarization corroded American hierarchies. At the end of the eighteenth century, military service affected only a small proportion of the population, and the impact of military reforms was felt much more strongly in some places than others. Coastal cities, such as Veracruz, Cartagena, Caracas, Lima, and Buenos Aires, saw the largest growth of regular forces and disciplined militias, without damaging loyalty to Spain. Even in such places where military and militias had a relatively prominent presence, there is little reason to believe that Bourbon military reforms systematically subverted civil authority or nurtured praetorian groupings primed for political intervention.[42]

Spain's Resurgence

Under Charles III, Spain not only recovered from the military humiliations of the Seven Years' War but entered into an expansive phase that lasted until almost the end of the century. During the American Revolution, Spain, with France, took revenge for its previous defeat by striking back against rival power in both North and South America. In 1776, Charles III launched a successful attack on Portuguese positions on the Banda Oriental, the region that flanked the increasingly important area of the River Plate. The attack was on an unusually large scale. Commanded by Pedro Antonio Cevallos, who became first viceroy of the newly established Viceroyalty of Río de la Plata, it was the largest military expedition that Spain had yet sent to America. A fleet of 96 merchantmen escorted by a substantial squadron of royal naval vessels carried some 9,500 troops across with Atlantic, consisting of 12 battalions of infantry and 12 companies of cavalry, with an appropriate support force of artillery. After landing in February 1777, Cevallos quickly forced the surrender of some 3,000 Portuguese troops and moved on to take the fortified town of Sacramento.[43] Diplomatic negotiations confirmed this territorial gain, and the treaties of San Ildefonso (October 1777) and El Pardo (March 1778) also brought further valuable concessions from Portugal. The new Portuguese king agreed that Portugal would henceforth respect established borders between Brazil and its Spanish American neighbors, stifle aggression from Brazilians, and prevent foreign powers (i.e., Britain) from using its ports as bases from which to attack Spanish interests.

Successful aggression in the Southern Cone was followed by an extraordinary military success in North America, when Spain went to war against Britain in 1779 as the ally of Bourbon France and the American revolutionaries. The subsequent reversal of roles between Britain and Spain was dramatic. Rather than suffering 'he invasion from British America that Spanish strategists had feared, Spain invaded British American territory. José de Gálvez, the minister of the Indies, appointed his nephew General Bernardo de Gálvez as governor of Louisiana and charged him with driving the British out of the Gulf of Mexico. This was to involve complicated combined operations by land and sea, using soldiers drawn from Peninsular Spain and from Mexico, Cuba, and Louisiana, including some militiamen. General Gálvez attacked British forces in West Florida and in 1781 took Fort St. George at Pensacola, with a force of about 7,500 men, most of them Spanish regulars sent from Spain and garrisons in Spanish America. This action, combined with a successful Spanish defense of New Orleans and the lower Mississippi Valley, had important consequences: it not only contributed to the North American rebels' defeat of Britain but also allowed Spain to attain a strategic goal to which it had long aspired. Both East and West Florida were restored to Spanish sovereignty, the Gulf of Mexico was cleared of British influence, and Spain secured its transcontinental frontier in North America.[44]

Such successes infused Spanish military policy with new confidence. The valuable contribution that the Cuban army contributed to operations in North America reflected very positively on the military reforms there, and, together with the operation to recoup Sacramento in the River Plate, gave Spain the appearance of an expansive, militarily effective power, able to carry out amphibious attacks of a kind that were vital for offensive operations in the Americas.[45]

The growth of the Spanish navy further boosted confidence. Indeed, such was the navy's strength in 1779 that Minister of the Indies José de Gálvez expressed confidence that the combined naval forces of France and Spain were capable of overcoming Britain's navy. Spain and France, he stated, would invade Britain with some 40,000 men and, by aiding the rebel colonies to secede, would reduce Britain's empire to a precarious niche in India, so that Britain would be "despoiled of its tyrannical empire of the seas."[46] In retrospect, Gálvez's high hopes seem exaggerated, but both he and his successors had grounds for greater confidence in Spain's capacity as a naval power during the closing decades of the eighteenth century, as the Spanish navy became the third largest in Europe, almost as big as that of France.[47]

The alteration of the balance of power in the Americas caused by North American independence also benefited Spain. Britain retained important colonies in Canada and the Caribbean, but British interest in territorial expansion in the Americas diminished as the English moved on from their "First Empire" to pursue commercial and colonial interests elsewhere, especially in India. The emergence of the United States was, on the other hand, of some concern to Spanish statesmen. They rightly feared that the new republic—where politicians talked of their future as a continental "empire"—would inherit British expansionist ambitions and encroach on Spanish American territories. However, in military and diplomatic terms, the United States was not a threat at this time, given that the new republic was anxious to avoid any confrontation with Spain that might weaken its position vis-à-vis Britain.

There were, on the other hand, frontiers that had to be guarded in regions that were either uninhabited or peopled by indigenous communities who might join with Spain's enemies. Thus, in the 1770s and 1780s, Spanish governments sought unsuccessfully to retain possession of the Falkland Islands in order to deprive Britain of a staging post in the South Atlantic from which it could also enter the Pacific. Meanwhile, to the north and west, Spain sought to secure the lands it claimed in California by supporting missionary expansion into Indian lands, while seeking to deter Russian and British expansion into the Pacific Northwest by a combination of diplomacy and a policy of friendly trading with coastal Indians.[48] A related element of Spanish strategy involved military "pacification" and colonization campaigns on Indian frontiers, aimed at subduing indigenous peoples, building up Hispanic settlement, and, in some areas, creating buffers against foreign invasion. Such frontier campaigns were justified as a way to evangelize and "civilize" Indian peoples, but their primary aim was to people frontiers that were permeable to foreign encroachment.[49] The northern frontier of Mexico was a key point for such activity; so, too, were frontiers in South and Central America during the 1770s and 1780s. In New Granada, the Guajiros of Riohacha and the Cunas of Darien came under attack; in Guatemala, Spain sought to exert sovereignty over the Miskitos.[50] In the River Plate region, the authorities also showed a fresh concern to guard its frontiers against incursions by hostile Indians with the construction of inland forts to protect settlement and trade, and measures to pacify Indians in both Río de la Plata and Chile intensified during the 1780s.[51]

On the whole, defense of frontiers was successful in the later years of Bourbon rule. Indeed, in sharp contrast to Britain and France, Spain enlarged its American empire in the later eighteenth century, particularly in North America where Spain continued to reach northwards into California and the Pacific Northwest.

Rebellion and Repression

Success on the edges of empire was reinforced by containment of challenges from within. Such was Spain's prestige among its own subjects that violent disaffection rarely disturbed the workings of the empire's institutions. There were, of course, localized riots and rebellions, but these were mostly extralegal forms of popular protest against administrative abuses and taxes, not attempts to reject the system of government.[52] There were, nonetheless, more potent threats against Spanish government in 1780–2, when the activities of inspectors sent by Minister of the Indies José de Gálvez to introduce administrative and fiscal reform provoked regional rebellions in Peru and New Granada.

The first of these took place in Peru, where the reforms carried out by Inspector General José Antonio de Areche triggered conspiracy in the city of Cuzco, riots in Arequipa, and a cluster of Indian peasant rebellions that spread throughout much of the southern Andes. The largely indigenous insurrection started near Cuzco, led by an Indian noble, who, by taking the name Túpac Amaru, last of the sixteenth-century Inca kings, evoked images of an Inca revival and reached out to indigenous communities beyond his own lineage.[53] Túpac Amaru began with dramatic defiance. He ordered the execution of a crown official, commandeered treasury funds, and mobilized thousands of Indian peasants to march on the city of Cuzco, apparently with the aim of establishing a new government there. The city of Cuzco resisted, and—with crucial help from Indian nobles—its hastily assembled militias defeated Túpac Amaru's short-lived siege and blocked the spread of rebellion northwards into Peru's central highlands. Rebellion swept south, however, to the basin of Lake Titicaca, La Paz, and beyond into Upper Peru. Fuelled by social unrest among the Indian peasantry, the rebellion became a bloody civil war in which Indian communities rose against their caciques and the rest of the property and office-holding elites, both Spanish and Indian.[54] Their attacks on the bastions of the social order encouraged Areche to pursue a fierce military repression, as he sought, with creole support, to extirpate the rebels' leaders and ideas.

A less violent but nonetheless formidable revolt took place in 1781 at the heart of the Viceroyalty of New Granada, when people from a cluster of provincial towns and villages joined in protest against the reforms introduced by Inspector General Juan Francisco Gutiérrez de Piñeres, another of Gálvez's commissioners. Taking the name of "Comuneros"—to signify their defense of the *común*, or commonwealth— the rebels demanded the expulsion of the inspector general and the reversal of his reforms. They swiftly overcame the tiny military force sent against them and, having amassed a force of some 20,000, threatened to overthrow the government in Santafé de Bogotá unless it acceded to their demands. The authorities in Bogotá were virtually defenseless, and with no garrison to fall back on, they were forced to negotiate an end to the rebellion by surrendering to Comunero demands.[55]

Both rebellions revealed gaping holes in Spain's capacity to deal with insurrection through military action. In neither case were local militias an effective instrument for repressing rebellion. In New Granada, provincial militias proved entirely incapable of halting the advance of the Comuneros from the provinces to the capital; indeed, where they existed, militias may have been more a help than a hindrance to the rebels.[56] The regular army was not much more useful, given that it was largely deployed on the Caribbean coast, hundreds of miles from the centers of rebellion, leaving the crown without forces capable of a quick response to revolt in the interior. Units drawn from the Cartagena garrison eventually reached the capital but only after the rebellion had been ended by peaceful negotiation. However, these units were essential to the postrebellion repression; indeed, regular garrisons were implanted in the interior for the first time to give military muscle to royal authority.

The Túpac Amaru rebellion also exposed flaws in Spain's military system of the Southern Andes, especially in its reliance on militias. Initially, the militias of the Cuzco region were unable to stand up to a rebel force that rapidly mobilized about 6,000 peasants. Only when the city of Cuzco was threatened did a coalition of Spanish officials, urban patricians, and Indian nobles join forces against the rebels and, helped by regulars sent by the viceroy, begin to defeat them in 1781. However, Inspector General Areche refused to confide in the militias. He referred to them as "unarmed gangs lacking any knowledge of tactics or discipline" and denounced the creoles, who should have provided leadership, as "cowards who fled to the cities and the coast" to avoid service against the rebels.[57] He was appalled by their lack of cooperation and suspected that in Cuzco some militia officers and men had sympathized, even colluded, with the rebels. Indeed, Areche so distrusted the Cuzco militias that he sought instead to build his own army at Cuzco, largely from Indian peasants whose leaders remained loyal to the crown, around a core of mulatto militiamen from the coast, some highland militias, and a few hundred regulars from Lima, all under the command of Spanish officers. Placed under professional military command, it was this force rather than the existing militias that defeated Túpac Amaru's "army" of untrained and poorly armed insurgents in the Spanish offensive of March 1781, and assisted by some contingents from Buenos Aires, finally extinguished the last vestiges of rebellions that cost thousands of lives as they spread into Upper Peru in 1781–2.[58]

Spain was fortunate that these insurrections did not offer a challenge comparable to that which Britain had faced in North America. The Peruvian and New Granadan uprisings were essentially antitax rebellions without any political program for home rule. They did not seek, nor did they attract armed support from foreign powers of the kind that had been so important in the American War of Independence, and their defeat owed as much to opposition among Spanish Americans as to repressive force from government armies.[59] However, while colonial governments succeeded in repressing the rebellions, they were made aware that military reform was insufficient to guarantee the internal security of the empire. The crown had learned that it could not rely on militias alone to defend its political authority. Indeed, arming the people entailed the risk of militiamen upsetting law and order, defying their social superiors, or even worse, turning their arms against colonial governments. In the wake of rebellions, the realization that governments needed greater powers of coercion within the colonies brought fresh changes to military organization in both New Granada and Peru during the 1780s, framed with an eye to ensuring armed support for political purposes.[60]

After the repression of the revolts of the early 1780s, the danger that the colonial militias might become instruments for opposing governments seems to have diminished. At the death of Charles III in 1788, the various reforms introduced during his reign appear to have done a good deal to strengthen the monarchy, and a period of international peace allowed Spain to enjoy some of the benefits. Internal unrest had been suppressed, the issue of policing domestic order addressed, and, despite some anxieties that the American Revolution was a portent of the future in Spanish America, Spain's colonies showed no signs of internal subversion.[61] External threats had also receded, chiefly because Britain turned away from America after negotiating a settlement with the United States in 1783. Previous proposals for invading Spanish America, such as Colonel Fullarton's innovative scheme of 1780 for an expedition against Spanish colonies on the Pacific coast using a force of British soldiers and sepoys sent from Madras, were shelved.[62] And, while Anglo-Spanish relations remained peaceful, Spain's reformist policies began to show some positive outcomes. Flows of colonial trade expanded considerably; American revenues and colonial fiscal remittances to Spain increased, and a mood of reformist optimism briefly flourished on both sides of the Spanish Atlantic, at least until the early 1790s.[63] This mood was then tempered by the appearance of new and unexpected dangers, emanating from the great political upheaval in France.

Crisis in the International System: Spain's Retreat

The first signs of trouble for Spain came within a few years of the start of revolution in France in 1789. The Spanish court watched the collapse of the French monarchy with mounting alarm for fear that the revolutionary movement might spread to Spain and its American colonies. To forestall such contagion, Bourbon ministers closed Spain's borders with France while also taking steps to insulate the colonies from seditious ideas and subversion by French agents. An extraordinary campaign of francophobic, anti-republican paranoia and political repression ensued.

In the Americas, colonial governments were instructed to be alert to French-inspired subversion, and the clampdown on any sign of seditious behavior, however mild, produced political witch hunts in several places.[64] Official anxiety was exacerbated by the spread of revolution to France's own Caribbean colonies, especially Saint Domingue, where in 1791, political crisis mutated into violent slave insurrections that sent a shudder throughout Spain's plantation colonies.[65] The execution of the French king and queen in 1793 was the last straw for Charles IV and his government. The judicial murder of the French Bourbons turned France from Spain's ally into its enemy and brought a temporary end to the century-long Bourbon alliance. It also had repercussions in Spain's internal politics: Charles IV now appointed his favorite, the young guard's officer Manuel de Godoy, as his first secretary of state. This in turn affected Spanish foreign policy, as Godoy maneuvered to find a way forward in a world where the old certainties were evaporating.[66]

Godoy's first foreign policy moved in the direction of radical change, as he allied Spain with Britain and declared war on revolutionary France. But the war (1793–5) did nothing to improve Spain's situation. Its navy barely left port, and its armies performed badly, bringing military defeats and territorial losses at considerable cost to the royal treasury. Having failed to intimidate the French regime, let alone reverse the fall of the old order, Godoy and Charles IV were forced to return to geopolitical realities. Thus, the Bourbon monarchy reverted from opposition to the French revolutionary state to alliance with its Napoleonic successor. The Treaty of Basle (1795) sealed the rapprochement, though not without loss: Spain recovered territory on its borders with France but had to relinquish one of its American colonies in return. The cession of Santo Domingo was a notable humiliation, given that it was Spain's oldest American colony and an important platform for Caribbean defense. Nor were the benefits of the Treaty of Basle obvious in other respects, for the agreement with France did not allow Spain to retreat into neutrality. On the contrary, having bowed to France, Spain soon found itself forced back into war with Britain, thereby entering yet another costly contest with Europe's strongest maritime power.

Spain's reversion to the old alliance in spite of French republicanism is largely explained by Godoy's hope that he could redeem himself by creating a partnership with France that would allow Spain to annex Portugal while also providing protection from British aggression. The alliance was, however, reestablished on terms that were disadvantageous to Spain and did not bring the rewards expected. France never treated the alliance as a partnership of equals, and by forcing Spain back into war with Britain in 1796, it imposed growing burdens on a country that, amid deepening economic and social difficulties, had little appetite for war. The two Anglo-Spanish wars of 1796–1808, separated by the brief Peace of Amiens (1802–3), did serious damage to Spain's economy and, what was worse, imposed increasing strain on the finances and defenses of the Spanish empire.[67]

In the Americas, Spain's loss of several territories signaled its military vulnerability. After the 1793–5 war with France, Spain not only lost Santo Domingo to the French but was also forced to make territorial concessions on its North American frontiers: Florida was ceded to the United States at the Treaty of San Lorenzo in 1795; Nootka was abandoned in 1795, which relaxed Spain's claims to exclusive possession of the Pacific Northwest, and Louisiana was handed over to France in 1802.[68] At the same time, the return to hostilities with Britain brought fresh dangers of external attack and internal subversion, as the British soon showed their intention to undermine Spanish colonial rule by whatever means possible. Spain's first serious loss of territory to Britain occurred in 1797, with the seizure of Trinidad. This was most unwelcome, since Trinidad had come to be regarded as a key point in the defense of the Spanish Main and in the previous year had been supplied with substantial military and naval reinforcements precisely in order to stave off British attack. And yet, when a British invasion fleet attacked, barely a shot was fired before the island's governor capitulated, on the grounds that lack of supplies, disease among his soldiery, and inadequate fortifications made his situation hopeless. The victorious British then moved on from Trinidad to attack Puerto Rico later in 1797, but there they were unsuccessful. In Puerto Rico, which was better fortified and manned than Trinidad, defense based on a preestablished, systematic "plan of defense" of the kind that the Junta de Generales had promoted following the Seven Years' War proved an effective barrier to British attack.[69]

Although balanced by the successful defense of Puerto Rico, the British occupation of Trinidad was a setback for Spain. Not only did it give Britain a base from which to attack the Spanish Main, but it also helped revive schemes for military expeditions that had been shelved in the 1780s. Such schemes now had a new dimension, provided by exiled creole revolutionists dedicated to the cause of emancipation from Spanish rule in their homelands. During the 1790s and early 1800s, these men sought to persuade British ministers that they shared an interest in overthrowing Spanish sovereignty in Spanish America. Creole revolutionaries—of whom the Venezuelan Francisco de Miranda was the most prominent—urged Prime Minister Pitt to launch military expeditions against Spanish colonies in the expectation that their inhabitants would welcome the British as liberators.[70]

While Pitt remained prime minister, these schemes did not prosper, partly because Pitt and some of his colleagues were reluctant to support revolutionary sedition and republicanism of a kind they associated with France, and partly because they harbored hopes of detaching Spain from its alliance with France. Lord Pelham also saw dangers in undermining Spain's empire. He feared that the emancipation of the Spanish colonies might rebound against Britain by making Spain even more dependent on France.[71] However, following the failure of Pitt's Third Coalition in Europe in 1805, followed by his death in January 1806, British ministers once again gave serious consideration to the case for a Spanish American military strategy as a means both to weaken Spain and to compensate for economic losses caused by Napoleon's Continental System.

In these circumstances, Spain's ability to deploy naval power became increasingly important. The crucial role of naval power was clearly expressed in a review of Spain's strategic situation written some years earlier: "As our possessions in America extend over a very great space," the author had remarked, "and as the many unpopulated areas between them impede the juncture of forces by land, for the purposes of their mutual defense they are best considered as though they were islands, and we must trust to naval forces to provide reinforcements and aid not only from Spain but also between the provinces themselves."[72] The Spanish navy was, however, shrinking from the mid-1790s, losing ships and men in a decline exacerbated by the losses suffered at Cape St. Vincent in 1797 and Trafalgar in 1805.[73] The fact that the Spanish battle fleet could no longer hope to defeat a British battle fleet did not, of course, mean that Spain lacked the means to protect its shipping and its coastlines; however, after Trafalgar, Spain became considerably more vulnerable to British seaborne threats, particularly when Britain began to make more determined efforts to attack Spain's colonies.[74]

This shift in policy away from the focus on taking French Caribbean colonies at the start of the French wars was reflected in two schemes implemented in 1806–7. One was concocted by Francisco de Miranda, the Spanish American soldier whose wide travels and colorful political experience in Europe and the

United States made him a welcome guest in influential London political circles. His access to powerful figures allowed him to become a plausible advocate for Spanish American independence in turn-of-the-century London, and in 1805, he tried to persuade Pitt to give him support for an expedition to Venezuela, aimed at overthrowing Spanish government in Caracas and establishing an independent government under British protection. When Pitt refused, Miranda turned to the United States for support, and, with tacit government agreement, raised a small private force, composed mainly of North Americans, to invade Venezuela. The ensuing expedition was a damp squib. Miranda failed to mobilize the local support that he had expected and never had the chance to establish a beachhead for Britain in Venezuela.[75] The people of Venezuela remained entirely loyal to the Spanish regime, and the militias quickly rallied against the potential invasion.

The other, much more formidable attempt to undermine Spanish sovereignty in America came from an adventurer of a different kind. Sir Home Riggs Popham had, like Miranda, been involved in planning for possible British military operations against Spain in America but had one vital advantage: as a serving British naval office, he had better access to military resources than his friend Miranda. After conducting a successful operation to capture the Cape of Good Hope from the Dutch in 1805, Popham persuaded himself that he was authorized to attack the Spanish in South America. He raised some 1,500 troops under the command of General William Beresford and transported them across the Atlantic to launch an attack on Buenos Aires, with a view to bringing the River Plate region under British rule or encouraging independence from Spain. Popham's expedition enjoyed an initial success by taking Buenos Aires in 1806, but local resistance soon pushed the British out. They also repelled reinforcements sent by the British government under Generals Auchmuty and Whitelocke in the second invasions of Montevideo and Buenos Aires in 1807.[76]

The most striking feature of these military actions in the River Plate was the fervent loyalty of the local population, which, led by Santiago Liniers, a Frenchman in the service of the Spanish navy, quickly formed volunteer militia companies to fight the invader.[77] These aroused great enthusiasm, attracting recruits from all classes and promoting a veritable *rage militaire* among creoles seeking to bask in the glow of victory. Their extraordinary display of loyalty was initially very reassuring for Spain, given that the *porteños* (people of the port) had rebuffed a very substantial British attack and thereby preserved Spain's position in the South Atlantic. However, the successful defense of Buenos Aires by local people could not conceal Spain's serious underlying weakness in naval power, and the victory in the River Plate was soon overtaken by fresh problems.

These problems stemmed from the changing situation in Europe, where Napoleon had, with Spanish collaboration, invaded Portugal and thereby forced the Portuguese court to flee to Brazil in December 1807. The re-centering of the Portuguese empire on Brazil changed the strategic situation in South America and gave Spain good reason to fear renewed British attack, especially in the River Plate region. Castlereagh had recommended the transfer of the Portuguese royal family to Brazil on the grounds that it would provide a platform for the extension of British commerce and political influence throughout South America, and in 1807, he even envisaged establishing a single friendly government for the whole of South America. Spain was probably aware that British government was making plans for an assault somewhere in Spanish America, particularly as Rear Admiral Sir Sidney Smith took his naval squadron from Portugal to Brazil in January 1808. Portugal was, moreover, a willing ally, eager to aggrandize territories bordering on the River Plate in revenge for Spain's participation in Napoleon's invasion and ready to use British naval support to do so.[78]

Meanwhile, while under attack from its enemy, Spain was also under duress from its ally; Napoleon's demands for subsidies of Mexican silver to pay for his campaigns imposed fresh strains on Spanish state finances, already desperately short of revenues to cover the costs of war. By the secret Subsidy Treaty of October 1803, Spain agreed to pay France 10 million silver pesos per year in specie, a sum that amounted to a large slice of the fiscal product of New Spain, the empire's greatest silver producer.[79] Caught between two aggressive powers, one its sworn enemy, the other its domineering ally, Spain was being pushed to the extreme of its fiscal and military capabilities, at the very time that intense strains on the international front were matched by economic difficulties and unstable politics at home.

The Onset of the Spanish Crisis

In Spain, the pressures derived from the intensifying international conflict had depressive effects on the economy and, by extension, on state finances. The contraction of colonial commerce, the decline of industry, and the periodic failures of agricultural production all contributed to worsening living conditions among large sectors of the rural and urban population.[80] The government's financial position also deteriorated sharply. Under Charles III, Spain had managed to increase tax revenues in Spain and paid for most of its domestic expenses while leaving the colonies to finance themselves; under his successor, taxes collected in Spain fell by over 40% in 1796–1808, and the state treasury was kept from bankruptcy only by American tax remittances and short-term fiscal expedients. However, these could not remedy the chronic imbalance between Bourbon revenues and expenditures. After several decades of international warfare, Spain's financial strength was approaching exhaustion, as, consequently, was its capacity to defend the monarchy and empire. Indeed, a leading student of Spanish state finances concludes that "imperial bankruptcy was the prelude to the wars of independence."[81]

In Spanish America, the impact of war with Britain was much less damaging. Few places came under direct attack, and the physical effects of war were consequently slight. Even where the British invaded, at Buenos Aires and Montevideo, casualties were low, and civilians did not suffer greatly from the war. Labor costs in Buenos Aires were forced up by payments to the militias, but trade was disrupted only temporarily, so that no lasting damage was done to the local economy.[82] In most major ports, the curtailment of trade with Spain was easily covered by a growing contraband trade, most of it with British traders operating out of Jamaica, and North American merchants sailing from United States' ports.[83] Although this exposed Spain's weakness as a naval power and economic metropolis and encouraged creole criticism of the Spanish commercial system, it did not of itself cause Americans to seek independence—proponents of economic liberalism called for reform of the commercial monopoly, not the overthrow of political authority.[84] Wartime taxation also appears to have done only minor damage to royal authority. Spain's voracious appetite for revenue produced unpopular fiscal measures, such as the appropriation of church funds and tax increases to meet the pressing needs of war.[85] But even in Mexico, where the appropriation of church funds had a strong effect on landowners, such measures did not provoke outright resistance. While no doubt unwelcome, they seem to have been borne stoically by peoples who accepted the crown's right to increase taxes without their consent.

The greatest political damage done by the Anglo-Spanish conflict was in Spain itself, where the reverses of war turned public opinion against the Bourbon regime. Part of the blame fell upon the army, which became very unpopular due to public dislike of the privileges of officers and the burdens the army imposed. But the main focus for opposition was the king's and queen's favorite, Prime Minister Manuel de Godoy, who had become deeply unpopular for his corruption, unsuccessful conduct of the war, and obsequious appeasement of Napoleon. In an effort to strengthen his position, Godoy entered into an agreement, by the Treaty of Fontainebleau (October 1807), to allow French troops to march through Spanish territory en route to conquer Portugal and then partition its territories between the partners: Portugal to Spain and Brazil to France. Spain earned no such benefit from collusion with Napoleon. On the contrary, Napoleon used the invasion of Portugal and the presence of French troops on Spanish territory as an opportunity to intervene in Spain's internal politics. Godoy, who was distrusted by Napoleon, thus became caught between an unfriendly French ally and his enemies at court, grouped around Prince Ferdinand, son and heir to Charles IV. The struggle for power at the center between Godoy and the *fernandino* faction came to a head when Godoy moved king, queen, and court to Aranjuez, apparently with the idea of decamping to Andalusia, then America. As the Caroline regime tottered, Ferdinand and his aristocratic supporters saw their chance. Ferdinand, who was anxious to come to an accommodation with Napoleon before he removed the entire Bourbon dynasty, joined with his aristocratic cronies to depose Godoy and open a way to his succession. They duly whipped up a popular riot at the court's residence at Aranjuez, ousted Godoy, and, backed by the army, enabled Ferdinand to force his father's abdication in mid-March 1808 and place himself on the throne.[86]

Ferdinand's accession did not rescue Spain from Napoleon's tightening grip. Rather, it aggravated the crisis of the Spanish monarchy by prompting Napoleon to seek closer control over his unruly ally. In May 1808, he lured Ferdinand VII and the rest of the royal family to Bayonne, announced the abdication of both Charles IV and Ferdinand VII, and dispatched them to *confortable* exile in a French chateaux. Napoleon's dethronement of the Spanish Bourbons and seizure of the throne was a coup de main intended to transfer power peacefully, but this ambition was soon thwarted. Spaniards rebelled against the intrusive French government—nominally led by Napoleon's brother, whom he thrust onto the throne as King Joseph I—and local rebellions gradually crystallized into a war of resistance that spread through the Iberian Peninsula.

This extraordinary tergiversation and the political crisis that it caused at the heart of Spain's monarchy changed everything. Until 1808, Spain had stood alone among the leading colonial powers of eighteenth-century Europe as the only major power that retained its empire intact at the turn of the century. The Bourbon monarchy had preserved its sovereignty over Spain's extensive American continental posses- sions and most of its Caribbean islands and had succeeded in suppressing internal rebellion in the few places where it appeared. The fact that Spain suffered relatively little from British aggression against its American territories was due partly to the fact that British governments did not pursue a consistent strategy for rebuilding their American empire at French and Spanish expense. After some success against French Caribbean colonies, Britain had to reconsider its imperial war strategy after suffering massive losses of men in the war for St. Domingue in 1796. However, although this meant that the British threat shifted to Spanish America—as British governments adopted a policy of seeking to take strategic points from which it might expand trade and territory—British plans during the next decade did not inflict much damage on Spain. After taking Trinidad but failing at Puerto Rico in 1797, Britain cut back on large overseas operations and tended to regard such plans as of secondary importance compared to operations in Europe.[87] This alleviated the British threat to Spain's empire but did not eliminate it completely—as the attack on Buenos Aires in 1806–7 showed—and British politicians continued to harbor ambitions for replacing the commerce and colonies lost in the north at Spain's expense in the south. However, the failure of both Miranda's plan to take Caracas and Popham's for taking Buenos Aires had displayed an important characteristic of the Spanish realms: their capacity for self-defense against external intrusion. Even as Spain's economy and government finances staggered under the strains of prolonged international warfare, the political bonds of the monarchy remained resilient.

Such resilience was to be undermined by changes in relations between the Eu- ropean powers after the French Revolution. Until then, the international system established at Utrecht, which aimed at a balance of power, had allowed the Spanish monarchy to sustain its position in Europe and, with some minor adjustments, its empire in America. When the French wars brought a breakdown in that interna- tional system, Spain was not saved by its alliance with France. Indeed, the collapse of the international system under pressure from an expansive French foreign policy also produced the breakdown of the Spanish political system in 1808. Little more than a year after Napoleon had forced the Portuguese monarchy into exile, the Spanish Bourbons suffered the same fate. The French occupation of the Peninsula was a cataclysm, which jeopardized the Spanish monarchy on both sides of the Atlantic, exposing political, administrative, and military structures that had served for so long to their greatest test. Until then, the central pillar of Bourbon strategy was to defend the colonies against the threat of attack from without; now it faced a quite different and more dangerous threat: that of disintegration from within, starting in Spain itself and spreading to the overseas territories. How did the political institutions and military establishments of the Spanish monarchy stand up to the challenges of this, its most profound internal crisis?

Notes

1. Henry Kamen, *The War of the Spanish Succession in Spain, 1700–1715* (Bloomington: University of Indiana, 1969), p. 135.
2. On the economic dimensions of inter-power rivalry in the War of Succession, see Stanley J. Stein and Barbara H. Stein, *Silver, Trade and War: Spain and America in the Making of Early Modern Europe* (Baltimore: Johns Hopkins University Press, 2000), pp. 109–16, 131–6.
3. First, the signatories recognized territorial states and gave priority to state over dynastic interests; second, they explicitly placed the balance of power in Europe as the prime objective of the treaty system; third, as Bolingbroke was the architect of this system, the European balance of power was connected to British power in the Atlantic. See Philip Bobbit, *The Shield of Achilles: War, Peace and the Course of History* (London: Penguin Books, 2003), pp. 129–32, 520–7. For analysis of the Utrecht settlement in relation to Spain and America, see Peggy Liss, *Atlantic Empires: The Network of Trade and Revolution, 1713–1826* (Baltimore: Johns Hopkins University, 1983), pp. 1–5.
4. The key introductions to the Bourbon succession and its place in Spanish history are John Lynch, *Bourbon Spain* (Oxford: Blackwell, 1989); and J.H. Elliott, *Imperial Spain* (Harmondsworth, UK: Penguin Books, 1970).
5. Henry Kamen, *Philip V of Spain: The King Who Reigned Twice* (New Haven: Yale University Press, 2001), pp. 8–9, 62–4, 81–4, 108–9.
6. The extraordinary weakness of Spain's navy is graphically documented by Pablo Emilio Pérez-Maillaína Bueno, *Política naval española en el Atlántico, 1700–1715* (Seville: Escuela de Estudios Hispanoamericanos, 1982), pp. 379–402.
7. On this phenomenon during the first half of the eighteenth century, see Francisco A. Eissa-Barroso, "'Of Experience, Zeal and Selflessness': Military Officers as Viceroys in Early Eighteenth Century Spanish America," *The Americas* 68, no. 3 (2012): pp. 317–45. The appointment of senior officers became even more pronounced under Charles III, when the system of intendants was introduced to Spanish America. On early military reform in Spanish America, see Allan J. Kuethe, "Decisiones estratégicas y finanzas militares del siglo XVIII," in *Por la fuerza de las armas: Ejército e independencias en Hispanoamérica*, ed. Juan Marchena Fernández and Manuel Chust (Castelló de la Plana: Universidad Jaume I, 2007), pp. 84–6.
8. Anthony McFarlane, *Colombia before Independence: Economy, Society and Politics under Bourbon Rule* (Cambridge: Cambridge University Press, 1993), pp. 102–12, 187–94.
9. On British policy, see William Spence Robertson, "La política inglesa en la América española," in *Historia de la Nación Argentina*, ed. Ricardo Levene, 10 vols, 3rd ed. (Buenos Aires: Academia Nacional de Historia), 5, pt.1, pp. 91–2. For British projects and campaigns, see Richard Pares, *War and Trade in the West Indies, 1739–1763* (London: Cass, 1963), pp. 65–127. On naval and military failings during the war, see Bruce P. Lenman, *England's Colonial Wars, 1550–1688: Conflicts, Empire and National Identity* (London: Pearson, 2001), pp. 67–78. On the limitations of British naval power revealed by the War of Jenkins' Ear, see Philip Woodbine, "Ideas of Naval Power and the Conflict with Spain, 1737–1742," in *The British Navy and the Use of Naval Power in the Eighteenth Century*, ed. Jeremy Black and Philip Woodbine (Leicester: Leicester University Press, 1988), pp. 71–90.

10. Juan Batista, *La estrategía española en América durante el siglo de las luces* (Madrid: Mapfre, 1992), pp. 116–30.

11. On the evolution of these defenses in the sixteenth and seventeenth century, see Julio Albi, *La defensa de las Indias (1764–1799)* (Madrid: Instituto de Cooperacion Iberoamericana, Ediciones Cultura Hispánica, 1987), pp. 9–29; and Juan Marchena Fernández, *Ejército y milicias en el mundo colonial americano* (Madrid: Editorial Mapfre, 1992), pp. 47–60. On the "keys to the Indies of Peru," see Juan Manuel Zapatero, *La Guerra del Caribe en el siglo XVIII* (San Juan, Puerto Rico: Instituto de Cultura Puertorriqueña, 1964), pp. 7–8.

12. There is a large literature on the Bourbon reforms. Two recent contributions that stress the novelty and importance of the reforms undertaken by Charles III are Stanley J. Stein and Barbara H. Stein, *Apogee of Empire: Spain and New Spain in the Age of Charles III. 1750–1789* (Baltimore: Johns Hopkins University Press, 2003); and Gabriel B. Paquette, *Enlightenment, Governance and Reform in Spain and its Empire, 1759–1808* (Basingstoke: Palgrave MacMillan, 2008).

13. For a reconstruction of Spanish strategy along these lines, see Batista, *La estrategía española*, pp. 145–6; for detail on the regional components of the strategy, see ibid., pp. 147–214.

14. On naval reforms, see Lynch, *Bourbon Spain*, pp. 127–9, 164–78. For more detail on improvements to the navy across the eighteenth century, in terms of organization, shipbuilding, manning, and the officer corps, together with an explanation of the reasons why the Spanish navy remained weak compared to the British, see José P. Merino Navarro, *La Armada Española en el Siglo XVIII* (Madrid: Fundación Universitaria Española, 1981), pp. 34–89. Also John D. Habron, *Trafalgar and the Spanish Navy* (London: Conway Maritime Press, 1988), pp. 29–39.

15. On these plans in general and the plan for Veracruz as an example, see Albi, *La defensa de las Indias*, pp. 57–9, 63–7. For analysis of a defense plan for the New World as a whole, drawn up by Colonel Francisco Crespo in 1784, see Christon I. Archer, *The Army in Bourbon Mexico, 1760–1810* (Albuquerque: University of New Mexico Press, 1977), pp. 21–4. For further comment on these defense plans, focusing on Antonio de Arévalo's plans for Cartagena, see Maria del Carmen Gómez Pérez, *El sistema defensivo americano: siglo XVIII*, (Madrid: Mapfre, 1992), pp. 17–24. For a closer appreciation of the characteristics of this plan, see the transcription of Arévalo's report on the defense of Cartagena in Enrique Marco Dorta, "Cartagena de Indias: riquezas ganaderas y problemas," in *Tercer Congreso Hispanoamericano de Historia* (Cartagena; Talleres Mogollón, 1962), 1, pp. 335–52.

16. Batista, *La estrategía española*, pp. 130–6.

17. Allan J. Kuethe, *Cuba, 1753–1815* (Knoxville: University of Tennessee, 1986), pp. 24–49. Also Kuethe, "The Development of the Cuban Military as a Sociopolitical Elite, 1763–83," *HAHR* 61, no. 4 (1981): pp. 695–704.

18. On the military planning conducted by the Junta, see Albi, *La defensa de las Indias*, pp. 57–9, 63–7.

19. The "Regulation of the Militias of Cavalry and Infantry of the Island of Cuba," officially promulgated in 1769, was followed by the introduction of similar regulations in New Spain in 1765; Venezuela, Cartagena, Panama, Yucatan, and Campeche in the 1770s; Peru and New Granada in the early 1790s; and Buenos Aires in 1802. See Marchena Fernández, *Ejército y milicias*, pp. 106–7.

20. José de Gálvez to Viceroy Manuel Antonio Flores, May 15, 1779: cited in Juan Marchena Fernández, "The Social World of the Military in Peru and New Granada," in *Reform and Insurrection in Bourbon New Granada and Peru*, ed. J.R. Fisher, Allan J. Kuethe, and Anthony McFarlane (Baton Rouge: University of Louisiana, 1990), p. 58.

21. My comments on military reforms in Spanish America draw (here and elsewhere) on the following key studies: Lyle N. McAlister, *The Fuero Militar in New Spain, 1764–1800*

(Gainesville: Florida University Press, 1957); Archer, *Army in Bourbon Mexico*; Allan J. Kuethe, *Military Reform and Society in New Granada, 1773–1808* (Gainesville: University of Florida, 1978); Leon G. Campbell, *The Military and Society in Colonial Peru, 1750-1810* (Philadelphia: American Philosophical Society, 1978); Juan Beverina, *El Virreinato del Río de la Plata. Su organización militar* (Buenos Aires: Círculo militar, 1935); Juan Marchena Fernández, *Oficiales y soldados en el ejército de América* (Sevilla: Escuela de Estudios Hispanoamericanos, 1983).

22. These figures are drawn from Marchena Fernández, *Ejército y milicias*, p. 128.

23. Ibid., p. 159.

24. One estimate suggests about 17,000 in 1800: see Jorge Dominguez, *Insurrection or Loyalty: The Breakdown of the Spanish American Empire* (Cambridge, MA: Harvard University Press, 1980), p. 76. Another suggests a similar figure for 1810: see Albi, *Banderas Olvidadas*, p. 65. These are too low. Regional estimates for the major areas of the empire suggest a rather higher figure. If the numbers of troops in the Spanish Caribbean are added, the total stands between 20,000 and 25,000.

25. Stephen Brumwell, *Redcoats: The British Soldier and War in the Americas, 1755–63* (Cambridge: Cambridge University Press, 2002), pp. 13, 19–20, 44–5, 51, 309.

26. Marchena Fernández, *Oficiales y soldados*, pp. 112–13, 300–1.

27. Archer, *Army in Bourbon Mexico,* pp. 223–33; Lyman L. Johnson, "The Military as a Catalyst of Change in Late Colonial Buenos Aires," in *Revolution and Restoration: The Rearrangement of Power in Argentina, 1776–1860*, ed. Mark D. Szuchman and Jonathan D. Brown (Lincoln: University of Nebraska, 1994), pp. 36–7. On the quality of the soldiery and garrison life, see Marchena Fernández, *Ejército y milicias*, pp. 244-72.

28. Francisco Andújar Castillo, *Los militares en la España del siglo XVIII: Un estudio social* (Granada: Universidad de Granada, 1991), pp. 425–9.

29. Francisco Andújar Castillo, *El sonido del dinero: Monarquía, ejército y venalidad en la Espana del siglo XVIII* (Madrid: Marcial Pons, 2004), pp. 419–20.

30. *Memoria sobre la táctica de infantería dirigido al gobierno de S.M. por la comisión encargada de revisar el actual reglamento* (Madrid: Imprenta de M. Rivadeneyra, 1856), p. 13.

31. Andújar Castillo, *Los militares*, pp. 59–64.

32. The following account of the disciplined militias draws on information in the studies by McAlister, Kuethe, Archer, and Campbell, all cited above. Also, for Río de la Plata, see Marcela González, *Las milicias, orígen y organización durante la colonia* (Córdoba, Argentina: Centro de Estudios Históricos, 1995), pp. 70–4.

33. For the "military participation ratio" and its scale in some regions, see Dominguez, *Insurrection or Loyalty*, pp. 75–6. Recent research indicates the 'militarization' of Chile has probably been exaggerated, due to overcounting of the numbers of militiamen: see Juan Luis Ossa, 'Armies, Politics and Revolution in Chile, 1780–1826' (D.Phil. dissertation, Oxford University, 2011), chap. 1.

34. See, for example, the report made by Francisco Douché, a high-ranking officer, who acted as a military inspector in Mexico and reported his views to Spain's Minister of War: Francisco Douché to Conde de Ricla, San Lorenzo del Real, October 25, 1772, Archivo del Servicio Histórico Militar (SHM), Madrid: Ministerio de Guerra, Ultramar 95. For analysis of Douché's report, see Anthony McFarlane, "Guerras e independencias en las Americas," in *Las Revoluciones en el Mundo Atlántico*, ed. María Teresa Calderón and Clément Thibaud (Bogotá: Taurus, 2006), pp. 178–80. Another report that expresses misgivings about the trustworthiness of American militias was written by the governor of Montevideo Joseph de Bustamante when reviewing the condition of the armed forces in the River Plate region in 1803: Joseph de Bustamante y Guerra to Principe de la Paz, Montevideo, August 31, 1803, SHM, Madrid: Ministerio de Guerra, Ultramar 129. For an account of this report, see Anthony McFarlane, "Los

ejércitos coloniales y la crisis del imperio español, 1808–1810," *Historia Mexicana* 58, no. 1 (2008): pp. 242–6.

35. This thesis was advanced by McAlister, *The Fuero Militar in New Spain*, pp. 5–15.

36. Archer, *Army in Bourbon Mexico*, p. 191.

37. For a synthesis of the history of slave and free-colored service in Spanish American militias, set in the comparative context of Euro-American colonies, see Peter M. Voelz, *Slave and Soldier: The Military Impact of Blacks in the Colonial Americas* (New York: Garland Press, 1993), especially pp. 111–28, 408–27.

38. An excellent example is the militia of Mexico's Gulf coast: see Juan Ortiz Escamilla, *El teatro de la guerra: Veracruz, 1750–1825* (Castelló de la Plana: Universitat Jaume I, 2008), pp. 80–99.

39. P. Michael McKinley, *Pre-Revolutionary Caracas: Politics, Economy and Society, 1777–1811* (Cambridge: Cambridge University Press, 1985), pp. 116–17.

40. Aline Helg, *Liberty and Equality in Caribbean Colombia, 1770–1835* (Chapel Hill: University of North Carolina Press, 2004), pp. 100–5.

41. Ben Vinson III, *Bearing Arms for His Majesty: The Free Colored Militia in Colonial Mexico* (Stanford, CA: Stanford University Press, 2001), pp. 3–6, 224–8.

42. For critiques of the McAlister thesis, see Archer, *Army in Bourbon Mexico*, pp. 299–300; Kuethe, *Military Reform and Society in New Granada*, pp. 187; Campbell, *Military and Society in Colonial Peru,* pp. 233–41

43. Albi, *La defensa de las Indias*, pp. 147–50.

44. On this campaign, see David J. Weber, *The Spanish Frontier in North America* (New Haven: Yale University Press, 1992), pp. 265–70; Albi, *Defensa de las Indias*, pp. 156–69.

45. Kuethe, *Cuba*, pp. 97–112, 117–18.

46. Joseph de Gálvez to Viceroy of Buenos Aires, August 30, 1779: reproduced in Beverina, *El Virreinato*, Anexo 11, pp. 407–9.

47. Michael Duffy, "World-Wide War and British Expansion, 1793–1815," in *The Oxford History of the British Empire*, ed. P.J. Marshall (Oxford: Oxford University Press, 1998), 2, p. 185, Table 9.1; Jaap R. Bruijn, "States and their Navies from the Late Sixteenth to the End of the Eighteenth Centuries," in *War and Competition between States*, ed. Philippe Contamine (Oxford: Clarendon Press, 2000), p. 71, Table 1.

48. On Spanish advances to the Pacific Northwest, see Warren L. Cook, *Flood Tide of Empire: Spain and the Pacific Northwest, 1543–1819* (New Haven: Yale University Press, 1973), especially pp. 41–199. On California: Weber, *The Spanish Frontier*, pp. 237–65.

49. Weber, *The Spanish Frontier*, pp. 215–30. For a wider examination of Spanish policy toward unconquered native peoples, which includes South America too, see David J. Weber, *Bárbaros: Spaniards and their Savages in the Age of Enlightenment* (New Haven: Yale University Press, 2005). Weber gives an overview of Bourbon policy towards independent Indian communities, stressing the pragmatic use of military force in combination with commerce and missionary activity see pp. 138–77.

50. On the New Granada campaigns, see Kuethe, *Military Reform and Society in New Granada*, pp. 130–44; on Guatemala, see Troy S. Floyd, *The Anglo-Spanish Struggle for Mosquitia*, (Albuquerque: University of New Mexico, 1967), chap. 11.

51. On the Indian frontiers of Río de la Plata and for Cevallos's plan to "pacify" them, see Beverina, *El Virreinato*, pp. 59–74; and Anexo 4, pp. 369–77. On plans to pacify the Indians in Chile, see Leonardo Leon, "La corona española y las guerras intestinas entre los indígenas de Araucania, Patagonia y las Pampas, 1760–1806," *Nueva Historia: Revista de Historia de Chile* 5 (1982): pp. 31–67.

52. Anthony McFarlane, "Civil Disorders and Popular Protests in Late Colonial New Granada," *HAHR* 64, no. 1 (1984): pp. 17–54; and "The Rebellion of the Barrios: Urban Insurrection in Bourbon Quito," *HAHR* 69, no. 2 (1989): pp. 283–330; William Taylor,

Drinking, Homicide and Rebellion in Late Colonial Mexican Villages (Stanford: Stanford University Press, 1979), pp. 113–51; Scarlett O'Phelan Godoy, *Rebellions and Revolts in Eighteenth Century Peru and Upper Peru* (Cologne: Bohlau Verlag, 1985).

53. For detailed narrative of the rebellions and a tendency to see it as a precursor to independence, see Boleslao Lewin, *La rebelión de Túpac Amaru y los orígenes de la independencia de Hispanoamérica* (Buenos Aires: Librería Hachette, 1957); and L.E. Fisher, *The Last Inca Revolt, 1780–1783* (Norman: University of Oklahoma, 1966). Jurgen Golte, *Repartos y rebeliones: Túpac Amaru y las contradicciones de la economía colonial* (Lima: Instituto de Estudios Peruanos, 1986) stresses the Indians' economic grievances; Scarlett O'Phelan Godoy's *Rebellions and Revolts in Eighteenth Century Peru and Upper Peru* focuses on the fiscal and economic contexts as well as the leadership and organization of rebellion; Ward Stavig, *The World of Túpac Amaru: Conflict, Community and Identity in Colonial Peru* (Lincoln: University of Nebraska Press, 1999) reflects historians' growing interest in the culture of the indigenous communities affected by the rebellion and the influence of millenarian ideas associated with the Inca past. For accounts and interpretations of the rebellion in Upper Peru, see Maria Eugenia del Valle de Siles, *Historia de la rebelión de Túpac Catari, 1781–2* (La Paz: Editorial Don Bosco, 1990). For a new emphasis on the importance of grievance and conflict within indigenous communities and peasant anticolonial consciousness, see Sinclair Thomson, *We Alone Will Rule: Native Andean Politics in the Age of Insurgency* (Madison: University of Wisconsin, 2002); and Serge Serulnikov, *Subverting Colonial Authority: Challenges to Spanish Rule in the Eighteenth-century Southern Andes* (Durham: Duke University Press, 2003).

54. On the role of Cuzco's Indian nobles and the different character of Indian insurrection in the Cuzco region compared with the regions in the Basin of Lake Titicaca, see David T. Garrett, *Shadow of Empire: The Indian Nobility of Cusco, 1750–1825* (Cambridge: Cambridge University Press, 2005), pp. 196–20.

55. A brief analysis of the causes and consequences of the rebellion is found in McFarlane, *Colombia before Independence*, pp. 251–75. For a full account of the Comunero rebellion, see John L. Phelan, *The People and the King: The Comunero Revolution in Colombia, 1781* (Madison: University of Wisconsin, 1978).

56. For the suggestion that the militias provided a structure for rebellion, see Marchena Fernández, "The Social World of the Military," in Fisher, Kuethe, and McFarlane, *Reform and Insurrection*, p. 92. For a brief description of the Comunero "army," which indirectly supports this view by demonstrating how rebel forces were built up in provincial towns and villages in the manner of militias, see Mario Aguilera Peña, *Los Comuneros: Guerra Social y Lucha Anticolonial* (Bogotá: Universidad Nacional, 1985), pp. 108–11.

57. Quoted by Leon G. Campbell, "The Army of Peru and the Túpac Amaru Revolt, 1780–1783," *HAHR* 56, no.1 (1976): pp. 45–6.

58. Ibid., pp. 47–9. Of this improvised army of some 15,000 men, about 14,000 were loyal Indians mobilized by the cacique Pumacahua and his allies.

59. On the similarities and differences between the main eighteenth-century rebellions, see Anthony McFarlane, "Rebellions in Late Colonial Spanish America: A Comparative Perspective," *Bulletin of Latin American Research* 14 (1995): pp. 313–39.

60. For the military responses to these revolts, see Kuethe, *Military Reform and Society in New Granada*, pp. 49–51; Campbell, "The Army of Peru," pp. 45–50.

61. For an assessment of the impact of the American Revolution in the Spanish world, see Anthony McFarlane, "The American Revolution and the Spanish Monarchy," in *Europe's American Revolution*, ed. Simon P. Newman (London: Palgrave MacMillan, 2006), pp. 26–50.

62. On Fullarton's scheme and its context, see Klaus Gallo, *Great Britain and Argentina: From Invasion to Recognition, 1806–26* (Basingstoke, UK: Palgrave, 2001), pp. 16–17.

63. For a detailed analysis of the expansion of Spanish transatlantic trade following the declaration of *comercio libre* in 1778, see John R. Fisher, *Commercial Relations between Spain and Spanish America, 1778–1796* (Liverpool: University of Liverpool, 1985). On the political optimism generated by the success of commercial reform and continuing commitment to reform in the early 1790s, see Barbara H. Stein and Stanley J. Stein, *Edge of Crisis: War and Trade in the Spanish Atlantic, 1789–1808* (Baltimore: Johns Hopkins University Press, 2009), pp. 3–30.

64. On the Spanish reaction to potential French ideological infiltration in Mexico, see John Rydjord, *Foreign Interest in the Independence of New Spain* (New York: Octagon Books, 1972), pp. 128–48; and for the views of Mexican viceroys, see Archer, *Army in Bourbon Mexico*, pp. 81–4. A striking example of official fears over French influence was the prosecution of creoles for seditious conspiracy in New Granada's capital in 1794: see McFarlane, *Colombia before Independence*, pp. 285–93, 307–9. For a French revolutionary scare in Buenos Aires, see Lyman Johnson, "Juan Barbarín: The 1795 French Conspiracy in Buenos Aires," in *The Human Tradition in Colonial Latin America*, ed. Kenneth J. Andrien (Wilmington, DE: Scholarly Resources, 2002), pp. 259–77. The influence of the French Revolution in the Caribbean and circum-Caribbean is assessed by David Geggus, "Slavery, War and Revolution in the Greater Caribbean, 1789–1815," in A *Turbulent Time: The French Revolution and the Greater Caribbean*, ed. David Barry Gaspar and David Patrick Geggus (Bloomington: Indiana University Press, 1997), pp. 1–50.

65. Spanish perceptions of the dangers of sedition and slave uprising and the concomitant need for military preparations are reflected in the correspondence conducted by military men with the Ministry of War during these years: examples abound in SHM, Madrid, Ministerio de Guerra, Ultramar 120.

66. On Godoy, see Lynch, *Bourbon Spain*, pp. 382–8.

67. Ibid., pp. 390–5.

68. Weber, *The Spanish Frontier*, pp. 285–91.

69. On Spain's defense against British attacks on Trinidad and Puerto Rico, see Albi, *La defensa de las Indias*, pp. 183–95.

70. John Lynch, "British Policy and Spanish America, 1763–1808," *Journal of Latin American Studies* 1 (1969): pp. 1–30.

71. Gallo, *Great Britain and Argentina*, pp. 22–31.

72. RAHM, Manuscritos sobre America, Tomo VI, 9/1922, *Observaciones sobre el estado actual de las Americas, y medios que parecen mas convenientes para el estado. Año de 1792.* fol. 261.

73. In 1795, Spanish naval strength was, by one measure, 264,000 tons; by 1805, it had declined to 138,700 tons, and by 1810, to just over 100,000 tons. See Duffy, "World-Wide War and British Expansion," in Marshall, *Oxford History of British Empire*, 2, pp. 204, Table 9.3. Another measure, by number of fighting vessels, shows a decline from 163 in 1795 to 90 in 1805 and to 52 in 1811: see Merino Navarro, *Armada Española*, p. 41. On the reasons for the defeat at Trafalgar, see Habron, *Trafalgar and the Spanish Navy*, pp. 120–1.

74. On British policy in 1806–7, see Martin Robson, *Britain, Portugal and South America in the Napoleonic Wars* (London: I.B. Tauris, 2011), pp. 83–100.

75. Karen Racine, *Francisco de Miranda. A Transatlantic Life in the Age of Revolution* (Wilmington, DE: Scholarly Resources, 2003), pp. 155–72.

76. On the emergence of the River Plate as a target for British attack, and the political maneuvering, motives, and interests behind Popham's expedition against Buenos Aires, see

Gallo, *Great Britain and Argentina*, pp. 33–40; on the vicissitudes of this expedition and the reasons for its failure to dislodge Spanish government, see ibid., pp. 40–50.

77. For a full explanation of the character and political implications of the popular mobilization in Buenos Aires, connecting it to the crisis of the city's labor force caused by imports of foreign goods and slaves, see Lyman L. Johnson, *Workshop of Revolution: Plebeian Buenos Aires and the Atlantic World, 1776–1810* (Durham: Duke University, 2011), pp. 248–82.

78. Robson, *Britain, Portugal and South America*, pp. 119–20, 197–213.

79. On the treaty and the reasons for it, see Carlos Marichal, *Bankruptcy of Empire*, pp. 154–8.

80. Lynch, *Bourbon Spain*, pp. 408–17; Charles J. Esdaile, *Spain in the Liberal Age: From Constitution to Civil War, 1808–1939* (Oxford: Blackwell, 2000), pp. 4–11.

81. Marichal, *Bankruptcy of Empire*, p. 255.

82. On the effects of crown expenditure in Buenos Aires, see Johnson, "The Military as a Catalyst," in Szuchman and Brown, *Revolution and Restoration*, pp. 41–8.

83. Adrian J. Pearce, *British Trade with Spanish America, 1763–1808* (Liverpool: Liverpool University Press, 2007), p. 1–32.

84. See, for example, the critique made by José Ignacio de Pombo, a prominent Cartagena merchant: McFarlane, *Colombia before Independence*, pp. 311–14. Also, for the famous petition made by Mariano Moreno in Buenos Aires in 1809 on behalf of landowners of the River Plate, see Diego Luis Molinari, *La representación de los hacendados de Mariano Moreno* (Buenos Aires: Facultad de Ciencias Económicas, Universidad de Buenos Aires 1939), pp. 280–377. For a translated extract of this document, see Mariano Moreno, "Free Trade versus Monopoly," in *Latin American Revolutions, 1808–1826*, ed. John Lynch (Norman: University of Oklahoma, 1994), pp. 137–42.

85. On the appropriation of church funds and its political repercussions in Mexico, see Brian Hamnett, "The Appropriation of Mexican Church Wealth by the Spanish Bourbon Government. The Consolidación de Vales Reales, 1805–1808," *Journal of Latin American Studies* 1 (1969): pp. 85–113. For the wider economic and fiscal implications of these fiscal pressures in New Spain, see Marichal, *Bankruptcy of Empire*, pp. 148–9, 237–49.

86. Lynch, *Bourbon Spain*, pp. 418–20; Charles Esdaile, The *Peninsular War: A New History*, (London: Allen Lane/Penguin Books, 2002) pp. 24–36.

87. Duffy, "World-Wide War and British Expansion," in Marshall, *Oxford History of British Empire*, 2, pp. 186–94.

2

KINGDOMS IN CRISIS

At the center of the empire, the crisis of 1808 seemed to paralyze the administrative and military institutions of the monarchy. When the king was deposed, Spain's military elite meekly recognized the new regime as senior officers apparently accepted that they owed allegiance to the crown, which had now passed to Joseph Bonaparte, rather than to the person of Ferdinand VII. The captains general, intendants, and provincial governors who commanded troops throughout the country also stood still. Such, it seems, was their blind obedience to authority that they did nothing to mobilize their forces against the French.[1] Even the Francophobes, it seems, preferred French rule to the breakdown of government.

When resistance emerged, it came chiefly from the provinces and the people. The first tremors of insurgency against the invader were felt in Madrid on May 2, 1808, in the violent outbursts that are so vividly depicted in Goya's celebrated images of the "Dos de Mayo." From Madrid, anti-French insurrection spread to the provinces. Peasants and plebeians joined with anti-French leaders among the gentry and middle classes, and new governments sprang up across Spain in juntas that proclaimed the rights of Ferdinand VII, now the symbol of freedom from foreign oppression. They were backed by an incipient, if disorganized national army.

The initial passivity of the political and military elites gave way to an anti-French war of liberation, and Spain entered a period of political transformation both at home and in the empire. A constitutional regime replaced an authoritarian Bourbon king, and Spain's relationship with its colonies was thoroughly disrupted. Creole leaders demanded autonomy in many Spanish American towns and cities, and as wars broke out between contending authorities, military men also became more conspicuous in Spanish American politics. In short, the imperial crisis meant that the politically passive armies of the old regime, obedient to the absolute monarch, were replaced on both sides of the Atlantic by military forces that were embroiled in politics and government.

War and Politics in Spain

To understand the character of the crisis in the Americas, we must first gauge its impact in Spain, for it was the Peninsular response to Napoleon's usurpation of the throne that set the agenda for Spanish Americans. The unique feature of the crisis of 1808 was that it decapitated the existing state. Not only were the king and royal family removed, but the traditional institutions of central and provincial government also broke down, leaving the authority and practice of government to a decentralized network of local authorities, led by the juntas.

The juntas were the great political innovation of 1808, even though they justified themselves by appealing to the old theory of a pact between the king and his people.[2] Their claim that without a legitimate king sovereignty returned to the people was based on a long-standing contractualist concept of monarchy, whereby the people had alienated their sovereignty to the king in return for order, security, and justice. The juntas abided by this long-sanctified political fiction; they presented themselves as temporary repositories of the king's sovereignty rather than sovereigns in their own right and did not initially envisage the creation of a new political order in which the "people" were an independent sovereign. The ideas that justified the foundation of juntas thus had nothing in common with the American and French revolutionary doctrine of popular sovereignty, which challenged the divine right of kings, dispossessed the monarch, and exalted the rights of the people. On the contrary, "the juntas acted like a collective prince rather than a revolutionary power."[3] Nonetheless, the 18 Spanish "supreme juntas" that proclaimed themselves as sovereigns and took up extraordinary titles, honors, and powers were to change the political climate within the monarchy, bringing a burst of creativity that was to have profound effects on political thinking and behavior in Spain and its overseas territories.

While the Spanish juntas all justified themselves by appeal to the concept that sovereignty reverted to the people in *vacatio regis*, their origins and membership varied widely. Often they were preceded by popular riots and local uprisings, though some stemmed from conspiracies of small groups that seized the chance to take power; others built on existing authorities, who kept power by creating juntas based on the local social hierarchy. On the whole, however, it seems that most reflected the practices of the old regime in both their composition and their behavior, though some had a more populist character than others.[4] Their creation reflected an extensive rebellion against the French in which Spaniards also fought fellow Spaniards. Local factions sought to take power or to settle old accounts, and peasants as well as townsfolk—many of whom had suffered badly from the economic downturn of the previous decade—arose against those whom they believed were their oppressors. The breakdown of the Spanish ancien régime thus brought considerable turmoil in its train, spreading fear among the propertied classes and hindering the formation of a unified movement against the French.

The rudiments of a national army were nonetheless created in 1808. Volunteers flocked to the flag, and while these new levies were too undisciplined, ill-trained, and unarmed to be of much practical use, they joined with the remnants of Spain's regular army to create forces that confronted the French.[5] After Spain's initial defeats in Galicia, these forces enjoyed some success. In July 1808, armies fielded by the Junta of Sevilla and led by General Castaños won a brilliant victory at Bailén, causing French losses of around 19,000 men, temporarily ending French plans to take Andalusia and prompting King Joseph to evacuate Madrid and retreat north.[6] By this time, the Spanish cause was also strengthened from another quarter. In August, British forces under Sir Arthur Wellesley, the future Duke of Wellington, arrived in Portugal and were shortly followed by the dispatch of an expeditionary force to Galicia under Sir John Moore.[7]

These advances provoked patriotic enthusiasm in the press and conjured hopes for the rapid expulsion of the French. But in practice they did little to enhance Spanish military effectiveness. While new levies raised fresh troops, they were untrained, badly supplied, and often reluctant to serve away from their localities. To make matters worse, political authority in patriot Spain was scattered among rival juntas so jealous of their independence that they were ready to go to war with each other: the Junta of Seville, for example, came close to sending troops against the Junta of Granada when the latter declared its autonomy. Such disunion prevented the patriots from exploiting the advantage gained at Bailén and allowed the French a respite in which to recover. It took months for a unified leadership to emerge. Encouraged by a British government that wanted to deal with a single government, the provincial juntas coalesced into a Central Junta. Composed of deputies from all over Spain, the Central Junta first met on September 25, 1808, at Aranjuez, and, under the presidency of the Conde de Floridablanca, declared itself the national government and established an infrastructure composed of five ministries.

The Central Junta was a body that reflected the political culture of Spain's ancien régime. The majority of its members were nobles, with a smaller group of clerics; its president, Floridablanca, was a figure from the past. The junta was representative insofar as it brought together delegates from several regions of Spain, but its members did not envisage a modern form of representation in which they held equal status, regardless of social position. Indeed, when Floridablanca conceived the convocation of a *Cortes* to bring together representatives of Spanish society in a deliberative assembly, he thought in terms of the traditional Spanish type, arranged according to the ranks of a society of estates. Even so, the Central Junta was a seminal institution. In the first place, the Central Junta opened a political space in which new political ideas could be proposed, including liberal ideas; this space was, moreover, considerably amplified by the appearance of a new press, which acted as a forum for debate and a means of disseminating ideas.[8] Second, the Central Junta not only brought the issue of representation to the forefront of politics but also committed to convoking a Cortes that would represent all Spaniards, whether Peninsular or American.[9] Third, it created a centralizing authority, placing the regional juntas in secondary roles, calling on deputies to act as representatives of national

rather than local interests, and seeking to coordinate the defense of Spain and mobilization of the Hispanic world against the French usurper.[10]

The Central Junta was, however, incapable of organizing effective resistance
to Napoleon. For reasons that were mainly outside its control, it was soon overwhelmed by military defeats. Despite the arrival of British troops in the Iberian
Peninsula, Spain's improvised armies were unable to contain French advances for
long. Before Bailén, Napoleon's army of Spain was a relatively weak force, clustered
in northerly areas, manned by untried troops, and with some 90,000 men, outnumbered by 114,000 Spanish regulars. In late 1808, however, Napoleon repaired these
shortcomings when he returned to Spain with a rejuvenated army and quickly
reversed the position. In December, the French retook Madrid, forcing the Central
Junta to flee to Seville; in January 1809, General Moore evacuated a shattered British army from La Coruña, losing his life in the process; in February, French forces
prevented General Blake from saving Zaragoza, and, though the junta could rejoice
in news of French defeats at Lugo, Santiago, and Puerto de San Payo, Napoleon's
troops broke the Spanish army and its main offensive at Ocaña in mid-November
1809, at the cost of some 10,000 Spanish dead and 26,000 prisoners. The French
then pressed southwards, sweeping through Andalusia in January, taking Seville on
February 1, and arriving at the outskirts of Cádiz, the last redoubt of Spain's national government, on February 5, 1810.[11]

Serial military defeat produced political altercation. Army officers and civilian
patriots each sought to blame the other, and the Central Junta had increasing difficulty in exerting its authority over army commanders in the provinces.[12] In these
circumstances, the Central Junta moved toward its demise. Its members, known as
the *centralistas*, had decided in May 1809 to convoke a Cortes—a national parliament composed of deputies elected by the Spanish provinces in proportion to their
populations—and the junta set March 1, 1810, as the date for the Cortes's inaugural
session. By January 1810, however, the French advance into Andalusia put these arrangements at risk. The centralistas fled south to Cádiz in great disarray, and in early
February, the Central Junta was replaced by a five-man REGENCY.

Besieged by the French in the city of Cádiz, the first Regency Council—a group
of old regime political notables led by General Castaños, the hero of Bailén—faced
formidable problems. The first of these was denial of its legitimacy by those who
argued that the Central Junta had no legal right unilaterally to appoint its successor.
A greater problem was that of simple survival. With the French on the outskirts
of Cádiz, the regency faced a very uncertain future. However, defended by British naval guns, it persisted in asserting its authority and by convoking the Cortes
promised by the Central Junta, took an important step towards creating Spain's new
constitutional monarchy.[13]

Colonial Complications

While Spain was convulsed by war in the Peninsula, its American possessions were
relatively secure from foreign military threat. Despite fears that Napoleon might extend the war in Spain across the Atlantic, military commanders in Spanish America

did not face any armed challenge from France. In 1808–9, Napoleon's strategy was to take command of government in Spain and thereby extend his political control over Spanish America. To this end, he sent emissaries to the main colonies, hoping to win over Bourbon officials and to encourage acceptance of the French takeover of the monarchy.[14] However, when these envoys achieved nothing, Napoleon had no serious alternative schemes for imposing French rule on Spain's colonies. There were rumors that the French were mustering expeditions to use against Spanish dominions and periodic alarms about the possibility of a Franco-American attack; in fact, Napoleon was too preoccupied with his plans for Europe to give much attention to American projects.

Spain did face other external challenges. Spaniards feared that the new Republic of the United States was one potential antagonist, particularly on the northern borderlands of the Viceroyalty of New Spain. The Portuguese monarchy, resident in Brazil after the flight from Napoleon in 1807, was another possible predator. Friction between Spain and Portugal in the Banda Oriental—on the frontiers between Brazil and the River Plate regions—had led to war on more than one occasion in the eighteenth century, and although the issue had been resolved by the Treaty of San Ildefonso in 1777, Portuguese ambitions remained unsatisfied. Indeed, after Spain had helped France to invade Portugal by allowing French troops to cross its soil in 1807, and thus forced the Portuguese monarchy to seek refuge in Brazil, the exiled Prince Regent Dom João had good cause to claim Spanish territory in America as compensation for the loss of Portugal.

Portuguese plans for aggrandizement focused on the neighboring Spanish Viceroyalty of Río de la Plata.[15] The Portuguese minister of war and foreign affairs, Rodrigo de Sousa Coutinho sought first to extend Portugal's hegemony over the Río de la Plata by diplomatic means. In March 1808, he sent a message to Buenos Aires, which, arguing that Spain had already fallen under Napoleon's yolk, offered "to take the Cabildo and People of the city of Buenos Aires and the whole Viceroyalty under his Royal Protection," with freedom of commerce and no new taxes.[16] When the brother of Viceroy Liniers passed through Rio de Janeiro en route to Buenos Aires, Coutinho prevailed upon him to warn Spanish officials that they should open negotiations immediately if they wished to avoid war with the Portuguese and British.[17] When these diplomatic efforts failed, rejected by Liniers, the cabildo of Buenos Aires, and Elío in Montevideo, Coutinho drew up other plans. On the arrival of a British naval squadron commanded by Rear Admiral Sir Sidney Smith at Rio in mid-May 1808, he proposed a joint military venture into the River Plate region, with Portugal supplying the troops and Britain the ships to carry them. He also suggested that the infantes Carlota Joaquina (the prince regent's wife and Ferdinand VII's sister) and her cousin Pedro Carlos, both present in Rio, might, being in the line of succession to the Bourbon throne, legitimately act as regents in Spanish America in Ferdinand's absence.

The possibility of Portuguese intervention took an unexpected twist when, buoyed up by Smith's enthusiastic support, Princess Carlota became active in promoting herself as a regent in Río de la Plata and, through her agents, made personal contact with interested parties in Buenos Aires. Smith was convinced that Britain's best interests were served by installing a limited monarchy at Buenos Aires. He saw this as a way to fend off Napoleon and preempt a popular revolution that might favor France, and he regarded Carlota as the natural candidate for this role. Creoles in Buenos Aires who wanted to remove viceregal government were also attracted by Carlota's proposal, since it seemed to offer the chance of a peaceful shift of power to a constitutional monarchy that enjoyed British backing.

Smith's plans to install Carlota at Buenos Aires backfired badly, however, and did not produce the early independence of the Río de la Plata that he and his creole allies wanted. Carlota became convinced that the *porteño* creoles were using her to camouflage their covert plans to establish a republic, and she switched sides.[18] After betraying the British agent whom Smith sent to Buenos Aires to negotiate on her behalf, Carlota tried to persuade the Spanish authorities in Buenos Aires and the Spanish ambassador at Rio (the Marqués de Casa Irujo) that they should accept her as regent. This worked no better, for her plans were opposed by the British ambassador in Rio, Lord Strangford. After news arrived that Spain had rebelled against France, Strangford committed Britain to defending the territorial integrity of the Spanish empire and thus opposed all the schemes for intervention in the River Plate that emanated from the Portuguese court, including Princess Carlota's schemes for acting as a Spanish American regent in place of the captive Ferdinand VII.[19] Thus, schemes to decide the political future of the Río de la Plata by an external intervention from Portugal's prince regent or through the idiosyncratic intrigues of the Spanish infanta went nowhere, largely because British statesmen were determined to avoid any action that might damage its relations with Spain and thus give an advantage to France.

Threats of foreign incursion into Spanish America generally diminished around this time, as Britain turned itself from enemy into ally of the Spanish monarchy. This was most obvious in the Río de la Plata, where the presence of a British ambassador in Rio de Janeiro and a naval squadron to patrol the Atlantic coast of South America gave Britain an unusual leverage. But it affected other regions in Spanish America too; from later 1808, colonial governments were relieved of the need to defend their territories from the British. Moreover, because Britain had been converted from predator into protector, British diplomacy and armed forces promised to become a guarantor of Spain's imperial integrity. British naval vessels now became the maritime shield against French attack, and as the Anglo-Spanish alliance lifted the threat of external assault from both the old enemy and the new, Spain's subjects in America could feel reasonably secure from foreign attack.

This reduction in external threats was, however, not entirely to the advantage of Spanish colonial governments, for it had an unwelcome side effect. Just as the removal of the French threat to Britain's American colonies in 1763 had made North American colonials less deferential to the metropolis in the 1770s, so the dramatic change in international alignments in 1808 gave Spanish Americans greater confidence in their ability to live outside the orbit of imperial rule. This was particularly evident in the Atlantic port cities, particularly Buenos Aires, where it seemed that Britain, although formally committed to defending Spain's empire, was keen to build commercial and political relations and ready to contemplate the creation of independent states. In short, Americans realized that flux in the international order had created a new asymmetry in the balance of power between Spain and its colonies, and as Spain's problems multiplied in 1808–10, they saw their chance to assert ambitions for home rule.

Towards Autonomy

The movements for autonomy in Spanish America developed slowly in response to political developments at the center of the monarchy. American reactions initially echoed those in Spain, with effusive declarations of fealty to Ferdinand VII orchestrated by royal officials and marked by elaborate public ceremonies.[20] However, although Americans shared Spanish dislike of Napoleonic France, discord soon developed. On the one hand stood those, including most government officials, who aimed at sustaining the existing structure of government and their authority over it; on the other side were those who wanted local representation in government and called for autonomous juntas on the model of those in Spain. The division left royal officials in a quandary about how best to sustain their authority; should they cultivate cooperation with local elites by allowing them co-government, or should they simply defend the status quo? The result was confusion and confrontation in several major cities during 1808–9, as disputes imported from Spain interacted with preexisting tensions and rivalries.

The first signs of instability surfaced in cities where the political elites divided over the issue of what constituted legitimate government in the king's absence. In July 1808, the political elites of Mexico City pressured Viceroy Iturrigaray to establish a congress of representatives from New Spain's leading cities to support his government, a proposal that was strongly opposed by the members of the *audiencia* (high court with administrative responsibilities) and other royal officials. Iturrigaray tried to compromise by convening meetings of the city's main corporate bodies but succeeded only in alienating the city's Peninsular Spaniards. Suspecting that the viceroy intended to establish an autonomous government in alliance with creoles, a small group of Spanish merchants and bureaucrats in Mexico City plotted his overthrow, and on September 15, 1808, they launched a coup against him.[21] The coup was carried out by private citizens led by a prominent Spanish merchant in league with other members of the city's social and political elite and with the collusion of the audiencia; its leaders also recognized the importance of the army as a guarantor of the new government by replacing the ousted viceroy with a senior army officer.[22] No doubt the fact that the viceregency passed to a military man, the old but eminent Mariscal de Campo Pedro Garibay, helped keep the army loyal, as did Garibay's appointment of trusted men to commanding roles and his creation of ten new companies of volunteers among Spaniards and creoles.[23]

Divisions among the social and political elites also polarized politics in Caracas. In July 1808, Captain General Juan de Casas seemed ready, like Viceroy Iturrigaray in Mexico, to share power with local notables. However, when a group of leading

citizens petitioned Casas to establish a junta in November 1808, he not only refused to do so but arrested its advocates.[24] This was evidently intended to restore his
control in a situation where, as the Intendant of Caracas put it, "zeal and ardour for
the sacred cause degenerated into a spirit of party," and the proponents of the junta
threatened to oust officials in the name of loyalism.[25] Fearful that they were losing
control, Casas and Juan Vicente de Arce also had the military means to impose their
will, for, although landowners had taken militia officerships for the prestige they
conferred, the Caracas elite did not attempt to use the militias for political purposes.[26] Hence the ease with which Casas stopped the juntistas short of their goals.

In Buenos Aires, the viceregal government was faced with comparable problems. Indeed, given that Viceroy Liniers was a Frenchman, the question of who
should hold power in the *vacatio regis* had an added urgency. The Governor of Montevideo, Francisco Javier de Elío, was the first to move against the viceroy. In September 1808, he accused Liniers of planning to turn the viceroyalty over to France,
and backed by leading citizens of Montevideo, he established a junta to repudiate
the viceroy's authority. Thus, the first autonomous junta in Spanish America was
the creation of an ultra-loyalist official aimed at defending, not overturning, the
royal authorities.[27] Spanish officials and merchants in Buenos Aires tried to follow
the same path. In October 1808, members of the city's cabildo plotted to depose
Liniers, and in January 1809, a pro-Spanish group, backed by Basque, Galician, and
Catalan militias, sought to seize control of the cabildo and eject Liniers from office.
Their forces were, however, met by creole militias led by the patrician Cornelio
de Saavedra that defended Viceroy Liniers.[28] Thus, unlike Iturrigaray in Mexico,
Liniers succeeded in defeating armed challenges to his authority largely because his
creole allies provided him with armed support.

During 1809, the Central Junta offered a solution to these disputes over who
should participate in Spanish American governance with an important innovation:
namely, the offer of representation at the heart of imperial government. In January,
crown officials were ordered to organize elections for deputies from America for all
Spain's subjects, so that American opinion would be heard in the government that
was taking shape in Spain. These elections obviously represented a novel departure
from the practices of absolutist government in the American colonies.[29] However,
the attempt to strengthen solidarities through representation did not silence creole demands for autonomy. Indeed, far from enhancing the authority of Spanish
governments in America, the Central Junta's efforts to bind the colonies to Spain
sometimes had the opposite effect. For, by indicating that a new form of government was taking shape in Spain, the elections to the Central Junta helped to make
American demands for self-governing juntas more vocal and more credible.[30]

Discord spread to new sites during 1809, as disputes of different kinds led to
the unseating of existing authorities in the Audiencias of Charcas (modern Bolivia)
and Quito (modern Ecuador). The first took place in Chuquisaca, capital of the
Audiencia of Charcas, on May 25, 1809, when the judges of the audiencia deposed
their president, León de Pizarro, on the grounds that he was preparing to recognize
Princess Carlota Joaquina as regent. They appointed Colonel José Antonio Álvarez

de Arenales, a Spanish militia commander, as overall commander of military forces in Charcas and ordered him to organize militias on their behalf.[31] This was a distinctly conservative coup, aimed at preventing change in the established order of government, and thus bears some resemblance to Montevideo's rejection of Viceroy Liniers the previous year. It was shortly followed, however, by a different kind of rebellion in another leading city of Upper Peru, when, in late July 1809, a group of creole radicals launched a popular uprising and established their own autonomous junta in La Paz. The La Paz movement was more radical and ambitious than that of Chuquisaca, for, although its proponents declared loyalty to Ferdinand VII, they called on popular support and issued plans for the organization of a new kind of government.[32]

These very distinctive political coups lasted only as long as it took to organize their repression. Both aborted when Viceroy Abascal of Peru took military action against them, in consort with Viceroy Cisneros of Río de la Plata. Abascal appointed Brigadier José Manuel de Goyeneche (then acting president of the Audiencia of Cuzco) to take regulars from Lima and militias raised in Arequipa, Cuzco, and Puno into Upper Peru, and, combining with forces sent from Buenos Aires, to crush the La Paz rebellion and restore the normal workings of government at Chuquisaca. The military intervention was immediately effective. The Junta of La Paz was unable to win support from other cities in Upper Peru and was quickly overwhelmed by the army of some 4,500 men, which Goyeneche brought from Peru.[33] He took the city on October 24, 1809, and extended the repression in the rural areas of the Yungas, capturing and killing rebel leaders who tried to keep the rebellion alive.[34] After La Paz, Chuquisaca was also swiftly restored to Spanish authority. On December 24, the new president of Charcas, Vicente Nieto, marched into the city with an army of 500 men brought from Buenos Aires, demobilized the militia companies raised by the audiencia, and placed himself in control. The status quo was thus restored in Upper Peru, partly because neither cities nor countryside joined the La Paz rebellion and partly because neighboring viceroyalties were ready and able to supply military forces to enforce royal authority.

The city of Quito, capital of the Audiencia of Quito, was the scene of another abortive rebellion in the latter half of 1809. In August, members of the urban patriciate removed the governor and audiencia and set up their own autonomous junta, aided in this instance by the commander of the city garrison, who used his troops to arrest leading government officials and take control of official buildings in the city. The junta failed, however, to secure support from the other provinces of the Audiencia, where royalists now mobilized forces against it. Peru's Viceroy Abascal again played a key role. He ordered the governors of Guayaquil, Cuenca, and Popayán to prepare forces to move against Quito, while also dispatching 400 men by sea from Lima to Guayaquil. Abascal had no jurisdiction over Quito, which came under the overall command of the viceroy of New Granada, but his initiative ensured that Quito's rebellion faced prompt military retaliation. Troops converged on the capital from several directions: Governor Aymerich of Cuenca led troops from the south, and Governor Cucalón of Guayaquil sent a vanguard expedition from the Pacific coast while he awaited reinforcements from Panama. Meanwhile, Viceroy Amar of New Granada mobilized forces in the north. Intimidated by these threats of armed action, the leaders of the Quito junta restored the audiencia president, Ruiz Castilla, disarmed their forces, and allowed the troops sent from Guayaquil to enter the city without resistance on November 25, 1809.[35] As in Charcas, the ability of royalist authorities to mobilize effective military forces had snuffed out a political challenge and showed that Spain, for all its weakness at the center, was still capable of wielding coercive force to defend its colonial governments.

At the end of 1809, Spanish governments in America had withstood the first shocks of political crisis in America; the old regime's officials remained in place, and their position was supported by the belief that Spain was still ruled by a legitimate government engaged in a justified war against France. Leading officials also had direct control of the military: garrison and militia officers took orders, not from a central commander in chief in Spain but from the viceroys, audiencia presidents, intendants, and provincial governors who were responsible for political, administrative, and military matters in their jurisdictions. Thus, army officers had to answer to the foremost regional political official—who was often an army officer himself—and were obliged to follow his orders. Colonial governments therefore kept the legal monopoly of force in their hands and, so long as their officials and their military remained loyal, could use their armed forces to suppress challenges to their authority.

This was a system that had evident strengths, since it put military force into the hands of political officials and allowed them to use force to sustain their authority. However, while the established system of government withstood the first tests imposed by imperial crisis, American colonial governments saw their authority drain away as Spain's resistance buckled under the force of French attack.[36] Royal officials insisted that, as the appointees of the supreme authority in Spain, they alone had the legal right to govern in America, but the propriety of their position was increasingly impaired. It was, in the first place, corroded by the suspicion that they would accept any authority, including that of Napoleon, so long as it enabled them to keep their jobs. Such slurs could easily stick. Those who had been appointed before 1808 were tainted by their association with the discredited Godoy regime, while those appointed after the French occupation in 1808 were vulnerable to accusations that they were *afrancesados* sympathetic to Bonaparte. Another problem for colonial governments was that the embattled Central Junta's direct appeals to Americans and offers of representation tended to undercut local authority. Most important, however, was the impossibility of dispelling dispute over the locus of supreme authority in the king's absence. Using the example of the juntas in Spain, some Americans argued that if sovereignty had reverted to the people in Spain, then the same applied in America.

The leading players in political conflict were officials of colonial governments and members of American cabildos. Royal officials invariably upheld the authority of Spanish metropolitan government as the sole possessor of sovereignty and source of law for the Americas and defended the status quo. Creole dissidents, on the other hand, used the cabildos as a vehicle for arguing that the best way to defend the sovereignty of Ferdinand VII and avoid falling under French domination was by American self-government, embodied in juntas through which Americans would direct their own public affairs. Initially, then, political conflict was confined to the small, politicized elites who occupied positions of political authority and influence within the main cities of Spanish America, whether as crown officials who held posts in royal government or as creoles associated with city cabildos. Both were very small minorities within larger populations that were mostly uninvolved in, or undecided on, the great political questions of the day. The limited social scope of political contention did not, however, prevent it from endangering the system of government. During 1810, a more widespread movement towards autonomy spread throughout Spanish America, for, as it became increasingly likely that Napoleon would crush Spain's government, the question of who should inherit its powers came to a head.

American Juntas

The debate over the locus of authority in America moved to a climax in early 1810, after the Central Junta passed its authority to the Regency Council. Desperate to legitimize itself and win support throughout the Hispanic world, the Regency promised to extend political equality and representative government to the colonies. By decree of February 14, 1810, it assured Americans that they were now free men, who, as soon as they elected representatives to the national congress, would no longer depend on viceroys and governors but take the future in their own hands. However, although such words and ideas "everywhere produced the most profound sensation,"[37] they did not necessarily translate into unequivocal support for government from Spain. As Spain's emergency governments scrabbled to hold onto authority in 1808–10, their pleas for American aid and promises of political reform dramatized the plight of the metropolis and precipitated a slide into confusion and conflict throughout Spanish America.

With the future of Spain's government in doubt, the argument that sovereignty should revert to the people in the king's absence took on new force. In administrative capitals and other towns, movements for autonomy proliferated. The proponents of autonomy usually won the argument by peaceful means, using the ancient institution of the cabildo to press for juntas, while taking advantage of doubt and division among royal officials to win allies and deflect opposition. Thus, power tended to pass from one elite group to another with little violence and limited popular mobilization, in processes that were more akin to coups d'etat than revolutionary insurrections.

The first juntas of 1810 were established in port cities on the Atlantic seaboard, where news of events in Spain arrived relatively quickly. Caracas took the lead. In April 1810, a group of prominent Spaniards and Americans convened an extraordinary meeting of the city's cabildo and used it to launch a coup against the captain general and governor, Vicente de Emparán. They secured a temporary consensus by bringing together the cabildo, the archbishop, members of the audiencia, and the city's merchant guild, while also winning over officers in the city's garrison. Emparán capitulated to what he evidently regarded as an insurmountable opposition among the elites and left his opponents to create a Supreme Junta that sought to rally Venezuela's other provinces to join in their bid for autonomy.[38]

In May 1810, a second major city broke with Spain's government when the established authorities were overturned at Buenos Aires. There, a situation comparable to that in Caracas developed during 1809–10, as a growing gulf opened between a government run by Peninsular officials and a group of creoles who wanted to establish a junta. Like the Caracas creoles, dissidents used the cabildo as their vehicle, and combining political action with the threat of force, they removed the viceroy on May 25, 1810, and installed their own junta in his place. The establishment of the Buenos Aires junta involved more use of military force than that of Caracas. The militias commanded by creole leaders were in the vanguard of the attack on the viceroy and audiencia, and seen from a contemporary royalist perspective, the Buenos Aires junta looked like a military coup. José María Salazar, the naval commander in neighboring Montevideo, described the overthrow of the viceroy as "more a military conspiracy than a movement of the people." Its leaders were, he said, no more than "a dozen subaltern officers of the kind who waste their time in cafés" and who had taken advantage of the "idleness, indiscipline and insubordination of their troops" to intimidate their opponents and drive the government out.[39]

It soon became clear, however, that the "May Revolution" was much more than a mere coterie of café revolutionaries. The Buenos Aires junta immediately moved to extend its authority over the whole of the Viceroyalty of Río de la Plata and, although Montevideo remained in royalist hands, its claims for autonomy attracted adherents across a very wide region, reaching into the Andean provinces of Upper Peru and across the Andes into Chile. Indeed, while the Regency Council struggled to survive at Cádiz, the beginnings of a more general movement against direct rule from Spain extended throughout the Americas during the second half of 1810.

From mid-1810, the example of Caracas echoed throughout the adjoining Viceroyalty of New Granada. The movement started at Cartagena de Indias, where the city's cabildo accused Governor Montes of being an *afrancesado* and deposed him on June 14, 1810.[40] Leading Peninsulars and creoles cooperated in his overthrow and negotiated with the pardo militias so they could back their political demands with the threat of force. The regular officers of the garrison were co-opted too; indeed, the cabildo promoted Montes's deputy, the lieutenant governor Blas de Soria, in return for overturning his chief. Having made itself the de facto power in Cartagena, the cabildo went on to establish a Supreme Governing Junta in August 1810. All this was done in the name of the king and acknowledged the authority of Spain's Regency, until, in November 1810, the REGENCY sought to impose a new governor on the city.[41] After the overthrow of the governor of Cartagena in June, juntas were soon set up in the towns and cities of New Granada's interior, notably in the viceregal capital of Santafé de Bogotá. Indeed, the overthrow of Viceroy Amar on July 20, 1810, followed a pattern that broadly resembled that of Cartagena;

a small group of creole juntistas used the cabildo to demand that the viceroy share power with a junta, and having secured the acquiescence of the commander and officers in the city garrison, the juntistas mobilized rioting crowds to intimidate the viceroy and force him to compromise, prior to ousting him completely.[42]

In August 1810, disagreements among military and political authorities undermined the royalist government in Quito. Viceroy Abascal of Peru had dispatched Brigadier Bartolomé Cucalón from Guayaquil, with reinforcements from Lima, to shore up the government of Quito, but Cucalón aggravated political tensions by trying to oust the civilian president from power. This not only revivified dissent within the city, whose leading citizens resented this attempt at a takeover by an outsider, but also provoked division within the ranks of the army. Soldiers from the old garrison mutinied on August 2, 1810, and when they killed one of Cucalón's officers, his troops raised havoc. The political damage was difficult to repair. Another junta was set up, led by Carlos Montúfar, a creole aristocrat from a leading Quito family who came from Spain as the emissary of the REGENCY, and a curious and confusing situation developed. Having taken power peacefully, the Junta of Quito recognized the REGENCY and elected a delegate to represent them in the Spanish Cortes, but it behaved as though it were autonomous. When the junta mobilized military force to impose its authority on the provinces of the Audiencia of Quito, several resisted, and royalist enclaves remained under the direct control of royal officials in both the highlands, at Cuenca, and on the coast, at Guayaquil. Thus, Quito was in the curious situation of having pro-Spanish governments that were at war with each other.[43]

In Chile, another territory on the periphery of the Viceroyalty of Peru, royal government also temporarily collapsed in 1810. For two years, Governor Carrasco had allied himself with a small clique of Peninsulars and used force to repress political dissent. However, after the May Revolution in Buenos Aires, the audiencia tried to take a more conciliatory approach, deposing Carrasco and replacing him with an octogenarian creole aristocrat in the hope that this would win local support. It did not. When the REGENCY called for allegiance, the cabildo of Santiago, Chile's administrative capital, responded by pressing for an autonomous junta, which was duly established, without violence, in September 1810. Although protesting loyalty to Ferdinand VII and integrating Peninsular Spaniards into government, the junta disavowed the regency and, conservative though it was, launched Chile on the road to separation from Spain.[44]

While governments fell in Venezuela, New Granada, Río de la Plata, Chile, and Quito, the Viceroyalty of New Spain also showed signs of serious internal stress. During 1809, the viceregal government had suppressed open creole dissent in Mexico City but could not contain creole opposition in the provinces. There, especially in the Bajío region north of the capital, hostility to the Spanish government had remained strong and active, particularly in the important provincial towns of Guanajuato, Valladolid, and Querétaro. Creole aims were essentially the same as those of creoles in other American cities; while pledging loyalty to Ferdinand VII, they demanded an autonomous government based in local representation. Their plans for achieving this goal were also broadly similar to those concocted by creoles in other regions. They aimed to create juntas of local notables, which would take power in urban centers using local military and militias in support, and then come together in a regional congress to decide on policy for the kingdom as a whole. The first significant plot along these lines took place in the city of Valladolid in 1809, where the authorities uncovered a conspiracy to create a congress of delegates from all the leading towns of New Spain to govern in Ferdinand VII's name.

The Valladolid conspiracy was mainly the work of two military men: Lieutenant José Mariano Michelena of the royal infantry and José María García Obeso, captain in the provincial militia, who, together with a group of creole associates, had solicited support in the neighboring towns and cities of Guanajuato, San Miguel el Grande, Querétaro, and Guanajuato for a general uprising against Spanish rule. Aware that their plans to change government would be opposed by force, the conspirators sought to ensure that they had the means to counter it. As creole militia officers were prominent among the conspirators, it is hardly surprising that their chosen weapon was the local militias. However, they did not plan to rely solely on military action. The Valladolid conspirators aimed to use the militias that some of them commanded, while also raising support from the Indian and mixed-race peasantry by promises to abolish tribute payments, thus combining popular participation with a military discipline that would bind the rebellion together.

Betrayed before they could move—they had planned to trigger the uprising on December 21, 1809—the Valladolid plotters and some of their allies were rounded up and tried. This did not discourage sedition among provincial creoles, however. During 1810, a fresh conspiracy was hatched in Querétaro, where a group of the city's creole notables joined with prominent creoles from nearby towns to resurrect the plans of Valladolid. Ignacio de Allende, captain of a cavalry regiment in San Miguel, and his fellow officers Juan de Aldama and Mariano Abasolo, were involved, together with Miguel Hidalgo, parish priest of the neighboring town of Dolores, and they embraced a plan to establish juntas in principal towns so that they might declare independence from Spain and expel Spaniards from Mexico.[45] This plan, akin to that of Valladolid, was to be effected by similar means: Allende and Hidalgo's correspondence shows that they aimed at a popular mobilization arraigned behind creole leadership. However, before their plans could be activated in a controlled manner, the conspirators were betrayed, prompting them, under Hidalgo's leadership, to declare open rebellion on September 16, 1810.[46]

Thus, precisely two years after European Spaniards had blocked a movement toward creole autonomy by overthrowing the viceroy and installing a hard-line loyalist government, American Spaniards reactivated demands for autonomy by launching a rebellion against that government. The attack on the viceregal government was politically similar to those that had taken place in other Spanish colonies, in that it arose from creole demands for self-determination, which echoed those voiced throughout the principal cities of Spanish America. However, the rebellion soon took on a very different shape when its creole leadership was overwhelmed by an enthusiastic, indeed uncontrollable, response from the lower classes, to whom they appealed for support. While the weakness of the state and the divisions among its elites allowed dissident creoles to mount a political challenge to the colonial regime, their challenge also inspired peasants and plebeians to vent their grievances in violent insurrection. The Hidalgo revolt was set apart from other American rebellions against colonial governments because it was underpinned by a great uprising among country people, who found in Spanish government and the Spaniards a scapegoat for their misery and a target for anger that was fuelled by apocalyptic rumor. Mexican rejection of Spain differed from the South American rebellions in another way, too: rebellion came from the provinces rather than the political capital and drew its initial impetus from the countryside, not the towns. Creole repudiation of Peninsular rule in Mexico thus assumed a very different form to those that had taken place in South America. When creole dissidents sparked rebellion at Dolores in September 1810, they ignited a social conflagration that swiftly outran their intentions in a spreading civil war.

By the end of 1810, then, the regency and Cortes in Spain had received the alarming news that the viceroys of New Granada and Río de la Plata had been overthrown and that most provinces in these viceroyalties were refusing to acknowledge the regency's authority; they also knew that New Spain, Spain's richest colony, was in the throes of a popular insurrection, which threatened the survival of its royal government. Only Peru remained stable: Viceroy Abascal was the sole surviving viceroy of the three who had governed Spanish South America at the beginning of the year, and free from serious threats from Lima or other important cities in Peru, was able to develop military responses to the rebellions in neighboring territories.

The movement towards autonomy in Spanish America had some common causes. One was their elites' loss of confidence in the Spanish imperial system. The patrician mercantile and landed families (mostly but not exclusively American) had suffered from the dislocation of transatlantic trade caused by international war and, as Spain proved incapable of reforming its economic system, wanted a chance to control their own affairs. The desire for autonomy was strongly reinforced by fear that the breakdown of authority in Spain might be reproduced in America, opening space for social disorder. And once autonomous government seemed a realistic prospect, the power struggles between rival families and factions that had long competed for office, wealth, and privilege, also came into play. As the deepening Spanish crisis raised questions about the future of existing authorities, these competing groups (often associations of Peninsular Spaniards or creoles) were anxious to create governments that would give them access to office and allow them to pursue policies that expressed their interests.

The juntas set up in 1810 sprang from the same ideological roots and had much in common. They were, in the first place, expressions of a shared Hispanic political culture.[47] Like their predecessors in Spain, they came into being simultaneously and with the same justification—namely, that in the absence of the king, sovereignty reverted to the *pueblo* (the "people"), who now had the right to establish their own self-government, embodied in the juntas. As they acted in the name of the captive king, they did not propose separation from Spain. The juntas were regarded as legal institutions that exercised self-government within the Spanish monarchy rather than being independent governments outside it, and they were built on the principles of corporate representation and defense of the *común* (common interest) that were characteristic of the ancien régime.

What was the "pueblo" that now exercised sovereignty by choosing representatives in whom to invest the authority of government? It was essentially the city and its associated province. Recently, historians have emphasized that in the Hispanic tradition, the "pueblo" was primarily identified with the city or town (in Spanish also the "pueblo").[48] After the conquest, villages, towns, and cities came to be recognized as a hierarchy of communities, which, as in Castile, structured the space around the principal city; the basic territorial structure throughout Spanish America consisted of the principal city and its dependent pueblos, usually denominated as a "province." These became "autonomous actors in social and political life, and even tended towards city-states if the state's authority were to disappear."[49] Thus, when a junta represented the "people," it referred to a specific place and saw itself as an autonomous political entity, free to govern itself within the monarchy.

These traditional qualities did not prevent the juntas from taking the first step towards independence. Once in power, the juntas behaved like independent governments, establishing new institutions (such as high courts, congresses, and civic militias) while also adopting liberalizing policies (such as free trade, abolition of state monopolies, the abolition of Indian tribute, an end to slave trading), which conflicted with Spanish law and interests. And while they generally started under the control of men who were determined to retain ties with Spain, they opened a space for the expression of local discontents and provided a forum for those who aspired to full independence.

When they became aware of the American movement towards autonomy, politicians and officials in Spain were unsure of how to respond. The flow of information and advice from America was uneven and sometimes contradictory, and the overall picture was blurred and confusing. The language of the autonomous juntas, which declared loyalty to Ferdinand VII while rejecting the regency, added to the confusion. It encouraged some loyalists to persuade themselves that colonials had moved against their governments in the belief that there was no legitimate government in Spain and that they would return to the Spanish cause as soon as they knew that a new constitutional regime was in being. Others saw the rebellions as a temporary aberration in another sense. When, for example, Brigadier Carrasquedo, the artillery commander in Caracas, reported on the April rebellion, he argued that the province would be readily restored to royal control with a few apposite military measures. Carrasquedo acknowledged that many creoles wanted independence, but he pointed out that whites feared the social effects of political revolution. One would have to be completely mad, he asserted, not to realize that the large numbers of free coloreds in the province of Caracas would demand equality, that the new government would have to accede to their demands in order to avoid civil war, and that this would inevitably lead to slave uprisings that would deprive landowners of their property and many of their lives. Most of the population would therefore support the restoration of Spanish rule if royalists mounted a swift, well-supported military operation, because creoles rich and poor would soon realize that only Spanish rule protected them from a social calamity of the kind that had occurred in Haiti.[50] Such an assertion, coming from an army officer who had been expelled from his post, raises an obvious question. If prompt military action would restore royal government, why had government military forces failed to prevent its overthrow in the first place?

Politics and the Military

Bourbon kings had, as we noted in the previous chapter, made unprecedented efforts during the later eighteenth century to strengthen Spain's ability to defend its sovereignty and authority in Spanish America, both by reorganizing the regular army and by enlarging the militias. Their reforms had mixed results. The regular units of the Army of America had, on the whole, proved their worth: Spain made gains in the American War of Independence, and although forced onto the back foot during the post-1790 French wars, it managed to sustain colonial defenses with few losses. The militias were less obviously successful, at least outside Cuba. They did not prove effective against the big regional rebellions of the early 1780s, and with the exception of militias in Buenos Aires during the British invasions of 1806–7, it was not obvious that they provided a reliable system of support and reinforcement in time of international war. How, then, did Spain's military forces respond to the sharp crisis of authority that occurred in 1810, when governments were most in need of armed forces to sustain them in power?

Given that Spain was unable to send armed forces from Europe, royalist officials who wanted to enforce their authority by military means had to rely on the army units available to them locally. The regular soldiers present in the major garrisons were the obvious choice; they were disciplined, armed, and ready for action, and led by officers under the direct command of viceroys and governors. Militias were less useful, since they did not share these attributes and being almost entirely composed of local men, were regarded as less reliable.

The responses of the regular army varied regionally. New Spain's major garrisons in Mexico City, Veracruz, and Puebla all supported viceregal government; so, too, did the Peruvian garrisons in Lima-Callao and Cuzco. In New Granada and Venezuela, smaller clusters of troops did the same, helping to preserve enclaves of loyalism in several provincial towns. In Caracas, Cartagena, Bogotá, Quito, Buenos Aires, and Santiago, by contrast, regular troops either failed to prevent, or participated in, the creation of autonomous juntas. These differences had some important long-term implications; where regular soldiers supported royal officials, governments tended to remain under Spanish rule, and where they supported opponents of colonial government, royalism retreated.

Militias generally played a lesser role. Despite being composed almost entirely of Americans, they were rarely a key force in politics. Buenos Aires was the exception.

The city had large, well-organized militias, which had already played a role in war and politics during the British invasions and were in 1810 mobilized to an unusual degree, far outnumbering the city's regular forces. While the regular army garrison counted only some 371 men in 1810, the militias numbered eight times as many, at nearly 3,000 men.[51] At first, the viceroy did not doubt their loyalty; when he needed forces to crush rebellion in Chuquisaca in 1809, he sent militia units from Buenos Aires. They were, however, less reliable in the political crisis of 1810. Indeed, thanks to the decisions of the creole militia officers, viceregal government was easily overturned, and Montevideo might have gone the same way had it not been for the prompt action of local commanders who mobilized soldiers and sailors to support the city's loyalist junta.[52] In Mexico, the position of the militias was much more mixed. Some supported rebellion and joined Hidalgo's insurrection; others remained firmly loyal to the crown and played a part in counterrevolution. On the whole, militias did not tip the balance one way or the other, rarely playing a key role in defending royalist officials or establishing juntas.

This does not mean that decisions made by army and militia officers determined the future of American governments. The key political decisions were taken by local elites, and it was their ability to mobilize support that decided whether Spain's authority was sustained or subverted. Nonetheless, officers and soldiers played a significant part in deciding contests for power in 1810 because, although their forces were small, their concentration in leading cities, especially capitals, meant that they could exercise a disproportionate influence over political decisions taken by both governments and their opponents. What, then, shaped the positions and behavior of these units, and why did they fail to provide unswerving support for Spanish government?

A possible explanation is that variations in army loyalty to Spain were related to the social composition of garrisons and their officers' relationship to local elites. All major garrisons had their quotients of regular soldiers from Peninsular Spain, especially officers, who might be expected to remain loyal to Spain. However, the majority of soldiers and many middle-ranking and junior officers were American-born and often had ties to the communities in which they served. A leading historian of Spanish American armed forces suggests that their political behavior in the crisis of 1810 reflected the balance between Spaniards and Americans.[53] Where Americans were preponderant, the behavior of officers and soldiers was strongly influenced by the political postures of the local creole elite. By contrast, cities where Peninsular officers were close to the political command tended to be less likely to break with established Spanish authority, especially where the existing authorities enjoyed support from creoles.

It would, however, be simplistic to assume that officers' origins were the sole determinant of their political allegiance in 1810. Like their peers in the bureaucracy and the Church, officers had identities other than those derived from place of birth; they had ties to particular cities, local networks of kin, bonds to their companions in military units, and, in the case of the pardos, to their own communities. They were, moreover, faced with circumstances that made their position more complicated than that of soldiers in Spain. In Spain, army officers chose between the intrusive, foreign King Joseph and the Spanish government that represented Ferdinand VII. In Spanish America, on the other hand, army officers, like their civilian counterparts, faced a more subtle choice. Should they accept the regency's claim to inherit the authority of the king, or should they side with Americans, who also claimed the right to exercise sovereignty in the name of the absent king? As both sides presented themselves as supporters of Ferdinand VII and both called themselves "patriots," the choice was not easy.

The Captaincy General of Caracas provides ample demonstration that the officer corps did not always split along a simple creole/Peninsular dividing line. There, the officer corps had not been heavily Americanized in the late eighteenth century, and yet both Peninsular and creole officers abandoned their commander and supported the Junta of Caracas in 1810. The first to transfer their loyalty to the new regime were the garrisons of the province of Caracas where the number of Peninsular officers was highest; Maracaibo, on the other hand, remained loyal to government in Spain even though nearly all its officers were Americans. In Cumaná, Peninsulars joined creole officers in supporting the Junta of Caracas, while Guayana, where numbers of creole and Peninsular officers were about the same, opposed the junta and remained true to the regency.[54]

According to Antonio Cortabarría, the Spanish envoy to Venezuela in 1810, the disloyalty of Peninsular officers in Caracas was due to their ties to *caraqueño* society; their marriages to local women and positions as local landowners, he observed, made them pay more attention to family and property than their duty.[55] This is, however, only a partial explanation, for, as a modern study tells us, we must also take account of differences in rank and, by extension, differences in officers' economic standing and career opportunities.[56] In Caracas, the highest-ranking army officers—brigadiers, colonels, and lieutenant colonels, who were sat alongside the upper echelons of the royal administration—were invariably loyal to the crown. The middle and lower ranks of officers—the captains, lieutenants, sub-lieutenants—were, whether they were Peninsulars or creoles, more likely to go over to the junta. And as these were the men who held direct command of troops through their leadership of companies, they had the greater influence over the common soldiers. Among the creole officers, social connections with civilians who supported the junta no doubt played its part, but there is good reason to believe that poor pay and promotion in the royal army undermined the allegiance of both creoles and Peninsulars, especially when the new government promised better. Under Spanish rule, Peninsular officers who were still connected to Spanish regiments had the best chances of promotion, while those who had long service in Venezuela, whether creole or Peninsular, had far fewer opportunities to achieve upward social mobility or good pay. Indeed, middle-ranking and junior officers saw their pay fall behind as costs of living rose at the turn of the century. When presented with an opportunity to improve their social and economic position, these officers, both Peninsular and creole, gave their allegiance to a junta that promised a better future.[57]

Another factor that complicated the position of army officers in Caracas was the conciliatory position taken by the captain general and governor, Vicente de Emparán. When he replaced Casas as captain general in May 1809, following Casas's arrests of leading creoles, Emparán presented himself as a mediator between political opponents.[58] He strongly criticized the audiencia for its repressive policy and advised the Spanish government that Caracas would remain in a "dangerous situation" while creole notables were kept under arrest, because their families had great influence over the people. He also noted that there was growing dissent among the "people of colour," and pointed out that this held great dangers for a province where such people outnumbered whites by a ratio of eight to one.[59] Clearly, Emparán believed that the use of force was counterproductive and preferred appeasement to intimidation.[60] This preference for political negotiation over military action was later identified as a cardinal error. For although he had a company of grenadiers from the Regimiento de la Reina in Caracas ready to act on his behalf, Emparán's willingness to negotiate allowed his enemies to isolate, then arrest him, opening the way to the removal of other leading officials. A later captain general, Juan Manuel de Cajigal, blamed Emparán for his inaction at a crucial moment, when "the Captain-General's slightest movement, his simplest order, his smallest gesture" would have stopped his opponents.[61] In fact, Emparán's position was almost certainly more difficult than Cajigal allowed. At the time of his arrest, Emparán knew that he had lost the support of *caraqueño* notables, some of whom were officers of the Aragua Valley militias, who had forces that they could turn against him. At the same time, he may have lacked confidence in the loyalty of the garrison's officer corps because of the animosities created by his expulsion of some of its leading officers in March 1809.[62]

Once Emparán had been arrested, the junta expelled senior officials and military officers and secured the allegiance of middle-ranking and junior officers by promoting them to the posts made vacant by the removal of the brigadiers, colonels, and lieutenant colonels.[63] These promotions, together with a doubling of pay for the common soldiery, were a powerful lure to officers who had few opportunities for promotion and had seen their social and economic status decline. In short, the garrison had not given active support to either side: it remained on the sidelines when the captain general did not call for armed support and then accepted a junta that quickly took steps to ensure its loyalty by improving officer pay and position.

Explaining the stance of the military in 1810 cannot, then, rest solely on analysis of the social composition of colonial armies and their officer corps. Nor does attention to institutional divisions within the officer corps offer a sufficient explanation of the positions taken by garrisons. For, although the problems of pay and promotion found in Caracas were no doubt also found elsewhere, not all garrisons split along the lines of rank or saw junior and creole officers default on their loyalty to the crown. On the contrary, for every garrison that accepted the authority of a junta, there was another that remained loyal to Spain. In Mexico and Peru—as well as in several provinces of the viceroyalties of New Granada and Río de la

Plata—officers remained loyal to the old regime and were indeed soon involved in fighting against those who rebelled against the regency.

There are good reasons to suppose that the decisions taken by army officers depended to a great extent on those made by leading government officials and urban elites. The general picture suggests that where elites accepted and defended existing colonial governments—as in Lima and other cities of Peru or in New Spain's capital and several important cities such as Puebla, Veracruz, and those of the Mexican south—military men tended to remain loyal to the established government. Where the civilian elites made decisive moves to establish autonomous juntas—as in Caracas, Cartagena, or Bogotá—they were invariably joined by some or all of the local officer corps.

Differences in army responses to the imperial crisis might therefore be best understood in terms of the overall command structure of colonial governments and armies. Unlike Britain's army in its American colonies at the time of the American Revolution, which had come under the single, centralized command of a British general, Spanish forces in America were divided between several commanders, all of whom also held civil posts. Viceroys, presidents of audiencias, and some governors were captains general and, as such, held overall military command in the regions under their civil jurisdiction. If these civil officials were removed and replaced by a junta, the result was often military paralysis, as army officers looked to the new government as their source of authority. This had happened in Spain immediately after the French invasion in 1808, and the experience was repeated, albeit in different circumstances, in several regions of Spanish America in 1810.

Where this paralysis occurred, it did not persist for long. While some officers and their troops went over to new governments, others resisted and rallied to the royal cause. Thus, from 1810, Spain's American armies tended to bifurcate, as two opposing sets of forces emerged from the military body put in place by the Bourbons: one sided with the groups who pursued autonomy and independence; the other remained committed to undivided Spanish sovereignty, exercised from the Peninsula. In short, the armed forces, which the Bourbons had created to shield Spanish sovereignty and authority, turned into the nuclei of armed forces that were to fight on opposing sides in the internal wars that extended for a decade and more after 1810.

Notes

1. E. Christiansen, *The Origins of Military Power in Spain, 1800–1854* (Oxford: Oxford University Press, 1967), pp. 10–12.
2. Antonio Moliner Prada, "El movimiento juntero en la España de 1808," in *1808: La eclosión juntera en el mundo hispano*, ed. Manuel Chust (Mexico City: Fondo de Cultura Económica, 2007), pp. 51–79.
3. José M. Portillo Valdés, *Crisis atlántica: Autonomía e independencia en la crisis de la monarquía española* (Madrid: Marcial Pons, 2006), p. 56.
4. For a description of the different juntas' composition, see Moliner Prada, "El movimiento juntero," pp. 62–8; also Antonio Moliner Prada, "De la Juntas a la Regencia. La difícil articulación del poder en la España de 1808," *Historia Mexicana* 58, no. 1 (2008): pp. 143–64.

5. Esdaile, *Peninsular War*, pp. 37–60; Miguel Artola, *La España de Ferdinand VII* (Madrid: Espasa Calpe, 1999), pp. 107–9. For a more detailed account of the organization and activities of the army in 1808–9, see David Gates, *The Spanish Ulcer: A History of the Peninsular War* (London: Allen and Unwin, 1986), pp. 50–81.

6. Esdaile, *Peninsular War*, pp. 71–86; Artola, *España de Ferdinand VII*, pp. 111–34.

7. On the British entry and early intervention, see Michael Glover, *The Peninsular War, 1807–1814: A Concise Military History* (London: Penguin Books, 2001), pp. 56–87.

8. Guerra, *Modernidad e independencias*, pp. 118–25.

9. Roberto Breña, *El primer liberalismo español y los procesos de emancipación de América, 1808–1824* (Mexico: Colegio de México, 2006), pp. 91–5.

10. Moliner Prada, "El movimiento juntero," pp. 70–4.

11. Esdaile, *Peninsular War*, pp. 109–39, 150–63.

12. Christiansen, *Origins of Military Power in Spain*, pp. 12–15. The clash of civilian and military groups continued throughout the constitutionalist period and impinged on the ability of Spain's government to fight an effective war against the French.

13. Artola, *España de Ferdinand VII*, pp. 339–50.

14. Rydjord, *Foreign Interest in the Independence of New Spain*, pp. 290–5.

15. Julián María Rubio, *La Infanta Carlota Joaquina y la política de España en América (1808–1812)* (Madrid: Biblioteca de Historia Hispano-Americana, 1920), pp. 36–8.

16. AHNM, Estado 55/1, Expediente del capitán general y virrey interino de Buenos Aires, April 4, 1807–October 5, 1809, document 1, Rio de Janeiro, March 13, 1808.

17. Ibid., document 2.

18. On Carlota's intrigues, see R.A. Humphreys, *Liberation in South America, 1806–1827: The Career of James Paroissien* (London: Athlone Press, 1952), pp. 21–36. Also Rubio, *La Infanta*, pp. 42–99.

19. John Street, "Lord Strangford and the Río de la Plata, 1808–1815," *HAHR* 33, no. 4 (1953): pp. 477–86. For a fuller account of the development of British policy in the region, see John Street, *Gran Bretaña y la independencia del Río de la Plata* (Buenos Aires: Paidos, 1967), pp. 95–136.

20. There are many examples of such declarations of loyalty and descriptions of municipal arrangements for the celebration of Ferdinand VII's accession to the throne in the Archivo Histórico Nacional (AHNM), Madrid, Estado 54.

21. Brian R. Hamnett, "Mexico's Royalist Coalition in the Response to Revolution, 1808–1821," *JLAS* 12 (1980): pp. 57–62. On interpretations of the coup and for an analysis of the investigation and indictment of Viceroy Iturrigaray, see Francisco A. Eissa-Barroso, "The Illusion of Disloyalty: Rumours, Distrust and Antagonism, and the Charges Brought against the Viceroy of New Spain in the Autumn of 1808," *Hispanic Research Journal* 11, no. 1 (2010): pp. 25–36.

22. On politics in Mexico City during 1808, see Anna, *The Fall of the Royal Government in Mexico City*, pp. 35–54.

23. Christon I. Archer, *The Army in Bourbon Mexico, 1760–1810* (Albuquerque: University of New Mexico Press, 1977), pp. 282–6.

24. Carraciolo Parra-Pérez, *Historia de la Primera República de Venezuela* (Caracas: Academia Nacional de Historia, 1959), 1, pp. 311–38. For further detail and a reaffirmation that the juntistas aimed to defend Spanish rule rather than assert independence, see Inés Quintero, "La Junta de Caracas," in Chust, *1808: La eclosión juntera*, pp. 334–55.

25. Juan Vicente de Arce to Francisco de Saavedra, Caracas, November 26, 1808, AHNM, Estado 60, document 58.

26. Michael McKinley, *Pre-Revolutionary Caracas: Politics, Economy and Society, 1777–1811* (Cambridge: Cambridge University Press, 1985), p. 85.

27. Ana Frega, "La junta de Montevideo de 1808," in Chust, *1808: La eclosión juntera*, pp. 251–63.

28. On the impact of the Spanish crisis of 1808 in Buenos Aires in 1808–9, see Tulio Halperín-Donghi, *Politics, Economics and Society in Argentina in the Revolutionary Period* (Cambridge: Cambridge University Press, 1975), pp. 135–48; Noemi Goldman, "Crisis del sistema institucional en el Río de la Plata," in Chust, *1808: La eclosión juntera*, pp. 230–3.

29. For a synthesis, see Rodríguez O., *The Independence of Spanish America*, pp. 60–4; and Guerra, *Modernidad e independencias*, pp. 177–98.

30. See, for example, Margarita Garrido, *Reclamos y representaciones: Variaciones sobre la política en el Nuevo Reino de Granada, 1770–1815* (Bogotá: Banco de la República, 1993), pp. 94–109; Jaime Rodríguez O., *La revolución política durante la época de la independencia: El Reino de Quito 1808–1822* (Quito: Universidad Andina Simón Bolívar-Corporación Editora Nacional, 2006), pp. 65–70.

31. On the rebellions of Chuquisaca and La Paz, see Charles W. Arnade, *The Emergence of the Republic of Bolivia* (Gainesville: University of Florida Press, 1957), pp. 11–31; Jorge Siles Salinas, *La independencia de Bolivia* (Madrid: Mapfre, 1992), pp. 139–95. The most detailed study is José Luis Roca, *1809: La revolución en la Audiencia de Charcas en Chuquisaca y en La Paz* (La Paz: Plural, 1998).

32. Roca, *1809*, pp. 95–107.

33. On Goyeneche, who subsequently became a key figure in the War of Independence in Upper Peru in 1810–13, see Luis Herreros de Tejada, *El Teniente General D. José Manuel de Goyeneche, Primer Conde de Guaqui* (Barcelona: Oliva de Vilanova Impresor, 1923), pp. 43–50.

34. On the repression of rebellion in La Paz in 1809 and pursuit of rebels in 1810, see Andrés García Camba, *Memorias del General García Camba para la historia de las armas españolas en el Perú, 1809–1821* (Madrid: Ed. América, Biblioteca Ayacucho, 1916), 1, pp. 39–44.

35. Robert L. Gilmore, "The Imperial Crisis, Rebellion and the Viceroy: Nueva Granada in 1809," *HAHR* 40, no. 1 (1960): pp. 2–24.

36. On the role of emissaries from Spanish juntas in undermining the authority of top officials in the colonies, see, for example, Viceroy Iturrigaray's fears that Juan Jabat, the envoy of the Seville junta, was plotting against him: Archer, *Army in Bourbon Mexico*, pp. 280–1.

37. The comment of a contemporary observer in New Granada, José Manuel Restrepo, *Historia de la Revolución de la República de Colombia*, 6 vols. (Bogotá: Bolsilibros Bedout, 1974), 1, p. 117.

38. Parra-Pérez, *Historia de la Primera República*, 1, pp. 377–88; McKinley, *Pre-Revolutionary Caracas*, pp. 153–6.

39. Salazar to Ciscar, June 23, 1810, Archivo del Congreso de los Diputados (ACD), Madrid, legajo 21, Expediente no. 7: document 72.

40. Archivo General de Indias (AGI), Cuba 2130: *Testimonio del proceso de purificacion . . . al Teniente Coronel Miguel Carballo*. This document gives an extensive account of Montes's governorship and his overthrow.

41. For the city's politics in these years, see Gabriel Jiménez Molinares, *Los martires de Cartagena de 1816*, 2 vols. (Cartagena: Imprenta Departmental, 1948–50), 1, pp. 38–120. For a recent synthesis that gives due weight to the importance of the pardo militias in these politics, see Alfonso Múnera, *El fracaso de la nación: Región, clase y raza en el Caribe colombiano (1717–1810)* (Bogotá: Banco de la República/El Ancora, 1998), pp. 140–61, 175–9.

42. On New Granada in 1808–10, see McFarlane, *Colombia before Independence: Economy, Society and Politics under Bourbon Rule* (Cambridge: Cambridge University Press, 1993), pp. 324–46.

43. For a brief introduction to events in Quito, an area often neglected in the historiography of independence, see Rodríguez O., *The Independence of Spanish America*, pp. 144–50; on the military action in Quito organized by the Viceroy of Peru, see Fernando Díaz Venteo, *Las campañas militares del Virrey Abascal* (Seville: Escuela de Estudios Hispanoamericanos, 1948), pp. 81–111.

44. Simon Collier, *Ideas and Politics of Chilean Independence, 1808–1833* (Cambridge: Cambridge University Press, 1967), pp. 44–57.

45. Contemporary reports of these plans are reproduced in J.E., Hernández y Dávalos, *Historia de la Guerra de Independencia de México*, 3 vols. (Mexico: José M. Sandoval, 1878), 2, pp. 63–72.

46. On the conspirators of Valladolid and Querétaro and their plans, see Hugh M. Hamill, *The Hidalgo Revolt: Prelude to Mexican Independence* (Gainesville: University of Florida Press, 1966), pp. 97–116.

47. Guerra, *Modernidad e independencias*, pp. 116–33.

48. Ibid., pp. 353–5.

49. Ibid., pp. 68, 71.

50. Brigadier Agustin Garcia Carrasquedo to Director General del Real Cuerpo de Artilleria, Philadelphia, June 13, 1810, SHM, Ministerio de Guerra, Ultramar Caja 129.

51. Albi, *Banderas Olvidadas*, p. 53.

52. John Street, *Artigas and the Emancipation of Uruguay* (Cambridge: Cambridge University Press, 1959), pp. 113–17.

53. Marchena Fernández, *Ejército y milicias*, pp. 273–6.

54. Gary Miller, "Status and Loyalty of Regular Army Officers in Late Colonial Venezuela," *HAHR* 66, no. 4 (1986): pp. 667–96, especially p. 695.

55. Antonio Ignacio de Cortabarría to Secretario del Despacho de Gracia y Justicia, Cadiz, August 21, 1812: in James F. King, "El comisionado regio don Antonio Ignacio de Cortabarría y la primera república de Venezuela," *Boletín de la Academia Nacional de la Historia* 37, no.146 (1954): Apendice documental 2, pp. 172–3.

56. Miller, "Status and Loyalty of Regular Army Officers."

57. Ibid., pp. 685–96.

58. For Emparán's conciliatory attitude, see the letter he wrote at the time of his appointment in early 1809: Archivo Histórico Nacional (AHNM), Madrid, Estado 60, document 72.

59. Vicente de Emparán to Crown, Sevilla, March 9, 1809: AHNM, Estado 60, no. 72.

60. On Emparán's policies, see Parra-Pérez, *Historia de la Primera República*, 1, pp. 367–71.

61. Juan Manuel de Cajigal, *Memorias del Mariscal de Campo Don Juan Manuel de Cajigal sobre la revolución de Venezuela* (Caracas: Archivo General de la Nación, 1960), p. 35.

62. Thibaud, *Repúblicas en Armas*, pp. 46–52.

63. Parra-Perez, *Historia de la Primera Republica*, 1, pp. 379–92.

3
PATHS TO WAR

The crisis of Spain's empire in 1810 contrasts sharply with the crisis of the British empire in 1776. In the latter, a group of North American colonies engaged in protracted disputes over their respective rights to authority until, after these disputes had escalated into violence in 1775–6, colonials joined together to declare a republic and fight for their independence. Although hopes of reconciliation persisted and colonials divided over their allegiances, the lines were clearly drawn. The American rebels affirmed their sovereignty by creating their own provincial governments, which in turn sent deputies to the Continental Congress. While the Continental Congress sought to unite opposition to Britain, it also created a unified military command, pooling provincial forces in the Continental Army under General Washington. Whitehall, on the other hand, responded to the colonial challenge by aiming to overcome the rebellion with overwhelming force. Britain, then at the meridian of its colonial power in the West, mounted a massive array of armed forces to assert its political authority. In late 1776, about two-thirds of the British army were deployed across the Atlantic: over 36,000 regulars, plus some 10,000 German troops, moved to North America, ready for large-scale, transregional campaigns. Supported by 70 naval vessels—about half the fighting ships of the large British navy—this represented the "largest projection of seaborne power ever attempted by a European state."[1] Thus, the political crisis shifted into an arena for war in 1776 when the British government determined that it would crush colonial defiance by an unprecedented use of force.

The Spanish crisis was of an entirely different kind. Its origins were external, and its first effect was to provoke Spanish Americans to affirm their loyalty to the captive monarch. It was only when Spain's survival was put in serious doubt by the French occupation that members of the American elites established their own autonomous governments. Even then, their claims were limited. The juntas refused to recognize the Regency on the grounds that it lacked legal standing, and they justified their seizure of power as consonant with Spanish law and po-litical traditions. Far from being breakaway movements seeking separation from the monarchy, they presented themselves as temporary depositaries of sovereignty, loyal to Fernando VII against the French tyrant and desiring independence from France, not Spain. The juntas were, moreover, far from presenting a united front of colonies against the metropolitan power. Like the Anglo-American colonies in North America a generation earlier, those who opposed the metropolitan govern-ment tried to form confederations within and between provinces. However, their vision was to retain the unity of existing administrative entities rather than join-ing together in war against the king, and this, together with the great distances that separated the colonial capitals, made an integrated "continental" movement inconceivable.

The rupture of Spain's relations with its American possessions did not, then, begin with transcolonial political organization against Spain. Nor did it lead to im-mediate armed conflict. This was partly because neither side took up arms against the other: the juntas were usually established with little violence and had no in-tention of making war on Spain, which was not yet regarded as an enemy. The government in Spain, on the other hand, had no military means to oppose them. Confined to the precincts of Cádiz, the beleaguered Regency was barely able to assert its authority at home, let alone project military might across the Atlantic. Unlike Britain, which was at the apogee of power when it went to war with its colonies in 1776, Spain was at its nadir in 1810, and had very few military or naval assets to spare for armed operations in Spanish America.

Why, then, were Spain's major colonies soon embroiled in wars? A key reason was that, though Spain was itself in military retreat and institutional disarray in 1810, substantial parts of the Spanish state in America remained intact. Loyalist governments were still in place in the viceroyalties of New Spain and Peru, and loyalist enclaves continued to mount resistance against the juntas established in the ex-viceroyalties of New Granada and Río de la Plata. Thus, despite Spain's weak-ness at the center, the new government in Cádiz was not entirely incapable of ex-ercising authority on the colonial peripheries. It did not see itself as making war on its American colonies but as restoring order in the face of rebellion, with support from surviving colonial governments and loyalist allies.

Understanding the movement towards war in the Americas thus requires at-tention to Spanish policies. Indeed, an important strand in the historiography of American independence—beginning with the Conde de Toreno, a contemporary liberal statesman—has attributed much of the responsibility for the loss of empire to the errors of governments in Spain. According to Toreno, Spain's politicians and state functionaries retained an outlook that was ultimately detrimental to the authority of Spanish state. Accustomed to seeing Spain's relations with America as those of a conquering and hegemonic power, such men refused to see that Spanish authority might be overthrown in America and were thus beguiled into policies that, by seeking to sustain that authority by force, produced fruitless and ultimately self-defeating conflict.[2] Toreno, of course, wrote with the benefit of hindsight and may have exaggerated the role of government at the center. As a Spaniard writing in Spain for a Spanish public, he tended to underestimate the significance of American actors in the crisis of the empire; as a liberal, he was naturally inclined to see policy errors as the mistakes of authoritarian government. His observations nonetheless carry some force. For although it was not the sole agent in developing conflict with the colonies, Spanish government was a key player in the politics of imperialism and independence after 1810, exercising power through its colonial surrogates, seeking to win hearts and minds by promises of reform, and, where it could, projecting military power to defeat American dissent. To understand how and why Spain and America entered into wars in the years after 1810, we must therefore take account of Spain's attitude towards the breakaway movements of 1810, the tenor of its policies towards them, and the consequences of those policies.

The Spanish Cortes and the American Rebellion

Recent studies suggest that the Regency blundered into war due to lack of information at the center and confused policy-making, then became committed to the pursuit of war when the Cortes wasted opportunities for compromise and reconciliation.[3] This is a persuasive interpretation. It is certainly clear that, in 1810, Spain's crumbling government was unable to exert much direct influence on American affairs. The Council of the Indies—the body traditionally responsible for advising on American affairs—had disintegrated when the French occupied Madrid, along with the other state councils, and in July 1809, the Central Junta had, as an emergency measure, hastily assembled a "Unified Council of Spain and the Indies" (the *Consejo Reunido*) from members of the four major state councils.[4] It was to this body that the Regency turned for advice when news of the first American rebellion, that of Caracas, arrived in early July 1810, and it was from this body that the first official response towards colonial rebellion emerged in a memorandum of July 12, 1810, concerning the action that should be taken to restore Spanish government in Caracas.[5]

This early policy statement about how to deal with American rebellion reflected the uncertainties of the time. The council did not know precisely what was happening in Caracas and was willing to acknowledge that the Caracas rebels might have acted in the mistaken belief that Spain had been taken over by Napoleon. For this reason, it favored conciliation, though without precluding the use of coercion. The council therefore recommended that one of its own members act as the *comisionado regio* (royal envoy) to deal with Caracas. Antonio Cortabarría was duly sent to Puerto Rico with instructions to negotiate with the rebellious provinces while also preparing to mobilize soldiers from the garrisons of Puerto Rico, Havana, Santo Domingo, and Cartagena in case they were not amenable to persuasion. Cortabarría was ordered to inform the *caraqueños* that there was a legitimate government in Spain and that disloyalty to this government would be punished. He was also told to collaborate with the governor of Puerto Rico and the recently appointed captain general of Caracas, Fernando Miyares, in preparing for a military strike and a naval blockade of the province of Caracas, should the junta fail to recognize the government in Spain.

This "carrot and stick" strategy did not take immediate effect. Cortabarría was delayed at Cádiz for two months by lack of resources and transport and did not arrive in Puerto Rico until mid-September 1810; many months then passed before he could take any effective action, using a few ships to blockade Venezuelan ports from January 1811, a task that was made more difficult by the need to avoid clashes with British vessels.[6] Armed confrontation between Regency Spain and the Junta of Caracas was thus avoided, despite the regents' determination to enforce their authority.

The difficulties that caused such delay did not, however, impede the formulation of a more generally aggressive policy towards Spanish American rebels. For while the Regency was formulating its first attempts to contain American rebellion, bad news from America accumulated. In October 1810, for example, the Spanish government received a full report on the May Revolution in Buenos Aires from the *oidors* (judges) of the audiencia, whom the junta had expelled together with the viceroy. They collectively urged the Regency to take immediate action to reimpose government in Buenos Aires, recommending as a first step the appointment of a new viceroy and his dispatch to Montevideo with troops, good officers, and 1,500 muskets. Meanwhile, the acting viceroy at Montevideo was to try to cajole the junta into accepting his authority and, if this failed, make arrangements with officials in the interior to reimpose Spanish rule by force. Such means might well be necessary, the oidors believed, because the "factious" in Buenos Aires wanted independence and were currently showing a great interest in the Constitution of the United States.[7]

The fiscal of the Regency Council concurred. On November 14, 1810, he advised the regents to wait to see whether official news of the installation of the Cortes would persuade the junta's members to end the "vicious system which they have established." In the meantime, the regents should prepare for war, since Spain could neither tolerate the secession of Buenos Aires nor leave unpunished outrages against its officials and violations of the law. Thus, the fiscal supported the recommendation that a viceroy be sent to Montevideo, together with the audiencia judges and "the number of troops which our current situation allows," in readiness for reimposing Spanish sovereignty.[8]

The regents' initial reaction to rebellion in Buenos Aires reflected the same ambiguity displayed in their policy towards the Junta of Caracas. Their instinct was to reimpose authority by force, spearheaded by a new viceroy using Montevideo as his political and military base. Governor Elío of Montevideo was appointed to the viceregency and issued with instructions to resolve differences between Buenos Aires and Montevideo, to impede Portuguese meddling, and to alert the public to the existence of a legitimate government in Spain by means of a general proclamation that appealed for their patriotic solidarity in the struggle against Napoleon.[9] Thus, the Regency again allowed for the possibility that the overthrow of the existing authorities stemmed from misunderstanding about events in Spain and might be mended as soon as porteños were aware of the existence of the Cortes. On these grounds, it instructed Elío to give Buenos Aires every chance to accept his authority before taking any military action.

At the outset of Fernando VII's interregnum, then, Spanish policy was deeply ambiguous, reflecting the two very different views of events in America propagated by officials, politicians, and the press. In one version, the American juntas were temporary aberrations, amenable to reconciliation with the monarchy. According to the other, they were challenges to Spanish sovereignty, which harbored ambitions for independence and consequently deserved to be crushed by force.

At first, the optimistic reading of events in America dominated policy. The Regency certainly had good reasons for caution: it lacked clear information, the transmission of news was slow, and, preoccupied by events at home, government had scant means to implement an interventionist strategy in its overseas territories. Moreover, throughout the early months of colonial crisis, the belief that Spain might recuperate its authority in America by peaceful means was fortified by the behavior of Britain, its new ally.

Previously a predator, Britain now proclaimed itself Spain's faithful friend. The transformation augured well for Spain, since it spelled an end to British efforts to subvert Spanish rule by supporting American separatists. Those tactics were now abandoned for a neutral position. On receiving news of events in Caracas from its own colonial officials in the Caribbean, ministers in London made a decision in June 1810 which announced Britain's new approach to Spanish America. After reading the dispatch from Governor Layard of Curacao on the Caracas Revolution, one British minister, Lord Harrowby, privately advised that it should be left to run its course. It was, he declared, the "the opening of a great Drama," on which "the curtain is indeed drawn up a little sooner than we expected: but all the materials of the Play have long been in preparation." His advice was: adopt the role of onlooker, neither encouraging the immediate independence of any Spanish colony nor discounting eventual independence. Lord Liverpool, secretary of state for war and the colonies, was of like mind, and this approach duly became the basis of public policy. On June 21, 1810, Liverpool made it clear to the Spanish government and the British government's own officials in the West Indies that Britain supported the integrity of Spain's empire and hoped that reconciliation and reunification might be achieved by negotiation.[10]

British policy was shaped by two main concerns. One was to sustain Spain's resistance to Napoleon and to prevent France or any other power from benefiting from the crisis in Spanish America; the other was to extract the maximum benefit for British merchants from the new possibilities for trade with the Spanish possessions. To achieve these goals, British ministers offered in May 1811 to mediate between Spain and its rebellious colonies, in return for commercial privileges. However, though mediation appealed to those members of the Cortes who favored a negotiated solution, the project foundered in 1812 because Britain refused to contribute men and arms to Spanish military reconquests, while Spain refused commercial access to Mexico. When Castlereagh put forward a compromise proposal in the summer of 1812, this did no better. Now the Cádiz Constitution had been published, Spain contended that its colonies had complete equality and needed no negotiations. Moreover, Spain continued to reject the argument that, as an ally who provided armies and subsidies, Britain deserved access to Spanish colonial resources.[11]

Britain's outward display of diplomatic solidarity strongly influenced Spain's initial responses to rebellion in the Americas, principally because it provided assurance that Britain would leave Spain to solve its own problems. Of course, Spaniards suspected British intentions: Britain had long coveted legal access to Spanish American markets and resources, and although British ministers refused to recognize the juntas of Caracas and Buenos Aires, emissaries from these juntas received a friendly informal reception in London in mid-1810. However, Spain also understood that Britain gave priority to supporting the Spanish war against Napoleon and would provide neither political succor nor military support for Spanish American dissidents.[12] So, despite its enfeebled state and preference for conciliation, the Regency was able to contemplate a military solution to the challenge from the colonies, even if it was unable immediately to implement it.

Constitutional Debate and the American Question

Was a policy of repression inevitable? Not necessarily. When the constituent assembly of the Cortes started on its inaugural sessions on September 24, 1810, new voices entered the debate about how to cope with Spain's crisis, and, as the Cortes looked beyond the task of defeating France to the more ambitious goal of establishing a constitutional monarchy, it conjured up a vision of a new political future in which Americans might happily find an equal place alongside Spaniards. The liberals who held sway in parliament boldly embarked on a political revolution, aimed at transforming the Spanish monarchy into a modern liberal state with all its key attributes: a written constitution based on the principles of popular sovereignty, individual civil rights enshrined in law, the division of powers between an elected executive, a representative assembly, and an independent judiciary, plus freedom of expression through an uncensored press.[13]

The liberal project completely changed the political climate of the Hispanic world and altered the terms of the debate about how to deal with American rebellion. Its paladins portrayed the territories of the Spanish monarchy as one people, united in a single *nación*, and sharing the same rights as citizens in a unified state.[14] Americans were therefore made free by the Cortes in the same way as Spaniards. They ceased to be subjects of kingdoms or colonies; instead, by a stroke of the constitutional pen, they became the bearers of equal rights in a single *patria*.

This message was conveyed in the Regency's famous proclamation of February 1810, when it informed Spanish Americans that they were "elevated to the dignity of free men." The Cortes repeated it in more ringing tones in October 1810, when it asserted that "the Spanish dominions in both Hemispheres are part of one and the same monarchy, one and the same nation, and one and the same family, and that . . . the natives born in the said dominions, whether European or overseas, have equal rights to those of this Peninsula."[15] And, having embraced Americans as equals, the Cortes appealed to the fraternal unity of "Spaniards" on both sides of the Atlantic and offered pardons to all those who, having rejected Spain's authority, now acknowledged it. The conclusion was clear: Americans now shared in self-government within the new state and had no need for locally improvised alternatives.

The chances that this conciliatory approach would provide a peaceful solution to the crisis seemed to be reinforced by the presence within the inaugural Cortes of a substantial body of representatives for the American provinces.[16] Their presence was palpable evidence that Spain intended to allow Americans a voice in governing the new unified state, and it also provided a phalanx of voices and votes that could influence the legislature's debates and decisions on key issues. On the other hand, the Americans were a minority in the Cortes, where two-thirds of the deputies were Peninsulars, most of whom were determined to assert Spain's ascendancy within the new state. Hence, despite invocations of unity and fraternity, there was an underlying fissure that was soon to surface in matters of principle and policy. The key issue of principle concerned equality of representation among the peoples of the monarchy, at home and overseas; the main issue of policy was how to deal with the regions in rebellion against Spain.[17]

The question of representation arose as soon as the Cortes convened and was a core issue in its debates for most of the year that followed. The American deputies immediately demanded that the American territories should be represented in the same way as those of Spain, with a deputy for each 50,000 free inhabitants. This proposal was unacceptable to most Peninsular deputies. On contemporary estimates, the American population outnumbered that of Spain; Spaniards therefore concluded that, if given equal representation, Americans would dominate the Cortes and take control of Spanish policy, an unwelcome prospect for Spaniards who believed that metropolitan control of American resources was essential to Spain's future. The conflict of views produced an uneasy compromise. The Cortes agreed that all free men should be treated as members of the Spanish nation and thus entitled to equal rights and representation as citizens; nevertheless, the constitution explicitly excluded those who could not trace their origins to either Spain or America, thereby depriving free people of color with African blood of the right to vote and keeping them off the electoral count.[18] The Cortes thus avoided full application of the principle of representation in America in order to ensure Spanish primacy. This was no doubt reasonable to the Spanish deputies, who believed that Spain had to retain a majority representation if it was to hold onto political and economic control of the empire, as well as to those who saw peoples of African descent as a potential source of conflict within their new polity. However, the constitutional provision harmed the Spanish cause in America. First, it contradicted the Cortes's assurances that all Americans were equal partners in the new Spanish monarchy and therefore had no cause to seek separation from it. Second, it allowed pro-independence creoles a chance to convince the pardos and free blacks to identify with their side in an independent patria that would offer full equality to people of all races. This was, as we shall see later, a way for the "patriots" to create a distinctive identity against the Spanish and a means to mobilize people of color on behalf of their cause.[19]

On the second question, concerning the "pacification" of regions in rebellion against the Regency, the Cortes initially took a conciliatory line, especially in its public sessions. On the rebellions, the Peruvian deputy Vicente Morales Duárez put the position succinctly. There were, he said, "only two measures available to the state in this case: the sword or the pen, the point of the bayonet or the spirit of persuasion."[20] He believed that negotiation was the only rational choice, and his belief was shared by a majority of the Cortes. There were, of course, powerful reasons for adopting this approach. It recognized the reality of Spain's military weakness; it encapsulated the liberals' belief that the offer of equal rights would reconcile Americans to Spanish rule; it fitted with the conviction, repeatedly expressed in official reports and the Spanish press, that the American rebellions were the work of a few troublemakers who represented nobody except themselves.[21] Moreover, intelligence from America suggested that peace still had a chance. Officials had reported the fervent expressions of loyalty made by Americans in 1808 and many continued to insist on their profound underlying loyalty, even in territories where dissidents had taken control. Added to this was another reason for optimism—the prospect that the concession of representation and further liberal reforms would assuage American grievances and persuade creoles that their interests were best served by maintaining ties to Spain.

The approach initially adopted by the Cortes was, then, to avoid confrontation and pursue conciliation.[22] This was not empty rhetoric but was a policy promulgated by the officials charged with reinstalling Spanish authority on the ground. Benito Pérez, the viceroy-elect of New Granada, provides a good example of the arguments deployed to cajole breakaway governments into accepting Spanish authority. After explaining that there was a legitimate government in Spain, despite news of Spanish defeats in the Peninsula, and that this government regarded Americans as an integral part of the body of the nation, Pérez urged New Granadans to recognize the Regency and accept the opportunity to be represented in the Cortes. Mexico had already done this; so too, he wrongly stated, had Buenos Aires; Bogotá, on the other hand, had behaved illegally in deposing its viceroy and audiencia and was causing dangerous division by forcing Cartagena to create its own government. If unhealed, this division would occasion a civil war and allow Bonaparte, the common enemy, to triumph in New Granada; he could then use it as a base from which to conquer other American provinces and thus destroy the "sacred religion and enviable peace from which these countries have benefitted for three centuries," as well as depriving Spain of means essential to its struggle against foreign domination. Pérez therefore appealed to the junta in Bogotá to accept the Regency's call for reconciliation on the understanding that "all that has happened will be consigned to the deepest oblivion and the just petitions of those provinces given preferential consideration."[23] For some months, Cortabarría in Caracas and Elío in Buenos

Aires also held back from military action and sought to persuade the juntas to restore Spanish administration with similar appeals to their patriotism.

The conciliatory approach did not last long. During 1811, the view that the juntas were in rebellion against Spain and could only be dealt with by force became increasingly influential in the Cortes, leading it towards a more aggressive stance and the dispatch of small military forces from Spain to America before the year was out.

Hawks and Doves: The Direction of Spanish Policy

Historians of Spanish policy in this period agree that the shift towards a military solution took place in 1811 but differ about precisely when and why the shift took place. One view is that the hawks gained ground during the secret sessions of the Cortes held during the opening months of 1811; as the Cortes received information and advice about events in America, the majority of deputies became convinced by June 1811 that peaceful reconciliation was impossible and a military solution required.[24] Another view is that the Regency and Cortes continued to cling to hopes for a peaceful settlement, possibly through British mediation, until in September 1811, the Consulado of Cádiz came up with a plan for sending troops to fight the rebels and the money to fund it.[25] A similar interpretation suggests that the choice of a military solution stemmed from the character of Spain's constitutional regime. In the first place, the Cortes was incapable of producing reforms that could satisfy American loyalist opinion in the Cortes itself, let alone the juntas in America. Second, because it was paralyzed by confusion of responsibilities for policy and incoherent management at the center, government policy for America was very vulnerable to influence from powerful private interests, notably the Consulado of Cádiz and the Spanish press, both which exercised a decisive influence in moving the Regency and Cortes onto a military track by providing the ideological and financial support for repression.[26]

If the military option was always on the agenda at Cádiz, it was because some reports from America reinforced the belief that a swift military response was the best means of dealing with dissent. During late 1810, the Regency's instinct for punitive action had been checked by the Cortes's preference for negotiation, but during 1811, the "hawks" exercised growing influence in the secret sessions of the Cortes, where reports from America were delivered and discussed. Most were written by Spaniards who were determined to present the rebellions as seditious movements led by small cliques of ambitious creoles, and thus tended to reinforce the view that armed action could restore Spanish sovereignty.[27] The first signs that the hawks were gaining ground appeared on December 30, 1810, when the Regency reported to the Cortes that the rebellions of Caracas and Buenos Aires, being seditious movements aimed at independence, could only be quelled by military action; it recommended that troops be sent from Spain for that purpose.[28] In January 1811, in an apparent effort to gather more information and develop a clearer policy, the Regency ordered the Council of the Indies to report in detail on political conditions throughout the colonies. The report was duly produced on January 30, 1811, but limited itself to descriptions that did little more than highlight the gaps in official knowledge of what was happening on the other side of the Atlantic.[29] Meanwhile, a further report was read to the Cortes on January 24, 1811, this time on rebellion in New Granada, and, with its references to the desire for independence and the outbreak of violence, reinforced the idea that Spanish military intervention was necessary to restore order.[30]

At this point, when news of Hidalgo's insurrection in Mexico had also reached Spain, the Cortes evidently began to reconsider its belief that Spain could be reconciled with the rebels. However, it still baulked at the use of force against the rebellious colonies in South America. Instead, the deputies called for more information and advice, requesting that the Regency advise on the best direction for policy while also setting up a special commission of the Cortes to propose new measures. The aggressive attitude of some of the deputies was revealed by the titles they suggested for this new body: they wanted a commission "for the American insurrections" or "for American pacification." In the end, the majority preferred the more diplomatic title of "Commission for Overseas Affairs" (*Comisión Ultramarina*), and while its five members—two peninsular and three American deputies—engaged in gathering information, the Cortes continued to maintain its conciliatory stance and prepare reformist legislation that was designed in part to reconcile Americans to the Spanish cause.

The division between hawks and doves soon resurfaced, however, and the hawks prevailed. In the secret sessions of the Cortes in early April 1811, deputies heard further reports from America that persuaded a majority to decide on April 10 that the moment for military action had arrived. As the Spanish press began to clamor for action against American rebellion, the Cortes's political options narrowed, and it became notably more bellicose.

The possibility of conciliation was not yet completely extinguished. The deputies who represented American provinces continued to argue for appeasement, and their voice had public resonance. A rambling presentation signed by 33 deputies and delivered at a secret session of the Cortes on August 23, 1811, staked out the arguments for a peaceful settlement.[31] The case was, quite simply, that Spain was at fault, not the Americans. If it was true that some Americans showed a desire for independence, the petitioners declared, this was a minority position without strong backing. The break with Spain, they argued, had been precipitated by the French invasion, which forced Americans to defend their own integrity against the threat of a French takeover, and was fuelled by experience of bad government by Spain and hopes for reform. Americans complained that, having been promised equality with Spain, they were treated with disdain. If this source of complaint were removed by reforms that allowed Americans to hold primary posts in the administration of their own countries and engage in free trade with other nations, then Americans would happily return to the loyalist cause. Military action, by contrast, would be both inhuman and inefficient and should be avoided at all costs.

This search for a peaceful solution enjoyed British support; in May 1811, the foreign secretary offered British mediation between Spain and the American insurgents.[32] The peacemakers had no effect on majority opinion in the Cortes, however, for two main reasons. First, the reforms which the Cortes had enacted had not persuaded the American rebels to recognize the constitutional regime; second, the majority of the deputies were not prepared to offer any further reforms to gain American acquiescence, nor were they ready to allow free trade with the British. Indeed, the merchants of Cádiz—always fearful of British commercial competition—were instrumental in supporting a policy of repression. When the merchants promised financial support, the Cortes approved plans in early September 1811 for a *Comisión de Reemplazos* (Committee for Reinforcements) that would finance military expeditions to America. Three months later, the new policy was carried into effect with the dispatch of the first 1,000 Spanish soldiers. The key policy-making body in Spanish government had, then, reversed plans for rapprochement with the rebel colonies by the late summer of 1811. Like the Central Junta before it, the Cortes blankly refused to acknowledge the claims for self-government demanded by American juntas and, while calling for negotiation, would accept reconciliation only on its own terms. And, with the creation of the Comisión de Reemplazos, Spain had found the means of providing military aid to the colonies without the government having to meet the whole cost. By blending government authority with private enterprise, the Regency was able to send over 1,000 reinforcements, distributed between Havana and New Spain, Montevideo and Puerto Rico, before 1811 was out, as well as another 12 expeditions of reinforcement during the remaining years of the interregnum, taking a total of over 12,000 men to various regions of royalist Spanish America.[33]

This intransigent attitude extended even to Spanish liberals who applauded the end of the old regime and the advent of representative government throughout the Spanish world. An outstanding example was Manuel Flórez Estrada, one of the leaders of the Asturian rebellion against the French, who, while in exile in London, denounced the autonomous American governments when their envoys arrived in London to seek recognition from the British government.[34] The juntas of Caracas and Buenos Aires were, he argued, illegitimate and their desires for independence unfounded, and he strongly objected to Britain's friendly reception of the envoys from Caracas. He conceded that the Central Junta had committed several serious errors, including its refusal to allow Americans to set up provincial juntas on the Spanish model; indeed, he censured the Central Junta for seeking to suppress provincial juntas in Spain itself, a policy he attributed to the conservative reflexes of its members, especially its first president, the Conde de Floridablanca.[35] But Flórez Estrada did not accept that the Central Junta's failings justified American refusals to recognize Spanish government in 1810. On hearing that the juntas of Caracas and Buenos Aires had rejected the Regency, he simply labeled them as seditious and oppressive bodies. The juntas were illegitimate, he argued, because they were based on a few families and did not express the will of the people; and, although they spoke in terms of liberty and popular sovereignty, they were oppressive because they had refused to allow neighboring provinces any rights to decide on their own allegiances and governments. Thus, using liberal arguments, Flórez Estrada depicted the juntas as illegal entities; he concomitantly criticized the British government for its willingness to receive emissaries from Caracas and Buenos Aires and to propose mediation with such rebels, since this was, he declared, analogous to Spain offering aid to foment rebellion against Britain in Ireland.[36]

This sharp opposition to appeasement of American dissidents was shared by most Peninsular liberals during the constitutionalist period.[37] Like Flórez Estrada, leading Spanish politicians clung to the opinion that the American juntas and their successors were the work of small, unrepresentative creole factions, which lacked any firm basis of support and had no prospect of permanence. This belief that the American rebellions were essentially ephemeral was, in the longer term, to have momentous implications, for it discouraged serious negotiation with American dissidents, promoted commitment to a military solution, and thus fuelled Spanish commitment to prolonged war in America.[38] But it does not mean that Spain alone was responsible for the drift towards war. For, although many American dissidents and their juntas had political views similar to those of Spanish liberals, such as Flórez Estrada, they spurned the olive branches held out by the Regency and Cortes. Instead, they decided that recognition of the Regency and Cortes meant subordination to metropolitan interests, and they saw the Cortes's refusal to negotiate on an equal footing as confirmation of a continuing Spanish authoritarianism.

These American demands for equality are clearly reflected in the position taken in a junta that initially recognized the Regency, that of Cartagena de Indias. In early 1811, the Cartagena junta declared that its future loyalty to Spain depended on the concession of equality of representation for Americans in the Cortes and recognition of the junta as an autonomous government, at least until the Cortes had framed a constitution. To justify this position, the junta argued that now "despotism" had been overthrown, Americans should make their own laws, end "military governments" by viceroys, replace audiencias and governors, and take measures to ensure that army commanders were prevented from making political use of military forces designed for external defense. If Spain was now more liberal than England, which had long allowed its colonies their own provincial governments, then at the very least the Cortes had to adopt a system of government that recognized Americans' rights to make their own laws and choose their own leaders. Anything less, the Cartagena junta avowed, "would be to re-establish the system of ancient Rome, in which citizens in the capital enjoyed full freedom, while the proconsuls and praetors devoured the provinces before returning in triumph to flout their profits."[39]

The issue that separated the Regency and the juntas was, then, essentially a constitutional question about the location of sovereignty in the absence of the king, an issue that, though it raised much contention, did not necessarily entail war. Nor was a move to war driven by a simple American opposition to Spain or hatred for Spaniards. Although Spanish Americans harbored resentments against Peninsular Spaniards, they rarely expressed a nationalistic hatred for the "other" and generally lacked the emotional motivations needed to die for a cause. They were, on the whole, ready to sustain their defiance of Spain because they believed that the international context favored their cause. After defeat in 1809–10, Spain had very few military or naval assets to deploy in Spanish America, aside from those already there, and it seemed clear that Britain would not intervene on Spain's behalf. Indeed, Britain's apparent willingness to mediate between Spain and its rebellious colonies, which implied treating Spain and the colonies as equal parties, encouraged Americans to believe that Britain might favor them. Confident that British statesmen were eager to open Spanish America for trade, the juntas of Caracas and Buenos Aires quickly sought recognition from the British government.[40] And, of more immediate importance, they had good reason to believe that Spain could take no effective military action against them without British acquiescence, since Britain commanded the seas.

In these circumstances, the chances of compromise diminished, and in early 1811, the Cortes moved away from conciliation towards repression, largely in response to the mobilization of force by American opponents. In late 1810, months before the Cortes formally adopted a policy of armed repression, the juntas of Caracas and Buenos Aires attacked cities and provinces where royalist authorities refused to recognize their authority. Even greater violence broke out in New Spain, where in late 1810, armed insurrection spread through the center and center-north of Mexico and posed a major challenge to viceregal government.

The move to war between Spain and its overseas dominions was, then, driven primarily by political divisions within American societies rather than repression from the metropolis. War arose from armed confrontations between the partisans of Spanish authority and the proponents of autonomous American governments, and once wars started, they were mainly fought among Americans. From their outset, these wars, which started in 1810–11, were dwarfed by those of contemporary Europe, including the war in Spain itself. But they were no less important. If Spanish American armies were small, so too were the populations where they fought. The shock of war was also considerable, given that these were societies that had very rarely, if ever, been exposed to warfare of the kind they experienced after 1810.

The emergence of autonomous juntas and their juxtaposition with royalist governments in America, as well as the decisions taken by the Regency and Cortes as they tried to recover Spain's undiluted authority, led to the breakdown of political relations between Spain and its overseas territories. The main cause of war was the dispute between those who defended Spain's authority, usually led by government officials, against those who claimed the right to form autonomous or independent governments. However, political disputes were not the sole ingredient of war. Once the bonds of civil order were loosened, social antagonisms also came into play as people of low social rank sought to improve their condition or vent their grievances. As the grounds of the old political order shifted, cracks appeared in the social and racial structures that ranked people according to European notions of social and racial hierarchy. Now the subordinate ranks of Spanish American societies, consisting of free people of color, Indians, and especially slaves, were drawn into politics. Indeed, slaves came to play a particularly important, sometimes crucial, role in war. This was, a recent study shows, not because they joined in Haitian-style uprisings but because they were recruited into contending armies in "the most extensive mobilization of black slaves for military purposes during the colonial period," which "in many instances . . . determined the difference between military success and failure."[41] Thus, in explaining the character and development of Spanish American wars, we must not only take account of the part played by social and racial enmities in stirring hostilities and polarizing loyalties but also consider the part played by subaltern groups in military operations.

To demonstrate the importance of wars in Spanish America during the years of Fernando VII's interregnum, we must now turn to some key questions about their spatial distribution and social contexts, and, of course, the reasons why people aligned with one side or the other. They were, as has long been acknowledged, civil wars rather than wars between Spaniards and Spanish Americans. It is true that the wealthy Peninsular Spaniards and rich creoles, who held preeminent social and political positions, tended towards royalism for fear that any substantial change might threaten their privileged place. But when we turn to the majority of Americans of all social groups, generalization becomes more problematic. Recent historiography has challenged the old belief that the lower classes were largely ignorant of, or indifferent to, the issues raised by political conflict among their social betters: we now know that peasants and plebeians became deeply engaged in political struggles in some regions, as allies for both royalists and patriots. But does this mean that we can detect patterns of allegiance related to race or class? And what of the differences between towns and countryside and the influence of local loyalties? Finally, when seeking to explain who became involved in political struggles and wars, we must also ask how war related to political developments, how it was organized and fought, and how patterns of warfare changed over time.

To answer these questions, we will now examine the major theaters of war that emerged from 1810 to about 1815, the period in which the Spanish empire entered and exited its first period as a constitutional monarchy. The overall purpose is to provide a unified account of the wars between Spain and its colonies during the constitutionalist period while also seeking to identify the distinctive features of warfare, its impact on society and politics, and resemblances and differences in the conduct of warfare in its main theaters. To do so, we will focus on the regions where political competition tipped into armed conflict in 1810–11 and led to prolonged armed struggles in succeeding years. There were three major theaters of war. First, the regions of northern South America, in Venezuela and New Granada, where political and social conflicts erupted into the vacuum left by the overthrow of royal authorities. Second, the areas of conflict in the south of the continent, where revolutionary Buenos Aires fought to overcome royalist forces in the Andes and on the Atlantic coast. Third, the regions of central New Spain, in Mexico, where the viceregal government confronted a violent plebeian insurrection that settled into a prolonged war of insurgency and counterinsurgency. Let us now examine each in turn.

Notes

1. David Hackett Fisher, *Washington's Crossing* (Oxford: Oxford University Press, 2004), p. 33.
2. See, for example, Toreno's comments on the measures the Regency took towards Venezuela: Conde de Toreno, *Historia del levantamiento, guerra y revolución de España*, 5 vols. (Madrid: Imprenta de Don Tomás Jordan, 1835), 3, pp. 445-6.
3. The significance of Spanish policy is recognized in three excellent studies of the breakdown of Spain's empire, which focus on the attributes and outcomes of policy under both the Regency and the restored monarchy: Heredia, *Planes españoles para reconquistar Hispanoamerica*; Anna, *Spain and the Loss of America*; Costeloe, *Response to Revolution*.
4. The Council of the Indies was not formally reconstituted until Sept 16, 1810. On the councils and the disruption of the old patterns of bureaucratic government in 1808–10, see Anna, *Spain and the Loss of America*, pp. 98–9.
5. Costeloe identifies this as an order of the Council of the Indies: *Response to Revolution*, p. 27–8. Anna refers to it as an order of the Council of State: *Spain and the Loss of America*, p. 97. Antonio Cortabarría, the commissioner to Caracas appointed by the body that drew up the July 12 document, refers to it as the work of the Consejo Reunido: see the instructions he gave to the captain general of Puerto Rico, published in James F. King, "El comisionado regio don Antonio Ignacio de Cortabarría y la primera república de Venezuela," pp. 156-7.
6. King, "El comisionado regio," pp. 125–40.
7. Ministros de la Audiencia de Buenos Aires to Consejo de Indias, Las Palmas, 1810, Archivo General de Indias (AGI), Buenos Aires 155, fols. 85–120.
8. Consejo de Estado: Expediente sobre los acaecimientos de la revolución de Buenos Aires en los meses de mayo y junio del presente año de 1810. Cádiz, November 19, 1810, AGI, Buenos Aires 155, fols. 167–177.
9. Instrucciones reservadas al General Javier Elío, AGI, Buenos Aires 40.
10. D.A.G. Waddell, "British Relations with Venezuela, New Granada and Gran Colombia, 1810–1829," in *Andrés Bello: The London Years*, ed. John Lynch (Richmond: Richmond Publishing, 1982), pp. 26–7.
11. William W. Kaufmann, *British Policy and the Independence of Latin America, 1804–1828* (New Haven: Yale University Press, 1951), pp. 66–74.
12. Wellesley told the Spanish ambassador to London of his meetings with the Caracas envoys, and the ambassador passed this information on to Spain in July and August 1810: see Iván Jaksic, *Andrés Bello: Scholarship and Nation-Building in Nineteenth-Century Latin America* (Cambridge: Cambridge University Press, 2001), pp. 30–1.
13. For an appreciation of the political revolution embodied in the Cortes, see Rodríguez O., *The Independence of Spanish America*, pp. 75–92.
14. The word *nación* has a wider meaning than that of the concept of "nation" subsequently popularized in the nineteenth century: it conveyed the sense of a history and culture shared by the realms of the Spanish monarchy rather than the idea of a people united within a single homeland.
15. Actas de las sesiones secretas, October 14, 1810: cited by Dardo Perez Gilhou, *La opinión pública española y las Cortes de Cádiz frente a la emancipación hispanoamericana, 1810–1814* (Buenos Aires: Academia Nacional de Historia, 1982), p. 95.
16. Marie Laure Rieu-Millan, *Los diputados americanos en las Cortes de Cádiz* (Madrid: CSIC, 1990), pp. 31–62.
17. Ibid., pp. 265–86.

18. Ibid., pp. 146–68. Also, James F. King, "The Colored Castes and American Representation in the Cortes of Cádiz," *HAHR* 33 (1953): pp. 33–64.
19. Marixa Lasso, *Myths of Harmony: Race and Republicanism during the Age of Revolution, Colombia, 1795–1831* (Pittsburgh, PA: University of Pittsburgh, 2007), pp. 36–49.
20. "Diario de sesiones," cited by Perez Gilhou, *La opinión pública española y las Cortes*, p. 101.
21. Costeloe, *Response to Revolution*, pp. 32–4; Perez Gilhou, *La opinión pública española*, pp. 79–85.
22. Rieu-Millan, *Los diputados americanos*, pp. 326–60.
23. Pérez to Justicia y Regimiento de. . . . Santafé de Bogotá, Merida de Yucatan, December 24, 1810, Archivo del Servicio Histórico Militar (SHM), Ministerio de Guerra, Ultramar, Mexico Caja 96.
24. The case for a decisive shift towards a military policy by mid-1811, based on records of the Cortes's secret sessions, is made by Perez Gilhou, *La opinión pública*, pp. 153–69.
25. Costeloe, *Response to Revolution*, pp. 52–9.
26. Anna, *Spain and the Loss of America*, pp. 96–9. For a similar view, less fully elaborated, see Heredia, *Planes españoles para reconquistar Hispanoamerica*, chap. 1. Also useful on the Cortes is Manuel Chust Calero, *La cuestión nacional americana en los Cortes de Cádiz* (Valencia: Fundación Instituto de Historia Social, 1999), especially chap. 1, though his account of the public debates in the Cortes from 1810 to 1813 provides a context for understanding the development of policy towards America rather than analysis of interactions with events in America or military policy.
27. These reports received from America are preserved among the papers of the Cortes and are found in Archivo del Congreso de los Diputados (ACD), Ultramar legajos 21 and 22; several are cited below. They are generally collections of letters from individuals in America reporting their observations of local and regional events rather than formal, dispassionate analyses written expressly for purpose of informing and advising the government or the Cortes. A characteristic view, portraying the American juntas as the work of a tiny minority of disaffected creoles is the "Memoria fiel de las turbulencias que la provincia de Venezuela ha sufrido por la ambición e inquietud de quatro familias de su capital Caracas empeñadas en dominar aquel distrito" in "Causas de la revolucion y sucesos de Caracas," ACD, Ultramar 22, no. 1. Perez Gilhou, *La opinion pública española y las Cortes*, chap. 5, gives an account of these reports in relation to the Cortes's secret sessions of 1810–11 and argues that they helped move the Cortes towards a policy of military repression.
28. "Informe de la Regencia del Reino acerca de los primeros movimientos de las provincias disidentes de América (1810)," ACD, Ultramar 22, no. 4.
29. "Certificación de lo que resulta en la Secretaria del Consejo de Indias sobre conmociones de América, Cádiz," January 30, 1811, AGI, Indiferente 1568.
30. "Exposición del Consejo de Regencia del estado de las alteraciones del Nuevo Reino de Granada, Real Isla de Leon," January 21, 1811, ACD, Ultramar 22, no. 6.
31. "Representación de los Diputados por América, sobre los medios que deben emplearse para la pacificación de aquellos Dominios," Cádiz, August 1, 1811, ACD, Ultramar 22, no. 14.
32. Kaufmann, *British Policy and the Independence of Latin America*, pp. 66–8.
33. Most went to New Spain and Montevideo; the rest were divided among royalist strongholds in South America: Costeloe, *Response to Revolution*, pp.52–9.
34. Alvaro Flórez Estrada, *Examen imparcial de las disensiones de América con España y de los medios de su recíproco interés* (London, 1810; Caracas, 1974). This work was first published in London in 1810, to put the case against British recognition of the new juntas, especially that of Caracas.

35. Flórez Estrada, *Examen imparcial*, pp. 61–74.

36. Ibid., pp. 93–101, 113–22, 384.

37. The *Examen imparcial* was passed to the Cortes's commission of mediation on September 1, 1811, and thus entered into the debate in Spanish governing circles. See Alvaro Flórez Estrada, "acerca de las disensiones de America con España y de los medios de su recíproco interés . . . A la comisión de Mediación," Cádiz, September 1, 1811, ACD, Ultramar 22, no. 13, D.

38. The view that the juntas in America were the work of small, unrepresentative minorities is strongly represented among the reports that reached the Cortes in 1810–11, cited above from the papers in ACD, Ultramar 21 and 22. Together with other unflattering opinions on America, this view was also publicly disseminated by the Spanish press: see Perez Gilhou, *La opinion pública española*, chap. 4; also Costeloe, *Response to Revolution*, pp. 20–35.

39. José María del Real to Diputados suplentes en Cortes, Cartagena, Expediente sobre las ocurrencias de Cartagena de Indias, February 1, 1811, ACD, Ultramar 22, no. 3.

40. On the Caracas mission, see Kaufmann, *British Policy and the Independence of Latin America*, pp. 49–51. On Buenos Aires's first envoy to London, see Street, *Gran Bretaña y la independencia del Río de la Plata*, pp. 170–5. Buenos Aires tried to cultivate relations via the British ambassador to the Portuguese court in Rio de Janeiro, as well as sending envoys on missions to London in 1810–11: see Gallo, *Great Britain and Argentina*: pp. 95–6, 99–101.

41. Blanchard, *Under the Flags of Freedom*, p. 2–3.

PART II

Theaters of War in
Spanish America, 1810–15

4

CIVIC WARS AND FIRST REPUBLICS
Venezuela and New Granada, 1810–12

The origins of war in Venezuela and New Granada can, in common with other regions of Spanish America, be traced to one original source: the breakdown of authority at the center of the monarchy and the subsequent fragmentation of the system of government into divergent parts. The primary source of conflict that led to warfare was not rooted in some general American opposition to Spain or hatred of Spaniards, nor in the opposition of plebeians to the privileged. While these played their parts in fomenting discord, the conflict initially issued from the dispute between towns that defended Spain's authority and those who claimed the right to form autonomous or independent governments of their own. Then, as conflict spread and persisted, armed struggle among the white elites spread to other social and ethnic groups. Such lower-class mobilization usually began, not as spontaneous uprisings by subalterns against the privileged groups, but as offshoots of struggles among elites who competed to win popular support for their opposing causes. It was, as we shall also see, to have quite different effects in Venezuela and New Granada, depending on the social composition of the communities that were affected by war.

Venezuela: Civic Wars and the First Republic

Caracas was the first Spanish American city to reject the Regency and establish a junta chosen by and composed of its leading citizens. The new governing body, set up on April 19, 1810, under the title of "Supreme Junta and Defender of the Rights of Ferdinand VII," quickly sent emissaries to other provinces (Maracaibo, Cumaná, Margarita, Guayana, and Barinas), urging them to follow its example. This assertion of leadership flowed naturally from the leading role the city had taken during the late eighteenth century, when the city and its province had become the largest and richest administrative region of the Captaincy General of Venezuela. The province of Caracas had more than half of Venezuela's 800,000 people, produced most of its exports of cacao, indigo, and coffee, and dominated external trade. At the hub of the province, the city of Caracas housed Venezuela's main institutions of government: the intendant and captain general were installed there in 1776–7, the audiencia in 1786, and the archbishop in 1803. It was also the home of its richest landowners, merchants, and crown functionaries, and the only university in Venezuela. Venezuela was in economic terms the only Caribbean region of comparable importance to Cuba; Caracas stood to Venezuela rather as Havana did to Cuba. The white aristocracy, moreover, was as unlikely to favor revolution as their counterparts in Cuba or other Caribbean plantation economies, given that their wealth and power were built on the labor of African slaves, and they were a very small minority among the poor whites, free blacks (*morenos*), and mulattos (*pardos*), who made up most of society.[1] However, while Cuba avoided violent conflict during Ferdinand VII's interregnum, partly because the whites feared that any fissures in their authority might provoke uprisings from below, Caracas saw a rapid political development from autonomous juntas to independent republic, and, with it, a movement into a widening war between separatists and their royalist opponents.

The provincial Junta of Caracas was soon followed by others. While Maracaibo refused to repudiate the Regency and, joined a little later by Guayana, remained under royalist control, the provinces of Cumaná, Margarita, and Barinas all established their own provincial juntas.[2] Like Caracas, they were neither seceding from Spain nor adhering to the liberal principles of the American and French revolutions. Indeed, for some, the juntas were the acme of Spanish loyalism, the means by which America was to save Spain. Ignacio Alvarez, a friar who lauded the Junta of Trujillo, gave clear expression to this attitude. He described Spain as a decadent power, unable to defend itself because it had been "pervaded for over forty years with French maxims, corrupted for twenty years by Godoy's scandals, and inseminated by atheist philosophers, libertines, materialists, freemasons and Machiavellians." America, by contrast, was filled with "loyal, enlightened, truthful men of integrity, devoted to their patria, religion and sovereign." In these circumstances, his city had acted in accord with the law, following the example of the other American cities that had created juntas "with the consent of all wise, holy and politic men of both estates, ecclesiastical and secular."[3]

Although this sense of legitimacy allowed the juntas to assert their sovereignty while pronouncing allegiance to the monarchy, the notion of distinctive sovereignties also generated centrifugal forces. This was hardly surprising. Geographically, the population of Venezuela was unevenly dispersed over a large area, and its provinces had little in common with each other. Venezuelan society was, moreover, composed of communities—cities, towns, and villages—that were marked by considerable variations in social composition, economic ways of life, and experience of government, and they saw themselves as autonomous entities rather than parts of an administrative hierarchy.

When provincial juntas proclaimed their sovereignty, they affirmed their independence of both the Spanish Regency in Cádiz and the Junta in Caracas. In addition to these differences between the provinces, there were also differences within them, as towns repudiated the authority of their provincial capitals. Barcelona, for example, separated from its provincial capital of Cumaná; Mérida and Trujillo broke away from Maracaibo; Puerto Cabello created its own junta, separate from that of Caracas; the city of Coro also refused to follow Caracas and remained under its existing authorities.[4] When other juntas showed the same tendency to behave as equal sovereigns between whom any larger unity had to be negotiated in the manner of separate states, it was evident that Venezuelan cities and provinces were not going to replicate the governmental system of the captaincy general. Caracas was, however, to retain a certain primacy in the new federation that emerged. In June 1810, the Caracas junta called for the election of provincial deputies to form a Constituent Congress that would decide on a central government; once this congress was installed, Caracas's large population would ensure its preeminence among its provincial peers.

Caracas's desire to bring the provinces into a federation took it closer to war with Spain because it brought confrontation with Maracaibo and Coro, towns where royalist officials remained in control. Spain's Regency Council had taken steps to reinforce the royalist position by promoting Fernando Miyares, governor of Maracaibo, to the position of captain general of Venezuela, while placing Antonio de Cortabarría in Puerto Rico in readiness to support an attack on Caracas if needed. The junta could not leave this challenge unanswered, and, in order to placate its critics and show that it could control its own province, it decided to confront the royalist challenge by mobilizing an army against Coro.[5] This was the first step towards the militarization of the political revolution inaugurated in April 1810.

Citizen Soldiers and Civic Wars

The junta embarked on war with a set of armed forces that combined regular soldiers from the old regime with new elements formed by urban militias of "patriotic volunteers." However, the plan for the defense of Caracas drawn up in July 1810 also envisaged a new kind of military establishment. Rather than rely on a professional army, the junta exhorted its citizens to give military service as an obligation to the community, a willing contribution to the public good rather than the reluctant shouldering of an onerous imposition.[6] This reflected contemporary ideas (loudly voiced in the American and French revolutions and expressed, too, in eighteenth-century "enlightened" military thinking) about the tendency of standing armies to become instruments of tyranny because soldiers were separated from citizens and unquestioningly obedient to the constituted authority, however corrupt. The Caracas plan, like other such plans for military organization drawn up in the neighboring provinces of New Granada, reflected instead the preference for military forces manned by the citizens themselves.[7] Recruitment of the people for the purposes of political education and preservation of social discipline were, indeed, just as important as military efficiency. For, at this stage, the junta was unwilling to use unrestrained force against its rivals, perhaps because it feared that outright war might lead to social upheaval of the kind that had devastated Haiti.

In its first military campaign, Caracas used methods that reflected the new political system and its assumptions. Its offensive against Coro was undertaken reluctantly after the junta failed to negotiate a solution through the bishop of Mérida. Led by the Marqués del Toro, a young creole aristocrat whose appointment reflected his social prominence rather than any military expertise, Caracas's forces moved against Coro with the aim of intimidating the enemy into surrender. At the start of November 1810, Toro concentrated the junta's army of 2,500 forces at Carora, then spent the entire month moving artillery over difficult terrain before finally moving against Coro. On arrival, he found that the Spanish commander Ceballos had prepared a strong defense for the city, and after a halfhearted attack, he quickly withdrew. He made a reasoned defense of his decision—the heavy caliber of enemy artillery, superiority of numbers of the defenders, lack of food and water, and danger of encirclement—but the fact remained that his campaign achieved nothing.[8] Some historians blame Toro's lack of military training for his languid campaign.[9] A more plausible explanation is that this was a "civic war," which, like eighteenth-century monarchies, used military operations to pressure the enemy into capitulation rather than seeking to destroy him by the unrestrained use of force.[10] It had, in effect, been more a display of force than a serious attack, or, to put it another way, "a semiotic war, an assembly of signs aimed more at persuading the civil authorities than at destroying their armed forces."[11]

The junta's preference for using its army as a diplomatic weapon rather than a means of annihilating the enemy reflected its political ideas. It aimed at a peaceful solution by presenting itself as the legitimate defender of Ferdinand VII, avoiding any hint of division between "Spaniards" and "Americans," and seeking to end the conflict with negotiation with the royalist enclaves. The new political leadership was, moreover, reluctant to build up its army for both financial and political reasons. While the pay increases and promotions made at the time of the April coup had substantially increased the army's cost to the treasury, the Caracas junta had a politically expedient alternative at hand in the form of civilian militias. These could build on existing urban militias and had the further merit of being attuned to the new politics; the *Gazeta de Caracas*, for example, publicized the arguments of "William Burke" that North American independence proved the superiority of patriotic militias over professional armies and showed that the new South American states should create well-trained militias to defend themselves.[12] This preference for militias was to have important implications in both Venezuela and New Granada. Most juntas and their successors preferred to create small armed forces in which citizens gave military service under local command rather than building strong professional armies under a central command. One consequence was military weakness, initially displayed in Venezuela, then repeated throughout the Viceroyalty of New Granada in the years that followed.

The attack from Caracas on Coro was the prelude to further conflict. From Puerto Rico, the royal commissioner Antonio de Cortabarría declared war in

January 1811, ordering a naval blockade of the dissident provinces, issuing licenses for privateers, and sending spies and provocateurs into their territories.[13] The Spanish blockade was ineffective, and the royalists remained on the defensive in their towns, but royalist aggression accelerated the movement into civil war. Seeing the royalist towns buoyed up by external support, their opponents in Caracas began to demand secession from Spain, and as the political divide deepened, the competing sides both began to seek popular support in order to overwhelm the other.

Race and the First Republic

The polarization of politics accelerated when proposals for an independent republic began to dominate discussion during early 1811. They emerged from the Patriotic Club, which, after its establishment by the Caracas Junta in August 1810 to encourage economic development, had been taken over by a group of white radicals who wanted independence. It wielded an influence that was disproportionate to its size, mainly because, following the arrival of Francisco de Miranda (whom the Caracas Junta reluctantly allowed to return in December 1810), it acquired a skilled and determined leadership. Miranda and his radical friends changed the scope and terms of the political debate by using the new press and public meetings to widen their support, bring the pardos to their side by promises of equality, and pressure the Constituent Congress for independence.[14]

These tactics secured their immediate aim. When the issue of independence was debated in the congress, most members were persuaded to break with Spain, albeit for different reasons. The congress duly declared independence on July 5, 1811, principally on the grounds that the French usurpation had broken the pact that bound Venezuela to Spain and thus left a government that had no consent from the Venezuelan people.[15] In 1812, it agreed on the constitution of the new "American Confederation of Venezuela," which grouped the autonomous provinces into seven independent sovereign states, while awaiting the later incorporation of those still under royalist control. The federal government in Caracas had a congress and senate, promised equal rights to all, abolished the slave trade, and ended legal discrimination against pardos.

This radical change did not, however, produce the fraternal republic promised. On the contrary, it weakened support for the republic among whites without firmly anchoring it in the allegiance of the free coloreds. Whites were angered by the pardos' assertions of their equality and feared that the new regime might go even further by emancipating slaves; pardos, on the other hand, were frustrated by the failure of the republican constitution to deliver what its proponents had promised. Although the Venezuelan Constitution of 1812 ratified the abstract principle of equality among all free citizens, it diminished pardo standing by requiring that voters and officeholders had to fulfill property qualifications.[16] Thus, having raised pardo expectations, the republic failed to fully satisfy them. Moreover, the formalization of the *Ordenanza de los Llanos* by the republican government made it clear to the *llaneros* (peoples of the plains) that their interests were to be subordinated to the great landowners of Caracas, for the new law stipulated that *llaneros* could not intrude into private land to graze or hunt the cattle they depended upon.

The failure to satisfy the pardos' aspirations was particularly damaging for the republic because it antagonized people who might otherwise have been allies. For although whites refused to acknowledge it, equal rights for pardos did not necessarily endanger the existing social order. That pardos wanted equality with whites did not mean that they sought social revolution, still less that they favored slave emancipation. Their ambition tended, as under Spanish rule, towards improvement of their position within the existing social hierarchy rather than equal rights for all. However, any modification of the social hierarchy was anathema to most whites, who were determined to defend their position of superiority. The new constitution thus lacked a broad social base.

The scope for social conflict within Venezuela's first independent state was further widened when the royalists recruited black slaves to fight for their cause. Ready to use any means to restore Spanish government, royalist leaders began in 1810 to actively encourage uprisings among pardos and slaves and to justify their rebellions as loyalty to the king. Some years later, José Heredia, an audiencia lawyer and leading royalist, denounced his fellow royalists for such behavior, arguing that their exploitation of the race issue was to blame for much of the subsequent violence: "We have," he said, "greatly lamented the results of these errors . . . because if Venezuela becomes another Algiers of *zambos* and blacks we will undoubtedly owe it to the seeds sown in this first period, and to the celebrity accorded the revolts, robberies and deaths which were carried out in the name of Ferdinand VII."[17]

The First Republican War

The use of military power assumed a new significance when the royalist enclaves on the coast began to draw support from outside Venezuela. In early 1811, the Spanish authorities in Puerto Rico stiffened royalist resistance at points west and east of Caracas with injections of men and materiel. In the west, at Coro, the Spanish navy captain Domingo de Monteverde arrived in March from Cuba, with some 120 soldiers for Governor Ceballos to add to his existing troops; two months later, Coro was further strengthened by the import of supplies in Spanish ships. To the east, the royalists also reinforced their position at the start of July by sending a flotilla from Puerto Rico to disembark a large force at Cumaná. Although repelled by local militias, this force strengthened the royalist cause by sailing south to the Orinoco to support the loyalists of Guayana. Thus, although Spain was unable to launch a direct military assault on the republic, the links between royalist bases on the coasts and islands of the Caribbean provided the network of resources needed to carry on a war against Caracas, which was thereby forced to sustain expensive armed forces at times when changes of regime made tax collection difficult.

The threats from royalists to the west and east were compounded by dangers closer to Caracas itself when, in mid-July, a small royalist rebellion broke out in the Sabana del Teque among Canary Islanders, creoles, and pardos opposed to the Caracas regime. Although the uprising was easily defeated, the government carried out a brutal repression in which rebel leaders were executed and their heads put on public display, an exercise that tarnished the republic's reputation without intimidating opponents. Indeed, there was a more serious upsurge of rebellion in the city of Valencia on July 11, 1811. Creoles, pardos, and Canarians rallied again in the name of Ferdinand VII, and this time they were joined by slaves from the Barlovento region, who wanted freedom in return for their loyalism. Governor Ceballos sent soldiers from Coro to support the rebellion, and royalist officials promptly rewarded the pardos with a promise of legal equality and slaves with a commitment to abolish slavery.[18]

Congress responded with a military crackdown. It replaced the ineffectual Marqués del Toro as army commander and appointed Francisco de Miranda to lead a 2,600-strong military expedition against Valencia. Miranda was an obvious choice, despite some misgivings about his politics. His training as an officer in the Spanish army, experience as a general in the French army, and political commitment to the republic meant that, although some members of the government distrusted him as a political extremist and social upstart, he now finally began to achieve the recognition he believed that his political and military experience deserved.

Miranda began his operation against Valencia with the usual tactic of civic warfare, using the threat of force to seek a negotiated solution. His first attack failed, however, to overcome the resistance of pardos and slaves, who held the city center, and his second attack, on August 12, 1811, took the republic closer to civil war. The republicans retook Valencia but at considerable cost; they reported 800 dead and 1,500 wounded from their army of 5,000 men after street-to-street combat against a much less numerous but very determined enemy.[19] Thus, within weeks of the declaration of independence, the republican government faced a resurgent loyalism, which, fuelled by social antagonisms, turned the war of words between cities into violent confrontation between social groups. The pardos and blacks were evidently not all persuaded by the republic's promises of political equality, and they displayed their dislike of creole privilege by becoming its militant opponents. Loyalist resistance was, moreover, still entrenched in Coro and Maracaibo, which, reinforced by contacts with officials and exiles in Puerto Rico, became bases for Spanish operations against Caracas. Although their forces were small, they reinvigorated the Spanish cause. In November 1811, soldiers from Coro repelled Miranda's forces, causing losses of some 300 men in a combat where they gave no quarter. Meanwhile, in the east, royalists struck out from Guayana in September, crossing the Orinoco to attack the republic's frontier forces at Soledad.

The damage inflicted by this and other royalist raids across the Orinoco forced the republican government to send an expedition against Guayana at the end of 1811, combining forces from Caracas, Barcelona, and Cumaná. But these forces failed to coordinate, and loyalist attacks on republican territory from Guayana continued, even reaching as far as the southern fringes of the province of Caracas at San

Fernando de Apure.[20] Independent Caracas was thus hemmed in by increasingly active opposition in its western, eastern, and southern boundaries.

The threat of military aggression against the republic might have been less serious had the new regime dealt with it more effectively. However, after briefly regaining the initiative by taking Valencia, the Caracas revolutionaries dissipated their authority. While Congress engaged in debates on constitutional issues, royalist forces encroached on two fronts. To the east, in Guayana, they defeated republican forces at Angostura in late March 1812 and took control of the Lower Orinoco, together with a considerable haul of boats, arms, munitions, and prisoners. In the west, royalist officials at Coro and Maracaibo opened a new offensive against Caracas, even though they had only small numbers of poorly equipped troops. In March 1812, Governor Ceballos dispatched Monteverde from Coro with a small expeditionary force of about 230 men to support a royalist uprising in the town of Siquesique, inspired by a local priest and led by the Indian cacique Reyes Vargas. This marked the start of the royalist revival led by Monteverde. Bolstered by the Indian irregulars who joined him at Siquesique, he advanced along the coast, enlarging his forces en route with other volunteers and men pressed into service, including soldiers who deserted from the republic's forces and slaves drawn from local plantations.[21]

These military maneuvers regained the political initiative for the royalists. Monteverde had taken a forward position that allowed him to strike against the communications of Caracas, and by doing so, he presented an alternative to a republican regime, whose support was hemorrhaging on all sides. The republic had lost credibility among the whites because of anxiety over the pardos' claim for political equality while gaining little compensatory support from the pardos because, although the republic's constitution gave equal political rights in principle, the government imposed property qualifications that ensured inequality in practice. Dislike of the republic was aggravated by mismanagement of the treasury and economic difficulties. Within months, the Caracas junta had exhausted the colonial treasury, mainly as a result of doubling army pay and creating new administrative posts, and left endemic fiscal problems. The republic sought to alleviate its bankruptcy by emitting a paper currency (1 million pesos in August and another 9 million in October 1811). However, when this led to a flight of specie and breakdown of trade, it not only compounded the government's fiscal problems but also generated widespread discontent.[22] But perhaps the most important problem facing the republic was its lack of legitimacy; the royalists exploited this to the full, appealing to entrenched beliefs in a natural social hierarchy presided over by throne and altar, against the godless, alien revolution of the republicans. In the words of a Spanish proclamation: "We are going to war against Caracas to defend the Christian religion . . . Here they want to introduce French ways and we shall die to defend God's law and our King."[23]

While the political tide was moving against the republic in early 1812, its position was further damaged by an entirely unpredictable event: a great natural catastrophe that devastated the country and stunned its people.[24] The vast destruction done by the earthquake of March 26, 1812, gave fresh impetus to the burgeoning royalist cause and shifted the military balance against Caracas. Monteverde took the city of Valencia against little opposition. Soldiers who were paid with worthless paper money deserted and often joined the royalists, thus further undermining the ability of republican commanders (usually chosen for their social prominence rather than their military ability) to mount an effective resistance. The republic's government sought to compensate by investing Francisco de Miranda with emergency powers. On April 26, 1812, Miranda was appointed as Generalissimo of the Confederation, and he used his martial authority to reorganize and enlarge the army. This included recognition of the importance of slaves as soldiers: Miranda offered freedom to slaves who fought for the republic.[25]

These were new steps towards republican militarization. Although Miranda had to limit slave recruits because of objections from slave owners on his own side, the patriot army grew to nearly 4,000 men; it also became a force outside political control, under a commander who was left largely to his own initiative. Miranda seems, however, to have lacked confidence in his position. Instead of attacking Valencia or going around Monteverde's royalist flank to attack Coro, he concentrated his forces along the route between Valencia and Victoria in order to block Monteverde's advance. If in principle this seemed a sound defensive move, it was nullified when Monteverde simply sidestepped Miranda's army. Aided by local rebels, Monteverde avoided the republican enfilade and forced Miranda to fall back on Caracas.[26]

Miranda's retreat towards Caracas might have been tactically justified because it conserved his forces, but it ceded territory and made the republican capital more vulnerable to attack. At the same time, republican morale and capacity to resist the royalist advance suffered another blow when the fortress and city of Puerto Cabello fell to a royalist uprising. On June 30, 1812, royalist prisoners conspired with disaffected troops to take the fortress and then bombarded the city, forcing the republican military commander, Simón Bolívar, to abandon Puerto Cabello. Miranda, seeing the enemy strengthened by the capture of Puerto Cabello while watching his own army disintegrate through desertion, decided that the situation was hopeless. Convinced that he could not prevent Monteverde from taking the capital, Miranda negotiated terms of surrender in mid-July and prepared for exile. On June 30, 1812, the royalists occupied Caracas and ended the first republic of Venezuela.[27]

The Fate of the First Republic

Why did the republic fall? It was certainly not crushed on the battlefield. Miranda negotiated surrender without fighting, and the republic went down not with a bang but a whimper. Indeed, several of Miranda's officers blamed him for defeat. Simón Bolívar, then a junior officer in the republican army, denounced the military commander in chief for defecting with republican funds while also blaming the republic's political leaders for pusillanimity.[28] Indeed, Bolívar and a group of fellow officers were so convinced of Miranda's dereliction of duty that they handed him over to Monteverde, who ensured that he ended his days in a Spanish jail.[29]

However, if Monteverde won by intimidation rather than destruction, overcoming an enemy who had lost the will to fight, the defeat cannot be wholly attributed to Miranda. The republican government had simply not secured sufficient political support; its confederal principles ensured that the cities remained intent on their own sovereignty and failed to cooperate. At the same time, the republic failed to broaden its political base; the refusal to grant full civil rights to the pardos neglected a constituency that might have been won over by concession of the rights that the Cádiz Constitution was reluctant to concede.

Miranda's attempt to create an army also reflected public unwillingness to support the republic. He had to impose draconian discipline because the army was vulnerable to mass desertion by men who did not want to serve. His soldiers were hastily assembled forced conscripts, men who were not united by a shared identity or by hatred of a common enemy, whom they were keen to kill. On the contrary, without exposure to battle, they had no sense of solidarity or purpose, and their unreliability discouraged Miranda from attacking the enemy at an opportune moment.

Another element in Miranda's defeat was the republic's failure to win support among slaves. He had tried to change republican policy with his proclamation of May 1812, promising freedom to slaves who joined his forces, but then allowed himself to be curbed by slave owners' protests, despite the military emergency. The royalists, on the other hand, were more successful in recruiting slaves, possibly because they were more desperate to augment their numbers and hence ready to promise freedom in return for military service. The slave rebellions that broke out in the Guarico and Curiepe valleys during May–July 1812 were, it seems, incited by royalist provocateurs, some of them priests, who incited slaves to overthrow their masters and fight for the king. Here, then, was another instance where royalist ability to recruit among the populace in the name of king and religion brought significant military and political advantage. For, as the slaves swept along the coast, spurred on by the royalists, creole landowners were concerned above all to stop slave insurrections that threatened their property and might undermine the institution of slavery itself. Thus, at the very moment that Miranda was preparing a last-ditch defense of the republic, the support he needed from the propertied classes diminished; Miranda himself also became alarmed at the prospect that war might allow the slaves to run out of control, thereby destroying the very interests that the republic was committed to protect.[30] War, it seems, was imposing social consequences that far outran the boundaries of political change envisaged by the revolutionaries and acceptable to the social elites.

Evidently, much had gone wrong with the creoles' first experiment in republican government. Despite the intense propaganda of its official press, the first republic failed to attract sufficient support either within the province of Caracas or among its provincial neighbors. On the contrary, the clique that took command of government made more enemies than friends. It was committed to reform but failed to create policies that would unite elite leaders with the lower classes. On the contrary, the uprising of slaves raised the specter of a servile revolt, which, even if it was a small threat compared to the great slave rebellion that had shattered Haiti around the turn of the century, further undermined the image of the republic as a stable form of government.

The weaknesses of the new republic were undoubtedly aggravated by the earthquakes of 1812. The republican government had no answer to the immense damage done by death, destruction of property, and dislocation of the economy. Providence, it seemed, had come to Spain's defense, and the republic could only take the blame. George Flinter reported, with a certain Protestant disdain, that:

> The effect which the earthquake had on this superstitious people is truly astonishing: they looked upon it as a signal mark of the divine vengeance for their rebellion, and the priests, who were in general addicted to the royal cause, employed themselves . . . in taking advantage of their present turn, to inculcate maxims unfavourable to the independent cause . . .[31]

But superstition and scheming priests were not solely responsible for the fall of the republic. Its leaders were also to blame, as their political and military ineptitude had stripped the Caracas government of defenses that might have been much more solid. The military weakness that allowed royalism to recover, for instance, was the result of decisions taken by republican politicians. The Junta of Caracas made the first error by hesitating to crush its opponents in a preemptive strike against provincial opposition, which was still weak in the latter half of 1810. The republican government did not make the same mistake when it faced rebellion in Valencia in mid-1811. However, having crushed the resistance there, it then squandered its military advantage by allowing resistance to regroup elsewhere, so that the royalist opposition, especially at Coro, was ready to take advantage of the confusion and demoralization caused by the earthquake of March 1812. Miranda was unable to restore any military advantage, mainly because of the inadequacies of his forces but also because of his own shortcomings as a commander. This was not for lack of military experience. He had fought with the Spanish army in North Africa and Florida in the 1770s and 1780s, taken part in campaigning with the French revolutionary army in 1792–3, and held substantial commands, notably at Valmy and the siege of Antwerp, which also exposed him to the problems of governing a captured city.[32] However, if these past triumphs set Miranda apart from his contemporaries, they were of little use in Venezuela, where he was without professional soldiers and the resources needed to train and support them.

If Miranda must bear most responsibility for the fall of the republic, it is because he secretly negotiated a surrender to Monteverde. He justified this on the grounds that it would avoid useless bloodshed, but his motives remain unclear. He might have been considering a tactical withdrawal to Cartagena but, if so, did not communicate the idea to his officers. Indeed, they believed that his relationship with the British had persuaded Miranda that while Britain was Spain's ally in the war against Napoleon, it was better to be reconciled with Spain.[33]

The immediate outcome of the fall of the First Republic was to reverse roles in Venezuela. The revolutionaries who had fought against royalist insurgents now became insurgents themselves. Forced into exile, they had neither the economic nor military means to continue their war with royalists, who now had the resources of the state at their disposal. However, the republicans' determination to carry the fight back into Venezuela ensured that Monteverde's regime did not enjoy its victory for long. The First Republic had scarcely been erased when its champions presented a fresh challenge, led by the handful of revolutionaries who went into exile in 1812. Several settled in Cartagena de Indias and, by joining the army of this independent polity, were able to regroup and reorganize their struggle for power.

The republicans' ability to fight back owed much to the spirit and resolution of these few intransigents, especially to Simón Bolívar, who entered exile determined to expiate the dishonor associated with defeat and flight. The republicans were also helped by sympathetic neighbors. Bolívar and other officers from the fallen republic found a congenial refuge in Cartagena, recently declared an independent state, and their sojourn in the city allowed them to enter a new phase of war. Cartagena's government was actively engaged in fighting royalist forces on the Magdalena River and in the adjoining province of Santa Marta, while independent governments proliferated in New Granada's interior. Here, then, was a chance for the exiled republicans to open another front and to yoke the revolutions of Venezuelan and New Granadan cities to a common cause.

New Granada: Multiple Sovereigns

During 1810, New Granada followed a pattern of political development that was broadly similar to that of Venezuela. The leading authorities and institutions of royalist government (the viceroy, the audiencia, provincial governors, and other such officials) were removed and replaced by juntas, which asserted their right to govern in the absence of a legitimate king. This movement against the established authorities began at Cartagena in June and then spread to the interior. In July, provincial authorities were removed in Cali, Pamplona, and Socorro, and on July 20, 1810, the juntista movement reached its high point with the overthrow of the viceroy and audiencia in Santafé de Bogotá and the installation of the Supreme Junta of Santafé. A few cities, notably Santa Marta in the north and Popayán and Pasto in the south, remained under their existing authorities, clung to royalist rule, and resisted demands that they should follow the example of the juntas.

The fragmentation of political authority reflected the tendency of the local notables who led the juntas, to assert sovereign rights in the name of their "pueblos" and to identify the province as the principal locus of sovereignty.[34] It also mirrored a country that encompassed a set of very distinctive economies and societies, and more than one "imagined community."[35] A coastal city such as Cartagena, for example, had a very different character from the cities of the Andean interior. Cartagena and its hinterland were peopled by large mulatto and black populations, with substantial numbers of slaves, and the white elites depended for their wealth on commerce with the exterior. The Andean communities, by contrast, were largely composed of white and mestizo populations, living from agriculture for domestic use, and were more isolated from the outside world.[36] Other variations were found in the west, where substantial cohorts of slaves worked in the gold-mining districts, and in the south, where slaves were used for tropical agriculture in the Cauca Valley and mining on the Pacific coasts, or where indigenous peasants made up the majority population in the region around Pasto.

There was some basis for unity among these disparate regions, given that they had been accustomed to the overarching authority of an audiencia and viceroy based in Bogotá. But the administrative structure established under Spanish rule had also nurtured localism. Whereas Venezuela had been brought under government by intendants towards the end of the eighteenth century, New Granada retained a much older structure based on its historic provinces. There were 22 provinces of varying size and political weight in New Granada compared to the 6 provinces of Venezuela's Captaincy General, and the communities in these many provinces tended to go their own way after the crisis of 1810.

One expression of divergence came from the towns that remained under royalist rule.[37] Their dissonance was not necessarily ideological; Santa Marta's allegiance to the Regency, for example, was mainly driven by rivalry with Cartagena, its principal competitor for maritime trade.[38] Popayán's royalism must also be seen in its regional context, as an affirmation of its position as administrative capital against the attempts by Cali to challenge its authority.[39] The same was true of the city and region of Pasto, which became the main prop of royalism in the Colombian south. Its royalism was partly an expression of ideological preference for Spanish rule, but more important was the desire of local communities to defend their autonomy; the Pasto elites wanted to fend off domination by Quito or Bogotá, while Pasto's Indian villagers wanted to preserve their communities from outside interference.[40]

Another expression of divergence arose among the provinces where juntas were established. Provincial capitals competed with each other as did towns within provinces, when secondary settlements tried to assert their autonomy from provincial capitals and other leading towns. Take, for example, the province of Cartagena. As soon as government changed in the city of Cartagena, the town of Mompós declared its independence from both Spain and Cartagena, prompting Cartagena to use its regular troops to cow the city into obedience early in 1811.[41] Conflicts also quickly emerged within the provinces of the interior, where towns and villages asserted their rights to self-government.[42] The crisis of the monarchy was, in short, frequently interpreted by the cabildos of secondary towns as an opportunity to break away from their provincial capitals, joining other provinces or even trying to turn themselves into new provinces.[43] The number of juntas established in New Granada is not known exactly, but, at around 30, it was far larger than the number in Venezuela and even exceeded the number of juntas in Spain.[44]

Finally, in addition to these fissures between and within provinces, there were also divisions within juntas over key political questions. These included issues of relations with Spain and other sovereign powers and, most important, whether they should seek full independence from Spain. There were significant differences, too, over issues of internal governance, such as who should participate, how delegates

.should be selected, and what policies governments should pursue. In some cities, notably Cartagena, conflict over such issues became an acute source of division, as rival factions competed for power by mobilizing the lower classes as their allies.

Conflicts in New Granada

In the mêlée generated by the proliferation of political sovereigns in New Granada, there were some moves towards unity, driven primarily by leading citizens in Bogotá. The members of the Junta Suprema established at Bogotá in July 1810 immediately proclaimed the junta to be the "interim supreme government of this kingdom" and called on the provinces to send delegates to Bogotá in order to form a General Congress that would act as constituent assembly and legislature for New Granada as a whole.[45] When convened, the General Congress faced difficult questions over what form the government should take. While Spain called on Americans to be part of a Spanish "nation," which encompassed all subjects of the Spanish monarchy, the juntistas of New Granada applied the term "nation" to their own lands. But problems of definition remained. How was the nation constituted, and how should it be governed? Some believed that a new government should have authority over the territory of the deposed viceroyalty; some believed that all New Granada's cabildos should send delegates to a federal congress; the majority favored the creation of a union in which autonomous provinces would cede some of their sovereign powers to a federal government.

Debate over these issues promoted more discord than concord as political leaders in capital and provinces aimed for different solutions. Within the Bogotá junta itself, there were marked differences of opinion. While the leading *santafereño* families, who had manned the colonial bureaucracy, wanted to perpetuate the hierarchy of provinces that they had known, others—especially the provincial lawyers, who had a strong representation on the junta—wanted to create a federation composed of provinces of equal standing.[46] This was a division that was to have powerful effects in shaping the system of government that emerged in New Granada. On one side were those led by Camilo Torres and a group of like-minded lawyers, who saw the traditional concept of the pluralist monarchy, composed of separate but equal kingdoms united under a single king, as the basis for a confederation sovereign states formed from the old provinces, each independent of and equal to the others.[47] On the other side were those who sided with Antonio Nariño in seeing Bogotá at the helm of a centralized government, which would unite the provinces under a single directorate.[48]

These differences between "federalists" and "centralists" immediately surfaced when the Junta of Bogotá attempted to convene a General Congress of representatives from New Granada's towns and provinces. The congress was something of a failure, however, because it failed to secure cooperation from the provinces. First, Cartagena objected, calling instead for a General Congress to be held at Medellín with the provinces represented in proportion to their populations and with the avowed purpose of establishing a federal government. Then, when the congress met for its first session (December 22, 1810–12 February 1811), it was attended by delegates from only six provinces and, after rancorous debates about who should participate, soon dissolved due to the absence of most of its potential members.[49] This failure reflected the combination of circumstances that frustrated Bogotá's bid for political leadership. In the first place, Bogotá did not have the authority of Caracas because the juntista movement had started in the provinces, thereby depriving the capital of the authority associated with taking the lead in the political revolution. Nor did Bogotá recover this lost lead, despite being a center for secular and ecclesiastical government with larger military resources than any other city except Cartagena. This was partly because the Spanish system of government did not leave a strong administrative and military platform on which to build a new state; for, despite Bourbon efforts to create a stronger chain of command from the center, governments of the provinces had continued to enjoy a good deal of autonomy. This was particularly true of large provinces, such as Popayán and Cartagena, whose governors could communicate directly with the king. Moreover, Bogotá had a further weakness as capital. Unlike Caracas, whose large population ensured that it always had a large number of delegates in any congress, the city had only a small jurisdiction, so that its hinterland of political authority and social influence extended to only a small number of secondary towns.[50] In these circumstances, the capital became one of the new sovereign powers that sprang up throughout New Granada, rather than their obvious leader.

The problem of promoting unity was accentuated by the activities of Bogotá patricians, who wanted their city to be the seat of a central legislature and executive, standing at the head of a hierarchy of provinces. This model emerged when the junta in Bogotá converted itself into the constitutional government of a new state based on the capital and its province of Santafé. In February–March 1811, guided by the creole aristocrat Jorge Tadeo Lozano, its constituent assembly created the sovereign state of Cundinamarca as a kind of constitutional monarchy. Its constitution was modeled on that of the North American republic but acknowledged Ferdinand VII as "King of the Cundinamarcans." While Ferdinand was absent, Lozano was chosen to be vice president to rule in his place.[51] Legitimation of the State of Cundinamarca was thus the same as that of other states: it was based on the assumption of sovereignty by the people in the absence of the legitimate king. But Cundinamarca was different. The presidents of Cundinamarca, especially Antonio Nariño, aspired to exercise greater influence in New Granada than that of a mere province. When Nariño was president, he tried to impose his political model on other territories through annexation of neighboring regions and municipalities, while also seeking to counteract the power of the two large provinces of Cartagena and Popayán.[52]

The contrast with Venezuela is again worth noting. There, the capital had taken the lead in creating a confederation of independent provinces, modeled on that of the United States. Caracas was, moreover, able to sustain its leadership because its relatively large population ensured that its deputies always formed the largest bloc in the federal congress. In New Granada, on the other hand, the capital of the viceroyalty was too small to carry such weight in congress and, rather than lead the new confederation, broke away to become the capital of the State of Cundinamarca. The patriot side thus quickly divided between those who saw the political future in a confederation of separate sovereign republics and those who wanted a single centralized republic.

This division sharpened in 1811–12, when the government of the State of Cundinamarca tried to create a unified government for New Granada, both by annexing the neighboring province of Mariquita to Cundinamarca and, more strikingly, by launching plans for restructuring New Granada into four large departments, which would enter into a general confederation with Venezuela and Quito.[53] During the same period, the bogotano revolutionary Antonio Nariño emerged as a vociferous critic of any kind of federalism and the champion of strong, republican government based in Bogotá.[54] Indeed, when Nariño launched his newspaper *La Bagatela* on July 14, 1811, it was largely for the purpose of demonstrating that federalism was hopelessly unsuited to conditions in New Granada. His criticism was not of the U.S. constitution per se, but of its irrelevance to New Granada: "We are told as if it were news," said Nariño, "that the Constitution of the United States is the wisest and most perfect known until today; its followers therefore conclude that we should adopt it to the letter . . . " But, he warned, "it is not enough that the Constitution of North America should be the best, it is necessary that . . . we should be able to use it . . . "[55]

Nariño's rise to political ascendancy and his subsequent spells as leader of Cundinamarca deepened divisions between capital and provinces. Shortly after congress reconvened for its second session, Nariño was elected president of Cundinamarca (September 19, 1811), and Cundinamarca became still more firmly entrenched in opposition to the congress. At the same time, the federalists' project took firmer form as the members of congress moved towards creating a confederation of sovereign states, with or without the cooperation of Cundinamarca. When the second congress started, it drew deputies from a larger number of provinces than had the first, with 11 representatives attending its opening session, and thus seemed to have more authority than its predecessor. The delegates also came under stronger pressure to act, if only to resist Nariño's design for centralized government. In these circumstances, the congress finally agreed to the Act of Federation of the United Provinces of New Granada, drawn up by Camilo Torres and signed by deputies from five provinces on November 27, 1811.

The Act of Federation formally structured New Granada into a set of equal and independent states formed from the old Spanish provinces. The states were to be the primary repositories of political authority and power with representative governments chosen by the people and exercised by legislative and executive powers. Some powers were ceded to the General Congress, which was charged with responsibility for matters of common defense, regulating international relations, and making war and peace. Congress was also allowed earmarked revenues from ports, post, and the minting of coinage to support these activities. Executive and legislative power were temporarily united in members of the congress; the creation of an independent judiciary was postponed until the danger of war was over.[56] The federation did not, however, have a standing army. For, with the concept of confederation came the conviction that the sovereign states should create, organize, and finance their own armed forces. And, as the concern of leaders in these small states was to limit the power of the military, their preference was for small forces, organized in militias composed of politically reliable citizens. Regional armed forces therefore proliferated, and the forces of New Granada's United Provinces were to be made up of companies of soldiers who were identified by their local origins: hence, the Battalion of Socorro, the Grenadiers of Cundinamarca, and so on.

The reconfiguration of political authority in New Granada during 1810–11 had created potential for conflict on several fronts. One was among the independents themselves, as the Federation of the United Provinces and the State of Cundinamarca struggled for ascendancy. Nariño and his centralists harassed the federal congress led by Camilo Torres until they moved out of Bogotá, first to Ibagué, then to Villa de Leiva, and finally to Tunja. Distance did not end their quarrels, however. In November 1812, war broke out between them, when Nariño sent a force under Colonel Antonio Baraya to assert Cundinamarca's sovereignty. Baraya defected to the congress, and an enraged Nariño redirected Cundinamarca's forces against Tunja, the seat of congress. When Nariño failed to take Tunja, congress counterattacked by sending Baraya against Bogotá. Baraya's siege of the city in January 1813 was in turn defeated, leaving Cundinamarca as the victor and ending war among the patriots.[57]

Royalists and Patriots in New Granada: The War for the South

While congress and Cundinamarca maneuvered against each other in 1810–12, the main fronts for war had opened elsewhere in conflicts between autonomous and royalist towns. One of these was in New Granada's south, where the governor of the Province of Popayán, Miguel Tacón, resisted demands that he establish a junta in the city of Popayán and created instead a force with which to defend royal authority. Tacón had already successfully defended this cause in 1809, when he mobilized military force against the first Quito junta, using his small detachment of 50 to 80 regulars together with militias raised in Popayán, blacks recruited from the Patía Valley, and Indians recruited from Pasto. His defeat of Quito's forces near Pasto strengthened the royalist authorities in the south before the crisis of 1810; it reinforced Pasto's sense of loyalty to the crown, showed that blacks and Indians could be recruited to the royalist cause, and thus encouraged Tacón to resist the juntas of the Cauca Valley towns when they pressured him to conform to their politics.[58] He also rallied some of the city's leading families and clergy within the city, playing to their desire to preserve Popayán's role as the major center of government in the south and prevent any political instability that might jeopardize social order.

Tacón's hold on Popayán and Pasto and his determination to defend royalist authority soon provoked a small-scale war in New Granada's south. In late 1810, delegates from seven Cauca towns convened at Cali under a "Provisional Governing Junta of the Allied Cities of the Cauca Valley" to defy Tacón and establish a mutual defense against him. Their willingness to go to war was strengthened by aid from Bogotá; in November 1810, the junta in Bogotá sent a force of about 170 soldiers under Colonel Antonio Baraya to support the Cauca towns against Popayán.

The ensuing campaign tested the capacity of New Granada's patriot provinces to undertake joint military operations, since it required Baraya to fuse his infantry and cavalry from Bogotá with the Cauca towns' militias and some Indian troops recruited en route. The campaign was slow to start because of the distances involved and the need to organize joint forces. Baraya took six weeks to march from Bogotá to Cali, where he combined with local forces; three more months then passed before he attacked Popayán directly. Like Caracas's campaign against Coro, Bogotá's offensive against Popayán was a display of force rather than the release of unrestrained violence. When Baraya finally advanced on the city, he had a rather rudimentary army of poorly trained men under inexperienced officers, but, with about 1,000 men, a sufficient number to force Tacón to retreat. Tacón's forces were small: he had only a few regulars and the militias of Popayán, and was so desperate for men that, in March 1811, he called on the free blacks and mulattos of the Patía Valley to join him and even offered freedom to slaves who fought for the king. He tried to strike back by taking 500 men to attack Baraya's vanguard but was driven back at Bajo Palacé on March 28, 1811, and he decided to retreat south, leaving bands of guerrillas in the Patía area as a rear guard.[59] This allowed the patriots to install a provincial junta in Popayán under Joaquin Caicedo y Cuero, leader of the confederate cities of the Cauca.

This first battle against the royalists in New Granada was acclaimed as a great victory on the juntista side. According to the victors' reports, the battle had involved infantry, artillery, and cavalry, and supposedly killed between 70 and 100 of Tacon's men with the loss of only nine patriots. But Tacón was not finished. He retreated to the town of Pasto and then fell back on the frontier zone of Barbacoas, where he established a royalist insurgency. Using treasury funds taken from Popayán and gold from local mines, Tacón kept royalist resistance alive in the south. He took advantage of coastal communications to sustain his forces, making contact with royalist ports in the Pacific, acquiring arms from royalist Guayaquil, and establishing communications with the viceroy of Peru in Lima and the viceroy of New Granada in Panamá. He was defeated again at Iscuandé in January 1812 and left for Guayaquil, but his allies continued to fight and to regain lost ground.[60] In late 1812, the rebels of the Patía Valley joined with Indian loyalists in an extraordinary coalition of peasant forces that took the city of Pasto for the crown, turning it into a royalist stronghold that was to defend the Spanish cause for years to come.[61]

This first phase of war in New Granada thus shared the same characteristics of the civic war of the First Republic in Venezuela. It was essentially a struggle between cities, carried out by improvised armies based on groups bound by local ties rather than a shared political identity. Volunteers were usually scarce, apart from those who, eager to win honor and reputation, became officers committed to military careers in the cause of independence. Some, such as Atanasio Girardot, Rafael Urdaneta, Antonio Ricaurte, and Francisco de Paula Santander, later became important commanders in Bolívar's campaigns in both Venezuela and New Granada. The armies in which they fought tended to be small in size—often only a few hundred men—and conflict was not fuelled by racial and class antagonisms to the same degree as in Venezuela. The royalist leader Tacón was, like Monteverde in Venezuela, ready to turn to slaves and Indians for support, and he stimulated the development of irregular forces among the runaway slaves and free blacks of the Patía Valley, the slaves of the gold-mining camps in Barbacoas, and the Indian communities of the Pasto region. In most of New Granada, however, mobilization along racial and ethnic lines was rare and did not play much part in the development of war.

Between Caracas and Cartagena: The Caribbean Theater of War

This was particularly evident in Colombia's Caribbean provinces where, despite the presence of slaves and large mulatto populations, war stemmed primarily from conflict between the cities of Cartagena and Santa Marta, which adopted contending systems of government. At first, in 1810, both established juntas, that recognized the Regency and retained ties to Spain. The solidarity of their elites (who shared family ties) had soon evaporated, however, and from early 1811, they followed diverging political paths.

Their divergence began when the junta of Cartagena repudiated the Regency at the end of 1810. The junta's refusal to accept a governor sent by the Regency, on the grounds that he had not been chosen by the people of Cartagena, shattered the fragile consensus among the city's notables. In February 1811, a group of Spanish merchants and army officers decided to reestablish royal authority without the junta and mounted a coup that was only narrowly defeated. In its wake, the city's political life became increasingly turbulent. Royalist sympathizers emigrated, often for Santa Marta, where loyalists remained in control, and left Cartagena's patrician factions to struggle for control of their government. Politics became polarized between an "aristocratic" group (led by the *cartagenero* patrician García de Toledo), which fought to fend off the challenge from a radical republican clique (led by the Gutierrez de Piñeres brothers, members of a prominent Mompós family that had fought and lost for their city's independence from Cartagena). Both sides tried to mobilize the pardos and free blacks on their side. In July, a republican clique seized the initiative, and in November 1811, Cartagena became the first province of New Granada formally to declare its independence from Spain.[62]

Cartagena's secession was a major military and naval setback for Spain, since the city's magnificent harbor, indomitable fortress and large forces of regulars and militias, together with its virtual monopoly of New Granada's foreign trade, made it a strategic key to New Granada. It was also an immediate threat to the loyalist government of Santa Marta, which now came under growing pressure to break with the Regency. Cartagena sought to bring down its royalist enemy by isolating Santa Marta, with some support from the congress in Santafé. The cartagenero strategy was initially aimed at winning allies among towns that wanted to throw off Santa Marta's authority, beginning in July 1811 with the creation of a "Confederation of the Magdalena" with a base at Guáimoro. Santa Marta responded by sending nearly 300 men to defend its sovereignty over the region and regained Guáimoro without a fight. However, while Cartagena temporarily retreated, Santa Marta came under pressure on another front. The junta in Bogotá entered its hinterland, sending a small force of 124 men to occupy the town of Ocaña.[63]

These actions were essentially political jousting, displays of force in which opposing sides exchanged insults and sought to impress the locals. At this time, neither side was ready to commit to serious warfare. Cartagena had the military resources inherited from the Spanish regime, but its internal politics distracted from the organization of war against Santa Marta. Santa Marta's leaders could hardly conceive of a direct attack on Cartagena, given its formidable defenses and larger forces. The balance between them was to shift during 1812, however, as both sides moved to the offensive.

Santa Marta's government initiated a systematic military offensive aimed primarily at taking towns along the Lower Magdalena River in order to cut Cartagena's communications with the interior. Governor Acosta started this campaign in December 1811; he seized the fortified river port of Tenerife with a force of about 250 men and followed this by taking a string of fortified bases along the Lower Magdalena. By April 1812, Santa Marta had succeeded in its primary goal—that of blocking Cartagena's river route into New Granada. Its offensive capacity was also strengthened by new developments. In February 1812, the new viceroy of New Granada, Benito Pérez, took up residence in Portobelo, thereby providing a fresh focus for loyalism and the potential for coordinated attacks. In May, 300 Spanish regulars, plus ships and financial support, arrived from Cuba, considerably enhancing Santa Marta's military capacity by placing a professional army corps at the center of Santa Marta's forces of about 1,500 men. And, of course, the loyalists of Santa Marta probably took heart during these months from the news of Monteverde's successful offensive against Caracas and Ramón Correa's occupation of Cúcuta, close to Santa Marta's southern border.

If Santa Marta's aggression against Cartagena was bolstered by its ability to acquire reinforcement and supplies from outside, by sea, it was also aided by weakness in Cartagena. In 1812, the newly independent state was experiencing serious financial difficulties—leading to the issue of paper money—and to deal with the crisis of confidence, a temporary dictatorship was installed. The dictator Manuel Rodríguez Torices took office in July 1812 and succeeded in recouping some ground, with raids along the Magdalena River to challenge royalist forces and a successful defense of Mompós in October 1812. But Cartagena's position remained insecure: in September–November, the royalist advance moved across the River Magdalena into the savannahs of Tolú (a major source of food supplies) and this, together with Correa's position at Cúcuta, threatened encirclement.[64]

Cartagena seems, then, to have entered a situation similar to that of Caracas. Small royalist forces from a neighboring province advanced against little resistance, gathering support while suffering few losses. The outcome was different, however, thanks partly to a new element in Cartagena's army, made up of the Venezuelan and European officers who had been forced out of Venezuela by the fall of the First Republic. On arriving in Cartagena in the closing months of 1812, they brought a fresh energy to the struggle against royalist Santa Marta, and their impact was soon more widely felt. In late 1812 and early 1813, a new phase of war opened on the Caribbean coast when Cartagena struck back against royalist Santa Marta and its allies. The war then spread into Venezuela, leading to the rise and fall of its Second Republic. And, while republicans engaged in a fierce struggle for power in Venezuela, the civic wars in New Granada were continued and extended, ending eventually in the dissolution of its autonomous states. We will examine these new phases of war in the chapter that follows.

Notes

1. Michael McKinley, *Pre-revolutionary Caracas*, p. 4. Venezuela had a population made up of about 15% slaves, 8% free blacks, 38% pardos, and 25% whites.
2. The following account of the Venezuelan juntas draws principally on Carraciolo Parra-Pérez, *Historia de la Primera República de Venezuela*, 2 vols. (Caracas: Academia Nacional de Historia, 1959), 1, pp. 403–34. This two-volume history, based on contemporary memoirs and political records as well as British reports, remains the key source for the history of the juntas and the First Republic.
3. Quoted by Parra-Pérez, *Primera Republica*, 1, p. 433.
4. Ibid., pp. 405–10.
5. McKinley, *Pre-revolutionary Caracas*, pp. 163–4.
6. Thibaud, *Repúblicas en armas*, pp. 52–3, 79.
7. On the meaning of the concept of the "citizen in arms" in Venezuela and New Granada in 1810–15, see María Teresa Calderón and Clément Thibaud, *La Majestad de los Pueblos en la Nueva Granada y Venezuela, 1780–1832* (Bogotá: Taurus, 2010), pp. 153–73.
8. For Toro's account, see Toro to Secretary of War, November 19, 1810, and December 8, 1810; for a supporting view from his artillery captain, see Diego Jalón, December 17, 1810. Both are reproduced in Pedro Grases and Manuel Pérez Vila, eds. *Las fuerzas armadas de Venezuela en el siglo XIX: La independencia, 1810–1830* (Caracas: Presidencia de la República 1963), 1, pp. 30–42.
9. Parra-Pérez, *Primera Republica*, 1, p. 473.
10. Gunther E. Rothenberg, *The Art of Warfare in the Age of Napoleon* (Bloomington: Indiana University Press, 1978), pp. 11–12. Use of the concept of "civic wars" is developed by Clément Thibaud in the first part of *La república en armas*, his innovative study of the wars of independence in Venezuela and New Granada.
11. Thibaud, *República en armas*, pp. 75–6.
12. "La organización militar por William Burke, 1811," in Grases and Pérez Vila, eds., *Las fuerzas armadas de Venezuela*, 1, pp. 64–86. The name William Burke was probably the pseudonym of James Mill: see Mario Rodríguez, *"William Burke" and Francisco De Miranda: The Word and the Deed in Spanish America's Emancipation* (Lanham, MD, University Press of America, 1994).

13. Parra-Pérez, *Primera República*, 1, pp. 473–4, 484–7; James F. King, "El comisionado regio don Antonio Ignacio de Cortabarría y la primera república de Venezuela," pp. 142–6.

14. On Miranda, the Patriotic Society, and the congress, see Parra-Pérez, *Primera República*, 2, pp. 25–36; McKinley, *Pre-revolutionary Caracas*, pp. 164–8.

15. The debates of July 3–4 on the question of independence are summarized in Parra-Pérez, *Primera República*, 2, pp. 55–75. On Miranda's contribution, see Karen Racine, *Francisco de Miranda. A Transatlantic Life in the Age of Revolution* (Wilmington, DE: Scholarly Resources, 2003), pp. 211–20. For a nuanced view of Miranda, which stresses his conservatism and abstention from involvement in the making of the 1811 constitution, see Parra-Pérez, *Primera República*, 2, pp. 121–2.

16. The debates on the pardo question and federalist case are set out with great clarity in Parra-Pérez, *Primera República*, 2, pp.113–20, 125–33.

17. J.F. Heredia, *Memorias del Regente Heredia* (Madrid: Editorial América, Biblioteca Ayacucho, 1916), p. 36.

18. Parra-Pérez, *Primera República*, 2, pp. 80–3, 96.

19. Ibid., pp. 85–9.

20. Ibid., pp. 96–111.

21. Ibid., pp. 240–53.

22. Ibid., pp. 134–40.

23. Quoted by Parra-Pérez, *Primera Republica*, 2, p. 251.

24. A striking account of the earthquake and its consequences is given by George Flinter, an English soldier who was stationed at Curaçao in 1812 and in close contact with Spanish exiles from Venezuela: see George Flinter, A *History of the Revolution of Caracas, Comprising an Impartial Narrative of the Atrocities Committed by the Contending Parties* (London: T. and J. Allman, 1819), pp. 29–35.

25. On royalist and republican attitudes and actions on slave recruitment during the wars of the First Republic, see Blanchard, *Under the Flags of Freedom*, pp. 23–7.

26. On Monteverde's maneuvers and Miranda's defeat, see Flinter, *History of the Revolution of Caracas*, pp. 36–8.

27. Parra-Pérez, *Primera Republica*, 2, pp. 413–34.

28. José de Austria, who was a junior officer in the republic's forces at this time, states that Miranda was responsible for the defeat because he accepted the British view that Spain sought to be reconciled with its colonies: José de Austria, *Bosquejo de la Historia Militar de Venezuela*, 2 vols. (Caracas: Academia Nacional de la Historia, 1960), 1, p. 358.

29. On Bolívar's difficult relationship with Miranda and the circumstances of Bolívar's denunciation, see Gerhard Masur, *Simon Bolívar* (Albuquerque: University of New Mexico, 1969), pp. 127–48.

30. Thibaud, *República en armas*, pp. 107–113.

31. Flinter, *History of the Revolution of Caracas*, pp. 33–4.

32. Malcolm Deas, "Some Reflections on Miranda as Soldier," in *Francisco de Miranda: Exile and Enlightenment*, ed. John Maher (London: Institute for the Study of the Americas, 2006), pp. 77–87.

33. Miranda's terms of surrender and the influence of his British connection are stated in the memoirs, first published in 1855, of an officer who served with him: Austria, *Bosquejo de la Historia Militar*, 1, pp. 340–3, 358.

34. On the new "sovereigns" and their conflicts, see Armando Martínez Garnica, *El legado de la Patria Boba* (Bucaramanga: Universidad Industrial de Santander, 1998), chapters 4–5. Also, Daniel Gutiérrez Ardila, *Un Reino Nuevo. Geografía política, pactismo y diplomacia durante el interregno en Nueva Granada (1808–1816)* (Bogotá: Universidad Externado de

Colombia, 2010), pp. 187–233. For a brief survey, see Isabela Restrepo Mejía, "La soberanía del 'pueblo' durante la época de la Independencia, 1810–1815," *Historia Crítica*, 29 (2005): pp. 101–23.

35. On the flaws in Anderson's concept of "imagined community" as applied to New Granada, see Anthony McFarlane, "Identity, Enlightenment and Political Dissent in Late Colonial Spanish America," *Transactions of the Royal Historical Society*, 6th ser., 8 (1998): pp. 309–35.

36. On New Granada's regions, see McFarlane, *Colombia before Independence*, chapters 2 and 3.

37. For an outline of the royalist enclaves, see Earle, *Spain and the Independence of Colombia*, pp. 36–54.

38. Steinar A. Saether, *Identidades e independencia en Santa Marta y Riohacha, 1750–1850* (Bogotá: Instituto Colombiano de Antropología e Historia, 2005), pp. 158–63.

39. Francisco Zuluaga, "La independencia en la gobernación de Popayán," in *Historia del Gran Cauca* (Cali: Universidad del Valle, 1996), p. 91.

40. Gutiérrez Ramos, *Los indios de Pasto contra la República*, pp. 158–64, 201–6.

41. Adelaida Sourdis de De La Vega, *Cartagena de Indias durante la Primera República, 1810–1815* (Bogotá: Banco de la República, 1988), pp. 36–41.

42. Sogamoso, Chiquinquirá, Leiva, and Muzo broke from Tunja; Girón and Vélez from Socorro; Ibagué and Tocaima from Mariquita; Timaná, Garzón, and Purificación from Neiva. Even Quibdó and Nóvita, sparsely populated towns on the far western mining frontier, set up in opposition to each other. See Garrido, *Reclamos y representaciones*, pp. 322–42.

43. On motivations, see Martínez Garnica, *El legado de la Patria Boba*, chap. 5.2.

44. The total number of juntas in Venezuela, New Granada, and Quito was about 38: Gutiérrez Ardila, *Un Reino Nuevo*, pp. 210–12.

45. "Cabildo extraordinario," in *Constituciones de Colombia*, ed. Manuel Antonio Pombo and José Joaquín Guerra, 2 vols. (Bogotá: Biblioteca Popular de la Cultura Colombiana, Ministerio de Educación, 1951), 1, p. 88.

46. On the influence of lawyers, see Victor M. Uribe Urán, *Honorable Lives: Lawyers, Family and Politics in Colombia, 1780–1850* (Pittsburgh, PA: University of Pittsburgh, 2000), pp. 45–59.

47. Gutierrez Ardila, *Un Reino Nuevo*, pp. 87–102.

48. Antonio Nariño, "Consideraciones sobre los inconvenientes de alterar la invocación hecha por la ciudad de Santafé en 29 de julio de 1810," in *Nariño periodista*, ed. Carlos Restrepo Canal (Bogotá: Academia Colombiana de Historia, 1960), pp. 157–65.

49. Restrepo, *Historia de la Revolución de Colombia*, 1, pp. 147–8.

50. Gutierrez Ardila, *Un Reino Nuevo*, pp. 231–3.

51. Pombo and Guerra, *Constituciones de Colombia*, pp. 123–95.

52. Gutiérrez Ardila, *Un Reino Nuevo*, pp. 237–78.

53. Restrepo, *Historia de la Revolución de Colombia*, 1, pp. 165–8.

54. Thomas Blossom, *Antonio Nariño. Hero of Colombian Independence* (Tucson: Arizona University Press, 1967), pp. 75–97.

55. *La Bagatela,* no. 16, October 20, 1811, in Restrepo Canal, *Nariño Periodista*, p. 312.

56. Acta de Federación, in Pombo and Guerra, *Constituciones de Colombia*, 1, pp. 208–36.

57. A participant's account of the war between Cundinamarca and congress is found in José María Espinosa, *Memorias de un abanderado* (Bogotá: Plaza & Janes, 1983), pp. 35–42.

58. Alonso Valencia Llano, *Marginados y 'Sepultados en los Montes': Orígenes de la insurgencia social en el valle del río Cauca, 1810–1830* (Cali: Universidad del Valle, 2008), pp. 71–4.

59. Francisco Zuluaga, "Clientilismo y guerrillas en el Valle del Patia, 1536–1811," in Colmenares et al., *La independencia: Ensayos de historia social* (Bogotá: Instituto de Cultura Colombiana, 1986), pp. 128–9.

60. On these campaigns in New Granada's south, see Restrepo, *Historia de la Revolución de Colombia*, 1: pp. 163–4, 174–7, 205–6. Also see Camilo Riaño, *Historia Militar: La independencia (1810–1815): Historia Extensa de Colombia,* vol. 18, part 1 (Bogotá: Lerner, 1971), pp. 75–95, 105–8.

61. Gutiérrez Ramos, *Los indios de Pasto*, pp. 177–81.

62. Múnera, *El fracaso de la nación*, pp. 180–91; Helg, *Liberty and Equality in Caribbean Colombia*, pp. 124–30.

63. Saether, *Identidades e independencia*, pp. 181–9.

64. Riaño, *Historia Militar*, vol. 18, part 1, pp. 175–97.

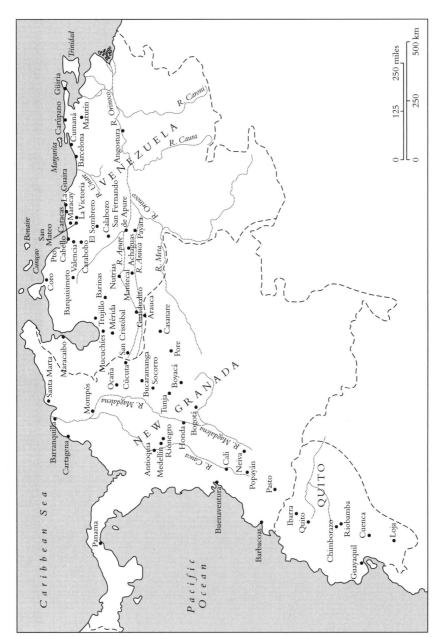

MAP 2. Venezuela, New Granada, and Quito

5

"WAR TO THE DEATH" IN VENEZUELA AND THE DISSOLUTION OF INDEPENDENT NEW GRANADA, 1813–15

During 1810–11, war in Venezuela and New Granada had started as "civic wars" in which contending towns mobilized armed forces to overawe rather than destroy the other. However, from 1812, wars in New Granada and Venezuela moved along new pathways. The pattern of limited "civic war" based in interurban and interregional competition persisted in New Granada, albeit with local variations. In Venezuela, by contrast, war took on more violent forms, as civic war turned into a more generalized civil war that unleashed social and racial conflict and mutated into a "war to the death."

The renewal of war in Venezuela began in New Granada, after the defeat of the First Republic sent a stream of refugees from Caracas to Cartagena. Exiled Venezuelan and foreign officers enlisted in Cartagena's forces and became an important new source of military leadership. Their most articulate and forceful member was Colonel Simón Bolívar, who, in his address to the Congress of New Granada in November and memorial to the citizens of Cartagena in December 1812, called for revolutionary solidarity in war against Spain.[1] His proclamations sought to persuade New Granadans that Venezuelans wanted to overthrow the royalist government in Caracas and that it was in New Granadans' interest that they should do so. According to Bolívar, the Venezuelan republic had not been defeated politically or militarily but betrayed from within, leaving its oppressed people waiting for liberation. He also insisted that the liberation of Caracas was the indispensable condition for the liberation of America and that the patriots in New Granada should subordinate their political differences to the pursuit of shared military goals. This meant centralized authority, total mobilization for war, and aggressive action to topple royalist regimes. For Bolívar, the priorities were clear: to defeat Spanish forces in New Granada, to build an army for the liberation of Venezuela, and, with New Granadan help, to retake Caracas and ensure the future of the region's independent republics.

Bolívar's ideas strongly appealed to Cartagena's leaders, since they feared that a resurgent royalist regime in Venezuela would support their enemies in Santa Marta. But his proposals resonated in wider political circles too, as the political leaders of Cundinamarca and the United Provinces became aware that Monteverde's counterrevolution was a potential threat to the independents in New Granada. From this situation, a new military nexus came into being, linking Venezuela and New Granada in wars against the royalist centers. First, war spilled over from Venezuela into New Granada in 1812–13, when army officers exiled from Caracas joined Cartagena's fight against royalist Santa Marta; it then rebounded into Venezuela, when Bolívar extended his military operations into a war to retake his homeland; finally, it ended in 1814–15, with Bolívar's defeat in Venezuela and return to New Granada to join the resistance against Spanish reconquest.

Republican Offensives in the Caribbean Provinces

The return to war in Venezuela started indirectly, in the civic war between Santa Marta and Cartagena in 1812. After receiving ships, money, and 300 Spanish regulars of the Albuera Battalion from Cuba, Santa Marta's royalist government launched an offensive aimed at overturning the independent government in Cartagena, and Cartagena responded with attacks on the city and province of Santa Marta. The forces of the two cities fought along, and on both sides of the River Magdalena, the main artery of communication between the coast and the interior. The main front was in the hinterland of the city of Santa Marta, where the French soldier Labatut (who arrived as an exile from Caracas and became the general commander of Cartagena's forces in the lower Magdalena) led 500 men into an offensive against the city. Bolívar, another exile who joined Cartagena's army, supported this operation by fighting on an associated front to the south of Santa Marta. Bolívar was sent to Barranca with 30 or 40 regular soldiers from Cartagena's garrison and orders to attack royalist strongpoints on the Magdalena River. The third front lay west of the river, in the region of Tolú, where Cartagena had to defend itself against rural rebellion and a military expedition sent from Santa Marta to support the rebellion. Here, the Spanish officer Antonio de Rebustillo, who led a force of 70 regular soldiers from the Albuera Regiment, was countered by forces under two more Venezuelan exiles: Manuel Cortes Campomanes led forces from Cartagena against the rebellion in the plains of Tolú, and Miguel Carabaño took 150 men to attack the rebels in the fort of Cispata on the Sinú coast.

Both sides tried to build their armies around a core of trained soldiers: Cartagena deployed regular soldiers from the remnants of the old Fijo Regiment of the royal garrison, together with white and pardo militia companies, while Santa Marta put together deserters from the Fijo with the Spanish regulars of the Albuera Battalion sent from Cuba.[2] Both sides also added untrained men, recruited by force or by promise of payment, but neither aimed at mass mobilization. They preferred to create disciplined forces composed of regulars and trained men, supported by local volunteers where necessary, and their forces remained small.

The military operations in which they engaged were on a correspondingly small scale. Campomanes, for example, set out to suppress the rebellion of Tolú with a couple of infantry companies, a company of patriot volunteers, some cavalry, and a few artillery pieces. To these, he added local recruits to make a force of over 500 men and went on the offensive against peasant forces which were larger but undisciplined and poorly armed. Campomanes's professional-looking force was sufficient to intimidate the enemy, and the rebellion fizzled out as soon as Rebustillo's Spanish soldiers moved back across the River Magdalena to the safety of Santa Marta.

Cartagena's military campaigns along the Magdalena River and in the province of Santa Marta were also small but effective. In November–December 1812, Bolívar took Tenerife from the royalists without much fighting and reopened upriver communications. At Mompós, he increased his forces from about 200 to 500 by local recruitment and continued to clear the Magdalena valley prior to moving inland to take Ocaña and Valledupar. While Bolívar was engaged in these operations, Labatut took the city of Santa Marta in an amphibious operation. In early January 1813, he attacked the city with about 500 men, backed by a flotilla of small armed boats; after forcing back a small force of defenders, mostly Indians armed only with bows and arrows, Labatut took the city without further resistance.[3] The leading royalists had already gone. At least 450 people, including whole households, fled by sea to royalist Portobelo, while an unknown number emigrated to other safe havens in the Caribbean. So, at the start of 1813, Cartagena had reversed royalist advances and, after taking the province's three main towns, seemed poised to eliminate the royalist enclave of Santa Marta.[4]

Cartagena's hold on Santa Marta was too brief to change the military balance on the Caribbean coast. Labatut's harsh behavior alienated the *samarios*, and they ejected his forces after a couple months, restoring the city to Spanish rule. This showed the mistake of assuming that the "people" would opt for independence. For, unlike the populace of Cartagena, which generally sided with independence, the people of Santa Marta tended to support governments that represented the crown. The difference is best explained by local rivalries rather than ideological commitments. In the provincial capital, the populace preferred royalism because the elites wanted independence; among the small towns in Santa Marta's provincial jurisdiction, the conflict was a way of improving their own standing. This led some to support outsiders, who promised to affirm their autonomy, but most followed the provincial capital and remained on the royalist side.[5]

Cartagena's defeat at Santa Marta had serious implications for the independents not only in Cartagena but throughout New Granada, since it returned an important port to royalist hands and thus provided a potential bridgehead for future royalist operations supported from Spain and its Caribbean possessions. The campaign against Santa Marta had some important indirect benefits, however, because Bolívar's operations had reopened the Magdalena and enabled him to restart the war in Venezuela. His chance came when Monteverde sent royalist forces under Ramón Correa to occupy the town of Cúcuta. Governor Manuel del Castillo of Pamplona interpreted Correa's advance as preparation for an invasion of New

Granada and called in January 1813 for Bolívar to bring his forces to the area. After joining Castillo, Bolívar further enhanced his military experience and reputation. They fought together at Cúcuta with a combined force of around 500 men and forced Correa to retreat back into Venezuela. This allowed Bolívar to take up a position where, to defend New Granada, he could return to the offensive in Venezuela, launching an extraordinary campaign to restore the Venezuelan republic.[6]

War in Venezuela

Historians correctly portray Bolívar as the main force behind the renewal of the war for independence in Venezuela.[7] He was a tireless promoter of such a war from the moment of his arrival in Cartagena, arguing publicly that the independence of Venezuela and New Granada were mutually reinforcing. He also made the war possible by building an armed force and commanding it to great effect in the field. His military successes in the Magdalena valley and at Cúcuta strengthened his reputation as a military commander, and he used this position to pressure New Granada's political leaders for action in Venezuela. In March 1813, after promotion to brigadier general of the United Provinces' army, he presented the Union's Congress with a plan that played to New Granadan interest in resisting the royalist government of Venezuela.

Bolívar's plan stressed strategic political aims above all, arguing that the restoration of the Venezuelan republic would destroy the Spanish military threat to New Granada and thus ensure its future security. He also argued that Correa's defeat presented a tactical opportunity that should not be missed. He told the secretary of state of the United Provinces that "in this month of March we should march into Venezuela (because) re-conquest is for the moment very easy but later will be impossible. Working with the greatest speed will produce the best result for both States."[8] At the end of March, he reiterated the need for urgency in the light of news of an uprising in Eastern Venezuela and of French military successes in Spain. Speed was essential, he argued, not only because Correa's force had retreated from the Cúcuta region but also because public opinion in Venezuela favored the republican cause. Bolívar countered his critics' charge that he was foolishly "rushing into a hopeless enterprise," by arguing that, on the contrary, it would be foolish not to seize the chance to take Caracas at a time when Spanish persecution had caused "a second earthquake [that] has destroyed public opinion," and when he had a thousand men with muskets, as many cavalry, and matching artillery.[9]

Bolívar had to use all his political skills to push his plan forward. His principal opponent was his second in command, the cartagenero Manuel de Castillo, who dismissed the plan to attack Caracas as the work of "delirious men, the principal authors of Venezuela's ruin," and did all he could to undermine Bolívar's authority. Indeed, when the campaign was about to start in April 1813, Castillo resigned, thereby dividing the army and bringing it to the brink of dissolution. Bolívar salvaged his scheme by persuading political supporters at the highest levels in the government of the New Granadan confederation. Camilo Torres, the president of the Congress of the United Provinces, supported Bolívar and steered congress into authorizing an offensive against Correa under Bolívar's command. Congress also sent artillery, arms, and munitions to Cúcuta, as did Antonio Nariño, president of Cundinamarca.[10]

Bolívar's "Admirable Campaign"

The priority of *neogranadino* politicians was to use Bolívar to defend New Granada against Spanish attack. He was therefore authorized only to conduct a preliminary campaign as far as the town of La Grita, and he was required to secure the agreement of his senior officers for any operation he undertook. But operations on the New Granadan border soon gave Bolívar the chance to press forward with his own plans for a more ambitious assault on Spanish Venezuela. He moved swiftly against La Grita, causing Correa's Spanish forces to fall back; then, after congress had authorized him to operate on his own initiative, he advanced on Mérida. When Correa again pulled back, Bolívar saw a way through to Caracas. Before the enemy had time to mobilize fully, Bolívar turned an exploratory expedition into a campaign that cut through royalist defenses to strike at their political heart. His advance acquired momentum when he took La Grita and Mérida in May, as this added another 1,000 men to his forces and provided a staging post for deeper penetration into Venezuela. He took Trujillo in June, Guanare and Barinas in July, Valencia and his final objective, Caracas, in August 1813. Within six months, Bolívar had not only restarted the war for Venezuelan independence but, with his lightning military strikes, had achieved a great political coup by taking the capital and restoring independent government.

The first question raised by this extraordinary operation—known to historians as the "Admirable Campaign"—concerns the reasons for its success. Here, explanations invariably focus on Bolívar's military vision and leadership, given that he had scant resources with which to attack a more numerous enemy. His "army" was a fragile force from its inception. Accounts of Bolívar's Magdalena campaign suggest that he relied on untrained fighting men who were prepared to fight in their own regions for pay and plunder but had limited staying power. The actions in the Magdalena were skirmishes in which neither side was committed to fight to the death; the losing side quickly retreated, mortality was light, and defeat prompted desertion. Plans to invade Venezuela were a different matter, however. When Bolívar expounded his plans at Ocaña, his appeals to patriotism fell on deaf ears, and many of his men promptly deserted. Motivation to fight evidently diminished with distance from home, and to compensate, Bolívar had to provide payment or at least a credible promise of future reward.

Bolívar nonetheless succeeded in building a force that resembled an army. It was, in essence, an assortment of small forces that reflected his recent victories. It included the 30–40 regulars he had brought from Cartagena, the 400–500 recruits whom he had picked up along the Magdalena, most of them from Mompós, some Venezuelan volunteers, plus about 500 men supplied by the congress, and another

100 or so provided by Cundinamarca. Officially, this became the combined army of Cartagena and the Union, with Bolívar formally appointed as commander. Its exact number is unknown, but it is likely that Bolívar started with fewer than 1,000 men, and although he added at least another 1,000 while campaigning, he was never able to match Monteverde's total forces of 10–12,000 (of whom about half were effectives).[11] Bolívar's army was, moreover, a motley crew, being a poorly integrated agglomeration of groups from different areas. Some deserted before the invasion of Venezuela, and Bolívar had to plunder funds from Spanish merchants at Cúcuta in order to assemble a credible force with sufficient firearms. Even then, he did not have a united command because the cartagenero Castillo refused to participate at the outset, and another New Granadan officer, Francisco de Paula Santander, only reluctantly agreed to provide Bolívar with his unit of 290 men and later refused to follow him into Venezuela.[12]

Bolívar overcame these disadvantages by his willingness to take risks and pursue his own goals. He was, in this sense, more like an armed chieftain than the officer of a conventional army. While broadly responsive to a chain of command that emanated from a political center, he and other commanders operated in circumstances that allowed a wide margin of autonomy. Slow communications over great distance demanded that commanders behave independently in the field, and, as they relied largely on their own resources, the civil authorities had little leverage over them. A military commander like Bolívar was, as an apt comparison has it, "a corsair on land."[13] Much, therefore, depended on Bolívar's strategy, tactical skills, and ability to persuade his men to execute his plans.

Bolívar's plan to strike quickly and adjust to circumstances was a key to success, but, although it relied on tactical improvisation, the offensive was shaped by a strategic vision.[14] His overarching strategy integrated political objectives with military means in a broad plan for seizing power at the political and economic heart of Venezuela. In this, Bolívar appears to have learned lessons from the French Revolutionary and Napoleonic wars. Rather than follow traditional ideas of war as a means of exhausting the enemy's resources and forcing negotiation, he aimed to seize the center of power and eliminate enemy forces.

His military strategy—that is, his plans for the movement of his forces—was also influenced by European examples, especially Napoleonic ideas for using speed and surprise to compensate for numerical inferiority. The campaign depended on avoiding battle with large forces, outflanking the enemy, and using the momentum of quick victories to force the enemy onto the back foot, disorganizing his responses. This emphasis on speed fulfilled a logistical imperative too—fast-moving forces could live more easily off the land and reduced the risks of desertion. His tactics in the field reflected late eighteenth-century practice. Bolívar deployed light infantry with muskets and bayonets, supported by flanking cavalry armed with lances and sabers. But the key to his campaign was speed. Whereas more conventional commanders, such as Castillo, preferred a military strategy of taking and holding territory, Bolívar decided to strike at enemy weak points and pass through the gaps between dispersed forces. Once in motion, Bolívar did not falter;

he maintained a brisk advance, driving onwards to his primary objective, the center of government at Caracas, and deviating only to defeat forces at Barinas that might threaten his rear.[15]

While historians usually agree that Bolívar's military vision, skill, and determination made key contributions to the success of the "Admirable Campaign," this consensus should not obscure the fact that Monteverde's regime made Bolívar's task easier. Bolívar no doubt exaggerated when he characterized the discontent caused by Monteverde as a "second earthquake," but comments from leading royalists confirm that Monteverde's arbitrary government weakened loyalty to the Spanish cause. The regent of the audiencia, José Francisco Heredia, gave a particularly damning account, portraying Monteverde's government as a disorganized quasi-dictatorship, which, far from restoring respect for royal government, exacerbated political and social discord.[16] Other royalists who were present at the time agreed that Monteverde had dispensed with the rule of law. On his way to power, it was said that Monteverde had sacked towns and violated treaties.[17] Once in power, he had violated the rule of law by allowing his supporters, particularly fellow Canary Islanders, to persecute their political opponents, subjecting creole families suspected of republican sympathies to arbitrary sequestrations of property, unjust imprisonment, and death threats.[18]

These portrayals of Monteverde as an intolerable tyrant were probably exaggerated; he did not conduct a campaign of systematic suppression, and he eventually released the great majority of his prisoners on orders from the Spanish Cortes in April 1813.[19] However, the comments of his contemporaries suggest that Monteverde's behavior made royalist government unpopular. This was partly for reasons beyond his control, as many parts of the country were still reeling from the damage done by the earthquakes. But Monteverde's reliance on military cronies, his favoritism towards Spaniards, and his arbitrary methods, all ensured that he took a good deal of the blame for Venezuela's ills. He also failed to use the proclamation of the Cádiz Constitution as a means of winning political support, despite the opportunities it offered for attracting Americans to Spain's side. The political failings of his regime were particularly evident in Eastern Venezuela, where a rebellion launched by Santiago Mariño in January 1813 quickly gathered pace and momentum and forced Monteverde onto the defensive even before Bolívar's invasion.

Monteverde's failure to build political backing was not, however, the main cause of his defeat. More important were his mistakes as a military commander. For although Monteverde recognized the possible threat from the Venezuelan exiles in New Granada, he did too little to guard against it. He showed that he was alert to the problem in November 1812 when he informed the Spanish minister of war that Venezuela was pacified and offered to conquer New Granada. However, he seems to have lacked confidence in the ability of his forces to carry out this mission and, instead of advancing into New Granada, simply waited for reinforcements from Spain. Thus, when Correa retook Cúcuta, Monteverde did not order him forward. Instead, he let the initiative pass to the republican forces in New Granada, who were gathering under Bolívar's leadership, and left them to strengthen their position.[20]

If Monteverde allowed the Caracas revolutionaries to use New Granada as the platform for an offensive into Venezuela, the willingness of New Granadan leaders to support them was another important reason for Bolívar's success in reinstalling the republic. New Granada provided both home and hope for the Venezuelan republicans, plus some invaluable material aid for Bolívar's military campaign. Its importance was such that Bolívar was henceforth convinced that cooperation of Venezuela and New Granada was essential to defeat Spain; indeed, he presented himself as a general of New Granadan forces and tried to bring Venezuela into the New Granadan Union.

A more indirect source of help to Bolívar came from an independent armed rebellion in the Venezuelan east, initiated by Santiago Mariño and a group of local notables who had their own grievances against Monteverde's regime. In January 1813, Mariño led a group of 45 officers from their refuge on Trinidad to the coast of Güiria and launched an operation aimed at removing Spanish control over Eastern Venezuela. Mariño quickly advanced to the plains of Maturín, where he found arms, skilled horsemen, and an abundance of horses and cattle. He and his insurgents made very effective use of these resources, and important new leaders and armed bands emerged. Most notable of these was Manuel Piar, who, in March 1813, defeated forces led by Lorenzo de la Hoz, the governor of Barcelona, at Maturín and thereby consolidated his standing as a local caudillo.

Piar's action at Maturín was an early sign of the new kind of warfare that was to sweep through Venezuela. The key to the insurgents' success was the use of llanero horsemen as cavalry and their dedication to war without quarter. While the royalists relied on foot soldiers, the patriot horsemen armed with long lances took the royalist officers by surprise and frightened the foot soldiers into flight, which led to heavy casualties on the royalist side.[21] This was an early instance of what was to become a common feature of the war: the use of large numbers of mounted irregulars against foot soldiers, followed by massacre when they broke and fled. Reprisal was also an ingredient. Piar's slaughter of the enemy followed the massacre of soldiers and civilians by the Spanish captain Zuazola some days previously. Thus, in its early stages, the armed struggle in the east signaled some of the traits of a new kind of warfare in Venezuela, characterized by fighters and combat of a distinctive kind.

While there had been some brutality during the First Republic's war, it became more commonplace as the men from the margins of society, particularly the llaneros, were drawn into the war and came to constitute a new kind of soldiery. These were men from the cattle frontier, who were accustomed to living in the tough environment of the tropical plains and who had skills that could be readily adapted to the needs of war. They were highly skilled horsemen, accustomed to using lances for hunting and herding cattle while living off the land and cooperating in small, highly mobile bands. Their leaders were chosen for military talent rather than social status and included blacks and pardos, such as Piar, a mulatto from the Dutch island of Curacao. Their way of life made them natural adepts at the guerrilla tactics of raiding and plundering, and, unconstrained by any sense of the laws of war, they were ready to fight without quarter. This was, in short, an army of a different stripe to Bolívar's, which was more conventionally organized with infantry, artillery, and smaller numbers of cavalry, and was commanded by white officers whose military leadership reflected their prominence in the social hierarchy.[22]

Mariño and his forces were active only in the Venezuelan East and constituted an independent force that was both different from, and uncoordinated with, Bolívar's army and operations. Nonetheless, Mariño's war in Cumaná made an important contribution to Bolívar's success because it distracted Monteverde from the military situation on the border with New Granada. At the end of April 1813, Monteverde judged Mariño's insurgents to be the main danger, and he sailed east to the port of Barcelona with an invasion force of 550 men, including 260 recently arrived Spanish regulars. He had, however, misjudged his enemy. Once again, the royalist forces were no match for Piar's horsemen, and they suffered a second heavy defeat at Maturín on May 25, with the loss of perhaps as many as 500 men.[23] This was a particularly bad blow to the royalists because, as Heredia later recalled, "there perished almost all the few European troops left in Venezuela."[24]

This royalist setback in the east coincided with difficulties in the southwest, where Bolívar was pressing forward from New Granada. Monteverde had assumed that he would withstand attack from New Granada because he had large forces in the territories west and southwest of Caracas. In Coro and Maracaibo, he had a few thousand men, and in the southwestern region of Barinas, straddling the route to New Granada, he had another 5,000–6,000. The Spanish commander in Barinas, Antonio Tiscar, had an entire division composed of 2,800 men organized in three battalions and six squadrons of horsemen. In the Apure River region, José Yáñez had about 1,200 men on foot and horseback, while Correa had another 1,000.[25] However, substantial though they were, these forces were insufficient to deal with Bolívar, who exploited lack of communication between them with his tactics of speed and surprise.

The significance of Bolívar's military skill is evident in his confrontation with Spanish forces in Barinas. When Tiscar, the royalist commander, got news of Bolívar's capture of Mérida, he took appropriate action, sending out forces under Yáñez and Martí with the idea of trapping Bolívar between them. But Bolívar successfully countered these maneuvers. He sent José Félix Ribas against Martí's force—of between 500 and 800 men—and defeated them at Niquitao, taking over 400 royalist prisoners together with a large haul of muskets and munitions. Then, in a clever maneuver, Bolívar wheeled back towards to the town of Barinas, against Tiscar's headquarters. After seizing the arms and munitions there, he joined with his lieutenant Atanasio Girardot in a pursuit that forced Tiscar's retreating forces to surrender, virtually without a shot, at Nutrias.

These actions meant that the large forces that Monteverde had planned to combine in an invasion of New Granada were scattered. The royalist commander was now left with small forces on the coast, which began to disintegrate in the face of Bolívar's advance, as men deserted en masse. Reinforced by recruiting of prisoners and captured caches of arms and munitions, Bolívar moved against Valencia and Monteverde's main forces. Rather than go into battle with a depleted army, Monteverde withdrew from Caracas on August 3, 1813, leaving the city's inhabitants to organize their own defense. Panic ensued among those who feared republican reprisals. Heredia, who joined the evacuation, captured the sense of fear that swept through the city: "children abandoned their parents, parents their children, husbands their wives and all their property and fortunes, to flee the death which awaited them in the capital."[26] Meanwhile, Monteverde retreated to the fortress of Puerto Cabello, leaving Bolívar to enter Caracas unopposed on August 6, 1813, and establish the second Venezuelan republic.[27]

Bolívar had scored an extraordinary victory with his "Admirable Campaign." Reports of Bolívar's entry into Caracas project an image of complete and comprehensive triumph: maidens crowned him with laurels amid cheering crowds, and Bolívar extolled the heroism of his forces, who, he said, had "triumphed seven times" in battle and "beaten five armies . . . of 10,000 men."[28] Such rhetoric was rather misleading, however, given that Bolívar had circumvented royalist forces rather than crushing them. By speed of movement, he had achieved surprise and thereby disorganized royalist forces, but his military actions were on a small scale—generally between forces of 300 to 1,500 men—and did not deliver a knockout blow. Contemporary battle reports suggest that casualties were generally low; many of the enemy preferred to change sides when caught unawares, sometimes even before fighting broke out, and, in the manner of poorly trained soldiers, they tended to break and flee when taken by surprise, abandoning their supplies and equipment.[29] One royalist observer contemptuously recalled that Bolívar's campaign scarcely merited the name of war: "there were no battles in the field but just ambushes . . . no armies but tumultuous throngs of undisciplined men."[30]

The campaign also fell short of achieving its political goals. Taking Caracas secured a valuable symbolic asset and, more important, gave Bolívar the material resources of the city and its hinterland. But it did not make his position secure. Monteverde had yet to be defeated in battle, and other royalist chiefs remained in the field with forces capable of defeating their republican adversaries. Moreover, the "people" did not flock to the republicans despite Bolívar's effort to force "Americans" to side with the republic by declaring a *guerra a muerte* (war to the death) at Trujillo on June 15, 1813.

The concept of guerra a muerte had originated with Antonio Nicolás Briceño, who, together with other Venezuelan émigrés in Cartagena, had, in January 1813, issued a public statement calling for a war of extermination. Briceño publicly declared that "the principal goal of this war is to exterminate in Venezuela the cursed race of European Spaniards, including the Canary Islanders," and he promised payment or promotion to soldiers in proportion to the number of severed Spanish heads they delivered to their commanders.[31] Although Bolívar did not sanction this gruesome system of rewards, his decree at Trujillo in June 1813 did declare that all Spaniards should be killed, whichever side they espoused.[32] Designed to promote the cause of independence by targeting Spaniards as the real enemy (a tactic that played on the anti-Spanish feelings stirred up by Monteverde's behavior), this was a political strategy that failed. Americans continued to fight together alongside Spaniards against the republic. However, the adoption of terror tactics undoubtedly escalated warfare. The civic wars in which the combatants fought for towns and villages with small forces and limited violence were increasingly displaced by a civil war in which violent reprisal and atrocity became commonplace. Violence was, moreover, aggravated by the royalists' tendency to criminalize the insurgents, whom they treated as morally flawed "traitors" and "bandits" who deserved to be eliminated.

One sign of the rising tempo of violence was the panic that gripped Caracas on news of the approach of Bolívar's army; government functionaries, soldiers, and thousands of civilians evacuated the city to seek refuge in the royalist towns of the Caribbean coasts and islands. Venezuela was, then, already gripped by spreading violence in mid-1813, as ideas of conciliation gave way to a mutual commitment to destruction of the opposing side. If Bolívar had fought an admirable campaign, he now became embroiled in an increasingly dirty war.

War for the Second Republic

The persistence of war in Venezuela was partly the consequence of Bolívar's failure to finish off the royalist forces, which he had sidestepped during the "Admirable Campaign." It soon became apparent that his strategic premise—that the capture of Caracas would provide the political support and economic means needed to finish off the royalists in Venezuela—was overly optimistic. As Rafael Urdaneta, one of Bolívar's principal lieutenants, later recalled: "the patriots had made only a rapid march, from victory to victory, terrifying the enemy and passing through his lines, in the hope of finding in the capital moral strength and the means to liberate a country which they had traversed, but not conquered."[33] Or, one might say, Bolívar had used the Napoleonic tactic of rapid advance only to put himself into a situation akin to Napoleon's in Spain; he held the capital and its hinterland but did not attract much political support beyond it, nor have the ratio of force to space needed to impose republican government by military means.

Bolívar responded to these problems by trying to create a viable government in the capital while striking out against his enemies before they could regroup. To achieve the first goal, he used diplomatic means, seeking to strengthen friendly relations with New Granada's United Provinces and with Cundinamarca, making overtures to Britain for recognition, and eliciting cooperation from Mariño in forming a single republic.[34] None of these measures yielded the material aid that Bolívar hoped for: New Granada had little to offer, Britain refused to allow an arms trade, and Mariño used his resources for his own purposes. Bolívar was thus thrown back on the resources of the region around Caracas, and, after assuming supreme political command, he concentrated on his central goal—that of building an army and an administration that could supply the means for making war.

Bolívar's conviction that the First Republic had been fatally weakened by its federalist form of government and reliance on militias meant that he immediately aimed at creating a centralized government and a professional army. Indeed, he soon went to the extreme of centralized power by becoming a dictator, giving priority to military over political imperatives. This might seem a sign of strength, since it showed that he could concentrate power at a moment of emergency and ignore the demands of the Venezuelan aristocracy for a share of power.[35] On the other hand, his dictatorship and draconian measures (especially against Spaniards and their property) can also be construed as symptoms of weakness, reflecting anxiety about enemies within and a desperate need to find resources to fight a war on several fronts. Whatever the case, Bolívar's assumption of command ensured an intensification of the war, together with a new phase of militarization. Convinced that he needed a larger, more organized army to defeat the royalist forces, he embarked on a new round of recruiting and military training. His aim was a European-style army of infantry armed with muskets, backed by squadrons of dragoons, hussars, and lancers. Such an army would, he hoped, enable him to defeat the regular soldiers who were at the core of royalist forces and to overcome their undefeated garrisons.

The royalists had three main strongholds. First, the strategic fortress of Puerto Cabello, a position from which Captain General Monteverde could threaten Caracas and rally royalist support along the coast and upland valleys where slaves had rebelled in the name of the king. Second, the coastal towns of Coro and Maracaibo, from which royalist commanders could launch offensives against Barquisimeto and Barinas as well as threaten Trujillo, Mérida, and even New Granada. Third, in virtually the entire southern part of Venezuela, stretching eastwards along the Orinoco River from its delta in Guayana, across the rolling plains of the Llanos and towards the Andean foothills, royalist enclaves challenged the republic's control. The royalist commander Cajigal held Guayana and was able to send reinforcements and supplies upriver to the western Llanos, where many pockets of royalist resistance remained under army officers, such as Tiscar, and irregular leaders, such as José Tomás Boves and José Yáñez. The region was rich in cattle and horses, its rivers provided lines of supply that connected east to Guayana, and its plains offered huge spaces in which llanero forces could concentrate, disperse, and reconvene. The plains around Calabozo and in Barinas were particularly important because they offered spaces for combining llanero forces with royalist armies from the west, in encircling movements against Caracas.

Royalist military operations against Bolívar's republic were initially cautious. Monteverde's strategy was to defend Puerto Cabello and promote resistance elsewhere while awaiting reinforcements from Spain. Bolívar, by contrast, took action to expand his radius of influence by eliminating the royalists who presented the most immediate threat. He declared a second "war to the death" in order to extirpate royalist bands around the coasts near Puerto Cabello, in the highlands around Valencia, at Guárico, and the valleys of Aragua, all of which stood close to his heartland. He then set up headquarters in Valencia, close to his seat of government, while also providing a position from which he could oversee military operations in several adjoining areas. He had up to 2,000 men, whom he dedicated to several purposes. One contingent of 130 men was sent to Calabozo to deal with royalist forces led by Boves; another of similar size went to the Tuy valleys to put down rebellious slaves, who were fighting in the king's name. A smaller contingent of some 50 men went south to Barinas as reinforcements for republican forces arraigned against Yáñez. Bolívar also planned two larger operations: he sent 800 men under Girardot to attack Puerto Cabello and gave García Sena a division of 600 to go west and attack Coro. He kept a reserve of 400 at his headquarters in Valencia, while the remaining troops were mostly in the garrison at Caracas.[36]

In the early days of the Second Republic, Bolívar deployed the largest contingent of his forces in a campaign against the royalist redoubt at Puerto Cabello. This was a key military objective because, as the English soldier George Flinter recalled, it was "the place of greatest strength and the most regularly fortified of any other town in Venezuela . . . surrounded by the sea . . . defended by a strong line of batteries . . . [and] the castle which . . . is bomb proof, and . . . considered to be impregnable."[37] Given these advantages, Monteverde's strategy was unsurprising; he sought to hold Puerto Cabello at all costs, harassing the republic by supporting guerrillas inland while awaiting reinforcements by sea. In August–September 1813, he withstood the attacks led by Girardot and Urdaneta and in the subsequent siege refused to surrender even when Bolívar threatened to execute 4,000 Spanish prisoners.[38]

Although Bolívar and his commanders fought some of their greatest battles inland, the struggle for Puerto Cabello was crucial. Monteverde's hold on the port constantly challenged the republican cause. It demonstrated that royalist government survived and was fighting back, provided a maritime bridgehead and acted as a base from which to launch attacks inland, while also forcing the republic to expend valuable military resources in frustrated offensives. Puerto Cabello was, moreover, the point of departure for a royalist military revival in late 1813, after the arrival of reinforcements from Spain. In mid-September, Colonel Salomón arrived from Cádiz with 1,200 regular soldiers of the Granada Regiment and prompted Monteverde to launch an immediate and substantial offensive, of some 1,800 men, against the republic's headquarters at Valencia. In the event, the royalist effort to rout the republic's main forces did not succeed. Bolívar launched successful attacks against royalist positions at Bárbula on September 30 and Las Trincheras on October 3, 1813, and severely punished Monteverde for his foray out of Puerto Cabello. The second action, at Las Trincheras, cost the royalists some 200 dead and captured, left Monteverde seriously wounded, and forced him back to Puerto Cabello, where he handed over command to Salomón. Final victory eluded Bolívar, however, for although the republicans sought to exploit their victory by renewing their siege of the fortress, they were again held at bay.[39] The military situation in this strategic zone thus returned to a stalemate in which neither side could overcome the other, but where the royalists retained the advantage of holding Venezuela's most important military stronghold.

Bolívar had blocked a royalist breakout from Puerto Cabello, but as royalist offensives started elsewhere, he was obliged to redouble the defense of the republic. At this difficult juncture, Bolívar showed that his military talents were matched by a capacity for symbolic warfare. At Bárbula, he had lost an outstanding officer,

Atanasio Girardot, who had led New Granadan troops to several victories and become a key commander on the fight into Venezuela. To honor Girardot and a depleted officer corps, he organized an elaborate funeral, deploying an extraordinary ceremonial display that served multiple purposes.[40] This was not only a moment to express grief at the loss of a close comrade; it also gave Bolívar an opportunity to bond his men together in a brotherhood of republican warriors. By proclaiming Girardot's warrior virtues, Bolívar sought to inspire his officers with a vision of themselves as heroic liberators, ready for glorious sacrifice in the name of liberty. And, while bonding his men together by funerary rites that gave a quasi-religious legitimation to the republican cause, the carriage of Girardot's embalmed heart from Valencia to the cathedral of Caracas also provided a public show of republican respect for religion and the Church.

If such rituals displayed Bolívar's skill as a propagandist for the cause of the republic, they also reflected his awareness of the need to heighten his men's emotional commitment to the cause at a time when enemy opposition was growing. For, with the failure to take Puerto Cabello, the republicans had lost a key campaign. Monteverde remained in place, and royalist forces began to organize against the republic in other regions of the country. As a result, the Puerto Cabello campaign was swiftly followed by several other important battles in late 1813, when republicans and royalists fought a series of actions in different parts of the country.

These actions—which took place on separate fronts to the south and the west of Caracas—reflected the growing intensity of the war, for they engaged larger forces, caused heavier casualties, and had a destructive impact on civilians caught in the theaters of war. The main fronts were south of Caracas, where the republicans had to fight the growing army of llanero irregulars led by Boves. To assure the republican grip on the region around Calabozo, Vicente Campo Elías went south with a force of around 1,800 men (1,000 infantry and 200 horsemen, plus 650 lancers) to fight Boves and his llanero warriors. On October 14, he defeated Boves's force of 2,000 horsemen and 500 footmen at Mosquiteros, in a battle that left a heavy toll of casualties (some 1,500 dead and wounded between both sides). Second, Bolívar moved against the royalist forces that lay to the west: he advanced against Ceballos at Coro and engaged in battle at Barquisimeto on November 9, 1813. His offensive was stopped, however, and when he withdrew towards Valencia, Bolívar then had to fight Colonel Salomón, who sallied forth from Puerto Cabello in an attempt to crush Bolívar's force on its line of retreat. Bolívar redeemed himself by repelling this attack and sustaining an army capable of moving onto the offensive. He then turned his attention to a third front, at Barinas, where Ceballos had joined his forces with those of Yáñez. In early December 1813, Bolívar joined Campo Elías to fight this royalist army, and leading 3,000 troops against a rather larger royalist force, Bolívar beat the largest army he had yet encountered, at Araure, in the biggest battle of the war so far.[41] Thus, when 1813 ended, the Second Republic had survived its most severe military tests, and the balance seemed to have tipped in the republic's favor.

At this point, the republican army was a much more effective set of forces than those that had defended the First Republic but was not without flaws. It was weakest when facing artillery and trained, well-organized infantry; for example, Bolívar was unable to overcome the fortress at Puerto Cabello because he had neither the artillery nor sufficient infantry to overcome a strongly fortified position, nor the resources to guard against the diseases that afflicted static encampments in tropical climates. Bolívar had also been defeated when he met a large force of disciplined infantry commanded by Ceballos at Barquisimeto, despite having 1,100 foot soldiers against 750 on Ceballos's side. The republicans seemed to do better against irregulars, at least when they were able to combine artillery, infantry, and cavalry against forces composed mainly of llaneros on horseback. The contribution of an increasingly battle-hardened infantry seems to have been crucial in the fight against the llaneros. In the action at Mosquiteros, Campo Elías deployed over 1,000 foot soldiers and 850 horsemen to beat Boves's 500 foot soldiers and 2,000 horsemen, However, Bolívar's battalions also showed themselves capable of defeating a large, well-organized royalist army, using European tactics and battle order. At Araure, the republic infantry played a key role in an intense battle of six hours, in which they repelled cavalry attacks and then overran the royalist infantry, showing a discipline and maneuverability under fire, which, according to the one contemporary account, was comparable to "the most battle-hardened European soldiers."[42]

The casualties in these battles corresponded to the larger forces deployed. At Mosquiteros, the royalists were reported to have lost 1,200 in dead and wounded, as well as many prisoners and horses. At Barquisimeto, the patriots were said to have lost 1,000 men in dead, wounded, and prisoners, while at Araure, the total of royalist and patriot dead and wounded was about 1,800.[43] And with these human losses, defeated forces also lost substantial quantities of arms, munitions, and equipment, an important byproduct of battle in a situation where it was difficult to get arms from outside Venezuela.

Bolívar's victory at Araure was important for the republic because it broke the main forces mustered against it; the royalists lost many of their European soldiers and saw their remaining forces dispersed. The outcome of the war was, however, still undecided. At the end of 1813, Secretary for War Tomás Montilla eulogized Bolívar's achievements and portrayed a republic in the ascendant, but he admitted that Bolívar had been forced to act "without the cooperation of the Venezuelans," that resistance remained, and that reforms were urgently needed to sustain the army.[44] In short, Bolívar's new republican order was still very much a work in progress. Although the republicans had succeeded in beating off royalist offensives, they had not eliminated the royalist enclaves nor eradicated the enemy's military potential.

The republic was, moreover, still as much the creature of a political minority as it had been in 1811–12. Despite his military prowess, Bolívar had wrought no great political change. Intent on restoring rule by enlightened liberals, he had plucked the capital from the royalists' grasp only to find that the Second Republic attracted no more enthusiasm than the first. Bolívar had, it seems, invented a republic that was forced to fight its own population. His call for a war to the death had tried to inspire a nationalist crusade by demonizing Spaniards but did not rally Americans to his side. Americans in Venezuela remained stubbornly divided in a civil war for and against the king, and Bolívar's adoption of terror tactics simply aggravated the violence, locking both sides into a war of reprisals and hindering reconciliation. The chances of compromise diminished still further in late 1813 when news that Napoleon had been forced out of Spain heartened royalists throughout Spanish America.

The demands of war accelerated political change on the patriot side. The revolution started in 1810–11 now became more authoritarian and more reliant on force. After his victory at Araure, Bolívar faced very adverse circumstances: the enemy was still at large, the treasury was empty, and trade and agriculture were badly damaged. He responded with emergency measures and more intense militarization. Martial law was decreed on December 21, 1813, partly in order to allow Bolívar to enlarge and reorganize his forces; all males were required to enlist in "civic militias" in order to strengthen his veteran battalions (some 8,000–10,000 men of whom about half were reckoned to be effectives). He ordered the construction within Caracas of a citadel for use in a last-ditch defense of the city, an act that reflected the republican sense of vulnerability. In January 1814, while deploying his army against enemy forces on several fronts, he also tried to slow the spiral of violence and to deplete royalist forces by suspending the "war to the death" decree and promising pardon to royalist partisans who gave up their arms and leaders.[45]

The royalist authorities were also in dire straits, as they too were disorganized and short of supplies. When Juan Manuel de Cajigal took over as captain general from February 1814, he found a confused system of command, an arbitrary, corrupt government, and an impoverished army. Many of those on the royalist side, he recalled in his memoirs, were using the royal cause to pursue their own nefarious ends; they called themselves "generals" and, with 20 or 30 men, undertook "conquests" in which they sacked and killed at will. José Tomás Boves was a prime example. According to Cajigal, Boves had the largest forces because of the ruthless and unlawful methods he used to recruit and sustain them.[46] Many areas of Venezuela were, it seems, at the mercy of roaming bands, which, in the name of one side or the other, lived from pillage.

To restore order and revive the fight against the republicans, Cajigal placed Ceballos in overall command of royalist forces, with orders to punish the freebooters, organize a disciplined army, and launch a new campaign against the enemy. The result was a fresh royalist offensive aimed against the republican cities, using conventional military methods but blending conventional and irregular forces. Most important, the royalist cause found new men to throw into battle when, under the leadership of Boves, irregular forces plundered the plains south of Caracas and, gathering strength, prepared to strike out against the republic's cities.

The Royalist Reconquest of Venezuela

The major royalist forces were grouped on three fronts. Ceballos reestablished an army at Coro by combining the Granada Regiment (now composed largely of

Americans) with local militias and Indians. Another, lesser nucleus was at San Fernando Apure, where Yáñez used his bands of irregulars to struggle for control of Barinas until he was killed in February 1814. His command was then taken over by a regular army officer, the Spaniard Sebastían de la Calzada. The third and more important concentration was at Calabozo, where Boves commanded growing numbers of llaneros in what was effectively a personal army.

When campaigning resumed in February 1814, offensives began on all these fronts. Ceballos advanced out from Coro into the province of Caracas, where he took Carora and Barquisimeto. Calzada came from the south to attack San Carlos. Then, in late March, their two forces—a total of about 2,000 men—took San Carlos and forced Urdaneta to retreat to Valencia. This was a crucial point in the outer defenses of Caracas: Bolívar feared that its fall would mean the loss of the republic, and he urged Urdaneta to defend it to the death, which he succeeded in doing. Ceballos made two abortive attempts to draw the republicans into battle outside Valencia but withdrew in early April in a clear sign of royalist weakness.

Boves meanwhile pursued his own objectives on a third front, moving northwards out of the Calabozo plains into the Aragua valleys close to Caracas, where his depredations caused panic among civilians and an exodus of refugees from areas where his forces operated. Ceballos called on Boves to join forces with him at Valencia, but Boves delayed sending forces until it was too late. Cajigal—who was present at these events—saw this as proof of Boves's insufferable pride and insubordination; he failed to participate because "he would never contribute to anything but his own glory."[47] Such criticism pointed to a serious problem of coordination in the royalist campaign. Ceballos had a very effective warrior in Boves, capable of raising very large irregular forces and using them to great effect on the battlefield, but Boves behaved like an independent warlord. He regarded his forces as a personal army, disobeyed orders that were not to his liking, and presented himself as the king's greatest champion in Venezuela.

José Tomás Boves was an outstanding example of a new kind of leader who rose to power in a society militarized by civil war. During his ascent to power, the war in Venezuela was marked by growing violence and greater destruction, deeper social fears, and sharper racial antagonisms. A plebeian Spaniard, Boves had first emerged as a local chieftain fighting in the frontier region of Calabozo against other local leaders who took the republican side. Appointed as royalist commander of the town of Calabozo, he rallied forces against Bolívar in 1813 and rose to a new position of prominence. He was, above all, the principal leader of the llaneros, the people of the vast plains of western Venezuela, cowboys and smallholders, who coexisted with the huge ranches owned by landowners who struggled to impose their authority over a frontier society. The poor llaneros' antagonism toward rich creole landowners made them enemies of a republic identified with such landowners, and their lifestyle as horsemen of the plains, herding cattle with lances, made them natural cavalrymen, who could be turned into soldiers against that republic.

Boves's genius was his ability to turn their grievances and skills to the royalists' advantage. By offering the llaneros the promise of plunder and merging them into improvised armies officered by their own leaders, he conjured a formidable force from the ranching communities of the plains. The llaneros' mobilization was not an unmixed blessing for the royalist cause, as they answered only to their own leaders and did not readily coordinate with other forces. However, under Boves's direction, they moved from defensive positions in frontier regions into attacks directed against the republican heartland and thus made a critical contribution to the royalist war effort.

Of all the royalist military campaigns of 1814, Boves's offensive was the single greatest threat to republican security. Its potency was revealed when Boves moved on the approaches to Caracas, where he confronted Bolívar's forces in several major military engagements. In early 1814, Boves showed again that he could concentrate large forces. With some 7,500 men of whom as many as half were llanero cavalry, he imposed severe pressure on republican defenses from late February to late March. To check his advance, Bolívar concentrated about 3,000 men, including over 2,000 infantry, at San Mateo (close to Victoria) and called on Mariño to bring reinforcements to attack Boves from the rear. At the first battle of San Mateo (February 28, 1814), Bolívar succeeded in halting Boves's advance from preprepared positions, using artillery and disciplined infantry to good effect against the undisciplined royalist horsemen. A second battle at San Mateo (March 25) was a much more closely run contest but eventually also turned in the republic's favor. For as Boves pulled back from his assault, he came up against Mariño's reinforcements and suffered another defeat. Republicans reported that they had inflicted heavy losses on Boves's forces in February–March, estimated at around 4,500 in total.[48] But Boves had not exhausted his resources: he now withdrew into friendly territory and concentrated on rebuilding his forces with fresh recruits.

While Boves was regrouping, Bolívar seized the opportunity to move back onto the offensive against Ceballos and the main royalist army in the west, while also uniting the republic's forces. He met Mariño at La Victoria on April 5, 1814 and transferred command of the army to him, with orders to attack Ceballos. The attempt to defeat the royalists in the west failed, however, when Mariño was defeated in battle at Arao, near San Carlos. After their long spell of combat, patriot forces now nearly disintegrated amid desertion and mutiny. The army's problems reflected the increasingly desperate state of the society around it, as hunger spread through the countryside to the towns, and Caracas filled with starving refugees. Bolívar took extraordinary measures to replenish his army (including compulsory conscription for males over 12) and to find food and money for arms. And, despite these obstacles, he scored an extraordinary military success. Ceballos had positioned his 6,000-strong army at Carabobo in the expectation of defeating the weakened republican forces, but despite having fewer men (about 4,000) and poor supplies, Bolívar again drove the royalists back, with a stunning victory on May 28, 1814.[49]

Bolívar's military talents had saved the day but did not win the war. Victory on one front was neutralized by reverses on others. While the republicans were fighting Ceballos, Boves had replenished his forces; by June, he had mustered some 3,000 men at Calabozo, mostly llanero cavalry, and was again ready for action. This time Bolívar was unable to stop him. When two armies of roughly equal size met at La Puerta on June 14, the llanero cavalry scattered the republican army, reducing it by about a third in dead and wounded. Bolívar had now to fall back on Caracas, pursued by Boves's swelling forces, and lost control of the city's hinterland as the peasantry flocked to the royalist banners and erupted in localized rebellions. Within a month, Bolívar was forced to abandon the capital completely, and in early July, he started an overland retreat towards Barcelona with his remaining 1,200 men. A great civilian exodus followed, with as many as 20,000 refugees fleeing in terror from Boves's approaching forces.

From Barcelona, Bolívar and Mariño played out the republic's endgame. In August, Boves crushed the final line of forces arraigned against him near Caracas, then headed east to Barcelona and into Cumaná. There was little left to stop him. In a campaign notorious for royalist atrocities, Boves swept all before him until he was killed in battle at Urica on December 5, 1814, having wiped out the last substantial patriot force.[50] On Boves's death, his deputy Morales was voted commander of the army by his fellow officers, and true to Boves's caudillo leadership, the officers agreed to recognize no other authority in Venezuela, including the captain general and the audiencia. The llaneros then proceeded to mop up in the east, killing patriots and, it was said, any whites they distrusted. Captain General Cajigal, who had concentrated on the west, now had to turn his attention eastwards, not to conquer, but to curb llanero atrocities and bring Morales under government control.

By this time, the patriots clung to a last piece of territory on the island of Margarita, where Arismendi still held sway, while other patriot chiefs—Monagas, Zaraza, Cedeño, and Páez—retreated into guerrilla warfare in the Llanos. These were mere remnants of a republic that had collapsed at its center. Bolívar and other leaders had once again fled into exile, back to Cartagena, and in April 1815, the last small redoubt of patriot government at Margarita fell into royalist hands. Captain General Cajigal later recalled that when General Morillo arrived in Caracas in mid-May at the head of 10,500 men, the largest expeditionary army that Spain ever sent across the Atlantic, he was able to hand over a country that had already been restored to Spanish rule.[51]

The Significance of the Venezuelan Wars

It is easy to see why the history of Venezuela's Second Republic in 1813–15 must be told in terms of war. The fate of the republic depended from its outset on military force, since Bolívar had seized the capital without fully defeating the royalist army or winning substantial political support. Like Monteverde before him, Bolívar was an invader who faced divided loyalties within the city and its hinterland, as well as outright opposition throughout the western provinces and in the Llanos. Thus, after taking Caracas, he faced the difficult tasks of imposing his government on a largely indifferent population while also fighting the substantial royalist enclaves that continued to oppose him. His political approach was based on military force; he assumed dictatorial powers and installed a government dominated by the imperatives of war. This militarization of political life was echoed by his opponents, who also saw war as their primary duty; indeed, although the royalist government was nominally under the authority of the Spanish parliamentary regime established by the Cortes at Cádiz, it was in practice run by warlords like Boves and his commanders. These caudillos mustered their peasant cohorts to deadly effect; they became the armed nemesis of the republic, the forces that drained Bolívar's resources and exhausted his armies. Indeed, in the end, it was essentially Boves who defeated Bolívar, not just by his triumph at the battle of La Puerta but because he created a more effective version of Bolívar's "war to the death."

War also looms large in the history of the Second Republic because it was much more violent and destructive than the fight for the First Republic. This was a war fought without negotiations and usually without quarter, and with devastating effects on civilian populations. When Bolívar's republic was overthrown in August 1814, it collapsed amid panic, flight, and carnage. Those who could fled from the wrath of the victors; long lines of refugees straggled towards friendly ports in the hope of escape. Those who could not suffered the depredations of royalist irregulars urged on by their leaders to exterminate the last of their enemies.

War left Venezuela a devastated land. In 1817, the official *Gazeta de Caracas* reported that 80,000 people (20% of the population) had died since 1810, about 10,000 in the earthquakes of 1812, the rest from war and its accompanying catastrophes.[52] These estimates may have been exaggerated, but contemporaries agree that war had inflicted deep wounds on Venezuelan society. The institutions of government had all but disappeared, the economy was wrecked, and vicious fighting continued in areas where insurgent and royalist bands struggled to overcome the other. Indeed, although the republicans had been defeated, violence persisted as irregulars on both sides refused to abandon the practices of plunder learned during the war.[53]

Why did the Second Republic founder? The explanations are not purely military. In terms of strategy and tactics, neither side had an obvious advantage. It has been argued that Bolívar lost because he was unable to import sufficient arms at a critical moment, due to the British government's refusal to allow an arms trade with British agents and ports.[54] But this lacks credibility, as it is not clear that the royalists were much better supplied in quantity and quality of arms. More important was the royalist mobilization of peasant forces under José Tomás Boves and other popular leaders.

While historians usually agree that Boves and his llanero warriors are central to explanation of the war, interpretation of the historical significance of Boves and his followers has involved greater controversy. One historical reading stems from the contemporary denunciations of Boves. Among patriot commentators, Boves became a byword for anarchic cruelty, a man who threatened the very essence of social order by leading pardos and blacks in a pitiless war against whites. Bolívar's aide-de-camp Daniel O'Leary literally demonized Boves, explaining his victories as "the diabolical course" of "this perverted soul," which no mere human power could have prevented.[55] Even royalists who hailed Boves's triumphs deplored his methods. Some suspected that he was less interested in defending the rights of Ferdinand VII than in building his own power by making himself "the idol of the people of colour."[56] Boves's Spanish chaplain, José Ambrosio Llamozas, informed Ferdinand VII that, while Boves had defeated the republicans, he had engaged in the systematic destruction of whites, putting thousands of men, women, and children to death and giving their property to his pardo followers. As proof, Llamozas listed many examples of the massacres that Boves had inflicted after his declaration of a "war to the death," observing that although his "insatiable thirst for blood" was not limited to whites, Boves had regularly incited the blacks and pardos to exterminate whites wherever they found them.[57] Archbishop Coll y Prat, a convinced royalist who was reluctant to condemn a man who had done so much for the "just cause," also told the king that Boves had behaved like an independent warlord and was notorious for devoting his men to "pillage and atrocities rather than military order and discipline." This, said the archbishop, had led to a destructive war, comparable to the barbarian assault on ancient Rome.[58]

There is little reason to doubt that Boves manipulated Venezuela's social and racial antagonisms, given the body of evidence that shows he aimed to secure the allegiance of blacks and coloreds by treating them as equals, proclaiming freedom from slavery on the lands he raided, and allowing them to plunder the towns they took.[59] However, there is some cause to question the stark characterization of Boves as a bloodthirsty scourge of civilization, leading a host of barbarous horsemen out of the wilderness to strike at Venezuela's helpless cities, spurred on by the lure of plunder and racial vengeance. In the first place, the damage inflicted by llanero plunder was not an irrational violence driven solely by hatred and greed. Boves and his men behaved in a manner that was neither novel nor notably different from that of their republican enemies.[60] Both sides faced the same problem of scarce resources and both turned to similar solutions. Sackings and sequestrations were the common means of compensating for scarcity of supplies and money, as neither royalist irregulars nor republican forces had adequate finances or a solid taxable base. Their forces lived off the land, and when they had exhausted the resources of one area, they moved to another, leaving behind a trail of devastation. The destruction of Venezuela by war was, in short, caused by the logistical needs of competing armies rather than the inherent barbarity of Boves and his troops.

If the belief that the llaneros were a host of barely distinguishable barbarians given to indiscriminate violence does not withstand serious scrutiny, there are also reasons to question their portrayal as "primitive rebels" engaged in constant rebellion against oppressive landowners in a lawless frontier.[61] Analysis of the sociology of the Llanos and its subregions, and the organization of the forces that emerged from them, suggests a more complex reality.[62] Closer examination suggests that the Llanos were composed of several distinctive geographical regions with different ecologies and socioeconomic structures, a pattern that cannot be reduced to a single region in which a single class of large landowners struggled to control a turbulent peasantry. While it is true that Boves and other commanders recruited largely among the mixed-race populations and used anti-white propaganda to win their support, the llanero armies were built on many communities, had a white component, and did not necessarily share a sense of racial or regional unity. Indeed, because historians have focused so tightly on Boves as the prime mover in the Llanos, they have overlooked the fact that three royalist armies emerged from the region, one led by Boves and the others by Yáñez and Rosete (both of whom, like Boves, had been small traders before the wars and had strong contacts throughout the areas in which they had worked).

These armies shared some essential characteristics. They responded to a personal leadership and were built on bands of men linked by ties of place or kin. Yáñez had a core of regular soldiers (the residue of Tiscar's forces left after the defeat at Mosquiteros in 1813), but the bulk of his recruits were irregulars, men who joined to fight back against republican forces that had plundered their settlements for food and forced recruits. The llanero adhesion to royalism was not, then, a rebellion arising from structural causes. It was more akin to the French counterrevolutionary uprisings in the Vendée against the depredations of the agents of republican government, an uprising promoted and manipulated by the agents of royalism and expressed in a series of localized wars rather than a fight for national power.[63] Here, in the special setting of the Venezuelan plains, we see the outlines of a phenomenon that we shall also find in other regions of Spanish America where political conflict led to warfare—namely, the readiness of peasants to defend the integrity of their own communities by exploiting the political competition between royalists and patriots.

How, finally, should we characterize the war for the Second Republic? Clearly, this was not a conventional "war of independence," which set "nationals" against a "foreign" colonial power, despite Bolívar's desire to make it so. Nor was it a race war: whites, pardos, and blacks were arraigned on both sides. It was, rather, a civil war, which split Venezuelan society vertically. The character and conduct of war in Venezuela was of course inflected by social and racial antagonisms. Political conflict had originated among the white elites, but politicization could not be confined to whites alone. Competition over political power brought into the open social and racial tensions that had previously been contained within the Spanish judicial system. Thus, pardos pressed for civil equality, and slaves became restive amid rumors of freedom. For the pardos, concessions were made; the 1812 Constitution gave them civil rights equal to those of whites. But this did not erase other conflicts. Despite the republican rhetoric of equality, the first governments of independent Venezuela were vehicles for white landowning supremacy, and as they eschewed popular support, they helped to fuel the royalist counterrevolution. People of color, especially those in the Llanos, responded to royalist recruiters as a way of asserting their rights against the republic's landowners and their hostile legislation, while slaves rebelled against creole masters in the name of the crown. Thus, the conflict between independent and royalist authorities turned into an internal war infused by social enmities. It stopped short of the generalized violence that had previously occurred in neighboring Haiti, which was shattered by prolonged slave insurrection and foreign invasions, but warfare nonetheless did lasting damage to

Venezuela's social order. Pardos and blacks learned that by fighting, they could escape the restraints of race and class, and when Spanish government was restored in 1815, they were to impede the reconstruction of the old regime for which they had previously fought.

The Dissolution of Independent New Granada

While Venezuela's republic was being battered to death in the bloody civil war of 1813–14, neighboring New Granada saw internal warfare of a more diffuse, polycentric kind. One element was the civic wars that continued on the Caribbean coast, where royalist Santa Marta remained at war with independent Cartagena, and in the south, where royalists at Popayán, then Pasto, fought against the independent towns of the Cauca Valley. Another source of armed conflict was the struggle for political dominance between the Congress of the United Provinces and the State of Cundinamarca and later between the congress and the State of Cartagena. Finally, there was war that interacted with that in Venezuela, as New Granada's Congress fought to contain the threat of royalist incursions from Venezuela on its eastern borders around Cúcuta and Pamplona.

These wars share some characteristics. They were all small in scale and, compared to the war in Venezuela, involved relatively limited militarization, less social violence, and had a more muted impact on civilian life. They were also separate conflicts fought on widely separated fronts, without any single political or military center. Indeed, their failure to create a unity of command, shared strategy, or co-ordination of forces was, as we shall now see, the Achilles's heel of New Granada's independent polities, exposing them to the same fate as Venezuela's republic.

Royalists and Republicans on the Coast

In June 1813, Francisco de Montalvo took over as captain general of New Granada and bringing 300 troops, turned Santa Marta into the principal center for royalist government and primary front for war in the Caribbean region. Montalvo's arrival seemed set to give fresh momentum to counterrevolution in New Granada. In his capital, the people backed the royalist side, as did the Indians of the neighboring rural areas and most of the towns and villages in Santa Marta's province; the port of Riohacha to the east of Santa Marta also continued in royalist hands and provided an armed base against incursions from republican Venezuela. However, the royalist military effort made little headway. Montalvo had a stable base and a relatively strong garrison, but he lacked the resources needed for counterrevolutionary war. He could count on the support of the city and the Indians of the neighboring Ciénaga, but they were unsuitable allies for fighting a wider war. The urban commoners were more concerned with enhancing their own position within local politics than fighting the enemy in Cartagena; as for the Indians, Montalvo considered them a risky ally, since they might turn their arms on whites.[64] Riohacha was also unreliable because, though solidly royalist, its leaders were more concerned to assert autonomy from Santa Marta than to join in a campaign against common enemies.[65] Montalvo was thus forced to hold a defensive position against Cartagena rather than seeking to eradicate its independent government or advance into the interior of New Granada.

The leaders of Cartagena also failed to pursue the war with much energy, mainly because they were distracted by political infighting within the city and popular opposition from its rural hinterland. At first, the creole political directorate seemed to establish a firm urban base for revolutionary war. They cultivated the city's substantial population of free blacks and coloreds, granting them legal equality and extending the military *fuero* to all who served in Cartagena's armed forces. However, the mulatto military units were controlled via vertical ties of patronage by the opposing parties of García de Toledo (*toledistas*) and the Gutiérrez de Piñeres brothers (*piñeristas*), who used them for party political purposes. Indeed, it seems that the city's creole leaders regarded the popular classes primarily as a support for their political struggles within the city rather than as a source for recruits to fight against the royalists outside it.[66] Political infighting extended beyond the city too. The 1812 peasant rebellion in the agricultural hinterland south of the city—known as the "Revolution of the Savannahs"—showed that support for the republic was tenuous in rural areas, where people were ready to rebel in the name of the king to defend local interests.[67]

In these circumstances, Cartagena's war effort faltered. In May 1813, President Rodríguez Torices tried to take Santa Marta with an ambitious operation that mobilized hundreds of men carried in gunboats. They were heavily defeated, however, both on this occasion and on their second attempt in August 1813.[68] In the recriminations that followed, Cartagena changed its military leadership amid further infighting among political factions. The Venezuelan Miguel Carabaño forcibly replaced the Frenchman Labatut as army commander and deported him. Carabaño then tried to regain the initiative against Santa Marta with a new offensive in February 1814 but had no greater success than his predecessor. The royalists defeated Cartagena's amphibious forces on the Ciénaga, strengthening Montalvo's position in Santa Marta while aggravating disunity among Cartagena's leaders.[69] Riven by internal divisions and unwilling to collaborate militarily with the Congress of New Granada's United Provinces, Cartagena had preserved its independence but failed to curb resurgent royalism on the Caribbean coast. Santa Marta thus continued to be a threat comparable to the royalist stronghold of Puerto Cabello, for it remained as a bastion of Spanish rule, a bridgehead for royalist reinforcements, and a potential threat to New Granada's interior.

War in the South

While war sputtered on and off on the Caribbean coast, the security of New Granada's independent governments was also threatened by war in the far south, where a resurgent royalist government in Quito reactivated military operations. In mid-1813, Toribio Montes, the Spanish president and captain general of Quito, decided to use Pasto as a platform from which to attack Popayán and the independent Cauca towns, with a view to opening a front against New Granada's independent provinces. To launch the war, he detached Brigadier Juan Sámano and a contingent from the royalist army in Quito and sent him to establish a forward base at Pasto. Sámano merged his troops with militias raised in Pasto and the Patía region, creating a force of some 1,550 men for his campaign, and in July–August 1813, he seized Popayán and several Cauca towns. The independents' troops—a small force commanded by the French soldier Manuel Serviez and another under Colonel José María Cabal—put up little resistance and, outnumbered, awaited reinforcements from Bogotá.[70]

Sámano's offensive was well-timed to exploit the divisions among the independents caused by conflict between the State of Cundinamarca and the Congress of the United Provinces in late 1812. While congress pressured Cundinamarca to join its confederation of states, the president of Cundinamarca, Antonio Nariño, sent a force against the Congress of the United Provinces in Tunja, and the Congress retaliated by sending forces to attack Bogotá.[71] This extraordinary dispute stopped only when the two sides became aware of the royalist threat from the south. After withstanding a siege of Bogotá by congressional forces, Nariño made an alliance with the congress in order to fight the royalists. He passed the presidency of Cundinamarca to his uncle, took up the role of commander in chief of a military expedition that was hastily assembled in Bogotá, and, with Cundinamarca supplying most of the troops, launched a campaign to retake Popayán and Pasto.

Nariño's campaign began in March 1813, when he led the 1,500-strong army of Cundinamarca from Bogotá southwards, with the aim of combining with forces from the Cauca towns and a 200-man force sent by the State of Antioquia under the command of José María Gutiérrez.[72] As Nariño did not leave an explanation of his strategy, his aims are not entirely clear. However, as Bolívar was on the offensive in Venezuela at this time, it is likely that Nariño saw his campaign as part of a larger strategy to push back the royalists in both Venezuela and Quito. He probably also hoped to enhance both the cause of Cundinamarca and his own prestige by leading a campaign that would coincide with Bolívar's. Certainly, this was an appropriate moment for coordinated action against Spain's military forces. By carrying the war back into Venezuela, Bolívar strengthened the independent provinces on New Granada's eastern boundaries; by attacking the other major royalist threat in Pasto, Nariño aimed to defend the south and, given the opportunity, to attack the royalist stronghold of Quito.

Nariño's campaign had a precedent in Baraya's 1810–11 expedition from Bogotá against Popayán and Pasto, and it followed a somewhat similar pattern of early success, followed by defeat and failure.[73] In December 1813, Nariño beat Sámano's vanguard at Alto Palacé and took the city of Popayán. In mid-January, he defeated Sámano again at Calibío, where the main bodies of the two armies met for the first time, with about 1,000 men on each side. Their two-hour battle was fought according to the conventional tactics of eighteenth-century armies: lines of infantry with muskets were arraigned in two files, artillery pieces positioned along the front, and cavalry stationed on each of the flanks. On this occasion, Sámano's troops broke and ran, but because Nariño did not pursue them, the majority were left to regroup and fight on another day.[74]

After a couple of months of recuperation at Popayán, Nariño headed for Pasto, intending to eradicate the main royalist stronghold. On arriving with his vanguard outside the city, he sought to achieve surprise by launching a quick attack without artillery, support, or clear lines of communication to the commanders of his supporting columns and reinforcements in the rear. The attack was blunted by *pastuso* militias, however, and Nariño's forces dispersed in disorder, leaving behind their artillery, most of their stores, and their general. Amid their disorganized retreat, Nariño was captured, leaving his army in disarray. His deputy José María Cabal managed to regroup about half of the army at Popayán, but, demoralized by defeat, those left lost the will to continue fighting. Soldiers from Cundinamarca mutinied and threatened to return to Bogotá, and Cabal conserved his forces only by pulling out of Popayán and dispersing them among several towns in the Cauca. The Army of the South thus ceased to be an offensive force capable of carrying the war into Quito; instead, Cabal had to concentrate on evading royalist operations aimed at finishing him off.[75]

We can get some sense of the character of this war in the south from the memoirs of participants on the patriot side, who give some telling details about the character of forces on both sides, the nature of their warfare, and the military situation that resulted from Nariño's defeat. The recollections of José María Espinosa, for example, suggest that Nariño's army was ill-prepared for the tough conditions that faced them in the south. In the war between Cundinamarca and congress in late 1812, they had been easily intimidated by the "thousand detonations of battle, the whistles of the balls through the air, the clouds of smoke that blind and choke, the noise of the cornets and the continuous beat of drums, not to mention the danger at every breath of falling dead or wounded."[76] Espinosa's account of the campaign also shows that the patriot forces ran into difficulties shortly after arriving in the south. Money ran out, supplies were difficult to find, and the advance on Pasto meant fighting in difficult terrain against peasants, particularly the "semibarbarous" people of the Patía Valley, who fought a war of attrition in which they gave no quarter.

The actions en route to Pasto were hard fought. The patriots used small artillery pieces, infantry muskets, and bayonets against entrenched enemy lines, against opponents who fell back in orderly retreats and inflicted significant casualties.[77] Nariño's men were sustained by the hope of taking Pasto, but when they failed and were forced to retreat, their physical state and morale deteriorated rapidly. Espinosa recalled a perilous flight by bands of men, who, amid the desperate pleas of wounded soldiers terrified of being left to the enemy's mercy, were constantly harassed by the pursuing pastusos and patianos. Their situation did not improve on returning to Popayán, as the city had emptied of people and supplies and was incapable of supporting the remnants of the army. The troops responded by plundering. Espinosa recalled that when they had first entered Popayán, the troops had behaved with great restraint; at that time, "property was treated as sacred. Nobody took anything."[78] By the end of the campaign, camp followers stripped the bodies left on the battlefield, and soldiers were accustomed to persistent "mistreatment, raggedness and short rations."[79] José Hilario López recalled this as a time when "we lacked everything," and without pay or food, soldiers were forced to cut wood or work as day laborers to feed themselves.[80]

Cabal saved what remained of his army by moving out into the Cauca Valley, where food supplies were abundant. Despite the rivalry among units made of men drawn from different places, Cabal's small army held together, mounting raids and ambushes and occasionally merging for larger actions in which liberal distributions of rum provided Dutch courage.[81] But the patriot forces of the south never fully recovered. They lacked local support and aid from the congress, which had to devote its meager military resources to fighting off royalist pressures elsewhere.

Endgame in New Granada

The wars fought by royalists and independents in New Granada, whether on the Caribbean coast or in the south, were all indecisive affairs, lacking the violence and impact of war in Venezuela. Both sides were capable of inflicting damage on the other, but their advances were invariably temporary and did not eradicate the enemy. Forces were small—usually fewer than 1,000 men on each side—and fighting was generally conducted by ambush, skirmish, and short actions, rather than organized battles. Local troops were reluctant to move far from their own regions, which made it difficult to sustain campaigns for long, and neither side fought with any coordinated, interregional strategy. And, whereas warfare in Venezuela's Second Republic shifted from limited civic wars to unrestrained civil war in populous provinces, war in New Granada was of lower intensity. It did not stir racial hatreds of the kind that affected warfare in Venezuela nor bring any great mobilization of the country against the city of the kind driven by Boves. New Granada's wars were fought mostly in border areas, brought only limited military mobilizations, and had little impact on the majority of the population. They were "games without winners, where, after fleeting successes, offensives ended in confusion and painful retreats."[82]

The tendency towards stalemate was broken during 1814, after Venezuela's republic was defeated and Spain's monarchy revived by the return of Ferdinand VII. Taken together, these events meant that Spain could concentrate larger resources on recouping power in Spanish America. The Congress of the United Provinces of New Granada responded to the threat by moving towards closer political union and more centralized military command. Its compromise with centralism was mirrored in the appointment of Simón Bolívar, once again in exile from Venezuela, as commander of the union's army, but it could not eradicate divisions among New Granada's governments. Indeed, before congress could turn its forces against the royalists, it sent them into military operations against independent provinces that refused to collaborate. In December 1814, congress declared war on Cundinamarca after its government refused to join the union, and Bolívar led congressional forces in a siege of Bogotá, which ended by defeating the city's defenders with a loss of some hundreds of lives.[83] Congress then turned Bogotá into the capital of the union and, in early 1815, mobilized its troops for an offensive against Santa Marta. However, this too ran up against provincial opposition: Cartagena refused to provide military supplies for the campaign, and congress ordered Bolívar to force the city to cooperate, using the forces he had taken to fight Santa Marta. When he failed to intimidate Cartagena, Bolívar despaired of fighting a successful war for an independent New Granada and left for exile in Jamaica.[84]

The failure to combine forces in a united front against Spain had dire consequences for New Granada's independent states. The delay in attacking Santa Marta depleted Bolívar's army, and the frontline on the Magdalena River was left exposed to royalist attack. The royalists of Santa Marta duly took control of the lower Magdalena, thereby ending the patriots' chances of carrying the war into royalist territory and leaving the city of Cartagena isolated and vulnerable. Nonetheless, under Manuel Castillo's leadership, the city's government continued to act without much consideration for the rest of New Granada. Confident in the defensive strength of Cartagena's fortifications, Castillo downplayed the royalist threat and did nothing to promote the coordinated operations needed to deal with a Spanish invasion.

Cartagena's recalcitrance was the extreme example of a larger problem: New Granada's provinces continued to deploy separate armies rather than creating a united command that might be capable of defeating an invading Spanish army. If multiple sovereignty in a loose confederation was a political arrangement that provincial elites preferred, it brought severe military disadvantages. For when in 1815, a large expeditionary army arrived from Spain under the command of General Morillo, the governments of New Granada's independent states had no unified military response.

Reconquest

Morillo's force of some 10,500 soldiers was the largest that Spain ever landed in America and presented a formidable challenge to the remaining independents. As Venezuela had already been reconquered by its own royalist forces, Morillo's task there was to restore peace rather than make war, and he soon advanced into New Granada. In July 1815, he took some 8,000 troops to Santa Marta and from there moved against Cartagena. The patriots in Cartagena appealed to Britain for help, even offering to accept the sovereignty of His Britannic Majesty.[85] Their resistance was in vain. In August, Morillo deployed the bulk of his army to besiege the city, while other units of his army moved inland to take the rest of New Granada. The siege of Cartagena was protracted and deadly. When it ended in early December 1815, about 7,000 people had died from starvation and disease within the city, while some 3,000 troops were lost to disease and desertion outside its walls—far greater losses than in any other military action in New Granada.[86]

The fall of independent Cartagena signaled the end of independent New Granada. It not only neutralized a formidable military stronghold but also placed the royalists in control of New Granada's principal point of communication with the outside world. During and after the siege, Spanish divisions fanned out across the country along key routes: from Santa Marta south to Mompós, from Cartagena westwards to the Chocó and Antioquia, and from Venezuela through the Llanos de Casanare into eastern New Granada. Some met strong local resistance, notably on New Granada's border with Venezuela. There, Calzada's force of some 2,000 men had to fight substantial patriot forces. He defeated Urdaneta at Cúcuta, Custudio García Rovira at Cachirí, near Pamplona, and their defeat opened the way to the capital. Calzada entered Bogotá along with the forces of Colonel Miguel de la Torre on May 6, 1816, and General Morillo joined them there later that month, amid public rejoicing.

By this time, the royalist army was subduing patriot forces in other major regions. In March 1816, Colonel Warleta defeated Andrés José Linares in Antioquia, in a battle that was finally resolved by the flight of most of the insurgents. The patriot army in the Cauca region, under Pedro Monsalve, was defeated first at Cuchilla del Tambo, outside Popayán, in June, and then at La Plata in July 1816. Meanwhile, as New Granada's First Republic collapsed, Santander and Serviez withdrew into the Llanos, where they were to join with Urdaneta and Manuel Valdés and proclaim for the republic in Villa de Arauca in July 1816. New Granada was thus restored to the royal authorities and only a handful of insurgents remained, isolated in the backlands of the Llanos de Casanare, where they had subsequently to accept the authority of the Venezuelan caudillo José Antonio Paéz.[87]

One historian has called Morillo's campaign a mere "military parade," conducted without serious military opposition.[88] This is an exaggeration; Spanish forces encountered pockets of organized armed resistance in several regions, and the reconquest took a year to complete.[89] Resistance was, however, constantly undermined by the failure of New Granada's independent governments to coordinate their military operations. Instead, each concentrated on defending its own territory, and scattered over distant regions, they were picked off one by one. Their defeats also owed something to the superiority of Spanish forces. Although the patriot armies had a core of veterans, the expeditionary soldiers from Spain presented them with a better-equipped, more disciplined, and battle-hardened opponent than they had ever faced from the forces mustered by royalist cities.

Another problem for the patriot cause was the lack of public enthusiasm for the political cause espoused by the independent states. Their leaders had tried to disseminate ideas of liberty and independence by various means and had some success in dislodging the widespread belief in monarchical rule.[90] But the new politics had generally failed to capture the popular imagination. The states that arose from the old Spanish provinces sometimes won strong local allegiance, but the confederation of the United Provinces was always short of symbolic capital. When Spain had been weak, its constituent states were able to survive within a loose federation, but larger loyalties were needed to thwart Spanish reconquest. Attempts to create popular armies failed, however, and in 1815–16, there was no powerful popular insurgency to harass the invaders as Spanish insurgents had harassed the French in the Peninsula. On the contrary, the populace shunned the small patriot forces that remained, and Spanish authority was restored throughout New Granada with much less resistance and bloodshed than Venezuela had suffered. Indeed, as we shall see in a later chapter, the next phase of war for independence in New Granada had to await the revival of the independents' military fortunes in Venezuela and Bolívar's return.

Notes

1. Vicente Lecuna and Harold A. Bierck, eds., *Selected Writings of Bolívar* (New York: The Colonial Press, 1951), 1, pp. 15–26.
2. On these armed forces, see Riaño, *Historia Militar*, pp. 21–2; Helg, *Liberty and Equality in Caribbean Colombia*, pp. 126–7.
3. For a description of these offensives based on reports from Cartagena's officers, see Riaño, *Historia Militar*, 1, pp. 201–22.
4. For Cartagena's position, see Sourdis de De La Vega, *Cartagena de Indias durante la Primera República,* pp. 77–81; for Santa Marta's, see Saether, *Identidades e independencia*, pp. 181–92.
5. Saether, *Identidades e independencia*, pp. 195–207.
6. Bolívar to Poder Ejecivo de la Unión, February 28, 1813, in Grases and Pérez Vila, eds., *Las fuerzas armadas de Venezuela en el siglo XIX*, 1, pp. 219–21.
7. See, for example, the early histories written by Bolívar's friends: Daniel Florencio O'Leary, *Memorias del General Daniel Florencio O'Leary: Narración*, 3 vols. (Caracas: Imprenta Nacional, 1952), vol. 1, pp. 141-72. The abridged English version of the *Memorias* is translated and edited by Robert F. McNerney as *Bolívar and the War of Independence* (Austin: University of Texas, 1970), chap. 4; José Manuel Restrepo, *Historia de la Revolución de la República de Colombia*, 6 vols. (Bogotá: Bolsilibros Bedout, 1974), chap. 5. Their line is followed in the standard work on Bolívar's wars: Vicente Lecuna, *Crónica razonada de las guerras de Bolívar*, 3 vols. (Caracas: Presidencia de la República, 1983), 1, pp. 15–24. Also John Lynch, *Simón Bolívar: A Life* (New Haven: Yale University Press, 2006), pp. 68–73.
8. Bolívar to Secretario del Poder Ejecutivo, March 19, 1813, quoted by Lecuna, *Crónica razonada*, 1, p. 17.
9. Bolívar to Secretary of State of the United Provinces of New Granada, Cúcuta, April 8, 1813, in Lecuna and Bierck, *Selected Writings*, 1, pp. 28–30.
10. Lecuna, *Crónica razonada*, 1, pp. 19–22.
11. Ibid., pp. 23–4, 33.
12. Riaño, *Historia Militar*, 1, pp. 265–6.
13. Thibaud, *República en armas*, p. 121.
14. For the definitions of strategy used here, see Archer Jones, *The Art of War in the Western World* (Urbana: University of Illinois Press, 1987), pp. 54–5.
15. Lecuna, *Crónica razonada*, 1, p. 24; Thibaud, *República en armas*, pp. 123–6.
16. Heredia, *Memorias*, pp. 84–117.
17. See the comments made by Francisco Yañes and Pedro Urquinaona, quoted by German Carrera Damas, *Boves: Aspectos socio-económicos de su acción histórica* (Caracas: Ministerio de Educación, 1968), p. 60.
18. Juan Manuel de Cajigal, *Memorias del Mariscal de Campo Don Juan Manuel de Cajigal sobre la revolución de Venezuela* (Caracas: Archivo General de la Nación, 1960), pp. 90–3. On the damage done by Monteverde's supporters, see the comments of the contemporary archbishop of Caracas, Narciso Coll y Prat, *Memoriales sobre la independencia de Venezuela* (Caracas: Academia Nacional de la Historia, 1960), pp. 246–7.

19. In Monteverde's defense, see Stoan, *Morillo,* pp. 42–7.
20. Lecuna, *Crónica razonada*, 1, pp. 32–3, 50–1.
21. Ibid., pp. 35–9; Mariño's account tells the story of the campaign but does not specifically mention Piar: see "Relación del General Mariño," in Grases and Pérez Vila, eds. *Las fuerzas armadas de Venezuela*, 1, pp. 276–81.
22. Thibaud, *República en armas*, pp. 136–40.
23. Lecuna, *Crónica razonada*, 1, pp. 39–41.
24. Heredia, *Memorias*, p. 172.
25. Lecuna, *Crónica razonada*, 1, p. 32.
26. Heredia, *Memorias*, p. 199.
27. Lecuna, *Crónica razonada*, 1, pp. 52–68.
28. Simón Bolívar . . . a los caraqueños, Caracas, August 8, 1813, in Grases and Pérez Vila, eds., *Las fuerzas armadas de Venezuela*, 1, p. 270.
29. See the reports on actions led by Girardot, Ribas, and Urdaneta in Grases and Pérez Vila, eds. *Las fuerzas armadas de Venezuela*, 1, pp. 241–50.
30. Heredia, *Memorias*, p. 215.
31. Plan de Antonio Nicolás Briceño, January 16, 1813, in Grases and Pérez Vila, *Las fuerzas armadas de Venezuela*, 1, pp. 216–20.
32. Decreto de guerra muerte, Simón Bolívar, Trujillo, June 15 1813, in ibid., pp. 239–41.
33. *Memorias de Urdaneta*, quoted by Lecuna, *Crónica razonada*, 1, p. 120.
34. Lecuna, *Crónica razonada*, 1, pp. 76–8, 93–105.
35. Lynch, *Bolívar*, p. 77.
36. Lecuna, *Crónica razonada*, 1, pp. 91–2.
37. Flinter, *History of the Revolution of Caracas,* pp. 50–2.
38. Lecuna, *Crónica razonada*, 1, pp. 113–19.
39. Ibid., pp. 123–8.
40. See the contemporary description cited by Lecuna, *Crónica razonada*, 1, pp. 132–4.
41. Ibid., pp. 135–8, 158–66.
42. José Francisco Heredia, quoted by Lecuna, *Crónica razonada*, 1, p. 168–9.
43. Ibid., pp. 136, 151, 165.
44. Tomás Montilla, Caracas, December 31, 1813, in Grases and Pérez Vila, eds. *Las fuerzas armadas de Venezuela*, 1, pp. 394–403.
45. Lecuna, *Crónica razonada*, 1, pp. 191–205.
46. Cajigal, *Memorias del Mariscal*, pp. 117–18.
47. Ibid., p. 120.
48. Lecuna, *Crónica razonada*, 1, pp. 224–31, 235–42.
49. Ibid., pp. 256–71.
50. Ibid.
51. Cajigal, *Memorias del Mariscal*, pp. 137–9.
52. McKinley, *Pre-revolutionary Caracas*, p. 170.
53. Stoan, *Morillo*, pp. 203–4.
54. For Lecuna, this lack of arms was "the principal cause of the collapse of the second republic": Lecuna, *Crónica razonada*, 1, p. 262.
55. Daniel Florencio O'Leary, *Bolívar and the War of Independence*, trans. and ed. Robert F. McNerney (Austin: University of Texas, 1970), p. 74.
56. Heredia, *Memorias*, p. 239.
57. "Memorial presentado al Rey en Madrid por el Dr. Don José Ambrosio Llamozas, vicario y capellan primero del ejercito de Boves," in Tomás Perez Tenreiro, *José Tomás Boves, Primera Lanza del Rey* (Caracas: Ministerio de Defensa, 1969), pp. 138–40.
58. Coll y Prat, *Memoriales*, p. 279.
59. Blanchard, *Under the Flags of Freedom*, pp. 28–9.

60. The thesis originated in Carrera Damas, *Boves*.

61. The portrait of "primitive rebellions" is found in Miguel Izard, *El miedo a la revolución: La lucha por la libertad en Venezuela, 1777–1830* (Madrid: Ed. Tecnos, 1979).

62. I rely here on Thibaud, *Republica en armas*, pp. 160–9, for geo-social analysis of the Llanos subregions.

63. Ibid., pp. 170–3, on the irregulars and their motives.

64. Saether, *Identidades e independencia*, pp. 197–207.

65. Earle, *Spain and the Independence of Colombia*, pp. 45–7.

66. Helg, *Liberty and Equality in Caribbean Colombia*, pp. 143–50.

67. Anthony McFarlane, "'La revolución de las Sabanas': Rebelión popular y contrarrevolución en el Estado de Cartagena, 1812," in *Cartagena y la independencia*, ed. Haroldo Calvo Stevenson and Adolfo Meisel (Cartagena: Banco de la República, 2011), pp. 215–47.

68. Riaño, *Historia Militar*, 1, pp. 253–9.

69. Ibid., pp. 468–71.

70. Ibid., pp. 310–14; José Hilario López, *Memorias*, 2 vols. (Bogotá: Biblioteca Popular de Cultura Colombiana, 1942), 1, pp. 25–34.

71. Riaño, *Historia Militar*, 1, pp. 147–72.

72. The latter arrived in the Cauca region but, due to the animosity of President of Antioquia Juan del Corral towards Nariño, it contributed nothing to the campaign: see Riaño, *Historia Militar*, 1, pp. 355–62.

73. My analysis of the military aspects of Nariño's southern campaign draws primarily on Riaño, *Historia Militar*, 1, pp. 325–440, a detailed account that incorporates the commentaries made by officers on both sides. I also use the two patriot memoirs that are important sources on the campaign. One was written in 1840 by José Hilario López, who served with Serviez in the Cauca before joining Nariño's army and participating in his Pasto campaign: see Hilario López, *Memorias*. The other was by José María Espinosa, a *santafereño* who had volunteered for the "national guard" established at Bogotá in 1810 and had some military experience in the Cundinamarca Grenadiers before joining Nariño's expedition: see Espinosa, *Memorias de un abanderado*. For comment on Nariño's qualities as a general, see Camilo Riaño, *El Teniente General Don Antonio Nariño* (Bogotá, 1973), pp. 155–208.

74. The action at Calibío is described by López, *Memorias*, 1, pp. 42–4.

75. Riaño, *Historia Militar*, 1, pp. 443–52.

76. Espinosa, *Memorias de un abanderado*, p. 36.

77. Ibid., pp. 47–56; López, *Memorias*, 1, pp. 46–62.

78. Espinosa, *Memorias de un abanderado*, p. 47.

79. Ibid., p. 87.

80. López, *Memorias*, 1, p. 80; Espinosa, *Memorias de un abanderado*, p. 47.

81. Ibid., pp. 62–83.

82. Thibaud, *Repúblicas en Armas*, p. 220.

83. Riaño, *Historia Militar*, 1, pp. 494–505.

84. Ibid., pp. 531–48.

85. Gustavo Bell Lemus, *Cartagena de Indias: de la Colonia a la República* (Bogotá: Fundación Guberek, 1991), pp. 39–67.

86. Earle, *Spain and the Independence of Colombia*, pp. 61–4.

87. Ibid., pp. 64–7. Also Jane M. Rausch, A *Tropical Plains Frontier: The Llanos of Colombia, 1531–1831* (Albuquerque: University of New Mexico, 1984), pp. 171–5.

88. Jorge Mercado, *Campaña de invasion del Teniente General Don Pablo Morillo, 1815–1816* (Bogotá: Ejército de Colombia, Estado Mayor General, 1919), p. 201.

89. Brian R. Hamnett, "Popular Insurrection and Royalist Reaction: Colombian Regions, 1810–1823," in J.R. Fisher, Allan J. Kuethe, and Anthony McFarlane, *Reform and Insurrection in Bourbon New Granada and Peru* (Baton Rouge: University of Louisiana, 1990), pp. 292–326.

90. Hans-Joachim König, *En el camino hacia la nación: Nacionalismo en el proceso de formación del estado y de la Nueva Granada, 1750–1856* (Bogotá: Banco de la República, 1994), pp. 203–74.

6

REVOLUTION ON THE OFFENSIVE

The Campaigns of Buenos Aires, 1810–11

In the Viceroyalty of Río de la Plata, the challenge to Spanish rule was led by urban revolutionaries in Buenos Aires, backed by the city's militias. Like their counterparts in Bogotá and Caracas, they mounted a coup at the center of viceregal government and transferred power to a junta with very little bloodshed. The Buenos Aires junta, led by Cornelio de Saavedra, then asserted its supremacy on the grounds that the junta was the legitimate successor to the viceroy and so inherited his authority over the defunct viceroyalty.

When the junta took power on May 25, 1810, it presented itself as an emergency government that represented the absent Ferdinand VII, eschewed major changes in the existing administrative structure, and exhorted the provinces of the interior to join it by sending deputies to participate in its deliberations.[1] It was, however, no easy task to impose the junta's authority, as it was unwieldy, divided internally, and faced obstacles in securing the cooperation of the interior provinces.[2] In the vast, sparsely populated territories of the old viceroyalty, the capital was separated from other centers of settlement by considerable distances and slow communications. To the west, the provinces stretched inland from the Atlantic coast for hundreds of miles across the pampas to the foothills of the Andes. In the northwest, over a thousand miles from Buenos Aires, in the very different geography and society of the Andes, the distant provinces of Upper Peru were established on high mountain plateaux and amid ancient Native American societies. To the east, the viceroyalty extended across the River Plate into the rolling grasslands of the Banda Oriental towards the contested border with Brazil. Finally, to the northeast, colonial governors held sway over the lands around the Paraná River system and the province of Paraguay, another distinctive colonial society built on Guaraní Indian communities and fringed by the old Jesuit missionary frontier.

The main points at which opposition to the new government emerged in this vast area were widely separated. The first focus was in the city of Córdoba, where ex-viceroy Liniers and the intendant Juan Gutiérrez de la Concha joined together to reject the junta and to try to stop the revolution from spreading inland. Another point of provincial resistance was in Paraguay, where the intendant, supported by the local elites in his capital at Asunción, refused to recognize the Buenos Aires junta. Much nearer to Buenos Aires, on the opposite bank of the Plate estuary, the cabildo and royalist officials in Montevideo also rejected overtures from Buenos Aires. This was a particular danger to the revolutionaries in Buenos Aires because Montevideo had a military garrison, a fortified position, and access to reinforcement by sea. There was, in addition, the danger that the royalists of Montevideo might link up with those of Paraguay, so taking control of the entire eastern bank of the River Plate and the Paraná–Paraguay river system that reached deep inland, with lines of communication that stretched as far as Upper Peru. Last but certainly not least, royalist government remained intact in the distant interior of Upper Peru, where the Audiencia of Charcas remained under the command of its president, Brigadier Vicente Nieto, and royal officials still held office in the intendancies of Potosí, La Paz, Charcas, and Cochabamba.

Faced with these enclaves of royal government, the junta embarked on military campaigns in Montevideo and the Banda Oriental (modern Uruguay), in Paraguay, and in Upper Peru, the distant Andean region, which had once formed part of Peru. Of these, the most important was Upper Peru (modern Bolivia). The latter was the most fiercely contested territory in the viceroyalty, for, while the Junta of Buenos Aires was determined to take it, the viceroy of Peru was equally determined to hold it. Viceroy José Fernando de Abascal y Sousa responded to the May Revolution by bringing the provinces of Upper Peru under his viceregency, not only to prevent their annexation by the revolutionary government but also to establish a platform from which to strike back against the heart of the revolution, in Buenos Aires itself. Both sides regarded Upper Peru as strategically central, and when the opposing sides sent armies to defend their claims, the region became a major theater for armed conflict. However, although the war in Upper Peru was a distinctive zone of conflict and had its own singular characteristics, it cannot be treated in isolation from warfare in other regions of Río de la Plata. The struggle to control Upper Peru constantly interacted with a struggle to control the Banda Oriental, where the royalist enclave of Montevideo gave Spain a military base that could be used in combination with Peruvian forces in a general campaign against Buenos Aires. For the Spanish Regency and the viceroy of Peru, the struggles for Upper Peru and Montevideo were elements of the same strategy. By controlling the Andean provinces and the Atlantic estuary, Spanish loyalists hoped to crush the Buenos Aires revolution in a pincer movement, using forces commanded from Lima and supplied from Peru in combination with forces commanded from Montevideo and supplied directly from Spain. By the same token, successful war in both areas was crucial to the government of Buenos Aires and, as we shall see, the need to sustain operations on the coast and in the Andes was to impose intense military and political strains on the new regime.

The First War for Upper Peru

War against the remnants of Spanish government in the viceroyalty began with an offensive from Buenos Aires. On May 25, 1810, the day it took power, the junta agreed to send a division of 500 men in an "auxiliary expedition" northwards through the interior provinces and into Upper Peru. When it set out in July, the primary target for this force was the city of Córdoba, where the intendant Juan Gutiérrez de la Concha had joined with the ex-viceroy Santiago Liniers to resist the new government of Buenos Aires.[3] The ex-viceroy was in touch with Nieto, the royalist commander in Upper Peru, and having assembled a force of some 700 men at Córdoba, Liniers planned to create a counterrevolutionary army by linking up with royalist forces sent from Potosí.

The first objective for the Buenos Aires junta was, then, to overcome the royalists at Córdoba. But this was not the expedition's sole purpose. Mariano Moreno's "plan of operations," drawn up at the behest of the Junta in July–August 1810, suggests that the extirpation of the loyalist threat in Córdoba was part of a wider scheme to take control of the whole viceroyalty.[4] While Moreno's suggestions were too radical for most junta members, his plan nonetheless reflected the shared assumption that the provisional government in Buenos Aires should extend its authority throughout the region, by force where necessary. Thus, after Córdoba, the expedition was to march into the heart of Upper Peru, high in the Andean altiplano, some 1,000 miles to the northwest. Its objective was to prevent the royalist officials who were still in control there from launching a counterattack, while also securing the region's rich resources for Buenos Aires. The expedition therefore marked the start of Buenos Aires's military efforts to take its revolution into the Andes, where its forces were to turn Upper Peru into one of the principal arenas of war in South America.

Buenos Aires's prompt move to bring Upper Peru under its political command is easily understood. Upper Peru's silver mining towns were the mainstay of the River Plate economy and Buenos Aires's government finances. They provided markets for Buenos Aires's imports from Europe and for the agricultural produce of the provinces of the Argentine interior; they were crucial to the new government because taxes on mining and control of the mint in Potosí were vital to pay for Buenos Aires's administration and armed forces. The towns of Upper Peru also occupied a strategic military position, since they were the obvious corridor for any royalist military expeditions that might be sent overland from the Viceroyalty of Peru. The highland provinces were, then, the most strategically important of the internal provinces as well as the richest in economic resources, and the Junta of Buenos Aires was determined to control them.

The junta had an instrument at hand in Buenos Aires's existing military units.[5] The Auxiliary Army was composed of 1,150 volunteers drawn from the militias.

They were placed under the command of Francisco Antonio Ortíz de Ocampo, colonel of the *Arribeños* (provincial) militias of Buenos Aires, and his second, Antonio González Balcarce, a regular soldier from a military family. Both these commanders had some experience of war, having seen action during the British invasions, and Balcarce was a professional soldier. Their force had a strong component of plebeian militiamen, who had been recruited from among the city's poor laborers and artisans during the British invasions and subsequently made a career of military life.[6] Though of modest size, its men had some military training but were short of arms. The royal arsenals, with their armories, artillery parks, and ammunition deposits, were few and poorly supplied. In 1810–11, the junta had to take a series of emergency measures to collect muskets, pistols, and swords from private citizens, using increasingly strong threats of punishment for those who failed to comply, while also trying to raise sufficient funds to import arms, particularly from North America.[7] Their designation as an Auxiliary Army reflected the image, which the Buenos Aires junta wanted to project, of a force for helping the provinces to join the revolution rather than an army of conquest.

The junta's aggressive plans to "help" the Andean provinces renounce Spanish government were opposed from their outset by Viceroy Abascal of Peru. Abascal knew that loyalty to the crown in Upper Peru was far from certain: Chuquisaca and La Paz had both shown signs of rebellion in 1809, and he feared that they might now opt to join with Buenos Aires. To prevent this, he annexed the provinces of Upper Peru in mid-June 1810, bringing them under his command as viceroy of Peru.[8] Having assured officials of his determination to recognize the Regency and defend the rights of Ferdinand VII, Abascal then prepared for war.

His first moves were defensive. He ordered arms and munitions to be transferred from Cuzco to Potosí and made Vicente Nieto, the recently appointed president of the Audiencia of Charcas, responsible for the immediate organization of military forces in Upper Peru, in coordination with the intendants of its provinces and with Goyeneche, president of the Audiencia of Cuzco. They were to do whatever they thought necessary to help Liniers in Córdoba and to launch a counterattack on Buenos Aires. As Abascal observed, this was a pressing matter, for the experience of events in La Paz the previous year had shown the error of delay in "a business which had in any case to be ended by arms."[9] In late July, José Manuel de Goyeneche had already mobilized forces in the Peruvian highlands, and in August, he was appointed as commander of the army that was to defend Upper Peru, with Colonel Juan Ramírez as his second. Together with other officers who had led the very successful campaign against the La Paz rebellion of the previous year, they began to assemble an army that was to guard the point where the southern shore of Lake Titicaca and the Desaguadero River marked the boundary between Peru and Upper Peru and formed a natural point for defense against an invader.[10]

While these preparations proceeded, Abascal developed a plan for action against Buenos Aires. On August 25, 1810, his Council of War decided to reinforce Nieto with 2,000 men from Cuzco and ordered Nieto to coordinate action against Buenos Aires from his headquarters in Potosí. Abascal later recalled that his primary intention at this stage was to defend the provinces of Córdoba and Salta at all costs.

He envisaged reinforcing royal officials in those provinces with forces sent from Chuquisaca, Cochabamba, Potosí, Paraguay, and Misiones, forming an army that would stop Buenos Aires's forces from advancing any deeper inland. He therefore told Liniers to remain at Córdoba, while ordering Nieto to create an appropriate "offensive and defensive plan" with Liniers and the governor of Potosí.[11] The viceroy also dictated measures for blocking all commercial and financial flows between Buenos Aires and the interior, while also taking steps to communicate with royal officials in Montevideo and with the Spanish ambassador in the Portuguese court at Rio de Janeiro, so that they could cooperate in the fight against the revolutionaries in Buenos Aires.

Abascal's initial plan was, then, to use Liniers's forces to resist the porteños at Córdoba, while government officials in Upper Peru mobilized forces for repression of the Buenos Aires's junta. This was evidently more than a passive defense of Upper Peru and Peru; it envisaged a bolder strategy for using Upper Peru as a springboard for striking back against Buenos Aires and crushing the revolution while it was still in its infancy. This seemed a credible approach: Liniers, Nieto, and other leading royal officials were confident of beating Buenos Aires because they believed its army to be a disorganized rabble, which, consisting of only about 500 men, would not stand up to serious military opposition; they also thought that the junta would be unable to deploy its forces outside the city for long for fear of attack from its internal enemies or from royalists in Montevideo. However, these calculations were based on imperfect intelligence or excessive optimism, and Abascal's plan soon started to unravel. His strategy for using Liniers to stop the expansion of Buenos Aires at a first line of defense was undermined when autonomists sympathetic to Buenos Aires took over government in Córdoba, depriving Liniers of his base and forcing him to retreat towards Upper Peru. He found his way blocked at Salta, and after being abandoned by his own men, Liniers and his fellow officers were captured. A few days later, on August 26, 1810, they were executed on the explicit order of the Junta of Buenos Aires, an act that sent a deliberate message to any other government officials who might have the temerity to hold out against it.[12]

Blame for this royalist defeat fell partly on Nieto, who had failed to implement Abascal's orders for reinforcing Liniers from the army in Upper Peru. He had not sent reinforcements because he feared for the reliability of his own forces— especially the men brought from Buenos Aires to suppress rebellion in Upper Peru in 1809, who had already shown signs of dissent—and because he believed that, to be effective, he needed an army of 8,000 men.[13] But Nieto was not entirely to blame. The decision of the local authorities in Córdoba to back Buenos Aires played a key part in Liniers's defeat, for it left him isolated and exposed. The lesson—that military mobilization was insufficient without political support—was to become increasingly obvious when the royal authorities were forced to defend their towns in Upper Peru.

Liniers's defeat was vital for the junta because it broke the first line of royalist resistance in the interior and cleared the way for the junta to advance on Upper Peru. The junta removed Ortíz de Ocampo when he protested at the execution of Liniers, and placed Antonio Gónzalez Balcarce in command of the army; the radical lawyer Manuel Castelli, an advocate of the executions, was confirmed as the junta's political commissar with joint responsibility for the expedition.[14] At the start of September, the junta then ordered the Auxiliary Army forward. Balcarce was to take a vanguard of 500 men to the royalist military outpost at Tupiza and there await the rest of the army to prepare for operations against the royalist army in Upper Peru.[15]

The first stage of this strategy—that of getting the army to the point of entry into Upper Peru—was relatively easy, since the three main towns en route—Tucumán, Salta, and Jujuy—were all allied to Buenos Aires. The expedition's advance into the interior was also favored by a topography that permitted relatively easy movement. Although towns were separated by long distances, the terrain was mostly undulating plains until the Andean foothills, and even there the march was not too demanding; Tucumán, and then Salta and Jujuy, higher in the Andean slopes, acted as points for rest, recuperation, and supply.[16] However, the difficulties involved in projecting military power from Buenos Aires became apparent as the expedition went further into the Andes. When the force that had left Buenos Aires reached Jujuy, it was much reduced. Many of those who started out from Buenos Aires had deserted, and the army barely maintained itself by enlisting men en route from the towns through which they passed. The expedition was able to continue only by employing a tactic that was to be crucial in the years to come—recruitment in the provinces that bordered on Upper Peru rather than dependence on men from Buenos Aires. When the dwindling Auxiliary Army was reorganized at Jujuy, more than half its men were from the Andean area.

The arrival of Balcarce's vanguard at Tupiza in mid-October 1810, some six weeks after his departure from Córdoba, marked the start of the war for Upper Peru. The intention of both sides was clear. The porteños intended to take control of Upper Peru not only for its economic potential but also as a base from which to challenge the viceregal regime in Peru. Abascal, on the other hand, was determined to defend Upper Peru and to hold the territory as a buffer against the revolution. In short, each side saw the occupation of Upper Peru as central to its own larger strategy for either promoting or preventing the expansion of revolution in South America.

Royalism and Rebellion in Upper Peru

If Viceroy Abascal's ambition to strike back against the Buenos Aires revolutionaries is perfectly understandable, his ability to turn Peru into the home of the counter-revolution requires further explanation. Interpretations of Peru's relative stability tend to stress the significance of regional differences in Peru, as well as the social and ethnic divisions that Spanish governments had long exploited by "divide and rule" policies.[17] Lima, the capital, was no home for revolution; on the contrary, it was generally amenable to Spanish rule, as its elites feared the plebeians and slaves of their city and its valleys, saw Spain as the foundation of their power, and did not dream of an independent Peru even when Spain collapsed in 1808–10. Though they paid lip service to the glories of the Inca past, they felt no kinship with Cuzco, the ancient capital, and the largely indigenous societies of the Southern Andes. On the contrary, they feared that Indian rebellion in the interior would derange the social and economic structures on which the stability of the Spanish regime, and thus their privileges, depended.[18]

Cuzco and the southern highlands were, by contrast, more propitious territory for rebellion. Its indigenous peasantry had taken part in violent uprisings during the Great Rebellion of 1780–2 and, after a brutal military repression, had no reason to regard Spanish government with any affection. Indeed, their fiscal and economic exploitation by government and landlords had intensified after the suppression of the rebellion, with more efficient tribute collection, the usurpation of indigenous political offices by mestizos and creoles, and appropriations of community lands and labor. Nonetheless, the southern sierra remained on the royalist side in 1810, providing an essential base for operations into Upper Peru and against the revolutionary government of Buenos Aires. The reasons for Indian quiescence are not entirely clear but were probably connected to the experience of repression during and after the Great Rebellion and the Indians' subsequent shift from violent revolt to judicial forms of protest; the usual divisions within and between Indian communities no doubt also hindered collective action.[19] The latter were particularly significant, for there was considerable internal heterogeneity among the groups labeled as "Indian" or "mestizo" as well as an absence of leaders capable of unifying them.[20] But whatever the reasons for Indian loyalty (or passivity) in the southern sierra, there can be no doubt that its outcome was crucial. Not only did it spare the viceregal regime the dangers of peasant rebellion in 1810, but it also allowed Viceroy Abascal to build a salient from which he could guard Upper Peru and create a platform from which to fight the revolution of Buenos Aires.

The balance of forces seemed initially to favor the royalist side. Faced with the threat from Buenos Aires, Abascal was able to draw on substantial military forces. To repel porteño incursion into Upper Peru at the likely point of entry in the south, he ordered Nieto to take up position in Potosí and from there to guard the approaches into Upper Peru. At the same time, he ordered Brigadier Goyeneche—who had displayed considerable efficiency in raising an army in Peru and deploying it against the rebels of La Paz in 1809—to muster Peruvian forces on the northern edge of Upper Peru, on the shores of Lake Titicaca, and the banks of the River Desaguadero. He also sent Goyeneche's deputy, Colonel Ramírez, with 1,500 troops into the region of La Paz, to secure its loyalty before moving south to join Nieto. The plan was, it seems, for Nieto's Army of Upper Peru to act as the forward army of operations, reinforced by Ramírez's soldiers, while Goyeneche's Army of the Desaguadero would provide a tactical reserve and, in the last resort, a line of defense for Peru.

The royalists aimed, then, to defeat the porteños by fortifying key points on the southern border of Upper Peru and using them as a base from which to attack the enemy. This was a sound military strategy, since it would force the army of Buenos Aires into combat before it could take advantage of resources in Upper Peru or find local allies. It was, however, heavily dependent on political stability in Upper Peru, where crown forces had to rely on the region's main towns to provide bases and resources, and required Indian villagers to provide material support along routes of supply and communication. The dangers of such dependence on the loyalty of Upper Peruvians soon became apparent when, on September 14, the city of Cochabamba rose in rebellion and declared allegiance to Buenos Aires.

Cochabamba's rebellion had multiple causes, but its timing was evidently determined by the porteño army's advance towards Potosí.[21] In August 1810, President Nieto had sent some 300 men from Cochabamba to Oruro to suppress an Indian leader connected with the La Paz rebellion of the previous year; he then ordered these men, led by Teniente Coronel Francisco del Rivero, a creole from Cochabamba, to join the royalist army at Potosí to oppose the expeditionary army from Buenos Aires. The *cochabambinos* and their leading officers promptly deserted, returned to their town, and, in mid-September, took its garrison, arrested the governor, and proclaimed for Buenos Aires.[22] The rebellion was particularly unwelcome for the royal authorities. Cochabamba had been famed for its military prowess since the victories of its militias over Indian rebels during the Great Rebellion of 1780–2 and could field many mounted men who were skilled in the use of the lance, the sling, the club, and the *chicote*, a kind of mace that the cochabambinos used to deadly effect.[23] It also set an example for others: on October 6, Oruro joined in an alliance against royal government and, reinforced by 1,000 men from Cochabamba, rose in support of Buenos Aires.[24]

These rebellions badly disrupted Abascal's plans for the defense of Upper Peru because they divided royalist forces at the moment they needed to coalesce against the porteño advance. Oruro's rebellion did particular damage, since it cut off contact between La Paz, Chuquisaca, and Potosí and delayed reinforcement of Nieto by Ramírez, who had moved into Upper Peru with a division of 1,500 men and was marching south towards Potosí. When news of the rebellions came through, Ramirez had not reached far beyond La Paz, due to logistical problems, and he promptly abandoned his march to Potosí in favor of a plan to attack Oruro with 1,000 men, followed by an assault on Cochabamba. To advance this plan, Ramírez sent Colonel Fermín Piérola forward with 600 men, while he prepared the rest of the division to follow. The objective was to overcome the rebels of Oruro and Cochabamba, then open the route south for the reinforcements that Nieto needed against the approaching porteño army.

The plan was reasonable but failed in its execution. When Piérola was confronted on the high plateau at Aroma by Esteban Arze and his force of 2,000 cochabambinos, he could not withstand the Cochabamba irregulars, who were both more numerous and, as about a third were horsemen, more mobile. Piérola's wing of Ramírez's forces were completely defeated at Aroma on November 14, 1810, with the loss of most of their arms and munitions, leaving La Paz open to rebel attack. There, Governor Domingo Tristán abandoned ideas of resistance and changed sides; on hearing of Piérola's defeat, he disarmed the 400 men of the city's garrison and led the city council in a proclamation of allegiance to Buenos Aires.

This left Colonel Ramírez little choice but to pull back. With the Cochabamba cavalry at his front and his flank uncovered by the defection of La Paz, Ramírez's advance turned into a hasty retreat to the Desaguadero River, and after this first serious reversal for royalist arms, he joined Goyeneche and the remaining body of the royalist army.[25]

Ramírez's defeat was damaging because of its character and implications. It had been inflicted by a large, organized force of men from a major town, and it showed that even though they had few firearms, such rebels could prevail over royalist troops led by regular soldiers. And, of course, their success had the political effect of encouraging the further spread of rebellion, this time to the city of La Paz. The delay of Ramírez's forces in the north also undermined the royalist strategy for defending Upper Peru against Buenos Aires's invasion force because it deprived Nieto of both reinforcements and an experienced military commander to help with his defense against the porteño advance.[26] Now, the security of Spanish colonial government in Upper Peru rested entirely on Nieto and his officers, who became solely responsible for stopping the invading forces led by Balcarce and Castelli.

Nieto's position was tenable in October 1810, when news arrived of Balcarce's approach. His main force was headquartered in Potosí under Nieto's overall command, and its vanguard was stationed at Tupiza under the naval captain José de Córdoba, on the route that the porteños had to follow to enter Upper Peru. Nieto's forces were substantial (1,500–2,000 men against Buenos Aires's smaller army); they also held a strong defensive position on the line of their enemy's advance, and had ample time to prepare their defenses. When Balcarce's forces approached in mid-October, Córdoba responded with appropriate caution; he made a tactical withdrawal from Tupiza to Cotagaita, where he established a strongpoint that commanded the route to Potosí. There, Córdoba entrenched his 700 riflemen, 200 lancers, and 8 artillery pieces in a defensive position behind earthworks; with reinforcements en route from Potosí, he was more than ready to repel Balcarce's 700 men and 2 artillery pieces.

The advantages of the royalist vanguard were demonstrated when Balcarce tested its strength. Finding himself unable to advance, he retreated to Suipacha, where he encamped his army. This was, however, a tactical retreat rather than a change of strategy; Balcarce recognized that there was no point in attacking a fortified defense without a large numerical or artillery advantage, whereas a retreat might tempt the royalists to come out from their defensive position and engage in open battle. This was, indeed, the effect. Shortly afterwards, the royalists were drawn from defense into attack, with the evident intention of engaging Balcarce's army in decisive combat.

Córdoba's reasons for moving onto the offensive have never been fully explained, but it would be wrong to think that he rushed into a reckless attack. He waited a week for Nieto to arrive at Cotagaita with reinforcements from Potosí on November 2 before taking a force of some 800 men in pursuit of Balcarce. On reaching Tupiza, he heard that Balcarce had been reinforced by 500 men, plus some additional artillery, and was encamped at Suipacha, some miles away. At this point,

Córdoba decided that he should confront his opponent and, on reaching Suipacha on November 7, launched an attack that was intended to destroy or disperse the enemy. According to a Spanish officer present at the time, Córdoba presented white, red, and black banners with a skull and crossbones—to indicate that no quarter would be given or taken—and sent four companies forward to probe the enemy position. It was at this stage that serious errors were made. Córdoba made little use of his artillery and after an exchange of shots for an hour and a half, sounded the retreat and left the field without giving any further orders. The troops then dispersed in a disorderly fashion, allowing the enemy to kill or capture about 100 men.[27] Outnumbered and outmaneuvered, the royalist vanguard broke into a disorderly flight back to their base at Cotagaita, where Nieto remained with 700 men armed with guns, lances, and 10 cannon. They did not have the chance to regroup; on the contrary, the arrival of the fleeing troops undermined the resolve of Nieto's remaining forces, inducing further panic. Indeed, Nieto was so alarmed by the news from Suipacha that he decided to abandon his well-fortified position, ordered that every man save himself, and beat a hasty retreat towards Potosí.

At the time, blame for the defeat at Suipacha fell on Córdoba. When Abascal wondered whether it was the fault of Nieto's "spirit weakened by old age" or Córdoba's "haste and inexperience," he concluded that the latter was more likely.[28] Córdoba's first mistake, Abascal lamented, was not to have returned to the defensible position at Cotagaita as soon as he heard of Balcarce's reinforcements. His second mistake came in battle, where, it seems, his enthusiasm to engage the enemy led him into a trap. While Córdoba failed to place his troops in effective battle positions, Balcarce's tactics enabled him first to deceive and then to overrun his opponents within a couple of hours, with the final half-hour attack deciding the day.[29]

There are, however, reasons to think that the most serious error, the mistake that turned a defeat on the field into a strategic setback in the entire campaign against Buenos Aires, was made by Nieto, not Córdoba. On a generous interpretation, Nieto's rushed retreat from Cotagaita could be construed as a rational attempt to preserve his forces to fight on another day. However, Nieto should have realized that the political repercussions of his retreat would nullify its military benefits. While he preserved his own life and that of his men, he lost the political authority vital to sustain his government. For as soon as Potosí's citizens were thrust into the front line, the political balance in the city shifted towards those who favored Buenos Aires. When Nieto and Córdoba arrived in Potosí on November 9, local support for the royalist cause had gone underground, and they were promptly arrested, along with the intendant Paula de Sanz, and imprisoned while the city awaited the arrival of the invading army.

The fall of Potosí, combined with Piérola's defeat at Aroma a week later, had sharply adverse consequences for Spanish authority over Upper Peru. The first defense against the incursion of revolutionaries from the south had failed badly, and Upper Peru's towns had learned that the viceroy in Peru was far from invincible. Losing battles was, of course, not the same as losing the war, and the royalists fought on; nonetheless, these early reverses left an impression that was difficult to eradicate.

The Spanish government in Peru had been shown to be vulnerable, and this lesson was to affect the politics of the region for years to come.

The immediate result of royalist defeat was to allow the new government in Buenos Aires to annex the provinces of Upper Peru. The porteño forces entered Potosí to an enthusiastic reception on November 25, 1810 and there established their first major base. Some weeks later, *potosino* ardor for the revolutionary cause cooled when, on December 15, Castelli presided over the public execution of Nieto, Córdoba, and Sanz in the city's main square, a merciless gesture that alienated many townspeople. Nonetheless, the Auxiliary Army had, with impressive speed, secured a key goal. Its victory at Suipacha was no great feat of arms: a few hundred men had been scattered by another small force with little loss of life; the defeated insurgents lost only 54 dead, and the royalists even fewer. Nonetheless, Suipacha had a political effect that was out of all proportion to its small scale because it opened the way for revolutionary forces to enter Upper Peru, secured the legendary city of Potosí, and strengthened Castelli's ambition to attack the viceregal regime in Peru.

Castelli's Regime in Upper Peru

The immediate consequence of Buenos Aires's success at Suipacha, when combined with the rebellions of Cochabamba and Oruro, was to jeopardize the royalist cause throughout Upper Peru. Castelli now seized the initiative and seemed perfectly positioned to take control of the entire region, as the junta had planned. Having eliminated the representatives of Spanish rule at Potosí, he appropriated the contents of its rich royal treasury, took control of the Potosí mint, brought Upper Peru's richest silver mines into the jurisdiction of Buenos Aires, and dispatched a large consignment of money to the junta. Buenos Aires thus combined a symbolic affirmation of its authority with an achievement of great practical value. In the short term, the mint provided essential funds needed to pay for further military advance; for the longer term, trade with Upper Peru promised a vital economic and fiscal support for the new regime.

Having secured Potosí with the cooperation of its people and some members of its social elite, Castelli moved northwards to Chuquisaca, with the intention of consolidating his hold on the central and northerly provinces of Upper Peru. A key part of his strategy was to win support from Upper Peru's large Indian population by promising what was, in effect, a social revolution. Influenced by progressive ideas, the junta aimed to convert the Indians from tributaries into full citizens, and Castelli accordingly sought Indian allegiance by promising rights to political participation and the abolition of Indian tribute. This approach was not purely ideological; it had a strongly pragmatic side, since Castelli had to have Indian support for his army, particularly for transportation. The promised reforms had drawbacks, however, for they were unwelcome to whites and many other non-Indians in a society where Indians were seen as natural inferiors and subordinates.[30]

While he resided in Chuquisaca, emitting proclamations and decrees designed to extend the Buenos Aires revolution to Upper Peru and enlarge his base of political support by promising to integrate Indians as citizens in the new system. Meanwhile his forces made preparations for pushing revolutionary war into Peru. At the end of 1810, Balcarce's army was were reinforced by about 1,000 men from Cochabamba, and in mid-March 1811, the combined forces of porteños and cochabambinos moved north to Oruro and La Paz, with the intention of undertaking the next stage of the campaign, aimed at defeating Viceroy Abascal's forces gathered on the border with Peru. From La Paz, Castelli and Balcarce prepared to invade Peru, setting up advance positions at Laja and Huaqui, a village on the shores of Lake Titicaca, close to the royalist encampments defending the bridge that was the key point for crossing the River Desaguadero into Peru.

At this point, in the opening months of 1811, the balance of power had clearly moved in favor of Buenos Aires, thanks in large part to active collaboration by Upper Peruvians. The five major cities of Upper Peru had declared allegiance to the Junta of Buenos Aires, recruits from Upper Peru had considerably strengthened the porteños' Auxiliary Army, and Castelli had gained substantial financial resources with which to back his military and political campaigns. Viceroy Abascal, on the other hand, was on the back foot. He had to switch from offensive operations in Upper Peru to defensive vigilance of the long border that ran from Lake Titicaca down the Desaguadero River and along the fringes of the Peruvian province of Arequipa, while watching his forces diminish through desertions.

The royalist regime in Peru thus faced a very disturbing prospect in early 1811. Not only were Upper Peru's towns under rebel control, but Castelli's forces were taking up position for an advance across the Desaguadero River, to carry the revolution into highland Peru. The prospect of such an advance was a nightmare for Viceroy Abascal since it would remove the viceroyalty's remaining line of defense in the southern highlands of Peru and expose the rest of Peru to military incursions and political instability that might topple the viceregal regime. The opening months of 1811 were, then, a key moment in the war between Buenos Aires's revolutionary government and Lima's colonial viceregency, with implications that extended beyond Upper Peru. For the royalists, much depended on General Goyeneche's leadership and on the strength of the army he commanded.

In early 1811, Castelli and Balcarce had good reason to be confident that the campaign was going their way, as they were received with acclaim throughout Upper Peru and met no further armed resistance. Buenos Aires's triumphant surge had flaws, however. In the first place, the porteños' success was not due solely, or even mainly, to their military prowess. Although Balcarce had defeated royalist forces at the border, his rapid capture of Potosí had been facilitated by the rebellions at Cochabamba and Oruro, which had split royalist forces, and by the royalists' poor military performance at Cotagaita. Once Potosí was taken and news of Cochabamba's rebellion spread, the subsequent collapse of royal government owed much to the decisions taken by Upper Peru's urban elites; they now found allegiance to Buenos Aires preferable to submission to the viceroy in Lima and were ready to join what looked to be the winning side. The interaction of military and political events is plain. First, the advance of the Auxiliary Army acted as a catalyst for the autonomist uprisings in Cochabamba and Oruro; then, by diverting royalist forces, these uprisings undermined royalist defenses against the porteños' advance; finally, the porteños' military victory at Suipacha was a catalyst for rebellion in Potosí, La Paz, and Chuquisaca, which joined with Cochabamba and Oruro in overthrowing royalist officials and turned the tide against royal authority throughout Upper Peru.

The combination of porteño military advance and local political rebellion had thus worked well in late 1810, but the installation of the May revolutionaries at the head of government in Upper Peru brought new difficulties. Although they had set themselves up as the leaders of Upper Peru, Castelli and Balcarce could not rely solely on their military forces to sustain their position, since they were far from their bases in Buenos Aires and the lower provinces, without any lines of supply except those found within Upper Peru. They relied almost totally on local support and, to keep it, had to persuade the inhabitants of Upper Peru that Buenos Aires not only offered a better political future but was also able to protect them against reprisal by royalist forces. Allegiance to Buenos Aires was, in short, neither unconditional nor unbreakable, and the porteños' political credibility depended heavily on their ability to retain the military advantage.

The Royalist Defense of Peru

The royalist position was even more heavily reliant on military success. Only armed victory could remove the porteños, reinstall royal government in Upper Peru, and defend Peru itself from attack. Abascal had therefore to invest his hopes in the skills of Goyeneche and the army at the Desaguadero. They were the only forces capable of reestablishing Spanish government in Upper Peru and all that stood in the way of the insurgents' advance into Peru.

The critical importance of Upper Peru as a theater of war was accentuated by reverses in other areas bordering the viceroyalty. While Peru remained quiet, its neighbors to the north and south were in turmoil. In Quito, a junta established in September 1810 recognized the Regency but refused to cooperate with the viceroy in Peru and displaced conventional royalist government until late 1812. In Chile, leading creoles also created a junta in September and followed a clearer path towards autonomy; they disavowed the Regency, called for the election of a congress, set up a correspondence with the Junta of Buenos Aires, and organized forces for defense against attack from Peru, whose viceroy they regarded as an enemy.[31] Thus, in late 1810, Abascal faced threats in all three territories that bordered on his viceroyalty, the greatest of which was in Upper Peru, where a rebel force had defeated royalist armies in battle and seemed poised to invade Peru or, at the very least, make common cause with Chile against Peru. For Abascal, the first priority was therefore to establish a defensive line against the porteños and to ensure in neighboring provinces that "the contagion of rebellion might not be propagated in their territories."[32]

Clearly, the rebellion of Buenos Aires was not merely a regional rising to be countered by customary modes of counterinsurgency. The threat was that of an organized revolutionary army, which, at a time when loyalties were weakened by the confusing situation in Spain, might trigger multiple uprisings, allowing the rebels of Buenos Aires to carve a revolutionary path into Peru, taking over the provincial governments in its way. Moreover, with both Quito and Chile under autonomous juntas, Viceroy Abascal had reason to fear that royalist Peru was being encircled by hostile regimes.

Military confrontation between royalists and insurgents on the borders of Peru and Upper Peru was therefore of enormous significance for both sides, since its outcome looked likely to determine not only control of Upper Peru but also the political future of Spanish rule throughout much of South America. For this reason, neither side sought to force an early confrontation, preferring instead to invest time in preparing their respective forces. While the royalists focused on training their untried troops at their camp on the shores of Lake Titicaca, Buenos Aires had its own reasons for delaying military confrontation and allowed the royalists their respite. The insurgents had arrived in a disorganized state and were not ready to push into Peru without consolidating their position and making further preparations. Castelli decided to strengthen his army by calling on volunteers from the towns, men who were not readily disciplined or molded into a single force. In early 1811, the porteños established their forward bases close to royalist lines and sought to integrate recruits from rebellious Upper Peruvian towns into their army, with the intention of consolidating their frontline forces into a disciplined whole.[33]

Goyeneche, commander of Peru's forces, focused on a similar task on the other side of the Desaguadero River. He set up his main camp at Zepita, on the shores of Lake Titicaca, established forward positions on the lake and river to prevent the enemy from crossing, and spent months in assembling and training a numerous army of disciplined troops.[34] Creating this army was no simple task. The viceroy supplied a contingent of regular soldiers, comprising a battalion of the Royal Regiment of Lima, of up to 680 men, plus 400 men from the Regiment of Pardos and 200 from the Regiment of Morenos. However, the majority of the army had been raised from the territories of southern Peru that bordered on Upper Peru, from often unwilling recruits. Those recruited did not inspire much confidence: in December 1810, Goyeneche told the viceroy that he despaired of ever building an effective force. He complained that desertions were running at an unsustainably high rate of 30 per day in spite of his efforts to cut off escape routes, to provide regular food and money, free rum on Sundays, and promises of home leave and enjoyment of the fuero militar. The problem was, in his view, deeply rooted in men who were "without honour, self-confidence . . . so downtrodden and apathetic that they wanted nothing more than to be idle," fit to be taught only by corporal punishment, and liable to desert when any attempt was made to discipline them.[35]

Comments of this kind, infused with social and racial prejudice, were common in the armies of the period and say more about the aristocratic disdain of the officer corps than about the character of the men in the ranks. Nonetheless, there is little doubt that Goyeneche faced serious difficulties in creating a disciplined fighting force from local recruits. These were mostly men without traditions of military service—men who were mainly coerced into service, deserted at the earliest opportunity, and had no obvious ideological commitments to the royalist cause. Loyalty to the king was an abstract concept for which few would sacrifice their lives, except perhaps among officers for whom memories of the Great Rebellion of 1780–2—when Indian insurrection had spread destruction through the southern Andes—were a reminder of the need to defend order and property. These men probably brought some recruits with them. As most were from Puno, Arequipa (Goyeneche's birthplace), and Cuzco (with which he was closely associated politically), loyalty to the royalist cause was no doubt reinforced by social ties, with soldiers aligned under officers whom they saw as leaders in their home communities. Pay, too, was an important consideration in regions where paid employment was scarce and precarious, and combined with punitive measures, a steady supply of money was a key to building the army. Indeed, it may be that Goyeneche made his most valuable contribution to the campaign by ensuring the regular payment, supply, and training of troops, all fundamental to creating a disciplined force needed to campaign away from home.

If Goyeneche delayed military operations for seven months, it was mainly because he had to invest time in turning raw recruits into an effective army. Despite his initial doubts about the quality of his recruits, he appears to have achieved a good deal at Zepita in the first half of 1811. He gradually assembled some 6,000 men and organized them into the three wings of a conventional army, including an artillery brigade of 260 men with a substantial train of some 30 pieces of light artillery. He also concentrated on drilling his men in disciplined maneuvers—no doubt adapted from those he had learned in Europe—and he expanded his previously weak mounted wing to a sizable force of some 1,000 men.

While Goyeneche struggled to strengthen his army, he was ably supported by Viceroy Abascal, who, despite his commander's constant complaining, recognized his key role in holding the army together and did all he could to meet Goyeneche's demands. Abascal also played for time, giving Goyeneche the luxury of months in which to train his men for battle. This was partly because he hoped Spain would reinforce the surviving royalist military enclaves in Montevideo and Chile, for, as he told the Spanish ambassador in Brazil, "without the despatch of troops from the Peninsula to the Viceroyalty of Buenos Aires and the Presidency of Chile, they will gain a great advance towards independence."[36] Hence, in the opening months of 1811, Abascal waited in the expectation that Elío, who had returned to Montevideo as the new viceroy of Río de la Plata, would launch an offensive on the Littoral. In March, the rumor that Elío had disembarked at Montevideo with 7,000 men caused Abascal to order Goyeneche to prepare for military operations in Upper Peru, taking advantage of Buenos Aires's need to defend its hinterland on the Littoral.

Abascal's desire for a swift strike against Buenos Aires was delayed, however, by Goyeneche and his officers. They sensibly decided to leave the cochabambinos to return home for the harvest and to wait and see whether Elío could take Buenos Aires.[37] Nature also played its part in delaying a return to war. For, as the author of a royalist memoir of the campaign stated, this was the season for gathering stores and supplies, not campaigning.[38] Castelli was also in no hurry to do battle and on May 13, 1811, agreed to a 40-day truce. Castelli was ready to explore the possibilities of a negotiated settlement, but Abascal would not tolerate any agreement that recognized the Buenos Aires junta as an independent government. Conscious of this impasse, both sides continued preparing for war. Castelli bombarded neighboring provinces with revolutionary propaganda and prepared to move across the Desaguadero into Peru, while his opponent Goyeneche concentrated on guarding against incursion across the river and readying his forces for action. As soon as the truce expired, the porteños began preparing to attack, aware that their contingent from Cochabamba would soon return home for the harvest. Their aim was, the royalists believed, to find a point on the Desaguadero where they could cross and outflank Goyeneche's forces. Goyeneche responded on June 20, 1811, with a carefully planned attack against the enemy's forward camp at Huaqui, close to Lake Titicaca.[39]

Royalist Counteroffensive in Upper Peru

Goyeneche's assault was, according to royalist accounts, a well-prepared, professional military operation, and not, as is sometimes said, an impromptu surprise attack. Having deployed his forces for an assault at dawn, he pushed two columns along the valleys that extended away from Lake Titicaca towards La Paz. Goyeneche took one column, consisting of an infantry regiment, plus 300 horse and 6 cannon, along the lakeside in order to attack the enemy's forward position and encampment at Huaqui. Colonel Ramírez was put in command of the other column—3 battalions, 350 cavalry, and 4 cannon—and went along the more southerly valley, towards Machaca, with orders to clear the enemy from their positions there. On successful completion, these columns, plus a smaller linking column, were to converge and then advance across the plateau towards La Paz.

Reports from the royalist and revolutionary sides indicate that the ensuing "Battle of Huaqui" was in fact two related actions.[40] First, Goyeneche dislodged the 2,000 men and artillery which Castelli, Balcarce, and Montes de Oca had set up in a defensive position outside Huaqui, and then took the village with all the enemy's supplies. Meanwhile, Ramírez led some 1,300 men against the defenses set up by Viamonte and Díaz Vélez along nearby hillsides and broke through when reinforced by Goyeneche. After six hours of battle, the porteños were forced to retreat. Once the retreat began, they scattered, losing their artillery, munitions, and equipment, as well as several hundred prisoners. Goyeneche's report stated that he had captured 250 prisoners and 400 muskets, and had seen many dead, while his own forces suffered only 7 dead and 14 wounded.[41] The cochabambinos took the retreat as a signal to leave the battlefield and head south to prepare for the defense of their own city.

Huaqui was not a major battle; it was more akin to a raid on the enemy's en-campments, which triggered a precipitous flight and caused the porteños to lose more men to desertion than by death or injury. Nonetheless, the royalists were right to claim an important victory because they had collapsed the porteños' primary position, with an ensuring "domino effect" in the rest of Upper Peru. As the Auxiliary Army retreated in disarray, so the porteños' political image suffered, causing potential allies to change sides. Huaqui may thus be reasonably regarded as the royalist reversal of the porteño victory at Suipacha nine months earlier, for it tipped the political balance back to the viceroy of Peru. For Abascal, it was an essential victory: Goyeneche's forces were all that he had to defend to the viceroyalty, as the royalists were without substantial reserves in 1811. Goyeneche's elevation to the Spanish aristocracy in recognition of his victory, as the Conde de Huaqui, was thus no empty gesture.

After Huaqui, Abascal's forces shifted onto the offensive and swept back across the Desaguadero River. Goyeneche's priority was to defeat the insurgents' remaining forces and to reimpose royalist control in Upper Peru's main towns, a task that was to take several months and involve a considerable military effort.[42] He entered the city on July 10, 1811, at the head of a force of 1,500 men and left a small garrison to ensure its submission. Peaceful pacification continued when, on July 22, he took Oruro without a fight.

The next step was more difficult. At Cochabamba, Goyeneche encountered strong opposition from local rebels and the remnants of the porteño army. Rebels led by Francisco del Rivero took up a defensive position at the River Amiraya near the village of Sipesipe with a large force of horsemen recruited from the vicinity and the promise of support from a detachment from the porteño army under Eustaquio Díaz Vélez. The latter did not arrive in time, however, and the cochabambinos succumbed to Goyeneche's forces. On August 13, 1811, Rivero was defeated, and Díaz Vélez retreated from the area; on August 16, Goyeneche entered the city and incorporated the rebels under Rivero into his army.

The capture of Cochabamba was an important moment in Goyeneche's counterinsurgency because it confirmed the royalist military superiority announced at Huaqui. A royalist report of the encounter at Sipesipe listed insurgent losses at 600 dead compared to 15 dead on Goyeneche's side, and, though this was probably an exaggeration of Cochabamba's casualties, such news was a discouragement to rebellion in other towns. The city council of Cochabamba still tried to assert some claim to autonomy, proposing to Goyeneche that he should bring the four provinces of Upper Peru into a captaincy general, comparable to that of Chile, with himself as its governor for life.[43] Goyeneche ignored this quixotic scheme and continued with his campaign of pacification, moving southwards to Chuquisaca and Potosí.

There was little further resistance from the porteños. Castelli had touched at Chuquisaca but left it undefended. Most of his fleeing soldiers headed for Potosí, foraging and plundering as they moved through the countryside. At Potosí, they joined the units commanded by Juan Martín de Pueyrredón, a Buenos Aires militia officer whom Castelli had installed as president of the Audiencia of Charcas.[44] Their regrouping was not, however, a concentration of strength, as Pueyrredón's regime was already unpopular. The unruly behavior of troops stationed in the city had already done much to poison relations between porteños and potosinos, and news of the royalist victories and the advance of Goyeneche's army strengthened the town's opposition to the porteños. Pueyrredón tried to censure news of the fall of Cochabamba, but the arrival of Díaz Vélez's unit confirmed that Potosí was the next likely target for royalist attack.

Recognizing their lack of support in Potosí, the porteño commanders saw retreat as their only alternative. Díaz Vélez headed south in order to regroup, while Pueyrredón remained in Potosí only long enough to organize confiscation of the funds accumulated in the Mint and the Bank of San Carlos, said to be about a million pesos. The town's citizens refused to cooperate with this plan, forcing Pueyrredón to flee by night with his plundered treasure on August 25, 1811. After fighting off a large pursuing force of potosinos, he eventually succeeded in retreating back to Salta with funds for a fresh campaign.[45] But his loot could not compensate for the severe defeat that Castelli's army had suffered. While Pueyrredón sought to regroup at Salta, the last contingents of the wounded struggled to find their way out of the Andes. James Paroissien (the English adventurer employed as the army's surgeon) recorded a sharp image of its ignoble end. Sent to find the last stragglers, he came across them moving painfully through the highlands at Humahuaca, "many of them with fractures, many with balls pass'd thro' their bodies . . . without medical aid . . . upon most occasions without bread . . . and swarming with vermin and filth."[46]

The porteño retreat meant that Goyeneche found Potosí despoiled but undefended. When he entered the city on September 20, he was given a tumultuous welcome akin to the celebrations afforded Castelli the year before. This blunted royalist vengeance. Although there were numerous arrests among those who had collaborated with the porteños, Goyeneche accepted Potosí's return to the royalist side and restored its role as a forward base for military operations in the south. From Goyeneche's new vantage point in Potosí, the prospect for royalist forward operations looked positive. Díaz Vélez and Pueyrredón had been rejected by their erstwhile allies in the southern town of Tarija, and their subsequent retreat gave Goyeneche the opportunity to pursue the porteño army southwards.

Thus, by late September 1811, Goyeneche had considerably strengthened the royalist cause in South America. By wrenching Upper Peru from the junta's hold, he had saved Peru from invasion, restored Upper Peru's towns to royalist rule, and established a position where Peru's military commanders could plan an offensive aimed against Buenos Aires itself. For the moment, at least, the military and political advantage in Upper Peru had clearly passed from the revolutionary regime in Buenos Aires to the royalist government in Lima. While Viceroy Abascal was vindicated, the government in Buenos Aires fell. Saavedra, the president of the junta, tried to blame Castelli for the failure of the northern campaign, but his position was fatally compromised by the army's defeat; he was removed from office, and in September 1811, the junta itself was replaced by a new executive, that of the triumvirate.[47]

The reasons for Goyeneche's triumph in Upper Peru are plain enough. He had, in the first place, conducted a very effective campaign, worthy of an officer with a far more sophisticated military background than any of his opponents. Before returning to Peru in 1808, Goyeneche had enjoyed a brilliant career in the Spanish army; he served as an officer in the prestigious corps of the grenadiers and the artillery, had seen action against the English at Cádiz, and, to complement his practical experience of war, had acquired an unusually wide theoretical knowledge. After leaving Cádiz, he was sent on a mission to study military tactics in Europe, which involved visits to Prussia, England, Holland, Switzerland, Germany, and Italy; this allowed him to see military maneuvers in Berlin, Potsdam, Vienna, Paris, and Brussels, and offered insights into the latest military thinking and practice. In 1805, Goyeneche presented Godoy, the king's chief minister, with a report on the institutions, conditions, and progress of Europe's best armies and was promoted to colonel as a reward for his efforts.[48] Here, then, was an officer with a breadth of knowledge of military institutions and tactics that was rare among Americans and which he evidently put to good use when leading his troops against less experienced antagonists. This did not mean that Goyeneche's generalship was unquestioned: some criticized him for spending too long at the Desaguadero and failing to take the initiative against the porteños. However, others believed that the time there had been well spent on training the royal army. Shortly after the victory at Huaqui, the governor intendant of Tarma informed the Minister in Spain that Goyeneche had transformed "a congregation of men who, taken from the plough, the loom and other artisan and rustic labours, feared to take hold of a musket." He had forged them into a field army of 8,000 men and had managed "to encourage, strengthen and confirm in their loyalty all his subordinate commanders, officers and soldiery." The result was plain for all to see in the victory at Huaqui; it showed that without Goyeneche, Peru would have suffered "irredeemable losses."[49]

When the principal officers of Buenos Aires's Auxiliary Army tried to explain their defeat, they blamed the *altoperuanos* (Upper Peruvians); with a hint of racist disdain, they condemned them for their "ignorance" and "servile spirit."[50] In fact, the leaders of the porteño army contributed much to their own defeat, as their army was less ready for battle and less effectively led than Goyeneche's. The high command was confusingly divided between Castelli and Balcarce, and soldiers were divided between supporters of Saavedra and Moreno, the leaders of political factions who were struggling for control of the junta in Buenos Aires. The forces drawn from Cochabamba, Oruro, and Indian villages were not unified under a single chain of command, and their officers were neither incorporated in Castelli's high command nor reliably informed of his plans.[51] The army's discipline was also lax and failed to consolidate support in Upper Peru's main towns. On the contrary, in several towns the soldiers from Buenos Aires alienated local people by their unruly and predatory behavior, at times turning potential sympathizers into outright enemies. The most famous incidents of opposition were in Potosí, where people became so enraged against the porteños that they rioted in protest in February 1811 and, in August, after Huaqui, rose against the porteño garrison, killing 145 of its soldiers.[52]

The antipathy aroused by the misbehavior of porteño troops was part of a broader problem caused by the incompatibility of liberal political views brought from Buenos Aires with social attitudes and practices in Upper Peru. Members of the Upper Peruvian propertied classes may have wanted greater political autonomy, but their political ideas did not usually encompass social and economic reform for the Indians; nor did those lower down the social scale necessarily want Indians to win equal status with them. Thus, when the revolutionary cause suffered military defeat, many watched with indifference or welcomed back the royalists, especially the landed gentry and mine owners who relied on Indian labor.

Although the porteños had been defeated, their first incursion into Upper Peru left an enduring mark. Antigovernment movements had developed in La Paz and Cochabamba; an autonomous government had emerged in the region of Ayopaya, and the spirit of rebellion in Upper Peru was not extinguished by Goyeneche's army of occupation.[53] Indeed, as we shall see later, rebellions broke out again in 1812 and were to play an important part in fighting the viceroy's counterrevolutionary army.

Second Front: Paraguay and the Banda Oriental

Buenos Aires's determination to impose its authority over the provinces of the old viceroyalty also provoked armed conflict in other regions. In addition to dispatching the Auxiliary Army to Upper Peru, the junta sent other forces to the Banda Oriental and Paraguay. On September 4, 1810, the junta resolved to send Manuel Belgrano with a military expedition across the River Plate and into the Banda Oriental to support the militias of its districts in a local resistance to royalist Montevideo. It subsequently extended his mission to include the regions of Santa Fe and Corrientes and then decided to send Belgrano and his forces further up the Paraná River to Paraguay in order to attack the royalist government in the city of Asunción.[54] There, the Spanish intendant Bernardo de Velasco had declared loyalty to the Spanish Regency, and the junta, believing that a couple of hundred men could defeat him, dispatched Belgrano's force to promote revolution in Paraguay and, if necessary, to occupy the province by military means.

Buenos Aires and Paraguay

The ensuing struggle set Buenos Aires against a society that had developed its own peculiar structure during the colonial period and had little in common with the outward-facing mercantile milieu of the capital. Paraguay's economy had limited exposure to the currents of Atlantic commerce that ran through Buenos Aires and, lacking mineral resources, relied for income on regional markets for the cattle and yerba maté produced by its small group of landowners. Its society also stood on the outer margins of the Spanish world; a tiny group of Peninsular officials and merchants controlled administration and trade, while its small population of some 100,000 people was largely divorced from the influences of eighteenth-century Spanish and European culture.[55] However, isolated though it was, Paraguay could not be ignored by Buenos Aires, mainly because of the risk that its Spanish officials might ally themselves with the royalist governments in Peru or Montevideo, or the Portuguese in Brazil.

When Belgrano, a man of political vision but scant military experience, arrived in the Paraná River region in September 1810, he soon came to grief.[56] He left Buenos Aires with a force of only about 200 men who were poorly equipped and mostly without military experience but managed to increase the size of his force en route to Paraguay by recruiting in the provinces through which he passed, so that when he crossed the Paraná River into Paraguayan territory, he had close to 1,000 men. Belgrano's plan was to confront the royalists before they could prepare adequate defenses, but despite his best efforts, the advance was slow. Hindered by the absence of settlements, roads, and trails, and by torrential rains and tropical temperatures, Belgrano's expeditionary force took two months to reach into the Upper Paraná. In the meantime, Governor Velasco, an experienced officer who had fought against the French in Europe and against the British at Buenos Aires, had plenty of time to assemble substantial forces and plan for a defense that would wear down the invaders as they struggled through a semiaquatic landscape of rivers, lakes, swamps, and forests. Thus, when Belgrano finally entered Paraguayan territory in late December 1810, he met with a well-prepared enemy.[57]

The first encounter between Belgrano and Velasco was at Paraguarí, where, on January 9, 1811, Belgrano's 700 men were stopped by Velasco's much larger forces. Although he lost about 150 men and some of his artillery, Belgrano's position was not irrecoverable. On the contrary, he was able to retreat with the bulk of his forces and could still call on a rearguard of some 600 men under Rocamora, which he left to guard the crossing point on the Paraná River. In these circumstances, Belgrano undertook an orderly retreat back towards the river with the intention of waiting for reinforcements from Buenos Aires before recommencing the campaign. After combining with Rocamora's forces, he eventually encamped in mid-February at Tacuarí, on the Paraguayan side of the Paraná, a position from which he could restart the campaign without having to repeat the dangerous river crossing.

His base at Tacuarí proved insecure, however, because he left himself with insufficient forces to defend it. Indeed, Belgrano made the mistake of dividing his forces, sending more than half his force with Rocamora to maintain communications with the settlements of western Misiones and win the allegiance of Indian communities. Thus, when on March 9, 1811, Colonel Manuel Cabañas led a well-organized, three-pronged attack on Tacuarí with a force of over 2,400 men, Belgrano was heavily outnumbered and, faced with a complete rout, was forced into an armistice with the Paraguayan commander. Under its terms, he agreed to withdraw from Paraguayan territory and moved back with his arms and equipment across the Paraná River. However, while Buenos Aires's military campaign to take Paraguay was over, all was not lost. During the retreat, Belgrano continued to press for Paraguay to join Buenos Aires—even contributing a substantial sum in gold for the widow and orphans of Paraguayans killed in the campaign—and Cabañas allowed him to leave Paraguay with much of his force intact.[58]

Buenos Aires's failure in Paraguay stemmed partly from the political choice taken by the local elite to back Velasco's royalist government, but also owed something to the junta's lack of military strength. Its forces were far too small and the terrain too difficult to ensure success against an enemy fighting on his own ground with larger forces. Without sufficient military capability, Belgrano was stopped far short of Asunción and failed to rally Paraguayans to the revolutionary cause. Instead, his expedition confirmed local opposition to domination by Buenos Aires, leaving Paraguay in the hands of a royalist government that might join with other provinces against Buenos Aires.

Belgrano's defeat was compensated, however, by the effects of his brief campaign on Paraguayan politics. Some Paraguayan creoles were attracted by the idea of an autonomous government, and while they did not openly oppose Governor Velasco, the attack from Buenos Aires gave them an opportunity to plot against him. To counter such subversion, Velasco dispersed the forces that had served him in the campaign against Belgrano—apparently for fear that their officers were potentially disloyal. His misgivings were justified. When he was about to call for Portuguese military support against Belgrano's forces on the outer periphery of the province, his internal opponents moved against him. On May 14–15, 1811, they overthrew royal government in Asunción and on May 17, 1811, declared Paraguay's independence, not only from Spain but also from Buenos Aires and the Portuguese monarchy; then, in early June, a General Congress convened in Asunción to decide on the country's new direction.

Paraguay's declaration of independence cut the province loose from its neighbors. The congress instituted its own governing junta and, while expressing interest in confederation with other independent provinces, insisted on self-government. Though this injured Spain, it did not work to the advantage of the Junta of Buenos Aires, as the new government of Paraguay was only prepared to acknowledge it as an equal. In 1811–13, government in Paraguay came increasingly under the idiosyncratic command of the creole lawyer José Gaspar Rodríguez de Francia, one of the members of the ruling junta. In 1814, he became "Supreme Dictator of the Republic," a position that he made permanent in 1816.[59] Although his government was independent of Spain and thus likely to intervene in regional politics to preserve its own position, Francia did all he could to keep Paraguay out of external conflict throughout his lifelong period of rule. Indeed, his policy of isolation, backed by armed forces that were accountable only to him, was so strict that Paraguay was all but sealed off from the outside world.

Paraguayan independence damaged the Spanish cause for an obvious reason: it removed a royalist government that might have provided an ally for royalists in Upper Peru and Montevideo. But it was not unequivocally advantageous to Buenos Aires either, since Paraguay's breakaway deprived the junta of a substantial territory with valuable resources and manpower. Nonetheless, Paraguay's isolationism offered an important consolation for the junta, for it left Buenos Aires free to pursue a struggle to control the Banda Oriental and its strategically vital capital at Montevideo.

The Royalist Defense of Montevideo

Montevideo had emerged as an opponent of Buenos Aires within days of the May Revolution of 1810. This position was consistent with the behavior of the city authorities since the inception of the Spanish crisis in 1808, when Governor Elío impugned Viceroy Liniers's loyalty and steered Montevideo's cabildo into establishing a junta under his leadership in January 1809. This damaging split between the leading officers of the crown was partly resolved by Liniers's successor, Viceroy Cisneros. After his arrival at Montevideo in June 1809, Cisneros dissolved the Junta of Montevideo, made Liniers and the Buenos Aires militias acknowledge his authority, and promoted Elío to second-in-command of the troops of the viceroyalty. But Cisneros's measures did not mend the rift between Montevideo and Buenos Aires, for he found Elío impossible to control. Indeed, such was Elío's insubordination that Cisneros ordered his recall to Spain early in 1810. Elío was consequently not in Montevideo at the time of the May Revolution, leaving Cisneros without a charismatic army commander at the time when his presence was most needed.[60]

Montevideo nonetheless remained under royalist control after the May Revolution in Buenos Aires. At first, on June 1, 1810, the town's leading citizens decided to recognize the Junta of Buenos Aires. Their decision was successfully contested, however, by a small group of royalists led by the commander of the naval station, José María Salazar.[61] Thanks to the chance arrival of news from Spain that the French advance had been stopped and that a Spanish government still existed, Salazar was able to swing the decision back towards the royalist party. On June 2, 1810, they recognized the Regency and spurned calls from Buenos Aires to send delegates to its new government. Backed by Peninsular merchants in the port, other royal officials, and some of the city's people, Salazar now used all the powers at his disposal, including his force of marines and sailors, to prevent Montevideo from aligning with Buenos Aires.

This refusal to ally with Buenos Aires was a crucial decision, for it gave Spanish officials the chance to turn Montevideo into a center for counterrevolution. Governor Soria of Montevideo had inherited Viceroy Cisneros's authority, but it was the naval commander José María Salazar who was the most energetic and effective royalist official in the city, using his well-armed contingent of Spanish marines and sailors to prevent the city's militias from going over to Buenos Aires. From the onset of crisis in May 1810, Salazar was especially vocal in denouncing the Junta of Buenos Aires and insisting that it could only be stopped by military means. He played a key part in carrying the decision against Buenos Aires, led the royalist political faction that dominated the Junta of Montevideo, and was the driving force in organizing the city's defenses. Here, then, was a town where a loyal garrison played a crucial part in determining political direction, an instance of a wider pattern of royalist resistance found in secondary cities, especially in places where Spanish officers were ready to provide political leadership and military organization.

The rift was followed by a phase of "phoney war." The Buenos Aires junta hoped to win Montevideo by attracting its citizens, particularly its militias, companies, and the *blandengues* (frontier horse soldiers) in its rural hinterland. The royalists, on the other hand, did not have the military resources with which to attack Buenos Aires and awaited instructions from the Regency. Thus, for six months after June 1810, the two sides settled into an uneasy truce. Salazar feared that the city would fall to internal enemies, and in July, he disbanded the creole militias in the city in order to deprive his political opponents of armed support. He told the minister of war in Spain that only the willpower of his military officers kept Montevideo from joining Buenos Aires. Indeed, in his frequent letters to the minister, Salazar regularly doubted the city's ability to defend itself against Buenos Aires, given that the population was not fully committed to Spanish rule. His complaints had several recurrent themes: Spain's failure to provide fresh resources to defend the city, the dubious loyalty of the townspeople, even the Spaniards among them, and the perfidy of the British, who, despite their alliance with Spain, used the revolution to promote their trade at Buenos Aires.[62]

The behavior of the British was a particularly sensitive point. Salazar tried to blockade Buenos Aires's trade but received no cooperation from the captain of the British naval station; this, he warned Spain, was deliberate duplicity, aimed at encouraging British merchantmen to enter Buenos Aires and engage in commerce with the rebels.[63] In fact, the British government's position was more complicated. It was reluctant to interfere with British trade in the River Plate but was also anxious to prevent war between Buenos Aires and Montevideo, for fear that war within Spain's dominions would not only weaken its Spanish ally but also afford the Portuguese an opportunity to appropriate Spanish territory on the Banda Oriental. This, British diplomats feared, would damage relations between its Iberian allies and thereby undermine Britain's strategy for fighting Napoleon in the Iberian Peninsula. Lord Strangford, the British ambassador at the Portuguese court in Rio de Janeiro, accordingly promoted negotiations that helped forestall war between Montevideo and Buenos Aires during 1810.

On the Spanish side, leading officials were ready to fight Buenos Aires, but they lacked the resources needed for a credible campaign. In the first place, Montevideo's royalist government was not entirely sure of the loyalty of its population or that of the Banda Oriental. Indeed, in seeking to impose authority on its hinterland, it was forced to adopt policies that alienated many of the province's inhabitants. When Gaspar de Vigodet took over as governor of Montevideo in October 1810, he set up a special treasury committee designed to maximize taxation, adding to the grievances of people who disliked a government that billeted soldiers on them, demanded donations, and heavier taxes to pay for Spain's wars, and, in a very unpopular revenue raising move, required landowners to buy titles to lands for which they could show no legal deeds.[64] The new burdens imposed by royalist government weighed heavily on the people of the Banda Oriental, which had a population of only some 20,000 inhabitants, and did much to turn them away from the royalist cause.

Lack of money and local support severely limited royalist military options. The dearth of military manpower and material was a constant theme in the correspondence of both Salazar and Vigodet, the city's governor, and at the end of 1810, Vigodet warned the Regency that it was much more likely that Buenos Aires would take Montevideo than vice versa. Like Salazar, Vigodet was appalled by the breakdown of Spanish trade, encouraged by its ally England, "whose subjects boldly refuse to comply with the blockade [of Buenos Aires], encourage criminals, and monopolize the wealth of the country, ruining Spanish commerce and destroying the sparse industry on American soil."[65] He distrusted the citizens of Montevideo, regarded many of his own troops as unreliable, and thus invested all his hopes in the arrival from Spain of the 4,000 men whom he had repeatedly requested as the only means to defend the city. Finally, Vigodet feared that negotiations with the Portuguese for money and arms were merely a cover for a Portuguese invasion. If that were to happen, he pointed out, his military weakness would be fully exposed, for he had no other weapons with which to defend himself than pen and paper, "pathetic arms . . . for one who would feel the stirring sounds of the cornet and the cannon's crash."[66]

In fact, the precarious peace was broken by the Spanish not the Portuguese. When ex-Governor Elío returned to Montevideo in January 1811 as the Regency's new viceroy of Río de la Plata, he soon moved onto the offensive. After Buenos Aires repudiated his claim to authority over the viceroyalty and reiterated demands that Montevideo submit to its authority, Elío responded aggressively: he closed all Banda Oriental ports to Buenos Aires, increased river patrols to hinder supply to Buenos Aires, and reinforced the garrison of Colonia. On February 12, 1811, he declared war on Buenos Aires with the intention of attacking it by land with 2,000 men. When this news reached Lima, coupled with the misleading information that Elío had brought thousands of Spanish reinforcements, it raised hopes that Buenos Aires might soon be crushed between the pincers of royalist military campaigns in Upper Peru and Montevideo. But Elío's arrival was a false dawn. He was unable to mount an effective, let alone a decisive attack, and was soon reduced to fighting for his survival. Indeed, rather than providing military help to the viceroy of Peru, he was soon looking to Abascal for money and arms.[67]

Rural Rebellion in the Banda Oriental: The Emergence of Artigas

Elío's planned offensive against Buenos Aires was abandoned because of rebellion within the Banda Oriental. The rebellion began shortly after his arrival and, as it spread among rural towns and settlements, threatened to encircle Montevideo at the very time when Elío was contemplating his offensive. By trying to extinguish the revolution at its source with a direct attack on Buenos Aires, Elío merely provoked stronger opposition. José Gervasio Artigas, a respected landowner and ex-militia officer from the Banda Oriental, quickly crossed over to Buenos Aires and, on offering his services to the junta, was given a military command, money, and

150 men to promote rebellion on the other side of the river. Captain José Rondeau, an army officer who had fought in Spain until returning to Montevideo in 1810, also defected to Buenos Aires and was rewarded with overall command of the junta's forces on the Banda Oriental. At the end of February 1811, the rebellion took a major step forward with the *grito de Asencio*, a proclamation of revolt against the Spanish colonial government by a group of landowners and ranchers led by Soriano Benavídez and Pedro José Viera. They gathered together some 300 volunteers, and having elected Ramón Fernández as their leader, they took the small town of Mercedes, en route to Montevideo. Fernández called on Artigas and Belgrano for support, and when Buenos Aires authorized these commanders to move, the first war for the Banda Oriental began.[68]

Buenos Aires's strategy for taking control of the Banda Oriental was akin to that employed in Paraguay and Upper Peru, where the junta hoped that the arrival of its forces would inspire and sustain local rebellions against colonial government. In this case, hopes rested on providing support from Buenos Aires for the rebels and integrating their forces into a single army commanded first by Belgrano, then by Rondeau. Belgrano was the first to move this strategy forward. He persuaded his government to allow him to move away from Paraguay, where he believed a long struggle was in prospect, in order to attack the strategic core of Spanish power at Montevideo. This would allow him to cut communications by river to Paraguay and win support among a rural population that was more amenable than their Paraguayan counterparts. The junta concurred, and in March 1811, they put Belgrano in overall command of revolutionary forces in the Banda Oriental, with orders to leave the border regions with Paraguay and to direct an offensive against Montevideo.

The shift away from the aborted campaign against Paraguay was timely. By the end of March, rebellion against the Montevideo royalists had spread throughout most of the Banda Oriental, and Viceroy Elío was forced to concentrate his defenses around Colonia and Montevideo while trying to cut communications between Buenos Aires and the Banda Oriental by a naval blockade. Montevideo received some money and gunpowder from Lima in late March but was under mounting pressure as the rural rebels continued to knock out small royalist outposts and to reduce the government's sphere of authority and radius of action. Belgrano also advanced from the north, backed by a force of about 1,200 men, more than half of them armed with muskets. Supported by Rondeau, who brought another couple hundred men, Belgrano took Arroyo de la China in early April, sent Artigas to raise more recruits, and set the course for an assault on Montevideo.

Cooperation between Buenos Aires and Artigas's insurgents worked well. The campaign was taken out of Belgrano's hands in early May (when he was recalled to Buenos Aires to answer charges arising from his failure to defeat the Spaniards in Paraguay), but combined operations continued under Rondeau's command. While Rondeau held men and artillery in reserve at Mercedes and Benavídez besieged Vigodet at Colonia, Artigas took a vanguard of 1,100 men into action against Elío's vanguard at Las Piedras. The engagement there was the most successful the rebels had yet had. Using his gauchos as cavalry, Artigas overwhelmed a royalist force of about 1,000 men, killing and wounding about 150, taking 482 prisoners, and capturing 500 arms as well as Spanish artillery. His own losses were far smaller—about 40 dead and wounded—and Artigas was ready to press his attack against Elío's disintegrating power at Montevideo. Having lost his army of operations, Elío was trapped in the city with depleted forces, while Artigas stood at the gates awaiting reinforcements and orders from Rondeau.[69]

The outcome of this first campaign is partly explained by Viceroy Elío's failings. According to his subordinate, the naval officer José María Salazar, Elío made a number of crucial tactical errors, not least of which was his delay in starting a serious offensive against the rebels. But the main reason was the mobilization of effective, motivated forces under Artigas. As in Upper Peru, Buenos Aires's ability to fight in the Banda Oriental depended heavily on regional allies, who had their own reasons for rejecting Spanish rule. Forces from Buenos Aires played a supporting role, and the success of the rebellion must be attributed mainly to its ability to recruit support among the *orientales* (or easterners, as the people of the Banda Oriental were known). For in contrast to Upper Peru, where local rebellions were separated by considerable distances and rarely coalesced for long, the rebellions of the Banda Oriental achieved coherence and unity.

This was partly a question of scale: the territory and population of the Banda Oriental was very much smaller than that of Upper Peru, more concentrated and hence easier to unite in a single movement. The character of its society was also significantly different, being more homogeneous than Upper Peru's sprawling society of Indians and castas, with a stronger sense of local identity, less obvious class divisions, and a core of gaucho horsemen, who, under leaders of their choice, were easily turned into highly effective mounted soldiers. Another striking feature of Artigas's forces was his willingness from the outset of war to recruit local slaves, principally for use in auxiliary roles, such as transport, but also as fighting men when they were willing. The offer of freedom to slaves in return for military service with the patriots was so potent that many hundreds joined the advance on Montevideo, when some 350 slaves belonging to Spaniards created their own separate unit of lancers with its own officers.[70]

Buenos Aires therefore found in the Banda Oriental rural allies who were better able to unite around the aim of overthrowing Spanish government and better organized to fight for that goal. Moreover, Artigas was a leader who unified local groups. He was supported by family networks among the landed class, accepted by minor leaders throughout the rural districts, and supported by the poorer orientales, who worked the land and drove the cattle. He also had a political vision, which attracted support because it reflected aspirations for local autonomy. Artigas had absorbed the idea that sovereignty reverted to the people in the absence of the king, and he concluded that provinces therefore had the right to set up their own governments and, as independent entities, to join in confederations of equals.[71] Here was a political orientation towards federalism that was, as in Venezuela and New Granada, to motivate war against Spanish rule. It was, however, also to generate conflict with Buenos Aires, where the creole political directorate was committed (like Bolívar and Nariño) to building political and military strength in a unitary state under central control.

The initial success that the alliance with Artigas's orientales brought to Buenos Aires in late 1810 to mid-1811 was not sustained for long. Artigas pressed Rondeau to bring the whole army against Montevideo but Rondeau delayed, allowing Elío to bring Vigodet and 600 men from Colonia to strengthen Montevideo's defenses. Artigas's "admirable campaign," was thus frustrated, and Montevideo remained intact as the sole remaining redoubt of royalism on the River Plate. With the moment lost, the earlier gains made against Viceroy Elío were gradually erased. For, although Elío was now shut into Montevideo with the port as his only exit, he was far from powerless. Access to the sea not only allowed him to supply the city but also enabled him to harass Buenos Aires with his own flotilla. And he had an important political card up his sleeve; in emergency, he was ready to call upon the Portuguese crown to help him defend the Banda Oriental by sending auxiliary forces across the border from Brazil. This was a risky stratagem because, once in, Portuguese forces might stay—whatever prior agreements were made. Nonetheless, Elío turned to Portugal's prince regent for help in April and, after his defeat at Las Piedras, urged General de Souza, the Portuguese captain general of Río Grande do Sul, to come to his aid with all possible speed. Souza entered the northern reaches of the Banda Oriental in July 1811 and began to move slowly southwards in the first Portuguese intervention against Artigas and Buenos Aires.[72]

In the short term, the risk that Elío took in invoking Portuguese intervention paid off for Spain. The entry of an army from Brazil provoked great alarm in Buenos Aires, where the junta was rightly concerned that the Portuguese would exploit the turbulence in the Spanish empire in order to absorb the Banda Oriental into Brazil. The junta responded by seeking to negotiate a truce with Elío, so that they might join together to push the Portuguese out of the Banda Oriental; it also looked to Britain to facilitate a negotiated settlement. The triumvirate, which took over in September 1811, took the next step: in October, Buenos Aires signed an armistice with Montevideo and made a major concession to Elío. In return for a promise that Elío would get the Portuguese out, Buenos Aires withdrew its forces and its challenge to the viceroy's authority over the Banda Oriental. Both sides promised to reopen normal relations in matters of trade, travel, and politics and to take joint action against any foreign invasion.[73] Thus, the siege of Montevideo was lifted, and the first war for the Banda Oriental ended.

If this was a setback for Buenos Aires, it was a crushing reverse for Artigas and his supporters. As part of the agreement, Rondeau took his forces back to Buenos Aires, while Artigas was to retreat across the Uruguay River into the province of Entre Ríos. Not only had Artigas lost the territory taken in his campaign, but, for fear of Spanish reprisals and Portuguese pillage, he now removed his men and their households from their homes in a great migration westwards. This "exodus of the easterners" was an extraordinary event. Some 4,000 civilians joined Artigas's 4,000 fighting men and, with their possessions loaded on ox carts and horseback, made the long trek to Entre Ríos, far from their homes. Undefeated, Artigas had retained his personal ascendancy over a force that retained solidarity and coherence. Here, among exiles expelled from their lands, was a guerrilla army in waiting, primed for reactivation when the circumstances were right.

The Balance of Power in 1812

What, then, were the achievements of revolutionaries and counterrevolutionaries in the first wars that stemmed from the May Revolution of Buenos Aires? Overall, the balance favored Spain in the sense that by early 1812, Buenos Aires's incipient war for independence had achieved few of the goals envisaged by the May revolutionaries. The strategy that the junta employed to spread its revolution had shaken the foundations of royal government throughout the old viceroyalty but had failed to consolidate the new regime's control over key regions. A royalist counterattack masterminded from Lima had forced the junta out of Upper Peru and exposed Buenos Aires to invasion by the forces of counterrevolutionary Peru. Another major segment of territory had been cut off when the Paraguayan royalists defeated Belgrano's forces and removed the region from control by Buenos Aires. The movement of Belgrano's forces from Paraguay, after failure there, had compensated with some spectacular successes in the Banda Oriental, almost leading to the capture of Montevideo; however, Portuguese intervention on the royalist side pushed the revolution out and left Spanish rule intact at Montevideo, the only fortified city in the entire region and the seat of an alternative government under Viceroy Elío.

The reasons for Buenos Aires's failures in both theaters of war were broadly similar. They stemmed partly from the political divisiveness found throughout Spanish America during these early years, due to the proliferation of provincial claims to sovereignty in the absence of the crown, the sole unifying institution of Spain's composite monarchy. When Buenos Aires sought to inherit the role of viceregal capital and to enforce political unity on the provinces, its government met with enclaves of opposition in Paraguay, the Banda Oriental, and Upper Peru that it lacked the diplomatic or military means to overcome. Although the militias of Buenos Aires provided a base for revolutionary war that was stronger than almost anywhere else in Spanish America, they could not take and hold territory without local support. This was particularly true when Buenos Aires's forces faced a determined military adversary, as they did in the region of Paraguay, which had been militarized in the late eighteenth century in order to defend against Portuguese incursions from Brazil.[74]

Another reason for Buenos Aires's failures was the intervention of counterrevolutionary governments from neighboring regions: in Upper Peru, the Peruvian army forced the porteños out; in the Banda Oriental, the Portuguese army did the same. Although these military setbacks were not terminal, they damaged the fragile unity of the city's political elites and their ability to project power over the old viceroyalty. The failures of the revolutionary government to achieve military success interacted with political factionalism in Buenos Aires, and cracks appeared in the new regime's political structure. The junta started to disintegrate when news of the ignominious retreat from Upper Peru was shortly followed by the setbacks caused by Portugal's intervention in the Banda Oriental. Its replacement by the first triumvirate reflected a hardening of the revolution in Buenos Aires, as power was taken by a faction that favored independence and a liberal constitution but wanted centralized and authoritarian government to ensure strength in time of war. After the triumvirate had dissolved the first junta and reorganized the army of the north, it abolished the provincial juntas, postponed convocation of the planned congress of deputies from the interior, and strengthened its own powers. The impulse in Buenos Aires was now to assert the leadership of the capital, to establish its primacy by strengthening the city's economy, and to place more power in the hands of army officers.[75] The triumvirate also changed the government's military strategy in 1812, shifting its emphasis from the Andean theater of war to a determined attack on Montevideo and its hinterland in the Banda Oriental.

For Spain, on the other hand, the counterrevolution had made strong progress in the second half of 1811. Viceroy Abascal of Peru had repelled revolution from the strategic zone of Upper Peru and, by so doing, had not only damaged the revolutionary regime in Buenos Aires but had also strengthened the royalist regime in Lima. The royalist victory in Upper Peru came at a time when Viceroy Abascal was grappling with constitutional reforms that tended to undermine his authority and undercut his revenues. In these circumstances, the recovery of Upper Peru was vital; it both reaffirmed Abascal's position as viceroy and provided him with sources of revenue that would otherwise have gone to the enemy in Buenos Aires. The preservation of the royalist enclave at Montevideo was also important because it frustrated Buenos Aires's annexation of the Banda Oriental and retained a Spanish base on the Atlantic coast.

Taken together, the preservation of these royalist strongholds in the Andes and the Atlantic littoral had another significant dimension of great importance to the Spanish counterrevolution. Although they were separated by great distance, Spanish positions in Upper Peru and the Banda Oriental offered the prospect of a strategic partnership between Spain and Lima. As an Atlantic port, Montevideo could provide a funnel for Spanish reinforcements brought by sea and thus offered a potential base from which forces sent from Spain might join with Lima's armies to crush the Buenos Aires revolution in a cross-continental pincer movement. Abascal and Elío had been unable to achieve this in 1811; indeed, the lack of communication and cooperation between them was such that Elío concluded his armistice with Buenos Aires without consulting either Abascal or Goyeneche, his two peers in the war for the Viceroyalty of the River Plate. (Abascal later professed that he had found the possibility that Elío might have entered into such a treaty without consultation so unlikely that he dismissed news of it as an enemy ruse.)[76] This lack of coordination did not, however, cause Abascal to abandon his grand strategy for restoring royalist control of the Río de la Plata via combined military operations. Indeed, with Upper Peru under Spanish control and a Portuguese army in the Banda Oriental, he remained firmly committed to a campaign designed to crush the core of political opposition at Buenos Aires by attack on two fronts. Whether it could be achieved was to be determined by the military operations to which, after a brief respite, both Buenos Aires and Spanish colonial governments returned in 1812. Their outcome was, as we shall see in the next chapter, to have an important effect on Spain's position in South America.

Notes

1. On the political positions taken by the provinces, see Ricardo Caillet-Bois, "La revolución en el Virreinato," in *Historia de la Nación Argentina,* ed. Ricardo Levene (Buenos Aires: Academia Nacional de Historia, 1939), vol. 5, pt. 2, pp. 93–240.
2. For a close analysis of the junta's problems in 1810–11, see Marcela Ternavasio, *Gobernar la Revolución: Poderes en disputa en el Río de la Plata, 1810–1816* (Buenos Aires: Siglo XXI, 2007), pp. 45–63.
3. On the counterrevolution in Córdoba, see Caillet-Bois, "La revolución en el Virreinato," in Levene, *Historia de la Nación Argentina,* vol. 5, pt. 2, pp. 155–70.
4. Moreno was commissioned by the junta on July 18 and delivered his report on August 30, 1810. In it, he responded to the junta's request for strategic guidance on a number of key issues by offering advice on policies for internal governance, war with royalists, and negotiations with foreign powers. While Moreno's responses were too radical for most of the junta members, his plan nonetheless reflects the chief concerns of the junta just two months after the overthrow of the viceroy. Copies of the original correspondence and orders of the junta and Moreno's plan are in AGI, Estado 78, no. 43: "Plano que manifiesta el metodo de las operaciones que el nuevo gobierno provisional de las Provincias Unidas del Río de la Plata debe poner en practica hasta consolidar el grande sistema de la obra de libertad e independencia," Manuel Belgrano, Buenos Aires, July 15, 1810. For a modern edition of Moreno's document and a defense of its authenticity, see Mariano Moreno, *Plan revolucionario de operaciones* (Buenos Aires: Ed. Plus Ultra, 1993).
5. For a synthesis of the expedition's organization and first campaign in 1810–11, see Juan Carlos Bassi, "La expedición libertadora al Alto Perú," in Levene, *Historia de la Nación Argentina,* vol. 5, pt. 2, pp. 247–72.
6. On the social character of the force, see Johnson, *Workshop of Revolution,* p. 286.
7. The armaments available in 1810 are listed in the various documents related to army organization in 1810–11 that are reproduced in the *Biblioteca de Mayo,* vol 14: *Guerra de la Independencia: Documentos relativos a la organización del Ejército, Buenos Aires: Senado de la Nación.* On arms shortages, see Emilio A. Bidondo, *La expedición de auxilio a las provincias interiores (1810–1812)* (Buenos Aires: Círculo militar, 1987), pp. 212–18.
8. For Abascal's initial responses, see José Fernando de Abascal y Sousa, *Memoria de Gobierno,* ed. Vicente Rodríguez Casado and José Antonio Calderón Quijano, 2 vols. (Seville: Escuela de Estudios Hispanoamericanos, 1944), 2, pp. 292–6. Written by Abascal at the end of his viceregency, this is a key primary source for information on royalist military campaigns and other elements of royalist policy during the years of Spanish crisis from 1808 until Abascal retired from his post in 1813.
9. Abascal y Sousa, *Memoria,* 2, pp. 295–6.
10. Herreros de Tejada, *El Teniente General D. José Manuel de Goyeneche Primer Conde de Guaqui,* pp. 242–4.
11. Abascal y Susa, *Memoria,* 2, pp. 296–300.
12. Díaz Venteo, *Las campañas militares del Virrey Abascal,* pp. 127–39.
13. Abascal y Susa, *Memoria,* 2, pp. 308–11, 313–15.
14. The harsh treaty meted out to royalist officials was recommended in Moreno's plan of operations, accepted by the junta in 1810: see Moreno, *Plan revolucionario de operaciones,* pp. 33–7.

15. Mariano Moreno stated that one of the main purposes of the expeditionary army was to try to take Upper Peru by surprise before it could be fully reinforced from Peru and that the advance of Balcarce's division to Tupiza was an element of this strategy. See Bassi, "La expedición libertadora," p. 251.

16. For a contemporary description of this route from Buenos Aires into Upper Peru and beyond into Peru, see Goyeneche to Floridablanca, Lima, April 28, 1809: Herreros de Tejada, *El Teniente General D. José Manuel de Goyeneche*, Appendix V, pp. 452–8.

17. For a brief review of the main currents in the historiography on independence, see Fisher, *Bourbon Peru 1750–1824*, pp. 106–9.

18. For a fuller analysis of the position of Lima's elites, see Anna, *The Fall of Royal Government in Peru*, pp. 26–42.

19. David Cahill and Scarlett O'Phelan Godoy, "Forging Their Own History: Indian Insurgency in the Southern Peruvian Sierra, 1815," *Bulletin of Latin American Research (BLAR)* 11, no. 2 (1992): pp. 127–40.

20. Walker, *Smoldering Ashes: Cuzco and the Creation of Republican Peru, 1780–1840*, pp. 116–19.

21. On Cochabamba's political position and its context, see José Luis Roca, *Ni con Lima, ni con Buenos Aires* (La Paz: Plural Editores, 2007), pp. 207–12.

22. Rivero gave an account of these events to the Junta of Buenos Aires at the time the cabildo of Cochabamba declared its allegiance to Buenos Aires: see "Informe de Francisco de Rivero sobre situación en Cochabamba," September 25, 1810, in Bidondo, La *guerra de la independencia en el Alto Peru*, Anexo 6, pp. 195–201.

23. Herreros de Tejada, *El Teniente General D. José Manuel de Goyeneche*, p. 249.

24. Siles Salinas, *La independencia de Bolivia*, pp. 200–2.

25. The importance of these events is reflected in their description by Viceroy Abascal to the minister for war in Spain: Abascal to Secretario de Estado, Lima, January 14, 1811, AGI, Lima 649.

26. Díaz Venteo, *Campañas militares*, pp. 144–6.

27. Narciso Batagoitia to Abascal, Tarapacá, November 25, 1810, AGI, Lima 649.

28. Abascal, *Memoria*, 2, p. 329.

29. For accounts of the engagements at Cotagaita and Suipacha from the royalist side, see Díaz Venteo, *Campañas militares*, pp. 147–52. For the porteño view, see Bassi, "La expedición libertadora," pp. 258–64.

30. On Castelli's policy, see Halperín-Donghi, *Politics, Economy and Society in Argentina in the Revolutionary Period*, pp. 241–4.

31. Rodríguez O., *The Independence of Spanish America*, pp. 138, 146–9.

32. Abascal y Sousa, *Memoria*, 2, p. 332.

33. Siles Salinas, *Independencia de Bolivia*, p. 210.

34. For information on the operational aspects of Goyeneche's military planning and information on his relations with Viceroy Abascal during late 1810 and early 1811, up to the battle of Huaqui, the following paragraphs rely on the detailed account, based on the reports of Goyeneche and his officers and the correspondence of Abascal, given by Díaz Venteo, *Campañas militares*, pp. 159–85.

35. Goyeneche to Abascal, Zepita, December 17, 1810, in Herreros de Tejada, *El Teniente General D. José Manuel de Goyeneche*, p. 462.

36. Abascal to Marques de Casa Irujo, Lima, January 8, 1811, and Abascal to Pérez de Castro, Lima, May 8, 1811: cited by Díaz Venteo, *Campañas militares*, p. 171.

37. Díaz Venteo, *Campañas militares*, pp. 174–5.

38. Ibid., p. 164.

39. Ibid., pp. 179–84, for the terms of the truce and the maneuvers that followed its expiry.
40. Goyeneche's and Ramírez's accounts of the engagement are transcribed in Herreros de Tejada, *El Teniente General D. José Manuel de Goyeneche*, pp. 268–73. For a synthesis from the royalist perspective, stressing royalist strengths, see Díaz Venteo, *Campañas militares*, pp. 185–9. For an analysis of Castelli's defeat seen from the porteño perspective, stressing porteño weaknesses and errors, see Bassi, "La expedición libertadora al Alto Perú," pp. 268–72.
41. Herreros de Tejada, *El Teniente General D. José Manuel de Goyeneche*, p. 270.
42. On Goyeneche's progress through Upper Peru in July to October 1811, see Díaz Venteo, *Campañas militares*, pp. 195–200.
43. Siles Salinas, *Independencia de Bolivia*, pp. 221–2.
44. Pueyrredón, like Díaz Vélez, had taken up a military career as a result of participation in the militias formed to fight the invading British in 1806–7. Their military experience and political sympathies ensured rapid promotion after 1810.
45. Arnade, *The Emergence of the Republic of Bolivia*, pp. 64–7.
46. Journal of James Paroissien, January 25, 1812, quoted by Humphreys, *Liberation in South America, 1806–1827*, pp. 56–7.
47. Ricardo Levene, "La formación del Triunvirato," in Levene, *Historia de la Nación Argentina*, vol. 5, pt. 2, pp. 539–83. The first triumvirs were Manuel Sarratea, Juan José Paso, and Martín Puerreydón; the secretary to the triumvirate was Bernadino Rivadavia, who exerted an important force in favor of creating a centralized independent state in which a political elite in Buenos Aires would promote enlightened reform.
48. Goyeneche, after attending university in Seville, had bought a commission in the Regimiento de Granaderos del Estado in December 1795. He was attached to the Real Cuerpo de Artillería at Cádiz in 1797 and saw action against the English in 1797 and 1800 at Cádiz. The report of his military mission has been lost, but Goyeneche's notes show that he had acquired a knowledge of the best military practices in Europe. He was promoted to colonel of Milicias Disciplinadas in 1805 and remained in Spain until sent back to Peru as the commissioner for the Central Junta in June 1808. See Herreros de Tejada, *El Teniente General D. José Manuel de Goyeneche*, pp.45–73.
49. Josef Gonzalez de Prada, Gobernador-Intendente of Tarma, to Minister of Gracia y Justicia, Tarma, Julio 27, 1811, AGI, Lima 649.
50. Roca, *Ni con Limas*, pp. 225–7. For explanations of the defeat given by officers who were present, see "Causa del Desaguadero," reproduced in *Biblioteca de Mayo*, vol. 13, pp. 11569–111850.
51. Bassi, "La expedición libertadora," pp. 257–8, 276–7; Bidondo, *La guerra de la independencia en el Alto Peru*, p. 55; Siles Salinas, *Independencia de Bolivia*, p. 210; Roca, *Ni con Lima,* pp. 218–20.
52. On dislike for Castelli and opposition provoked by the excesses of his army in Upper Peru, see Arnade, *Emergence of the Republic of Bolivia*, pp. 59–63.
53. Roca, *Ni con Lima*, pp. 241–3.
54. Emilio Loza, "La campaña de la Banda Oriental (1810–1813)," in Levene, *Historia de la Nación Argentina*, vol. 5, pt. 2, pp. 837–8.
55. John Hoyt Williams, *The Rise and Fall of the Paraguayan Republic, 1810–1870* (Austin: University of Texas Press, 1979), pp. 3–15.
56. Leopoldo R. Ornstein, "La expedición libertadora al Paraguay," in Levene, *Historia de la Nación Argentina*, vol. 5, pt. 2, pp. 273–304, gives an account of Belgrano's campaign based on primary sources and offers a graphic impression of the environment in which the Paraguayan campaign took place.

57. Ibid., pp. 277–82.
58. Ibid., pp. 288–302.
59. Williams, *Rise and Fall of the Paraguayan Republic*, pp. 24–33.
60. Street, *Artigas and the Emancipation of Uruguay*, pp. 101–11.
61. Salazar is also an important historical source on Montevideo and its struggle against Buenos Aires. Between June 1810 and December 1811, he conducted a steady stream of correspondence with Spain, comprising more than 200 hundred letters, some of which provided detailed reports on events and conditions in Montevideo and Buenos Aires. The correspondence is found in three Spanish archives: AGI, Buenos Aires 155; ACD, Ultramar, legajo 21, no. 7; and Biblioteca Nacional, Madrid, Manuscritos de América, no. 7222 and no. 7225.
62. Salazar to Ciscar, no 71, June 22, 1810, ACD, Ultramar 21, Expediente 7; no. 90, July 20; no. 92, July 21, 1810.
63. Salazar to Ciscar, June 24, 1810, AGI, Buenos Aires 156, no. 77; Salazar to Secretario de Estado, October 17, 1810, BNM 7225, fols. 173–5.
64. Street, *Artigas*, pp. 123–4.
65. Gaspar Vigodet to Ministro de Estado, Montevideo, December 27, 1810, AGI, Buenos Aires 47.
66. Ibid.
67. Abascal y Sousa, *Memoria*, 2, pp. 346–7.
68. Loza, "La campaña de la Banda Oriental," pp. 840–1; Street, *Artigas*, pp. 118–20, 127–9.
69. Loza, "La campaña de la Banda Oriental," pp. 842–51; Street, *Artigas*, pp. 130–6.
70. Blanchard, *Under the Flags of Freedom*, pp. 40–1.
71. Street, *Artigas*, pp. 154–6.
72. Ibid., pp. 140–6.
73. Loza, "La campaña de la Banda Oriental," pp. 857–8.
74. Nidia R. Areces, *Estado y frontera en el Paraguay: Concepción durante el gobierno del Dr. Francia* (Asunción: Universidad Católica, 2007), p. 82.
75. The crisis of *juntismo*, which led to this change, is recounted in Ternavasio, *Gobernar la Revolución*, pp. 63–76. On the struggle within Buenos Aires and the reasons for the increasing political influence of army officers, see Halperín-Donghi, *Politics, Economics and Society in Argentina in the Revolutionary Period*, pp. 209–17.
76. García Camba, *Memorias del General García Camba para la historia de las armas españolas en el Perú*, 1, p. 114.

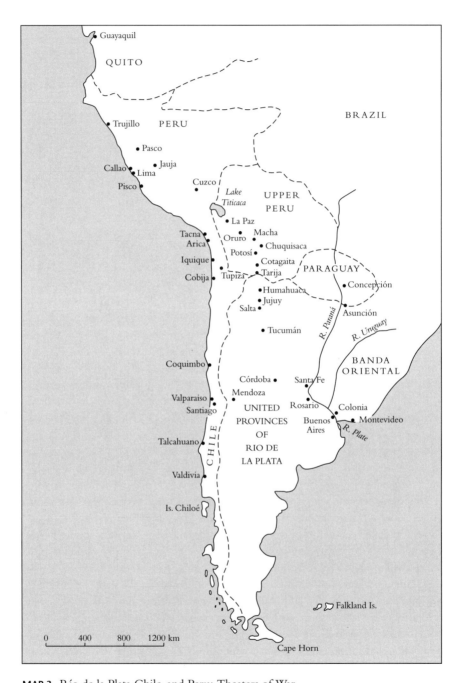

MAP 3. Río de la Plata Chile, and Peru: Theaters of War

7

COUNTERREVOLUTION AGAINST THE UNITED PROVINCES, 1811–15

The struggle between Lima and Buenos Aires entered a new stage after the royalist victory at Huaqui and Goyeneche's occupation of Upper Peru in the latter half of 1811. Now, Upper Peru became the principal theater of war in the southern Andes, the pivot on which the opposing sides set their military strategies. Their reasons remained the same as in 1810. For Viceroy Abascal in Lima, the region was a vital outwork for the defense of royalist Peru and a platform for an assault on revolutionary Buenos Aires; for the governments of Buenos Aires, Upper Peru was equally vital, both for its economic resources and as a bridgehead for war against the viceregal regime in Peru.

Upper Peru was, however, difficult for either side to take and hold. Its tortuous mountain landscape not only impeded the movement of armies but made it a mosaic of subregions which resisted military occupation and political control. Its political and social geography was also complex. Like other Spanish American territories, Upper Peru had no preexisting sense of "national" identity. It was, rather, a composite of towns, regions, and communities with disparate histories and interests, where loyalties to community or city could override identities of race or class. Indian peasant communities, for example, might prefer the stable relationships of the traditional tributary and landholding regimes to the promises of *rioplatense* revolutionaries, who imported an unfamiliar political language and culture. However, the deep divisions of a society and culture in which the majority indigenous population was subordinated to small white minorities also provided great potential for political conflict to extend into the social sphere, especially as the contending sides sought to recruit support for their armies. Indeed, as social mobilization for war widened, Upper Peru became one of the most contested areas and intensive battlegrounds of revolution and counterrevolution in Spanish America.

The resumption of war stemmed principally from Viceroy Abascal's plans to press ahead with a transregional counterrevolution backed by military force. After retaking Upper Peru, Abascal aimed to rebuild royalist government in all the regions that bordered on Peru. One facet of his planning involved expeditions to restore full royalist government to Chile and Quito, but his main strategic aim was to destroy the revolutionary epicenter at Buenos Aires by combining his army in Upper Peru with royalist forces in Montevideo.

Buenos Aires, on the other hand, remained equally committed to bringing all the provinces of the old viceroyalty under a single independent government and, after retreating from Upper Peru and the Banda Oriental, changed its government without altering its objectives. Power was transferred from the junta to a triumvirate, which, in November 1811, renamed the old viceroyalty as the United Provinces of the Río de la Plata. The new *rioplatense* leadership retained the same basic political goals—to spread revolution throughout the Southern Cone and into the Andes and to establish in Buenos Aires a single, centralized government—but revised its military strategy. The focus of the revolutionaries temporarily turned away from Upper Peru and centered instead on defeating the Spanish government in Montevideo and the Banda Oriental.

The first revision of military strategy shifted the emphasis of military operations from the Andean to the Atlantic front. This was driven by several considerations. First, the triumvirate had inherited an Army of the North that had been so disorganized by defeat that it was incapable of a retaliatory offensive in Upper Peru; second, Buenos Aires had to deal with Montevideo because, though politically and economically much less important than the cities of Upper Peru, it posed a potentially deadly military threat. For, despite being the smaller of the two cities, Montevideo had not only resisted conquest by Buenos Aires, but, with its hinterland secured by the Portuguese army, had become capable of aggression against Buenos Aires. It had a naval force that attacked porteño trade and impeded Buenos Aires's communications with the interior along the Plate and Paraná rivers; as a port with unchallenged access to the Atlantic, it could sustain itself by external supply; and last but not least, Montevideo had the potential to become the base for a Spanish counterattack reinforced from the Peninsula.

In these circumstances, the First Triumvirate had good reason to concentrate on defeating the Spanish enemy at its closest point, on the coast, while slackening its war effort in the distant Andes. It could not completely abandon operations in the north, however, as Goyeneche still threatened to launch an offensive onto the plains via Salta and Jujuy. Thus, while Buenos Aires regarded Montevideo as its military priority in 1812, Spanish pressure in the north forced Buenos Aires to sustain operations on two fronts.

Each of these wars was conditioned by the environments in which they took place, and the clearest way to explain their military shape and impact on the politics of revolution and counterrevolution is to treat them separately. Nonetheless, we must bear in mind that, although they were set apart by great distances and fought in very distinctive terrains, the military campaigns in Upper Peru and the Banda Oriental constantly interacted. Indeed, as we shall now see, both sides found that military success on one front tended to be balanced by failure on the other, frustrating the achievement of wider political goals and producing a recurrent stalemate.

The Andean Theater of War

Goyeneche and the Peruvian Counterinsurgency

In later 1811, the Upper Peruvian theater of war was dominated by the Peruvian royalists, and their success sharpened Viceroy Abascal's counterrevolutionary ambitions. In August, Abascal decided to push Goyeneche's forces into an offensive southwards towards Jujuy and Salta and thence to Tucumán. His military strategy was, as we have noted, designed to crush Buenos Aires in a pincer movement by combining the Army of Peru in operations with Viceroy Elío at Montevideo. In September, Goyeneche took the first step towards implementing the plan by establishing his headquarters at Potosí; in November, he began to concentrate troops at Tupiza; in December, he reinforced those troops and ordered Brigadier Picoaga to advance towards Jujuy. Díaz Vélez tried to rally the remnants of porteño forces in the area in a surprise attack at Suipacha on January 12, 1812, but Picoaga soundly defeated the porteños, inflicting heavy casualties.[1] This effectively ended Buenos Aires's first war for Upper Peru. Faced with the arrival of Major General Tristán with further royalist reinforcements, the remaining units of the porteño army retreated south to Salta; then, under Pueyrredon's command, they fell further back towards Tucumán in the belief that the royalist army was on their tail.

The Buenos Aires government reacted to the royalist advance with desperate measures. In February 1812, the First Triumvirate appointed Belgrano to replace Pueyrredón and to salvage the remnants of the northern army, whose 1,500 men looked incapable of dealing with Goyeneche's much larger forces, said to be 4,000-strong. But, believing that there was little that Belgrano could do, Buenos Aires gave him orders simply to save the army and slow the royalist advance. In these circumstances, the porteño forces were in a poor position to resist, and Abascal's plans for an assault on Buenos Aires from Upper Peru might have succeeded if Goyeneche had pressed on. However, royalist pressure relented at this critical moment because Goyeneche was distracted by rebellions that broke out at La Paz and Cochabamba in late 1811. These induced Goyeneche to hold all his troops in Upper Peru rather than pushing south against Buenos Aires.

The revival of rebellion in the Andes was very significant, for it showed how far Upper Peru had been destabilized by the revolution in Buenos Aires. The cities of Chuquisaca and La Paz had already shown signs of political instability in 1809, before the May Revolution, but the revolutionary potential of the region was considerably accentuated by Castelli's "liberation" of 1810–11. The porteño presence in Upper Peru detonated smaller rebellions, which, though incapable of coming together into a single coherent force that could challenge the royalist regime in Upper Peru, were able to keep open the fronts of revolutionary war first established by the army of Buenos Aires. Several foci for resistance remained, based on people who had their own reasons for fighting the royalist authorities. Animated by local conflicts, they became avatars of the revolution that had started in Buenos Aires and, for years to come, were to play an important part in keeping civil conflict alive in Upper Peru, acting either in conjunction with, or in the absence of, forces from Buenos Aires.

The crucial role of Upper Peruvian rebels and insurgents in the war against the Viceroy of Peru became clear immediately after Castelli's defeat at Huaqui. In La Paz, there had been strong popular support for the forces from Buenos Aires when they arrived in 1810 because they provided an ally for those who wanted the reform or removal of the Spanish regime. This continued after Huaqui. On news of the defeat, the city erupted in a vengeful uprising. On July 29, 1811, angry crowds of Indians and mestizos, suspecting complicity among the whites with Goyeneche's invading forces, demanded death for Spaniards and killed the governor when he refused to hand them over. This lower-class insurrection dissolved when Goyeneche entered the city at the head of a 1,500-strong army, but resistance continued in the rural hinterland. As soon as the general and his army left La Paz, it was besieged by rebellious Indians from the areas of Ayo Ayo, Calamarca, and Sicasica, led by Juan Manuel Cáceres, a mestizo leader who had evaded capture since his involvement in the La Paz Junta of 1809. He was soon joined by other revolutionary leaders, and La Paz became the focus for revived rebellion in Upper Peru.[2]

The months of siege at La Paz (August–September 1811) were a sharp reminder of older social conflicts in the city and its hinterland. The siege echoed that which the city had suffered 30 years earlier during the Great Rebellion of 1780–2 and was propelled by an insurgent Indian peasantry with many of the same grievances. The risk that such Indian rebellion might become a widespread assault on the established order was not lost on contemporary observers. The priest Ramón de Mariaca, who saw it firsthand, described the signs of incipient civil war and feared that worse was to come:

> while war is an unfathomable abyss of evils, civil, internal, revolutionary war is especially so . . . in it one sees a much more terrible face, bloody and ferocious; it is like a devastating monster with many heads, which, when cut off, are replaced by others, perhaps different in appearance but similar in terms of horror, destruction, and ruin to the homeland . . .[3]

In fact, the threat was cauterized, at least in the short term. The La Paz rebellion was contained by a royalist military campaign that lifted the siege and drove the Indian rebels back. Moreover, like the Great Rebellion of the 1780s, insurrectionary Indians were counterbalanced by loyal Indians, drafted in from neighboring regions. The regular soldiers who led the assault that lifted the siege of La Paz in late September 1811 were supported by 2–3,000 Indians from the Cuzco and Puno regions. Led by their caciques, the Inca nobles Mateo Pumacahua and Manuel Choquehuanca, both of whom were commissioned as colonels in the Spanish army, these Indian warriors were another reminder of the Túpac Amaru rebellion, when

Indians from different ethnic groups fought on opposing sides and Pumacahua had made a key contribution to the defeat of Indian insurgents.

Surprisingly little is known about the rank and file of Indians from Cuzco who fought for the king in 1811, and it is difficult to explain why they remained loyal to the Spanish monarchy. Although it is tempting to compare them to the indigenous troops whom the British recruited for their wars against native kingdoms in India during the late eighteenth and early nineteenth century, in fact, they bear scant resemblance to the *sepoys* drawn from South Asian communities and cultures that had their own distinctive traditions of martial action, where a caste system afforded high status to the warrior, and where native warriors, though dressed and trained to fight with firearms like European infantry, understood their role in terms of their own values.[4] Such a warrior tradition is difficult to detect among the natives of the Cuzco region, the heartland of the old Inca empire, for they were never incorporated into Spain's armies in the manner that the professional sepoys of eighteenth-century India or Native Americans peoples in North America became auxiliaries for British and French armies. On the contrary, Indians in Spanish realms were barred from carrying European arms unless they were nobles or members of militias. The people in and around Cuzco did, however, have a special relationship to the crown through the privileged position that their hereditary leaders, the Inca nobles, had long enjoyed in return for their support of Spanish rule. This relationship was badly disturbed by the Great Rebellion of 1780–2, for, even though the great majority of the Inca nobility of Cuzco had remained loyal, the crown subsequently attacked the power and influence that Inca nobles and other Indian caciques held in their native communities. Nonetheless, in Cuzco, some key connections remained. There, Indian nobles who had joined the war against Túpac Amaru were rewarded by the crown and allowed to increase their wealth and power. Prominent among them was Mateo Pumacahua, who became the most powerful Indian leader in Cuzco, indeed in the whole of Peru, after his part in saving the city from Túpac Amaru.[5] He was to remain a pillar of royalist support in 1810, participating as a military commander and bringing other Inca nobles into the war against rebels in the basin of Lake Titicaca in 1810–11.

If the Inca nobles and other caciques remained loyal when they judged that it might bring personal reward in privileges, titles, and land as well as strengthening their political position in the Spanish political order, it is harder to explain why Indian peasants fought for the crown. Traditional loyalties, as well as memories and customs that encouraged animosity towards other indigenous ethnic groups in neighboring areas, no doubt played a part in persuading them to join their leaders on the side of the king and viceroy, just as they had during the rebellion of Túpac Amaru. The allegiance of Indian *alcaldes* (mayors) was crucial, as they could use their authority to recruit from their communities. Indian peasants were no doubt as susceptible to the promise of material reward as their leaders: war provided chances for plunder and for taking resources from local competitors, whether creole and mestizo landowners or other Indian communities, particularly where there was a history of conflict over land and labor.[6] Whatever their motives, they certainly made a useful addition to the royalist army because, though insufficiently trained to fight in European-style warfare, they were invaluable as a counterinsurgency force against other Indians. Without them, the siege of La Paz might have done much greater damage to royal government in Upper Peru.

The rebellion at La Paz was one of several Andean uprisings that arose in response to news of the revolution in Buenos Aires, even after Castelli's defeat at Huaqui. At the end of October 1811, Cochabamba rose for a second time, led by Esteban Arze, and reasserted its role as a focus for insurgency in other areas. This time, royalist forces were unable to effect a rapid repression and, at the end of 1811, Arze and the Cochabamba rebels had a significant impact on the progress of the royalist counterrevolution. While Picoaga and Tristán stamped Spanish military ascendancy on southern Upper Peru, in preparation for a royalist advance into porteño territory, the Cochabamba rebellion, together with uprisings in other towns, held up their offensive against Buenos Aires.

The upheaval caused by Castelli's invasion of Upper Peru also had repercussions in highland Peru, in the rebellions of Tacna in June 1811 and at Huánuco in February 1812. The Tacna rebellion joined creoles and Indians in the overthrow of the city's authorities but was quickly suppressed when news arrived of the porteño defeat at Huaqui. The Huánuco rebellion was more alarming for the authorities; it mobilized thousands of Indian peasants under a creole leadership of small landowners and priests and seized the city in the name of "King Castel" (Castelli).[7] The Indians apparently envisaged Castelli as a new Inca or a figure who would restore rule by the native dynasty, echoing millenarian beliefs that had permeated Indian rebellion since the days of Túpac Amaru. They, too, were suppressed by the viceroy's troops, sent from Tarma and Lima.

If these Andean rebellions were short-lived, they were not inconsequential. Indeed, they saved Buenos Aires from a royalist offensive. For they persuaded Viceroy Abascal to postpone his campaign against Buenos Aires and thus gave the porteños a breathing space in which to recover from Castelli's defeat. Belgrano, his successor, took command of the Army of the North at Yatasto and had time to rebuild. He found much to do, as support for Buenos Aires was waning. Throughout the trek from Rosario across the interior and into the province of Salta, Belgrano encountered not just a lack of enthusiasm for the revolutionary cause but "complaints, laments, coldness, total indifference, and even mortal hatred."[8] Then, on arriving at Yatasto, he found an army that was in no condition for combat. He informed Buenos Aires that desertion was chronic and all but uncontainable; that the remaining troops were ragged, sick, and undisciplined; that their officers were militiamen with little training; and that the troops were regarded with indifference, if not outright hostility, by the towns through which they marched. At the end of April, his forces remained small and unfit for operations; he had around 1,500 men, but half were sick and many were raw recruits, leaving him unable to offer aid to the rebels of Cochabamba. In May, Belgrano moved north to Jujuy but could not attack the royalist forces on the frontier. Without sanction from Buenos Aires to do more than save the army from defeat, he concentrated all his efforts on training and organization while also awaiting news from Cochabamba. Some support came from Buenos

Aires, which sent the Austrian officer, Baron von Holmberg to train artillerymen plus a consignment of 400 muskets from Buenos Aires, though these did little to improve Belgrano's position. Desertion continued to reduce army numbers, which sank to 1,225 by June 1812, while the continuing presence of the Brazilian army in the Banda Oriental kept alive the threat that Goyeneche might at any moment decide to join in combined operations with Montevideo.[9]

In fact, the royalist strategy was shelved for many months due to Elío's failure to break out of Montevideo and Goyeneche's campaign against Cochabamba. Deploying detachments of royalist troops from all the main garrisons, Goyeneche finally moved against Cochabamba in May 1812, in an offensive designed to push the rebels back towards the city and there to crush them completely. This concentration of several thousand troops under Goyeneche's direct command overcame the rebel forces—said to number 6,000 men—and retook the city on May 27, 1812.[10] After sacking the city and executing captured leaders, Goyeneche left a garrison to hold the territory gained and moved south to return to the strategic objective of destroying the porteño army outside Upper Peru.

When Goyeneche prepared to push the Peruvian counterinsurgency southwards into the territory held by Buenos Aires, his rearguard in Upper Peru was stable but not yet completely secure. Jerónimo Lombera, the Spanish army commander at Cochabamba, reported that rebel leaders were still at large in the countryside and that military service in Cochabamba was "that of a rigorous campaign, not an ordinary garrison."[11] Such was the ongoing threat to security in the area that the viceroy subsequently ordered royal troops to be separated from the local population in a fortified garrison, thus to strengthen their position against any future local rebellion.

These conditions—where defeated and resentful rebels were evidently waiting for fresh opportunities to take power locally—spelled danger for the future but did not deflect the long-planned royalist offensive. While royalist military commanders realized that while the repression of rebellion in Upper Peru was an essential prelude to a successful campaign against Buenos Aires, they also knew that peace in Upper Peru depended on crushing the porteño army, which, so long as it existed, was an incentive to rebellion throughout the Andean provinces.

The Royalist Offensive of 1812

The royalist southern campaign finally began in August 1812, a full year after Abascal had issued orders to advance against Buenos Aires. Goyeneche's first move was to send Major General Pío Tristán, his cousin and trusted aide, to take Jujuy and Salta prior to an advance on Tucumán. This impact of the vanguard augured well for the royalists, as it prompted a porteño retreat. At the end of August, Belgrano was forced into a hurried evacuation of Jujuy, taking many of the townsfolk with him, and he headed directly south towards Tucumán. His instructions from Buenos Aires were to avoid battle and to salvage the army, even if this meant allowing the royalists to penetrate deep into the lower provinces. When he found Tristán in close pursuit, however, Belgrano decided to take a stand at the city of Tucumán and draw the royalists into battle.

The decisions of the two commanders to seek battle at this early stage stemmed from a clash between Tristán's cavalry vanguard and Belgrano's rearguard at the river crossing of Las Piedras on September 3, 1812. This action, though short of a battle, caused both sides to change their strategies. The porteños were encouraged by the fact that they fought well at Las Piedras, and in the light of this, Belgrano decided to defend Tucumán. His opponent Tristán also decided to fight as soon as possible, despite his instructions to do no more than establish a base at Salta and await orders. So, in response to Belgrano's halt, Tristán moved onto the attack with his whole army in the belief that he could use his numerical superiority (some 4,000 men against 2,000) to crush Belgrano and create a base that would enable the Army of Peru to move against Buenos Aires itself.

Tristán's decision to confront Belgrano's army at Tucumán was based on the assumption that the porteños would take up a defensive posture in the city and allow themselves to be encircled. Belgrano proved, however, to be a more astute commander than Tristán believed. Rather than barricading his forces within the city, Belgrano prepared a strong position on its outskirts and, with a newly formed cavalry of 600 gauchos pressed into service for the occasion, was ready to attack the royalists as soon as they approached. Thus, when Tristán arrived on September 24, he confronted an enemy who held well-prepared positions and was not easily surrounded. Nonetheless, Tristán proceeded with his attack. Confident in his superior numbers, he sent four battalions of infantry against the enemy formation, while keeping 1,200 men, including most of his cavalry, in the rear as reinforcements.

From the outset, the royalists' battle strategy faltered. The forward probe was quickly blunted, its advance undermined by tactical errors and poor coordination. Accounts of the battle suggest that Tristán made some elementary mistakes, unsurprising perhaps in an inexperienced commander. He sent in his Peruvian infantry without artillery support and failed to maintain communications with their commander. When Belgrano's artillery fired on them, their commander Colonel Barrera ordered his lead battalions to fix bayonets and advance in the dispersed formations that they had used against Indians in Upper Peru. This might have reduced their vulnerability to artillery fire, but it cost Tristán control of the battlefield. When other officers followed Barrera's example, they divided the infantry into separated sections, and, without a firm order of battle, were vulnerable to a surprise attack by part of Belgrano's army that had been hidden from view. This force (some 200 skirmishers with firearms and 600 gauchos armed with swords, lances, and machetes) outflanked and then drove back into the rear of the royalist infantry, causing the flight and desertion of entire companies of Peruvian soldiers. At this stage, the royalists might have been overwhelmed completely had the gauchos not fallen to plundering the royalist baggage train. The battle then broke into a series of actions led by unit commanders without control from their generals, and, though the royalists recovered some ground, Tristán now encountered another problem: a shortage of munitions needed for an attack on the city. By nightfall, it was evident that Tristán's attack had failed. He admitted the loss of 462 deserters or prisoners and 152 dead, but other observers put his losses at closer to 1,000 between dead, wounded, and prisoners. The fact that he had lost a very substantial part of his army, as well as much of his artillery and ammunition, explains why Tristán refused to be drawn into any further fighting and, after rejecting Belgrano's offer of an armistice, retreated under cover of darkness on the night of September 25–26.

For once, the outcome of the battle was agreed by both sides. After being drawn too deep into enemy territory, Tristán had gone into battle too hastily, organized his forces ineptly, and allowed himself to be surprised by the enemy's cavalry. Indeed, he might have suffered even greater losses had Belgrano sent a larger force to pursue him. As it was, Belgrano decided he lacked sufficient men to deliver a coup de grâce, and Tristán's army was left to fall back on Salta.[12]

The battle at Tucumán was the most substantial and bloody engagement of the royalist and rebel armies so far, and it had powerful short-term effects on the northern theater of war. For the porteños, it gave a much needed fillip to the morale of soldiers who had retreated for much of the previous year and boosted confidence in Belgrano, the army's new commander. Now that the royalist army had been forced to turn on its heels, it also set the scene for porteños to return to the offensive with an attack on Salta.

For the royalists, on the other hand, the significance of Tucumán was entirely negative. Goyeneche reported that he had lost about 1,000 men of his vanguard, and he refused to move again without reinforcements to replace them. Not only had the army been diminished by losses, especially through desertion, but, after encountering the ferocious combat tactics of the gaucho horsemen who had joined Belgrano to defend their home territory, it became less confident of its ability to crush the enemy. The defeat was also, as García Camba later observed, a badly missed opportunity to defeat the porteños at a time when they were weak and retreating, and when the destruction of the northern army might have struck an irreparable blow to the revolution.[13]

The defeat at Tucumán damaged the royalist cause in another sense too, in its effect on relations between Viceroy Abascal and Brigadier Goyeneche. This was clearly reflected in their growing divergence over strategy, where differences were soon to lead to a complete rupture in relations. The viceroy had seen Goyeneche's successes in Upper Peru and Tristán's advance to Salta as confirmation that his strategy for defeating the revolution was working. He reported that he had ordered communication to be opened with Paraguay and Montevideo in order to prepare for combined operations and affirmed that, if Tucumán were taken, this would, when combined with the loss of Upper Peru, deprive Buenos Aires of a great part of its resources and lead to its defeat. He also noted that, so far, much had been achieved with "little loss of blood . . . and the peace of more than a million souls with the loss of only some troops and some 30 executed rebels leaders."[14]

Goyeneche, on the other hand, took a much less sanguine view. In the course of his counterinsurgency campaigns in 1811–12, the general began to suspect that he had entered a political quagmire where there were neither firm footholds nor a clear way forward. In a report he wrote in October 1812, before receiving news of Tristán's defeat at Tucumán, he was already voicing doubts about achieving a military solution to the challenge caused by the Buenos Aires revolution and, despite his achievements since leaving the Desaguardero, Goyeneche seemed to be losing faith in the long-term prospects of counterrevolution.

His report began on a positive, even complacent, note.[15] Goyeneche claimed that since Buenos Aires had declared "this bloody civil war against Peru," he had played a crucial role in winning the war. He had turned raw recruits into "valiant conquerors who, on sixteen battlefields against a rebellious people and thousands of ferocious Indians, had succeeded in overshadowing the reputation of the Pizarros and the Almagros." He also claimed his share of glory for the army's success. Everything, he boasted, had been accomplished without guidance from Spain or Lima, without any chance to combine forces with Montevideo and Brazil, with just the resources of conquered provinces, and an army of only 8,000 men, which he could not expand due to lack of money and arms.

Goyeneche's triumphant tone was muted, however, by the doubts that he voiced about the crown's future ability to hold its own, not just in Upper Peru but throughout Spanish South America. For, despite all his successes, "the great apparatus of South America" was, he said, "moving towards ruin because of insufficient strength to maintain its enormous weight, failure to understand the ills of its character, or the remedies that might revive the paralysed parts of this vast empire."[16] His fear was that war had irrevocably changed the political environment, as people lost "the simple ideas with which they had once been imbued" and seemed to be changing into "different nations which wanted nothing more than to live for themselves and without union with the Metropolis." In these circumstances, "fear is the only curb; without it, rebellion is immediately reborn." He was not confident, however, that he could instill sufficient fear, since he was the sole source of royal authority in the huge area from the Desaguadero to Jujuy and could not create local defense forces among people who were too unreliable to be given arms. In Goyeneche's view, the only sensible strategy was to sustain a defensive position in Peru, preventing the porteños from returning to Upper Peru by closing the passes of Tucumán "like the Thermopylae of Thessaly," while waiting for improvement in the situation in Europe or the Río de la Plata.[17]

The reference to the ancient Greeks' historic defense of their homeland against overwhelming odds was more than a rhetorical flourish. While lauding the heroic qualities of the royalist army, it simultaneously implied that the royalist position might turn into a desperate last stand if the enemy continued to grow in strength. At this juncture in late 1812, Goyeneche did not admit a purely defensive future. He accepted that it was still possible to halt the spread of revolution by defeating Buenos Aires because, "if Buenos Aires falls, all these peoples will immediately surrender, [being] satellites that spin in the field of that malignant comet." He doubted, however, that this could be accomplished without an extraordinary military investment from Spain, helped by Britain and Portugal. Goyeneche estimated that to undertake an offensive against Buenos Aires, he needed reinforcements of 4,000 troops from Spain, 3–4,000 muskets brought upriver through Brazil, and help from the English navy to transport 2,000 men up the Paraná to Rosario in order to attack Córdoba. Without these measures, it would need 8,000 European troops to take Buenos Aires by "blood and fire."[18] To reinforce his message, Goyeneche sought Abascal's permission to respond to Belgrano's offer of a truce in late October 1812, unless the viceroy could supply 2,000 reinforcements.

Abascal ignored Goyeneche's pessimism. He insisted that Buenos Aires was vulnerable because it had fewer troops and was unable to divert forces from the coast to the Andes, and he restated his belief that Buenos Aires could be defeated. He demanded that Goyeneche hold the passes at Jujuy and Salta while they awaited news from Montevideo and, in mid-December 1812, he ordered Goyeneche to reject Belgrano's overtures and to defend every inch of territory.[19] Although Goyeneche had no choice but to follow Abascal's orders, he continued to harbor serious reservations about the credibility of the viceroy's strategy. In January 1813, he again warned Abascal that the revolution was more dangerous than it had seemed. The royalist loss of Upper Peru in 1810–11 was, he pointed out, not caused solely by Nieto's mistakes, nor had victory at Huaqui dissolved Buenos Aires's army. The danger was more deeply rooted. It lay in "the spirit of liberty and independence," which had appeared in Buenos Aires with the deposition of Viceroy Sobremonte in 1807, reappeared in Chuquisaca and La Paz in 1809, and blossomed most malignantly at Buenos Aires in 1810. Since then, he affirmed, it had become clear that the towns throughout the old Viceroyalty of Río de la Plata would side with the porteños whenever the latter had the military advantage; indeed, he predicted that this was likely to happen soon in Salta and Jujuy if the rebels managed to mobilize larger and better-armed forces. The royalist position was, in short, much more precarious than the viceroy allowed, not because people loved the porteños, but because they wanted "to throw off the yoke of any overseas government."[20]

Goyeneche was right to be anxious about the future course of the war, partly because the government in Buenos Aires showed signs of rejuvenation during the closing months of 1812 and became more openly committed to independence. This was partly because the Cádiz Constitution of March 1812 ended the ambiguities of the *vacatio regis*, and the Cortes rejected negotiations with Americans. The First Triumvirate's policy of formal allegiance to Ferdinand VII—a policy designed to sustain informal British support—and its authoritarian treatment of political opponents thus became less easy to sustain, and those who wanted to affirm independence from Spain came to the fore.[21]

The principal vehicle for political renewal was the *Logia de los Caballeros Racionales* (later the *Logia Lautaro*), a secret society established by Carlos María de Alvear, José de San Martín, and José de Zapiola, military officers who had recently arrived from Europe after fighting in the Peninsular War.[22] The Lodge recruited into its conspiratorial ranks those who wanted a more open commitment to independence, and its members conducted a carefully orchestrated political campaign to bring about a change of government.[23] On October 8, 1812, Alvear and San Martín, the two leading army commanders in the city, removed the triumvirs and established a Second Triumvirate that was committed to move towards full independence. This new executive power sought to rally the provinces to its side by calling a general constituent congress at Buenos Aires, and it raised the tempo of war in both Upper Peru and the Banda Oriental.

Belgrano's Defense

The shift in power in Buenos Aires had important implications for the royalist position in Upper Peru. In early December 1812, Tristán told Goyeneche that Buenos Aires might soon be sending substantial reinforcements to support an attack on Salta, and in early January 1813, Viceroy Abascal ordered Goyeneche to reinforce Salta with 1,000 men from Tupiza and Cotagaita. He also suggested that Goyeneche replace Tristán with Ramírez, who was then acting as interim president of Charcas. Goyeneche preferred his kinsman, however, and decided to keep Tristán as his commander at Salta on the grounds that he was a more able officer. Left in charge of the defense of Salta, Tristán made no special arrangements. With reinforcements of 400 men from Tupiza, he had an army of about 2,700 men and 11 artillery pieces and, assuming that campaigning was unlikely during the rains, believed that Belgrano was still far to the south. This proved to be a serious misapprehension, with major repercussions for the royalist campaign.

Belgrano was more dangerous than Tristán thought, despite his lack of military experience. In the four months after his victory at Tucumán, Belgrano had concentrated on training his army, reinforcing it with men, arms, and other supplies provided by Buenos Aires, as well as raising a regiment of dragoons from the Tucumán militia. He also organized the manufacture of fire arms and munitions, built large carts for transporting supplies, rafts for river crossing, and provided his men with shoes and clothing. José María Paz, one of his junior officers, recalled Belgrano's exemplary leadership at this time; he checked rivalry among his officers, raised the morale of his men, and sought to win over the uncommitted by identifying the revolutionary cause with religion. Paz applauded Belgrano's willingness to use religious beliefs for political ends, since it helped bond his soldiers while ensuring that the revolutionary cause blended with local customs. It was perhaps also a necessary antidote to the promises that Goyeneche made to royalist soldiers, that those who died would be recognized as martyrs and, as such, guaranteed immediate entry into Heaven.[24] At Tucumán, Belgrano dedicated his army to the Virgin of Mercy and, after engaging his troops' devotion through ceremonies and rituals, ordered a solemn distribution of badges carrying the Virgin's image to all his men as they marched out to advance on Salta.[25]

Here, for the first time, the porteño campaign began to engage the provincial population in its army, incorporating local militias under symbols, which unlike the constitutional discourse of politicians in Buenos Aires, resonated with popular culture. Until now, Buenos Aires's government had tried to secure support in the towns of the interior by giving leading families political and administrative posts rather than seeking to mobilize the populace. The royalist threat forced Belgrano to change that conservative approach, and with the attack on Salta, he began to broaden the basis of military participation. From this time, the revolution began to stir a popular insurgency in the north, as gauchos were recruited to the revolutionary cause around Salta and Jujuy. For this reason, in this region, "the political revolution stressed, rather than hid, the simultaneous social revolution."[26]

Belgrano's months of preparation were crowned with success in early 1813. His army made an orderly advance from Tucumán on January 12, 1813, moving in several separate contingents towards the River Pasaje, where they made a difficult but unopposed crossing in early February. Once over the river, Belgrano had the opportunity to bring substantial forces to bear against his enemy, together with an element of surprise. On February 13, he united his forces, moved quickly towards Salta, and on February 17, he made camp near the city; on February 20, after maneuvering some 4,000 men into position, he attacked. The fight for Salta was brief, and Belgrano's victory decisive. After a few hours, the royalist troops were broken by a cavalry charge and fled back into the city, where, splintered into intimidated groups, they were persuaded to surrender.[27]

Contemporary explanations of the outcome of the battle for Salta were, as usual, influenced by the allegiance of the observer. The porteño version stresses Belgrano's achievement in battle. Paz praised the general's intelligent tactics and the valor of his men while acknowledging that the royalist defenders did not put up much of a fight; after breaking in the face of mounted attack, the royalists were so demoralized that they hid in houses and churches and were easily persuaded into premature surrender.[28] The official royalist account tended to blame Tristán, whom Viceroy Abascal accused of insubordination and incompetence. At Tucumán, Tristán had gone into battle when his orders were simply to establish a vanguard position at the River Pasaje, and he had then made serious blunders on the battlefield by attacking a strong position without sufficient use of artillery or cavalry. By subsequently establishing a base at Salta, he had ignored orders to fortify Jujuy and then allowed himself to be surprised by the porteños and unable to retreat to Jujuy.[29] Francisco Javier de Mendízabal, who was on Tristán's staff at this time, took another view. He did not hold Tristán wholly responsible for his army's inadequacy in battle at Salta but blamed that on the cowardice and disloyalty of his men, many of whom had had their loyalty undermined by their "indecent relations" with the town's "many very attractive and manipulative women," who favored the cause of Buenos Aires. However, Mendízabal did find Tristán guilty of failing to invigilate the porteño advance and, then, when he was aware of danger, allowing his personal feelings to prevent him from calling on Brigadier Picoaga, who was stationed at Suipacha, to provide the reinforcement required to support a retreat to Jujuy.[30] García Camba, who joined the army a few months later, echoed this judgment, blaming Tristán for failing to coordinate with Picoaga and for not taking sufficient precautions against "the pernicious influence of a society that was filled with women who . . . had decided for the new system and whose methods it was prudent to fear."[31] Royalist military power was, it seems, unable to withstand subversion from communities committed to independence.

Belgrano's victory at Salta was an instance of action on the battlefield that had a marked effect on war and politics, for it changed both the military and political situation in the Upper Peruvian theater of war. The battle cost the royalist army around 500 in dead and wounded, while the terms of surrender meant that the remaining 2,200 troops were forced to lay down their arms and promise not to fight again. These tactical losses were compounded by a major strategic setback, for the loss of Salta led to an immediate withdrawal from Jujuy and thus deprived Goyeneche of two essential bases. It also startled him into an abrupt shift from offense to defense. On receiving Tristán's warning that Belgrano, having taken Salta, had 4,000 armed men poised to advance on Potosí, Goyeneche threw his army into reverse with a rapid withdrawal to the city of Oruro. There, deep in the center of Upper Peru, he planned to concentrate against a porteño invasion while negotiating a ceasefire with Belgrano.

The immediate effect of the battle of Salta was, then, to open a way for the army of Buenos Aires to reenter Upper Peru and to rekindle its internal rebellions. This in turn was to propel Goyeneche into adopting a defensive posture based on Oruro, abandoning Abascal's strategy for advancing on Buenos Aires. Goyeneche had, it seems, lost all faith in the idea of rolling back the Buenos Aires revolution. Indeed, by emphasizing defense in Upper Peru, he tacitly disowned the viceroy's strategy for overcoming Buenos Aires by joint operations with Montevideo.

The Reorganization of the Royalist Army

Goyeneche's withdrawal to Oruro had considerable repercussions on the royalist side, for it opened a rift with the viceroy that led to months of stasis, if not crisis, in the army. After Goyeneche's retreat from Potosí and suggestion of a parley with the porteños, Viceroy Abascal doubted the resolve of his leading general. In Abascal's eyes, Goyeneche had made a tactical blunder by retreating so rapidly from Potosí and then shown a lack of commitment to the strategy of counterrevolution by contemplating conciliation of Belgrano. These were wounding accusations, particularly the former with its implication that Goyeneche had been too timid. Goyeneche angrily rejected the idea. He argued that his retreat from Potosí was essential to save the army and had been backed by a consensus among his leading officers. He pointed out that 4,000 armed men were moving against his much smaller forces and that the potosinos were likely to turn against him as soon as the porteño army approached. In short, Goyeneche pointed to the persistent problem for the royalist army: its inability to rely on Upper Peruvians' loyalty and constant fear that locals would change their allegiances as circumstances dictated. He also argued for a military strategy that did not aim at holding the whole of Upper Peru, including Potosí. Oruro, he argued, was a central point for communications and a place where troops from garrisons in Upper Peru and reinforcements from Peru could be more easily assembled. Oruro was to the four provinces of Upper Peru, said Goyeneche, as Mantua to the rest of Italy.[32]

In fact, memoirs of Spanish army officers suggest that opinion among his officers may have been divided over the question of retreat. Some thought that Goyeneche could have united his forces with those of Picoaga at Cotagaita and awaited the arrival of reinforcements from the garrisons of Oruro and Cochabamba, and that, had he done so, he would have had an army of 4,000 that could easily have stopped Belgrano from entering Upper Peru.[33] But whatever the truth of the matter, the royalist retreat from Potosí signaled the start of a new phase in the war for Upper Peru. A porteño army now found the way open for a second campaign to take the territory, while the royalists fell back on defensive lines.

The political implications were obvious to Viceroy Abascal, who, while trying to control elections of Peru's representatives to the Spanish Cortes in March 1813, suppressed publication of news from Upper Peru and immediately disowned Tristán's treaty.[34] In fact, the changing situation in Upper Peru did not have an obviously negative impact effect on political opinion in Peru where, in Lima at least, fear of rebellion among the Indians and castes remained the dominant emotion. As one observer testified, "most people are frightened of the horrors they would experience in case of a revolution . . . and of what the immorality and barbarism of the castes . . . would cause."[35] Nonetheless, the return to war in Upper Peru was a significant setback for the royalists in both political and military terms: it not only left the source of revolution intact at Buenos Aires but also weakened the stature of the viceregal government in Lima and had a serious impact on the Army of Peru. These strains were immediately reflected in relations between Viceroy Abascal and Brigadier Goyeneche. In mid-April 1813, the viceroy told the minister for war that the general had to be replaced. Goyeneche, he said, was petulant, self-centered and arrogant, a Peruvian "native son" who ran the army by favoring his friends and clients. Abascal complained that he tolerated the general for so long only because the army was built on personal connections and loyalties and might disintegrate without him; he therefore had to take the utmost care to make his removal seem a response to the general's repeated requests for release from his post. He also explicitly asked Goyeneche to ensure that his troops extend their loyalty to his successor.[36]

In the event, the risk that the army might disintegrate during the handover of command was overcome. Goyeneche took his transfer badly but accepted the viceroy's decision and helped hold the army together until his departure on May 22. A period of careful consolidation followed. Under the temporary command of Mariscal Ramírez, the army remained in position at Oruro to await the arrival of Joaquín de la Pezuela, who eventually took his place on July 27, 1813.[37] In the two intervening months, Ramírez concentrated on stabilizing the army and strengthening its position by establishing a forward position at Ancacato. When Pezuela finally took command at Ancacato on August 7, 1813, his army consisted of 3,177 men, almost all foot soldiers, and, after some reorganization to incorporate the 360 men and many munitions he had brought with him, he moved back onto the offensive.[38]

The Second War for Upper Peru

General García Camba later observed, with the benefit of hindsight, that "the defeat at the battle of Salta . . . could not of itself produce the dissolution of Peru . . ."[39] However, in mid-1813, Abascal's strategy for defeating the revolution and the future of Peru seemed to have reached a tipping point. Two key questions faced the royalist side. The first was whether it was possible to restore control over Upper Peru by military means; the second was whether the crown could retake the offensive against Buenos Aires and kill the revolution in its cradle. Abascal did not deviate from his belief that both were possible, and he tasked Pezuela with reactivating his offensive strategy. To explain why Upper Peru—and Peru more generally—remained in royalist hands, requires closer examination of the military operations conducted by both sides.

On the royalist side, Pezuela adapted his tactics to the prevailing circumstances. His first concern was to improve the army. In Oruro, he found a force that, he reported, was on the brink of dissolution after the desertion of 2,000 men and was "without clothing, shoes, food supplies and money in its treasury." The main force, which numbered some 3,000 men in Ancacato, was in what Pezuela thought was a state of considerable disorganization. The troops were without uniforms and many without shoes; they were only passably trained in the use of the musket and maneuvers by battalion; and, overall, they lacked the discipline Pezuela expected in a regular army. Nor was there much that was Spanish about them—most were Indians and mestizos who spoke native languages; only the minority, from Lima and Arequipa, spoke Spanish. They did not even eat together, but relied on their women to provide them with the potatoes, *chuño* (dessicated potato), and maize that were their preferred foods. When the army was on the move, these women moved ahead and stole food from Indian villages; when the army was encamped, they ranged over long distances around the camp in search of supplies. The army did not have a commissariat that supplied food, nor a centralized means of obtaining food, since Indian villagers fled before the advance of the army and there was no possibility of sustaining long supply lines. "And thus," Pezuela observed, "the Army lived entirely by marauding. It did not control more territory than that on which it walked. The Indians hated the soldier, the officer and everything connected to the King."[40] Here, in short, was a force that was appropriately named "the Army of Peru," since it consisted almost entirely of men and women drawn from the Indians and mestizos who were the majority of Peru's population. And, for lack of a better alternative, it carried European eighteenth-century military doctrines for living off the land to an extreme degree.

Pezuela had to face a robust enemy. Belgrano's army was well established at Potosí; his vanguard had entered in early May 1813 to a warm welcome and was probing forwards into royalist territory. Having a presence at Potosí had considerable strategic value. It allowed Belgrano to revitalize his treasury and create collaborating governments in the provinces of Potosí, Cochabamba, and Santa Cruz. Belgrano had other assets too. By decree of May 31, 1813, the constituent assembly of Buenos Aires ordered the establishment of a regiment of slaves, whose owners would be compensated from government funds, and began a policy of recruiting slaves by promising freedom to those who fought for the revolution. This was partly an ideological matter; liberals favored an end to slavery, and the government had passed a free womb law early in 1813. But it was also recognition of the effectiveness slaves had shown as soldiers for the revolutionary cause in the Banda Oriental and had the important effect of opening up a new vein of recruits for an army that frequently required new cohorts.[41] More important at this stage, however, was the allegiance of rebel juntas at Cochabamba and Chuquisaca and the support from the various *republiquetas* (little republics), which emerged in the wars between the armies of Buenos Aires and Lima.

The activities of these foci of rebellion point to an important, if neglected, aspect of the war for Upper Peru—namely, the part played by local insurgents who rose against royal government, identified with the revolutionary cause of Buenos Aires, and continued to fight when the porteños had to retreat from Upper Peru. By 1813, six main republiquetas existed in backland areas throughout Upper Peru. In the north, the priest Ildefonso Muñecas operated out of Ayata, close to Lake Titicaca, within reach of La Paz and threatening royalist communications between Peru and Upper Peru. In central Upper Peru, the area of Ayopaya, north of Cochabamba, was controlled by guerrillas, mostly recruited from Indian peasants whose communities had a long history of conflict with government tax collectors and were organized under leaders who had links with Buenos Aires, such as José Miguel Lanza, and local men opposed to Spanish government, such as Eusebio Lira and José Manuel Chinchilla.[42] The area to the south of Ayopaya was held by Álvarez de Arenales (the Spanish soldier who had taken part in the 1809 rebellion of Chuquisaca and had escaped from royalist prison to join the porteños at Tucumán in 1812). Adjacent to his domain was that of another leading insurgent chieftain, Ignacio Warnes, a porteño professional soldier who had gone into Upper Peru with Belgrano in 1813 and subsequently carved out his own base of popular support in Santa Cruz de la Sierra. Closer to Potosí, the Padillas, a creole couple with a background among radical students in Chuquisaca, dominated the area based on La Laguna. Further south, within reach of the Spanish fortress of Cotagaita and the entry into Upper Peru along the royal highway, Vicente Camargo operated out of a base at Cinti.[43]

The scant information available on these guerrilla bands suggests that their members crossed the social spectrum. Their caudillos tended to be educated creoles, some with a military background either as militia captains or regular soldiers, who opposed Spanish rule by reason of their commitment to the idea of independence, from some personal resentment against the authorities, or a combination of both.[44] Their followers were mestizo and Indian peasants whose motives are often obscure. The extraordinary account left by José Santos Vargas, a young mestizo from Oruro who fought in the republiqueta of Ayopaya under the creole commander Eusebio Lira, suggests that few knew much about the revolution outside their small worlds or had ideas about alternative government beyond their immediate environment.[45] Their idea of a patria was linked to the political initiative of Buenos Aires; they looked to the armies of Buenos Aires to provide leadership and wanted autonomy for local communities as part of the independent provinces of the River Plate. They justified their rebellion by talk of Spanish tyranny and kept to their Christian beliefs and practices (sometimes with the aid of priests who accompanied them).Their primary loyalty was to the caudillo, who led them in war.They fought with guns and swords, often stolen from defeated enemies, lived by plunder and exactions, and occasionally enlarged their numbers for military operations by making alliances with Indian caciques, who could mobilize members of their communities to fight at specific times. Santos's diary suggest that the guerrillas lived a precarious existence, always on the move, fighting for survival while constantly "on the brink of death," bound together by personal ties but also prone to fight among themselves as rival leaders competed for local supremacy.[46]

The importance of these republiquetas and guerrilla groupings has been underestimated by historians who focus solely on the contest between the armies of Buenos Aires and Lima.[47] Although the rebel caudillos were situated in isolated areas, they usually operated separately from each other and found it difficult to sustain any coordinated action; they were, nonetheless, a constant problem to the royalist regime because, with their raids on commerce and communications, they kept rebellion alive and forced the authorities into expensive counterinsurgency operations.There were also occasions on which they contributed directly to the campaigns and actions of Buenos Aires's army, acting as auxiliary forces that were temporarily absorbed into the army or joining in combined operations with it. Arenales and Warnes were particularly valuable to the revolutionary cause, since they had professional military experience and close political connections with the revolutionary regime in Buenos Aires; Muñecas and the Padillas also had strong ideological commitment to the revolution against Spain and a proven capacity for mobilizing Indian peasantries.

The existence of these irregular forces helped persuade Belgrano to move onto the offensive in September 1813, when he advanced north from Potosí in search of the royalist army. As the two sides maneuvered around each other, Belgrano seemed to have the advantage. Pezuela's royalist army was still recovering from the defeats of Tucumán and Salta, and Pezuela believed that Belgrano's force was much larger than his. He estimated his own forces at about 3,200, and Belgrano's at about 7,000 disciplined men, plus a division of some 2,000 Indians and mestizos under the Indian caudillo Baltazar Cárdenas.[48] Thus, when Belgrano advanced towards him, Pezuela initially took up a defensive stance at Condocondo and avoided battle. Belgrano failed, however, to press forward, and his hesitation handed the initiative back to Pezuela. For, while Belgrano held back, royalist forces defeated the irregulars led by the Indian Cárdenas, not only putting them to flight but also capturing correspondence that revealed Belgrano's intention to attack at Condocondo later that month.

Knowing that the insurgents had reinforcements en route to bolster their numbers and aware that his own retreat would be very difficult in the bleak terrain of the high Andes, where settlement was very sparse, movement slow, and food in short supply, Pezuela decided that the best form of defense was to attack Belgrano's position at Vilcapugio. He sought the element of surprise by taking an unexpected route across the mountains under cover of darkness in the freezing Andean night, so that his forces could be in position to mount an assault at dawn on October 1,

1813. The difficulties of moving troops in these conditions meant Pezuela lost the full shock of surprise, but his unexpected advance nonetheless forced Belgrano into a hurried, poorly prepared defense.

The numbers of the forces that fought at Vilcapugio is uncertain, since each side gave different estimates. Pezuela reported that the insurgents held the numerical advantage, with some 4,600 infantry, 1,300 cavalry, and 16 artillery pieces against the royalists' 3,000 infantrymen, 410 cavalry, and 12 artillery pieces. He was less certain about the amount of Indian support each side had, except that the insurgents had more: he tallied some 3,360 Indian auxiliaries on his side and "a multitude" of Indian auxiliaries on the enemy's. Accounts of the fighting suggest, however, that effective soldiers were probably closely matched in both number and expertise, for the battle was hard fought, lasted for many hours, and, according to testimonies from both sides, was closely run. At first, when Belgrano's forces withstood the initial royalist assaults and forced some of Pezuela's men back, they were convinced that they had won.[49] Then, however, Pezuela personally rallied his men to fight on, forced Belgrano to fall back, and caused heavy losses of officers, arms, and equipment.[50] Belgrano saved what he could in the circumstances. His deputy, Díaz Vélez, returned to Potosí to ransack the city for supplies while Belgrano regrouped his depleted forces at a defensive position at Ayohuma, closer to Potosí. Thus, although Vilcapugio was reported as a great victory, celebrated in Lima's famous theater by a play called *The Battle of Vilcapugio*, Pezuela had not yet removed the porteño army from Upper Peru.

Vilcapugio was, however, to be the first step towards royalist victory in the second war for Upper Peru, for it pushed the porteño invaders into a desperately difficult position from which they were unable to recover. A letter from Díaz Vélez to Belgrano, which fell into royalist hands, showed that the porteños had few options after the battle at Vilcapugio. According to Díaz Vélez, the only reasonable course of action was for Belgrano to join him in Potosí as soon as possible, to defend the city and its essential resources. Without reinforcements, he stated, he could not hold Potosí; most of the propertied classes and the priests were against him, and his only allies were the "mob" and the Indians. Neither of these was reliable; the mob was given to robbery and lawlessness, while the Indians had been reduced by long exploitation to "little more than machines," who might easily change sides. If Potosí were lost, Belgrano would not be able to retake it and would jeopardize alliances with other provinces that had sided with Buenos Aires. Any retreat back into the lower provinces was unthinkable because it would invite a royalist offensive that, by linking with Montevideo, could encircle Buenos Aires. Díaz Vélez therefore insisted that Belgrano take up a defensive position at Potosí and avoid at all costs another engagement with the royalist army.[51]

Belgrano's options were, however, closed down by Pezuela, who pursued Belgrano until finally cornering him at Ayohuma on November 14, 1813, where he inflicted a more complete defeat than that of Vilcapugio. Pezuela reported that the army of Buenos Aires lost 600 dead on the battlefield, and many more were cut down by Spanish cavalry as they fled towards Potosí.[52] Belgrano's army now dispersed, with the loss of thousands of men, and its rump withdrew to Jujuy and Salta. Buenos Aires's second attempt to take control of Upper Peru had been soundly defeated.

The outcome of this second war for Upper Peru was largely determined by the qualities of the opposing armies and their commanders. Although it is difficult to make a systematic comparison, there is evidence to suggest that the contending forces were more evenly matched than those of Goyeneche and Castelli in 1811. Both sides now had more experience of combat, and Belgrano's army was better able to fight battles using European-style tactics in which commanders maneuvered for position, made tactical use of artillery, and deployed soldiers who were sufficiently armed and disciplined to hold linear formations and give and receive heavy fire. There was no great disparity in the size of their forces, and both sides had a core of veterans. Pezuela had been able to rebuild his army around a nucleus of experienced officers and men who were capable of fighting a coordinated battle for position. The porteños also had a core group of experienced officers and men who, at Salta and Jujuy, had enjoyed victory over a royalist army. And, it seems, they had the added advantage of support from Upper Peru's indigenous peasantry.

The Indian peasantry seems to have been more willing to fight on the side of the porteños than the royalists. Although Pezuela used his Indian auxiliaries, he and other royalist officers tended to regard Indians as inveterate enemies.[53] For example, when leaving Condocondo after the battle of Vilcapugio, Pezuela sent all his wounded and supplies back to Oruro to avoid their destruction by Indian villagers. Then, when he returned to the advance, he found the Indians deeply uncooperative; villagers of the few communities in his path fled from the royalists' approach, taking all their food and animals.[54] Although a local priest recruited and paid Indian carriers to move supplies and artillery for his army, they were so eager to desert that they had to be guarded at all times. So, even when the royalists had Indians on their side, they proved an unreliable resource. The Spanish found this impossible to understand. According to García Camba, the Indian inclination to desert was "irresistible, amazing and inexplicable"; he also thought it entirely incorrigible since "neither persuasion, nor the stimulus of honour and glory, nor the most severe punishment" affected Indian attitudes.[55]

If Belgrano enjoyed greater sympathy among the Indians and was better able to recruit them, the creole chroniclers of the war judged their contribution slight, at least on the battlefield. José María Paz, who fought as a captain of dragoons in Belgrano's army, stated that Indians "never gave any service in the fighting, nor entered into combat, nor did it occur to anyone to have them do so."[56] According to Paz, Indians were useful for moving artillery when draft animals were not available but were so terrified by enemy artillery fire that they were a liability in battle.[57] He attributed their tendency to flee the battlefield as cowardice that was inherent in the Indian character rather than seeing it—as we now would—as the natural reaction of men who were untrained to stand fast under fire. However, his comments underscore the fact that, although the Indian peasantry was generally reluctant to commit to war for royalists or republicans, it was at the very least vital to keeping armies moving and supplied.

The skills and abilities of the commanders and soldiers who fought in Upper Peru were also crucial. While the porteños had more local support, the army of the crown had the military edge. Pezuela had undertaken a bold attack at Vilcapugio, where his timing, positioning, and vigorous assault had offset his disadvantage in numbers and lack of cavalry. He did not succeed in eliminating the enemy's forces because he lacked sufficient horses for effective pursuit, but he fruitfully used the following weeks to strengthen his forces for the next assault. Belgrano's forces showed discipline by withdrawing from Vilcapugio in an orderly manner that allowed about 1,500 infantrymen and 500 cavalry to regroup at Ayohuma. However, Belgrano's generalship was inadequate. According to one of his own officers, he exposed himself to attack by allowing Pezuela to find his position, then committed the error of being drawn back into battle too soon, only to make several tactical blunders that paved the way to defeat.[58] Belgrano himself accepted that his military experience played a part in the defeat, for, as he admitted to San Martín, "By chance, or God's will, I find myself a general, without knowing where I am . . . I was completely beaten in the pampa of Ayohuma when I thought I was on the point of victory."[59]

The actions at Vilcapugio and Ayohuma were highly significant for both sides. On the eve of battle at Vilcapugio, Pezuela told his officers that, if they lost, people throughout Peru, as far as Lima, would "declare for the revolutionaries of Buenos Aires, unite with them, and finish off all Europeans and loyal subjects of the King in this South America, in order to attain their independence."[60] After the battle of Ayohuma, he marked the providential character of his victory by attributing it to the intervention of the Virgen del Carmen, whom he made the *Generala*, or official patron of his army.[61]

Pezuela's claim that victories at Vilcapugio and Ayohuma saved South America for the crown was wildly exaggerated, but Belgrano's defeat was, without doubt, a body blow to Buenos Aires. It had discredited Belgrano and again exposed the problems faced by Buenos Aires in sustaining an effective army at long distance and in the face of defeat. When José de San Martín arrived to take over from Belgrano at Tucumán in January 1814, he found "only a few sad groups of a defeated army . . . Troops so naked it offends decency . . . Officers ashamed to appear in public . . . and everyone shouting for their pay."[62] For the second time in two years, the viceroy of Lima had fielded armies that scattered the forces of Buenos Aires with apparent ease, taking control of resources that would otherwise have fuelled the insurgents' war effort, and revealing the disparity in the effectiveness of the rival armies.

While royalist victory in the Andes strengthened the viceregal regime in Peru, it caused political consternation in Buenos Aires. The Second Triumvirate was overturned in January 1814, and authority passed to one of the triumvirs, Gervasio Antonio Posadas, in the hope that, given emergency powers to act as supreme director, he might focus the energies of government on coping with an increasingly difficult situation. For, not only had Buenos Aires suffered a major defeat in the Andes, but its political elite was alarmed by news of successive French defeats in Spain. According to a British observer in Buenos Aires, this "produced a very considerable abatement in the tone of the leading party here," so that "the visionary and extravagant ideas of liberty and independence . . . were beginning to give way to a more reasonable plan of accommodation with the mother country . . ."[63]

By the same token, Belgrano's defeat was a tonic for Viceroy Abascal, who at the beginning of 1814, had reasonable cause for self-congratulation. In Pezuela, he had found a military commander who was more amenable and successful than Goyeneche. Moreover, having recovered the royalist hold on Upper Peru and thoroughly defeated rioplatense forces, Pezuela now seemed poised to resume Abascal's counterrevolutionary strategy by moving into rebel territory and taking the war to Buenos Aires. To trace the outcome of his counterrevolutionary project, we must take account of events on several fronts: first, Pezuela's efforts to capitalize on his victory in Upper Peru; second, the war between Buenos Aires and Montevideo; third, the outbreak of rebellion in southern Peru; and, finally, events in Spain.

Pezuela on the Andean Front

In seeking to expand the counterrevolution, Pezuela established his headquarters at Tupiza, sent his vanguard to Jujuy and Salta in January 1814, and in February, prepared a plan to concentrate his army at Salta in order to carry the war south into the lower provinces of the Río de la Plata. His purpose was to sweep down from the Andes onto the plains, carrying the war deep into the United Provinces and eventually linking up with royalist forces from Montevideo. However, for all his fine words about saving South America, Pezuela was not confident that he could proceed safely from the mountains to the pampas, and he soon encountered formidable difficulties.

His first problem was the usual one of manpower. He pressed the viceroy to provide thousands of reinforcements but found the flow of fresh recruits hindered by Peru's *cabildos constitucionales* (municipal councils which had acquired more power under the terms of the 1812 Cádiz Constitution). Pezuela was forced to demand 1,000 conscripts from regions in Upper Peru, whose men were known to oppose militia service and had a reputation for deserting rather than fighting. Half of those raised duly deserted en route to Tupiza, and Pezuela managed to create two new battalions of about 800 men only by the expedient of joining those who arrived with men recouped in a prisoner exchange and a couple of hundred veterans already in service. The pressure on the army in Upper Peru had not wholly abated, however, and to ensure the security of his rearguard, Pezuela had to send troops to Santa Cruz de la Sierra and neighboring areas to deal with the guerrilla leaders who were still undefeated. Nonetheless, by May 1814, he had formed an army of 4,000 men and moved forward to Jujuy with the intention of opening an offensive against Tucumán as soon as he received reinforcements from Peru. However, no sooner had Pezuela ordered the first regiment to march to Salta in mid-July than he was forced to rethink his plans.[64]

The chief obstacle that stood in his way was a small but very effective resistance around Salta. Although the city of Salta had a small population (about 7,000 in a province with only 30–40,000 people), its hinterland became a strong buffer for Buenos Aires. Opposition came from across the social spectrum, led by a local elite that had created large estates (*estancias*) used for raising livestock (cattle, horses, mules), much of which was traded into Upper Peru. Through intermarriage, the *estancieros* had established webs of kinship that gave them local political power in the urban cabildos and a capacity for united action in a common interest. In 1810, the four leading families had sided with Buenos Aires and given impressive support in men, money, and livestock to the Balcarce-Castelli expedition into Upper Peru. They then continued to provide very effective military support for the revolutionary cause, thanks to their ability to mobilize informal armies from the men who worked their estates. These were the gauchos, mounted livestock herders who were harnessed to the revolutionary cause in return for the chance to fight and plunder the intruders from Peru.[65]

The gauchos were essentially peasants of scant means who lived on the great estancias of the region, where they rented land in return for seasonal labor or worked for wages. Some owned a few head of cattle and some engaged in trade, but the great majority were landless peasants who worked as herders and had unusual skills with horse and blade. These were, as the Spaniards found in Venezuela too, skills that could be turned to martial use, especially when gauchos united under a leader with military training and the support of the local elites. In the words of General La Serna, Pezuela's successor as commander in Upper Peru, the gauchos sprang from an environment that made them natural horse soldiers and guerrilla fighters:

> The peoples who inhabit these vast and almost empty lands are scattered around in the manner of nomadic hordes, without any occupation other than the care of their herds; they live on horseback and throw the lasso and *bolas* with singular ability, making them not only the best but perhaps also the most skilled horsemen found in these lands. The people of towns and villages share these attributes to a greater or lesser degree depending on the distance and character of their haciendas, which they call *estancias*; but in general all are large, robust, agile, well-made, generous, open and lively, and with the independent spirit found among half-civilized peoples. . . . They always carry a knife as long as a bayonet, which they wield expertly and use to kill and butcher their cattle . . . In sum, they are people entirely made, bred, and trained for war.[66]

The effectiveness of the gaucho war owed much to its principal leader, Martín Güemes. A *salteño*, who had fought against the British at Buenos Aires in 1806–7, with Balcarce in Upper Peru, and at the siege of Montevideo, Güemes became the key commander in Salta when he returned to serve with San Martín in 1814. In the years that followed, he became Buenos Aires's outstanding military chief and indispensable political ally in the Andean border region. Güemes proved hugely successful in bonding the gauchos into a hard-hitting military force, not only by drawing on the ties of clientelism and patronage of landowners but also by rewarding his soldiers with the military fuero, which gave freedom from local judicial authorities, exemption from rent payments, the right to take stock from the haciendas to sustain their military activities, and the chance to plunder their enemies.[67]

Here, then, was a popular insurgency that was crucial to the rioplatense independents. In 1814, the gauchos' hit-and-run tactics slowed the royalist army to a virtual standstill; they made it extremely difficult to get the cattle, horses, and mules needed for the army's food and transport while at the same time picking off royalist soldiers who strayed beyond well-defended lines. The inhabitants of Jujuy and Salta also opposed the royalist cause, albeit in a less direct way. The majority of these inhabitants were women, left by men who had gone to join Belgrano in Tucumán, and they acted as spies and agents for the insurgents, providing them with a constant stream of information on the royalist army and its dispositions. The royalists, in short, felt themselves to be deep in enemy territory once they had reached Jujuy, exposed to guerrilla harassment and popular animosity, and at the tenuous outer limits of their lines of supply and support in Upper Peru.[68]

To make matters worse, Pezuela's problems were compounded by the continuing peasant-based insurgency in Upper Peru. Much of eastern Upper Peru was in the hands of insurgent caudillos, of whom Arenales, Warnes, and Padilla were the most effective. In May 1814, these men united behind Arenales and virtually wiped out a royalist army unit of 300 men at Piray (La Florida), thus raising again the possibility of a general uprising.[69] Knowing that the royalist army was far to the south, guerrilla bands mobilized in a war of many small engagements, which, though incapable of defeating the royalist army, imposed severe strains on its capacity to hold the towns and countryside that Pezuela had previously recovered. Officials throughout Upper Peru warned that unrest would spread throughout the provinces of Cochabamba, Chuquisaca, and Potosí, and called for military reinforcements. In such circumstances, the royalist strategy for an offensive into the United Provinces was again thrown into doubt.

Abascal's offensive strategy was further damaged by military problems on the Atlantic coast, far beyond the military reach of royalist Peru. In mid-May 1814, Pezuela was told of the defeat of Montevideo's navy and, with it, the likelihood that the Spanish stronghold would fall to a siege. Pezuela understood that this would jeopardize any further advance in the interior. He therefore decided to remain in Salta and Jujuy in the hope that an amphibious expedition from Spain might relieve Montevideo by sea. However, on receiving confirmation of the fall of Montevideo in July 1814, Pezuela promptly discarded plans for an offensive southwards and turned back to the borders of Upper Peru.[70] For, not only had any possibility of joint operations with Montevideo disappeared, but Pezuela feared that 6,000 men under General Rondeau, armed with the thousands of muskets and plentiful munitions seized at Montevideo, might now restart the war on the Upper Peruvian front.

War in the Banda Oriental

The Fall of Montevideo

The immediate consequence of the fall of Montevideo in June 1814 was, then, to stall the trans-Andean royalist offensive planned by Lima. But what of its causes? Why, after five years of resistance and at the very moment when Abascal held the initiative in the Andes, did the royalists lose their only port in the South Atlantic and their only stronghold close to Buenos Aires?

The royalist position at Montevideo was, in fact, always precarious. In 1810–11, the city was saved from the assaults of Buenos Aires and Artigas by the intervention of a Portuguese army from Brazil, and its security was then underpinned by the continuing presence of these forces. Artigas and his followers meanwhile remained in Entre Ríos, outside the conflict zone, while the government of Buenos Aires sought a diplomatic solution to the Portuguese occupation. In May 1812, Manuel Sarratea, the president of the First Triumvirate, succeeded in getting agreement from Portugal to withdraw its troops, a peaceful solution that merely opened the way to a new war between Buenos Aires and Montevideo.[71] For, once the threat of Portuguese intervention was removed, Buenos Aires and Artigas moved back onto the offensive against the royalists.

The war restarted in September 1812, when Rondeau advanced across the Uruguay River and towards Montevideo. His forces entered a devastated countryside where neither side dominated. Bands of irregulars, operating without any central command, kept the Spaniards from establishing any stable authority. Montevideo lacked the military manpower to maintain garrisons outside the regional capital and quickly lost control of its rural hinterland. Rondeau was thus able to establish formal siege of the city and make a concerted effort to remove its royalist government. This should have been easy, but mutual distrust between Artigas and Buenos Aires impeded full-scale military operations. Royalist Montevideo therefore survived because Buenos Aires could not take the Banda Oriental on its own. Artigas's cooperation was essential because of his authority as the *jefe de los orientales* and his ability to provide Rondeau with the forces needed to strengthen his own small army. But Artigas would cooperate only on his own terms. While Buenos Aires insisted on imposing its authority over the Banda Oriental, Artigas demanded autonomy within a loose federation. This difference blocked the way to a unified war effort. Indeed, after the Second Triumvirate took power in October 1812, the centralizing tendencies of the porteño political directorate worsened relations with Artigas. Alvear persuaded him to join Rondeau's siege of Montevideo in early 1813, but his contribution was halfhearted, and political relations did not improve.

The campaign against Montevideo made little progress in these circumstances. The only notable military achievement secured by Buenos Aires was stopping

Montevideo from taking the offensive. In January 1813, when Viceroy Vigodet sent a convoy of ships and some 350 troops upriver, Buenos Aires responded by sending San Martín with his Regiment of Mounted Grenadiers to find and defeat this force, which he duly did in a masterly attack at San Lorenzo. This was an important victory because it prevented Vigodet from establishing a strategic enclave on the Paraná River for use as a base for royalist attacks in the interior; it also preserved an important route for communications between Buenos Aires and its army in the north.[72] However, it inflicted only slight damage on Montevideo's forces and did nothing to improve relations with Artigas. Indeed, these deteriorated to the point where Viceroy Vigodet thought it worth trying to persuade Artigas to change sides and join the royalists.[73]

Buenos Aires sought a political antidote: to allow Artigas a voice at the political center, its government called a General Constituent Assembly of the United Provinces for January 30, 1813. In April 1813, Artigas declared allegiance to Buenos Aires and accepted Rondeau as commander in chief, but unity did not ensue. After the ultracentralist Alvear was elected as president of the assembly, Artigas's plans for provincial autonomy were openly rejected. The rift now turned into a complete breakdown of relations in December 1813, followed by Artigas's withdrawal of his army from the siege of Montevideo in January 1814.[74]

The persistence of the royalist enclave at Montevideo owed much, then, to the transformation of war in the Banda Oriental into a complex plural conflict, involving Spain, Portugal, Buenos Aires, and the insurgent orientales under Artigas. Although Buenos Aires was determined to take the city, Montevideo posed a number of problems. First, Portugal's ambitions meant that it might use war as the excuse for reinvading the region and expanding its Brazilian empire southwards. Second, the regime in Buenos Aires was, in the wake of its military defeats, distracted by internal reorganization. The appointment of Posadas as supreme director in January 1814 did little to improve matters; in theory, it enhanced the authority of government, but in practice, his emergency dictatorship was shallow and unstable. Thus, when Posadas tried to negotiate with the Spanish government in Montevideo, the royalist governor Vigodet, seeing his besiegers weakened by Artigas's withdrawal, refused to cooperate. Posadas was also unable to restore the alliance with Artigas; indeed, Artigas aggravated Buenos Aires's weakness during 1814, when he set out to organize a "Federal League" that would oppose Buenos Aires as well as Spain and Portugal.[75]

Montevideo thus remained a potential platform for a royalist counterattack against the revolutionary government in Buenos Aires, but Spain proved unable to exploit the divisions between Buenos Aires and Artigas. One obstacle was Spain's failure to supply sufficient forces. After sending only 87 men to Montevideo in 1811, the Regency made a serious effort to reinforce the city in 1812, with the dispatch of 681 troops. Unfortunately for Spain, nearly two-thirds were drowned in a shipwreck in the Plate estuary.[76] The following year, in August 1813, Spain succeeded in landing another 446 men in Montevideo, but their arrival did little to strengthen the city; instead, they brought disease that further debilitated a population already weakened by the blockade imposed by Buenos Aires's flotilla. A further problem was that Pezuela's victories in Upper Peru in late 1813 came too late to allow him to mount the long-planned strategic offensive into Tucumán, which would have forced Buenos Aires to redeploy forces from Montevideo to the interior.

While Spain delayed, Buenos Aires modified its strategy. Instead of relying on land forces alone, it built a fleet to fight Montevideo's flotilla and cut off the port's maritime supply routes. These naval forces succeeded where army campaigns had failed and weakened the city by intercepting its supplies. In May 1814, Posadas increased the pressure by sending reinforcements of 1,500 men into the siege, under the command of his nephew Carlos María de Alvear, but the porteño flotilla played the decisive role. Commanded by the Irishman William Brown and staffed largely by officers released by the British navy as the war in Europe came to an end, it defeated Montevideo's fleet, closed the port completely, and forced Vigodet to come to terms. Vigodet surrendered on June 23, 1814, and Alvear took the city in the style of a conqueror, repudiating the terms of a treaty that had included safeguards for Spanish sovereignty and loyalist property.[77]

The subjugation of royalist Montevideo was a considerable triumph for Buenos Aires in its struggle against Spain. Although Artigas and his allies continued to oppose domination by Buenos Aires, even to the point where they went to war with Buenos Aires itself, the loss of Montevideo was very costly for Spain. Having held the city for nearly five years, Spain lost Montevideo at a crucial moment. It removed a platform for invasion of the River Plate at the very time that, due to the end of the Peninsular War and the restoration of Ferdinand VII, Spain was in a good position to use Montevideo as a pivot on which to hinge the pincer movement that could crush Buenos Aires between Spanish forces sent west across the Atlantic and Peruvian royalist troops sent east from Upper Peru.

Nor was this the only setback to Viceroy Abascal and the royalists in 1814. Despite Pezuela's victories at Vilcapugio and Ayohuma, the royalist position in the Andes became more insecure as a result of popular rebellion in the Andean heartland. In August 1814, rebellion broke out in Cuzco and spread to regions that had previously been in royalist hands.

The Cuzco Rebellion

If the loss of Montevideo deprived the Peruvian counterrevolution of an important outwork, the rebellion in Cuzco threatened a key bastion in Peru's political and military infrastructure. Since the crisis of the monarchy began in 1808, Viceroy Abascal had been able to fight his war against Buenos Aires (as well as other enemies in Chile and Quito) from a politically stable Peruvian base, including the southern Andean region that had seen the great rebellions of the early 1780s. Although he faced many financial and economic difficulties, Abascal had not previously faced serious insurgency within Peru. There were some small-scale revolts, but not in the southern highlands, despite the fact that their history and proximity to Upper Peru seemed to make them vulnerable to the contagion of revolution.[78] On the contrary, the regions around Cuzco and Puno had supplied the viceroy with many of the troops needed to fight against the insurgents in Upper Peru and their porteño allies.

News that rebellion had broken out in the city of Cuzco first reached General Pezuela as he was pulling back to Suipacha on the southern edge of Upper Peru, in a temporary withdrawal from an offensive into the territories of Buenos Aires. Faced with the fall of Cuzco, the city that had been the rampart from which the Lima government supervised the security of neighboring Upper Peru, and amid fears that rebellion would engulf the whole of southern Peru, Pezuela immediately abandoned his previous plans and withdrew into a strictly defensive strategy that took his forces back into Peru.

The most immediate threat was that the upheaval in Cuzco would destroy the essential instrument of Peru's counterrevolution by subverting the Army of Peru— for, as Pezuela later recalled, "five sixths of the force" of the royalist army and most of the officers were from Cuzco, Puno, and Arequipa. If they refused to fight against people from their own cities, he would have had only 300 men, drawn from Lima and other parts of Peru, on his side.[79] Despite a plot to depose him by one of his officers who was in league with the Cuzco rebels, Pezuela managed to secure the loyalty of his army and detached a force of 1,200 men under his deputy Juan Ramírez for service against the Cuzco rebels. He meanwhile moved back to a fortified position at Cotagaita in September 1814, ready to defend the south of Upper Peru while Ramírez engaged the rebels in Peru.[80]

The Cuzco rebellion posed a threat to the integrity of Spanish rule that was as serious as any that the royalist army had hitherto encountered in neighboring Upper Peru. The rebellion was triggered by disgruntled creoles, who believed that they had been deprived of full enjoyment of the rights conferred by the Cádiz Constitution, but it quickly threatened to become a movement for independence that would overturn all that Abascal and the Army of Peru had achieved in five years of fighting rebellion in Upper Peru. From being a vital base for royalist operations in Upper Peru, Cuzco now became the vanguard of an insurgency that threatened to engulf the whole of royalist southern Peru, to reignite rebellion in Upper Peru, and thus create a new revolutionary front with Buenos Aires.

Explanations of the rebellion have invariably stressed its urban character and creole leadership, portraying it either as an expression of *cuzqueño* autonomism against Lima or as a movement for independence.[81] Whatever the intentions of its leaders, the Cuzco rebellion certainly had considerable political and social potency. Politically, its creole leaders had a message with widespread appeal, They manipulated the Inca symbolism, which had infused several conspiracies and rebellions in eighteenth-century Peru, especially the revolt of Túpac Amaru, and, playing on a mythologized Inca past, rallied followers across ethnic and class lines. Cuzco's leading ideologue—the Spanish cleric Francisco Carrascón, of the Cuzco cathedral chapter—revived Túpac Amaru's vision of a polity built on a Lima-Buenos Aires axis, albeit in a distinctive form: he proposed that the rebellion aim for a "Peruvian

Empire" that would combine Lima, Cuzco, and Buenos Aires in a single southern state, a creole-dominated republic, independent of Spain.[82]

Although Carrascón found no room for an Inca king, the Cuzco leadership was able to give their rebellion real force by mobilizing Indian allies. They incorporated the cacique Mateo García Pumacahua, who had led Indians to fight against Túpac Amaru's rebels in the Great Rebellion of 1780–2 and against the Indian peasants who had besieged La Paz in 1811. Now, the Inca noble, who had previously been the crown's most notable ally among the indigenous community leaders, joined with the creole revolutionaries to fight the government he had previously defended. Under the combined leadership of creole cuzqueños and the cacique Pumacahua, who was given a military command, the rebels expanded their control far beyond the Cuzco hinterland, spreading southwards over an area comparable to that of the Great Rebellion. The Junta at Cuzco sent forces in three directions: to Puno and La Paz under Ildefonso de las Muñecas and José Manuel Pinelo, to Huamanga under José Gabriel Béjar and Manuel Hurtado de Mendoza, and to Arequipa under Pumacahua and Vicente Angúlo. As their forces advanced, local populations joined the rebellion, often in large numbers.[83]

This ability to arouse mass participation across the populous, economically important, and strategically located southern sierra of Peru turned the rebellion of Cuzco's creoles into a serious threat to Spanish rule; the viceroy's Council of War unanimously agreed that the viceroyalty had entered "a highly critical state" and called for emergency measures to save it.[84] This was the first major eruption of Indian peasant revolt since the rebellion of Túpac Amaru, and it brought large forces into action against the viceregal regime, including men who had previously been among the crown's firm allies against Buenos Aires's incursions into Upper Peru. In 1815, Indian communities in the region around Cuzco—in the areas of Quispicanchis, Canas y Canchis, Paucartambo, Carabayo, and Azángaro, all of which had participated in the Túpac Amaru rebellion—took advantage of the turmoil in regional society to express their grievances and seek resolutions to their local conflicts.[85]

As Cuzco's armed columns pushed forward into adjacent regions, they seemed set to reverse Abascal's counterrevolution. However, the social and political energy of the rebellion could not be converted into military effectiveness. Despite its potential for attracting widespread Indian support, the fighting capacity of the Cuzco rebellion was undermined by internal divisions and lack of military experience among leaders and followers.[86] By inspiring rebellion among the Indian peasantry, it divided those who were ready to support an anti-Spanish movement. At the same time, its large popular underpinning worked against unity. Although the mobilization of Indian villagers seemed to resemble the Great Rebellion of the early 1780s, they tended to remain tightly tied to local politics and did not achieve a great deal.

Peasant rebels were, moreover, inadequate when faced with regular soldiers led by professional army officers. The rebel column under Pinelo and Muñecas was initially successful; during September 1814, it took the region between Cuzco and Lake Titicaca, seized the strategic Desaguadero crossing, and then occupied La Paz, inflicting considerable bloodshed on the city's royalist defenders. But it could not withstand General Ramírez when he marched against them. Pinelo and Muñecas withdrew to Puno to avoid engaging with the royalist troops but were defeated at Achacolla. Muñecas retreated further north to the shores of Lake Titicaca, where he created a republiqueta in Larecaja, defended by Indian recruits whom he organized according to Christian principles in a "Holy Battalion."[87] By November, Ramírez had suffocated the rebellion in this area, to considerable strategic effect. By recapturing La Paz and Puno, he stemmed the advance of rebellion into Upper Peru, reestablished royalist control of the strategic bridgehead between Peru and Upper Peru, and kept open communications with Lima.

Nor did Cuzco's other armed expeditions do any better. The rebels who marched on Huamanga suffered several defeats in combat with forces reinforced from Lima and by early October had been decimated. The rebels who went to Arequipa followed a similar trajectory—from an enthusiastic start to a sad end. They advanced from Cuzco to Arequipa in early November and brought the whole intervening area under their sway; however, when Ramírez moved south against them, they were unable to withstand his offensive. In early December, he entered Arequipa; three months later, on March 11, 1815, he completed the military defeat of the Cuzco rebels in a battle with Pumacahua's forces at Umachiri, near Lampa, and followed it with the exemplary executions of the principal rebel leaders.

This action demonstrated, once again, how well-armed, well-trained, and experienced soldiers could overcome much larger numbers of indisciplined and poorly armed peasant rebels. Ramírez had only about 1,300 men in a battle where he faced more than ten times that number, and he won with minimal losses. The rebels' main force (estimated at between 15,000 and 20,000 men) had some 40 artillery pieces and at most about 800 muskets; the great majority used slings, clubs, and lances, the traditional weapons of the peasantry. The only members of the rebel forces with experience in the use of artillery and muskets were deserters from the Army of Peru, and they were few. They were, moreover, unable to bring these weapons to bear as they were quickly outmaneuvered. Once they were penetrated by Ramírez's troops, Cuzco's peasant rebels broke and ran, suffering heavy losses (perhaps 1,000 men) among those cut down in flight or executed arbitrarily on capture.[88] Finally, after Ramírez's relentless attack, in a remarkable campaign that crossed and recrossed the Andes in months of marching, the Cuzco rebellion disintegrated. With it went the threat, indeed the nightmare for Peru's royalists, of an insurgent bloc in southern Peru that would link with the insurgents of Upper Peru and create a territorial bridgehead for the armies of Buenos Aires.

Lima and Buenos Aires: The Balance of Power in 1814–15

By the end of 1814, then, the revolutionary and counterrevolutionary wars had reached an impasse where both sides were still far from achieving the breakthrough they had been seeking since 1810. In Upper Peru, the Spaniards held the advantage. Lima's royalist forces had beaten back two offensives from Buenos Aires and retained their hold on a region that acted as both a buffer to defend Peru and a base for attacks on Buenos Aires. Buenos Aires, on the other hand, had achieved little at considerable cost. The Army of the North lived mostly off the land, like its royalist counterpart, but troops had to be paid and sustained with military materials, imposing a financial burden without the compensating flows of trade and revenues that made silver-rich Upper Peru such coveted territory. Repeated military failures also had dire political effect, since they helped to undermine the authority of Buenos Aires and hindered the attainment of unity and stability in the provinces of the old viceroyalty. Buenos Aires clung to its ambitions in Upper Peru and could draw some comfort from the fact that the local guerrillas continued to challenge the royalist occupation there. However, in 1815, all the signs suggested that Buenos Aires was losing and Spain winning the war for Upper Peru. Indeed, far from being a point of penetration into Peru, the region remained a barrier to the advance of Buenos Aires and a bastion from which the royalists might reverse the revolution.

Military strategies, and the mobilization of resources needed to implement them, had played a crucial part in determining this outcome. On the royalist side, Viceroy Abascal had defined clear objectives and pursued them with consistent determination. He realized in 1810 that the projection of armed forces from Peru was the only way to defend Upper Peru against subversion by porteño forces and their sympathizers, and he clung to Upper Peru because he saw it as the strategic key to counterrevolution throughout the lands under his authority, from Peru itself to Quito in the north and Chile in the south. Abascal consequently did all in his power to maintain a strong army in Upper Peru, even at the time when the Cuzco rebellion fanned out over the southern Peruvian heartland. The armies that his officers raised, and which he sustained at enormous cost to the Peruvian treasury, had proved their worth. Based mostly on recruitment among the Indian and mestizo populations of southern Peru, from Puno to Arequipa, this army proved surprisingly loyal and increasingly effective, and under Spanish and creole officers became the spearhead of Abascal's strategy for defeating the Buenos Aires revolution. By keeping a military grip on Upper Peru, Abascal was able to assure its political loyalty or at least its quiescence, preventing the insurgents from uniting into an articulated rebellion, which might merge into a single assault on power. And by keeping Upper Peru, Abascal and his generals achieved the more important goal of sustaining Spanish rule in the Viceroyalty of Peru.

There were, of course, other reasons too for the survival of the vicegeral regime. Abascal's political leadership and creole fears of Indian and plebeian rebellion were both important in sustaining loyalism in Peru. But the military successes of Abascal's commanders were crucial. Not only did the Army of Peru hold Upper Peru and sustain an image of impregnability, but the very specific form of militarization that absorbed Indians and mestizos into a disciplined regular army no doubt helped to inhibit lower-class rebellion in Peru's southern highlands.

By the same token, Buenos Aires's military failure in Upper Peru undermined its plans to extend the May Revolution. The Junta of Buenos Aires had, like Abascal, set out with clear political objectives and pursued them stubbornly. But successive governments were unable to project their power into Upper Peru with a military effectiveness comparable to Abascal's. Nor could they secure firm alliances with local insurgents or merge them into a coordinated force. Whereas the caudillos of the Banda Oriental brought a small population together under a unified leadership of Artigas and did much to damage the power of the royalist military center in Montevideo, the insurgent leaders of Upper Peru focused on their localities and did not merge into a force capable of defeating royalist field armies. Like most guerrillas recruited from local rebellions, their preference was for defending small territories, raiding, and retreating rather than seeking a decisive contest with the enemy. Their cause was linked to that of the porteños, but Buenos Aires was unable to provide sufficient support to bind the local insurgents into their army. This was partly because Buenos Aires was under considerable military strain, since it was also fighting on another front in the Banda Oriental. It was also because the porteños and altoperuanos never identified sufficiently strongly with each other. The fact that porteño armies lived off the land ensured that they were not widely regarded as liberating forces; indeed, it seems that the populace often failed to distinguish one occupying army from another. There were also political reasons for Buenos Aires's failure in Upper Peru. On entering the region, they had promised Indian emancipation to secure Indian support for their army, but this attempt to turn the Indians into a weapon of war proved counterproductive, since it alienated whites and mixed-race groups without stimulating a widespread adherence of Indian communities to the revolutionary cause.[89]

Royalist successes in Upper Peru gave the Lima government a very plausible claim to victory over the forces of revolution in the year that followed Ferdinand VII's restoration in early 1814. Viceroy Abascal's counterrevolution had not only frustrated Buenos Aires's project of revolutionary expansion via Upper Peru but had also defeated revolution on the northern and southern borders of the viceroyalty. To the north, Abascal's military aid supported the provinces of Guayaquil and Cuenca, and by 1812 had helped to reestablish a royalist government under General Toribio Montes in the Audiencia of Quito. The provinces of Quito (Guayaquil was treated as part of Peru) were then brought into the new system of Spanish government established by the Constitution of Cádiz and elected deputies to the Cortes in 1814.[90]

To the south, in the Captaincy General of Chile, Abascal's military intervention played a key role in repressing the groups that had established independent government. It began in early 1813, when Abascal sent Brigadier Pareja with a small contingent to the Chilean south. Pareja made little military headway, but the entry of his forces encouraged royalists in Chile to rally to the Spanish cause, while also accentuating divisions among the patriots. Their military weaknesses were exposed by a second military expedition sent from Peru in early 1814 under General Gavino Gainza; his offensive forced the patriots to sign an armistice (the Treaty of Lircay) on May 3, 1814, accepting Ferdinand VII's sovereignty and the Constitution of Cádiz in return for some concessions on autonomous government and freedom for trade. This truce was rejected by Viceroy Abascal, who sent another force into Chile to impose his authority, led by General Mariano Osorio. When O'Higgins and the Carrera brothers came together to oppose the advancing royalist army, they were too late. On October 1–2, 1814, they were defeated at the battle of Rancagua, and Chile's first independent regime disappeared, leaving the small remnants of its armies, no more than about 1,000 men, to retreat across the Andes.[91]

The losses of revolutionary forces in Upper Peru and Chile were to some extent counterbalanced by Buenos Aires's seizure of Montevideo in June 1814. By removing Spain's only base on the River Plate, this reduced the threat of a military strike from Europe as well as undermining Abascal's strategy for crushing Buenos Aires in a pincer movement from Upper Peru and Montevideo. Spain's advances in the Andes were therefore neutralized by Buenos Aires's advance on the Atlantic coast. This was not an uncomplicated benefit, however, for two main reasons. In the first place, Artigas became a formidable enemy of Buenos Aires and mobilized his forces to push the porteños out of the Banda Oriental. Second, circumstances in Europe no longer favored independence in Spanish America. Posadas, who became supreme director in January 1814, expressed this setback in pungent terms:

> That damned Napoleon ruined the best of times: he lost his empire, something which our descendants will never believe possible, and has left us on the bull's horns . . . our political situation has changed a great deal and we must consequently change our policies.[92]

Such was the sense of uncertainty that Posadas lost hope for a military victory and sought instead to find a negotiated solution. In November 1814, he sent Belgrano and Rivadavia to London to ask the British to prevent Spain from launching a new offensive and, covertly, to negotiate a peaceful solution in which the Río de la Plata would become either an independent constitutional monarchy under a Bourbon prince or an autonomous state within a reformed Spanish monarchy. This willingness to compromise took another twist in 1815, when Buenos Aires was losing its grip on the Banda Oriental. After Carlos María de Alvear was made supreme director in January 1815, he decided that the best hope of defending the United Provinces was to attach them to Britain, and he wrote to Lord Strangford in Río de Janeiro to propose that Britain send troops to Buenos Aires to enforce British sovereignty. In London, meanwhile, Manuel Sarratea—another Buenos Aires envoy in Europe—contacted the former king Charles IV of Spain in the hope that he would persuade his youngest son to take the throne of an independent monarchy in the Río de la Plata.[93]

Nothing came of these efforts to placate Spain and engage international support for a negotiated independence. Indeed, after Alvear was deposed in April 1815, the revolutionaries of Buenos Aires despaired of defense by negotiation and sought instead to concentrate their political and military resources on repelling Spain. They convened a national congress, which met at Tucumán, and declared independence in July 1816. The outcome of that declaration was uncertain: Spanish governments remained committed to sending a military expedition against Buenos Aires, while conflict among the provinces made the Río de la Plata an unstable platform for securing international recognition or winning the war against Spain. In these circumstances, much hinged on Spain's capacity to exert military pressure on Buenos Aires and on Buenos Aires's ability to respond to the permanent royalist threat in Peru and its satellites. The first was decided by Spanish policy and will be discussed in Chapter 10. The second was decided by General San Martín, who, as we shall see in Chapter 12, spent these difficult years far from Buenos Aires at Mendoza, where he fashioned a new strategy for advancing the war against royalist Peru.

Notes

1. Díaz Venteo, *Campañas militares del Virrey Abascal*, pp. 204–7.
2. Roca, *Ni con Lima,* pp. 239–41.
3. From Father Mariaca's diary of the siege, cited by Siles Salinas, *La independencia de Bolivia*, p. 218.
4. John Lynn, "Victories of the Conquered: The Native Character of the Sepoy," in *Battle: A History of Combat and Culture*, ed. John Lynn (Boulder, CO: Westview Press, 2003), pp. 145–77.
5. Garrett, *Shadow of Empire*, pp. 211–40.
6. For a good discussion of the reasons that influenced Indian peasant alignments in Peru's internal wars, see Méndez, *The Plebeian Republic*, pp. 102–10.
7. Marie-Danielle Demélas, *La invención política: Bolivia, Ecuador, Perú en el siglo XIX* (Lima: IFEA, 2003), p. 211.
8. Emilio Loza, "Yatasto, Tucumán y Salta," in Levene, *Historia de la Nación Argentina*, vol. 5, pt. 2, pp. 782–4, quoting Belgrano's correspondence from the field with the government in Buenos Aires.
9. Loza, "Yatasto, Tucumán y Salta," pp. 785–9.
10. On military affairs in Upper Peru from late 1811 until the sack of Cochabamba in May 1812, see Díaz Venteo, *Campañas militares*, pp. 206–18. On the Cochabamba campaign, see Siles Salinas, *Independencia de Bolivia*, pp. 231–5.
11. Quoted by Díaz Venteo, *Campañas militares*, p. 222.
12. This account of the battle is based on the following Argentine and Spanish contemporary sources: for the porteño version, drawn from Buenos Aires documents, see Loza, "Yatasto, Tucumán y Salta," pp. 800–7; for a summary of Tristán's account, see Díaz Venteo, *Campañas militares*, pp. 239–44. For another contemporary royalist account, critical of Tristán, given by a royalist officer who drew on eyewitness accounts of fellow officers, see Francisco Javier de Mendizábal, *Guerra de la América del Sur, 1809–1824* (Buenos Aires: Academia Nacional de Historia, 1997), pp. 45–7.
13. For his account of the battle, which generally follows that of Mendizábal, and his assessment of its consequences, see García Camba, *Memorias*, 1, pp. 124–7.
14. Viceroy Abascal to Secretario del Estado, October 13, 1812, Archivo General de Indias (AGI), Estado 74: no. 8.
15. Goyeneche to Abascal, Potosí, October 20, 1812, in Herreros de Tejada, *El Teniente General D. José Manuel de Goyeneche*, Document xii, pp. 466–9.
16. Ibid., p. 466.
17. Ibid., p. 467.
18. Ibid., p. 468.
19. Díaz Venteo, *Campañas militares*, pp. 257–60.
20. Goyeneche to Marqués de la Concordia, Potosí, January 31, 1813, in Herreros de Tejada, *El Teniente General D. José Manuel de Goyeneche*, Document xvi, pp. 491–6.

21. On the repercussions of the Cádiz Constitution in Buenos Aires and on the political reasoning and maneuvers of those who moved against the First Triumvirate, see Ternavasio, *Gobernar la Revolución*, pp. 100–26.

22. This Lodge was not a Masonic lodge tied to international Masonry. Like other South American lodges in this period, it used the structures, secrecy, and discipline of the Masonic lodge as a model for the pursuit of specific political goals, especially independence from Spain. See Patricia Pasquali, *San Martín: La fuerza de la misión y la soledad de la gloira,* (Buenos Aires: Emecé, 2004), pp. 119–32.

23. On the roles of the Logia Lautaro, Alvear, and San Martín in the creation of the Second Triumvirate, see Pasquali, *San Martín*, pp. 135–41; John Lynch, *San Martín: Argentine Soldier, American Hero* (New Haven: Yale University Press, 2009), pp. 45–9.

24. José María Paz, *Memorias póstumas del General José Maria Paz*, 2 vols. (La Plata: Imprenta La Discusión, 1892), 1, pp. 50–1.

25. Ibid., pp. 61–3.

26. Halperín-Donghi, *Politics, Economics and Society in Argentina in the Revolutionary Period*, p. 264.

27. Loza, "Yatasto, Tucumán y Salta," pp. 819–29.

28. Paz, *Memorias*, 1, pp. 73–7. For Belgrano's more formal description of the battle, see *Biblioteca de Mayo*, vol. 15, pp. 13174–9.

29. Díaz Venteo, *Campañas militares*, pp. 277–8.

30. Mendizábal, *Guerra de la América del Sur,* pp. 51–3.

31. García Camba, *Memorias*, 1, pp. 133–5.

32. Goyeneche to Abascal, Oruro, April 25, 1813; Goyeneche, Quinta del Pacallar, March 30, 1814, in Herreros de Tejada, *El Teniente General D. José Manuel de Goyeneche*, document xiv, p. 471 and document xvi, pp. 473–505. The latter is Goyeneche's lengthy justification of his retreat in 1814. It included an analysis of the virtues of Oruro as a headquarters, offered evidence that his officers had supported him, and argued that Abascal's statements criticizing his retreat were based on errors, lack of military experience, and falsehoods.

33. Mendizábal, who was with Tristán at Salta and narrowly missed capture there, took this view: see Mendizábal, *Guerra de la América del Sur,* pp. 53–4. García Camba also believed that Goyeneche erred in retreating from Potosí: see García Camba, *Memorias*, 1, pp. 136–7.

34. García Camba, *Memorias*, 1, p. 137.

35. On politics in Lima at this time, see Anna, *The Fall of Royal Government in Peru*, pp. 76–93; quotation from Felix de la Rosa, director of the mails, referring to the critical situation in Upper Peru, p. 93.

36. Díaz Venteo, *Campañas militares*, pp. 282–8.

37. Ibid., pp. 293–311.

38. Ibid., p. 315. These were divided between 2,236 infantry, 659 cavalry, and 282 artillerymen.

39. García Camba, *Memorias*, 1, p. 134.

40. Joaquín de la Pezuela, "Compendio de los sucesos ocurridos en el ejército del Perú y sus provincias desde que el General Pezuela tomó el mando de él," in *Colección de Documentos de la Independencia del Perú*, XXVI, vol. 1, pp. 248–9. This is the first part of Pezuela's account of his activity as commander of the Army in Upper Peru, subsequently referred to as CDIP, Pezuela, *Compendio*.

41. Blanchard, *Under the Flags of Freedom*, pp. 46–7.

42. Roca, *Ni con Lima*, pp. 241–8.

43. Arnade, *Emergence of the Republic of Bolivia*, pp. 32–4.

44. For brief biographies of Arenales, Muñecas, Manuel Ascencio Padilla, Juana Azurduy de Padilla, and Warnes, see Siles Salinas, *Independencia de Bolivia*, pp. 371, 375, 377–8, 379–80. On Padilla, also see Roca, *Ni con Lima*, pp. 326–33.

45. José Santos Vargas, *Diario de un comandante de la independencia americana, 1814–1825*, ed. Gunnar Mendoza (Mexico: Fondo de la Cultura Económica, 1982).

46. On Santos Vargas, see Arnade, *Emergence of the Republic of Bolivia*, pp. 37–53. For a summary of the guerrillas of Upper Peru, see Lynch, *Caudillos in Spanish America*, pp. 44–51.

47. For evidence of the effectiveness of the guerrillas and a comparison with the role of the army of Buenos Aires, see Roca, *Ni con Lima*, pp. 301–34.

48. The discrepancy in numbers of trained men was probably not so great. At Buenos Aires, Belgrano's army was reported to total about 6,000 men, about half of whom were disciplined soldiers and the rest "militia of the country." Captain William Bowles to Croker, Buenos Aires, July 28, 1813, in G.S. Graham and R.H. Humphries, eds. *The Navy in South America, 1807–1823: Correspondence of the Commanders-in-Chief on the South American Station* (London: Navy Records Society, 1962), p. 102.

49. For accounts from the insurgent side, see Belgrano's report in *Biblioteca de Mayo*, vol. 15, pp.13255–6; a much more vivid portrait of the battle by a participant, acknowledging that Pezuela achieved some degree of surprise and expressing bewilderment at the defeat, is given by Paz, *Memorias*, pp. 119–27.

50. For Pezuela's account of his maneuvers, his estimates of opposing forces, and the conduct of the battle of Vilcapugio, see CDIP: Pezuela, *Compendio*, pp. 250–8. Pezuela reported 85 officers lost on the insurgent side, most to death and wounding, compared to 25 royalist officers; the insurgent losses of firearms and munitions were also considerable, suggesting that they were abandoned on the battlefield. He gave no estimate of casualties among the ordinary soldiery.

51. Eustaquio Díaz Vélez to Belgrano, Potosí, October 7, 1813, AGI, Estado 78, no.36.

52. CDIP: Pezuela, *Compendio*, p. 266.

53. According to Pezuela, Indians contributed much more to the insurgents than to the royalists, primarily because the insurgents treated them more harshly; they served as porters and spies and were easily mobilized by priests sympathetic to the insurgents' cause: see CDIP: Pezuela, *Compendio*, p. 249.

54. Ibid., pp. 260–1.

55. García Camba, *Memorias*, 1, p. 115.

56. Paz, *Memorias*, p. 146.

57. Ibid., p. 121.

58. Ibid., pp. 161–3. For Belgrano's account of Ayohuma, see *Biblioteca de Mayo*, vol. 15, pp.13274–6.

59. Cited by Lynch, *San Martín*, p. 56.

60. CDIP: Pezuela, *Compendio*, p. 252.

61. Ibid., pp. 266, 275.

62. Cited by Lynch, *San Martín*, p. 58.

63. Bowles to Croker, Buenos Aires, January 26, 1814, in Graham and Humphries, *The Navy in South America*, p. 102.

64. CDIP: Pezuela, *Compendio*, pp. 276–8.

65. Robert M. Haigh, "The Creation and Control of a Caudillo," *HAHR* 44, no. 4 (1964): pp. 481–90.

66. "Campañas del Perú: Extracto de los diarios de E.M.G. del Ejército del Alto Perú, años de 1816 y 1817," in *Documentos para la historia de la guerra separatista en el Perú*, ed. Conde de Torata (Madrid: Imprenta de la viuda de M. Minuesa de los Rios, 1895), 2, p. 165.

67. Gustavo Paz, "'El orden es el desorden.' Guerra y movilización campesina en la campaña de Jujuy, 1815–1821," in *Desafíos al orden: Política y sociedades rurales durante la Revolución de Independencia*, ed. Raul Fradkin and Jorge Gelman (Rosario: Prohistoria, 2008), pp. 83-101,

68. CDIP: Pezuela, *Compendio*, pp. 276–80.
69. On the battle of La Florida, see Roca, *Ni con Lima*, pp. 363–75.
70. CDIP: Pezuela, *Compendio*, pp. 280–6.
71. Street, *Artigas*, pp. 158–61.
72. For an account of the battle of San Lorenzo and its implications, see Pasquali, *San Martín*, pp. 149–57; Lynch, *San Martín*, pp. 49–52.
73. Street, *Artigas*, pp. 163–74.
74. Ibid., pp. 174–8, 187–93.
75. Ibid., pp. 243–6.
76. Figures for troop movements from Albi, *Banderas Olvidadas*, pp. 401–2.
77. Street, *Artigas*, pp. 199–201.
78. For an outline of rebellions in Peru in 1810–15, see Fisher, *Bourbon Peru*, pp. 112–15.
79. CDIP: Pezuela, *Compendio*, p. 288.
80. For Pezuela's comments on the state of army loyalty and Colonel Castro's plot against him, see CDIP: Pezuela, *Compendio*, pp. 289–93. For a historian's account of Pezuela's predicament, see Díaz Venteo, *Campañas militares*, pp. 341–4.
81. For interpretations of the Cuzco rebellion, see John R. Fisher, "Royalism, Regionalism and Rebellion in Colonial Peru, 1808–1815," *HAHR* 59, no. 2 (1979): pp. 232–57. Also, arguing that this was a movement for independence, see Brian R. Hamnett, *Revolución y contrarevolución en México y el Perú*, pp. 183–92.
82. David Cahill, "New Viceroyalty, New Nation, New Empire: A Transnational Imaginary for Peruvian Independence," *HAHR* 91, no. 2 (2011): pp. 203–35.
83. For a full and detailed narrative of the rebellion, see Jorge Cornejo Bouroncle, *Pumacahua: La revolución del Cuzco de 1814* (Cuzco: Editorial H.G. Rozas, 1956). A concise account is given by Walker, *Smoldering Ashes*, pp. 97–101.
84. CDIP: Pezuela, *Compendio*, pp. 298–9.
85. The social impact of the Cuzco rebellion is illuminated in a study of the revolts that it triggered in the Indian towns of Ocongate and Marcapata in 1815–16. On these rebellions and their different meanings, as well as some illuminating comparisons with the rebellion of Tupác Amaru, see Cahill and O'Phelan Godoy, "Forging Their Own History: Indian Insurgency in the Southern Peruvian Sierra, 1815," pp. 140–67.
86. On the reasons for its failure, see Hamnett, *Revolución y contrarevolución*, pp. 193–99; Walker, *Smoldering Ashes*, pp. 102–3.
87. Roca, *Ni con Lima*, pp. 343–6.
88. On the disparate forces at Umachiri, see Nuria Sala i Vila, *Y se armó el tole tole: Tributo indígena y movimientos sociales en el Virreinato del Perú, 1784–1814* (Huamanga: IER José María Arguedas, 1996), p. 237.
89. Halperín-Donghi, *Politics, Economics and Society in Argentina*, pp. 242–3.
90. Rodríguez O., *La revolución política durante la época de la independencia: El Reino de Quito*, pp. 81–8.
91. Collier, *Ideas and Politics of Chilean Independence*, pp. 98–101.
92. Posadas to San Martín, July 28, 1814: quoted by Pasquali, *San Martín*, p. 205.
93. Mario Belgrano, *Rivadavia y sus gestiones diplomáticas con España (1815–1820)* (Buenos Aires: Editorial Huarpes, 1945).

8

INSURRECTION IN
MEXICO, 1810–11

Creoles in New Spain initially responded to Spain's 1808 collapse in much the same manner as creoles in the South American viceroyalties, by peaceful pressure for home rule through self-governing juntas modeled on those of Spain. However, the resemblance did not last for long. After Spaniards in Mexico City seized control of the viceregency by coup d'etat in late 1808, creole dissidents were forced underground, where they continued to conspire until, in September 1810, Father Miguel Hidalgo and his co-conspirators raised provincial rebellion against the authorities in Mexico City. Their intention was to intimidate the government into surrender by seizing control of provincial centers of government and setting up a junta, which would exercise sovereignty in the king's absence. But plans for a relatively smooth transition were soon subsumed by a popular mobilization that was of far greater scale and violence than they had anticipated, and quite different from the movements against the crown that occurred in other regions of Spanish America.

By raising rebellion among peasants and plebeians in the provinces, Hidalgo and his companions opened a Pandora's box from which those at the bottom of Mexican society burst forth and, in their insurrection, exposed the mutual incomprehension, disdain, and hatred that separated white and Indian cultures and communities. Unlike the creole leaders of South American cities who overthrew Spanish officials in largely bloodless coups in towns and cities, the leaders of Mexico's rebellion stirred a surge of peasant rebellion. In 1810–11, demands for autonomy interacted with plebeian and peasant grievances, generating a turbulent, often contradictory, coalition of forces that convulsed much of central Mexico.

Hidalgo's Revolt

The revolt broke out in the small town of Dolores on September 16, 1810, when its parish priest Miguel Hidalgo incited local people to rise against the viceregal government in the name of the captive Ferdinand VII, the Church, and the Catholic religion. From Dolores, the rebellion rapidly swept through the villages and towns of the Bajío region. It then gained even greater momentum by spreading to other regions, going westwards to Guadalajara, northwards to Zacatecas and San Luis Potosí, east into the Llanos de Apan, close to Mexico City, and southwestwards into the Pacific lowlands, where rebels moved against Acapulco, Mexico's most important Pacific port. During late 1810, the rebellion reached its greatest intensity in the center/north region between Mexico City and Guadalajara and thus affected the most important centers of Mexican economic and political life. During the four months between September 1810 and January 1811, Hidalgo and his comrades mobilized thousands of supporters, sacked cities, ousted provincial governments, and at one point even threatened to take the capital city itself. Here, then, was the greatest rebellion seen in Spanish America since the great Andean insurrections launched by Túpac Amaru in 1780, this time in a country that had never seen a rebellion on anything approaching such a scale.

To explain why political crisis tipped over into insurrectionary warfare in Mexico requires an understanding of why Hidalgo and his co-conspirators decided to propagate popular rebellion and why they were able to do so. It was not their first choice. Their preferred method was to use the provincial militias to commandeer provincial governments and to force the authorities in the capital to relinquish power. However, they were forced to appeal to the lower-classes because they could not count on widespread support among their fellow creoles. That Mexican creoles had grievances against Spanish government is not in doubt. Many felt that Peninsular Spaniards in Mexico were accorded privileges that Americans were denied, particularly in access to government office. Educated creoles had also developed a strengthening consciousness of their identity as "Americans" during the later eighteenth century and had constructed a version of Mexico's past that expressed their sense of a history and destiny separate from that of Spain.[1] And among the landed classes, Bourbon government created specific grievances because of its appropriation of church capital through the *consolidación de vales reales* in 1804, a measure that appears to have struck hardest at large landowners, who financed chantries, and parish clergy, who relied on such chantries for income.[2]

Creoles in Mexico were, however, as divided by the imperial crisis as their counterparts elsewhere in Spanish America. Many, perhaps most, identified with Spain in its hour of need. In 1808–10, Mexico was inundated with proclamations, periodicals, and pamphlets from Spain, which denounced Napoleon, called for Hispanic solidarity across the empire, and drew creoles into vigorous political debate; Mexican writers also became active propagandists for the royalist cause, regaling public opinion with accounts of French atrocities, ridiculing Joseph Bonaparte, and depicting Napoleon as a force for untrammeled evil.[3] Political debate was cut short, however, when anti-creole Spaniards sought to block creoles from power-sharing in a self-governing junta. In late 1808, a group of Peninsulars, members of the merchant guild of Mexico City, deposed a viceroy whom they thought overly sympathetic to creole participation in government and went on to construct a regime designed to quash aspirations for political change.[4]

The immediate effect of the coup was to drive creole opposition from the capital into the neighboring provinces, a shift that had important implications for the development of political conflict in Mexico. First, it diminished the prospects of a peaceful creole accession to power of the kind that had occurred in Caracas, Buenos Aires, or Bogotá. Instead, during 1809 and 1810, the Mexico City cabildo was subdued, opposition moved underground, and its main locus shifted from the capital to the towns of the Bajío, where provincial creoles plotted to overthrow the viceregal regime by raising rebellion in the provinces, principally at Valladolid and Querétaro. Second, it encouraged the regime's opponents to consider a violent, insurrectionist solution to the problem of overthrowing the viceroy. For, although both the Valladolid conspirators of 1809 and the Querétaro conspirators of 1810 envisaged a movement that was led from above rather than driven from below, they recognized that their plans were much more likely to succeed if they attracted peasants and plebeians to provide the weight of numbers needed to oppose loyalist military forces. Indeed, the Querétaro group planned to start their rebellion among the masses concentrated at the December fair in San Juan de Lagos, and when Hidalgo was inducted into the conspiracy, he organized the accumulation of rudimentary weapons for arming lower-class volunteers. These preparations for rebellion did not include contact with the peasantry, much less the design of a detailed choreography of popular uprising; nonetheless, Hidalgo and his companions were poised to incite rebellion among the Indians and castes and did not hesitate to do so when the moment arrived. This came suddenly and prematurely when their conspiracy was betrayed. After the arrest of leading conspirators in Querétaro, the militia officers Ignacio Allende and Mariano Abasolo joined with Hidalgo at Dolores and launched the rebellion in the hope that sympathizers in provincial militias would join them.[5] Hidalgo's decision to mobilize popular support was soon vindicated. From its slender stem at Dolores, the revolt swiftly mushroomed into an insurrection that swept across the Bajío, gathering thousands of recruits and acquiring such momentum that, within scarcely six weeks, it threatened the viceregal capital.

Rapid recruitment was driven by incitement of plebeian discontents, which were recently sharpened by economic distress. Those close to Hidalgo in his own small community were his first followers and were motivated more by personal ties than ideological conviction or social hatred.[6] But as he moved beyond Dolores, Hidalgo found many willing followers, particularly among the poor. For in the Bajío, political crisis intersected with environmental and social crisis. In 1808–10, drought, famine, and other economic dislocations had brought widespread hardship to the laboring classes of central Mexico, but those in the Bajío had been particularly exposed to the effects of high and rising food prices. This was not, of course, the first occasion on which the Bajío's poor had suffered hunger caused by drought and frosts: famine had caused tens of thousands of deaths in 1785–86.[7] However, in the circumstances of 1810, when creole dissidents were ready to exploit the economic desperation and bitter social resentments of the rural and urban poor, the situation was much more conducive to rebellion from below.

The appearance of a creole leadership with a political agenda was the crucial catalyst for rebellion. Creole leaders were confident that they could manipulate the discontents of peasants, particularly Indian peasants, despite the gulf between their political views. Ignacio Allende recalled that, "as the Indians were indifferent to the word liberty, it was necessary to make them believe that the uprising was carried out solely on behalf of King Ferdinand."[8] The tactic of justifying rebellion as a defense of the king's rights—the so-called "mask of Ferdinand"—was accompanied by an appeal to another potent source of legitimation, that of defending true religion against heresy and decadence. Mariano Jiménez denounced Peninsular Spaniards for adopting French ideas and called upon his fellow Americans to "exterminate that pernicious weed which, sown in the fertile lands of our obedient and religious nation, seeks . . . to suffocate the inestimable heritage of Jesus Christ . . ."[9] Hidalgo also censured Europeans for their moral laxity and readiness to bow to the French, making it his mission "to conserve for our king these precious possessions which were handed over [by Europeans] to an abominable nation."[10]

Creole leaders thus addressed the populace in resolutely traditional terms. They called upon "Americans" to join Spain in defending the "patria," the king, and the Church against attack by the impious French. They declared that they were raising forces to repel a French invasion of Mexico and played to popular sentiments by presenting themselves as defenders of religion, deploying a rhetoric that exalted Hidalgo's followers as champions of religion against heresy, impiety, and the other works of the Devil.[11] Hidalgo's added weight to these religious claims with promises of material and social improvement: the abolition of Indian tribute, an end to caste distinctions, tax reductions, and, later, the suggestion of a redistribution of lands to Indian communities.

These were powerful pledges in regions where social divisions had deepened over the previous half-century. Changes in the agrarian economies of the Bajío and central Guadalajara, together with recession in the mining centers of Guanajuato, San Luis Potosí, and Zacatecas, had made lower-class life more precarious, while periodic drought brought bouts of deeper immiseration. Throughout these areas, demographic and economic trends worked against the peasantry; growing urban demand for food encouraged large landowners to expand commercialized agriculture, to force higher rents and lower wages on their tenants and workers, and to encroach on Indian community lands. The grievances of the poor were further aggravated by difficulties in the textile industry after 1802, when imports from Europe caused recession, and in silver mining, where rising costs brought closures and large-scale unemployment in the famine years of 1808 and 1809.[12] Such poverty and hunger were of themselves potent provocations to break the law and created circumstances propitious to Hidalgo's purposes.

The readiness to strike out against the authorities and European Spaniards was particularly acute in the Bajío, where peasants were aware that their suffering was manufactured for the profit of landlords, who drove up prices by hoarding grains.[13]

Hidalgo also found enthusiastic support among Indian villagers because, for many communities, the rebellion offered a timely opportunity to defend community lands and cultures that were under growing pressure. During the latter half of the eighteenth century, the incidence of localized peasant riot and revolt had multiplied as Indian villagers struggled to preserve their lands and communal identities amid the political turmoil of 1810, their practices of protest readily transmuted into violent insurrection as they blended with ideas, projected by Hidalgo, of a struggle of good against evil driven by loyalty to crown and church.[14] This confection of religious fervor with royalism and rebellion with xenophobia is reflected in a rebel slogan, reported in an early piece of insurgent propaganda:

> Everywhere nothing is heard but long live Religion, long live the Patria, long live Ferdinand VII, long live Our Most Holy Queen and Mother of Guadalupe, and death to bad government and that the wealth of the *gachupines* shall serve to defend our Kingdom against the French, against the English, and against all the Enemies of God.[15]

Defense of the king and the Church was, then, coupled with abhorrence of foreigners, particularly the small minority of European Spaniards resident in Mexico (popularly known as *gachupines*). Hatred of Spaniards was deeply rooted in Mexico and, though particularly acute at the base of the social scale, transcended local differences and class lines. Among creoles, immigrant *gachupines* were resented for the economic success they derived from their dominance of the import and export trades, for the preference they received in appointments to government posts, and their arrogant sense of superiority towards Americans. Among the downtrodden Indians and *castas* in the towns and villages of rural Mexico, this dislike could easily turn into violent Hispanophobia, manifested in murderous assaults on Spaniards by peasant insurgents.

Violence of this kind was rooted in social antagonisms. Because Spaniards were often merchants, shopkeepers, and government functionaries, who lived from trade and taxation, they could be identified all too easily as the enemy of the poor, in the same way that Jews had been singled out for persecution in medieval Europe.[16] They were thus a target that allowed Indians to unleash their hatred against those of Spanish descent without requiring them to engage in a more generalized war of extermination against whites.[17] There were, moreover, religious images that informed and justified rebellion against Spaniards. For, while the gachupín personified the immigrant whose success and standing was an affront to the native-born and whose wealth was a curse to the poor, his European origins also linked him to a metropolis where respect for the Church and its doctrines had supposedly been corroded by secular ideas, and which had succumbed to domination by the godless Napoleon. The popular religious belief, propagated by leaders such as Hidalgo, that Spaniards were heretics, who threatened the purity of Mexican Christianity, was one potential source of religious righteousness.[18] Indian peasants may have also found a religious justification for their rebellion in Catholic messianic traditions which, at times of economic difficulty and social dislocation, conjured dreams of an inversion of the existing social order and a return to a mythical golden age, purged of the imperfections spread by intruding Europeans.[19] In these circumstances, the *gachupín* quickly became a convenient target against whom creoles and castas alike could direct their anger. Scapegoating of this xenophobic kind not only encouraged violence but, once the insurgency was in motion, created a cultural gulf between Indians and whites that fuelled further hatred and violence.

Organizing Insurrection

After raising popular rebellion, Hidalgo and his companions had a clear strategy. They aimed to overthrow the viceregal regime and replace it with an autonomous, Mexican-led regime of some (initially undefined) sort, and they sought to do so using a mass movement that would overwhelm centers of authority and undermine the ability of the government to resist. To achieve these goals, the rebel leadership began by building support within the towns and villages of Bajío and bringing their followers into a single force under hierarchical command.

The reported pace of recruitment was phenomenal. During the opening weeks of the rebellion, Hidalgo's invocation of the Virgin of Guadalupe and Ferdinand VII attracted thousands, and the rapid accumulation of popular support gave the movement an unstoppable momentum. The 700 or so Indian rebels who marched out from Dolores with Hidalgo on September 16, 1810, soon won over the neighboring town of San Miguel el Grande, home of Allende and other leaders. Then, with additional recruits from San Miguel, they moved on to Celaya, where the cabildo negotiated the peaceful surrender of their town, only to see it plundered. At this point, the rebel leadership paused to impose a rudimentary military organization upon its swelling forces. Hidalgo was proclaimed captain general, while Ignacio Allende became lieutenant general and Juan de Aldama was given the exalted military rank of Mariscal del Campo. After two or three days in Celaya, these commanders marshaled their "army"—said at this time to total 25,000 men—for an advance on Guanajuato, the rich mining town that was also the seat of the intendant and headquarters of regional political authority. After a five-day march, the rebels arrived in Guanajuato on September 28, 1810, and encountered their first armed resistance.[20]

The rebels' entry into Guanajuato quickly escalated into a bloody encounter, which exposed undercurrents of social war.[21] A town resident described in appalled tones how the small force of royalists led by the intendant Juan Antonio Riaño attempted resistance by fortifying the city's Alhóndiga (the large public granary), only to be overrun and massacred, how surviving Spaniards were rounded up and imprisoned, and how the city was sacked with losses estimated at 1.5 million pesos. On the day after the attack, the naked corpses of the royalists slaughtered at the granary—most of them, it was said, castrated by the Indians—were flung into common graves, and the city was given over to the invading rebels and their local allies until order was restored a couple of days later. "All has been horror and fear," the writer reported, and he warned that as the soldiers charged with upholding order either turned tail or joined the rebels, the rebellion was spreading fast. It was rumored that the rebels were planning to march on Valladolid to free the Bishop, and he warned against opposing them for fear of suffering the same fate as Guanajuato's Spaniards.[22]

The significance of the attack on Guanajuato was unmistakable. Hidalgo had scored his first major military victory and taken an irretrievable step into war against the viceregal authorities. To win that war, he sought to extend the rebellion and so sent out envoys to recruit allies in regions beyond the Bajío. Some of these envoys were eminently successful, particularly in areas where antigovernment feeling could be grafted onto local disputes and conflicts, and the rebellion developed several distinctive regional nodes, each under local leadership.

These were positioned throughout Mexico's provinces. In the north, Aguascalientes and the important mining town of Zacatecas were brought under rebel control in October–November 1810, and San Luis Potosí became the seat of a rebel government between November 1810 and March 1811. While the fall of these cities and their hinterlands virtually destroyed government authority in the north, rebel emissaries had similar successes in the west. Hidalgo's agent José Antonio Torres took the rebellion into the Jalisco region and after raising recruits from rural areas, captured the strategic city of Guadalajara on November 11, 1810, thus establishing an important base for rebel operations throughout New Galicia, including its Pacific coast. Another of Hidalgo's men, Miguel Sánchez, went south, in the direction of Mexico City, to Huichapan, where, by winning over the local Villagrán clan, he created a locus of insurgency that caused severe problems for the authorities there and in the neighboring mining complex of Pachuca and Real del Monte. Mariano Aldama, whom Hidalgo sent to the Llanos de Apan, on the eastern edges of Mexico City's hinterland, also succeeded in raising and unifying support for the rebellion by winning the allegiance of a dominant local clan, the Osornos, whose members were eager to take advantage of political turmoil to extend their own local wealth and power.[23] Finally, the priest José María Morelos was sent to spread the rebellion southwards into Michoacán and the tropical coasts of the Pacific. He concentrated first on attacking the fortress-port of Acapulco in November–December 1810; after failing to take it, he turned inland to probe the southern boundaries of the Intendancy of Puebla, still a royalist stronghold. Thus, in the closing months of 1810, Hidalgo's envoys created a network of regional and local uprisings that projected the rebellion far beyond the Bajío, generating attacks against the governing authorities and their allies throughout much of Mexico, and initiating an armed insurgency that was to outlive Hidalgo himself.[24]

While insurrection was spreading through the provinces, Hidalgo moved against the center of royal government by driving southwards towards Mexico City. From the stronghold of Guanajuato, Hidalgo marched confidently against the city of Valladolid in mid-October; then, backed by fresh recruits—who, it was said, brought up his numbers to some 60,000 people—he directed his forces towards the viceregal capital. Mexico City was an obvious goal for the rebels. As the viceroy's seat, it was the apex of authority and power and, as such, the symbolic heart of the

Kingdom of New Spain. Moreover, Hidalgo and his co-leaders were fully aware that the viceregal government was unusually vulnerable at this time, given that command had just passed to a viceroy who was fresh from Spain and had yet to establish himself.

Hidalgo's rapid advance sustained the momentum of the rebellion and exposed the government's military weakness. The new viceroy, Francisco Javier Venegas, had arrived in Mexico City just two days before the outbreak of the rebellion and found only small regular forces in a capital that lacked fortifications or other fixed defenses.[25] In theory, Venegas could count on provincial militia companies, but such militias were not available for the defense of the capital. They were in any case unreliable; the militias in Hidalgo's primary area of operations had either failed to oppose him or gone over to his side. Venegas was therefore forced back on men and material within the city and its immediate hinterland. He had around 2,000 regular troops in Mexico City, supplemented by ten recently raised companies of Spanish and creole civilian volunteers. Other reliable soldiers were further away in the garrisons of Veracruz and Puebla. To supplement his forces, Venegas broke with the tradition that Indians should not be armed and agreed that Indian communities close to the city should, at the request of their leaders, be mobilized as militias to fight against Hidalgo.[26]

Facing invasion from the countryside, Venegas had little choice. He was not ready to negotiate—nor had Hidalgo offered any such option—and so had to fight. His preferred strategy was to avoid battle, but he did not contemplate evacuating the capital. Venegas tried instead to seize the military initiative by ordering the militias of Querétaro to move against the neighboring insurgent town of San Miguel while at the same time taking steps to create an army capable of doing battle in the field. To fulfill this need, he ordered the creation of a new force, the Army of the Center, which was made up of two main elements. The first was to be established by Brigadier Félix María Calleja, commander of the Tenth Brigade of Militias in San Luis Potosí, who was also made commander in chief of the new army of operations. The second was to be formed from forces at the center of Mexico, brought together by Manuel de Flon, the Spanish intendant of Puebla and commander of the Third Brigade of Milicias; Flon was also appointed as Calleja's second-in-command. The viceroy's plan was for Calleja to marshal forces in the north and Flon at the center and then to converge in rebel territory and destroy Hidalgo's forces at the earliest possible opportunity.

Venegas's creation of an army of operations was of crucial importance, as was his choice of Félix María Calleja as its commander. While many militia officers had either joined the rebels or remained passive, Calleja's mobilization of forces shows that the military system created under the Bourbons could, in the right hands, provide a robust prop for the Spanish regime. Calleja proved to be an excellent appointment. He was a career officer of impeccable military background, extensive military experience, and, equally important, strong local connections. After seeing action at Algiers, Minorca, and Gibraltar, he had arrived in Mexico in 1789 and became a leading figure in its army. In 1810, after years of organizing the defense of the northern frontiers of New Spain, Calleja was commander of the regular and militia forces over a huge area of northern Mexico and a highly respected figure in the society of San Luis Potosí, where he had married into the local aristocracy.[27] His response to the rebellion showed that he was soon to become a very considerable asset to the royalist cause as a "proto-caudillo," who used his position in local power networks to undergird his role as an army commander and provide the means to raise an army.[28] His influence at San Luis Potosí helped him to assemble a force of 2,000 cavalry and 500 infantry to take into the field against Hidalgo, and within a month, he was able to lead his army into operations against the rebels.[29] He headed south from San Luis Potosí in early October in order to rendezvous with Flon in the Bajío; Flon was meanwhile engaged in tentative operations against the rebels in the region around Querétaro.

Viceroy Venegas's strategy was to defend territory against further rebel advances while awaiting an opportunity to strike back. He had little choice: Calleja was far from the flashpoints of rebellion, while Flon found it difficult to recruit and retain troops; indeed, when he began to move against insurgent-occupied towns, many of his men deserted, leaving him with very few loyal soldiers.[30] Government officials and military officers were, moreover, forced onto the defensive by the rebels' rapid progress; understandably, they preferred to concentrate on defending their own towns rather than going onto the offensive outside them. The intendant of Valladolid, José Alonso Terán, disparaged such static defense and called for a more aggressive approach. The rebels, he said, had neither order nor discipline and were interested only in pillage: they would "disperse like a swarm of flies at the first cannonades."[31] At this stage, however, it was easier to demand a quick offensive than to deliver one. Coherent royalist military operations could not be conjured up without strong leadership and an army of operations, and neither materialized quickly. The delay cost Terán his life; the rebels, whom he had dismissed as an undisciplined rabble, took Valladolid in mid-October, and Terán was among those captured and executed.

If the royalist strategy was to defend and delay, Hidalgo's was to remain on the offensive and to move forward as quickly as he could. During late October 1810, he moved the mass of his forces towards Mexico City with the evident intention of taking the capital. This was a potent threat, since the forces available to defend the capital were hopelessly outnumbered by the oncoming rebel hosts. Venegas mustered the forces that were immediately available in the city and its hinterland, but these were few compared to the size of Hidalgo's advancing forces. Hidalgo was said to have between 60,000 and 80,000 people, of whom perhaps about 5,000 were part-time soldiers from provincial militia companies. Venegas had about 6,000 men, of whom about 2,000 were regulars and the rest militias, including the newly created Distinguished Patriotic Battalions of Ferdinand VII.[32] He also had the Army of the Center, which was taking firmer form at the end of October when Calleja and Flon met at Dolores and joined forces in pursuit of Hidalgo. However, they were still too far north to come between Mexico City and the rebels, and for the vital task of holding the capital, Venegas had to rely on the forces he had managed to concentrate there. The significance of the task was evident to all. The city was the key strongpoint of royal government, and its loss would inflict a strategic and symbolic defeat of potentially catastrophic proportions. The balance of forces and their use by opposing sides were therefore of paramount importance to the rebels and the royal government.

What decided the outcome of this key confrontation? On the royalist side, Venegas, an army officer who had fought in the Peninsular War and acted as governor of Cádiz, brought military experience and decisive leadership. He had little to work with but made the best of his forces by combining defense and attack. To defend Mexico City, he barricaded the streets and distributed arms to hastily assembled militias; at the same time, he sought to slow the rebel advance by sending a force of between 1,300 and 2,500 men under Colonel Torcuato Trujillo towards Toluca in order to stop Hidalgo's forces from closing on the capital.[33] Given the rebels' weight of numbers, this was a risky maneuver because it exposed a substantial element of the viceroy's forces to defeat. This risk seemed to be realized when, on October 30, Colonel Trujillo clashed with the rebels in the mountain pass at Las Cruces. After fighting throughout the day, Trujillo was forced to yield to the pressure of larger numbers, and his retreat allowed Hidalgo to advance to the town of Ixtlahuaca, a mere 30 miles from Mexico City. Viceroy Venegas suppressed news of the royalist retreat at Las Cruces for fear of its repercussions in the capital, for Trujillo had not only failed to halt the rebel advance but had weakened the city's defenses by his losses of men and artillery. Having expended their offensive energy, the viceroy and his government were left to await Hidalgo's attack.

Hidalgo's entry into the Valley of Mexico was an extraordinary moment. From its origins in a small revolt in an insignificant Indian town, his rebellion had proliferated into a force that was sufficiently powerful to move against the viceregal capital. While Hidalgo's people massed around Ixtlahuaca, Viceroy Venegas could only draw up his remaining forces to guard the environs and entrances to Mexico City and hope that Calleja would arrive in time to attack the rebels from the rear. In the event, and to the amazement and relief of the governing class in Mexico City, there was no contest. On November 3, 1810, Hidalgo turned away from Mexico City and retreated northwards, taking the rebellion back to its birthplace in the Bajío.

This retreat is harder to explain than the advance that preceded it. Hidalgo had abandoned an opportunity to attack the heart of viceregal government and by moving away from the capital, seemed to relinquish the chance to bring his rebellion to a decisive victory. He said later that he wanted to avoid bloodshed, and it may be that his conscience prevailed. However, Hidalgo had sound tactical reasons for avoiding battle. He was not confident that Mexico City would flock to his banner as other cities had, and he was unsure that his followers could take the city by force. He later justified his retreat on the grounds that the battle at Las Cruces had cost so much ammunition that he lacked the means to fight a way into Mexico City.[34] Hidalgo's people had suffered heavy casualties too. Colonel Trujillo believed that continuous accurate fire from his artillery and muskets had killed a couple of thousand rebels.[35] García Conde, a royalist captive with Hidalgo at this time, put the figure far higher. He recalled that when he and other prisoners were taken forward after the battle, they were "treading on corpses," some of whom he feared were his own army friends. He believed, however, that the rebels had suffered far more than the royalists, estimating that death, injury, and desertion at Las Cruces cut the rebel force of 80,000 in half.[36] García Conde's figures were guesswork and probably highly inflated. Nonetheless, the losses inflicted by the viceroy's forces must have persuaded Hidalgo to change his strategy, as did the knowledge that, as Calleja was moving southward, he risked being caught between Calleja's army and the viceroy's forces in the capital.[37] Thus, Hidalgo turned from triumphant advance to cautious retreat, hoping to conserve his resources for another day.

Insurrectionary Warfare

The consequences of Hidalgo's decision were felt almost immediately, for his volte-face gave Calleja time to intercept the rebel forces. Calleja had marched south towards Toluca with the intention of attacking the main body of the rebels near Mexico City, only to be delayed by a deviation to Querétaro to defend it from rumored rebel attack. However, when he left Querétaro on November 1, 1810, for a forced march towards the capital, he came into contact with Hidalgo's retreating army. On November 6, his men skirmished with a small insurgent force and, from the prisoners taken, learned that Hidalgo and his forces were close by near, the village of Aculco. Calleja decided to attack them at dawn the following day, bringing to bear the largest concentration of royalist troops that the rebels had yet faced.

The action that followed showed Hidalgo's military ineptitude, for he was evidently unable to take advantage of his pre-prepared defensive position and considerable superiority in numbers. If we are to believe contemporary reports that the rebels counted some 40,000 men, then Calleja, with about 7,000 men, was outnumbered by a factor of nearly six to one. He was also facing an enemy that held a positional advantage: Hidalgo had chosen a protected hillside above the village of Aculco and marshaled his main force behind two lines of battle and two artillery batteries.[38] But Calleja did not hesitate to attack. He arraigned his forces in a classic attack formation: the infantry made a frontal assault on enemy lines; the cavalry attacked the rebels' right flank and attempted to get behind them, and at the same time a mixed force of horsemen and infantry attacked their left. The plan was executed with considerable efficiency. Calleja noted with satisfaction that his forces maneuvered in "such unison, silence and speed to the sound of drums and other military instruments, as though on parade, that this contributed not a little to surprising the enemy and making him realize our superiority."[39] The cavalry movement on the right flank was stalled by difficult terrain, but Calleja's infantry burst through the center, virtually unscathed by inaccurate fire from the rebels' ill-positioned artillery.

This breakthrough decided the action. Already intimidated by the display of military efficiency given by Calleja's army, the rebels mostly turned tail and fled in disarray, losing many of their officers, much of their arms and equipment, and suffering many casualties. Just how many were lost is impossible to say. The official report stated that the countryside presented a "horrible spectacle" after the battle, littered with the corpses of thousands of the dead and wounded, who were cut down in the chase. Calleja estimated enemy losses at 10,000, compared to his one dead and one wounded, a comparison that so obviously strained credulity that he felt constrained to note that this was "not strange in view of the fact that great losses are usually in flight."[40] Another, equally unverifiable, contemporary estimate gave a much more realistic assessment of rebel casualties, listing 85 dead, 53 wounded, and 600 prisoners, and listing the very considerable amounts of arms, munitions, and food supplies that the rebels had abandoned.[41]

Hidalgo was, of course, anxious to play down the defeat at Aculco. He denied that this engagement was the "total defeat" that was rumored, and he reported that his men had retreated with few losses and only because their artillery had proved unusable. It would, he affirmed, not be long before he returned to the capital of Mexico with forces that were "larger and more terrible to our enemies."[42] This seems an unconvincing attempt to save face. It is difficult to see Aculco as anything other than a defeat, which, whatever the actual casualty figures, had amply demonstrated one simple fact: the rebel forces were unable to cope with attack by disciplined troops under an experienced commander and, in hasty retreat, were vulnerable to heavy losses.

The revolt was, however, far from finished. Hidalgo's envoys had raised rebellion throughout the provinces to the north and west of the capital and as revolt spread "over all the wide space between one ocean and the other . . . [making] the revolution stronger and more terrible," it became all but unstoppable.[43] Calleja's cautious behavior after Aculco reflected his appreciation of this reality. Instead of trying to capitalize immediately on his victory by pursuing the rebels, Calleja preferred to rest his army at Querétaro, prior to moving across the Bajío towards the town of Celaya, en route to Guanajuato. This marked the start of a fresh phase in the royalist military campaign, taking the war northwards into the heart of insurgent territory.

While the royalist military was recovering strongly from its initial paralysis, the rebel directorate was seeking a countervailing strategy. This was made difficult, however, by the division of forces and disagreements between the leading commanders. After pulling out of the Valley of Mexico, Allende went north to rally the rebels and returned to Guanajuato, while Hidalgo went northwest to Valladolid. When Allende knew that Hidalgo planned to go to Guadalajara, he warned him that this could be construed as a concern with his own safety and pleaded that he bring his forces to Guanajuato instead, where they might join in common cause. As it was, Allende pointed out, the army of operations under Calleja and Flon was entering "our conquered towns as though into its own home," thereby doing great damage to the rebellion's image and prospects. It was, he insisted, essential to stop the rot by defending Guanajuato and keeping control of its important resources. He therefore called upon Hidalgo and the rebel leaders Iriarte and Huidobro to join him there with all the forces at their disposal, with a view to attacking Calleja and reopening the way to Querétaro and Mexico City, or at the very least, creating a cordon to the north of the capital to cut off its supplies. Allende's strongly worded letters accusing Hidalgo of both military stupidity and personal cowardice did not deflect him from his course; Hidalgo ignored Allende's pleas and concentrated on his own political activities in Valladolid.[44]

This division among the rebels gave Calleja a chance to push into the rebel heartland. During November 1810, he moved through the Bajío, taking the towns of Celaya, Salamanca, and Irapuato without resistance, and thus considerably narrowing the rebels' hinterland. Then, on reaching Guanajuato, Calleja continued to attack, launching an offensive against the insurgents' defenses on November 24–25, 1810.

Guanajuato, an important administrative, political, and economic center for the region, was a strategic target for both sides. The insurgents had held it for nearly two months, and Allende was convinced that it had to be held for both its material resources and symbolic value. Calleja and Flon also had powerful motives for wanting to retake Guanajuato. First, they needed its resources, which included the richest silver mine in the world (the Valenciana) and a royal mint; second, they were eager to avenge the massacre of the city's notables and its leading official, the intendant Riaño, who was also Flon's brother-in-law; third, they were leading an army whose morale was boosted by their prior victory over the rebels. There was, however, the usual disparity in the numbers and battlefield advantage of rebels and royalists, as the former were much more numerous and well-entrenched. What, then, decided the outcome of this, the third of the major military encounters between the Army of the Center and the insurgents?

Calleja did not anticipate an easy victory; on the contrary, he approached Guanajuato with considerable care. The mountainous terrain made the town easy to defend, the rebels had large forces and plenty of time to prepare their defenses. Calleja's estimate of 70,000 men on the rebel side was a considerable exaggeration, but even at half that number, the rebels had a very sizeable advantage over the royalist army of some 5,000 men. The insurgents had, moreover, put time and thought into preparing their defenses. They had organized a network of fortified points in the hills around the city, where they positioned men and artillery to await the intruder, and, using local miners' skills and abundant supplies of explosive, had mined the canyon that was the main point of entry to the city, intending to bury the approaching enemy under a shower of rocks.

Calleja overcame these defenses thanks to his military skill and the rebels' military inexperience. He probed rebel defenses by dividing his army into two columns. He led one force of cavalry and dragoons towards the northeast in order to take the great Valenciana minehead overlooking the city; Flon, his second, approached from another angle, via the southeast side, avoiding the mined canyon and taking without much difficulty the defensive points that stood in his path. Armed only with stones, staves, and lances, the rebels were unable to withstand royalist artillery fire and skirmishing attacks by disciplined infantry, and they fell back in panic. They had artillery of their own but, as at Aculco, failed to turn it to good use: the guns were stuck in fixed positions, unable to vary trajectories of fire, and had little if any impact on the advancing enemy.

Thanks to the combination of good leadership on the royalist side and military incompetence on the rebel side, the royalist columns overran rebel positions in a six-hour advance through the hillsides and canyons on which the city was built, and ended their first day of battle encamped in two hillside positions, dominating Guanajuato from opposite sides. All that remained was a clearing-up operation. Calleja and Flon entered Guanajuato the following morning with little further fighting, though amid high tension. For, having heard that royalist prisoners held in the city granary had been massacred, Calleja gave the order to sound the signal for no quarter, so that his troops would take Guanajuato "by fire and blood," sparing no one. As he and Flon rode into a silent city, where people hid in their houses and only a priest emerged to call for mercy, Calleja withdrew his order to sack Guanajuato and kill its people; instead, he took a more measured revenge, with executions of rebel prisoners and decimation, by choice of lots, of townspeople suspected of complicity in killing Spaniards. This concluded an attack, which, though it had been more difficult than the previous action at Aculco, had further demonstrated the military effectiveness of Brigadier Calleja and his Army of the Center. The attack had been impeded more by the difficult terrain than the opposition of the insurgents, and the balance of casualties showed that the well-armed and well-organized royalists again inflicted disproportionate damage on their opponents. According to official reports, the rebels suffered heavy losses, possibly some 1,500 men, while there were very few among the royalists. Indeed, the heaviest loss on the royalist side came not in battle but in the massacre of some 200 civilian prisoners, mostly Spaniards, held in the city's granary.[45]

The consequence of Allende's defeat at Guanajuato was to put the insurgents under growing military pressure, stemming from both the capital and Calleja. From his seat in Mexico City, Viceroy Venegas opened an offensive on November 16, 1810, aimed at clearing a corridor northwards. He placed Brigadier José de la Cruz in command of an infantry division and 250 dragoons and ordered him to march on Huichapan. The purpose was to eliminate the rebel caudillo Julián Villagrán and his insurgents in that area, to open the road to Querétaro, and to establish communications with Calleja's Army of the Center. Cruz, the commander chosen for the task, had recently arrived in Mexico after fighting in the Peninsular War, and he soon proved brutally efficient in applying lessons learned from fighting the French in Spain.

Cruz failed in his attempt to capture the insurgent leader Villagrán, but his entry into the Huichapan area inaugurated a counterinsurgency strategy that was a template for the future. Cruz ordered that the general population should surrender anything that might be used as an offensive weapon, including knives, scissors, and other tools used in homes or trades; he also threatened to kill and raze to the ground communities that harbored insurgents. On December 14, 1810, he then marched to Querétaro where, after meeting with other contingents of royal forces sent from Mexico City under the naval captain Rosendo Portlier, he moved against Valladolid. When Cruz entered Valladolid on December 28, after threatening to destroy the city "by fire and blood" in reprisal for any killing of Spaniards, he found that Hidalgo and his supporters were long gone, and the city put up no resistance. Shortly afterwards, the conversion of Valladolid from insurgent stronghold into royalist military base was consolidated by the arrival of another force from Mexico City, under Colonel Trujillo.[46] The stage was now set for royalist forces to concentrate on an offensive against the one major rebel stronghold that remained, at Guadalajara.

After defeating Allende's forces at Guanajuato, Calleja immediately turned his attention to finishing off Hidalgo's insurgents at Guadalajara. In two months of campaigning, Calleja had driven his men over hundreds of miles of forced marches and was left with a force of some 5,000 men, mostly cavalry, depleted by illness and desertion, with exhausted mounts and worn-out equipment. However, now that reinforcements were en route with Brigadier Cruz, Calleja did not delay. While at León in mid-December, he conceived a plan for a major assault against the main body of insurgents concentrated at Guadalajara, and he set down a timetable for a campaign in which he aimed to combine his army with forces sent by the viceroy from Mexico City. To bring together these forces, Calleja ordered Cruz to set out with his 2,000 troops, mainly infantry, from Valladolid on January 1, 1811, while he himself moved his force of some 5,000 men, mainly cavalry, towards Guadalajara.[47] Thus, scarcely three months after the start of the insurrection, the royalist military had moved from desperate defense of the capital to a full-scale offensive operation in the provinces: Calleja's Army of the Center was now poised to converge with Cruz's reserve army in an attempt to crush the insurgent forces in a decisive military action. Their battle ground was to be at Guadalajara, and the battle took place in mid-January 1811, deciding the fate of Hidalgo's revolt.

The Battle of Calderón

Hidalgo chose Guadalajara for good reasons. He left Valladolid because he believed that his forces were too few to withstand an attack there and took about 200 infantry and some 7,000 horsemen north to Guadalajara to combine with the rebels who had recently seized the city. When he entered the city on November 26, 1810, Hidalgo and his followers received a splendid reception from its authorities and people, orchestrated by his envoy José Antonio Torres. Judging by the warmth of this welcome, Guadalajara looked set to provide the strong base from which to rebuild the revolution, which the insurgents had so far failed to find.[48] All that remained was to create an army that could overcome Calleja's army and, by defeating the royalists, restore the morale and momentum of the rebellion.

Hidalgo set out to achieve this goal with a straightforward plan. He aimed to amass sufficient men, artillery, and munitions to overwhelm Calleja's pursuing army. He had a good supply of artillery—most of it captured from the Spanish garrison at the Pacific port of San Blas—and he had no difficulty in mobilizing large numbers of men. It was, however, much more difficult to arm his recruits and turn them into soldiers. Muskets were in such short supply that the rebels tried to compensate by making large numbers of lances, hand grenades, and rockets tipped with iron spikes; many relied on more traditional weapons, such as the contingent of 7,000 Indians who exercised with bows and arrows. Men were divided up into divisions for training, and many new officers were commissioned to impose discipline and provide rudimentary military instruction. Such was the boom in promotions that even the long scale of rankings taken from the Spanish army was insufficient for the rebels' swollen officer corps, and their leaders had to invent fanciful titles, such as "colonel of colonels" and "brigadier of brigadiers." Hidalgo's critics also suggested that the leader himself was losing his grip on reality. He assumed the title of "Serene Highness," and, it was said, he went about with a corps of bodyguards and musicians, appearing at official functions bedecked in an ornate uniform, preceded by guards with blazing torches and with a beautiful young woman on his arm.[49] These incongruities were, of course, not necessarily the signs of corruption supposed by Hidalgo's enemies; they were designed to conjure the image of majesty needed to express the charisma of the leadership, to strengthen the sense of a collective identity, and to build morale in the face of the oncoming struggle.

Whatever the eccentricities of insurgent organization and the differences among its leaders, Hidalgo made detailed preparations to meet Calleja in open battle, taking care to ensure that his forces were advantageously positioned and that the enemy's options were limited. Thus, when he became aware that Cruz was bringing up additional troops, he sent a force of some 10–12,000 men to block these reinforcements at Urepetiro. At the same time, against advice from Allende (who had seen the results of battle with the Army of the Center at Aculco and Guanajuato), he aimed to position the main body of his army outside the city to meet Calleja. On January 14, 1811, Hidalgo put this plan into action, only to receive news the following day that his troops at Urepetiro had been badly defeated by Cruz. The bad news spurred Hidalgo into action, for he now wished to attack Calleja before Cruz's reinforcements arrived. To do so, Hidalgo occupied the ground at the Calderón Bridge, the main passage into Guadalajara, with a force said—no doubt with the usual exaggeration—to have numbered some 100,000 men. It included some 20,000 horsemen, 7 uniformed and disciplined (though poorly armed) regiments, a mass of irregulars, and 94 artillery pieces of various calibers together with plentiful ammunition.

Hidalgo's initiative prompted Calleja to attack without further delay on January 17, 1811. This was, perhaps, because he wanted to stop the rebels from further strengthening their position, or perhaps to ensure that he did not have to share command with Cruz, who was his equal in rank and senior in length of army service. Calleja's readiness to move was no doubt also underpinned by the confidence he and his troops had acquired at Aculco and Guanajuato. On both occasions, they had faced far larger forces embedded in firm defensive positions, and on both occasions, they had won without difficulty and with few casualties.

Hidalgo's people had no such experience of victory but they doubtless drew confidence from their large numbers and commanding position. Hidalgo and his commanders had taken all possible advantage of the terrain. They chose a site where the advancing enemy had to cross the river at a narrow point overlooked by hillsides, then move into a narrow valley flanked by hillsides and the river. This seemed an easy place to hold with strong artillery and large numbers, and the insurgent leaders did their best to create sound lines of defense. They placed their main artillery battery on the steep slopes overlooking the Calderón Bridge, positioned smaller artillery positions on the hillsides to extend the field of fire against approaching troops, and blocked the advance of any troops who crossed the bridge by massing their forces in the valley below. This made frontal attack very difficult. To come to grips with the insurgent army, Calleja's forces had to traverse the river, neutralize the artillery firing down from the hillsides, and then push into the ranks of the insurgents who were massed in the valley and outnumbered them, if contemporary estimates are to be believed, by a ratio of ten to one.

Calleja's solution was to adopt a simple plan of attack. He sent Flon with infantry, cavalry, and some artillery to cross the river above the bridge and to attack the main insurgent battery from that flank. Meanwhile, Calleja moved toward the bridge with another body of troops to provide covering artillery fire for Flon's men as they scaled the opposing slopes and to test the way forward on the other side of the river. He opened his attack by establishing a small gun battery to fire across the river at the enemy and ordering various mounted units to ford the river under this covering fire. These thrusts met with strong resistance, mostly from the stones and arrows of insurgents who came down the hillsides to defend the pass, and on a couple of occasions, the royalist soldiery had to be forced forward by their commanders to keep them from faltering.

The decisive moment came when the royalist cavalry charged the rebels' batteries, dispersing the insurgents and capturing all their artillery. Some said that the rebels broke and fled under unremitting gunfire and cavalry attack; others said the explosion of rebel munitions carts, hit by a stray grenade, caused the rout. Whatever the cause, the panic was such that the chasing royalist horsemen had difficulty in forcing their way into the fleeing mass of insurgents to chop them down. The casualties of battle were highly uneven, as was common in such circumstances. Royalist losses were counted in tens and, though these included some important officers like Flon, they were slight in comparison with insurgent losses, which, though never accurately assessed, were said to have been in hundreds if not thousands of casualties.[50]

The military defeat at Calderón and the fall of Guadalajara effectively ended Hidalgo's revolt. Hidalgo and other leaders fled northwards and hoped, no doubt, to regroup in friendly territory. However, betrayed by one of their own, they were ambushed and captured near Aguascalientes in March 1811 and subsequently tried and executed. Hidalgo's hope of overthrowing the viceregal regime in a short, forceful rebellion thus disappeared in what seemed a total defeat. The rebellion had spread with unexpected rapidity, recruited large numbers of supporters and sympathizers, and implanted the seeds of defiance against authority that the royalists could not everywhere eradicate. However, Hidalgo's revolt had not become a war for independence. The rebel leaders did not plan for a war, nor, after it became clear that they would have to defeat royalist armies to achieve their political goals, did they succeed in creating an efficient military organization. Indeed, despite the early pretensions of the leadership to establish a unified force under proto-military command and discipline, the rebels remained an inchoate insurrectionary mass rather than becoming an orderly revolutionary army.

Hidalgo's Defeat

Explanations of the failure of Hidalgo's revolt tend, rightly, to stress the incompetence of its principal leaders and their armed forces.[51] It is clear that the creole directorate that initiated the rebellion was unprepared for a major armed struggle. They hoped to turn the existing military structure to their own ends and to overwhelm the viceregal authorities by taking control of provincial governments, rather than by fighting a war against them. Men like Allende and Aldama had been present at the large army and militia exercises held at Jalapa in 1807, and they were consequently fully aware that Americans were an overwhelming majority in New Spain's armed forces and that their fellow creoles held key positions as militia officers. They were, moreover, convinced that opposition towards Spaniards and the government in Mexico City was widespread among middling creole groups as well as the lower classes, and they believed that, once a wave of resistance started, it would carry all before it, collapsing the infrastructure of Spanish rule in the provinces and opening a path for creoles to take power in the capital. In short, their strategy did not allow for strong military resistance and, when they met with such resistance, they had no serious plans for dealing with it.

Associated with the failure to plan for war was another, equally grave weakness: the leadership's inability to make effective military use of its mass popular following. Initially, the rebellion's host of plebeian followers was its greatest strength. Preponderance of numbers ensured that the advance through the Bajío met little effective resistance, and, as its numbers swelled, so the rebellion gained credibility as a political opposition. Many towns quickly surrendered when faced with invasion by unruly masses, particularly where the local authorities feared collusion from among their own populations, and the rebellion soon acquired an apparently unstoppable momentum. In several places, both creoles and plebeians joined the rebels, sometimes with entire militia units going over to Hidalgo's side, thereby adding to rebel forces while the crown's military forces were still struggling to organize a response. Opposition was usually slight, as critics were silenced by fear of suffering the same fate as the gachupines, who were killed or stripped of their property.

The rapid extension of rebellion and the fear that it induced was not, however, a guarantee of its success. When the rebels swept authority aside amid destruction of life and property, it was increasingly easy for the royalists to persuade the public, especially in urban centers, that this rural, largely Indian insurrection was an affront to civilization and a threat to social stability. Faced with the specter of an impoverished horde, believed to be intent on the overthrow of all social order, even those who sympathized with creole claims for self-government became supporters of the viceregal regime.[52] This was, perhaps, unavoidable because, politically, Hidalgo faced an invidious choice. To raise support among the masses, he had to allow them to vent their hatreds; to keep their support, he had to permit pillage. When Ignacio Aldama warned him that the Indians' excesses were harming the cause, Hidalgo reminded him that "we have no other arms but theirs . . . and if we start punishing we shall not find them when we need them."[53] Such willingness to countenance the violence, murder, and pillage that rebels sometimes visited upon civilians, especially Spaniards, inevitably aroused aversion. Nor was antipathy to the rebellion confined to the respectable classes. Although the plebeian population might join the rebels if they succeeded in taking command of an urban space, cities generally did not rebel.[54] Moreover, the rebellion failed to inspire peasants outside the Bajío and the Guadalajara region, even where they were exposed to hardships comparable to those that drove the Bajío peasantry into revolt.

It seems, then, the viceregal government, having been caught unprepared, with neither a strategy to combat insurrection nor forces ready to oppose mass rebellion, owed its salvation partly to the internal contradictions of the rebellion itself. Hidalgo tried to build a coalition that incorporated Mexicans from all social classes, but his ability to attract creoles dwindled as rumors of rebel outrages spread. Spaniards, both European and American, fled from his path and sought refuge in royalist areas, carrying tales of terror and atrocity. Hidalgo also failed to win significant support from the Church, despite his status as a cleric and his recourse to religious rhetoric.[55] Even so, widespread creole reluctance to support the rebellion was not Hidalgo's greatest difficulty. For, despite flagging creole support, he still had a formidable popular following and a loose ascendancy over large areas of the country. His problem was converting social and political support into military strength and using that strength to defeat royalist forces.

Hidalgo and his companions quickly recognized the need to mold their supporters into a fighting force, and they tried to turn them into an army, grouped around the core of militiamen who joined the rebellion in its early stages. The rebel leaders took military titles and placed themselves at the head of a hierarchy of ranks taken from the structure of the Spanish military. They also adopted and displayed the trappings of martial command. Witnesses to their entry into Guadalajara described in some detail, and with a certain admiration, the costumes in which Hidalgo and Allende were attired as they rode into the city, and several testimonies refer to Hidalgo's accompaniment by a band of musicians, who provided the ceremony required by his high rank. The creole directorate aimed, too, at giving substance to their army by providing arms and training. Thus, they arraigned their forces in a military hierarchy with officers to provide a chain of command and quickly took steps to acquire and manufacture arms. In the latter, they enjoyed apparent success. In 1810, the rebels were able to make cannon at the cities of Guanajuato, San Miguel, and León while also producing their own muskets and gunpowder and were, according to Calleja, at least as well-armed as their opponents.[56]

In reality, however, Hidalgo's army was a simulacrum. Behind the bright façade of its high command was an untrained, badly armed mass of people, who were soldiers in name only. If militiamen joined the rebels, they were but a small minority of the total force. This might seem no great loss; after all, professional soldiers had for many years repeatedly criticized the militias for their poor training, lack of arms, and absence of discipline. But it meant that the rebel forces were largely composed of men who were even less trained and disciplined, as well as lacking firearms or experience of using them. Indeed, as most of Hidalgo's men were Indians, they were even more ignorant of military ways than other Mexicans, having been exempt from militia service and discouraged from using arms, even horses. Clearly, Hidalgo's forces were an army in little more than name. The "colonels" appointed by Hidalgo were chosen for their ability to raise numbers rather than their military aptitude or experience—any man who could bring 1,000 men was made a colonel and went on the rebel payroll at 6 pesos a day—and the bulk of Hidalgo's forces were correspondingly an improvised, untrained, badly armed mass. While they may have been bound together by social and ethnic solidarities, animated by enthusiasm for the cause, and excited by the prospect of adventure and reward from plunder, en masse the rebels were prone to disorder and, in battle, repeatedly showed themselves liable to panic under sustained gunfire and cavalry attack.

The deficiencies of Hidalgo's forces were matched by the inadequacies of their commanding officers. Hidalgo was a complete novice in military matters, and his fellow commanders had scant military expertise or experience. Among the upper echelons of the rebel leadership, men such as Allende and Aldama had received some militia training but had no previous experience of leadership in combat.[57] As for the lower-ranking officers, they were generally chosen for their ability to attract recruits rather than for their military skills. Royalist troops were, by contrast, in much more practiced hands. Brigadier Calleja, commander of the Army of the Center, was a professional soldier of relatively considerable experience: he had fought in European theaters of war before arriving in Mexico in 1789, against Indians on the northern frontiers of Mexico, and had held prolonged command over both regular soldiers and militias.[58] Calleja's second-in-command, Manuel de Flon, had less experience of war but was accustomed to military command over both regular and militia forces in Puebla. Other leading officers were regulars, who, in several cases, had recently participated in war in Europe: Brigadier José de la Cruz, for example, had fought against the French in Spain and thus brought to the royalist side particularly pertinent experience of unconventional warfare.

The disparity of knowledge and experience between opposing commanders was soon exposed. When Calleja was appointed as field commander with orders to defeat Hidalgo's forces, he used his past experience to set about organizing a trained force in San Luis Potosí, a city where, through marriage and long residence, he had built strong connections with the local elite. Using his influence to recruit from neighboring haciendas and farms, Calleja spent weeks recruiting and training the men whom he planned to take into battle, while he also put the city's artisans to work producing arms. Hidalgo, on the other hand, had been preoccupied with spreading the rebellion and replacing municipal authorities with his sympathizers and had paid little or no attention to organizing the defense of the towns that came under his control. This neglect was exposed when the Army of the Center penetrated the Bajío. Flon entered from the south and Calleja from the north in late October 1810, and both quickly took towns previously committed to the insurgents. Then, in November and December, a new division of loyalist troops entered the fray, when Viceroy Venegas ordered Brigadier José de la Cruz to conduct his own campaign of counterinsurgency en route to joining Calleja. Cruz arrived at Guadalajara too late to contribute to Calleja's victory there, but he weakened Hidalgo by smashing his forces at Urepetiro. Other professional military men, such as Captain Rosendo Porlier and Lieutenant Pedro Celestino Negrete of the Spanish navy, who, when pressed into emergency service against the rebels, also contributed to defeating the insurrection by bringing to bear an experience of military action and command that was unknown to the insurgent leaders.

While historians have recognized Hidalgo's military incompetence, they have been less clear about why his forces as a whole seemed so incapable of using their superiority of numbers to better effect. To approach these questions—and thus to understand more fully Hidalgo's defeat—it is worth considering first an aspect of the rebellion that has received relatively little attention—namely, the severe organizational difficulties that the inexperienced rebel leaders faced in sustaining large forces in the field and deploying them as an efficient military force. Indeed, having large forces had some serious disadvantages when they were ill-trained; their instability put commanders under pressure to bring them quickly to battle only to find that, when engaged in battle, they resisted structured deployment in combat and tended to break down under determined and orderly attack.

Consider, first, the question of rebel numbers. Contemporary estimates suggest that Hidalgo commanded huge forces, far greater than above those available to the royalists. Hidalgo was reported to have mustered some 25,000 supporters in the first few days after setting out from Dolores, and it is said that this number climbed to 60,000 after the fall of Guanajuato, swelled to 80,000 people on his march towards Mexico City, and rose again to a comparable figure at Guadalajara (even Calleja accepted that the figure of 100,000 was exaggerated). Such figures must be treated with skepticism—they came from government officials who had no means of accurately measuring rebel numbers and were inclined to exaggerate in order both to emphasize the threat and to magnify their own achievements against it. At best, then, such figures may reflect the order of magnitude of support for Hidalgo at its peak rather than forces at his disposal for military use at any given time. Indeed, rather than seeing Hidalgo's forces as a swelling multitude, which accumulated while on the march, it is more realistic to think of them as a wave, rising to a peak at certain points, then breaking and flattening out, before gathering again to repeat the process until its energy was finally dissipated.

If we assume that contemporary estimates provide rough indications of the size of Hidalgo's following, what is their significance for understanding the rebellion's military capacity and failures? In the first place, large numbers were not necessarily a military advantage. Many of Hidalgo's following would have been noncombatants, as the rebel forces no doubt included whole families, perhaps even substantial segments of village communities, who joined the rebellion without any clear intention to fight. The very large numbers said to have been involved in the march on Mexico City must, however, have imposed a serious logistical strain. Although contemporary sources say little about the logistics of Hidalgo's army, we know from the experience of eighteenth-century military campaigns that feeding large numbers of people on the move for days or weeks required an enormous effort to supply food and drink, provide transportation, organize distribution, and to set up orderly encampments where an army might be fed in a reasonable time.

We have little information on how Hidalgo's forces moved, camped, and fed when on the march or in the towns through which they passed. However, though their numbers were sometimes comparable to that of a medium-sized European army, we can assume that they were not supplied in the manner of a conventional army and that their logistical problems were probably fewer. It is likely that most of the rebels carried their own food; if each person carried two and a half pounds of food—maize and maize flour, tortillas, and beans being the likely staples—their load would have been about 21 pounds for a week.[59] This would have diminished as it was consumed over the days and, as the rebels did not have to carry heavy weapons, was a reasonable burden to bear. And when passing through towns, villages, and agricultural estates, the rebels would no doubt have taken advantage of local foodstuffs, either by paying local traders or plundering local stores. So long as the distances between towns did not exceed a week's journey, which they rarely did in the course of the rebels' perambulations, then it was possible to sustain large numbers as long as they kept moving and regularly called at towns that had sufficient supplies to feed them.

Even so, this did not release the rebel command from the need to provide some supplies, as we can see in the rare glimpse of rebel logistics provided by capture of the rebels' supply train after the action at Aculco. On this occasion, the royalists seized a cart of foodstuffs, 1,250 head of cattle and 1,300 calves, 200 horses and mules, 16 carriages, a crate of cigars, 6 crates of shoes, clothing, papers, and baggage. They also took some muskets, some silver plate, and 13,550 pesos, which, being carried in reales at 8 per peso, constituted over 100,000 coins.[60] The captured supply train included a lighter element, too: "eight good-looking girls," whom Calleja described as the "insurgents' seraglio." Clearly, many of Hidalgo's people must have been involved as drovers and carriers of supplies, which had to be turned, day after day, into food for the entire force.

It is, of course, possible that their leaders ensured that food distribution and preparation was carried out in a disciplined manner. But with the impromptu character of the rebellion and the magnitude of the organizational tasks involved in providing central supplies for large forces, it is more likely that rebel recruits were left simply to forage for themselves, whether by spending the daily wage they were supposed to receive, at the rate of four reales (half a peso) per day for a man on foot (twice the daily rate of pay for an agricultural worker in central Mexico and in itself an incentive to join the rebels) or by stealing from the estates, communities, and towns through which they moved. Getting food was in all probability the principal daily preoccupation for the mass of the rebels, absorbing much of their attention and energy while inhibiting both their mobility and their readiness for combat. The rebellion is, then, best pictured as a kind of migratory movement, a wave that waxed and waned as it moved through towns and villages, taking in recruits and losing deserters, scouring the countryside as it went, and always concerned more with the source of the next meal than with preparation for military action.

Imagine, too, the means by which the rebels moved through the countryside. While some had horses, mules, or wagons, the vast majority were on foot and, given the rough conditions of Mexican roads at the time, must have formed long, straggling columns that stretched for many miles. The captured Spaniard Diego García Conde provides a rare glimpse of the rebel host on the move when recalling his time with them on the journey towards Mexico City. He observed that an order for the rebel army to advance was, "given the great disorder in which it always marched and the great queue that it made . . . an operation that took many hours, because the Indians marched with their children and their livestock . . . and from their plunder they carried doors, tables and chairs, and even house beams on their shoulders."[61] Unfortunately, García Conde did not paint a more detailed portrait of Hidalgo's force beyond making rough guesses about its size and derogatory comments about the brutishness of its members. He probably had little real information. As a hostage in fear of his life, carried with other prisoners in coaches that moved in the vanguard, he was in no position to form a clear picture of the masses moving behind. However, despite the paucity of contemporary description, we can create some sense of how the rebels were arraigned on their marches by taking into account the factors that military historians identify as determining the movements of premodern armies.

First, their progress tended to be very slow. Armies in eighteenth-century Europe could sometimes achieve high march rates, even as much as 20 miles per day, but depending on the terrain, they could also be as low as 5 miles per day. It is reasonable to assume that Hidalgo's forces were at the slower end of the spectrum, as they were moving over the narrow dirt roads, probably single-file tracks, which linked towns. If they moved in single file, then (assuming that each individual occupied about a square meter), numbers of the order of 60,000 to 80,000 would have created long columns that snaked back for many miles. A single-file column of 8,000 troops would, it has been estimated, stretch for some 15 miles and take many hours to unify into a force capable of military maneuver and action.[62] Given the larger numbers and undisciplined nature of the rebel forces, which probably did not march in any formal order and tended to spread out as they moved, Hidalgo's rebels must have presented an extraordinary spectacle when on the move, with long files of people that constantly formed and reformed in lines that took many hours to assemble in any one place. Hidalgo's army was an enormous straggling caravan of men and women whose numbers were sometimes swollen by the hope of food and plunder, particularly as they approached towns and settlements and attracted new recruits, but quickly depleted when supplies were short or attack threatened. If rebel numbers did reach the magnitudes reported—80,000, 60,000, 40,000—it is unlikely that these numbers would have been sustained for long, given the sheer difficulty of organizing and moving them, particularly as they were not trained for campaigning nor subject to military discipline.

In addition to these organizational and logistic difficulties, Hidalgo's insurrection was impeded by its shortcomings as a fighting force. At first, it advanced at a rapid rate as the rebellion swept across the Bajío, carrying all before it. This was, however, the effect of massing large numbers against small opposing forces rather than the military achievement or martial qualities of Hidalgo's "soldiers" and "officers." They had done little fighting before meeting royalist forces at Aculco and Calderón, and on the one occasion when they did encounter and overcome entrenched resistance—at Guanajuato in September 1810—they had faced opponents who were both far fewer and at a serious tactical disadvantage because of their defensive position. The decision by the intendant Riaño to convert the city's stone-built granary into a defensive refuge had the unintended effect of handing the political and military initiative to Hidalgo's rebels. For, although the fortress-like structure of the granary made it the town's obvious stronghold, the royalists' retreat to its shelter alienated the townspeople, who felt that they had been deserted by their protectors and left them either to join the rebels or simply to watch the spectacle of attack on the granary. It also allowed the rebels time to gather and concentrate their forces for an attack on a fixed point, which they could assail from several sides, including the high ground on flanking hillsides.

The action at Guanajuato bore no resemblance at all to war between opposing armies in eighteenth-century style. It was conducted without use of artillery or firearms and was akin to a medieval peasant insurrection against a fortified manorial house, except that in this case, the insurgents faced a building that, however solid, was not designed for defense against determined assault. To take the granary, Hidalgo's forces did not have to behave like an army acting under the orders of commanders and facing mobile opponents in open country. Because Guanajuato's loyalists had taken refuge in the granary—possibly hoping to negotiate with the rebels rather than fighting them—the target was clear to all: by its very immobility, this pocket of resistance invited attack. Such an attack was, moreover, made all the easier by the fact that many of Guanajuato's plebeian population welcomed the rebels and, far from resisting Hidalgo, joined in the sacking of the city. Even under these favorable conditions, the rebels suffered disproportionate losses. They defeated the royalists and put at least 300 to death, but they were said to have lost some 2,000 of their own people in the attack.

It was not long before the weaknesses of rebel forces became more obvious and more damaging to Hidalgo's cause. At Las Cruces, the rebels appeared to have won another victory, their first against a royalist commander in the field, as they pressed towards the capital. Colonel Trujillo noted, as he prepared to do battle, that there were about 5,000 men with some military training among Hidalgo's cohorts. And, after clashing with these forces, Trujillo reported that they had shown a knowledge of military organization and tactics in their attack. The royalist positions had been attacked by columns of uniformed soldiers from the provincial infantry battalions of Celaya, Valladolid, and Guanajuato, flanked by dragoons and lancers, and backed by masses of Indian auxiliaries armed with sticks and stones. This description of the action suggests that, at this stage, Hidalgo made good use of the trained militiamen who had joined his cause; infantry from the provincial militias armed with firearms and supported by artillery and horse formed the vanguard of an attack on Trujillo's force, with a great mass of Indians armed with slings and sticks coming up behind them. Their advance was irresistible; Trujillo's men held out for some hours but were eventually forced to retreat in such haste that they were unable to take their arms and artillery with them.

Although Trujillo's defeat left the way open to Mexico City, the advantage gained was offset by heavy costs to Hidalgo, since it was achieved at great cost to men and morale.[63] One of Hidalgo's men reported that many Indians had died because they clustered together and were mown down by the enemy; this he attributed, with characteristic creole racial arrogance, to their "low intelligence" rather than to their obvious lack of military experience and discipline.[64] Whatever its cause, the consequence of Las Cruces was clear. Worried by his losses at Las Cruces and fearing that viceregal forces were advancing against him, Hidalgo not only turned away from Mexico City but divided his forces in a withdrawal that took him back to Valladolid and Allende to Guanajuato.

Hidalgo's decision had such fatal consequences for the rebellion that it demands a full explanation. Historians have invariably attributed it to his lack of military experience and, given the evidence that his military talents were slight, this view has much to recommend it. But it is not entirely convincing. Hidalgo had by this time already experienced the difficulties of marshaling his forces in battle against a trained enemy army and must therefore have had some misgivings about meeting Calleja so soon after the defeats of Aculco and Guanajuato; he also received strong warnings from Allende, who opposed the defense of Guadalajara because of the danger that it would allow Calleja to corral rebel forces and destroy them in a single blow. Allende had, however, lost most of his influence by this time, and Hidalgo, supported by his war council, persisted with his determination to take a stand at Guadalajara.

Hidalgo's willingness to do battle with Calleja led to the most severe loss in battle that the rebels had yet suffered and brought an end of his leadership and his hopes. It is, nonetheless, simplistic to blame this loss on Hidalgo's lack of military expertise. For, although we have no direct record of Hidalgo's reasoning, it is not difficult to see why he decided to concentrate his whole force at Guadalajara and do battle at Puente de Calderón. In the first place, Calleja's army was in hot pursuit, and Hidalgo faced the danger that, if he dispersed his forces in order to regroup later, he would lose his credibility and their loyalty. With reinforcements from Guadalajara and its hinterland, he had recovered his numerical advantage and thus seemed to be in a good position to recover the prestige lost by the reverses of the previous weeks. Second, Guadalajara was a defensible space where Hidalgo could quarter his people in a friendly environment, find provisions to sustain them, and defend a strategic position in the heartlands of rebel territory. Third, if contemporary reports are to be believed, Hidalgo had at his disposal substantial quantities of money and precious metal seized from public and private funds (perhaps as much as 420,000 pesos at Guadalajara). This gave him the means to finance immediate large-scale recruitment at the four reales per day promised to rebel foot soldiers.[65] Cash was, of course, of limited value if food ran short, and the problems of feeding his army were an additional pressure to opt for a large-scale military engagement; the advantage of numerical superiority could only be retained so long as Hidalgo had the means to pay and feed his soldiers, and neither could be sustained indefinitely. To Hidalgo, then, it must have seemed better to stand and fight rather than allow his forces to hemorrhage and his prestige to dissolve.

As in previous encounters on the battlefield, weight of numbers was of itself an inadequate defense. Hidalgo was better prepared for battle than on previous occasions; he had advance notice of Calleja's coming, chose a defensible site, and took some elementary military precautions when selecting the ground on which to fight and deploy his men. The insurgent leadership sensibly chose a position where the enemy could neither arraign incoming columns of troops in a full line of battle nor make efficient use of cavalry, and where they were also vulnerable to artillery and other projectiles discharged from above. But these advantages were wasted. The insurgents, lacking firearms for all their soldiers, relied too heavily on captured artillery pieces, which they did not use effectively. They placed cannon in fixed positions at high points in the hope that they would cover the surrounding countryside and left their men to adopt static positions around these guns while allowing the enemy freedom to maneuver. The battle at Calderón thus followed the pattern Calleja had seen work to his advantage at Aculco. The royalists advanced in attack; the insurgents let fly with random salvoes from badly aimed cannon, stones, arrows, and their few firearms—all to little effect. Meanwhile, the royalist officers multiplied the strength of their much smaller forces by maneuvering them around the battlefield, shifting troops to points where they could exploit insurgent vulnerability or where they needed to counter insurgent attack. At the same time, more accurate fire from disciplined soldiers, advancing under command from officers who led from the front and operated under the direction of a single general commander, inflicted heavy casualties and further compensated for the royalists' smaller numbers.[66] The Battle of Calderón was an unequal contest, where the insurgents' military incompetence contributed much to their own defeat.

Hidalgo's military defeats were, of course, also royalist victories and owed much to commanders who displayed the will and skill to save Mexico's Spanish regime. In the first month of the insurrection, the military system of New Spain seemed incapable of dealing with the rebellion, as several major towns fell in quick succession and royalist forces were unable to stop their advance. This was partly attributable to an almost complete lack of readiness on the government side. Government forces had never previously faced any substantial challenge to central or provincial government, and, though viceroys Garibay and Lizana had taken steps to increase the garrison in Mexico City, it was in no position to counter the massive challenge that appeared in 1810.

Fortunately for the viceregal government, its military commanders had time and space to recover from the setbacks of 1810. Their successes owed much to the leadership of professional soldiers, who insisted on adequate training for their troops, pursued the rebels with energy, and punished them ruthlessly. Indeed, by actively pursuing rebel forces and taking retaliatory measures to discourage potential adherents, Calleja and other commanders inflicted such cumulative damage on the condition and morale of Hidalgo's forces that, six months after the outbreak of the insurrection, the rebellion was much reduced in its territorial scope. The royalist victory at Calderón was the clearest example yet of the superiority of relatively small numbers of well-armed and well-managed soldiers against plebeian irregulars, and this was demonstrated by its decisive military effect, knocking out the mass of Hidalgo's forces in a single, intensive action. Moreover, by showing that the viceregal government could cope militarily with the rebellion, the action at Calderón had an important political consequence: it demonstrated to the authorities that they had no need to parlay with the rebels, who, now that they were defeated and disunited, were no longer the terrible threat they had been a month before. Indeed, royalist propaganda could represent the rebels as merely the rump of Hidalgo's insurrection, a few scattered bands of malcontents and criminals, who could be treated as a problem of law and order rather than the avatars of an alternative government.

The first attempt to secure autonomy for Mexico was, then, much more like an ancien régime rebellion than a modern war for independence. Hidalgo and his companions had not initially intended to fight the forces of government, and they proved incapable of mounting an orderly military campaign. They had planned neither a regular war aimed at destroying government armies on the battlefield, nor did they organize an irregular war of guerrillas making hit-and-run attacks against government forces. In this sense, the Hidalgo rebellion was quite unlike the rebellion of Britain's North American colonies. A better parallel, perhaps, is with the French Vendée in 1793. There, peasant uprisings driven by intensely local concerns but united by some common interests, coalesced into a single great rebellion that briefly seemed to sweep all before it, until large, inchoate peasant forces were stopped by small, well-organized military forces.[67]

To conclude, as one historian has, that "Hidalgo accomplished nothing" is, however, to understate his significance.[68] Despite his defeat and the dispersal of his forces, Hidalgo's rebellion continued after his death, as the many smaller regional uprisings raised by his envoys mutated into a persistent insurgency that continued to challenge Spanish government. Indeed, the end of Hidalgo marked the beginning of a new phase of conflict in which rebel leaders abandoned mass uprising and turned to guerrilla warfare. With this development came a new pattern of regionalized, low-intensity warfare. Insurgents harried government supporters and forces in the provinces by attacking towns and villages, disrupting trade and communications, seeking to operate outside the law, and even setting up alternative forms of government. The viceregal authorities, for their part, doggedly defended their control of the capital and all major regional cities, including the vital Atlantic port of Veracruz, while pursuing a controlled counterinsurgency strategy designed to extirpate rebellion in the countryside. This pattern was punctuated by periodic clashes in which rival armies engaged in major battlefield actions where both fought to inflict permanent damage on the enemy's military capacity. How this pattern of insurgency and counterinsurgency developed after Hidalgo, as well as its impact on the course of Mexican political and social life in the years after 1810 are questions for the next chapter.

Notes

1. A sense of "national" identity and potential seems to have been particularly well-developed in Mexico, where creole authors had, since the later seventeenth century, claimed that Mexico had a special status in the Spanish world, assured by the sophistication of its ancient civilization and the privileged character of its evangelization and Christian experience. See Jacques LaFaye, *Quetzalcóatl and Guadalupe: The Formation of Mexican National Consciousness, 1531–1813*, trans. Benjamin Keen (Chicago: Chicago University Press, 1976); David A. Brading, *The First America: The Spanish Monarchy, Creole Patriots and the Liberal State, 1492–1867* (Cambridge: Cambridge University Press, 1991), pp. 343–61.
2. Brian R. Hamnett, "The Appropriation of Mexican Church Wealth by the Spanish Bourbon Government. The Consolidación de Vales Reales, 1805-1809," *JLAS* 1 (1969): pp. 85–113; Stein and Stein, *Edge of Crisis*, pp. 314–16.
3. Hugh M. Hamill, "'Vencer o morir por la Patria!' La invasión de España y algunas consecuencias para México, 1808–1810," in *Interpretaciones de la Independencia de México*, ed. Josefina Zoraida Vázquez and Jaime Rodríguez O. (Mexico City: Nueva Imagen, 1997), pp. 88–99.
4. Anna, *The Fall of Royal Government in Mexico City*, pp. 58–61, 67.
5. On the launch of the rebellion and its first six weeks, see Hamill, *The Hidalgo Revolt*, pp. 117–23.
6. A strong impression of the importance of personal ties in shaping loyalty is found in the statement by an artisan of Dolores, who had been patronized by Hidalgo and, like other members of the community of Dolores, joined the rebellion out of affection and respect for the priest. See "Memoria del último de los primeros soldados de la independencia, Pedro José Sotelo," in *Historia de la Guerra de Independencia de México*, 2, pp. 320–30.
7. John Tutino, *From Insurrection to Revolution in Mexico: Social Bases of Agrarian Violence 1750–1940* (Princeton, NJ: Princeton UP, 1989), p. 74.
8. Quoted by Hamill, "'Vencer o morir por la Patria!,'" p. 83. On Hidalgo's views of independence and his strategy towards the populace, also see Hamill, *Hidalgo Revolt*, pp. 121–3.
9. Proclama de Mariano Jiménez, Matehuala, December 14, 1810, quoted by Juan Ortiz Escamilla, *Guerra y gobierno: Los pueblos y la independencia de México* (Seville: Universidad de Sevilla et al., 1997), p. 32.
10. "Primera proclama formal de don Miguel Hidalgo," quoted by Ortiz Escamilla, *Guerra y gobierno*, p. 33.
11. On monarchism and messianism among the poor and its influence in the Hidalgo revolt, see Eric Van Young, "Quetzalcoatl, King Ferdinand and Ignacio Allende go to the seashore, or Messianism and Mystical Kingship in Mexico, 1800–1821," in *The Independence of Mexico and the Creation of the New Nation*, ed. Jaime E. Rodríguez O. (Los Angeles: University of California Press, 1989), pp. 109–27.

12. Brian R. Hamnett, *Roots of Insurgency: Mexican Regions, 1750-1824* (Cambridge: Cambridge University Press, 1986), pp. 4–13; Tutino, *From Insurrection to Revolution*, pp. 79–98, 119–24.

13. Tutino, *From Insurrection to Revolution*, pp. 125–6, 178–82.

14. Like Tutino, Eric Van Young argues that economic deprivation alone cannot explain the rebellion. However, he rejects Tutino's thesis that differences in the relations between peasants and landlords explain the geographical distribution and intensity of revolt, points out that insurrection and insurgency were more widespread than Tutino allows, and argues that the peasant participation that underpinned the rebellion should be understood primarily in cultural terms, related to the defense of Indian community identities and culture. See Van Young, *The Other Rebellion*, especially pp. 496–503.

15. Hamill, *Hidalgo Revolt*, p. 127.

16. Hamnett, *Roots of Insurgency*, pp. 26–30.

17. On the reconciliation of Indian respect for Spanish kingship and hatred of the Spaniards in Mexico, and a psychosocial explanation of the scapegoating of gachupines, see Van Young, *The Other Rebellion*, pp. 463–6, 471–5.

18. LaFaye, *Quetzalcóatl and Guadalupe*, p. 28.

19. For a full discussion of messianism and its relationship to Indian insurrection in Mexico, see Van Young, *The Other Rebellion*, chap. 18, especially pp. 475–82.

20. On this opening phase of rebellion in the Bajío, see Hamill, *Hidalgo Revolt*, pp. 123–6.

21. For detailed description of the rebel attack on Guanajuato, see ibid., pp. 137–41.

22. "Carta de Guanajuato detallando lo occurrido al ser atacada y tomada la ciudad por el Sr. Hidalgo," in Hernández y Dávalos, *Historia de la Guerra de Independencia*, 2, pp. 126–9.

23. Virginia Guedea, *La insurgencia en el departamento del norte: Los Llanos de Apan y la Sierra de Puebla 1810–1816* (Mexico City: Universidad Nacional Autónoma de México, 1996), pp. 19–27.

24. For a synthesis of the network of rebellion created by Hidalgo's envoys into the regions to the north, west, and south of the Bajío, and a pioneering analysis of its significance, see Hamnett, *Roots of Insurgency*, pp. 125–49; also Lucas Alamán, *Historia de Méjico*, 4 vols. (Mexico City: Editorial Jus, 1942), 2, pp. 7–23.

25. On Spanish forces in 1810, see Christon I. Archer, "The Army of New Spain and the Wars of Independence, 1790–1812," *HAHR* 61, no. 4 (1981): pp. 705–14; see also his "La revolución militar de México: Estrategía, tácticas y logísticas durante la Guerra de Independencia, 1810–1821," in *Interpretaciones de la Independencia de México*, ed. Jaime Rodríguez O. and Josefina Zoraida Vázquez (Mexico City: Nueva Imagen, 1997), pp. 123–35.

26. Virginia Guedea, "Los indios voluntarios de Fernando VII," in *Estudios de Historia Moderna y Contemporánea de México* (México: Universidad Nacional Autónoma de México, Instituto de Investigaciones Históricas, 1986), 10, pp. 11–83.

27. Archer, *Army in Bourbon Mexico*, pp. 22–3.

28. On Calleja as a caudillo, see Hugh M. Hamill, "Caudillismo and Independence: A Symbiosis?" in Rodríguez, *The Independence of Mexico and the Creation of the New Nation*, pp. 171–4.

29. Carlos María Bustamante, *Campañas del General D. Felix Maria Calleja, comandante en gefe del ejercito real de operaciones, llamado del Centro* (Mexico: Imprenta del Aguila, 1828), p. 11, gives grudging admiration to Calleja for his alacrity and decisiveness at this time. In the rest of this account, which uses Calleja's correspondence and is a supplement to Carlos María de Bustamante, *Cuadro histórico de la revolución mexicana* (Mexico City: Comisión Nacional para la celebración del seisquicentenario, 1961), Calleja is presented as the key military figure of the period 1810–12.

30. Archer, "The Army of New Spain and the Wars of Independence," pp. 705–6.

31. Terán made these comments in a letter to Flon dated October 2: quoted by Archer, "La revolución militar de México," p. 132.

32. Timothy Anna states that Venegas had forces of some 7,000 men to defend the city. This is a speculative figure, unsupported by direct evidence from official sources. It is, however, a reasonable estimate, since 5,930 medals of the Virgin de los Remedios were distributed to officers and soldiers as the city awaited Hidalgo's attack. For these figures, see Anna, *Fall of Royal Government in Mexico City*, pp. 69, 71.
33. Ibid., p. 70 gives the sources for these estimates.
34. Miguel Hidalgo, Quartel General de Celaya, November 13, 1810, in Hernández y Dávalos, *Historia de la Guerra de Independencia*, 2, p. 221.
35. Torcuato Trujillo to Viceroy Venegas, Chapultepec, November 6, 1810, in ibid.
36. Diego García Conde to Viceroy Venegas, Guanajuato, December 8, 1810, in ibid.
37. Hamill, *Hidalgo Revolt*, pp. 177–9.
38. Calleja's map of the battlefield is given in "Plano de los terrenos inmediatos al pueblo de San Geronimo de Aculco, Mejico, en que fue batido y dispersado el ejercito insurgente el 7 de noviembre de 1810 por el Brigadier D. Felix Calleja," Archivo del Servicio Histórico Militar (SHM), Ministerio de Guerra, Ultramar, Caja 107. For a reproduction, see Bustamante, *Cuadro histórico*, 1, p. 79.
39. Calleja to Venegas, Querétaro, November 15, 1810, in Hernández y Dávalos, *Historia de la Guerra de Independencia*, 2, p. 225.
40. Ibid., p. 226.
41. Bustamante, *Cuadro histórico*, 1, p.78.
42. Miguel Hidalgo, Quartel General de Celaya, November 13, 1810, in Hernández y Dávalos, *Historia de la Guerra de Independencia*, 1, p. 121.
43. Alamán, *Historia de Méjico*, 2, pp. 23–4.
44. See Allende's letters to Hidalgo of November 19 and 20, 1810, in Alamán, *Historia de Méjico*, 2, pp. 31–2. Full transcripts are also found in Hernández y Dávalos, *Historia de la Guerra de Independencia*, 2, pp. 232–4.
45. Alamán, *Historia de Méjico*, 2, pp. 34–45. For a map of Calleja's attack and the insurgents' defensive positions, see SHM, Ministerio de Guerra, Ultramar Caja 107: Plano de las inmediaciones de la Ciudad de Goanaxuato, Mejico, en que tuvo lugar la accion librada el 24 de noviembre de 1810 por el Brigadier D Felix Calleja contra el ejercito insurgente. This and other maps of the period are interesting not only for the information they provide on battle formations but also because they reflect the professionalism of the Spanish officer corps.
46. Alamán, *Historia de Méjico*, 2, pp. 51–7.
47. Ibid., pp. 77–8.
48. The entry is described in "Relasion de la entrada del Serenicimo Señor Generalísimo del Exercito Americano . . ." in Hernández y Dávalos, *Historia de la Guerra de Independencia*, 1, pp. 123–4.
49. On Allende's marginalization from power, Hidalgo's continuing rise to prominence at Guadalajara and his preparations for battle, see Alamán, *Historia de Méjico*, 2, pp. 58–64.
50. Alamán, *Historia de Méjico*, 2, pp. 81–8. For Calleja's letter with his official battle report, printed by the government, see SHM, Ministerio de Guerra, Ultramar, Caja 96: Detalle de la accion gloriosa de las tropas del Rey en el Puente de Calderón, Mexico, 1811.
51. See, for example, Hamill, *Hidalgo Revolt*, pp. 141–8; and Ortiz Escamilla, *Guerra y gobierno*, pp. 42–50.
52. On royalist propaganda against the rebels and its impact, see Hamill, *Hidalgo Revolt*, pp. 151–66, 170–5.
53. Quoted in Alamán, *Historia de Méjico*, 1, p. 470.
54. On cities, see Eric Van Young, "Islands in the Storm: Quiet Cities and Violent Countrysides in the Mexican Independence Era," *Past and Present*, no.118 (1988): pp. 120–56.

55. On the role of the clergy during the insurrection and the insurgency that followed, see chapter 9, this volume.

56. Hamill, *Hidalgo Revolt*, pp. 148–9; Ortiz Escamilla, *Guerra y gobierno*, pp. 47–8.

57. Allende had been sent to the northern frontier to fight Indians, but it is not known whether he ever engaged in combat.

58. For an overall assessment of Calleja's importance during 1810–11 and subsequent role in counterinsurgency, see Christon I. Archer, "New Wars and Old: Félix Calleja and the Independence War of Mexico, 1810–16," in *Military Heretics. The Unorthodox in Policy and Strategy*, ed. B.J.C. McKerchar and A. Hamish Ion (Westport, CT: Greenwood Press, 1993), pp. 33–56.

59. These figures are based on soldiers' rations in eighteenth-century Europe: see Jones, *The Art of War in the Western World*, p. 273.

60. Bustamante, *Campañas del General D. Felix Maria Calleja*, pp. 22–3.

61. Diego García Conde to Viceroy Venegas, December 8, 1810, in Hernández y Dávalos, *Historia de la Guerra de Independencia de México*, 2, p. 271.

62. Ross Hassig, *Aztec Warfare: Imperial Expansion and Political Control* (Norman, OK: University of Oklahoma Press, 1988), pp. 65–6.

63. Bustamante recorded the battle of Las Cruces as a victory for Hidalgo's rebels, but even this supporter of the insurgent cause was forced to admit that it did great damage to morale, particularly among Hidalgo's Indian followers, who were unaccustomed to withstanding artillery fire: see Bustamante, *Cuadro histórico*, 1, pp. 67–8.

64. "Memoria del último de los primeros soldados de la independencia, Pedro José Sotelo," in Hernández y Dávalos, *Historia de la Guerra de Independencia de México*, 2, p. 327.

65. On the importance of payments for recruiting to Hidalgo's rebellion, see Hugh Hamill, "Royalist propaganda and 'La Porción Humilde del Pueblo' during Mexican Independence," *The Americas* 36 (1980): pp. 437–8.

66. For reflections on the military disparities of royalists and insurgents at the battle of Calderón, see Alamán, *Historia de Méjico*, 2, pp. 88–91.

67. On the social and political aspects of the comparison, see Hamnett, *Roots of Insurgency*, pp. 52–3. For further comparison with peasant insurrection during the French Revolution, see Van Young, *The Other Rebellion*, pp. 507–9.

68. This judgment is given by Anna, *Fall of Royal Government in Mexico City*, p. 76.

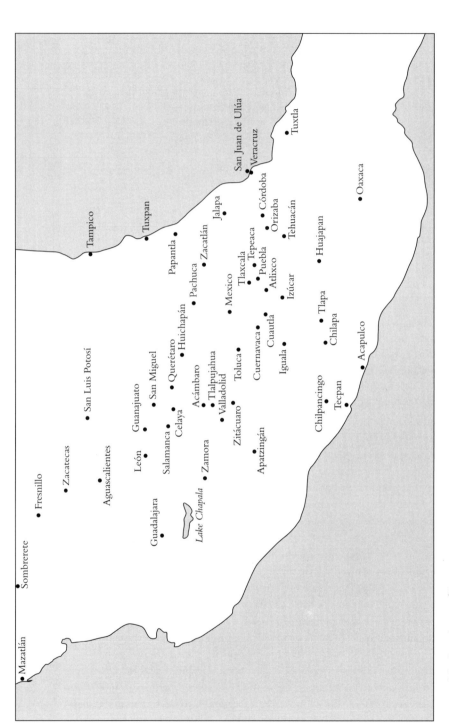

MAP 4. Mexico: Areas of Insurgency

9

INSURGENCY AND COUNTERINSURGENCY IN MEXICO, 1811–15

The transformation of Hidalgo's explosive insurrection into a prolonged insurgency was possible for a number of reasons. One was the survival of a tier of leaders ready to take the place of Hidalgo and the other principal commanders. Before heading north in March 1811, Allende had promoted Ignacio López Rayón to command the movement, with José María Liceaga as his second, and sent these men southwards with a force of several thousand to continue the rebellion. Their first attempt to rally the insurgents was at Zacatecas, where they tried to establish an autonomous government—a Junta Nacional—in the second half of April 1811. This seat of rebel government lasted barely two weeks: Calleja retook the city on May 3, and the insurgent leaders had to move on. While their followers in Zacatecas took refuge in the mountainous backlands outside the city, Rayón moved to Zitácuaro where he sought to convene a provisional government that would provide a political directorate and represent the insurgents abroad. The eleven leaders who attended accepted Rayón as "Minister of the Nation," agreed to establish a "Supreme National American Junta," and chose three of their number, led by Rayón, to run this government and direct its military operations. In their pronouncements, the insurgent leaders courted public support by recognizing Ferdinand VII as sovereign and embracing Catholicism as the only true religion, thereby retaining at least a symbolic allegiance to the two great pillars of the old regime. However, they also declared America "free and independent," and their purpose was clear: to replace the Spanish authorities in Mexico City with an autonomous government of their choosing.

The commitment of these regional leaders was underpinned by the persistence of rebellion in many areas. Although the authorities offered pardons to rebels who gave themselves up, there was no widespread surrender. Indeed, because Calleja's victory persuaded the government that the rebels could be defeated by military means, it blankly refused to consider anything less than unconditional surrender from rebel leaders and thus ignored an opportunity for appeasement. Ignacio Rayón and others who refused to submit were isolated from legal political activity and left with little choice but to continue their struggle. Here, then, was one reason why rebellion continued: by failing to offer a sufficiently generous settlement to surviving rebel leaders, the viceregal government left the most committed rebels beyond the pale, without incentive or opportunity to abandon their cause.

Popular support for rebellion also persisted in many rural areas. If the rebellion lost momentum when the mass of Hidalgo's followers were defeated in open battle, it sustained an underlying strength. The turbulence generated by Hidalgo's revolt continued to convulse rural society long after his death, for it had opened a space for political dissent and social violence that the viceregal government could not easily shut down. Many rebels, who had been inspired by Hidalgo, remained at large, and the surviving rebels and their sympathizers were not readily vanquished.[1] Rebellion had, moreover, spread beyond the Bajío to other regions, and Brigadier Calleja soon abandoned his hope that he could quickly restore order by defeating the rebels in open battle. Indeed, in August 1811, he admitted that the insurrection "sprouts up like the Hydra as fast as its heads are cut off."[2] To prevent "a spirit of ferment which, once it takes hold of a country's inhabitants, devours everything" required an army of comparable force. However, even such an army, Calleja conceded, might easily be overstretched and outdone by bands of mounted insurgents, who, "like Arabs, fall indiscriminately on settlements, robbing and plundering, and quickly retreating when troops are sent to punish them."[3]

The Hydra's Head: Regional Insurgencies

The insurrection started by Hidalgo thus entered a new phase and took on a new character. It fragmented into many parts, dispersing among local guerrilla bands, which, although they did not aim to overthrow the entire system of Spanish government, constituted a serious threat to the image and authority of the royalist regime. Striking at local political officials and institutions, plundering property, attacking trade routes and communications, and generating a climate of local insecurity that hindered economic activity, these guerrillas forced the royalist regime to engage on many fronts. In the Bajío and Guanajuato-Querétaro, the central areas of Michoacán, and the central districts of Guadalajara, the insurgents continued Hidalgo's revolt and threatened important towns that the government could not afford to lose. Insurgency also sprang up where Hidalgo's rebellion had made no mark, notably in the regions of Puebla and Oaxaca. In 1811–12, these areas became important theaters of war, where opposing sides struggled for control of key cities.

In addition to the insurgencies in rich and populated areas, there were peripheral zones where insurgency was even more difficult to erase. The Llanos de Apan to the east of Mexico City, the northern and southern borders of the Intendancy of Puebla, the southern sierras, the Altos de Jalisco and the area around Lake Chapala, and the backlands behind Veracruz were among the most important zones of persistent insurgency that lay beyond the hinterlands of major cities.[4] Sparsely populated and in mountainous terrain, they provided bases for insurgents to attack richer neighboring areas or trade routes and acted as safe havens to which they could retreat when necessary.

The stamina of the insurgency showed that its leaders had learned some important lessons from the debacle of Hidalgo's revolt. Prominent among these was their recognition of the need for a coherent political program with a coordinated military arm. The "Suprema Junta Nacional Americano" established at Zitácuaro in August 1811 aimed at those goals. It sought to establish political legitimacy and credibility by drawing up a draft constitution for an alternative system of government; it proclaimed principles such as the abolition of slavery and tribute, and freedom for trade and agriculture; it also announced a foreign policy aimed at winning support from the United States.

Military cohesion was harder to achieve. The mass popular uprising associated with Hidalgo's leadership was now supplanted by disparate rebel bands operating under local leaders who engaged in guerrilla warfare. Rather than seeking confrontation in open battle, guerrilla leaders favored hit-and-run attacks, raiding centers of population and evading royalist retaliation by taking refuge in backland bases that were difficult to attack. These tactics impeded Calleja's efforts to snuff out the rebellion, but they also made it difficult for the heirs of Hidalgo's movement to coordinate and concentrate force against the royalists. Nonetheless, the insurgency continued to flourish throughout 1811, due largely to the prowess of José María Morelos, who emerged as the outstanding leader in the south and, after a series of striking military successes, eclipsed Rayón as the most prominent leader of the independents' cause.

Morelos: The "Second Mohammed"

Morelos, like Hidalgo, was a priest, though of more lowly social origins. A mestizo from a poor provincial background, he worked on haciendas in the *tierra caliente* (tropical lowlands) of Michoacán and as a mule driver on the "China trail" between Acapulco and Mexico City. He then entered the Colegio de San Nicolás in Valladolid in 1790 (when Hidalgo was its rector), subsequently became a seminarian and took Holy Orders in 1795. On becoming a priest, Morelos spent some years in obscurity, living as a curate of impoverished Indian parishes in the backlands of Michoacán, far from the comfortable clerical livings that went to well-connected Spaniards and creoles. It was from this environment that Morelos made contact with Hidalgo in 1810, apparently hoping to become his chaplain. Hidalgo, however, saw leadership potential in the mestizo priest and, in October 1810, commissioned him to raise rebellion in the Pacific tierra caliente and to take the Spanish fortress at the Pacific port of Acapulco.[5]

Morelos soon had an impact, opening a new front for the rebellion in the south. Although he had no military training, his first campaign as an insurgent displayed a talent for armed leadership. Within a few weeks of leaving his parish at Carácuaro, he swept south towards Acapulco, seizing arms and ammunition and multiplying his force from about 25 to around 3,000 men, as local militias in the tierra caliente enthusiastically took his side. His rapid advance was helped by the absence of any strong garrison forces except at Acapulco, where the royalists concentrated their strength.

Morelos was unable to overcome the Acapulco fortress, which was one of the strongest in New Spain and, being reinforced by sea, was capable of withstanding prolonged attack. Nonetheless, Morelos showed sound military sense by isolating Acapulco, taking control of its hinterland, and moving his campaign inland. Well-supplied with men and captured munitions, Morelos opened a new front by moving northwards through the passes of the coastal sierras to take the towns of Chilpancingo, Tixtla, and Chilapa, and in so doing he established forward bases for a future offensive into the Intendancy of Puebla, close to the heart of the viceroyalty.

His advance also brought important new recruits to the cause. As his reputation grew, Morelos won the support of leading creole families and access to their extensive networks of kin and retainers. The Galeanas of Tecpan, the leading family of the coastal region, joined him in 1810, adding to his cadre of leaders, swelling his forces with workers from their haciendas, and providing support throughout the hinterland of Acapulco. In May 1811, he absorbed the Bravo family into his military command, which brought him both ascendancy over the Chilpancingo region, where the family had a large hacienda, and the allegiance of five brothers, who were to provide outstanding military leadership in future campaigns. An alliance with the guerrilla chief Vicente Guerrero brought more armed followers, and, as Morelos moved deeper into the interior in 1812, he further reinforced his military and political strength by alliances with local leaders.[6]

Morelos's first campaign from October 1810 to August 1811 was flawed in the sense that he failed to capture Acapulco, his prime target. But this defeat was compensated by his achievement of dominance in the southern coastal area and his consequent ability to build a platform for fresh offensives into neighboring regions. At the end of 1810, Morelos had been an obscure, impoverished priest leading a couple of dozen men in an unimportant region of southwest Mexico, far from the main theater of conflict in the north-central plateau. By August 1811, he had created a substantial and efficient armed force, turned the tropical coast and its hinterlands into an insurgent zone, and had advanced north to the boundaries of Puebla, thereby preparing a way for an advance into a region contiguous to the viceregal capital. Morelos had also asserted himself as a political leader. He spread the ideals of Hidalgo's movement by proclaiming an end to slavery and the caste system and provided crucial political support for Rayón and the insurgent government in Zitácuaro at a time when the tide of insurgency was ebbing in its old strongholds. In short, Morelos was the military and political chieftain who did most to keep the insurgency alive, carrying it from the north and central regions into the Pacific coastlands and then, after taking control over the Michoacán tierra caliente, using this terrain as a base from which to take the struggle back towards the center of the viceroyalty.

Morelos's early success owed much to his ability to win support across a social spectrum ranging from slaves to substantial local landowners. He appealed to the lower classes by promising an end to slavery and discrimination against the castas (in a decree of November 1810), and took advantage of cotton farmers' animosities towards Spanish merchants who dominated the cotton trade of the coast to win wider adherence to his cause. Morelos also won over prominent landowning families, who, as local *caciques* (rural bosses), had networks that served for the recruitment and mobilization of irregular forces. The Bravo brothers probably joined the insurgency initially to resist repression from local royalist officials, then stayed on out of dislike for peninsular privilege in Mexico and a concomitant conviction that creoles had the right to independence.[7] The Galeana family had more direct grievances: like other farmers on the Pacific coastal lowlands, their antagonism towards Spanish cotton merchants was an incentive to join the insurgent cause.[8]

Morelos's ability to attract such people showed his skills as a leader. His display of military prowess—helped perhaps by his charisma as a priest—helped him to win respect from the leaders of insurgent bands, and he was able to insinuate himself into local power structures and thereby sustain popular recruitment. Morelos's capacity to organize his fighters ensured, too, that he wielded an increasingly effective instrument of war. Rather than aiming to overwhelm the enemy by weight of numbers as Hidalgo had done, Morelos trained his men carefully and imposed strict discipline.

This approach was shaped partly by the terrain within which he operated, where the density of population was much lower than on Mexico's central plateau and large forces thus more difficult to assemble and sustain. But it also reflected Morelos's good political sense; he wanted broad support for his cause and, by avoiding the anarchic behavior attendant on Hidalgo's mass mobilizations, aimed to win over the propertied and educated creoles who were unnerved by plebeian violence. Morelos grasped that, to achieve his political goals, he needed more than mass uprising or guerrilla war by insurgent bands; he saw that a revolutionary army was required both to defeat royalist armies and to nurture an embryonic alternative to the existing government, with its own identity, political goals, and administration.[9] He therefore did not limit his military operations merely to raids against the enemy, but he embarked on what military historians call a "combat strategy" designed to take and hold territory and to seek battle with the enemy, using a fast-moving force of 2–3,000 men, his preferred instrument of war.[10]

Morelos in Central Mexico

To advance these aims, Morelos launched a second campaign in November 1811, aimed at extending northwards from Chilapa and the tierra caliente in order to fight for territory in the populous and prosperous regions south of Mexico City. He started with offensives on three related fronts: Morelos himself took about 2,000 men towards the city of Puebla, Miguel Bravo went to support Rayón at Zitácuaro, and Galeana took the rebellion south, in the direction of Oaxaca. The key aims were to bring other regions into the rebellion and create blocks of rebel territory from which to threaten the capital. The first priority was to take the city of Puebla, at the heart of government and economic life in one of the viceroyalty's richest agricultural areas. Indeed, Morelos's second campaign is best understood as a "struggle for Puebla" for, although insurgents continued to fight elsewhere, the Intendancy of Puebla became the main theater of war during 1811–12, where both sides invested their main effort and greatest resources.[11]

The campaign started well for the rebels. On December 10, 1811, Morelos employed his army of some 2,600 men to take the town of Izúcar. This not only brought fresh recruits to the rebellion—including Father Mariano Matamoros, soon one of Morelos's leading commanders—but also opened the way north towards the city of Puebla. Puebla was very vulnerable because its authorities had done little to protect it. Even after Colonel Ciriaco de Llano took frantic measures to strengthen the city's defenses, the royalist position was still weak against Morelos's larger forces. However, Llano did enough to discourage Morelos by blocking the approach to the city at Atlixco, where he prepared a defensive position to resist assault by the insurgents. The expected battle at Atlixco did not take place, however, as Morelos preferred not to do battle. Instead, he turned away from Puebla and moved west to the town of Cuautla, which he took on December 26, 1811.

This was a critical decision. By diverting from Puebla at a time when its defenses were weak, Morelos missed an opportunity to take one of the viceroyalty's leading cities and turn it into a base for a revolutionary government. The reasoning behind this decision—regarded by some historians as a mistake of the first order—is not entirely clear. Morelos said that he fell back to defend insurgent areas that were threatened by royalist attack; his collaborator Carlos María Bustamante glossed this by stating that Morelos went to support Rayón's forces at Zitácuaro, which was about to come under attack from Calleja and the Army of the Center.[12] As Zitácuaro was the headquarters of the insurgents' Supreme Junta, its defense was important. But if Morelos intended to deflect assault from the city, his maneuvers were ineffectual. On January 2, 1812, Calleja took Zitácuaro and a few days later razed it to the ground. Morelos's chances of a successful attack on Puebla had, it seems, been sacrificed for nothing.

The sack of Zitácuaro was a setback for the insurgents, as it forced the putative revolutionary government to flee and cost Rayón the credibility he needed to build a unified movement. Nonetheless, it was not an irredeemable defeat, militarily or politically. Rebel bands were very active in the province of Tlaxcala, and although their assault against the city of Tlaxcala failed on January 2, 1812, they continued to control most of the province. Other rebels were meanwhile on the offensive to the southeast of the city of Puebla, at Tepeaca, and to the north, at Huejotzingo. And, while the insurgents still threatened Puebla with encirclement, Morelos and Galeana opened a new front against Mexico City. In late January, they defeated Colonel Porlier at Tenancingo, and Morelos moved closer to Mexico City by taking Cuernavaca on February 4, 1812. This forced Calleja to concentrate on shoring up the capital's defenses rather than reinforcing Puebla. He pushed Morelos back from Cuernavaca, but the insurgents continued with a plan to cut off the capital from neighboring regions. Morelos and Rayón sought to stir up an insurgency east of the capital, in the Llanos de Apan, and Morelos took up a fixed position at Cuautla.[13] His plan, according to royalist spies, was to use Cuautla as a base from which to return to the offensive against Atlixco and Puebla while also blocking food supplies to Mexico City.[14]

The viceregal government faced a difficult military position in early 1812. Morelos was little more than 50 miles south of the capital, with an experienced fighting force of some 3,000 men, and, according to Viceroy Venegas, Morelos had become the "guiding genius" of an insurgency that represented a growing threat. In early February, Venegas reported that the insurgency was spreading on all sides, compromising vital routes for trade and communications and setting up bases (at Izúcar and Cuautla) that threatened to isolate Puebla from the capital and cut trade and communications with the south. Aware that an encirclement of the capital could be fatal, he responded with an aggressive combat strategy. Venegas ordered attacks on Izúcar and Cuautla in the hope that, once defeated, the insurgent forces would be forced to turn southwards, where they could be pursued and finished off by the royalist division that was defending Puebla.[15] This plan set the stage for the first great confrontation between Calleja and Morelos, as the main royalist and insurgent forces came into collision at Cuautla.

The battle for Cuautla came at a critical moment. In March 1812, the dire state of the silver mining industry provoked an intense debate in the capital's influential Mining Tribunal over a proposal that the viceroy should be encouraged to enter into peace talks with the rebels.[16] The proposal was rejected—probably because the offensive on Cuautla had just begun—but it shows that influential voices were ready to call for a political solution. The outcome of Cuautla was therefore going to be critically important to the government. Both sides brought substantial forces and artillery into the field and prepared to risk a decisive battle. For Venegas, victory was essential to show that the insurgents were not a serious military force capable of defeating a professional royalist army and that a military solution to the insurgency was therefore possible.

The Battle for Cuautla

The confrontation at Cuautla was on a different dimension from other military operations at the time, both in duration and scale.[17] The royalist campaign began with twin operations against Izúcar and Cuautla, to which the viceroy assigned some 3,000 men. At first, about half were assigned to the newly formed Army of the South under Ciriaco de Llano and sent against Izúcar; the other half went with Calleja to attack Cuautla. Later, Llano joined forces with Calleja in the siege of Cuautla.

The precise size of Morelos's force is not known; he may have had as many as 3,000 men of his own forces and when preparing for the first royalist attack, added another 500 cavalry and about 1,000 Indians from neighboring villages. These were supplemented during the siege by reinforcements, which increased his numbers to an overall total of about 5,500, possibly more. A higher figure came from the captured North American Nicolas Cole, who in mid-March, just a few weeks into the siege, told his royalist interrogators that Morelos had "about eight thousand men between blacks, Indians and boys, about two thousand muskets [and] that the blacks from the coast were the bravest and the rest cowards." While Cole's estimate inflates the size of Morelos's force, his comment on the quality of the men shows that quantity was not necessarily an advantage. His portrait of the besieged town shows, nonetheless, that its defense was well-organized. Cole revealed that the plaza and streets of the town were guarded with cannon, as was the Hacienda de Buenavista, an important source of food and forage on the southern side of the city. He also reported that the rebels were well-supplied with basic foods and ammunition and were not intimidated by the royalist artillery bombardments.[18]

The Cuautla siege seems initially to have inflicted most damage on the insurgents. Interrogations of those who were captured by, or deserted to, the royalist side show that their position deteriorated throughout March and April 1811, as food stocks ran down, water supplies dried up, forage for animals all but vanished, and casualties from royalist artillery bombardments increased. However, these testimonies also reflected the resilience of Morelos's forces. In late March, for example, deserters from Cuautla agreed that, although supplies of all kinds were very low, the spirit of resistance was strong; the blacks and mulattos had firearms and, supplemented by many men with slings and lances, were ready to repel any attempt at entry by the royalist army.[19] Other testimonies taken in late March give a similar picture of a city subject to deepening hardship, but where rebels with about 2,000 firearms, 30 artillery pieces, and plentiful munitions remained ready to resist attack. Indeed, it was said that they were waiting for reinforcements from Izúcar in order to break out of Cuautla against the besieging royalist army.[20]

Here, then, was an insurgent force that was very different from those that had followed Hidalgo. While it no doubt included many reluctant recruits, such as Cuautla townsmen pressed into service and peasants forcibly recruited from local villages, Morelos's army had a strong core of 2,000–3,000 men, who were well armed and committed to the insurgent cause. We get a glimpse of this force from the memoir of Lucas Alamán:

> This was not now a matter of a rabble of undisciplined and unarmed Indians on foot, nor of rustics on horseback who were easy to scare with artillery fire and whose leaders gave the example of flight even before combat began. Except for a few people from the environs of Cuautla, the rest were blacks and mulattos from the coast, men of strength and resolve, armed with guns and skilled in their use, emboldened by an almost uninterrupted series of successes, and led by men of honor and heart, such as the Bravos and Galianas.[21]

With such men, Morelos was able to conduct a campaign that drained royalist resources. Cuautla offered a good defensive position; its location made it difficult for an enemy to attack under cover, and the rebels made adroit use of fortifications, trenches, and careful positioning for their 30 artillery pieces. This reduced Calleja's scope for effective use of the artillery and cavalry contingents that were the main strength of his army and forced him to rely on infantry columns in his first attack on the city on February 19, 1812. After six hours of intense fighting, the rebels repelled these forces with heavy fire and, it seems, confirmed Morelos's decision to take a stand at Cuautla. At the same time, the demonstration of rebel strength convinced Calleja that it was essential to take the town. To fail to do so, he informed the viceroy, would be to persuade the enemy that they should set up fortifications in strategic places and use them as bases for recruiting, intercepting trade and communications, attacking villages and haciendas, and confronting royalist forces. In short, it would give the insurrection a new and unwelcome vigor. Hence Cuautla had to be demolished and the rebels of the area buried with it, so that the insurgent leaders would never again dare to use fortified towns as a stratagem of war.[22]

Viceroy Venegas accepted Calleja's assessment of Cuautla's strategic importance and duly diverted Llano's forces from Izúcar into the operation against Cuautla. This removed pressure on the insurgents at Izúcar, who had managed to fight off attacks from Llano's forces on February 23–24, 1811, but at the expense of Morelos at Cuautla, where the royalists now settled down for a lengthy siege. Viceroy Venegas agreed with Calleja that "to avoid as far as possible bloodshed and army losses and to reconcile this essential measure with the extermination of the enemy, we must prefer a siege . . . to an assault," at least until there were signs that an attack could achieve a sure success with few costs.[23]

When Llano arrived in late February, the addition of 1,500 to 2,000 men complicated Calleja's logistics, as he now had larger forces to feed, but allowed him to tighten the blockade and to pursue classic siege tactics. On March 10, he began a four-day artillery bombardment, while also trying to cut off the town's water supply. Neither tactic was decisive, and the combatants settled into a prolonged struggle in the area around the town, with frequent skirmishes over fortified positions, access to water, and supply lines. Calleja occasionally ordered actions against insurgent positions on the outskirts of the town, sometimes involving hundreds of men, and had to maintain permanent vigilance to protect his own supply lines against insurgent horsemen. His basic strategy was, however, that of the simple siege: he aimed to starve Morelos's forces into submission.

Calleja's tactics cost him dear, for the defenders of Cuautla were not easily dislodged. Indeed, as the siege moved into late April, Calleja expressed reluctant admiration for their fortitude, stating that, had they been fighting in a just cause, they might have deserved a distinguished place in history. He observed that despite their desperate position, "they show good cheer in all circumstances, bury their dead on their return from their frequent sallies, with battle cries, dances and drunkenness whatever the outcome, [and] with pain of death on whomsoever speaks of misfortunes or surrender." The priest Morelos was, Calleja added, able to beguile them, like "a second Mohammed, who promises bodily resurrection for his happy Muslims, followed by Paradise with the gratification of all the passions."[24]

This intriguing comparison shows the powerful links between religion and politics in the contemporary mind. Calleja's parallel between Morelos and Mohammed was clearly intended both to denigrate the insurgents by relegating Morelos to the role of a religious outcast, while also appropriating an heroic myth of Spanish history for the royalist cause. In Calleja's formulation, Morelos was the heretic who had broken faith with true religion, while the royalists were akin to Christian Spaniards fighting against the Moors and thus firmly situated in the crusading tradition.[25]

The identification of insurgency and Islam might also have been a means to neutralize the claim to Christian inspiration by the rebel camp, particularly when it was discovered that Morelos's men claimed that the priest had with him a miraculous child, known as the *adivino*, who had the power to raise insurgent soldiers from the dead after three days. The story had surfaced when a captured Indian, facing execution as a rebel, begged that his body be sent back to Cuautla after his execution, apparently so that he might have a chance of resurrection.[26] Clearly, the struggle of royalists and insurgents was fought on more than one plane, and the claims of rebel priests to special powers may well have provided an important source of inspiration to their followers.[27]

While the religious meanings with which both sides invested their struggle no doubt played a vital role in justifying their causes and sustaining soldiers' morale, the contest at Cuaulta was decided by material factors. By late April, the town's food supplies were exhausted, deaths and desertions were increasing, and the rebels had to try to break the blockade. Morelos began by sending out a force of over 100 horsemen on the night of April 21 in the hope that they could rally rebel bands outside Cuautla and lift the siege. He then launched his main attack a week later, throwing thousands of men into action on April 27 in order to clear a way for supplies into the town. The combined attack of rebel forces was repulsed on various fronts, however, and Calleja calculated enemy losses at 800–1,000 men.[28] Morelos's options now narrowed dramatically. Conditions were bad for the besiegers, too, as they were whittled away by disease; some 800 were hospitalized at the end of April, and the numbers of deaths were rising by the week. But conditions for those besieged inside Cuaulta were much worse. The townspeople and the rebel garrison suffered a rising death toll from malnutrition and disease and were reduced to scavenging like animals. Knowing of the terrible conditions inside the town, Calleja was convinced that so long as he husbanded his resources and the rains were delayed, he would triumph. Morelos, meanwhile, came to the conclusion that escape was his only option. Although pardon was possible under the terms offered by the Cortes of Cádiz, Morelos expected no mercy for himself or his men in a conflict where prisoners were routinely executed. Rather than remain trapped in Cuautla, he evacuated the town under cover of darkness on May 2, 1812.

According to royalist sources, Morelos's retreat from Cuautla involved heavy insurgent losses. Escape was certainly difficult, given that Calleja expected such a move and had his troops on full alert. It seems that Morelos managed to cross the river undetected until his men clashed with royalist pickets; then the alarm went up and fighting broke out. Morelos had prepared to fight his way out. He had placed his best infantry in the vanguard, followed by a couple of hundred horsemen; his main force, armed with lances and slings, followed, together with a large body of people of all ages and both sexes; the rear of the column was covered by some small artillery pieces. Calleja sent his main cavalry force in hot pursuit, and it soon rode down the rebel force, cutting through to their advance guard and almost taking Morelos himself. Casualties were considerable. Eyewitnesses reported that the roads taken by the insurgents were strewn with dead and dying, as royalist soldiers hacked their way to the front of the column, killing indiscriminately. Morelos succeeded in reaching Izúcar, however, and there regrouped the forces that survived the retreat. Meanwhile, the Army of the Center returned to Mexico City, where Calleja retired from command, leaving his army under another officer.

The significance of the battle for Cuautla was unclear at the time. Not surprisingly, the loyalists claimed it as a victory. For Venegas and Calleja, it had contributed to their one overriding goal: the survival of the royalist cause. However, Calleja had expended a great military effort at enormous financial cost without managing to eliminate Morelos and his forces. He was consequently criticized, even ridiculed, in Mexico City, and the Army of the Center disbanded.[29] Morelos, on the other hand, emerged bloodied but unbowed. Although his losses were considerable, he had tied Calleja down, damaged royalist arms and morale, and, by absorbing the attention of the main royalist army, allowed rebel leaders to strike at targets elsewhere.

Provincial Insurgencies

While Calleja was engaged in a static war with Morelos at Cuautla, insurgent leaders conducted raids against royalist towns, communications, and supply lines. The damage they inflicted was considerable and affected many regions. Mexico City's route to the sea was a particularly sensitive target. During the first half of 1812, insurgents closed the road from the capital to Veracruz and, though forced back by a military expedition from Mexico City, quickly retook it once the royalist troops had passed. By July 1812, the Mexico City-Querétaro road was also closed; in August 1812, a force of 600 men led by Nicolás Bravo, one of Morelos's commanders, destroyed a royalist force sent to reopen the Veracruz road and closed it to all but small armed convoys for many months.[30] Serious insurgent offensives also took place in the mountains north of Puebla, where Juan Francisco Osorno and others took place a force of some 2,000 horsemen plus many Indians against the town of Huamantla and by taking the town acquired a commanding position on the trade route to Veracruz. Other actions in this area did not bring comparable gains, but they tied down royalist troops and showed that the capital had little control in the region.[31]

By the end of 1812, most of the coastal region north of Veracruz and the sierras behind the Gulf coast were also in the hands of insurgents. This region (the Huasteca) was less strategically important, since it had a relatively small, scattered population of some 70,000 people and was poorly connected to the rest of Mexico; its insurgency was essentially a network of village rebellions led by local leaders, who, though nominally under the orders of the caudillo José Francisco Osorno, were concerned almost exclusively with village matters.[32] Nonetheless, the spread of the insurgency to this area shows the extent to which rebellion engulfed substantial areas on the periphery as well as challenging for control of core cities and regions.

Insurgents were active further north too, especially in the vital mining zone of Guanajuato. In November 1811–May 1812, the guerrilla chieftain Albino García made repeated attacks on the city of Guanajuato, which he briefly seized on two occasions, while also attacking and sometimes sacking neighboring towns held by royalists. In his main attacks, he mustered as many as 5,000 to 6,000 men and was a major threat to Spanish control of the region until his capture and execution in June 1812. Even then, the threat did not recede: later in 1812 and early in 1813, there were further attacks on Guanajuato.[33]

Although 1812 was a bad year for the royalists, the government had survived fighting on several fronts and still held the key regions of the central plateau. At the same time, the insurgents were still divided and unable to coordinate their activities. Morelos appealed to rebel leaders for reinforcement during the siege at Cuautla, but they preferred to pursue their own plans and, by failing to conduct joint operations, missed the chance to attack the viceregal government at one of its most vulnerable moments.[34] The struggle at Cuautla was thus an important moment in the war. For the royalists, it had stopped an insurgent offensive in a key area, dispersed Morelos's forces, and deprived him of the base from which he might have coordinated insurgency in the hinterlands of Mexico City and Puebla. But Cuautla also had some positive results for Morelos. He had lured Calleja to a battlefield of his choosing, proved that he could withstand an assault by the royalist army—something that Hidalgo had never achieved—and had for months held the royalists to a draw. These months also saw Morelos's emergence as a primary leader among the insurgents. With his operations near Puebla and Mexico City, he became the nearest and greatest threat to the viceregal regime at a time when social and political conditions in Mexico City were aggravating its difficulties. His activities from mid-1812 therefore merit close attention.

Morelos's Third Campaign

After Cuautla, Morelos returned to the offensive with a third military campaign, starting in June 1812. His primary intention was to renew the attack on the heart of New Spain, in Puebla and Mexico City. As a preliminary, he sought to secure his position to the south; he reinforced the insurgent town of Huajuapan on the mountainous borders between the provinces of Puebla and Oaxaca, and then he moved west against Tehuacán, which he took on August 10, 1812, with some 3,500 men. The capture of Tehuacán achieved a strategic advantage because it commanded the major routes from Puebla to Oaxaca and through Orizaba to Veracruz. The question was how best to exploit it.

Morelos had several possible choices. He could move directly against Puebla or divert his forces towards the Caribbean coast, against the port of Veracruz; alternatively, he might go south into the Intendancy of Oaxaca. His initial instinct was to link up with the insurgents surrounding Veracruz, probably as a preliminary to moving against Puebla. To do so, he advanced from Tehuacán towards the coast, but when faced with royalist forces outside Orizaba in late October, he fell back on Tehuacán. His royalist adversaries had meanwhile improved their position at Puebla. Ciriaco de Llano, the Spanish officer in command of its defense, had broken through the insurgent cordon around Veracruz and extracted a force of Spanish regulars, and on returning to Puebla, he commenced an offensive against Tehuacán and Izúcar. Confronted by this royalist army, Morelos again responded cautiously. Rather than do battle, he evacuated these towns and left the royalists to recover their control over the Puebla region. Thus, at the end of 1812, Ciriaco de Llano had effectively won the battle for Puebla. By preventing the insurgents from encircling and taking the city, he stopped Morelos from turning Puebla into a center for revolutionary operations and the seat of a provisional government that might challenge the capital from close range.

This was a setback for Marelos, but was compensated by an advance elsewhere. Indeed, Morelos's retreat was tactical, allowing him to strike at a point where royalist forces were weaker. He shifted military operations southwards, and on November 25, 1812, led a force of some 5,000 men in an attack on the city of Oaxaca. The capture of Oaxaca on December 4 seemed to give Morelos what he had been seeking—namely, a provincial capital in which to install a revolutionary government and a resource base to finance the cause. It was, he told Rayón, "the first capital which we have taken which has a unity of its own" and would, he affirmed, "serve as a basis for the conquest of the whole kingdom."[35] However, the establishment of a revolutionary base at Oaxaca had some drawbacks, which Morelos had to remedy. First, the movement southwards took Morelos away from the core area of the viceroyalty in Mexico's central valleys, and second, it removed his main forces from easy contact with the insurgents who continued to hinder contact between the capital and Veracruz, the viceroyalty's main link to Europe.[36] This might explain why Morelos did not remain long at Oaxaca nor turn it into a permanent base for an alternative government. Instead, in January 1813, he returned to a terrain with which he was more familiar, moving southwest to attack the Spanish fortress at Acapulco and to extend his control over the huge coastal zone that reached from the Pacific up into Michoacán.

The implications of Morelos's successes in late 1812 were not lost on the royalist government. Indeed, a sample of Calleja's correspondence with the minister of war suggests that when Calleja replaced Venegas as viceroy on March 4, 1813, he believed that the central regions of the viceroyalty were in great danger. He informed the minister that he found a country "destroyed by thirty months of an impolitic and disastrous revolution," which had undermined the wealthy, deepened divisions between Europeans and Americans, perverted public opinion, seduced an ignorant population, paralyzed agriculture, industry and commerce, and exhausted the treasury.[37] The royalist military position was also weak. In the center and south, the army was thinly spread over a huge area, divided into small detachments, which did little damage to the enemy, had scant communication among themselves, and were surrounded by numerous insurgent bands; its soldiers were poorly clothed and armed and so badly paid that even the troops sent from Spain were deserting.

Morelos, by contrast, was doing well in the south. Calleja believed he had an army of 14–16,000 men and was maneuvering for a strike on Puebla. The royalist situation north of Mexico City was also bad. Rayón and his Junta Nacional de América were positioned with a respectable force between the capital and Querétaro, blocking trade and communications and besieging important towns. Meanwhile, leaders such as Liceaga, Verduzco, Cos, Velasco, and many others of lesser rank were operating throughout the provinces of Valladolid, Querétaro, Celaya, Guanajuato, and others, "burning and sacking towns, killing honorable people, and recruiting those greedy for robbery and pillage." The siege of Veracruz had been lifted, but the capital's communication with the coast was still very difficult, as was its commerce and communication with the interior. The sole consolation was that the northern provinces of San Luis Potosí, Guadalajara, Zacatecas, and the broad northern interior were at peace, though even in the distant north there was some danger. There, the rebel Bernardo Gutiérrez had joined with a group of adventurers from the State of Louisiana to threaten Texas, invading the frontier at Nagodoches.[38]

To confront the most serious dangers at the heart of Mexico, Calleja proposed a new military strategy and inaugurated a fresh phase in military policy, enlarging the army and focusing on the threat from Morelos. His first move was to concentrate the royalist army's divisions in the province of Puebla—which he described as "the principal theater of war"—under a single command. The Conde de Castro Terreno was put in charge of this Army of the South. His mission was to contain Morelos and fight him wherever he appeared, to secure the tobacco revenues produced by Orizaba and Córdoba, and to protect the convoys between Mexico City and Veracruz. Calleja proposed a similar plan for the north, establishing an Army of the North with headquarters in Querétaro or Guanajuato under a single commander, who was tasked with keeping open trade with the silver mining regions, dislodging the forces of Rayón and other insurgent leaders, and securing the sources of royal revenue vital for paying for the war.[39]

Calleja had very slight success with his strategy in the short term. At the end of May 1813, he reported gloomily about the difficulties of fighting a war while implementing the liberal political reforms brought by the new Constitution of Cádiz, complaining about his extreme financial problems, and the reluctance of the wealthy to provide funds. There were some bright spots: Villagrán and his cohorts had been forced from Zimapán and Huichapan, Rayón from Tlalpujahua, and Osorno from Zacatlán, while Verduzco and Liceaga had also suffered defeats in the province of Valladolid. These were, however, not necessarily permanent gains, and Calleja understood that they could be reversed as long as Morelos remained active. Indeed, in mid-1813, he believed that Morelos planned to renew his attack on the center; rebel correspondence intercepted by the royalists indicated that, after enlarging his forces with blacks recruited on the Pacific coast, Morelos intended to advance on the capital via Izúcar and Cuernavaca while joining with Rayón, Villagrán, and Osorno to encircle the city.[40]

In fact, while Viceroy Calleja prepared for an attack on the center, Morelos was engaged in a siege on Acapulco that lasted for six months, from mid-April until the starving garrison finally capitulated on August 20, 1813. This campaign on the Pacific coast had significant repercussions, both military and political. It delivered an important military victory to the insurgents' cause. Morelos was now able to control the city and fortress that had defeated him two years earlier, and with this came some strategic advantages. In military terms, the capture of Acapulco eradicated the sole stronghold of royalist resistance in the Pacific lowlands and allowed Morelos to consolidate his control over a vast region that stretched southwards down the Pacific shoreline from the Intendancy of Guadalajara to the Isthmus of Tehuantepec, while reaching into the interior to embrace Oaxaca, a key city in the Mexican south, and still potentially threatening Puebla, a strategic city on the central plateau. The political consequences were equally significant. With this victory, Morelos had secured a position of primus inter pares among the insurgent leaders, and he sought to turn his military triumphs to political advantage; in September 1813, he convoked a national congress at Chilpancingo with the intention of unifying political and military opposition to the Spanish regime. In short, during 1813, Morelos not only recovered from his setback at Cuautla but had done much to strengthen the insurgent position against the viceregal regime.

The Climax of the Insurgency

By the end of 1813, it was clear that Morelos was the single most dangerous threat to the viceregal regime, a fact fully recognized by Viceroy Calleja even before the fall of Acapulco. On the eve of the Congress of Chilpancingo, Calleja described Morelos as "the body and soul of the whole insurrection," who might soon be formally elevated to the position of its supreme leader. To prevent this, Calleja aimed to eliminate Morelos by concentrating forces against him. The viceroy called for the muster of two divisions of the greatest strength and best possible leadership to attack Morelos wherever he might be found and to take Oaxaca, his capital. Immediate action was imperative, Calleja insisted, in order to take advantage of Morelos's current preoccupation with "preparing and assuring the sovereignty that is now within his reach."[41]

The viceroy's chances of defeating Morelos did not, however, look any better in 1813 than they had seemed the previous year. On the one hand, royalist war-making capacity was under great strain, as the government was caught between collapsing revenues and rising military costs, while disruption of trade and production was shrinking the economy of the Mexican heartlands.[42] The capital was particularly hard hit; it was suffering spiraling food prices, rising unemployment, and, to make matters much worse, from April 1813, it was hit by a typhoid epidemic that caused heavy mortality and, together with rising crime and the collapse of urban services, deeply damaged the city's social fabric.[43] At the same time, the introduction of the Constitution of Cádiz in September 1812 created conditions that, according to Venegas and Calleja, did nothing to help the royalist cause. They believed that its liberal measures damaged the security of the realm, and they accordingly obstructed freedom of the press, free elections, and any civil liberties that stood in the way of counterinsurgency.[44] On the other hand, Morelos's stature as a military commander and his support among prominent creoles in Mexico City was growing, and his convocation of an insurgent congress promised to harness other rebel leaders to a shared strategy. Certainly this was Morelos's purpose when he took up residence in Chilpancingo, and having assured his dominance in the south and southwest, he seemed to be well-placed to attain it.

Morelos's position was not without its flaws, for his Acapulco campaign incurred opportunity costs. He eventually captured the royalist stronghold, but in so doing, he had diverted force from more important areas. The move southwards took him away from the central plateau, lifted the insurgent threat against Veracruz and Orizaba, and gave the royalist army time to recoup territory in the Puebla region and to regroup, thereby exposing Oaxaca to a future attack. Some historians therefore conclude that the six-month-long siege may have been a serious strategic error.[45]

Was the time spent in the siege of Acapulco wasted? Did it fatally distract Morelos from applying pressure against royalist cities in the more strategic arena of the central plateau and Gulf coast? It is difficult to come to a clear conclusion on this issue, partly because we know little about Morelos's thinking about strategy and tactics. However, as Morelos was a thoughtful commander, it seems likely that his Acapulco campaign was the start of a considered strategy for refocusing the insurgent war by recouping energy in the south, then turning back against the royalists' main armies in the center. It also displays the characteristics of what has become a classic guerrilla strategy—namely, the long game of wearing down enemy military strength by evading major engagements, forcing the enemy to use up resources in fruitless pursuits, and striking only where success was assured, while slowly building and widening political support. Seen from this perspective, it is not obvious that Morelos's move back to the Pacific coast was an error. It enabled him to remove the last vestiges of government power in the great coastal region, and, having secured Acapulco, gave him time to consolidate his strength and to focus on building his political influence. It also allowed him to avoid battle with Calleja's army, which had so far shown itself superior, and thus to conserve his forces for battle on an occasion of his choice.

During the six months after the capture of Acapulco, Morelos remained at Chilpancingo. While there, in a setting closer to the Mexican heartlands than either Acapulco or Oaxaca, he carried out an essential political task: the organization of a new political assembly to represent the insurgent cause. This was an important project, for, by convoking a national congress, Morelos was putting down the foundations of a revolutionary government that could seek recognition at home and abroad. As an assembly of provincial representatives elected by the parishes of insurgent areas, the congress would embody the sovereignty of the people and choose an executive to act in its name; it would also provide a body that could negotiate with other governments, vital at a time when the insurgents looked to the British and the Americans to supply aid and recognition.

In the event, the congress did not fulfill Morelos's expectations. The turnout of deputies for the inauguration of congress on September 14, 1813, was disappointingly small and could not provide Morelos with the broad mandate he wanted; nonetheless, he proceeded to install the congress and drove his political plans forward. He insisted that the new government be strong and centralized; he wanted its executive to be chosen from the principal military leaders and selected this role for himself by accepting the position of commander in chief. He was also unequivocal about relations with Spain. On November 6, 1813, he oversaw the declaration of independence from "the arrogance and tyranny of Spain, with her extraordinary Cortes, which is so lacking in reason."[46] Thus, Morelos briskly renounced Ferdinand VII and openly espoused independence.

Did the establishment of a government for an independent Mexico enhance the prospects of an insurgent overthrow of the viceregal regime? Morelos's plan was reasonable; he had to give a clearer political identity and more coherent organization to the insurgent cause in the political and propaganda war against the Spanish regime, especially since the introduction of the Cádiz Constitution. Now that Spain had made serious concessions to Americans, allowing them representation in an imperial parliament and a greater degree of participation in local and regional government, the insurgent leadership had to raise the political stakes, shifting towards a position that could compete with the Spanish constitutionalists. However, while Morelos trumpeted independence, it was harder to turn rhetoric into reality, particularly on the military front.

The main task was, as always, to destroy the military power of the royalist regime and thus force its surrender, a goal that would require a considerable concentration of force. However, in the later months of 1813, the insurgents did not come close to achieving this goal. Their problem was that although royalist forces had lost at Oaxaca and Acapulco, Calleja's armies made significant gains in their counterinsurgency campaigns of late 1812 and 1813. When the insurgent caudillo Sixto Verduzco brought together a force of about 6,000 to attack Valladolid in January 1813, he was repelled with heavy losses. In April, the royalist commander Agustín de Iturbide defeated Ignacio Rayón at Salvatierra and captured his base at Tlalpujahua. In June, Iturbide killed Albino García, the leading insurgent leader in the Guanajuato area.[47] In late June, the viceroy also reported the capture of Julián Villagrán, whose clan dominated the region around Huichapan.[48]

The balance had not, however, tipped entirely in the royalists' favor, since the insurgents were still operating in several regions and using guerrilla tactics to strike military blows and disrupt social and economic life. Indeed, their impact was felt very close to Mexico City, in the Llanos de Apan. There, close enough to the capital to threaten its food supplies, the insurgent movement had gathered considerable strength and controlled many of the region's villages and most of its haciendas and farms.[49]

While the military contest remained in the balance, both sides faced critical tests. Morelos took the initiative by seeking to carry the fight back into the core of the viceroyalty. In November 1813, he left Chilpancingo and marched on Valladolid, the city that been the cradle of Hidalgo's rebellion. His aim was clear: to establish a base in royalist territory and to take up the insurgent challenge back towards the Mexican heartlands. And with an army of over 6,000 men and some 30 cannon to attack a garrison of only 800 royalist troops, Morelos seemed well-equipped to succeed. Confidence in a quick win was shattered, however, when the insurgent attack was interrupted by the arrival of substantial contingents from the royalist army. At the moment that Morelos's men made their first assault on the city, two veteran royalist officers, Ciriaco de Llano and Agustín de Iturbide, arrived with some 3,000 royalist reinforcements and joined the garrison's resistance to the insurgent attack. Taken by surprise, Morelos's troops broke and ran.

The experience of unexpected and bloody defeat in their first major encounter since Acapulco was a trauma from which Morelos and his insurgents never fully recovered. Although Morelos quickly adopted a fresh plan of attack, he was forestalled by another surprise assault from Iturbide and was again forced to retreat. His subsequent attempt at an orderly withdrawal to Puruarán, a hacienda in Valladolid's hinterland, was also scuppered by Iturbide and Llano; they overtook him and on January 5, 1814, inflicted heavy losses in battle. Morelos escaped with his life but without his forces or his reputation. He was subsequently unable to muster more than one in six of the men he had started with, and his defeat brought discredit in the congress that had so recently acclaimed him. Indeed, the congress was itself forced into flight by an advancing royalist army and, under intense pressure, became divided and ineffectual. Morelos's political achievement at the Congress at Chilpancingo was now erased by his army's failures, and the balance of military power shifted away from the insurgents.

Morelos's defeat not only diminished the independents' army but also undermined their political movement. On reuniting with Congress at Tlacotepec in February 1814, Morelos was deposed from the military high command and marginalized from the leadership. Ordered south to sack Acapulco before it fell into royalist hands, he carried out this task and then continued to maraud along the coast north of Acapulco, exacting reprisals in revenge for his losses. The remaining members of congress meanwhile retired to Apatzingán and, in an effort to revive the rebellion, proclaimed Mexico's first constitution on October 22, 1814. By now, however, the insurgent cause looked increasingly desperate: Oaxaca had fallen to the royalists without a struggle, the insurgent leaders of the center/north were being culled by royalist offensives and pardons, and the royalist government was given a new lease of life by Ferdinand VII's restoration in March 1814, following the end of the Peninsular War.

The struggle was not yet over, but the end was at hand. Under mounting pressure from the successful royalist generals in Mexico, the insurgency continued to shrink into an uncoordinated and increasingly discredited residue of the rebellion, which had previously presented such a serious threat. The congress persisted, moving from place to place to evade pursuing royalist forces, but it could not escape discovery indefinitely. In November 1815, a Spanish force came upon the itinerant insurgent government while it was travelling under an escort led by Morelos and, though the congress escaped in the ensuing mêlée, Morelos himself was captured and taken away for trial.

Responsibility for this eclipse may be attributed partly to the insurgent leadership itself. Morelos, for example, can be blamed for failing to make the key contribution needed from the insurgency's principal leader—namely, to forge a revolutionary army that was capable of taking and holding territory, supporting a revolutionary administration, and creating a credible political alternative. But this is to misapportion blame. Morelos not only put the viceregal government under continuous pressure but his combinations of military campaigns and political initiatives ensured that the insurgents presented a real challenge to Spain's monopoly of power. The fact that he was unable to take Mexico City or to create an alternative government with clear chances of success was not his responsibility alone. As we have seen, the "insurgency" was never a single movement; it was, rather, a series of local rebellions following courses that sometimes crossed but never fused into a single stream. This diversity weakened the cause espoused by the major political leaders of the insurgency. The many smaller leaders of rebellion—the *cabecillas* as they were known by the authorities—derived their authority from local connections, local knowledge, and a localized constituency of support, and their concern with parochial issues and personal interests had far greater meaning than the big "national" issues espoused by the movement's largely creole directorate. Such leaders and their followers were invariably unwilling to move beyond the areas that they knew and in which they were known; indeed, some actively opposed attempts to create coordinated campaigns under a united, "national" leadership and pursued only their own goals, while others were brigands for whom war became a way of life.[50] Morelos, whose military achievements made him the plausible leader of a larger movement, was thus impeded in his efforts to mount concerted military actions capable of defeating royalist armies in battle or holding major cities for any length of time.

Calleja and Counterinsurgency

The fragmented character of the insurgency was not the sole reason why Morelos and the insurgents were unable to overcome the viceregal government. If insurgent leaders remained as far from achieving independence in 1815 as they had been four years earlier, this was mainly because many Mexicans still saw them as a violent threat to social order rather than a reasonable political alternative. The political reforms introduced by the 1812 Constitution of Cádiz had also probably strengthened support for the Spanish regime, despite problems of implementation. While many Mexicans embraced the new system, confident that it promised greater autonomy, the viceroys and audiencia judges did all they could to oppose it. Indeed, it has been argued that the high-level resistance to reform—by officials who insisted that elections and freedom of the press would undermine the war effort—undermined confidence in Spanish rule.[51] On balance, however, it is likely that the reforms helped to limit support for the insurgents because they promised—and to some extent delivered—the prospect of greater self-government by Mexicans, via elections to the Cortes, provincial deputations, and elective municipal governments. Certainly, there is little evidence that the new constitution inhibited the royalist military effort or gave the insurgents a more favorable political climate in which to operate.

However, while the reforms set in motion by the Cádiz Constitution might have curbed the growth of support for the insurgency, they certainly did not end it. For the insurgents, Spanish rule remained illegitimate, and the settlement offered by the new Constitution did not address, nor could it resolve, their demands for independence. Fighting therefore continued in spite of the concessions offered by the Cádiz Constitution, and the future of Mexico still hinged on the outcome of the internal war. In short, the royalist military effort was crucial to assuring the future of Spanish rule, since it was only by eradicating the enemy's armed forces that the viceregal regime could restore unchallenged political authority.

In that sense, the defeat and death of Morelos appears to be a turning point, for it removed the only leader capable of providing the unity of command and clarity of political direction that were essential to defeating Spanish government and installing a new regime. His execution on December 22, 1815, was, moreover, a tremendous propaganda coup for the royalist regime. By eliminating its outstanding military and political leader, the viceroy could now plausibly claim that the insurgency was defeated. Historians have thus reasonably regarded Morelos's defeat as the moment at which Spain won the war of Mexican independence, and they have identified Calleja as the chief architect of that victory. To a contemporary conservative, he was a "second Hernán Cortés," who had reconquered Mexico for the crown. From the insurgent perspective, he was the "Spanish Tamerlaine," who had mercilessly crushed the movement for national liberation.[52] When Calleja left office in 1816, royalist forces had, in the words of a more recent historian, achieved "one of the Spanish empire's greatest victories."[53]

Calleja had undoubtedly made a tremendous contribution to saving royalist Mexico, for he had presided over the defeat of the two great phases of Mexican insurgency led by Hidalgo and Morelos. Victory was not complete, however, when he handed over to his successor. As Calleja observed, while Mexico was recovering well from its internal war, it would continue to do so only "if the methods that have served me well are continued."[54] This cautious coda to his viceregency was perhaps to be expected of a man who had seen many setbacks in a long struggle, where military progress in one area was so often countered by setbacks in another. Nonetheless, it suggests that Calleja was unsure that his success on the battlefield had destroyed the insurgency, and it therefore raises the question of whether Spain had at this stage won the war in Mexico.

By winning on the battlefield and capturing Morelos, Calleja had certainly eliminated the main challenge to Spanish rule in Mexico and thus prepared the way for royalist government to be fully restored following Ferdinand VII's return to the throne in March 1814. But conventional military victory, important though it was, was only one element of the struggle between insurgency and counterinsurgency. War in Mexico was fragmented and regionalized, and for this reason, it was difficult to eliminate completely. The insurgents fought a guerrilla war under leaders who were usually only recognized in their own region and had no ambitions to figure beyond it; in fighting them, royalist forces also took on a decentralized character, with military commanders often acting with considerable autonomy in what were essentially local wars. We must therefore pay attention to Calleja's strategy of counterinsurgency, since this provided the framework for the struggle to eliminate rebellion in the countryside and rebuild government authority throughout the territories that harbored insurgents. Given the fissiparous nature of the insurgency, was the government capable of eliminating rebellion entirely, even after the victories of the army in battle? And, for the same reason, were the insurgents ever likely to defeat the viceregal regime?

Counterinsurgent Strategy

The strategy and tactics of counterinsurgency reflected a situation in which the royalist army had to combat proliferating rebel bands and respond to their attacks on communities and communications over a huge geographical area. They also had to deal with insurgents of different kinds. Some, notably Morelos, were overtly nationalistic and had clear political aims; they tried to establish autonomous territories with their own administrations and systems of support—based on plunder, confiscations of property, and sometimes taxation. Others were more concerned with local quarrels than national emancipation, or combined insurgency with making a living, or took advantage of the breakdown of order to practice banditry. But whatever the character of the insurgency, its wide spatial diffusion guerrilla tactics posed great problems for the royalist army. For, though the army might be better armed, better trained, and better disciplined, it was simply too small to combat an insurgency of many regions; it also had to find ways to separate insurgents from the communities among which they moved and where they often enjoyed sympathy and support. Counterinsurgency measures and tactics thus had to function on more than one level and to adjust to changing circumstances.

Crown policy to combat the insurgency was, on one plane, an ideological and political struggle involving persuasion by propaganda and policy. Viceroy Venegas quickly realized the need to shape public opinion, and during and after Hidalgo's defeat, he deployed all the means at his disposal to extirpate rebellion. In the capital, the government launched a strident propaganda campaign, using the official press to spread the image of the rebellion as a monstrous assemblage of miscreants driven by their own depravity. It had the advantage since all printing presses were in government hands, while the rebels had to make do with handwritten pasquinades and a few printed bills, neither of which had much circulation. Hidalgo captured a printing press at Guadalajara and used it to publicize his cause in the first rebel newspaper *El Despertador Americano (The American Awakener)*, produced by a fellow insurgent cleric. With only a half dozen issues, this was too little and too late to be of much use, but it was a precursor to the insurgent publications of 1812–13 that were also produced by clerics.[55]

If the government had the advantage in the war of the printed word, it had a potentially even more powerful weapon for shaping public opinion in the alliance of throne and altar. The Church was not, of course, a homogeneous body, and the clergy were neither universally nor unequivocally committed to defending Spanish government. Indeed, clerics played important roles in the insurgent leadership; aside from Hidalgo and Morelos, several priests played key parts as leaders of armed revolt and more sympathized with the insurgent cause.[56] Nonetheless, a recent estimate of those who actively committed themselves to the insurgency suggests that they were a small proportion of Mexico's clergy, in the region of one in twelve, and were heavily concentrated in two areas.[57] Broadly speaking, it seems that while some individuals from the lower clergy actively supported the rebellion, most of Mexico's priests either responded pragmatically—by shifting their allegiances according to the proximity of royalists and rebels—or they joined the upper echelons of the ecclesiastical hierarchy in outright rejection of the insurgency. Certainly, the upper echelons of the Church hierarchy were strongly in favor of the Spanish regime, even if individual bishops sometimes criticized viceregal and even royal policy. Their steadiness ensured that the alliance of throne and altar held firm.

The wrath of the Church was visited first on Hidalgo and other rebel leaders in September 1810, when the bishop of Michoacán, Manuel Abad y Quiepo, decreed their excommunication. This was subsequently confirmed by Archbishop Lizana in Mexico City in October 1810, and the Inquisition heaped anathema on Hidalgo by finding him guilty of heresy and apostasy. It was not long before the Church was called upon to condemn its own clergy more widely, as the government sought to punish priests who sided with the insurgents. This led to the extraordinary measure of June 1812, when Viceroy Venegas removed rebellious priests from the ecclesiastical jurisdiction that protected them from trial by civil or military courts; he instructed that military commanders who issued a proclamation of "blood and fire," could arrest, try, and if necessary, execute clerics suspected of rebellion.[58]

Political and ideological measures were, of course, paralleled by the development of military and policing policies designed to eradicate armed rebellion and its supporters. These had three main elements. The first involved the deployment of conventional military power and was delivered by royalist armies that grew in strength: in 1812, some 4,600 soldiers were sent from Spain and in 1813, another 2,600.[59] Periodically replenished by American conscripts and volunteers, these troops provided field armies to defend Mexico City and go into battle against any large-scale insurgent offensive in the strategic central regions. From the action at Zitácuaro onwards, the royalist high command was prepared to put large forces into the field, of several thousand men, to prevent the insurgents from building fortified urban bases anywhere close to Mexico City or attempting encirclement of the capital; it also wanted to ensure that the rebels did not coalesce under a single military command.

The second element of counterinsurgency, also of Calleja's making, aimed at the insurgent bands that had proliferated in the wake of Hidalgo's revolt, and that were difficult to eradicate by conventional military means because of their dispersion and mobility. These bands, numbering in tens, hundreds, and occasionally thousands, struck at unprotected settlements and means of communication and preyed on farms and villages for supplies but generally avoided the risks of open battle. In guerrilla style, they simply melted away when threatened with attack, often into difficult terrain, only to return when the army had left. Because the army was too small to deal with these multiple threats, Calleja aimed to create a decentralized system for defense against them. In June 1811, he issued a *Reglamento Político-Militar*, a fourteen-point set of rules that was in effect a blueprint for dealing with the low-intensity, localized guerrilla war waged by insurgents in the provincial countryside. And with the implementation of the *Reglamento* went another, third level of policy. This addressed the need to prevent subversion within urban centers and to curb communications with rural insurgents, and it led to the introduction of new systems for controlling movements in urban areas, especially in Mexico City.[60]

Calleja's *Reglamento* stood at the core of the crown's emerging counterinsurgency strategy. It complemented the use of the field army for military operations against large rebel concentrations with an everyday system of security that protected people from insurgent assault, represented royal authority throughout the land, and reduced the range of insurgent operations. It also mobilized Mexicans into action as self-defense forces. In his plan, Calleja acknowledged that people "want the King's troop deployed everywhere" so that "each town, estate and farm have a garrison to defend them." He also pointed out that this was impossible: the army was simply unable to deal with all those "gangs of thugs," who were "taking advantage of the vastness of the countryside to disrupt public order . . . threaten everyone and sometimes coalesce [into] larger forces by recruiting rabble from other gangs."[61] Mexico's communities therefore had to take some responsibility for their own defense by supplying men and money.

To ensure that they did so in an ordered and effective way, Calleja laid out a plan that was, in effect, a system of military government that gave army officers unprecedented authority over the civil population. He created new regional commandancies in areas that were particularly affected by guerrilla activity and divided part of his army into small garrisons of infantry and dragoons, equipped with artillery and usually with a mobile detachment for hunting down rebels. The *Reglamento* also provided for army garrisons to be supported by local defense forces conscripted from the local population and armed and paid for from special local taxes. Each town was to supply units of 100–150 men, who were to be enlisted by town magistrates and placed under the command of the district army commander. Similar militias were to be raised in the districts around towns, with haciendas and farms supplying units of between 30 and 150 men, depending on their size. The district army commander was to oversee these units and deploy them for local security; if the need arose, he could unite them for military operations against insurgents. All members had to carry signed identity papers; anyone who failed to report to their units would be treated as an insurgent. No one could carry arms unless they had the appropriate documents; anyone found with unauthorized arms of any kind was treated as an insurgent.[62]

Here, then, was a counterinsurgency strategy that in some ways resembled that used by the French in Spain. Conditions in Mexico were different in one important respect, of course, in that Spanish officers fighting insurgents did not confront guerrillas who were backed by foreign allies, as the French did in Spain. The operational characteristics of counterinsurgency were, however, broadly similar. Calleja aimed to hold towns and cities, to isolate the insurgents, and gradually to recover control over the countryside. The methods that his officers used also bore a resemblance to those used by Napoleon's army, notably in the use of terror to kill off insurgents and undermine their civilian support.

Counterinsurgent Tactics and Impact

The recourse to terror tactics started early. Royalist officials justified the use of violent summary justice when dealing with insurgents on the grounds that they were traitors, not ordinary criminals, and thus liable to severe corporal punishment. Punishments for political crime, which came before judicial and military authorities, ranged from hanging, shooting, whipping, running the gauntlet, hard labor in prison camps, and various combinations of hard labor and physical punishment, to exile and confiscation of property.[63] The systematic use of violence against individuals and communities was, moreover, widely used in operations against insurgents as a means of discouraging rebellion and as reprisal.[64] Venegas, who had seen action in the Peninsular War, recommended such tactics as a means of eliminating rebels and intimidating the civilian population, and it was not long before they were put into action by his commanders. Calleja, for example, not only routinely killed insurgents taken by his forces but also destroyed the town of Zitácuaro and stripped its people of their lands, a punishment for insurgency suffered by many other towns and villages in New Spain. Other royalist commanders were also given to brutal exemplary punishments. Most notorious was one of Calleja's officers, Brigadier José de la Cruz, who began his military service in Mexico as a recent veteran of the Peninsular War. While operating in Huichapan and its region, Cruz ordered public executions and the public display of rebel corpses, and he boasted to Calleja that "I have already caused suffering in this infamous race and I am going completely to terrorize them." True to his word, he left his mark on the territories through which he moved, persisting with the use of violent repression even though Calleja advised him to show some restraint. Cruz later described his methods as aiming to "shoot hundreds, punish towns, and make the word soldier as fearful as death itself."[65]

Cruz's determination to extirpate rebellion also prompted him to develop fighting tactics designed specifically for dealing with guerrillas. Like the French in Spain, he realized that if the army was to match the mobility and flexibility of insurgent movements, it had to respond with comparable speed and dexterity. To achieve this, he created "flying detachments" (*destacamentos volantes*) of mounted men to patrol highways, launch attacks on insurgents in the countryside, and prevent small rebel bands from coming together into more dangerous groupings. As early as December

1810, he had three such squads in action, sowing terror in districts that he suspected of harboring rebellion and stripping the countryside of arms and resources that might be useful to the insurgents. Though initially regarded as a temporary measure, these "flying detachments" became an established part of the counterinsurgent repertoire. During the years of war that followed, army and militia garrisons used them to strike out against rebels in their districts, to guard trade and communications, and to discourage civilians from supporting the insurgents.[66] They were, in short, an ideal means of "showing the flag" outside the garrison towns and contesting territory that might otherwise have been claimed by the guerrillas.

These counterinsurgency techniques had some contradictory effects. On the one hand, the plan for coupling army garrisons with local vigilantes addressed the shortage of regular troops. But these measures did not always work. First, they met with problems of local implementation. Even in regions with large estates, they placed heavy burdens on local resources; other, poorer regions simply could not meet the demands without damaging economic activity. And in regions like Veracruz, where there were many absentee landlords and a strong sympathy for the insurgents among the peasantry, these measures barely worked at all. Indeed, there were large areas around Guadalajara, Valladolid, and Mexico City where the insurgent presence predominated except on the occasions when the army conducted sweeps through them. This was perhaps acceptable while the government held the main town and cities and could envisage a long-term attrition of insurgency from its bases. However, there was an ever-present danger that the army would become hopelessly overstretched, excessively subdivided, and thus unable to prevent the insurgents from coalescing into more formidable forces.

Calleja recognized this risk and called for dispersed garrisons to be concentrated into two substantial forces, an Army of the North and an Army of the South. However, despite the arrival of nearly 7,000 Spanish regulars in 1812–13, the army was always overstretched. On becoming viceroy, Calleja established a strong army presence in areas of insurgent strength: in Puebla (for control of territory south of the capital), in Querétaro, Zacatecas, San Luis Potosí (for the north), and Guanajuato, Valladolid, and Guadalajara (for the northwest). But the regiments and battalions stationed in those cities were still subdivided into small units that spread out over the areas in which insurgents operated, and this had disadvantages. As army commanders knew, regiments that were parceled up for long periods could lose their identity, their discipline, and their military effectiveness. Setting troops up in small garrisons also had the disadvantage of nurturing a "blockhouse mentality," whereby soldiers became attached to their static defensive positions, reluctant to hunt down insurgents, and ready to accept that the countryside beyond their walls was the enemy's domain.[67]

These shortcomings in counterinsurgency strategy were mirrored in the persistence of regional insurgencies. The insurgents in the Veracruz area continued to be a serious problem, especially when in 1814 the guerrilla chief Guadalupe Victoria reestablished a unified leadership among competing bands. Under his command, strongholds were built in the backlands and lived off supplies plundered from neighboring areas; arms were manufactured as well as being imported from the United States; the insurgents concentrated, too, on obstructing Mexico's trade and communications with the exterior via the road to Veracruz. Such was their impact that the viceroy had to make special arrangements in 1815–16 for the creation of a "military road" that was regularly garrisoned and patrolled. Such was the importance of this task that the Spanish government sent some 2,000 Spanish troops to Veracruz under Pascual de Liñán and Fernando Miyares, rather than their planned destination in Peru. This effort succeeded in restoring stability to the region's economy and to communications between the coast and interior, but it did not wipe the slate clean. Guadelupe Victoria remained at large, as did small guerrilla bands hidden in the sierras.[68]

The insurgents also retained strength in other areas along the Gulf coast, especially where villagers had joined in the rebellion as a means of taking local power, whether from larger communities or from the state, and creating autonomous communities. The Papantla region to the north of Veracruz is a case in point, for there villagers continued to resist royalist forces even as the latter made more determined attempts to occupy and subdue the region. When they could no longer defend their villages and towns, some rebel combatants took to the hills where they built new communities based on insurgent camps. These even entered the commercial economy, producing hot-country products, which could be exported through the port of Boquilla de Piedra. Thus, the insurgency survived by spawning new communities that stood outside the royalist-occupied spaces and forged an identity of their own.[69]

On the Pacific coast, the commitment of poor villages to the insurgent cause was also undiminished, despite the disappearance of Morelos's army. When royalist forces advanced into tierra caliente and Tlapa in 1814, they met strong resistance from villages that had sided with the insurgent cause; on the Costa Grande, a land of haciendas, they were opposed by mulatto sharecroppers, who, after being inspired by Morelos, continued to defend themselves in a guerrilla war. The royalists employed counterinsurgency tactics—such as concentrating the population in defensible villages, making individuals responsible for community behavior, and killing those who failed to cooperate—which were effective in suppressing rebellion but could not eliminate it. Where they could, villagers simply withdrew to the backlands, out of reach of the colonial state but ready to mobilize again when an opportunity arose. In these circumstances, war continued at a low level in which royalists occupied ground only to lose it when they withdrew.[70]

Popular commitment to the insurgent cause continued in the regions north of Mexico City, too, in places where Hidalgo's revolt had made some of its deepest inroads. Insurgents continued to hide out in the mountains around Guanajuato and from there to strike into the hinterlands of Valladolid and Guadalajara. Close to Guadalajara, indigenous insurgents had fortified the island of Mezcala on Lake Chapala and fought off royalist assaults for several years before they were finally dislodged in November 1816. Even then, resistance persisted. In 1818, José de la Cruz (military commander of the Guadalajara region) continued to warn that the remaining insurgent bands in his area might well come together in a renewed challenge to government.[71]

Insurgency also persisted in the north around Zacatecas and Aguascalientes and in the large southwestern region, which had been Morelos's territory, where a number of leaders refused compromise with the government. Guerrilla bands continued to operate, too, in zones between the regional army commands, where royalist officers had difficulty in coordinating their forces or were reluctant to take responsibility for filling gaps between areas of operations.[72] Clearly, then, the defeat of Morelos had not ended armed conflict. Many regions continued to experience low-intensity guerrilla warfare, which disrupted local economic and social life, drained government resources and authority, and kept alive the idea of independence.

What, then, did Venegas and Calleja achieve by their defense of Mexico? By dividing the country up into a series of armed encampments, composed of cities, towns, and villages, which acted as defensive centers against a rural insurgency, they secured their overriding objective. For the first two years of the insurgency in 1810 and 1811, the royalist regime managed to survive; in 1812–13, it continued to suffer serious setbacks but won back some ground; in 1814–16, Calleja's counterinsurgency strategy continued to improve the royalist position, cutting the insurgency back to more peripheral regions and smaller numbers. The defeat and execution of Morelos in 1815 marked a turning point, for it destroyed the insurgent's only large army and most respected general, leaving in its wake a fractured and diminished rebellion. By 1816, the insurgency was weakening—geographically, it was reduced to guerrilla bands operating out of inhospitable terrain; militarily, these bands were only capable of small operations, usually plundering raids on roads and small, ill-defended villages and towns, but not attacks on substantial towns or cities; socially, the insurgents could often be plausibly characterized by the authorities as mere criminals and bandits; and politically, the insurgency lacked clear, central direction and faced an uncertain future. However, the victories won in battle by Spain's forces could not guarantee the future, for Mexico had been profoundly changed by the effects of war. Indeed some regions, war had become a way of life for both sides and continued to disrupt economic activity as well as straining government finances. Thus, when Calleja handed over the vice-regency to Juan Ruíz de Apodaca in September 1816, he passed on command of a country where the civil war was changing its character but where the end was not yet clearly in sight.

Notes

1. On the spread of insurrection in 1810–11, see Hamnett, *Roots of Insurgency*, pp. 125–49.
2. On the insurgency during the year after Hidalgo's capture, see Hugh M. Hamill, "Royalist Counterinsurgency in the Mexican War for Independence: The Lessons of 1811," *HAHR* 53, (1973): pp. 472–6, quotation from Calleja, p. 474.
3. Calleja, quoted by Alamán, *Historia de Mejico*, 2, p. 185.

 4. Hamnett, *Roots of Insurgency*, p. 52.
 5. On Morelos's life before 1810, see William H. Timmons, *Morelos of Mexico. Priest, Soldier, Statesman* (El Paso, TX: Western Press, 1963), pp. 1–30.
 6. On the first campaign, see Timmons, *Morelos of Mexico*, pp. 44–9; Hamnett, *Roots of Insurgency*, pp. 142–9.
 7. Eduardo Mirando Arrieta, "Los Bravo del Sur: Relato de una familia insurgente, 1810–1821," in *Las ciudades y la guerra, 1750–1898*, ed. Salvador Broseta, Carmen Corona, Manuel Chust, et al. (Castelló: Universitat Jaume I, 2002), pp. 47–59.
 8. Hamnett, *Roots of Insurgency*, pp. 144–6. For a more detailed account of subregional responses to Morelos and the insurgency in the area of modern Guerrero, and the social and cultural background to political allegiance, see Guardino, *Peasants, Politics, and the Formation of Mexico's National State*, pp. 48–54. For brief sketches of the Bravo and Galeana families, Morelos's crucial allies among the region's landowners, see pp. 56–7.
 9. On the fusion of military and political organization in Morelos's first and subsequent campaigns, see Ortiz Escamilla, *Guerra y gobierno*, pp. 90–9.
10. On combat strategy, see Jones, *The Art of War in the Western World*, pp. 691–2.
11. The identification of the "struggle for Puebla" as a vital campaign and the best account of its significance is Hamnett, *Roots of Insurgency*, pp. 150–77.
12. Timmons, *Morelos of Mexico*, p. 64, citing Morelos and Bustamante.
13. Hamnett, *Roots of Insurgency*, pp. 158–61.
14. Conde de Colombini to Viceroy Venegas, February 8, 1812, in Valentín López González, ed., *Documentos sobre el sitio de Cuautla*, (Mexico City: Porrúa, 1992), p. 2.
15. Venegas's assessment of the situation and his orders to Calleja on February 8, 1812, are quoted at length by Alamán, *Historia de Méjico*, 2, pp. 308–12; for an abbreviated version in English, see Timmons, *Morelos of Mexico*, p. 66.
16. Alamán, *Historia de Méjico*, 2, p. 355. Alamán suggests that this debate was stimulated by news in the government's gazette that Viceroy Elío in Montevideo had come to an agreement with the Junta of Buenos Aires.
17. The following account of the siege of Cuautla relies on Lucas Alamán, who used contemporary correspondence from both sides to write what remains the best brief history of the siege and its outcome. See Alamán, *Historia de Méjico*, 2, pp. 308–41. Some of that correspondence is reprinted in López González, *Documentos sobre el sitio de Cuautla*, to which I refer where necessary.
18. Interrogatorio del norteamericano Nicolas Colée, in López González, *Documentos sobre el sitio de Cuautla*, pp. 14–18, quotation from p. 15.
19. Interrogatorio de los individuos José Valeriano, Vicente Ortiz y José Laureano, March 23, 1812, in ibid., pp. 28–30.
20. Interrogatorio de José Cirilo González y Felipe Villanueva, March 25, 1812, in ibid., pp. 30–6.
21. Alamán, *Historia de Méjico*, 2, p. 313.
22. Calleja to Viceroy Venegas, February 20, 1812, in López González, *Documentos sobre el sitio de Cuautla*, pp. 6–7.
23. Venegas to Calleja, March 2, 1812, in López González, *Documentos sobre el sitio de Cuautla*, pp. 9–10.
24. Calleja to Venegas, April 24, 1812, in López González, *Documentos sobre el sitio de Cuautla*, pp. 67–8; also Alamán, *Historia de Méjico*, 2, p. 328.
25. Another instance in which Spain's struggles were likened to the Christian wars with Islam is found in a sermon preached and printed in Cuba in 1808. Dr. Don Sebastian de

Rives y Noriega, the chaplain of the Royal Tobacco Factory, likened the war against Napoleon and the French to the eighth-century war in which Don Pelayo had forced the Saracens from Asturias, aided by the intercession of Virgin of Covadonga. See "Sermon de María Santísima con el título de Covadonga, Restauradora de España . . . predicado el dia 8 de septiembre del año de 1808," Archivo Histórico Nacional, Madrid (AHNM), Estado 59, document 42. This had become an important myth in Spanish history, regarded as the starting point for the reconquest of Spain from the Moors and the origin of the Christian Kingdom of Asturias, and it is interesting to see it used to legitimate the Spanish struggle against France. Parallels between the religious imagery of the Spanish War of Independence against France and the American wars of independence against Spain deserve some further exploration by historians.

26. The tale is told by Alamán, *Historia de Méjico*, 2, p. 339.
27. For an analysis of the "Cuautla Lazarus," see Van Young, *The Other Rebellion*, pp. 467–9.
28. Calleja to Venegas, April 28, 1812, in López González, *Documentos sobre el sitio de Cuautla*, pp. 69–73.
29. The cost of the siege was huge—more than half a million pesos—and its outcome badly damaged relations within the royalist government: see Anna, *Fall of Royal Government in Mexico City,* p. 87.
30. Anna, *Fall of Royal Government in Mexico City*, p. 148.
31. Guedea, *La insurgencia en el Departamento del Norte*, pp. 40–4.
32. Michael T. Ducey, *A Nation of Villages: Riot and Rebellion in the Mexican Huasteca, 1750–1850* (Tucson: University of Arizona Press, 2004), pp. 72–3.
33. Hamnett, *Roots of Insurgency*, pp. 180–2.
34. Alamán, *Historia de Mejico*, 2, p. 371.
35. Morelos to Rayón, Oaxaca, December 16, 1812, in *Morelos of Mexico*, p. 79.
36. Hamnett, *Roots of Insurgency*, pp. 165–8.
37. Calleja to Minister of War, no. 1, Reservada, March 15, 1813, Archivo del Servicio Histórico Militar (SHM), Ministerio de Guerra, Ultramar 97.
38. Ibid.
39. Ibid.
40. Calleja to Minister of War, no. 6, Reservada, May 31, 1813, SHM, Ministerio de Guerra, Ultramar 97.
41. Calleja quoted by Ernesto de la Torre, *La independencia de México* (Madrid: Mapfre, 1992), p. 113.
42. Anna, *Fall of Royal Government in Mexico City*, pp. 144–57.
43. Ibid., pp. 162–71.
44. Ibid., pp. 106–29.
45. Timmons, *Morelos of Mexico,* pp. 82–3. For a fuller statement of this position and appreciation of the implications of the Puebla campaign and the shift to Oaxaca and Acapulco, see Hamnett, *Roots of Insurgency*, pp. 168–71.
46. Timmons, *Morelos of Mexico*, pp. 112–24, quotation from p. 122.
47. Hamnett, *Roots of Insurgency*, p. 186.
48. Calleja to Minister of War, no. 11, Reservada, June 22, 1813, SHM, Ministerio de Guerra, Ultramar 97.
49. Guedea, *La insurgencia en el Departamento del Norte*, pp. 107–8.
50. On leaders and followers and the *cabecillas*, see Van Young, *The Other Rebellion*, pp. 141–3, 166–78.
51. Anna, *Fall of Royal Government in Mexico City*, pp. 134–7.

52. The conservative Mexican historian Lucas Alamán likened Calleja to Cortes: see Alamán, *Historia de Méjico*, 4, p. 308. The Tamerlaine epithet came from the insurgent politician and historian Carlos María de Bustamante, who, among other works, wrote the first book on Calleja's campaigns: *Campañas del General Don Félix María Calleja, Comandante del Ejército Real de Operaciones, llamado del Centro* (Mexico City: Imprenta Aguila, 1828).

53. Anna, *Fall of Royal Government in Mexico City*, p. 179.

54. Ibid., p. 181.

55. Karl M. Schmitt, "The Clergy and Mexican Independence," *HAHR* 34 (1954): pp. 300–1.

56. Farriss argues that a large proportion of the Mexican clergy supported the insurgency actively and that the majority were in favor: see Nancy M. Farriss, *Crown and Clergy in Colonial Mexico*, 1759-1821 (London: Athlone Press, 1968), pp. 198–9. This is disputed by more recent research, which provides both new data and persuasive arguments to the contrary: see William Taylor, *Magistrates of the Sacred: Priests and Parishioners in Eighteenth-Century Mexico* (Stanford, CA: Stanford University Press, 1996), pp. 452–60; also Van Young, *The Other Rebellion*, pp. 201–2. Both stand closer to the view advanced by Schmitt, "The Clergy and Mexican Independence," albeit with more evidence and a greater emphasis on priestly neutrality. For an exceptionally enlightening analysis of the position and motives of priests caught up in the insurgency, see Van Young, *The Other Rebellion*, pp. 243–66.

57. Taylor, *Magistrates of the Sacred*, p. 453. The two areas were the Bajío and its adjacent highlands and the tierra caliente behind the Pacific coast and its neighboring highlands.

58. Hugh Hamill, "Early Psychological Warfare in the Hidalgo Revolt," *HAHR* 41 (1961): pp. 206–35; Anna, *Fall of Royal Government in Mexico City*, pp. 67–9, 79.

59. These figures are from Julio Albi, *Banderas Olvidadas*, p. 402. Archer gives a slightly lower figure of about 6,400 for troops arriving 1812–15, 3,500 in 1812, 1,100 in 1813, and 1,800 in 1815: see Christon I. Archer, "Soldados en la escena continental: Los expedicionarios españoles y la guerra de la Nueva España, 1810–25," in *Fuerzas militares en Iberoamérica, siglos XVIII y XIX*, ed. Juan Ortiz Escamilla (Mexico City: Colegio de Mexico et al., 2005), p. 156.

60. Hamill, "Royalist Counterinsurgency in the Mexican War of Independence," pp. 470–89.

61. These quotations are from the translated text of Calleja's *Reglamento*: "Political-Military Regulations that must be observed, New Spain, 1811," in *The Wars of Independence in Spanish America*, ed. Christon I. Archer (Wilmington, DE: Scholarly Resources, 2000), pp. 87–92.

62. The leading student of the Mexican counterinsurgency is Christon I. Archer, who has analyzed its structures, development, and impact in a number of overlapping articles covering the period between 1810 and 1821. One group of these articles is dedicated to showing that the counterinsurgency failed to crush the rebellion completely and that the war of independence was by no means over, as historians from Alamán to Anna have affirmed, when Morelos was defeated in 1815. To sustain this argument, Archer analyzes the correspondence of leading royalist officers in various regions in several articles, all of which point to the difficulties of the counterinsurgency strategy and failure to eliminate its enemies. These are: Christon I. Archer, "'La Causa Buena': The Counterinsurgency Army of New Spain and the Ten Years' War," in *The Independence of Mexico and the Creation of the New Nation*, ed. Jaime Rodríguez O. (Los Angeles: UCLA Latin American Center, 1989), pp. 85–108; C.I. Archer, "Where did all the Royalists Go? New Light on the Military Collapse of New Spain, 1810–1822," in *The Mexican and Mexican Experience in the Nineteenth Century*, ed. Jaime Rodríguez O. (Tempe, AZ: Bilingual Press, 1989),

pp. 24–43; C.I. Archer, "The Cutting Edge: The Historical Relationship between Insurgency, Counterinsurgency and Terrorism during Mexican Independence, 1810–1821," in *Terrorism: Roots, Impact, Responses*, ed. Lawrence Howard (Westport, CN: Greenwood Press, 1992), pp. 29–45; C.I. Archer, "Politicization of the Army of New Spain during the War of Independence, 1810–21," in *The Origins of Mexican National Politics, 1808–1847*, ed. Jaime Rodríguez O. (Wilmington, DE: Scholarly Resources, 1993), pp. 11–37; C.I. Archer, "Insurrection-Reaction-Revolution-Fragmentation: Reconstructing the Choreography of Meltdown in New Spain during the Independence Era," *Mexican Studies/ Estudios Mexicanos* 10 (1994): pp. 63–98; C.I. Archer, "Fighting for Small Worlds: Wars of the People during the Independence Ear in New Spain, 1810–1821," *Cuadernos de Historia Latinoamericana* 6 (Leiden: Asociación de Historiadores Latinoamericanistas Europeos, 1998), pp. 63–92. This body of work provides the foundations for my account of the counterinsurgency, and I make direct reference only when necessary to show the source of specific points or quotations from contemporary sources.

63. On political crimes and their punishment during the insurgency, see Antonio Ibarra, "Crímenes y castigos políticos en la Nueva España borbónica: Patrones de obediencia y disidencia política, 1809–1816," in *Las guerras de independencia en la América española*, ed. Marta Terán and José Antonio Serrano Ortega (Zamora, Michoacán: El Colegio de Michoacán et al., 2002), pp. 255–72.

64. On terror tactics, see Moíses Gúzman Pérez, "Los métodos de represión realista en la revolución de independencia de México, 1810–1821," in Terán and Ortega, *Las guerras de independencia,* pp. 323–35.

65. Christon I. Archer, "The Royalist Army in New Spain: Civil-Military Relationships, 1810–1821," *JLAS* 13 (1981): pp. 68–9.

66. On Cruz and his terror tactics, see Archer, "'La Causa Buena,'" pp. 93–5; and Archer, "The Cutting Edge," pp. 37–9.

67. Archer, "Insurrection-Reaction-Revolution-Fragmentation," pp. 73–4.

68. Escamilla, *El teatro de la guerra: Veracruz*, pp. 134–56.

69. Michael Ducey, "Village, Nation, and Constitution: Insurgent Politics in Papantla, Veracruz, 1810–1821," *HAHR* 79, no. 3 (1999): pp. 463–93.

70. Guardino, *Peasants, Politics and Mexico's National State*, pp. 70–4.

71. Archer, "Politicization of the Army of New Spain during the War of Independence, 1810–21," pp. 21–7.

72. Hamnett, *Roots of Insurgency*, pp. 188–97.

10

RESTORATION AND RECONQUEST

When Ferdinand VII returned to Spain in March 1814, he was restored to the throne of a monarchy that had been badly warped by wars on both sides of the Atlantic. In Spain, the struggle against Napoleon had inflicted huge damage. The Peninsular War had mobilized tens, sometimes hundreds of thousands of British and Spanish soldiers against French occupying forces of up to about 240,000 men. It had involved major offensives conducted by conventional armies fighting under British and Spanish officers, while multiple bands of Spanish partisans fought prolonged guerrilla wars in the countryside, inflicting heavy human and material losses. And while Spaniards were fighting Napoleon at home, the American territories of the monarchy had plunged into civil wars, which undermined Spain's prestige and system of rule in its most important possessions.

Ferdinand VII's restoration seemed at first to offer a new way forward, given that peace in the Peninsula coincided with successes for royalist arms in Spanish America. Spain had not eliminated its American opponents, but by the end of 1814, royalist officials and armies had made considerable progress in that direction. In Mexico, the viceroy's forces had defeated the main insurgent army and, although pockets of insurgency remained, had by 1815 clipped the military wings of the independence movement. The royalist regime in Peru looked even more solid. In 1813, Viceroy Abascal had restored Quito to its royal authorities and made it a platform for attack on New Granada; in October 1814, a military expedition from Lima crushed independent Chile at Rancagua; by the end of 1815, Abascal had stifled the threats that emanated from Buenos Aires by defeating rioplatense armies and local insurgents in Upper Peru, while also crushing the rebellion of Cuzco. The restoration also intersected with royalist advances and republican reversals in Venezuela, where the royalist chieftains Boves and Morales had all but eliminated the Venezuelan revolution, scattering republican forces. In New Granada, too, patriot forces failed to defeat the royalist challenge in 1813–14 and soon succumbed to

Morillo's invading army in 1815–16. Only the Río de la Plata region escaped Spanish reconquest. There, the revolutionary government of Buenos Aires remained in place, as did independent governments in Paraguay, the Banda Oriental, and the interior provinces. However, their position looked insecure in 1814–15, when Spain was actively considering an attack on Buenos Aires and Portugal stood ready to seize any territorial advantage offered by the conflict within Spanish territories.

Ferdinand VII's return to government took place, then, in a comparatively promising setting: Spain was at peace, the currents of war in America seemed to have moved in Spain's favor, and the leading European powers supported the territorial integrity of Spain's empire. However, great challenges remained. Now that the king had been restored, the issue of first importance concerned Spain's political system. Was the constitutional system implanted during the interregnum to be retained or removed, and, if the latter, what was to replace it? Of comparable importance were questions of how to rebuild authority and power in the areas where people had abjured Spain's authority and gone to war with crown officials and their armies. How, then, did Ferdinand VII deal with these problems? What shaped his policies on the American question, how did his policies evolve during the early years of the restoration, and what did they achieve?

Restoration Politics

When Ferdinand VII reentered Spain in March 1814, the Cortes required that he swear fealty to the Constitution. However, the king's reactionary entourage, backed by opinion in elite circles, encouraged him to overturn the constitutional regime and reimpose an authoritarian monarchy. Conservative deputies in the Cortes (whom their opponents labeled the *serviles*) petitioned the king to replace the existing Cortes with another, based on medieval traditions; bureaucrats wanted the old administrative system restored, and leading army officers pressed the king to dissolve the Cortes completely. Against this background, and with army support, Ferdinand VII launched a coup d'état in May, proclaiming his return as an absolutist monarch. Welcomed by his allies and popular among the many Spaniards who had no sympathy with the liberals or the Cortes, Ferdinand VII opened the way to a purge of the liberals identified with the constitutionalist regime and a program to expunge their reforms.[1]

The constitutional interlude of the interregnum was not easily erased. The liberal reforms introduced by the Constitution of Cádiz had brought important changes in both Spain and Spanish America, while entirely new political forms had been fashioned in the independent American regions, usually along republican lines. Throughout the empire, new groups had entered political life, bringing ways of thinking and behaving that were impediments to the revival of the old political order. Thus, although Ferdinand VII overturned the constitutional regime, he entered a political arena crowded with new actors, whose expectations were difficult to meet in straitened times. Even the Spanish army, whose generals backed the restoration, was a destabilizing presence in politics, as liberal army officers opposed the king's coup against the Cortes. The upheaval of war thus extended in a series of political aftershocks between 1814 and 1820, in conspiracies and rebellions involving army officers, liberals, regional leaders, and malcontents among the serviles, who had initially presented themselves as the king's firmest friends.[2]

The political turmoil of the interregnum had also altered political attitudes in Spanish America and American relations with Spain. In areas where the Cádiz Constitution had been introduced, the practice of elections, freedom of the press, and other liberal reforms had changed political expectations and behavior. The loss of these new freedoms revived old resentments. With the closure of the Cortes, Americans who had been loyal to the royalist cause lost their representation in the imperial parliament and with it their ability to influence policy. At the same time, the suppression of provincial deputations and elected municipal councils reduced American participation in domestic politics in the regions, thus removing another political safety valve. And, of course, the restored king faced even greater problems in the many regions where Spain's authority had been overthrown and where his government officials consequently had to reinstall royal authority in communities that had experienced alternative forms of government.

Ferdinand VII was not chosen because his talents or experience suited him for these difficult tasks. Indeed, he was deficient in both. He had entered politics when prince of Asturias to give vent to his adolescent jealousy of the favorite Manuel de Godoy and in response to manipulation by a faction at court. This brought scandal in 1807 when he was accused of conspiring in a coup d'état and led to his untimely succession to the throne when Charles IV abdicated amid the anti-Godoy riots of Aranjuez in March 1808. Little more than a puppet for his aristocratic mentors, Ferdinand VII's accession was too short to offer any significant experience of kingship. During his years in exile, he gained in popularity as the *deseado*, or the "beloved" symbol of Spanish popular resistance, but this did nothing to remedy his inexperience or his disconnection from the forces that were reshaping politics in the Spanish world. He was a stranger to Spanish political life when he returned from France and had no clear plans beyond an urge to return to the status quo ante 1808. Fiercely anti-liberal, Ferdinand sided with the reactionaries of the Church and army who yearned to turn back the clock, destroy the institutions of representative government, and erase liberalism.[3] Though not the doltish despot of Spanish liberal historiography, Ferdinand nonetheless invites the sardonic epithet applied to the Bourbon émigrés who returned to France after Napoleon's fall: he seems, like them, to have "forgotten nothing and learned nothing."

Ferdinand VII favored the "ministerial despotism" of his Bourbon predecessors and exercised his power through ministers whom he chose personally. At the apex of government stood the MINISTER of STATE and the KEY COUNCIL of STATE, where the king or his brother Don Carlos presided over his chosen group of ministers, ex-ministers, and personal appointees. American issues were briefly the domain of a new Ministry of the Indies (or Ultramar), reestablished in May 1814, and the Council of the Indies, which was revived in July. The Ministry of the Indies under Miguel de Lardízabal did not last long, however. In 1815, the king abolished it and redistributed its responsibilities among other ministries. He also addressed the American question directly by instituting a new Junta of Pacification and a Military Junta for the Indies, to give specific political and military advice on how to deal with the American rebellions. The Council of the Indies continued to advise on matters of American government and justice, while the Ministry of State also played an important part in shaping American policy, since it had to ensure coherence between colonial, domestic, and foreign policies. Indeed, as American policy loomed ever larger among the important issues of state, the Council of State became an increasingly important forum for discussion and decision on American matters.[4]

A description of the upper tiers of government that made policy, tends, however, to create a false impression of order and stability. In fact, ministers were subject to sudden dismissal at Ferdinand's whim and on average served only about six months. And behind the ministers and their councils was an informal tier of advisors, a *camarilla*, or private inner grouping of men from outside government who had personal access to the king, whom he trusted to keep him in touch with public opinion, and who, it was said, exercised greater influence than his ministers. Some historians believe that Ferdinand chose his own political course; others think that it was mapped out for him by the camarilla. What is undeniable is that the anti-liberal tenor of his monarchy and its most important decisions were heavily marked by their influence.[5] Urged on by these men, Ferdinand extended his anti-constitutionalism from a campaign of repression against liberals in Spain into a counterrevolutionary revanche in America.

Ferdinand VII and the American Question

Ferdinand VII's attitude towards Spanish America was in one respect unequivocal; he believed that Spain could only recover from the prostration caused by war by restoring control over its American possessions. However, at the outset of his restoration, the king had no specific plans for Spanish America. The framework for policy was set by his decision to eliminate the political and administrative innovations made by the Cortes and reestablish the institutional structures of prewar Bourbon government; then, after removing all traces of the constitutional system, Ferdinand proceeded to search for measures to reanimate American loyalty and secure the permanent pacification of rebellious provinces.

His approach to the American problem started with a statement of conciliation. In May 1814, Miguel de Lardízabal, the Minister of the Indies, was ordered to inform Americans of the king's benign intentions and assure them that Ferdinand VII would end the discord caused by his absence. In a proclamation to Americans, Lardízabal duly echoed these sentiments: the king, he stated, had been "miraculously returned by the visible hand of Providence to reign in peace and justice" and had shown his good intentions by appointing men born in America to important government posts. Ferdinand VII, said Lardízabal, was keen to forgive and forget: he would "always look with singular appreciation on those who had been faithful to him . . . and receive like a father those who had gone astray, totally disregarding their crime if they gave themselves up to be pardoned."[6]

The promise of conciliation was backed by a process of consultation on the issues of American policy in which the king solicited and received advice from many royalist officials, ex-deputies of the Cortes, and others with relevant experience. The first group of experts consulted by the king in the summer of 1814 tended to favor conciliation, though they did not discount the use of force: Francisco López Lisperguer, José Baquíjano, General José de Zayas, and the Conde de Puñonrostro all talked of the need for reform of one kind or another; only Antonio Pérez, who focused on Mexico, demanded a military solution requiring the sending of large reinforcements from Spain.[7] However, the old refrain that the rebellions were the work of small cliques of malefactors resurfaced, allowing Ferdinand VII, who knew virtually nothing about Spanish America, to cling to the belief that "love for the king" would reunite the monarchy.[8] This view was presented in its most credulous form by the Quiteño noble, Arias Dávila y Herrera, the Conde de Puñonrostro, who averred that the king's American subjects were, "due to the nature of their climate and temperament . . . docile, submissive and gentle, and above all admirers to the point of idolatry of the name and persons of their sovereigns."[9] Puñonrostro's notion of a restorative peace was a pious hope with perverse effects. For given the implicit assumption that there was no serious disaffection nor reason for it, it precluded other political viewpoints and impeded consideration of reforms that might have won support among Americans.

For a couple of years after his return, Ferdinand VII's American policies showed considerable continuity with those of the Cortes in that they combined the use of coercion with the promise of reconciliation. While military resources were mobilized to show Americans that Spain was sufficiently strong to use violence, discussion of political reform and British mediation continued. However, military methods of pacification soon took center stage. Now that Spain was free from war in Europe and had large forces at its disposal in the Peninsula, military intervention in Spanish America seemed a more viable prospect. It also offered employment for the huge army that Ferdinand VII inherited from the Peninsular War and was unable to fully demobilize. The king duly sanctioned the development of a military policy designed to impress Americans with Spain's ability to wipe out rebellion by force. This impulse to take military action took firm shape in September and October 1814, when the Council of the Indies recommended that the king send one or more army expeditions to South America. The main result of their decision came six months later with the dispatch of a large expedition to Caracas and New Granada under the command of General Pablo Morillo.

The source of this decision is difficult to identify precisely, but the most plausible source is the proposal for military action in Venezuela made directly to the king in early June 1814 by Pedro de Urquinoana, secretary of the Ministry of the Indies.[10] When Ferdinand turned to the Council of the Indies for its opinion, a larger plan emerged in the form of 21 recommendations related to Caracas and New Granada. First among them was the proposal that the king send an army to

Caracas, led by a distinguished general who was to assume political as well as military command and take all the measures needed to restore order. The council also recommended the appointment of a Junta of Generals "of land and sea," who could offer informed advice on these regions. This set of recommendations were sent to the king on October 3, 1814, swiftly followed by another on October 4, which commented on the consequences of the fall of Montevideo to the insurgents of Buenos Aires and recommended dispatching an expedition against Buenos Aires, perhaps by rerouting the expedition the council had previously suggested should go to Caracas.[11] After various administrative delays, orders were given in November 1814 to dispatch an expedition before the year was out.

While these decisions were being taken, Buenos Aires appeared to be the chosen target. The strategic case for an urgent expedition to the River Plate was clear: the revolution of Buenos Aires had not only taken a key port in the Spanish Atlantic but also posed a significant threat to Spanish rule in Upper Peru, Peru, and Chile. The merchants who financed the Comisión de Reemplazos were, moreover, particularly keen to recover and defend their commerce with these key regions. When the plan went belatedly into action in mid-February 1815, the expedition was a suitably impressive force; it carried 12,254 men in 20 warships and 59 other vessels, stretching Spain's naval forces to its limits. The army of some 10,500 men was commanded by General Pablo Morillo and the naval force by Brigadier Pascual de Enrile. Its destination was, however, a complete surprise. When General Morillo opened sealed orders at sea, his soldiers found themselves bound for Venezuela, not Buenos Aires.[12]

The decision to divert from Buenos Aires to Venezuela and New Granada was not improvised. It seems that the decision had been taken in October 1814 after news that Montevideo had fallen to Buenos Aires in June. The porteños' capture of Montevideo made a critical difference to the destination of Morillo's expedition because it removed the obvious base for an attack on Buenos Aires and left Spain dependent on Portuguese agreement to an invasion via the Banda Oriental. However, ministers maintained the pretense that the expedition would go to the River Plate in order to ensure that the Comisión de Reemplazos continued to provide financial support, to confuse American enemies, and perhaps to prevent desertion by Spanish soldiers, who feared the dangers of campaigning in the Caribbean.

The decision to send the expedition to South America was an important strategic development. Sending military expeditions was not of itself entirely novel, given that the regents and Cortes had since 1811 used the Comisión de Reemplazos to send to America as many troops as Spain could spare. But the Morillo expedition was nonetheless more than just an extension of the military policy of the constitutionalist period. It also had a symbolic significance in demonstrating to Americans that Spain had recovered its capacity to project military power across the Atlantic and was ready to take war to a new stage. Behind it lay a new group around the king, which, in the words of Juan Antonio Yandiola, believed that "force . . . is the only thing that can suffice in the state at which things have arrived."[13]

This approach was reflected on the diplomatic as well as the military front. Ferdinand hoped to use his alliance with Britain to help restore relations with the colonies but soon rejected British mediation. In this, he sustained the stance taken by the Regency and Cortes, for the impasse was the same. The Spanish were ready to allow British mediation only if Britain was prepared to commit armed force against rebels who refused to accept Spanish terms; the British, on the other hand, were prepared to mediate only if Spain was ready to allow its American subjects political autonomy and commercial freedom.[14] The question of mediation was therefore shelved in 1814–15 but did not disappear, for while Ferdinand VII and his ministers were taking their first steps to formulate policies for restoring the old equilibrium, leading officials in Spanish America were still fighting wars against insurgents. In principle, the restoration improved their chances of winning, for peace in the Peninsula allowed Spain to concentrate on stabilizing the empire while also removing liberal reforms that had constrained colonial officials from violent repression. In practice, however, hopes of a return of peace and prosperity under Ferdinand VII were confounded by the economics and politics of an empire that had been severely disrupted by war.

The Impact of War

In Spain, the Peninsular War had inflicted huge damage; the march and counter-march of contending armies had laid waste to much of the country, while the practice of "la guerrilla" left a legacy of widespread banditry. Guerrillas were often men who had no political purpose; they simply lived from war and were as likely to prey on Spaniards as Frenchmen. Banditry was only one feature of the social up-heaval caused by war. In some regions, peasants also seized the opportunities offered by the breakdown of government to challenge the power of landlords. These were features of a larger social and economic crisis: towns and cities had been exposed to ruin and sometimes reduced to rubble by repeated attack; rural areas were subject to the constant predation of competing forces that lived off the land, leaving agri-culture, industry, and trade all badly disrupted by war. As many as a million people (about 10% of the population) may have died from famine, epidemic, and massacre during a war, which for many Spaniards, had consequences that were "well-nigh apocalyptic."[15]

Spain's overseas trade had, of course, been exposed to considerable losses, as commercial contacts between Spanish and Spanish American ports were cut down by foreign interloping and insecurity at sea. Spanish investments in America were also endangered by war, particularly in areas where Spaniards and their property had been singled out for violent attack or subject to heavy financial exactions. A contemporary calculation gives a sense of the large scale of losses during the years 1810–14: in January 1815, the Spanish merchant Juan Antonio Yandiola esti-mated that Spain had lost 183 million pesos in public and private capital and ship-ping seized by the insurgents, as well as 440 million pesos of trade diverted into the hands of the English, not to mention unknown losses of trade to the United States.[16] These very large figures were probably exaggerated. Yandiola represented Cádiz merchants who were pressing for measures to restore the old commercial monopoly, including military action against Buenos Aires, and thus had every reason to stress the tribulations of the American trade. Nonetheless, the evidence gathered by economic historians confirms the depth of the crisis. Recent estimates indicate that at the time of the restoration, Spanish exports to America had fallen from their peacetime peaks by between 60 and 80%.[17]

The state of the royal treasury reflected this economic devastation. As war strangled American trade and stemmed the flows of tax revenues, it provoked an acute financial crisis in Spain. Financial problems were no novelty, of course. Before 1808, Spain could not come close to matching Britain in generating the state revenues needed to fight large-scale wars; indeed, the Spanish state was already on the brink of financial meltdown before it was convulsed by political crisis. However, while the empire was intact, its access to American revenues in silver had at least provided collateral for credit. The postwar situation was quite different. American revenues contracted sharply during the wars of the interregnum, while at the same time revenues from ordinary taxation in Spain declined. Fernandine Spain thus carried a structural debt, which could only be addressed by borrowing to cover short-term deficits, while cutting expenditure and increasing taxation in the longer term. Borrowing was a problem, however, for, with queues of creditors clamoring for payment, investment in state loans was hard to obtain at anything but the most exorbitant rates of interest. Cutting expenditure was problematic while large armed forces were still required, and changes in the tax system were difficult to contemplate because of the certainty that they would provoke opposition at all social levels.

The plans for fiscal reform put forward in 1817 by Minister of Finance Martín de Garay addressed these problems but brought no lasting solutions. His recourse to periodic extraordinary contributions was merely a short-term expedient, incapable of sustaining the regime's fiscal future, while his schemes for a new tax system and plan to fund the public debt by sales of land foundered in the face of opposition. Indeed, Garay's failure points to the central contradiction of Ferdinand VII's regime—namely, that to rebuild and conserve the old regime required financial resources of a kind that could only be obtained by radical economic and fiscal reforms that were incompatible with the political character and aims of that regime.[18]

If the war in the Peninsula had upset Spain's political structures, convulsed its society, unhinged its economy, and emptied its treasuries, the wars in the Americas had also had deeply disruptive effects. It is impossible to give an accurate assessment of their financial and economic impact due to the shortage of data for regions where Spanish government broke down. However, it is obvious from the accounts of regional warfare given in previous chapters that violent conflict had inflicted damage of several kinds.

One was demographic. In some places, there were considerable casualties of war among soldiers and civilians. They were almost certainly greatest among military forces; participation in battles and other armed encounters exposed combatants directly to death and injury, and life on campaigns made them vulnerable to sicknesses, especially in tropical zones. Given that armed forces were generally small, their losses usually did not entail lasting demographic damage, but war could and sometimes did inflict much larger loss of life. In Venezuela, probably the most extreme example, the combatants in war inflicted heavy losses on the civilian population. The *Gazeta de Caracas*, an official publication, calculated that about 220,000 people had lost their lives by 1815—that is, around a third of Venezuela's total population and about half of its white population.[19]

In other regions, civilian casualties were almost certainly smaller, but the movement of armies, the operations of insurgent guerrilla bands, and the increased criminality that came with internal war all damaged economic activity. The production of commodities that required fixed capital investments, were particularly vulnerable. Mexican and Peruvian silver mining, Venezuelan cacao and coffee plantations, and Mexican sugar and tobacco plantations all suffered badly. So, too, did the ranching economies of the great plains in Venezuela, Río de la Plata, and the Banda Oriental, where herds of livestock were the main wealth; horses and cattle were simply appropriated by warring bands and sometimes hunted down on a scale that devastated whole regions. Internal trade was, likewise, disrupted by the predations of armed forces that lived off the land, taking or taxing commerce that passed along internal routes. War was not necessarily a cause for general impoverishment; as old fortunes were lost, new fortunes were created. In Río de la Plata, for example, landowners who supplied armies with food, men, and livestock began to enter, even replace, the older provincial elites. In Mexico, military men, such as Iturbide, found opportunities for personal enrichment through war; in Venezuela and New Granada, confiscations of property by contending sides also led to transfers of wealth that were not always recovered.[20]

The impact of American wars reverberated throughout the Spanish monarchy through its effects on Spain's commerce and state finances. Transatlantic trade was already declining sharply before 1810, but the years of internal war severed more or less completely the trading ties between Spain and its colonies. While Cádiz merchants struggled to uphold Spain's claim to monopolize its colonial commerce by trade with loyalist ports, the British made considerable inroads into Spanish American markets in independent regions, to the point where British trade supplanted Spain's. These fissures in the Spanish commercial monopoly exacerbated the crisis of Spanish government finances. Before 1810, the great silver-producing economies of Mexico and Peru provided the bulk of the funds Spain needed to fight its international wars, channeled through a network of fiscal transfers to the metropolitan treasury and fiscal subsidies to poorer American regions. After 1810, this financial web was torn apart by war. Governments faced with a sudden spike in military expenditures were forced to suspend revenue transfers to Spain, and rich treasuries, such as that of New Spain, also cut or curtailed subsidies for American defenses outside their regions.[21] Thus, fiscal crisis not only hit the richer regions but spread to poorer areas too, further undermining Spain's ability to fight its colonial wars.

The extent and depth of the financial problem was revealed in a report to the king in 1814, which spelled out region by region the damage done to Spanish American royal treasuries by the diminution of taxpayers, the extraordinary costs of war, the decline of commerce, and the inability of Spain to provide subsidies to its colonies.[22] With few resources to spare, the restoration of Spanish rule in America was to depend heavily on the ability of colonial officials to sustain their counter-revolution not only by overcoming armed resistance but by reconstructing colonial administration and winning back loyalty. To what extent were they able to achieve these goals?

Restoration Mexico

In Mexico, Ferdinand VII's return and his suppression of the constitution were welcomed by the propertied classes who feared the social threat of insurgency and yearned for a return to the old order. However, the problem of how to eradicate the insurgency remained. In August 1814, Viceroy Calleja observed that even though all the principal towns and cities were in royalist control, a major military effort was still needed if the government were to recover control of rural areas, communications and transport, and the resources that had fallen into the hands of the "bandits." He stated that it would be possible to begin this task of reconquest only if Spain sent 6–8,000 reinforcements with large supplies of arms.[23] Others agreed with Calleja, albeit for a different reason. They blamed the failure to extinguish the insurgency on Calleja and his fellow officers, whom they accused of corruption: Bishop Abad y Quiepo, for example, accused Calleja and his commanders of keeping the war going in order to profit from it, and ex-viceroy Venegas recommended that Calleja be replaced.[24] These doubts about Calleja probably reflected a growing nervousness among the civilian elites about the expansion of the army and its powers. The formidable army built up under Calleja brought huge financial costs and a seepage of power away from the center, and after the king's return, the civilian elites were concerned to redress the balance. For those who wanted to return to normality, it was vital not only to finish eliminating the insurgency but also to cut back on the army—hence, the recommendations to Ferdinand VII, which undermined Calleja's credibility in Spain and led to his replacement by a new viceroy, Juan Ruíz de Apodaca.

On arriving in September 1816, Apodaca immediately found that the insurgency still had sharp teeth. As he travelled from Veracruz to Mexico City, his convoy came under insurgent attack, a rude reminder that guerrillas could still operate wherever difficult terrain hindered royalist penetration, even on the key route from the coast to the capital. While this prompted the viceroy to undertake a vigorous pacification campaign in the Veracruz region, he also had to deal with threats from insurgents and from adventurers who used the United States as a platform for attacks in the north of New Spain.

The best-known of these attacks came from the Spanish liberal and ex-army officer Francisco Javier Mina, who, after falling foul of Ferdinand VII's regime, left Spain for exile in England. In London, he was persuaded by the Mexican revolutionary Servando Teresa de Mier to continue his opposition against Ferdinand VII from Spanish America. Mina duly raised a cosmopolitan expedition of about 235 men in the United States and Haiti (where he tried to persuade Bolívar to join him) and sailed to Mexico with a plan to raise a rebellion among Mexicans. His plan was to secure not independence but the resurrection throughout the monarchy of the Cádiz Constitution of 1812. He landed far to the north of the main centers of insurgency however, and on heading inland found that recruits were scarce. Viceroy Apodaca was nonetheless sufficiently alarmed to send substantial Spanish forces against him for fear that he might revive revolution in the province of Guanajuato. Commanded by the very experienced Brigadier Pascual de Liñán, these forces hunted Mina down, and some six months after his landing, Mina was captured and executed.[25]

Mina's expedition was not the only threat in the north: Viceroy Apodaca also had to defend against incursions by foreigners, particularly from the United States. In 1815, Luis de Onís, the Spanish ambassador in Philadelphia, warned his government about the risk that North American adventurers might help the insurgents, introduce republicanism, and take Spanish territory for settlement. Over the next few years, Onís prevailed upon his government to mitigate these risks by negotiation with the United States and suggested more radical solutions should this fail to work, including the dispatch of a large army to Mexico under the command of a Bourbon prince.[26] The king took no action, but the viceroy had to remain alert for threats from the north and commit resources to containing them.

The threats that stemmed from the United States were twofold. First were the ambitions of the United States to expand its territory at Spain's cost. The Louisiana Purchase from Napoleon had given the new republic a strategic position for expansion west of the Mississippi, and the need to guard New Orleans meant that its governments also wanted to take Florida from Spain. North American ambitions were, moreover, supported by a public opinion that tended to favor Spanish American independence for political and economic reasons; press and politicians wanted to cultivate republican allies and promote commercial opportunities that would strengthen the United States against Britain and the reviving monarchies of post-Napoleonic Europe.

If this geopolitical setting gave Spain cause to fear that the United States would aid Spanish American insurgents, another problem arose from the influx of foreign adventurers into the United States after the end of the European wars and their use of United States' territory as a base from which to attack Spain. One site of pressure was in Florida where, in 1817, Gregor MacGregor (who had previously fought for Bolívar and the insurgents of New Granada) continued his fight against Spain by establishing the very short-lived Republic of Florida on Amelia Island.[27] Although this venture was unsuccessful, the United States' ambition to acquire Florida demanded constant Spanish vigilance in this distant and sparsely populated territory, imposing further strains on Spain's overstretched resources.

Another point of pressure that required vigilance was in the northern reaches of the Gulf of Mexico, where New Orleans and the Texas coast became a breeding ground for illegal trade, insurgent-flagged privateering against Spanish shipping, and plots to invade and take territory in the Mexican north. After Napoleon's defeat at Waterloo, the exodus of French refugees to the United States added a fresh ingredient to the pool of international adventurers and insurgents. As enemies of Britain, these Bonapartist exiles were welcomed into the United States. The rich and well-connected—Joseph Bonaparte among them—settled into comfortable lives and avoided controversy; others, especially career soldiers, looked for ways of making a living from the wars of Spanish American independence. In one unusual case, a group of prominent French refugees secured a grant of land from the United States government, supposedly for the cultivation of vines and olives but in fact to guard a difficult internal frontier and to pressure Spain into ceding Florida. From this group emerged one of the more extraordinary ventures of the period when in 1817–18, the Bonapartist general Charles-Francois-Antoine Lallemand tried to establish a French settlement in Texas, apparently in the hope that he could secure its future either by persuading Spain that it would act as a buffer against North American invasion or convincing the United States that it would give North Americans a foothold in Spanish territory.[28] Unsuccessful though this was, it shows that the insurgency within Mexico was not the viceroy's only problem; he also had to guard borderlands that Spain's perceived weakness made vulnerable to external attack.

While maintaining a militarized Mexico, Apodaca took a political track too. His approach is reflected in a remark he made when referring to the war against insurgents in the north: "I will not relax my iron fist from the cursed rebels," he told the minister of war, "until either they are annihilated totally or pacified after they have received royal amnesties."[29] His attention to military repression was thus accompanied by an effort to bring those outside the law back into the fold. He abandoned Calleja's terror tactics and tried to rebuild goodwill by a generous dispensation of pardons, perhaps as many as 17,000 during his four-year term of office. This had notable effect in northern Mexico, where thousands took up the chance to return to peace.[30] Apodaca interpreted this as evidence that the crown could overcome the insurgency, and some historians have agreed that his viceregency brought a lull in Mexico's ten-year war.

Although the insurgency fragmented, this did not end the war nor greatly reduce the pressures on royalist forces.[31] The army could conduct successful lightening campaigns against guerrillas and concentrate recalcitrant peasants in fortified villages, but it lacked sufficient forces to hold territory. No sooner was one campaign over than another was needed, and from around 1818 the morale and organization of the royalist army started to deteriorate due to lack of pay and adequate supplies. Here, then, was a core problem. Not only did the government lack sufficient force to hold territory, but it lacked the resources to meet existing military needs, let alone pay for significant reinforcement. In these circumstances, it was crucial to find a political means of winning the cooperation of the tax-paying population. This, too, was a hugely difficult task, given the economic disruption caused by war and loss of respect for the royalist regime.

Apodaca's regular reports to the crown suggest steady general improvements in reestablishing government authority, stimulating economic growth, particularly in the silver mines, and improving the income of a deeply indebted treasury.[32] But this was recovery from a low base; the destruction done by war to key areas of Mexico's mining and commercial agriculture, combined with a flight of Spanish capital, made reconstruction a Sisyphean task.[33] War had also pushed government to the brink of bankruptcy. Stretched to the limit before 1810 by Spain's demands for tax remittances to pay for its international wars, the Mexican treasury was broken by internal war after 1810. Total revenues declined from 28 million pesos in 1809 to less than 9 million pesos in 1817 (a fall of nearly 70%), and the whole system of remittances between treasuries broke down as provincial governments kept local revenues to finance their rising military expenditures. The central government responded with emergency measures; it cut nonmilitary expenses and remittances to areas outside Mexico while turning to the wealthy and propertied sectors for loans and donations.[34] But these expedients could not relieve a structural imbalance in its funds, for without larger streams of revenue, the government was unable to service its debts and restore its creditworthiness.[35]

The problems of rebuilding the old order were exacerbated by changes that had undermined respect for the legitimacy of the royal government in Mexico City. First, the constitutional regime had proffered important reforms, but the idea of a new pact with Spain, which gave Mexicans greater autonomy, did not have time to flourish. Having been undermined by viceroys who refused fully to implement reform in wartime, the prospects for autonomy diminished further after Ferdinand VII's restoration.[36] Second, when fighting the insurgency, Mexico's viceroys had contributed to a process of militarization, which made regional military groups into virtual fiefdoms that could (and in 1820–21 would) challenge the power in Mexico City that they were supposed to defend. The restoration of the king had not, in short, restored the Viceroyalty of New Spain to its previous equilibrium.

Peru and the Challenge of Buenos Aires

The Viceroyalty of Peru was, like Mexico, still embroiled in war when Ferdinand VII returned. Indeed, the viceregal regime had to redouble its military efforts in order to deal with multiple threats: the rebellion of Cuzco in August 1814; the threat that Buenos Aires's forces would return to Upper Peru after the fall of Montevideo in June 1814; and the continuing defiance of an independent Chile. However, little more than a year after the restoration, the military position was transformed. Viceroy Abascal's armies crushed the Chilean rebels in October 1814, delivered the coup de grâce to the Cuzco rebellion in March 1815, and repulsed Rondeau's offensive in Upper Peru in November 1815. They also succeeded in capturing and killing some key leaders of the guerrilla republiquetas in Upper Peru, such as Muñecas and Padilla, thereby depriving Buenos Aires of valuable Andean allies. Nonetheless, unlike Calleja in Mexico, when Viceroy Abascal retired in mid-1816, he could not report that the worst of the war was over. The Army of Peru still faced defiance in Upper Peru, and Abascal's generals had not achieved his goal of crushing the core of the revolution in Buenos Aires. Indeed, the Peruvian royalist regime, unlike that of Mexico, had to confront a neighboring revolutionary state which, though riven by internal dissension, remained a threat to Peru's royal government and its satellites. The great question that faced General Pezuela, Abascal's successor, was, then, whether he could defeat the enemy on his borders or, at the very least, prevent it from importing revolution into Peru.

While Abascal was viceroy, military repression had been the central axis of policy. Abascal believed that force alone would persuade the rebels to give up their cause, and, as he would not parley with them, he informed the authorities in Spain that "war is my only salvation."[37] His approach to governing Peru was equally militant. During the era of the Cortes and constitution, the viceregal government of Peru, like that of Mexico, had tended to weaken Spanish authority, as viceroys intent on winning wars evaded inconvenient constitutional constraints and reforms. While the authority of the king was damaged by his relegation to the role of constitutional monarch, the viceroys' tendency to disobey or ignore the provisions of the constitution also undermined confidence in and respect for the new constitutional regime. Abascal undermined the rule of law by his routine interference with elections and neutralization of liberal reforms at the same time that the Cortes's failure to offer equality between Spaniards and Americans and refusal to contemplate commercial reform added to the sense of disillusion. When Pezuela took over, the constitutional regime had contributed little to preserving the Spanish regime; indeed, the Cuzco rebellion showed the confusion it had sown.[38]

Pezuela, like his contemporary Apodaca in Mexico, was more inclined to seek a political solution than his predecessor. His experience of fighting in Upper Peru told him that military action could not of itself win the war against the insurgents. Because the army could only hold the territory on which it stood, it was vital to win loyalty by conciliation and amnesty. This was not a view shared by the Spanish soldiers who arrived in Peru after the restoration. They believed that their experience of war against Napoleon would ensure the swift defeat of colonial insurgents, whom they regarded as inferiors, and their new commander, General José de la Serna, dismissed Pezuela's Army of Peru as mere "armed peasants." La Serna even regarded Pezuela himself with some disdain, asserting that his rank as a *general en jefe* (commander in chief) allowed him to operate independently of the viceroy's orders. These officers were, moreover, supported by an important group of merchants in Lima whose fortunes depended on transatlantic trade and who were consequently unwilling to see any deviation from the regulations of external commerce. Rather than make concessions to freer trade, they demanded the use of military force even when the viceroy lacked the means to fund it.[39]

Hindered by dissent among key groups on his own side, Pezuela also had to face the resurgence of the revolutionaries of the Río de la Plata on both land and sea. Although the third porteño offensive into Upper Peru failed in late 1815, Buenos Aires had strengthened its military position by capturing Montevideo. The scale of this naval action was slight, but its short- and medium-term significance was considerable. It marked the onset of naval war that emanated from the estuary of the River Plate, as Buenos Aires became an increasingly important port for privateering against Spanish shipping in the Atlantic and Pacific.

More immediately relevant, however, were the effects of the loss of Montevideo on Spanish military strategy. When the news reached Pezuela in Upper Peru, he realized that Buenos Aires could now shift forces from the coast to the interior, and, confronted by this possibility, he postponed his offensive into the United Provinces. In Spain, news that Buenos Aires held Montevideo also discouraged plans to retake Buenos Aires by means of a military expedition sent from Cádiz. When this postponement became obvious in the latter part of 1815, it altered the strategic balance in the Southern Cone. On the revolutionary side, release from fears of Spanish invasion relieved military and political strains on the government of Buenos Aires and allowed it to return to the prime purpose of combating the forces of the Peruvian viceroy. On the royalist side, it pushed responsibility for counterrevolution in the Southern Cone firmly back onto the viceroy of Peru, imposing fresh strains on his already overstretched financial and military capacities.

Pezuela was in a poor position to shoulder this responsibility, as his financial position went from bad to worse. In 1815, Viceroy Abascal had staved off bankruptcy with sweeping tax reforms that were designed to maximize revenues without putting excessive pressure on the poorest taxpayers. The treasury's solvency remained delicately balanced, however, for the economic damage done by war made Peru too poor to pay for the army and navy it needed. Silver mining had been very badly hit by the curtailment of mercury supplies from Spain, labor shortages, and flooding of the mines; at the same time, Lima's trade was throttled by the contraction of Spanish commerce, pressure from foreign interlopers, and, from 1816, the assaults of insurgent privateers operating in the Pacific.

While the cash flows from taxation were drying up, so too was the regime's credit, particularly among the Lima merchants, who were an indispensable source of loans and donations. The Consulado of Lima could occasionally be relied on to provide large sums when its members' interests were at stake—it financed six armed merchantmen to counter the activities of privateers from Buenos Aires in 1816—but could reasonably claim to have exhausted its resources by 1817. Pezuela thus faced a structural financial problem in the shape of huge debts, insufficient tax incomes, and the concomitant difficulty of raising new loans. He could not, however, escape heavy military expenditures because he still had to maintain large operational forces in Upper Peru, as well as defend the outlying territories in Chile and Quito.[40]

Before becoming viceroy, Pezuela had tried to stabilize the position of the army by remaining on the defensive within Upper Peru, despite Abascal's call for a march on Buenos Aires. The memoirs of Francisco Javier Mendizábal, a staff officer in the Army of Peru, show that throughout 1816, the army's activities were focused on more defensive goals: to block fresh invasions by the porteños and to eliminate insurgency within Upper Peru.[41] When La Serna took over as army commander, Viceroy Pezuela expected more. The general had brought reinforcements from the Gerona Battalion in Spain, plus a new group of officers experienced in war, and after he had established his headquarters at Cotagaita in November 1816, Pezuela urged him to advance against Tucumán as soon as possible. La Serna was, however, quickly caught up in the increasingly bloody war for Upper Peru against the insurgent bands led by Camargo, Lamadrid, and Warnes. He eventually advanced on Salta in April 1817 with a well-armed force of around 1,500 men, but, harassed by the gauchos, he could not sustain this position and was forced back to Jujuy and then to Tupiza.[42] Thus, like previous Spanish commanders, La Serna learned the lesson that repression of the guerrillas of Upper Peru was a necessary but not sufficient condition for an offensive against Buenos Aires. His failure was, moreover, to cause a rift with the viceroy akin to that which had previously divided Goyeneche and Abascal. As their already tense relationship worsened, it not only impeded collaboration on military operations but also had a wider significance. For after Pezuela blamed La Serna for the failure of 1817, La Serna retaliated by blaming Pezuela for all subsequent military problems.

Pezuela's viceregency was, from its outset, dominated by military issues, which he saw from the perspective learned while commanding the Army of Peru. Fearing attack from Buenos Aires and insurgency in Upper Peru, he continued to concentrate his military strength on the Andean provinces, sending reinforcements and preparing for a fresh assault from Buenos Aires. His previous role as military commander was also reflected in his approach to administration, which he sought to militarize. In December 1816, Pezuela ordered that officers with experience of war should be given priority in appointments to civil posts as recognition for their services and, no doubt, because their record of wartime service made them reliable officials of state. This ran counter to the practices of Spanish government and was offensive to the civilian professionals who saw such posts as their prerogative, but it recognized that Spain's position in Peru relied above all on the army. Officers had to be rewarded and, once this was made explicit by Pezuela, military men took an increasingly prominent role in political life.[43] The infiltration of military men into government did not, however, solve Pezuela's principal problem, which was to find the resources needed to sustain his army. Indeed, this problem became much worse in 1817, with the emergence of a new threat from the forces of revolutionary Buenos Aires, not in Upper Peru as expected, but in Chile, a region vital to the defense of Peru.

This threat came from José de San Martín, the soldier and revolutionary politician who had fought for Buenos Aires and served in its government since 1812. Disillusioned by repeated failures against the royalist army in Upper Peru, San Martín used his appointment as the governor of Cuyo to plot a new course for war and to build the army that it required. His strategy aimed at overcoming royalist Peru by attacking its Pacific flank rather than continuing to batter against its Andean defenses; his plan was to take Chile in order to deprive Lima of a vital trading partner while also providing a base from which to attack Peru by sea. This would take war between Peru and revolutionary Buenos Aires into a new phase, away from the Andean borders defended from Cuzco and to the Pacific coast defended from Lima. San Martín's military campaigns and their implications for the future of South America are matters considered later. For the moment, suffice to say that San Martín's campaigns were to reveal how far the Peruvian viceregal government remained from ending the civil wars of the interregnum or stifling the desire for independence.

Morillo and Military Government in Venezuela and New Granada

While the viceroys of Mexico and Peru struggled to assert Spanish authority under Ferdinand VII, royal officials in Venezuela and New Granada also faced great challenges. They had to reimpose the king's authority on societies where war had caused considerable economic and fiscal damage, with the additional difficulty of doing so in regions where independent governments had held sway for five or six years. From the outset, the military were to play a central part in the reconstituted government, as leadership passed to General Pablo Morillo, the veteran of the Peninsular War who commanded Spain's invading army.

Morillo's military responsibility was easily accomplished in Venezuela because Boves and his lieutenants had already destroyed Bolívar's Second Republic. He had little more to do than remove the insurgent enclave at the island of Margarita before concentrating on two main tasks: restoring public order in Venezuela, where the rapine of royalist partisans was a serious problem, and preparing an army to reconquer New Granada, most of which remained under independent governments. Morillo dampened violence in Venezuela by demobilizing the llanero irregulars and incorporating some into the army that he raised for the invasion of New Granada. His plan involved a considerable military effort, as he had to take the fortified city of Cartagena de Indias and face the forces of independent governments in New Granada's interior. However, for the reasons given earlier (in Chapter 5), this was accomplished quite quickly, and royal government reestablished on the back of military occupation. In April 1816, Montalvo was promoted to viceroy and set up his government in Cartagena, while Morillo entered Bogotá in May and continued to mop up resistance in New Granada's interior. He had scarcely accomplished this when he was ordered back to Venezuela in December 1816 to deal with renewed insurgent threats there; Morillo remained in Venezuela until, after a dozen attempts to resign, he was finally relieved of command and returned to Spain four years later, in December 1820.

The reconquest of Venezuela and New Granada was the most distinctive of the military campaigns undertaken during the restoration. It was a signal that Spain was determined to crush opposition by war, whatever the cost; it deployed an army from Spain, under a commander to whom the king gave powers amounting to those of a military dictator; it aimed to rebuild civil institutions of government but was always to retain strong characteristics of a military occupation, even when most of the Spanish soldiery had died or deserted and been replaced by American recruits. Its capacities were, however, constrained by conditions similar to those that afflicted the governments of New Spain and Peru: first, defiance from rebels, who had been weakened in 1814–16 but continued to fight for their cause; second, damaged economies, which could not provide sufficient resources for war;

and third, an ongoing financial crisis, which led to fiscal measures that alienated a resentful population.

Morillo initially aimed, above all, at eliminating rebellion. In 1815–16, he achieved his main military goals. His forces brought all the main cities and regions of Venezuela and New Granada back under royal authority and placed occupying forces in strategic areas. He also set up military governments—one under Brigadier Salvador Moxó in Venezuela and the other under his own command in New Granada. Military occupation did not, however, facilitate political renewal. Morillo's military governments were designed primarily to punish those who had participated in or colluded with the rebellion against the king, while also raising resources to pay for his occupying army by confiscation of their property. His arbitrary use of authority to achieve these goals soon brought conflict with the institutions of civil government. The audiencia of Caracas was the first to complain, after Morillo's decision to suspend it in June 1815 and his attempt to transfer its judges elsewhere. To the judges' protests, many others were soon added, from officials accused of complicity with the republicans, from those suspected of "infidelity," and from communities saddled with paying for Morillo's armies. Military and civil authorities in Venezuela were therefore soon at loggerheads and their inability to cooperate was to drain the reinstated royal governments of their energy and direction.[44]

Similar problems arose in New Granada. There, again, government was bedeviled by the question of how to deal with the insurgents and the larger grouping of *infidentes*, a diffuse, ill-defined category, which ranged from those who had actively colluded with independent governments to those who had simply temporized. The confusion caused by lack of legal clarity about how to gauge loyalty was compounded by contention over how to eliminate rebellion. In New Granada as in Venezuela, the key issue was how to win back the loyalty of the population so that the insurgency could be thoroughly eradicated. While Morillo and his army commanders believed that force and discipline were indispensable, Viceroy Montalvo blamed them for alienating the population by disrespectful attitudes and excessive demands for resources.[45]

Straitened economic times made cooperation between the military and civil authorities doubly difficult. After 1815, Venezuela and New Granada were required to sustain armed forces that were considerably larger than those present before 1810, but in an economy diminished by war. The export agriculture of Caracas had been almost entirely upset by losses of labor and disruption of trade; the gold mines and commercial agriculture of New Granada were less afflicted but had also been exposed to damage that diminished their fiscal yield. Taxation, which had barely covered government spending before the wars, was lost during the wars and could not be easily reintroduced.[46] The consequent financial difficulties not only forced governments into extraordinary levies that angered Americans, but they also exacerbated the divisions between civilian officials who wanted to return to the rule of law and army officers whose priority was to win the war.

The problems of rebuilding the royalist order were especially severe in Venezuela. The Spanish authorities controlled Venezuela's major regions and main towns but had not prevented insurgent forces from regrouping in frontier areas. In the southwest, the patriot leaders Rafael Urdaneta and Pedro Zaraza remained at large in the Llanos of Caracas, while José Antonio Páez continued to hold the plains near the River Apure. In the east, Arismendi had reestablished a stronghold on Margarita Island, Monagas threatened the port of Barcelona, and Piar was gathering an attack aimed against Guayana. Moreover, behind the presence and activities of these various forces was an additional, greater threat: that they might come together in a coordinated campaign.

Morillo decided that the threat to the east had to be given priority, because the insurgents' recapture of Margarita Island and advances in Guayana threatened to give them a strategic position at the mouth of the Orinoco, from which they could extend westwards into the Llanos and even reach towards New Granada. He therefore concentrated his first efforts at military reconquest on retaking Margarita Island, combined with a flanking movement by his deputy Brigadier Miguel de la Torre into Guayana. This did not dislodge the insurgents. On the contrary, Morillo was tied down on Margarita and Torres was badly beaten by Manuel Piar, who took the town of Guayana in July 1817 and quickly established control over its hinterland. Morillo was now forced to retreat from the east, leaving the rebels in control of the entry to the Llanos, with their huge supplies of horses and cattle, and vast spaces for refuge and maneuver.

While these successes kept alive the possibility of independence from Spain, the rebel forces were still far from realizing it; indeed, they had yet to merge under a unified command. That was to change in 1817–18, when Bolívar reemerged as a supreme leader. Bolívar had returned to Venezuela in March 1816 only to be forced back to Haiti after an abortive attack on royalist Margarita; he returned in December 1816 to attack the port of Barcelona but managed to penetrate inland only with aid from Mariño. As one patriot caudillo among several, Bolívar had no special authority. However, for reasons we shall explore in Chapter 11, he succeeded within a year or so in taking the war to a new level, resurrecting a new threat to Spanish control of both Venezuela and New Granada.

The Contradictions of Spanish Policy under Ferdinand VII

As viceroys and generals struggled to rebuild Spain's authority from Mexico to Chile, it became increasingly obvious that punitive measures alone could not resolve the imperial crisis. The framework for royal government had been badly shaken: the administrative chain was broken, crown institutions were altered or entirely suspended, the fiscal system was riddled with holes, and military mobilizations had damaged economic life and undermined respect for the social hierarchy. Spain's ability to defend the empire at sea had suffered badly too, with the loss of ships, sailors, and port facilities in America. During the interregnum, the money and men needed to support the Spanish navy, already weakened by Trafalgar, were directed into war in the Peninsula rather than mobilized to blockade enemy ports or mount amphibious operations against them, and the Armada was seriously weakened.[47]

Given the great expense involved in building and maintaining ships, this was difficult to remedy in times of financial emergency and had serious repercussions on Spain's ability to defend its coasts and its trade in America.

The impact on Spain's commercial monopoly was a central problem, as the inflow of British goods subverted Spain's claim to commercial exclusivity. Spain retained commercial connections with America, mainly through Cádiz, but they never recovered the scale and value reached during periods of peace in the late eighteenth century. Indeed, instead of being a means by which Spain could rebuild its position in America, the conduct of external trade became a source of damaging political contention among royalist supporters, splitting them into those who advocated free trade in order to stimulate economic and fiscal recovery against those who defended Spain's monopoly at all costs.

Difficulties such as these pointed to the larger obstacle to Spain's efforts to rebuild its empire after 1814—namely, the huge damage done to the country's economy by the Peninsular War and the parallel decline of Spanish American commerce. Its agriculture and industry ravaged, Spain became incapable of supplying American markets with the goods they wanted during or after the war and was therefore starved of the silver that paid for such goods. Foreign commercial competition had meanwhile become ineradicable. With only a negligible Spanish navy to oppose them, insurgent privateers did great damage to Spain's trade, and foreign interloping became uncontrollable. This shrinkage of resources created the central dilemma for Ferdinand VII's governments: to recover America, it needed solvency, but without American trade and revenues it could not achieve it.

The struggle to rebuild Spanish administrative and commercial systems was further complicated by the fact that Spain could not eradicate internal armed opposition completely nor eliminate foreign threats to its territory and trade. While patriot caudillos accumulated forces and grew more aggressive in Venezuela and New Granada, the Río de la Plata remained outside Spanish control and could not be reconquered while Spain's military assets were overstretched elsewhere. In May 1816, the Council of the Indies informed the king that "the rebellion in the Americas is a more terrible and disastrous event than he perhaps had thought," and called for a political solution. This proposal was given added weight by Portugal's seizure of Montevideo in June 1816. This was a vivid revelation of Spain's weakness, as Portugal invaded at the very time that Ferdinand VII and his brother were arranging marriages with the daughters of King João and Queen Carlota in order to improve Luso-Spanish relations. In these circumstances, it was crystal clear that the restored monarchy lacked the international leverage as well as the political authority and military power to renew Spain's dominance in America. Indeed, Minister of State Cevallos concluded that Portugal's invasion in the River Plate made Spain appear incapable of controlling its overseas territories, and he felt constrained to seek help from Britain. The hope that British mediation might produce solutions reopened debate over the direction that Spain's American policy should take. This was conducted under the auspices of José Pizarro, a pragmatic politician whom Ferdinand VII appointed as the new minister of state in October 1816 to search for a strategy that would deliver a negotiated peace.[48]

Pizarro initially lacked the power to determine American policy, but his ministry saw a definite shift of opinion among members of the Council of State and Council of the Indies. As military reports became increasingly pessimistic, recognition of Spain's weakness encouraged statesmen to seek a new approach, combining force with international diplomacy. British mediation seemed to be the best hope, but, as before, it aroused sharp opposition in Spanish political circles. The British government insisted that mediation required Spain to offer concessions to its American opponents, particularly on the thorny issue of free trade. However, if free trade seemed to some a price worth paying, to others it meant handing over the riches of Spanish America to foreigners, and thus deprived political ties of any economic meaning.

To resolve this dilemma, Pizarro had devised a policy for the pacification of America based on wide-ranging reform coupled with targeted warfare. He offered various concessions: a general amnesty for dissidents, reform of commercial regulations, careful selection of government officials and appointment of Americans, an end to Spanish rivalry with Americans, open immigration, the employment of foreigners in the king's forces, the use of missionaries to promote reconciliation, and the use of agents to turn European opinion in Spain's favor. At the same time, Pizarro aimed to show that Spain could still wield force. He therefore recommended implementation of the long-promised military expedition to Río de la Plata in order to save that region and protect Peru, Upper Peru, and Chile from revolution. He also suggested that Spain's naval power be improved by arming privateers to combat the insurgent corsairs, while also investing in the development of military and merchant shipping.[49]

In the event, the proposals made, debated, and addressed to the king met with prevarication. This indecision points to the persistent flaw in Ferdinand VII's regime: the lack of clear and consistent direction at the center, due partly to the organizational and procedural failings of Ferdinand's style of governance. Until Pizarro took control of American policy in November 1817, there was no single organizing vision to shape American policies. Ministers were deeply divided on the American question, and incoherence in policy-making was compounded by a king who changed his ministers frequently and often failed to inform them of important policy initiatives. Behind the gyrations and contradictions of policy was, of course, the fundamental dilemma facing Spanish statesmen: how to find a political settlement in America without ceding Spain's claim to monopolize colonial resources. British mediation did not provide the solution; for, as Spain's control of Spanish American ports diminished, British merchants informally acquired the open access they wanted.

As a result, Ferdinand VII swung back towards a military solution. Recognizing that effective military action in America would require naval strength, the king tried to repair Spain's naval weakness by buying a flotilla of Russian warships from the Czar in 1817. In principle, this was a sensible move, for it addressed the chronic neglect that had so drastically diminished the navy's effectiveness. After 1814, the negative consequences of such neglect became increasingly obvious as American insurgents began to build their own navies, chiefly by commissioning privateers to plunder Spanish trade, blockade Spanish ports on both sides of the Atlantic, and occasionally assemble for amphibious operations. However, when the Spanish government awoke to the vital need for dominance at sea, the recuperation of naval power was beyond its reach. Ferdinand VII's first minister of the navy, José Vásquez Figueroa, made it plain as soon as he took office in 1816 that naval power had to be the keystone of an American military strategy. He succeeded in improving his budget, but it still fell far short of the finance needed to combat insurgent privateers, convoy merchantmen, and cut off trade to American rebels. As for the king's Russian transaction, it was a military and political disaster. Because most of the eight ships sent by the Czar were unseaworthy and required extensive repair, the deal caused a huge political scandal while doing nothing to rebuild Spanish naval strength.[50]

The Spanish government also tried to reinforce the military position in Spanish America by dispatching several regiments of regulars—about 2,000 men—to Chile and Peru in May 1818. This too met with failure, as one group mutinied en route and most of the others were captured on arrival in Chile. Finally, in late 1818, the king confirmed the commanders of a large army that was to be sent from Cádiz to the Río de la Plata, finally implementing the plan to crush Buenos Aires, which had been on his agenda in 1815.[51] By this time, however, Spanish hopes for a military solution in Spanish America were fast disappearing, and the expedition was aborted in early 1820 amid a political crisis in Spain, which, once again, reverberated throughout Spanish America.

By 1819–20, it was increasingly obvious that imperial reconstruction was a chimera. If it had seemed possible to recreate Spanish authority at the start of the restoration, that prospect had rapidly receded in the years that followed. Addressing the king, the Peruvian judge Manuel Vidaurre captured the problem:

> The American today is the same as a Spaniard. He knows that if they are not so naturally strong as the European, fire arms level out the difference . . . They have excellent artillery and can forge as much as they wish in a few months. Their cannon are as good or better than European cannon. Muskets are being manufactured, and mortars . . . Emigrants from Europe teach ancient and modern tactics . . . It is impossible for Europe to dominate America by the use of force.[52]

Though Vidaurre's judgment was based on his observation of the war between royalist Peru and independent Buenos Aires, it had a wider relevance. For although warfare in Spanish America had diminished around the start of the restoration, nowhere in America were the roots of insurgency easily destroyed. Even in Mexico, where insurgency contracted after the death of Morelos, the recession of rebellion did not bring a return to a peaceful civil order. On the contrary, regional warfare left a strong residue of violence, evident in the armed bands that continued to operate in several areas. These insurgents were less politically threatening, as they were without unified leadership or political coordination and incapable of realizing Morelos's ambition to build an alternative state. The continuity of violence was, however, a danger that continued to stand in the way to the normalization of royal government. It meant that the royalist army had both to continue with operations against insurgent bases and to sustain the self-defense system created under General Calleja, requiring the maintenance of a large military apparatus at crippling expense to civil society and government. Mexico thus remained in a state of crisis with a civil government that was increasingly dependent on the military officers who effectively controlled local government in many regions.

In South America, royalist officials had even less success in extirpating the roots of rebellion. In several regions, the wars started during the interregnum continued to present a serious threat to royalist regimes and were, from 1816, to build into conflicts, which gradually came to resemble wars between rival states. The main sites of resistance were at opposite ends of the continent: Venezuela and New Granada in the north and the Río de la Plata in the south. In the first two regions, the republics had fallen and the soi-disant patriots were forced to take refuge in either overseas exile or backland regions where they continued to fight using the tactics and techniques of guerrilla warfare. In the Río de la Plata, on the other hand, the government of Buenos Aires was unconquered and continued with wars on fronts where it had been fighting for some time. The future of these nuclei of resistance remained uncertain for several years, as patriot leaders struggled to survive in a counterrevolutionary climate. They were often disunited; they faced strong opposition from royalist forces within Spanish America, and they had to adjust to an international diplomatic context, which was largely hostile to their cause. Spanish American enclaves of resistance were nonetheless able to develop into increasingly plausible movements for independence during the decade after Ferdinand VII's return, due largely to three factors.

The first, which we have seen in this chapter, was Spain's economic weakness, fiscal penury, and political instability. The second was the determination of Spanish American patriot leaders and their followers not only to continue but also to extend their wars against Spain. The third was an international climate, which, though initially favorable to Spain, gradually became more favorable to the patriots, allowing them to find foreign resources to fight their wars and eventually to persuade foreign governments to recognize their independence.

These factors constantly interacted with each other. As Spain's weaknesses provided chances for American patriots to fight back, so the changing balance of power in Spanish America further weakened Ferdinand VII's regime. Its debility encouraged foreign powers to rethink their support for Spain, and the Spanish American patriots accordingly blended their military offensives with diplomatic initiatives aimed at undermining Spain's position in the international arena. My contention is, however, that the primary driver of change was the resurgence of patriot forces in South America under leaders who revived the war against Spain and, from unpromising beginnings, created ambitious political and military strategies.

The outstanding leaders were in Argentina and Venezuela, where José de San Martín and Simón Bolívar built new armies, created new strategies, and took the struggle against Spanish military and political power in new directions. From the Orinoco basin of Venezuela and the Andean interior of the Río de la Plata, these leaders developed what were later to become the vanguards of continental offensives against Spanish rule. Why, then, after multiple defeats and setbacks in 1814–15, did patriot military revivals gather pace in South America during 1817–18, and what did they achieve?

Notes

1. Artola, *España de Fernando VII*, pp. 408–30. On the sectors of the army involved and the support given by Wellington in support of this coup, see Brian R. Hamnett, *La política española en una época revolucionaria, 1790–1820* (Mexico City: Fondo de Cultura Económica, 1985), pp. 184–201. On the role of the army, the "Persians," and popular acclaim, see Anna, *Spain and the Loss of America*, pp. 115–32. On the purges of Spanish and creole deputies to the Cortes, see Hamnett, *Revolución y contrarrevolución en México y el Perú*, pp. 203–21.
2. Esdaile, *Spain in the Liberal Age*, pp. 45–50, 199.
3. For sketches of Ferdinand VII, see Raymond Carr, *Spain, 1808–1939* (Oxford: Clarendon Press, 1966), pp. 120–2; Esdaile, *Spain in the Liberal Age*, pp. 42–3.
4. A useful study of the role played by the Council of State in American policy, seen through the documentation it generated, is Enoch F. Resnick, "The Council of State and Spanish America, 1814–20," (PhD thesis, The American University, 1970), especially chapters 1 and 2.
5. Anna, *Spain and the Loss of America*, pp. 118–32; Artola, *España de Ferdinand VII*, pp. 430–5.
6. A los habitantes de las Indias el Ministro Universal de ellas, July 20, 1814, cited by Heredia, *Planes españoles para reconquistar Hispanoamerica*, p. 115.
7. Heredia, *Planes españoles*, pp. 124–45.
8. Anna, *Spain and the Loss of Empire*, pp. 134–9.
9. Conde de Puñonrostro to Duque de San Carlos, Madrid, May 22, 1814, Archivo General de Indias (AGI), Estado 88, no. 39, p. 2.
10. Heredia, *Planes españoles*, pp. 151–61.
11. The first recommendations came from the Council on September 13 and were sent to the king on October 3. The second were recorded by the council meeting of October 4: AGI, Ultramar 780.
12. Earle, *Spain and the Independence of Colombia*, pp. 57–8.
13. Quoted by Anna, *Spain and the Loss of America*, p. 143.
14. On the question of mediation between 1811 and 1815, see Anna, *Spain and the Loss of America*, pp. 104–10.
15. Esdaile, *Peninsular War*, p. 505.
16. Juan Antonio Yandiola to King, January 29, 1815, AGI, Estado 87, no. 30.
17. In 1784, the best year of the eighteenth century, Spanish exports to America peaked at 22.8 million pesos; during the Peace of Amiens, they reached a high of about 17.5 million; they then fell precipitously in 1811–15 to an average of 4.9 million pesos per year: See Fisher, *Commercial Relations between Spain and Spanish America in the Era of Free Trade*, p. 61; *Trade, War and Revolution: Exports from Spain to Spanish America, 1797–1820* (Liverpool: Institute of Latin American Studies, 1992), pp. 80–1. The decline of trade through Cádiz, traditionally the major port for American trade, deepened after 1816 as

the chances of recovering colonial trade were wiped out by the revival of war in Spanish America: see Antonio García-Baquero González, *Comercio colonial y guerras revolucionarias* (Seville: Escuela de Estudios Hispanoamericanos, 1972), pp. 228–42.

18. For a full account of Spain's fiscal problems during the restoration and the reasons for the failure of Ferdinand VII's restoration governments to resolve them, see Fontana, *La quiebra de la monarquía absoluta*, pp. 51–82, 101–2, 158–77. For confirmation of Fontana's thesis and an analysis of Spain's fiscal crisis and reform in a longer perspective, see Juan Pan-Montojo, "La construcción del nuevo Estado y la fiscalidad: España, 1808–1845," in *Las nuevas naciones: España y México, 1800–1850*, ed. Jaime E. Rodríguez O. (Madrid: Mapfre, 2008), pp. 169–90.

19. Stoan, *Pablo Morillo and Venezuela*, p. 70.

20. For evidence of the economic impact of war in these key regions, see Street, *Artigas and the Emancipation of Uruguay*, pp. 214–5; Earle, *Colombia*, pp. 92–6; Stoan, *Morillo*, pp. 73–4; José Luis Roca, *Ni con Lima*, pp. 308–9, 387–8; Halperín-Donghi, *Politics, Economics, and Society in Argentina in the Revolutionary Period*, pp. 245–61; Hira de Gortari Rabiela, "La minería durante la guerra de independencia y los primeros años del México independiente," in Rodríguez O., *The Independence of Mexico and the Creation of the New Nation*, pp. 129–49.

21. Marichal, *Bankruptcy of Empire*, pp. 255–65.

22. Heredia, *Planes españoles*, pp. 116–22.

23. Ibid., pp. 147–8.

24. Ibid., pp. 228–33.

25. Harris G. Warren, "Xavier Mina's Invasion of Mexico," *HAHR* 23, no. 1 (1943): pp. 52–76; William F. Lewis, "Simón Bolívar and Xavier Mina: A Rendezvous in Haiti," *Journal of Inter-American Studies* 11, no. 3 (1969): pp. 458–65.

26. Heredia, *Planes españoles*, pp. 208–11.

27. On MacGregor, see Matthew Brown, "Inca, Sailor, Soldier, King: Gregor MacGregor and the Early Nineteenth-Century Caribbean," *Bulletin of Latin American Research (BLAR)* 24, no. 1 (2005): pp. 44–71.

28. These comments are based on Rafe Blaufarb's illuminating account of French exiles in the American south, set in the context of United States' policy towards Spain and Spanish American independence: see Rafe Blaufarb, *Bonapartists in the Borderlands: French Exiles and Refugees on the Gulf Coast, 1815–1835* (Tuscaloosa: University of Alabama, 2005), pp. 33–43, 51–7, 61–77, 87–116.

29. Juan Ruíz de Apodaca, "An Update for the Minister of War on the Military Occurrences of the Kingdom of New Spain during the Month of March, 1818," in *Wars of Independence in Spanish America*, ed. Christon I. Archer (Wilmington, DE: Scholarly Resources, 2000), p. 148.

30. Archer, "The Cutting Edge: The Historical Relationship between Insurgency, Counterinsurgency and Terrorism during Mexican Independence, 1810–1821," p. 37.

31. Archer, "'La Causa Buena,' The Counterinsurgency Army of New Spain and the Ten Years' War," pp. 102–5. On the erosion of army organization and morale under the Restoration, see Archer, "Where did all the Royalists go?," pp. 30–7.

32. Anna, *Fall of Royal Government in Mexico City*, pp. 182–7.

33. Van Young, *The Other Rebellion*, pp. 75–86.

34. John Jay TePaske, "The Financial Disintegration of the Royal Government of Mexico during the Epoch of Independence," in Rodríguez O., *The Independence of Mexico and the Creation of the New Nation*, pp. 63–83; Marichal, *Bankruptcy of Empire*, pp. 237–54.

35. Hamnett, *Revolución y contrarrevolución en México y el Perú*, pp. 94–105, 109–17.

36. On the political contradictions of the Restoration in Mexico, see Anna, *Fall of Royal Government in Mexico City*, pp. 184–7.

37. From a letter of May 1812, cited by Marks, *Deconstructing Legitimacy: Viceroys, Merchants, and the Military in Late Colonial Peru*, p. 184.
38. Anna, *Fall of the Royal Government in Peru*, pp. 76–108.
39. Marks, *Deconstructing Legitimacy*, pp. 171–203, La Serna quotation from p. 185–6.
40. For analysis of the fiscal and economic crisis that Pezuela inherited from Abascal, see Hamnett, *Revolución y contrarrevolución*, pp. 122–8; Anna, *Fall of Royal Government in Peru*, pp. 109–22.
41. Mendizábal, *Guerra de la América del Sur, 1809–1824*, pp. 103–27.
42. Ibid., pp. 130–6.
43. Hamnett, *Revolución y contrarrevolución*, pp. 289–96.
44. Stoan, *Morillo*, pp. 64–118.
45. Earle, *Spain and the Independence of Colombia*, pp. 75–88.
46. Ibid., pp. 107–23; Stoan, *Morillo*, pp. 145–76.
47. On the decline of the navy in 1810–14, see Cervera Pery, *La marina española en la emancipación de Hispanoámerica*, pp. 119–21, 128–37.
48. Anna, *Spain and the Loss of America*, pp. 156–9.
49. Ibid., pp. 190–6.
50. Costeloe, *Response to Revolution*, pp. 66–7; Anna, *Spain and the Loss of America*, pp. 177–8, 204–5.
51. Anna, *Spain and the Loss of America*, pp. 200–6; Costeloe, *Response to Revolution*, pp. 76–83.
52. Manuel Vidaurre to King, Lima, April 2, 1817, AGI, Indiferente General 1568.

11

REPUBLIC REARMED

The Birth of Colombia

In 1815–16, the independent states in New Granada and Venezuela had vanished, overwhelmed by a combination of internal royalist opposition and Spanish armed invasion. In their wake, only pockets of resistance remained. The patriots who refused to surrender scattered into local groupings dedicated primarily to surviving the royalist counterinsurgency. Their position was precarious. By mid-1816, Spain had retaken control of all the major cities and regions of New Granada and Venezuela, and Morillo's expeditionary army, replenished by American recruits, provided unprecedented military support for resurgent royalist governments.

Morillo's arrival brought new factors into the military equation. Royalist propaganda proclaimed Morillo's troops as seasoned warriors, who, having defeated Napoleon's armies, would make short shrift of American rebels. That this was exaggerated soon became clear; the expeditionary army included many malcontents, suffered low morale, and was prone to desertion.[1] It was, nonetheless, a larger, more disciplined force than any the patriots could muster and had a core of veterans hardened by experience of war in Spain.[2] Once in place, Morillo and his fellow commander Pascual de Enrile also developed an ambitious strategic vision, which had New Granada at its center. They saw New Granada as the "natural route" to Peru, Chile, Buenos Aires, and Montevideo, and a hub from which to direct military operations in South America. Their plan called for the establishment of a network of garrisons and arms dumps in New Granada to supply war zones in neighboring regions. Soldiers in Bogotá were to be potential reserves for Venezuela; troops from Venezuela could be sent to Peru, together with two battalions from New Granada, to reinforce Pezuela's offensive against the Río de la Plata. In the future, New Granada might even reinforce points to the north, in Guatemala and Acapulco. Enrile's influence showed in the emphasis on building up naval forces, both on rivers and on the coast, and curbing the growth of insurgent naval power.[3]

Morillo's grand strategy was, then, to turn New Granada into the core of royalist counterinsurgency across the continent, the center for coordinated warfare against insurgents in Venezuela and New Granada, as well as on the Pacific coast to Peru and even Central America. It counted on local resources but also depended on metropolitan government to provide logistical, diplomatic, and political support. Morillo and Enrile expected regular troop rotations and reinforcements from Spain; they wanted Madrid to pressure foreign governments into cutting off trade with the insurgents, and, most important, they called on ministers to use New Granada as the point of departure for the pacification of South America as a whole.

This grand strategic plan was not well received in Spain, however, and after his initial meetings with ministers, Enrile was largely ignored. Moreover, at the time when Morillo and Enrile unveiled their strategy in mid-1817, the possibilities of putting it into practice were already receding, as an insurgent revival in Venezuela required more localized responses.[4]

Caudillos and Guerrillas in Venezuela

The revival of republican insurgency in Venezuela formed around three principal points. One nucleus of opposition was in Eastern Venezuela at Margarita Island. Another was far to the west in the great plains close to the headwaters of the River Orinoco. A third was outside Venezuela in the independent state of Haiti, where Simón Bolívar gathered forces with which to restart the war against Spain.[5]

Of these, the resistance in Eastern Venezuela was the most complicated, as it was arraigned under several leaders at different locations. On Margarita, the caudillo Juan Bautista Arismendi continued to resist Spanish occupation, while on the mainland several combatants from the previous war also fought on. Santiago Mariño, José Tadeo Monagas, and Pedro Zaraza operated in the sparsely peopled plains in the provinces of Barcelona and Cumaná, out of range of the royalist towns on the coast; Manuel Piar and Manuel Cedeño continued with their resistance further south in the plains of the lower Orinoco in the province of Guayana. These men were of mixed origins: some were from humble backgrounds, others were local notables; the great majority were from the region itself and closely identified with the interests of leading landowners. All had acquired military experience while fighting for independence during the Second Republic as officers under Bolívar's command. They were not a united group, however; Bolívar had lost much of his authority over them while he was in exile in Jamaica and Haiti, and they were not immediately brought to heel. Indeed, Mariño and his allies, having asserted their autonomy during the First Republic, continued to be more interested in creating an independent eastern state than restoring the republic ruled from Caracas. Manuel Piar, the Curaçao mulatto who had fought with the patriots since 1812, emerged as an important autonomous chief, fighting at the head of his own army and guided by his own political vision. Like Bolívar, Piar envisaged an offensive against Caracas and a political revolution, but his primary interest was in securing a place for the pardos and blacks who made up most of his army and with whom he closely identified. Initially, these eastern bands had no overall commander, and though they communicated with each other, they did not act in concert.

The resistance in the west was also made up of disparate groupings. One was composed of the refugees from the armies of New Granada's federation around 800 men led by white officers of superior social rank. In flight from royalist pursuit, forces under the Frenchman Serviez and the neogranadino Santander had retreated from the highlands of New Granada and the plains of Casanare to the area around the River Apure, a territory dominated by the llanero chieftain José Antonio Páez. The llanero bands led by Páez, about 700 men in total, were the core of independent resistance in the plains. Recruited from the simple rural societies of the region, these men were free of the formalities of military hierarchy; they chose leaders from within their ranks and were bound to their leader by ties of personal loyalty, forged in the companionship of war. The distinctive feature of this nucleus of resistance in the west was that it quickly gelled around one paramount leader, the warrior caudillo Páez. The refugees from New Granada elected their own leaders when they arrived at the town of Arauca, but the well-born creoles, who had previously held military and political command, were swiftly swept aside by Paez's llaneros, who would answer only to the orders of their charismatic chieftain. Páez thus assumed undisputed control; he suspended the civil government, rewarded Santander, Serviez, and Urdaneta with commands in his army in return for their declarations of loyalty, and proceeded to direct his own operations, independently of the leaders in the east and unconnected to Bolívar and his supporters.[6]

The nucleus of resistance around Bolívar was militarily the weakest of the three. Bolívar had no army. He was supported by a few hundred New Granadan and Venezuelan officers and political sympathizers who joined him in Caribbean exile, and he intended to make them the core of a new republican army, which he would command. His international contacts helped him to sustain this entourage and prepare for military action. Credit from British merchants in Jamaica provided the means to buy arms, and when he arrived in Haiti in January 1816, Bolívar received aid from President Petión in return for a commitment to end slavery in the future republic. These external contacts fed his dream of a republican revival, for they showed that it was still possible to muster some international support for the cause of independence and find the material means for relaunching the republican revolution.

Rebellion against the Spanish regime in Venezuela restarted because these disparate groups of patriots, or "insurgents" as the Spaniards preferred to call them, took advantage of Morillo's move to New Granada in 1816 to restart an organized anti-Spanish war in Venezuela. From their bases in the backlands, Mariño and Bermúdez took points along the coast of Güiria and advanced on Cumaná; Piar established his base at Maturín and made plans to advance on the royalist outposts in the towns of Guayana and Angostura. From his base in Haiti, Bolívar reestablished his connections with the leaders in the east and joined them in March 1816, leading a military expedition from Haiti to the mainland. He had only about 240 men, mostly officers, and his purpose was to establish a foothold on the coast of eastern Venezuela, to ally with other patriot forces, and to organize a larger offensive against the royalists.[7]

While Bolívar sought to revive his leadership in the east, Páez emerged in the west as paramount leader of the forces there and an important potential rival. He entrenched his leadership by defeating royalist forces sent to obliterate the patriots in the Western Llanos, not only holding off attacks from Barinas but also overcoming the royalist forces sent from New Granada against him. He dispersed Brigadier La Torre's Spanish regulars in several attacks during late 1816 and a few months later, in January 1817, defeated La Torre again on the plains at Mucuritas, when he led 1,100 horsemen into an attack on 1,500 Spanish infantry and 800 cavalry and forced them to retreat before the repeated charges of his llanero lancers. Morillo saw for the first time that he was facing a formidable enemy rather than the "small band of cowards" he had been told to expect. And now that he was master of the Apure region, Páez sought to strengthen his position by collaboration with Bolívar. In February 1817, he told Bolívar that he had 4,000 men at his disposal as well as huge herds of horse and cattle and that all he needed for victory was firearms and munitions, which he asked Bolívar to supply.[8]

The third revolutionary war in Venezuela was, then, launched by clusters of irregulars led by armed caudillos. Bolívar commanded a loose allegiance among the caudillos, no doubt because they shared his commitment to independence and recognized his ability to bring them together for mutual benefit. He could not, however, create an immediate unity of purpose among them. While he enjoyed some prestige from his past position, he found it difficult to assert his authority while he had neither an army nor a territorial power base of his own.

Bolívar and Republican Leadership

Bolívar received a sharp lesson in the problems of merging the military actions of patriot leaders into a coordinated insurgency shortly after he returned to Venezuela in 1816. When he landed at Margarita, Bolívar was acclaimed by an assembly of caudillos who voted for a unified Venezuela and confirmed him as their leader, with Mariño as his deputy. This affirmation of loyalty was, however, conditional on Bolívar's military success and soon proved a fragile pact. From Margarita, Bolívar immediately moved to consolidate his position by initiating a military campaign, taking about 300 men to seize the nearby port of Carúpano. Having established a position on the mainland, he then struck out on a surprise attack against Caracas. In a daring amphibious operation, he landed with about 800 men at Ocumare in July 1816, intending to make a lightning strike on the capital that was, in effect, a repetition of the strategy of his 1813 "Admirable Campaign."[9]

These actions showed Bolívar's strategic vision and his adroit use of a new arm in the war against Spain—the ships provided by his naval commander, the Dutch privateer Luis Brion. Brion's ships enabled him to enhance his relatively small forces by making a surprise attack from seaward. Unfortunately for Bolívar, he overreached himself. After sending Soublette and MacGregor inland to link up with patriot forces in the Llanos, Bolívar had to beat a hasty retreat by sea. This was a potentially fatal setback. He had not only failed to rejuvenate his authority by displaying military skill but also made himself vulnerable to his rivals, Mariño and Bermúdez, who promptly tried to arrest him.[10] Had he not escaped their attempt to depose him, Bolívar's career might have ended at this point, with incalculable effects for the republican cause in Venezuela and New Granada. In the event, however, he returned to Haiti and continued to contribute to the war, first with a second expedition from Haiti at the end of 1816 and, second, with a new military strategy for the revolution. Conceived in 1817, his strategy aimed at taking control of the great plains of the Orinoco basin in the southern half of the country and converting these llanos regions into the base for a long-term offensive against the royalists.

Bolívar's shift to a new strategy was driven by necessity. On his second return from Haiti at the end of December 1816, he carried arms and munitions to Barcelona and tried to bring Mariño and Piar into his strategy for attacking central Venezuela. But they had their own plans and refused to reinforce him. Without adequate forces, Bolívar lost Barcelona to Morillo in early January 1817 and decided to retreat south into Piar's domain in Guayana.[11] There, he gradually reasserted his authority by combining military engagement alongside Piar with diplomacy among the caudillos. While Piar wanted a firm regional base for himself, Bolívar recognized the larger strategic importance of Guayana for a war to liberate Venezuela from Spanish rule. Thus, after joining Piar's camp near Angostura in early May 1817, he established the base on which to build both his military operations and his political system.

For Bolívar, the war in Guayana was a pressing military priority, but it was not his sole concern. He was acutely aware that the recovery of the republic needed clarity of political purpose and a constitutional system, but he feared that both were absent from the cockpit of patriot warlords wrestling for dominance. He therefore sought for a means to harness their military energy to his political goals. The risk was that the caudillos would, if left to themselves, bring only destruction. "Arms," he said, "will destroy the tyrants in vain if we do not establish a political order capable of repairing the damage done by revolution. The military system is that of force, and force is not government."[12]

The "military system" that Bolívar criticized was, however, to become the essential foundation of the republic he aimed to rebuild. When he started, the armed bands led by local caudillos were essentially private armies fighting for survival rather than ideologically committed cadres seeking a new political order; nevertheless, they identified with the republican cause and, by keeping up military pressure, were to play a crucial part in the establishment of Bolívar's Republic of Colombia. To understand how the republicans turned from the defensive to the offensive and what they contributed to recreating the republic, we must first examine their adaptation to guerrilla warfare and their gradual unification under a single leadership. For it was in the regional wars of Venezuela that new republican forces were formed, Spanish armies stretched and depleted, and the balance of military power gradually altered.

The republicans had continued to fight after their defeat by Boves because they had no choice; it was their only means of defending themselves against a bloody repression. They did so from places of refuge because they simply lacked the means to make conventional war.[13] In this, their struggle bears some resemblance to the Spanish guerrilla war against the French.[14] Venezuela's guerrillas, like Spain's, emerged from armies that had abandoned regular war because they were unable to engage a superior enemy in battle. Instead, soldiers dispersed into groups that followed classic guerrilla tactics. They lived off the land and evaded the enemy by constant movement, ceding territory to conserve their capacity for combat; they created bases from which to operate but, unlike militias, did not identify with specific communities; they recruited from soldiers and civilians of all social ranks. They also had features that set them apart from Spanish guerrillas, stemming from the very different character of Venezuelan society. They relied heavily on horsemen recruited from ranch hands organized by landowners or their administrators (such as Páez) and from disaffected llanero fighters who changed sides when Morillo discharged them from the royalist army. Indian bowmen were also sometimes pressed into fighting, as were escaped slaves. The Venezuelans were more autonomous and less nationalistic than the Spanish guerrillas, too; they did not have to coordinate with a regular army, as their enemy was not a foreign army of occupation but forces made up largely of fellow Americans. They were, moreover, drawn mainly from the distinctive pastoral society of the western plains, from communities that had long been on the fringes of colonial society and were less subject to the rule of law.

The war in Western Venezuela developed along its own distinctive lines, dominated by a single outstanding leader, the llanero chieftain José Antonio Páez. The forces grouped around him included elements of the defeated republican forces led by republican officers from the previous war, but his llanero horsemen were the major force, and their mode of warfare dominant. Irregular war replaced direct war, and llanero cavalry tactics supplanted the use of infantry formations, leading to the formation of a new kind of guerrilla army.[15] The basic unit was the small band, from a few dozen to around 100 horsemen who subsisted by moving around, taking supplies and arms by raiding or trading, behaving like bandits but attacking a political enemy rather than merely plundering. The individuals who made up the band were free from regular military discipline; these were communities of men who came and went as they pleased and obeyed their leader from personal respect and loyalty.

These disparate bands were in turn the building blocks for another level of guerrilla organization, formed from their merger into groups of about 1,000 men or more. Such larger groupings united under a charismatic leader like Páez and operated from settled bases that were built to provide refuge for those escaping royalist persecution. They included refugees from different regions and social classes, men, women, and children, and they worked together to supply food from a communal agriculture, supplemented by meat supplied from the cattle herds of the plains. Here, the law of force counted for more than the force of law. Officers of the republican army were supplanted by popular leaders, and formal political institutions were absent. But a republican identity was nonetheless nurtured in these communities and their associated guerrilla bands, not only because creole officers and guerrilla leaders shared a desire to fight and destroy the royalist regime but also because the combination of people from different social groups under leaders of their choice erased colonial hierarchies and nurtured an "egalitarian republic in arms."[16]

The resistance in the east differed from Páez's western war in that it arose under several leaders rather than being bound to a single one. Patriot leaders such as Mariño, Monagas, Cedeño, and Piar had no immediate reason to recognize a single command; each had their own forces, mostly horsemen armed with lances and some firearms, and they sustained themselves from cattle and horse rustling on the plains of Cumaná and Barcelona, occasionally converging to attack royalist forces and to raid or capture towns. Bolívar intended, from the time of his arrival, to impose his leadership on these caudillos, but his depleted military prestige and uncertain political standing made this difficult. He favored a direct form of war, of concerted attack on the royalist heartlands, but when this was unsuccessful, was forced to adopt a more indirect approach. After defeat at Barcelona, he withdrew from the coast to the plains of the Orinoco, where he joined forces with Piar near Angostura in May 1817 and, with Piar's essential help, turned to developing another theater of war in Eastern Venezuela.

Bolívar had opted to join Piar because he recognized Guayana's strategic potential: control of the Orinoco not only provided access to maritime trade but also opened a channel deep into the interior as far as the western Llanos and the foothills of New Granada's Eastern Cordillera. General Morillo also recognized the strategic importance of Eastern Venezuela and Guayana, and on returning from New Granada to confront the insurgency in December 1816, he immediately focused his military activities on those areas. He led the campaign against the insurgents on Margarita Island and the eastern mainland and sent Brigadier La Torre to defend royalist positions at Angostura, the principal port of the Orinoco and provincial capital of Guayana. It was, in the event, the patriots who managed to take the advantage in both areas; they were successful in resisting Morillo's forces in both Margarita and Guayana.[17]

The fall of royalist Guayana was particularly important, as it gave Bolívar a stable base on which to rebuild the republic under his leadership. Piar had laid the foundations for Bolívar's project. He had converted the Caroní River missions into a source of the supplies needed for war, laid siege to Angostura and, in April 1817, used his infantry to defeat La Torre at San Felix. But Bolívar brought a new dimension to the struggle by combining operations on land, sea, and river. Recognizing that the royalists were immovable from their fortified river ports as long as they controlled navigation on the Orinoco, he built gunboats to harass Spanish shipping and, more important, ordered his "admiral," Luis Brion, to bring a flotilla of armed vessels from the Caribbean. Brion's domination of the river forced the royalist evacuation of Angostura and of the troops who manned its fortifications. The royalist defeat was orderly: La Torre moved out with 2,000 soldiers and mariners, plus some 1,800 civilians, in early August 1817, in "a spectacle never seen on the proud Orinoco at any time since the creation of the Universe."[18] However, hundreds perished as they fought their way down the Orinoco towards the sea, and a substantial number of vessels, artillery, muskets and munitions, plus a large sum of treasury money, fell into insurgent hands.[19]

Much more important than immediate gains and losses were the strategic consequences of the campaign. Bolívar had not only taken the key royalist strongholds on the Orinoco but removed Spain's command of important coasts and rivers. This brought a tremendous advantage. Control of navigation along the Orinoco strengthened the insurgents' economic base by opening up free trade with foreigners in the Caribbean, allowing the exchange of livestock and agricultural goods from Guayana for arms, munitions, and other material for war. Brion's operations also did much to strengthen the insurgents' naval power because, by exposing Spanish naval weaknesses, it enhanced the attractions of privateering under the banners of the republic, thereby further undermining the royalists' ability to control the coasts.

If the capture of Angostura and Guayana gave Bolívar a territorial base on which to rebuild the republic, control of the Orinoco allowed him to develop his larger strategic vision. He saw the river as the axis on which to extend republican control far to the west, towards Páez's area of operation in the plains of the Apure and Casanare rivers, and beyond, across the Andes, into New Granada. "This decisive blow against the enemy navy," he told Páez,

> gives us a perpetual predominance and irrevocably determines the destiny of Guayana, Barinas and even New Granada. The Orinoco will always be ours, and nothing will block this channel through which we will receive from the exterior and send into the interior the elements for making war, however long the Spaniards sustain their unjust project for suppressing us.[20]

Building the Republic

In addition to its military implications, Bolívar's success in Guayana had important political repercussions. Men who had previously accepted orders from Mariño and Piar now turned to Bolívar, and Bolívar, having established his own base at Angostura with some 3,000 men under his command, felt able to strike back against his rivals and crystallize his competition with Piar. For although Piar nominally accepted Bolívar's command, he was insubordinate and threatened to divide the forces that Bolívar intended to integrate into a single army. Piar was, moreover, accused of plotting to start a "race war" against the whites.[21] Bolívar's accusations were sufficient to damn him in the eyes of the other caudillos and army officers. He was duly arrested and in October 1817 formally executed by firing squad "for proclaiming the odious principles of race war . . . for inciting civil war, and for encouraging anarchy."[22]

The accusation of fomenting "race war" directed against Piar reflects the racial tensions that came into the open during the revolutionary wars. Recruited by both royalists and republicans, pardos and blacks took advantage of the wars to express their grievances and engage in politics. They joined both sides, but, as they became empowered by warfare, royalist and republican leaders worried that they might displace and dominate the white minority. For whites, racial war was a real concern. Bolívar expressed strong anxiety that participation in wars would give pardo leaders the ideas, weapons, and organization to fight for their cause alone, giving rise to a "pardocracy" that would displace rule by whites. Spanish leaders had comparable worries: General Morillo was told that Piar and Petión were plotting to destroy the white ruling class throughout the Caribbean and to create a series of black republics, and Morillo shared Bolívar's fear that people of color might take over if not curbed.[23]

It is, in fact, difficult to be sure that there was any substantive threat of "race war." Pardos and blacks, including slaves, fought alongside whites on both sides, and there is no sign that pardos developed a clear political agenda or organization directed specifically against whites. This was partly because the republicans offered people of color a place in the new political order. Rather than shut them out (as the republic of the United States had done), Venezuela's republican leadership offered equal civil rights for pardos from 1812 and, after Bolívar returned in 1816, added the manumission of slaves in return for military service. However, having thus identified the republic with racial equality and harmony, white republican leaders then used the threat of "race war" to impose unity on their terms. By raising the specter of race war, they reminded whites that they should concede pardo equality and slave manumission in order to avoid racial conflict, while also reminding pardos and blacks that they had to conform to the rules of the creole-led republic in order to be accepted.[24]

Whether or not Piar had planned a war against whites, his execution was a milestone in the revival of the republican insurgency. On the one hand, Bolívar's assertion of authority strengthened his plans to reestablish the republic and bring the independents' forces under his leadership. On the other, the caudillos' willingness to acknowledge a higher authority showed that, far from being anarchic warlords, they recognized the need for a stable authority, if only to preserve the rank and honor they won in war.

This combination changed the organization of the patriots' insurgency. In the first place, it enabled Bolívar to reform the republic's armed forces. From September 1817, he created a General Staff in order to train officers, bond them in a chain of command, and provided a single source of orders for the army as a whole. He sought, too, to create a more disciplined soldiery, which acknowledged loyalty to the republic and behaved reliably on and off the battlefield. This meant encouraging officers to recruit widely in order to create units composed of men who were not tied to particular regions and to foster their allegiance to the republic rather than their local patria.[25] It also meant establishing court martial to punish indiscipline, particularly the murders, assaults, and unrestrained plunder that besmirched the republic's reputation, as caudillos such as Piar and Páez—as well as most local leaders—continued with the exterminationist "war to the death."

The establishment of a system of military justice signaled Bolívar's intent to transform the patriot soldiery from clusters of insurgents identified with their local caudillos into a disciplined army with shared values and an identification with the republic. It also reflected a move to curb the extraordinary brutality that had come to characterize war in Venezuela. While the royalist commanders Boves and Morales had acquired terrifying reputations for cruelty in 1814, several leaders on the republican side also became notorious for ruthless treatment of enemies. Accounts of their operations suggest that they, like the royalists, routinely executed wounded soldiers and prisoners. Richard Vowell, who joined the patriot forces at Angostura in early 1818, blamed the Spaniards for instigating indiscriminate violence. However, he soon found that the patriots had adopted their methods, so that "every prisoner was massacred in cold blood; villages and farms were ravaged and burned; and every species of cruelty and insult, without compassion for sex or age, was practised on an unresisting, and often unoffending population."[26] Like Vowell, other English officers who joined Bolívar and Páez in the course of the 1818 campaign reported their shock at the routine killing of prisoners and in some cases sought to transfer out of the forces responsible for them.[27] However, attempts by both sides to limit violence were slow to take effect. Bolívar's repeated declarations of an end to the *guerra a muerte* suggest that it was still widely practiced by the patriots and matched by reprisals from the royalists. The Spanish tendency to see the insurgents as traitors and criminals who deserved death gave way only slowly to the notion that they were combatants worthy of civilized treatment.[28]

Strategies and Campaigns, 1818–19

The creation of a unified structure of command among the insurgents took time to take effect. The patriots remained divided into forces that had their own identity under chosen leaders, and their separation was reinforced by the great distances between them. Nonetheless, Bolívar's renewed authority, embodied in his headquarters at Angostura, enabled him to forge a more cohesive set of armed forces and pursue a more ambitious strategy for war.

This development was reflected first in his initiation of combined operations with Páez, undertaken for the purpose of consolidating control over the Orinoco and opening a new front against Morillo's forces. Command of the Orinoco offered indispensable advantages. The great river was a channel for the arms trade and maritime communications with the exterior; it provided access to food and livestock that was vital for sustaining armies; it facilitated the movement of forces deep into the interior and was thus a means of building a platform from which to advance northwards into the sierras, which protected Spanish positions on the coast. The latter was, indeed, a primary consideration for Bolívar. Rather than simply consolidating control of the Llanos, he aimed to take immediate tactical advantage of the merger with Páez by taking their forces northwards against Morillo. In January 1818, Bolívar pressed forward with his new strategy by moving the fulcrum of patriot campaigning westwards. He took 3,000 men from his headquarters in

Angostura to Páez's base in the Apure River plains and joined with the leader of the llaneros into a new campaign and a new phase of the war.[29]

The course and outcome of the campaign—which set Bolívar directly against Morillo for the first time—showed that the patriot and royalist forces, though different in composition, were evenly matched in operations against each other.[30] Morillo opened his campaign with a misjudgment, due to his ignorance of enemy movements. In early February 1818, he decided to move to the Llanos in order to defend San Fernando de Apure against attack from Páez and his llaneros, and he took a force of around 1,800 men, mostly infantry, to establish his campaign headquarters at Calabozo. Knowing nothing of Bolívar's advance up the Orinoco or his merger with Páez, Morillo was unaware that he was moving towards a larger force and so was vulnerable to surprise attack. Bolívar and Páez were ready to take advantage. As soon as they learned of Morillo's position and strength, they drove rapidly forward to Calabozo with a joint force of 4–5,000 men, mostly mounted llaneros, who could be used to great effect against infantrymen on the plains. Outnumbered and without hope of adequate reinforcement, Morillo seemed trapped at Calabozo and in danger of being eliminated. However, thanks to his skill in marshaling his troops and to Bolívar's inexplicable delays in pursuit, Morillo succeeded in fighting an effective rearguard action. On reaching a defensible point in the foothills of the mountains, where his infantry stood a better chance against the patriot cavalry, he took a stand at Sombrero and broke the momentum of the patriots' advance. His opportunity lost, Bolívar turned back to Calabozo to regroup, and Páez concentrated on taking San Fernando.[31]

After this failure to take advantage of their superior forces, the independents' leaders considered two alternatives. Páez wanted to consolidate control of the Llanos and Orinoco basin; Bolívar clung to his plan for attacking northwards through the sierra to the coast and Caracas. Though this fulfilled the prime purpose of war—to destroy enemy forces—the offensive was risky. For, while Bolívar was reorganizing the forces that had dispersed after his defeat at Sombrero, Morillo had time in early March 1818 to prepare his defenses on home territory. He placed La Torre to guard the approach to Caracas with 900 men, while taking the main royalist force of about 3,000 men forward to Valencia, to meet the republican advance. In the maneuvers that followed, Bolívar and Morillo finally met on March 16 at the Semen gorge, where Bolívar chose to fight on ground near La Puerta, scene of one of his earlier defeats. The choice was poor, as the broken ground curbed cavalry action and gave the royalist infantry an advantage that Morillo fully exploited. The battle was hard fought; it lasted for several hours until finally decided by Morillo's adroit deployment of infantry and artillery. The remains of the patriot army, mostly horsemen, beat a hasty retreat back to Calabozo, having lost at least 1,200 men against smaller losses to the Spanish.[32]

The consequences of this defeat were, unsurprisingly, felt largely within the patriot camp. Blame stuck to Bolívar and very nearly cost him his command. Several of the British officers who had recently joined his army questioned his competence and sought to install Páez in his place. Gustavus Hippisley was particularly scathing. He not only deplored the insurgents' murder of prisoners and wounded but decried Bolívar's military ability and failure to discipline his army. "Tactics, movements, and manoeuvre are as unknown to him as to the lowest of his troops," said Hippisley, a point on which several other British officers agreed, leading to their withdrawal or dismissal from Bolívar's army.[33] They were no doubt expecting too much. As regulars from the highly drilled, socially hierarchical, battle hardened British army, British officers found it difficult to accept the irregular organization and style of warfare they found in Venezuela, particularly when their cultural prejudices and sense of superiority were sharpened by a shortage of the deference, drink, and pay that they believed were due to them.[34] There is, nonetheless, some cause for blaming the failures of the 1818 campaign on Bolívar's shortcomings as a military commander. His tactical mistakes on the plains of Calabozo and at Sombrero cost him the chance to overrun Morillo when the Spanish general was at his most vulnerable; his inflexible focus on taking Caracas then lured him into operations and battles that would, as Páez understood, have been better avoided. At Semen, for example, he allowed himself to be drawn into battle where the enemy's infantry and artillery could neutralize the impact of his llanero lancers. He had no clear plan for retreat, and the demoralization and desertion that followed the battle effectively dispersed his army, leaving him with little to show for months of costly campaigning.

The human and material costs of the campaign were borne largely by the patriots. Morillo lost about 500 killed and wounded and was himself severely injured by a lance thrust to the belly. But Bolívar lost far more: about 1,200 men and a good deal of war material, including large quantities of much-needed arms. His confidence also suffered, and though he tried to disguise defeat as victory, he withdrew from the offensive and returned to Angostura to rethink his position and strategy. The strategic impact of the patriots' defeat at Semen/La Puerta was thus considerable. It halted their offensive, forced them back to prior positions, and consolidated the royalists' hold on Venezuela's key cities and their hinterlands.

The royalist victory had also come at a high cost. Morillo suffered substantial losses of men, particularly among the European officers and soldiers who were difficult to replace, and his campaign rendered little in territory or resources. At its end, his army had not recovered control of the Llanos and remained chronically short of the horses and other livestock that were essential for an army on the move. The problems of financing and supplying his troops had also become a constant source of anxiety. In April 1818, Morillo reported that the army was miserably clothed and underfed: soldiers' uniforms had not been replaced for three years and were falling off their backs, many were forced to go barefoot, and even the sick and wounded had inadequate food and poor housing. Indeed, the food supply was so poor that Morillo ordered his troops to take up farming corn, rice, and beans for their own subsistence.[35]

Bolívar and his generals, on the other hand, continued to dominate southern Venezuela and, though they had failed to penetrate the royalist heartlands, were better able to hold their position and replenish their losses.[36] They were also aware that support for their cause was reviving in neighboring New Granada. Most of the viceroyalty was quiet, but the mountains of the Eastern Cordillera and its adjacent plains harbored local insurgents, who added to Morillo's problems. In 1817, the landowning Almeyda brothers of Cúcuta, resentful of royalist confiscation of their property, led a guerrilla campaign, which brought together about 300 men and linked with the more important enclaves of resistance led by Santander in the plains of Casanare. This troubled the royalist authorities sufficiently to send Colonel Carlos Tolrá with a force of some 600 men to terrorize the region, a campaign that forced the insurgents to retreat during 1817 but failed to eliminate them completely.[37]

One evident difference between royalist and insurgent forces at this stage in the war was the highly irregular composition of the latter, caught in Richard Vowell's portrait of the men he fought with at Semen. They were, in the first place, an unusual sight because, unlike the uniformed Spanish troops, most of them "wore literally what they could get" and resembled nothing better than a rabble, clothed in "small ragged blankets and pieces of carpet, which they had plundered on the retreat, with holes cut in them for the head to pass through." As for arms, their "firearms . . . were all very old and generally speaking in a very bad condition. Some muskets were absolutely without locks, and were apparently carried for show, until the fall of a few friends or foes should give their owners the opportunity of exchanging them for more effective weapons." The cavalry had "as ill-assorted accoutrements and apparels as the infantry. All had lances of different lengths, and some few carbines . . . which were muskets cut short in the barrel." The baggage train was guarded by Indians with bows and arrows.[38] It seems, then, that stabbing weapons continued to be the soldier's main arm. The infantry used bayonets and swords, and most of the larger actions involved bayonet charges and hand-to-hand fighting. Lances were the key weapon of the cavalry, particularly the llaneros, who were especially adept in using lances adapted from cattle herding.[39] Battles tended to be brief and bloody, often decided by the initial shock of cavalry and infantry charges, which broke and turned the enemy's lines. With infantrymen fighting on foot with lances and Indian bowmen in attendance, such actions more closely resembled European warfare of the seventeenth than the early nineteenth century.

A related difference between royalists and patriots, at least until around 1820, was in their strategies for war. Morillo and his commanders tried to take and hold territory and bring it under royalist control; the patriots on the other hand were able to strike at will where royalist forces were weak and thus gradually wear down the royalist cause. As Morillo informed the minister of war, his troops had many victories but could not eliminate elusive enemies:

> Any of their caudillos who arrives in a place where they are no soldiers of the King can call the inhabitants to arms, free slaves and form a new army in a few days. When swept out of one province Paez, Bolívar, Cedeño and all the other ringleaders move on to subvert another, without fear of obstacles and sure of the goodwill of its inhabitants. For this they can also count on the open

protection of the [foreign] colonies where, in exchange for the prizes taken from our traders and the livestock and products they steal, they find shipyards where they can careen their vessels and acquire as much armament, munitions, clothing and material for war that they need for their infantry; for the horseman or the llanero no more is necessary than a wooden stave with a piece of iron . . . and a horse which can be ridden perfectly without bridle or saddle.[40]

The insurgents' ability to conduct this kind of warfare grew considerably stronger during 1817 when llaneros once loyal to Boves transferred their allegiance to Páez.[41] This amplified the advantages that the patriot generals derived from the region. It gave them recruits accustomed to guerrilla fighting, combined with the ample supply of horses needed to elude the enemy, to constantly harass enemy foot soldiers in open spaces or confine them to defended positions, and, above all, to strike at will. The Spanish, on the other hand, were weak in cavalry; they lacked their enemy's ready access to horses, mules, and cattle, their familiarity with the terrain, and their ability to use guerrilla tactics. The Spanish infantry were capable of resisting llanero attacks but were unable to hold much more than the ground they occupied, leaving royalist towns as oases of Spanish rule in plains patrolled by hostile forces.

The differences in the military strengths and weaknesses of each side were such that the royalist infantry maintained its grip on the hill country and fortified positions of the coasts, while patriot horsemen dominated the plains.[42] This balance was difficult to break. Like the French army in Spain during the Peninsular War and Spanish forces fighting rural rebellions in contemporary Mexico and Upper Peru, Morillo's army was unable to dominate territories where the enemy operated and prevent the build-up of rebel forces. The guerrillas, by contrast, had the advantages of attack and of striking where they chose. The royalist defensive problem was, moreover, harder to solve in Venezuela than in other parts of Spanish America. In Mexico, for example, the royalist army used landowners and villages to organize defenses against insurgents, something that was not easily done in Venezuela. There, insurgents controlled large territories, and it was much more difficult to prevent them from coalescing under a unified leadership capable of moving from guerrilla to conventional warfare.

The deadlock was broken during 1819, not by guerrilla war but by Bolívar's successful implementation of a new strategy. This was designed to shift the theater of war once again, this time into neighboring New Granada. Bolívar's logic was straightforward. Morillo had moved most of his forces to Venezuela in 1817 to cope with the revived insurgency and left only relatively small garrisons to defend New Granada. Since then, neogranadinos had become increasingly opposed to Spanish rule, while Morillo's forces were pinned down in Venezuela. Bolívar concluded that Morillo was unable to defend Venezuela and New Granada simultaneously and so began to prepare for an invasion.

Preparations began in mid-1818, when Bolívar made Santander commander-in-chief of Casanare and gave him the task of creating a vanguard for the liberation of New Granada. Once secured, a liberated New Granada promised the patriots a tremendous strategic advantage, greater even that than secured by taking Guayana, because its central provinces would provide new sources of men and material for patriot offensives within New Granada and against royalist Venezuela. This would in turn considerably augment Morillo's existing problems of finding sufficient force to defend and dominate large territorial spaces. As Bolívar explained to Páez, an invasion would force Morillo "to choose between evacuating Venezuela in order to march to New Granada, or accepting that the latter be completely lost."[43]

This logic was reinforced by the political and military developments on the patriot side during early 1819. On returning to Angostura at the end of the 1818 campaign, Bolívar had called a National Congress, prepared a law for electing its deputies, and drafted his proposals for a constitution. The constituent congress met for the first time at Angostura in February 1819, adopted a constitution based largely on the model proposed by Bolívar, and elected Bolívar as president, with the neogranadino Francisco Antonio Zea as vice president.

The adoption of the Angostura constitution was an important political move because, by uniting the various constituents of the patriot insurgency, it gave greater legitimacy to Bolívar's government. Its claim to represent the "people" was, of course, largely fictional. Since elections were possible only in areas under patriot control, the "people" were composed mostly of members of Bolívar's armed forces, and the representatives they elected were mainly officers in those forces. But if the congress was partly a convenient cover for a military dictatorship, it was also more than that. By participating in elections, the army acted as the matrix of the republic, with military men entering into political life rather than merely taking power by force. First, soldiers became citizens (reversing the prior assumption that citizens would become soldiers); they were the principal electorate for the congress and, as unlettered caudillos were eliminated by literacy requirements for candidacy, their voting did not necessarily coincide with caudillo loyalties. Instead, loyalty to local community began to be supplemented, if not yet supplanted, by loyalty to the concept and institutions of the republic. Thus, the army became the embodiment of the republic and its institutional vanguard.[44]

The political consolidation of the republic was followed by a fresh military offensive in early 1819. This time, the opposing forces were more evenly matched. In March 1819, Bolívar launched another campaign with Páez in the Apure region of the Western Llanos, where Morillo had concentrated an army of over 6,000 men (mostly infantry) with the intention of reestablishing royalist control. The patriot forces held back the royalist counterinsurgency. Páez, in particular, scored some important victories, displaying a virtuoso ability to deploy his horsemen against larger forces and displaying the llaneros' superiority over the royalist cavalry.[45] However, Bolívar admitted that his infantry was inferior to Morillo's, and that, despite having inflicted heavy casualties on his enemy, he was obliged to adopt a cautious "Fabian" strategy, which left Morillo in control of the core regions of Venezuela.[46]

Morillo's position was, nonetheless, becoming increasingly uncomfortable as his command of the coastal regions was challenged by threats of attack by sea. The maritime war that Bolívar had started in 1816, when he placed Brion in charge of attacking Spanish ships and ports, enabled the patriots both to hinder Spanish military operations and to undermine government revenues from commerce. By 1818, Spain lacked a naval presence on the Venezuelan coasts, and the royal treasury in Caracas lacked the funds to build one. Without a fleet, Morillo could not mount an offensive in the east against the key insurgent bases of Margarita and Guayana, nor find the naval support needed to repress the privateers commissioned by Bolívar's government. He saw "the vast coasts of these provinces, from the mouth of the Orinoco to the Isthmus of Panama . . . entirely at the mercy of the pirates, without a single warship cruising on them."[47] Brion's insurgent navy and the privateers inflicted serious damage on the royalist cause; their attacks on Spanish merchant shipping and their blockades of Venezuelan ports paralyzed economic life and further undermined government finances, obstructed Morillo's supply lines, and facilitated the patriots' trade in arms and other goods.[48]

The war could not be won at sea alone, however, and in early 1819, patriot forces were very far from their goal of defeating Morillo's army and taking the capital. Indeed, it seemed that neither side could overcome the other. Bolívar's plan to take Caracas by coordinated campaigns from the east and south was stopped by Morillo's army, but Morillo was unable to overcome the patriots' dominance of the strategic southern plains that stretched from Guayana to Casanare.

At this juncture, the strategies of the opposing sides diverged. Morillo continued to hold New Granada and decided to focus on the elimination of the patriot forces that threatened him in Venezuela.[49] With the rainy season on the way, he withdrew from the Llanos in order to rest his exhausted troops, build up his cavalry, and amass supplies for a renewed campaign in the following year. Bolívar, by contrast, adopted an aggressive strategy aimed at undermining the royalist war effort by opening a new theater of war in neighboring New Granada. Thus, while Morillo pulled back towards his coastal strongholds, Bolívar stayed in the Western Llanos and in May 1819 prepared to strike across the Andes at royalist positions that seemed vulnerable.

Bolívar's New Granadan Campaign

The idea of moving the war into New Granada was not new to either the patriots or Morillo. The unexpected element was that of timing. Bolívar decided to open operations at the start of the winter season, when an assault from the Llanos would be least expected. Bolívar persuaded his staff officers that, rather than weaken the army by wintering in the Llanos, it was better to deploy into a region where the Spaniards were unprepared for imminent attack; they therefore agreed on a two-pronged trans-Andean offensive, aimed at the heart of New Granada and the Spanish army that guarded the viceregal capital at Bogotá.

The initial plan was for Santander to take one force by the more difficult approach via Casanare, while Bolívar and Páez brought their forces together at Cucutá, an easier but better-guarded point of entry. In the event, Bolívar decided to lead the more difficult expedition himself. On May 26, 1819, he left the Apure

River with close to 2,200 soldiers (1,332 infantry, 814 cavalry, and 40 artillerymen), plus porters and camp followers, and set out on a hazardous journey. He
planned to cross the flooding plains to Casanare, to join with Santander's force of
around 1,200 and then to climb the Cordillera into New Granada, via remote and
icebound Andean trails.[50]

The expedition was a gamble. It involved moving a large body of men with
their mounts and supplies across long stretches of difficult terrain during the rainy
season, a time when movement across the flooding grasslands and into the mountains was at its most arduous. In addition to the sheer difficulty of getting into
the highland basins of New Granada without suffering irreparable losses en route,
Bolívar's soldiers had to be ready to fight well-supplied and well-positioned forces
on the other side of the Cordillera. They overcame both obstacles. The journey
of about five weeks caused losses of men, mounts, and equipment and exhausted
the survivors. However, after joining with Santander's forces on the plains at Tame,
Bolívar pushed on into the highlands and, in early July, arrived in royalist terrain,
ready to face Morillo's Third Army division under the command of Colonel José
María Barreiro.[51]

The royalists were ill-prepared.[52] When Barreiro had first received news of
insurgent movements into New Granada in mid-June 1819, he doubted that
they intended to invade, given that their strongholds were far away, in the Llanos
and Guayana.[53] When the invasion was confirmed, he decided to concentrate his
forces at Tunja in order to avoid meeting the enemy without the benefit of greater
numbers.[54] Barreiro's reluctance to throw his strongest forces into an early attack
on the invaders allowed Bolívar to rest his men and recruit among the peasantry,
capitalizing on support from locals who saw their chance to throw off an oppressive regime.[55] He suffered some setbacks in July and early August but also fought
several successful actions. Of these, the action at the Pantano de Vargas was most
promising, as the patriot army succeeded in overcoming a well-defended enemy
position with a combination of British infantry and llanero cavalry charges. It
did not, however, dent Barreiro's confidence. Indeed, he recorded the action as
a royalist success because of the casualties inflicted on the enemy and the lessons
learned about Bolívar's battlefield tactics.[56] Barreiro's strategy was basically defensive: he had good intelligence on Bolívar's army but was unsure of his intentions. In mid-July, he believed that Bolívar would avoid battle and decided that
the appropriate response was to concentrate his forces and await the opportunity
to attack.[57] At the end of July, he called on Viceroy Sámano to provide artillery
and reinforcements but observed that his troops did not fear the large numbers
that Bolívar was amassing because they understood that "the mob does not make
war but contributes to undermining the order of good soldiers, making their
annihilation easier."[58] Bolívar was, however, confident in his enlarged army and
moved quickly to draw the royalist army into battle at a point of his choosing and
before Barreiro could be reinforced. His opportunity came when he intercepted
the royalist army at Boyacá, on the road to Bogotá, and deployed his forces for an
all-out attack.

The battle of Boyacá (August 7, 1819) was fought between soldiers of similar quality using conventional battlefield tactics. The opposing forces were more or less matched in size. Each had close to 2,800 troops, nearly all Americans, and roughly divided between veterans and conscripts. Bolívar seized the initiative by entering into battle when he saw that Santander had separated Barreiro's vanguard troops from the main body of the royalist army. While Santander held them down, Bolívar launched an assault on Barreiro's main force. The battle that followed was typical of actions of this kind. Barreiro drew up his infantry in line on higher ground, with three field cannon in the center and his cavalry on both flanks, ready to fend off attack. Bolívar sent Anzoátegui with an infantry division and cavalry squadron directly against the enemy front line, holding back a reserve of infantry and cavalry to exploit any break. In the ensuing mêlée, Anzoátegui crashed through the enemy's right, opening a gap for Bolívar's cavalry and allowing encirclement of the royalist center and left. Barreiro tried to counter with his cavalry, but they were beaten by the patriots' lancers. Depleted by large losses—about 200 dead and some hundreds wounded or fleeing the battlefield—Barreiro decided to end the slaughter and after a couple of hours of fighting, surrendered himself and 1,600 soldiers.[59]

Barreiro left no explanation of his defeat. He did not survive long enough to justify himself to his superiors because, contrary to his expectation of clemency, he and 38 other officers were executed after a short imprisonment. Barreiro nonetheless took most of the blame. Several royalist officers suggested that Barreiro's tactics, particularly the use of infantry columns, were at fault; they also mentioned that his artillery broke down at a critical moment and that his badly organized infantry fled precipitately when charged by the insurgents' cavalry.[60] Certainly both Viceroy Sámano and General Morillo found Barreiro a useful scapegoat; by blaming his incompetence, they limited their own responsibility and avoided attributing success to Bolívar.[61] In reality, however, Bolívar had been the architect of his own victory. As Daniel O'Leary, the Irish officer who became the Liberator's aide-de-camp, friend, and livelong admirer, explained, Bolívar played the crucial role in mounting the expedition, leading it across the Andes, and taking it into battle. O'Leary's judgment may well have been biased, but others less friendly to Bolívar agreed. Santander, for example, attributed success to Bolívar above all, for his "extraordinary energy and determination" in reviving the "moribund body" of the army and leading it to victory.[62]

These are plausible judgments. Bolívar's vision and leadership brought the army across the Andes, and his organization of patriot forces into an efficient fighting force, capable of better performance in conventional battle than they had been a couple of years previously, paved the way to his victory in New Granada. The improvement in his forces may have owed something to the contribution of British infantry officers, but it stemmed mainly from Bolívar's focus on training officers and men after he had established his base at Angostura. His creation of a General Staff provided a stable command and a source of instruction for a hierarchy of commanders, officers, and soldiers, and he integrated the caudillos and their private armies more tightly into his army by appointing them to field commands and to

the General Staff. It was a slow and difficult process to instill discipline and training into soldiers, who, being motivated by personal bonds and promises of plunder,
were prone to desert when defeated. Bolívar's efforts appear to have paid off, however, because at the start of his New Granadan campaign, he regarded his Army of
the West as a force capable of dealing with Spanish infantry, and, as such, he recommended it as a model for the forces of the eastern caudillos. Although the enemy
believed that the patriots were incapable of working on tactical principles or engaging in disciplined movement on the battlefield, Bolívar observed, the Western
Army had learned to do so. "It is thus necessary," he told his commanders, "that
they find in the Army of the East the same as in the West: valour, tactics and discipline." This meant an ability to cope with Spanish army tactics, which consisted of
attacking in closed columns that were rapidly unfolded into lines on the battlefield
in order to gain an element of surprise. To counter these tactics, Bolívar ordered
that commanders always take the greatest care to follow the enemy's movements in
order to deploy their columns in an equal or larger front in battle. He added that
they should ensure that their lead companies consist of selected soldiers, as these
decided the forward momentum of the rest of the column, its fate, and even the
outcome of the battle.[63] Bolívar evidently had confidence in his soldiers' ability to
achieve more exacting military standards than those of earlier times, and their performance at Boyacá reflects his success. He had turned patriot forces dominated by
mounted irregulars into an army built on a core of infantrymen, who were capable
of fighting ordered actions against a disciplined enemy.

The organization of the army was matched by high morale, as Bolívar himself
observed after Boyacá.[64] The hardships of the Andean expedition bonded men from
diverse backgrounds into a single fighting force; their confidence was boosted by
victory at the Pantano de Vargas; their motivation in battle was strengthened by
knowledge that they had no easy escape route. They were, moreover, supported
by the people of the province of Tunja. As Santander recognized, the locals made
a vital contribution to Bolívar's war effort by replenishing the supplies of his exhausted army and supplying sufficient recruits to create a force of equal size to the
royalist army. The quality of the republican forces was as good, probably better, as it
had ever been: Bolívar's soldiers were battle-ready, thanks to their prior experience
of war in the Llanos, and the presence of experienced British infantry officers was
also of some help in battle.

The British military contribution should not be exaggerated. While officers in
the *Legión Británica* made some important individual contributions to the battles at
the Pantano de Vargas and Boyacá, English and Irish soldiers were generally a great
disappointment. After the arrival of the first batch in early 1818, Bolívar was so disillusioned with them that he told his London agent López Mendez to seek recruits
from Spain instead—they would at least speak Spanish.[65] When they continued
to come, his misgivings were confirmed. Both the British and Irish Legions were
subsequently involved in violent mutinies and on balance did more to damage than
to advance the republican military effort. High rates of death and desertion among
such men also meant that they never became the professional core that Bolívar

wanted for his army.[66] Fortunately for Bolívar, the royalist army that faced him in New Granada was not great competition. Before the campaign, Barreiro had complained that his New Granadan conscripts resented military service and were of doubtful loyalty, while Bolívar believed that Barreiro's Venezuelan troops could easily be persuaded to change sides.

Enemy errors undoubtedly benefited Bolívar. First, Morillo guessed wrongly that the insurgents would avoid a winter campaign and rest their forces before returning to fight after the rainy season. Then, when he received news of Bolívar's movements, he sent Brigadier La Torre to New Granada with forces that were too little and too late. The relief expedition was delayed by harassment from enemy guerrillas around Cúcuta, and while La Torre waited for reinforcements, Bolívar was able to push forward and expand his forces to the point where he could engage Barreiro's Third Division.[67] Second, Barreiro made tactical errors, for he was slow to engage the patriot army and missed chances to strike when, at the end of the mountain crossing, it was at its weakest. Barreiro was reluctant to engage his army for a good reason: he had the only force capable to stopping the invaders and did not wish to risk it in a single action. But he evidently spent too long in gathering intelligence and maneuvering around the enemy. When he did engage, he was forced into battle and, after only a couple of hours of fighting, decided to surrender despite having substantial forces. His capitulation is difficult to explain, given the custom of killing prisoners of war. It was, perhaps, influenced by an expectation of clemency from Bolívar, who had announced an end to the guerra a muerte and was seeking to impose civilized rules of war. However, if the reasons for Barreiro's decision are obscure, its consequences are plain: his surrender eliminated Morillo's main army in New Granada, forced the flight of the viceroy, and allowed Bolívar to take Bogotá.

After Boyacá

The battle of Boyacá evidently had considerable impact on the course of war in Venezuela and New Granada. Politically, Bolívar's victory undermined the Spanish regime in New Granada. The viceroy escaped from Bogotá to Cartagena, but left Bolívar in possession of the capital and the populous regions of Colombia's Eastern Cordillera, where people rallied to the patriots and the cause of independence. By overturning the Spanish regime, Bolívar was also able to strengthen his republican project. He announced the establishment of the Republic of Colombia, accepted the presidency, and formed a provisional government. Then, on this base, he returned to Venezuela to reaffirm his authority and tighten the connections between the two regions. In December 1819, Bolívar outmaneuvered his Venezuelan rivals at Angostura and presided over the congress, which formally created a Republic of Colombia that was to comprise New Granada, Venezuela, and Quito. The Angostura Congress also confirmed Bolívar as president of the Republic and called a Constituent Congress to meet at Cúcuta a year later. This settled, Bolívar then returned to Bogotá before moving to the border region at Cúcuta to prepare for a final struggle in Venezuela.[68]

The military significance of Boyacá was also considerable. The royalists still had forces in New Granada and held Western Venezuela, but Boyacá moved the balance of armed power strongly against them. The consequences were most pronounced in New Granada. There, the main royalist army in New Granada was eliminated, its officers executed, and most of the surviving soldiers incorporated into Bolívar's army. The remaining forces were isolated from each other. Sámano retreated to the Caribbean coast; Calzada went south to join Governor Aymerich in the defense of Pasto and Quito, and Morillo was confined to western Venezuela. None of these generals could easily collaborate with his colleagues given the distances that separated them, while Bolívar, dominating the territory between them, could turn on either at will. The collapse of the viceregal regime also gave Bolívar resources needed for war both within New Granada and neighboring regions. Sámano's hasty departure provided an immediate windfall, since it gifted the patriots a treasury of more than half a million pesos, but more important was possession of a territory that could provide for the armies needed to turn Bolívar's Republic of Colombia into a reality.

These advantages worked slowly in Bolívar's favor. He did not make the mistake of rushing into action, nor attempt to replay the "Admirable Campaign" of 1812. Rather than turn immediately against Morillo's substantial Venezuelan forces, Bolívar concentrated instead on eliminating remaining royalist forces on New Granada's Caribbean coast, in the Magdalena Valley, the western province of Antioquia, and the southern province of Popayán. Morillo, on the other hand, took up a defensive position in Venezuela, disillusioned by the ruin of the grand strategy that he had presented to the Spanish government in 1817.

Before Boyacá, Morillo's strategy was dormant; after Boyacá, it became completely moribund. In late 1819, the position of royalists and patriots returned to that of early 1812, when royalist power in New Granada was limited to a few defensive enclaves and patriot forces contested Spanish rule in Venezuela. As Morillo told Spain's minister of war, Bolívar had reaped the reward of five years of campaigning in a single battle, cancelling everything that the crown's soldiers had won in all their previous engagements. In addition to the resources of New Granada, the insurgents had acquired an army of ex-government troops and access to Pacific ports for their privateers. While Spain sent no reinforcements to Morillo, large numbers of foreign soldiers had arrived to join the insurgents, who were becoming stronger in Guayana, Cumaná, and various parts of the Llanos, and had plentiful supplies of arms and uniforms from the Guayana warehouses of English merchants. Foreign merchants were, moreover, now even more willing to supply the insurgents, confident that their victories would provide the means of payment.

Morillo blamed Madrid for his predicament. He reminded the minister of war that he had been chronically short of men for years and observed bitterly that the loss of New Granada might have been averted had Spain sent the 4,000 men he had requested in April 1816. These reinforcements, Morillo argued, would have allowed him to defend Guayana and thus block the insurgents' avenue for attack on New Granada; without them, he had been outflanked and his position overturned at Boyacá. Then, after Boyacá, he confronted the dire prospect that Bolívar might turn that strategy against him, using New Granada as the platform from which to extend insurgent warfare into neighboring regions. His only hope was that Spain would immediately send an army of 7,000 to 8,000 men, together with sufficient naval forces to combat insurgent dominance at sea. Without such measures, he predicted that the region would be lost forever, even if the king were later to send 30,000 men.[69]

Morillo was right to emphasize the importance of armed strength. Without substantial reinforcement of his land forces and naval deployments to discourage privateers and smugglers, he could not hope to hold Venezuela and recover New Granada. Experience had already shown the impossibility of guarding both territories with limited forces, and in early 1820, the best that Morillo could do was to prepare to resist Bolívar's burgeoning forces. The royalist military position was, however, under growing strain due to problems of payment and supply in a country where the economy and treasury were exhausted by years of war. Morillo frequently reminded the minister of war of the diminution and impoverishment of his army. It was, he stated, short of everything. Its European cohorts were reduced to a small minority; the troops were rarely paid; officers and soldiers wore the same tattered uniforms; all lived amid unprecedented shortages. The problem was that after nine years of war, Venezuela was economically prostrate and unable to produce more than a tenth of the revenues needed to meet the most urgent expenses; the costs of the garrison at Cumaná alone ate up 50% of total revenues. There was no obvious solution internally; forced contributions would finish off what was left of the economy. It was therefore essential that Cuba fulfill the orders the king had already issued and provide the support needed to save the army, not in kind, as the contractors preferred, but in cash.[70]

Another strategic problem was that of sustaining naval power on the shores of Spanish territories. Spain had lost maritime dominance in the Caribbean, the Atlantic, and the Pacific, where privateers licensed by Bolívar, Buenos Aires, and San Martín operated freely. Among the consequences was Spain's inability to cut insurgent contacts with foreign trade, or stem the trade in arms and influx of British soldiers of fortune. In early 1820, Morillo warned the crown that he could not cope much longer. He pointed out that if Bolívar moved armies against him, he would have to concentrate his forces and leave the insurgents to take areas previously under his control; then, as the insurgents advanced, he would be forced into battle with a larger and better-supplied army, thus gambling the future of royalist Venezuela on a single action. The only way to improve the odds was for Spain to strengthen his army with reinforcements and find a sustainable method of financing its operations.[71]

These options were unavailable because Ferdinand VII had other plans. While Morillo was calling for reinforcements to save Venezuela, the king and his ministers had their eyes fixed on another military target. In 1819, the long-delayed plan for a military expedition against Buenos Aires became an urgent priority, overriding all others. It was, ministers believed, the only way to recover a valuable commercial and strategic point in the South Atlantic and the best means of defending the Vice-royalty of Peru, still Spain's greatest stronghold in South America. To explain why Spain's position in southern South America had reached this point, we must now return to the theaters of war that lay between the Atlantic coasts of Argentina and the Pacific shores of Peru.

Notes

1. Margaret Woodward, "The Spanish Army and the Loss of America," *HAHR* 48 (1968): pp. 589–90.
2. On the composition of Morillo's army, see Albi, *Banderas Olvidada*, pp. 147–8.
3. The strategy was presented by Enrile to the king and several key government commit-tees in June 1817. See Enrile to Minister of War, June 19, 1817, reproduced in Antonio Rodríguez Villa, *El Teniente General Don Pablo Morillo, Primer Conde de Cartagena, Marqués de la Puerta (1778–1837)*, 4 vols. (Madrid: Real Academia de Historia, 1908–1910), 3, pp. 321–7. For a discussion of the plan, which mistakenly presents Enrile as the sole au-thor, see Juan Friede, *La otra verdad: la independencia vista por los españoles* (Bogotá: Tercer Mundo, 1972), pp. 27–8.
4. Costeloe, *Response to Revolution*, p. 75.
5. My principal sources for the wars in Venezuela and New Granada are the key contem-porary account by the young Irish officer O'Leary, *Memorias del General Daniel Florencio O'Leary*, vol. 1–2. The English translation gives an abridged version of the main cam-paigns; see O'Leary, *Bolívar and the War of Independence*. A key secondary source is Lecuna, *Crónica razonada de las guerras de Bolívar*, vols. 1–2. For an assessment of Bolívar's contribu-tion seen from a biographical perspective, see Lynch, *Bolívar*.
6. On Páez, see Lecuna, *Crónica razonada*, 1, pp. 484–6.
7. On the Haitian exile and expedition, see Lecuna, *Crónica razonada*, 1, pp. 416–29; Lynch, *Bolívar*, pp. 92–7.
8. Lecuna, *Crónica razonada*, 2, pp. 3–5.
9. Lecuna, *Crónica razonada*, 1, pp. 438–45.
10. Bolívar was blamed for the failure of the operation at Ocumare because, as Soublette politely put it, like Antony, he lost precious moments at the side of Cleopatra (his mis-tress, Pepita). For a full account of the operation and the extent of Bolívar's responsibility for its failure, see Lecuna's detailed narrative based on contemporary documentation: *Crónica razonada*, 1, pp. 455–83.
11. On Bolívar in the Barcelona campaign and his withdrawal to Guayana, see ibid., pp. 507–45.
12. Bolívar, quoted in ibid., p. 497.
13. de Austria, *Bosquejo de la Historia Militar de Venezuela*, 2, pp. 385–6.
14. For an outline of the Spanish "guerrilla," see Artola, *España de Fernando VII*, pp. 197–202.
15. Thibaud, *República en armas*, pp. 276–87.
16. Ibid., p. 287.
17. The royalist explanation of the loss of Guayana is laid out at length in a report made to Morillo two years later: see "Expediente instruído de orden de Morillo para averiguar ... la pérdida y retirada del Ejército de la ciudad de Guayana en 1817," in Rodríguez Villa, *Morillo*, 4, pp. 116–54.
18. Ibid., p. 145.
19. For description of the operations of Piar and Bolívar, see Lecuna, *Crónica razonada*, 2, pp. 7–18, 36–7, 44–56.

20. Ibid., p. 58.

21. On the conflict between Piar and Bolívar, and Bolívar's views on the race issue, see Lynch, *Bolívar*, pp. 102–10.

22. Bolívar, "Manifesto to the Peoples of Venezuela, 5 August, 1817": cited by Lynch, *Bolívar*, p. 107.

23. Stoan, *Morillo*, pp. 212–13.

24. Lasso, *Myths of Harmony: Race and Republicanism during the Age of Revolution*, pp. 154–5.

25. On army reorganization, see Thibaud, *República en armas*, pp. 322.

26. Richard Vowell, *Campaigns and Cruises in Venezuela and New Granada and in the Pacific Ocean; from 1817 to 1830*, 3 vols. (London: Longman, 1831), 1, p. 130.

27. For example, O'Leary, *Memorias*, 1, p. 491.

28. Thibaud, *República en armas*, pp. 394–400.

29. Lecuna, *Crónica razonada*, 2, pp. 101–19.

30. My main sources for the 1818 campaign are O'Leary, who joined Bolívar's forces in March 1818: O'Leary, *Memorias*, 1, pp. 465–94, and two military histories, both focused on the role of Bolívar in the the 1818 campaign. The most detailed analysis is by the nineteenth-century Colombian military historian, F.J. Vergara y Velasco, *1818: Guerra de independencia*, 2nd ed. (Bogotá, Editorial Kelly, 1960), which draws on the memoirs of leaders and the operational records of the Spanish forces to argue that Bolívar was entirely responsible for patriot military failures. The Venezuelan historian Vicente Lecuna draws on similar sources to give a similar account but reaches different conclusions, spreading the blame between Bolívar and Páez: see Lecuna, *Crónica razonada*, 2, pp. 121–208. A good summary of the controversy over Bolívar's military mistakes, favoring Vergara's interpretation, is given by Stoan, *Morillo*, pp. 214–19.

31. Vergara y Velasco, *1818*, pp. 119–50.

32. Accounts of the battle are given by Vergara y Velasco, *1818*, pp. 193–202; Lecuna, *Crónica razonada*, 2, pp.172–7. Morillo's personal report is reproduced in Rodríguez Villa, *Morillo*, 3, pp. 525–31.

33. Quoted by Stoan, *Morillo*, p. 220.

34. Matthew Brown, *Adventuring through Spanish Colonies: Simón Bolívar, Foreign Mercenaries and the Birth of New Nations* (Liverpool: Liverpool University Press, 2006), especially chapters 3 and 4.

35. Stoan, *Morillo*, pp. 184–5.

36. Santander to Bolívar, San Fernando, May 13, 1818, *Escritos del Libertador*, 13, p. 239.

37. Hamnett, "Popular Insurrection and Royalist Reaction: Colombian Regions, 1810–1823," pp. 314–19; Rausch, *Tropical Plains Frontier: The Llanos of Colombia*, pp. 178–9; Earle, *Spain and the Independence of Colombia 1810–1825*, pp. 105–6.

38. Vowell, *Campaigns and Cruises*, 1, pp. 83–4.

39. O'Leary, *Memorias*, 1, p. 350.

40. Morillo to Minister of War, July 22, 1818: Rodríguez Villa, *Morillo*, 3, pp. 591–2.

41. Thibaud, *República en armas*, pp. 332–9.

42. Vergara y Velasco, *1818*, pp. 33–46.

43. Bolívar to Páez, August 19, 1818: cited by Lecuna, *Crónica razonada*, 2, p. 234.

44. For this argument in full, see Thibaud, *República en armas*, pp. 400–6.

45. See the action at Las Queseras, reported in Boletín del Ejército Libertador, April 3, 1819, in Grases and Pérez Vila, eds, *Las fuerzas armadas de Venezuela en el siglo XIX*, 3, pp. 43–4.

46. Bolívar to Vice-president, March 28, 1819; April 4, 1819; in ibid., 3, pp. 41, 49. The Fabian strategy to which Bolívar referred was that of Fabius against Hannibal's invading army in Italy, of harassing it while refusing to engage in battle: see Jones, *The Art of War in the Western World*, p. 67.

47. Morillo to Minister of War, July 22, 1818: Rodríguez Villa, *Morillo*, 3, p. 590.

48. Lecuna, *Crónica razonada*, 2, pp. 228–9, 251.

49. Morillo to Minister of War, May 12, 1819: Rodríguez Villa, *Morillo*, 4, pp. 25–32.

50. For a full account of the campaign of early 1819 and the decision to invade New Granada, see Lecuna, *Crónica razonada*, 2, pp. 249–94, 300–2.

51. The most graphic contemporary account is by Daniel O'Leary, the young Irishman recruited in London who accompanied the expedition as one of Bolívar's junior officers. See O'Leary, *Memorias*, 1, pp. 555–69. A similar account from an English officer in Bolívar's forces is Vowell, *Campaigns and Cruises*, pp. 153–70. For a modern synthesis based largely on O'Leary but also using Morillo's correspondence, see Lecuna, *Crónica razonada*, 2, pp. 307–32.

52. The state of royalist preparation can be gauged from the correspondence of army officers and government officials in 1819 found in two collections of documents: Juan Friede, ed., *La batalla de Boyacá, 7 de agosto de 1819, a través de los archivos españoles* (Bogotá: Banco de la República, 1969); and Alberto Lee López, ed., *Los ejércitos del Rey, 1819*, 2 vols. (Bogotá: Biblioteca de la Presidencia, 1989), vol. 2.

53. Barreiro to Sámano, Tunja, June 16, 1819: in Friede, *La batalla de Boyacá*, pp. 20–2.

54. Barreiro to Sámano, Tunja, June 25, 1819: ibid., pp. 22–4.

55. The relationship between royalist oppression and Bolívar's recruitment is fully and explicitly identified in the account of the state of New Granada written by the fiscal of the Audiencia of New Granada: see Augustín de Lopétedi to King, Cartagena, September 25, 1819: ibid., pp. 274–83.

56. Barreiro to Sámano, Pantano de Vargas, July 26, 1819: ibid., pp. 96–7.

57. Barreiro to Sámano, Paipa, July 19, 1819: ibid., pp. 83–7.

58. Barreiro to Sámano, Paipa, July 29, 1819: ibid., pp. 98–9; July 31, 1819, p. 101.

59. For description of the battle, see Lecuna, *Crónica razonada*, 2, pp. 345–8. For the patriot version, see O'Leary, *Memorias*, 1, pp. 577–80. For a royalist account, see "Diario histórico de la division, 4–7 August 1819," in Friede, *La batalla de Boyacá*, pp. 116–19.

60. Lee López, *Los ejércitos del Rey*, 2, pp. 425–34.

61. Earle, *Spain and the Independence of Colombia*, pp. 142–3.

62. Cited by Lecuna, *Crónica razonada*, 2, pp. 333–4.

63. O'Leary, *Memorias*, 1, p. 550.

64. Earle, *Spain and the Independence of Colombia*, p. 137.

65. Lecuna, *Crónica razonada*, 2, pp. 215–6.

66. Brown, *Adventuring through Spanish Colonies*, pp. 113–8, 214.

67. Morillo to Minister of War, Valencia, September 12, 1819: Rodríguez Villa, *Morillo*, 4, pp. 49–50.

68. Lynch, *Bolívar*, pp. 132–4.

69. Morillo to Minister of War, Valencia, September 12, 1819: Rodríguez Villa, *Morillo*, 4, pp. 50–55.

70. Morillo to Minister of War, Tinaco, September 30, 1819: Rodríguez Villa, *Morillo*, 4, pp. 74–8.

71. Morillo to Minister of War, Pao, February 10, 1820: Rodríguez Villa, *Morillo*, 4, pp. 162–5.

12

WARS IN THE SOUTHERN CONE

At the time of Ferdinand VII's restoration, the wars in the Río de la Plata followed a different course from wars elsewhere in Spanish America. Whereas the independent governments of Venezuela and New Granada were swept away in 1815–16, that of Buenos Aires remained intact. Indeed, after capturing royalist Montevideo in mid-1814, Buenos Aires was able to return to rebuilding its position in the war against royalist Peru. It did not, however, continue to be the main stronghold of independence in Spanish America during the years of Ferdinand's restoration. On the contrary, the political directorate in Buenos Aires gradually lost its position as the leading force for revolution in South America's Southern Cone, and its independent regime moved in a diametrically opposite direction from that of the incipient Republic of Colombia. In Venezuela, Bolívar moved from a position where unified leadership and central authority were weak to one where they were strong; thanks to his military success, Bolivar managed to impose a single authority on the regional caudillos of Venezuela and establish the foundations of a unified republic on the old Viceroyalty of New Granada. The Supreme Directors of Buenos Aires, on the other hand, were forced to abandon their ideal of a centralized government exercising authority over the old viceroyalty and had instead to acknowledge the multiple sovereignties of autonomous provinces linked in a loose confederation. In short, whereas Bolívar took Venezuela and New Granada from federalism to an authoritarian centralism, the Supreme Directorate of the United Provinces moved in the opposite direction.

The dilution of Buenos Aires's authority was closely related to its continuing internal wars. After taking Montevideo in mid-1814, Buenos Aires became embroiled in another war in the Banda Oriental and the Littoral against local opponents and Portuguese armies. It also remained heavily committed to war for control of Upper Peru, which the viceroy of Peru continued to contest. And Buenos Aires was also drawn into a new war from 1817, when it opened a front against royalist Chile, the prelude to a new attack on Peru.

The War for Independence in the Banda Oriental

The war on the Atlantic Littoral developed out of Buenos Aires's campaigns to take Montevideo and the Banda Oriental. The capture of Montevideo gave Buenos Aires a crucial victory over Spain, but it also led indirectly to an interprovincial war, as those who had previously united against Spain now went to war among themselves. This civil war began when Buenos Aires tried to impose its authority on the peoples of the Banda Oriental, only to find that José Artigas and other leaders from the cattle-ranching regions of the Littoral wanted freedom from the economic domination and fiscal exactions of Buenos Aires and were willing to resist porteño centralism by force.

Artigas, the rural caudillo who had previously been Buenos Aires's ally against royalist Montevideo, turned against Buenos Aires because, he said later, he had to "reply with war to the shady manoeuvres of the Directory and to the war which it was making on me because it considered me the enemy of centralism . . ." He claimed that "the Pueyrredóns and their acolytes wanted to make of Buenos Aires a new Imperial Rome, sending its proconsuls as military governors of the provinces and despoiling them of all public representation . . ." He wanted independence for the Banda Oriental in a federation modeled on the United States, "giving each state its own government, constitution, flag and the right to elect its representatives, its judges and its governors from among the citizens native to each state."[1] Here, in the conflict between capital and provinces, centralists and federalists, was a major cause of the warfare among the independent provinces of the Río de la Plata that was to go on for years to come.[2]

Interprovincial war began when, in August 1814, Buenos Aires sent Carlos María de Alvear into the Banda Oriental to enforce its authority. When Alvear tried to extend his control beyond Montevideo, Artigas and his lieutenants responded by mobilizing thousands of men against him. Like the Spaniards before him, Alvear faced strong rural resistance, especially when he adopted tactics designed to terrorize the interior into submission and to make the people pay for the war against Artigas. Artigas, by contrast, was on much firmer ground; he was fighting on familiar territory with loyal followers recruited from the gaucho horsemen who had already shown themselves to be effective warriors. These advantages soon showed. In January 1815, Artigas ambushed the porteño army at Guayabos and broke Alvear's offensive. The remaining porteño forces retreated to Montevideo but, besieged by Otorgués, found their position untenable. Isolated in an unfriendly city, they were forced to evacuate in February 1815, leaving Otorgués to convert Montevideo into the capital of an independent government led by Artigas.[3] A few months later, Artigas further extended his domain by taking Santa Fe and Córdoba, and as his power grew, he threatened to invade Buenos Aires. This prompted another crisis in the capital's leadership and, in April 1815, Alvear was forced to relinquish his military dictatorship and seek exile aboard a British frigate.

These events resonated throughout the Río de la Plata by loosening the bonds between the provinces and Buenos Aires. They also marked a critical moment in the history of the Banda Oriental, inaugurating a period of independence under Artigas's leadership. This did not involve any complicated state-building. Artigas spent little time at Montevideo, preferring his rustic headquarters in the interior at Purificación. However, he started to create a polity that was quite different from that preferred by the political elites of Buenos Aires, not only because it was based on federal autonomy but also because it aimed at an unusual degree of social equality, based on redistribution of land among poor settlers.[4] He extended his commitment to federalism beyond the Banda Oriental, too, by assuming leadership of the Banda Oriental and the neighboring Littoral provinces under the title of "Protector of Free Peoples."[5] This created a formidable alliance, backed by regional gaucho forces mustered under local caudillos from the neighboring provinces of Entre Ríos, Santa Fe, Córdoba, and Corrientes, all pastoral economies whose cattle ranchers shared Artigas's desire for independence from Buenos Aires.

The federalist wars were a serious impediment to Buenos Aires's larger struggle against Spain. Buenos Aires tried to resolve the conflict by inviting representatives from all provinces to a congress at Tucumán in March 1816, but this attempt at political palliation did not get far. The representatives from 13 provinces (some from Upper Peru, still under Spanish rule) were dominated by men from Buenos Aires who duly elected the porteño Juan Martín de Pueyrredón as supreme director. Then, on July 9, the congress declared the United Provinces of South America independent of Spain. This was, however, a statement of aspiration rather than an affirmation of achievement, for war continued on several fronts, and the leaders of the May Revolution seemed no closer to achieving their goals. In Upper Peru, the armies of Buenos Aires and Lima had reached a temporary stalemate. On the Atlantic Littoral, provincial federalists fought Buenos Aires's centralists, while in the Banda Oriental, Artigas and his followers also fought back against Portuguese invaders from Brazil.

The Portuguese invasion started in June 1816, captured Montevideo in January 1817, and from there sought to subjugate the rest of the Banda Oriental. The government in Rio de Janeiro argued that its invasion was necessary to stop the "anarchy" in the Banda Oriental and prevent revolution from spilling over into Brazil, but in reality, the occupation reflected Portugal's long-held expansionist ambitions. With the end of war in Europe, Portugal also had the means for intervention. King João drew on the Portuguese troops who had fought the French in the Peninsular War and in early 1815 transferred some 5,000 regular infantrymen and cavalry to Brazil, together with a substantial artillery park, under the command of the veteran General Carlos Federico Lecór. Portugal had, furthermore, the benefit of collusion from Buenos Aires, which secretly cooperated with the Portuguese invasion in the hope of neutralizing Artigas.[6]

The course taken by the war reflected Portugal's superiority over its diminutive neighbor. The Portuguese had much larger forces and easy access by land and sea. General Lecór's army was made up of some 6,000 men, including veterans from the Peninsular War and Brazilian cavalry, which he deployed for an invasion of the

Banda Oriental along the Atlantic coast. To these, he added another 4,000 who were carried by sea to a rendezvous near Montevideo, to meet up with the forces he brought overland.[7]

In addition to this 10,000-strong army of invasion (about half of whom were experienced in European warfare), Portugal had around 6,000 local men on Brazil's southern frontier, ready to defend against invasion or to mount offensives overland into the Banda Oriental. Lecór's army was, one might say, a surrogate for the expeditionary army that Spain was planning to send to Río de la Plata: it was exceptionally large, delivered from outside the territory, and set a European army against American irregulars.

Federalists and Guerrillas

The war in the Banda Oriental stands out for its markedly popular character. While the Portuguese invader brought a well-organized regular army, Artigas relied on irregulars fighting guerrilla wars of attrition. Here we find another example of the guerrilla warfare that had been so important in central Mexico, the Venezuelan plains, and the Argentine Andes, where local communities joined in resisting external governments. In the Banda Oriental, as in those other regions, social rebellion blended with the political ambition of local leaders and set a course towards the creation of a series of mini-states under caudillo rule.

The character of Artigas's warriors is graphically illustrated by the British merchants W.P. and J.P. Robertson, who encountered them when selling arms and supplies to the insurgents in the Banda Oriental. In the Robertsons' eyes, the followers of Artigas (artigueños) were more like brigands than soldiers. William Robertson described the first artigueños he encountered as "really savage and fierce-looking men." They had an unkempt look in their worn-out jackets, dirty shirts, kilts and drawers, and toeless calf's-leg boots, and they were heavily armed with a carbine in the hand, a long knife in the belt, and a saber dangling by the leg.[8] His brother John Robertson also saw the artigueños as semi-savage; after suffering the terrifying experience of kidnap by a plundering gaucho band loosely affiliated to Artigas, he described them as "marauders, ungovernable by any system of civilized discipline, held together somewhat as pirates are, by privileges tacitly understood as appertaining to each, and corresponding to the relative merits of his services."[9]

Robertson subsequently formed a rather more favorable impression of Artigas and his movement when he visited the caudillo's headquarters. He drew a vivid picture of Artigas's camp at Purificación, where he found "the most excellent Protector of half of the New World, seated on a bullock's skull, at a fire kindled on the mud floor of his hut, eating beef off a spit, and drinking gin out of cow-horn!" There, Artigas communicated far and wide, dispatching correspondence as "couriers dashed up on steaming horses every half hour and galloped away again." Robertson noted, too, the extraordinary mobility of Artigas's forces and their ability to move over long distances at short notice. Artigas and his men were capable of 75-mile forced marches by night, and all had horses ready for immediate departure.

Officers and men treated each other as equals, "except that all, in addressing Artigas, did it under the endearing and at the same time familiar appellation of 'Mi General'—My General."[10] An inspection of the camp at Purificación also left a strong image of the backwoods society over which Artigas presided:

> He had about 1,500 tattered followers who acted in the double capacity of horse and foot soldiers. They were chiefly Indians, taken from the decayed establishments of the Jesuits, admirable horsemen, and inured to every species of privation and fatigue. The sloping hills and fertile plains of the Banda Oriental and Entrerios furnished abundant pasture for their horses, as well as numerous herds of cattle for slaughter. They wanted little more. A scanty jacket, and one poncho tied around the waist in the form of a Highlander's kilt, while another hung over their shoulders, completed, with a foraging cap and a pair of potro boots, large spurs, a blunderbuss and a knife, the Artigueños' attire. Their camp was made of rows of mud huts and hide hovels, and these, together with a few dozen cottages of somewhat better description, constituted what was called the "Villa de la Purificacion."[11]

Artigas had evidently created an irregular army that had much in common with those of insurgent caudillos in other parts of Spanish America. Drawn from poor whites, slaves, free coloreds, and Indians from the frontier regions, it was held in a skein of personal ties, united by the leader's charisma and armed prowess rather than his social rank or legal authority and strengthened by his willingness to allow plunder.

The artigueños' arms and tactics were typical of irregular forces raised in the pastoral economies of South America. They used muskets and pistols but relied more on lances, machetes, and swords. Like the Venezuelan llaneros, their tactics were simple; they tried to envelop the enemy by attacks in semicircular cavalry formations, with a few infantry at the center, and withdrew and regrouped if faced by superior forces. They were organized in small groups, ranging from a few dozen to a couple of hundred men. They sometimes coalesced in brief campaigns but avoided battle unless they had a clear advantage. They lived off the land and relied on local support, operating out of bases that were difficult to find and attack and that served as platforms for their raids and offensives. These were, in short, tough irregulars recruited from the peoples of the plains and the Indian missions, men who had learned war on their own terrain, often fighting American enemies, who were not so different from themselves.

In the eyes of respectable, property-owning society, Artigas and his men seemed little more than bandits. "People of property and any consideration," an English observer noted, were against Artigas because of his popularity among "the lower orders," to whom he permitted "every excess and disorder."[12] In fact, Artigas and his followers were much more than rustic bandits who grabbed what they could without thought for the morrow. Artigas attracted recruits not just for plunder but also because he had a larger plan for social change, set out in 1815. His political purpose resembled that of other caudillos insofar as his prime concern was to achieve regional autonomy, allowing local people to live as they wanted without external interference. However, unusually among rural caudillos, Artigas also aimed for permanent social change by granting lands confiscated from his enemies to poor settlers, without discrimination by color.

Artigas's War and its Aftermath

Artigas's strategy reflected the character of his forces. He abandoned Montevideo without attempting to defend it and directed the war from his rural headquarters at Purificación, where he could command operations in the interior. He mounted some static defenses against Lecór's advance of columns, using small concentrations of troops and artillery (taken from Montevideo). But his main strategy was to avoid fighting against the Europeans on their own terms and to engage instead in a mobile war aimed at hitting Portuguese forces wherever they were vulnerable.

The "Protector" succeeded for a couple of years. He dominated the interior by controlling the River Uruguay, vital for supplying his forces and keeping open contacts with the federalist provinces inland. However, although for a while Artigas managed to confine the Portuguese to Montevideo and a corridor along the Atlantic coast, he was gradually forced to withdraw. In 1818, the Portuguese sent a naval squadron into action on the Plate estuary and the River Uruguay to stop insurgent corsairs from attacking Portuguese shipping and to cut Artigas's communications and supply lines. Artigas countered by setting up artillery batteries along the river's western banks while also raising forces from his federalist allies and launching attacks into the Banda Oriental. But the strength of the Portuguese army proved too great, particularly when Buenos Aires's attacks on Artigas's allies forced him to divert some of his forces into the centralist-federalist war. Under growing pressure, Artigas tried in December 1819 to lure the Portuguese from the south onto his terrain in the north, where he was backed by forces from his allies in Corrientes and Entre Ríos. The strategy failed, however, when his main force was crushed by an army that unexpectedly entered from Brazil. He hoped to fight on from Entre Ríos, but his principal allies were unwilling to continue fighting. As a result, Artigas took refuge in Paraguay in 1820—an exile from which he was never to emerge—and the first war for independence in the Banda Oriental was over.

Artigas's war against the Portuguese had shown some of the key strengths of a guerrilla campaign: the ability to live off the land, to concentrate rapidly for surprise strikes on the enemy, and to disperse equally rapidly to avoid meeting forces that were better trained and better armed. But it also had the weaknesses of guerrilla campaigns: an inability to hold territory, to defeat the enemy in decisive battle, and to maintain alliances with those whose territory was not occupied by the enemy. Lecór, on the other hand, had forces that were sufficiently large to take and hold territory, as well as viable supply routes by land and sea, and support from a government that was willing to invest heavily in converting the Banda Oriental into Portuguese territory. Lecór also practiced a policy of conciliation, which won over parts of the population on whom Artigas's guerrillas had to depend; where they could not provide protection, many were persuaded to collaborate with the Portuguese rather than go on suffering the insecurity and depredations of war.[13]

While Artigas's war in the Banda Oriental was drawing to a close, the civil war of the rioplatense provinces continued. In 1819, the congress promulgated a centralist constitution and sent Pueyrredón to enforce it in Santa Fe, whose caudillo Estanislao López was a leading federalist. But Buenos Aires did not have forces sufficient to overcome its provincial opponents or occupy their territory. López promptly repulsed Pueyrredón's invasion and rallied Francisco Ramírez of Entre Ríos and other provincial caudillos in a combined offensive against Buenos Aires. The city's army of 2,000 men, led by José de Rondeau, was unable to resist the federalists' combined cavalry forces and was defeated at the Battle of Cepeda in early 1820. This battle ensured the triumph of Artigas's federalist principles at the very time, ironically, that the "Protector" himself was nearing political extinction. Indeed, it ensured that the Banda Oriental remained under Portuguese rule for another decade (until, after British diplomatic intervention, it eventually became the independent state of Uruguay.) But if Artigas's project for independence was frustrated, so too was the political project born in Buenos Aires in 1810. For after the battle of Cepeda, the government of the capital was forced to abandon claims to central authority and take its place as one province among others.

War in Upper Peru: Buenos Aires's Third Offensive

Throughout the war with Artigas and his confederates, Buenos Aires also had to sustain its preexisting war in Upper Peru. This continued to be an area of strategic importance not only because of the wealth of Upper Peru but also because Belgrano's defeat in late 1813 had decimated the Army of the North and made Buenos Aires vulnerable to royalist attack. In 1814, the Spanish commander General Pezuela was planning to press south into the provinces governed by Buenos Aires, and the Supreme Directorate in Buenos Aires had therefore to concentrate on rebuilding its northern army at Tucumán under new commanders. In December 1813, José de San Martín was sent to replace Belgrano and ordered to stop incursions by the royalist Army of Peru; in May 1814, he was in turn replaced by Rondeau, who took up the task of reviving Buenos Aires's campaign to capture Upper Peru.

When Belgrano handed over command to San Martín, Buenos Aires's position in the north was far from secure. Belgrano made it clear to his successor that the ambitions of Buenos Aires depended heavily on provincial opinion. This was, he told his successor, a different world, where it was essential to cultivate local support and overcome the cultural chasm that separated the revolutionary elites with their European ways and liberal leanings from the mass of the people. He told San Martín that "you have to wage war not only with arms but also with principles, always holding fast to moral, Christian and religious virtues, for our enemies have been calling us heretics and with this argument alone have recruited uncultured people, telling them we were attacking religion."[14]

During his few months in command, San Martín became aware that the war could only be sustained by mobilizing popular forces, while Buenos Aires learned the lesson that it had to devolve authority on local urban oligarchies and caudillos in order to sustain war in the interior. His principal instrument was the *guerra gaucha* in which he used local leaders and their bands of gauchos to harass the enemy. Foremost among these were the gauchos organized by Martín Güemes around Salta. While San Martín was reorganizing his depleted army, Güemes's tactics kept the enemy in constant fear of attack and restricted their access to supplies, with the added virtue of being much cheaper than regular army operations.

While Güemes's horsemen blocked Pezuela's advance beyond Salta, insurgents led by Arenales and Warnes harassed the Spanish rearguard in Upper Peru. San Martín told Arenales that his plan was "to complete the reorganization of this army under my command, increase its strength, improve its discipline, and equip it with everything necessary to advance with firm and sure steps into the interior of Peru."[15] He therefore consolidated his position at Tucumán while keeping communications open with the insurgents and supplying military support where he could. However, before San Martín could advance into Upper Peru, Rondeau took his place. In August, San Martín left Upper Peru for the last time, moving to Mendoza on the border with Chile, where he incubated his own plans for war in the Andes. In the meantime, Rondeau planned another offensive aimed at taking control of Upper Peru and defeating the Spanish army, which occupied this strategic territory.

In early 1815, several important developments favored the renewal of Buenos Aires's northern campaign against Peru. First, Buenos Aires's seizure of Montevideo had removed a steppingstone for Spanish amphibious attack and released resources for war elsewhere. Buenos Aires duly stepped up its propaganda war, spreading rumors that Spain had no troops to send to America, that Ferdinand VII had fled to Lisbon, and that the English were supporting independence. According to General Pezuela, the caudillos of Upper Peru "believed all these things as though they were Gospel" and enthusiastically returned to the offensive in their operations in Upper Peru.[16] Second, the Cuzco rebellion indirectly strengthened Buenos Aires's military position because it drew royalist forces out of Upper Peru and left the royalists more exposed to the guerrilla campaigns of Buenos Aires's allies.[17] In his memoirs, Pezuela recalled that these were very dangerous times for the royalist cause, as his forces were beset by guerrilla attacks that caused many casualties and forced significant retreats.[18] Patriot guerrilla commanders made particularly important gains in early 1815. In April, Arenales inflicted a bloody defeat on Spanish forces at La Florida; Güemes's gauchos massacred royalist forces at Punto del Marqués and forced their commander Pedro de Olañeta to retreat from Cotagaita; Arenales and Padilla took Chuquisaca some weeks later, and Zárate and Betanzos seized Potosí. Taken together these attacks did much to improve Buenos Aires's position in Upper Peru and smoothed the way for Rondeau to restart the contest for its territory and resources.

If guerrilla support in Upper Peru demonstrates once again the importance of popular insurgency for the ambitions of Buenos Aires, the advance of Rondeau's army did not produce the results anticipated, principally because Rondeau failed to take full advantage of the ground prepared by the guerrillas.[19] He wasted time after his entry into Upper Peru by spending seven months between Potosí and Chuquisaca rather than mounting a vigorous campaign against Pezuela. This had several adverse consequences. While Rondeau's soldiers alienated the towns and villages they plundered in order to support the army and enrich its officers, Rondeau's military inactivity allowed Pezuela time to pull royalist forces out of the vulnerable cities of Potosí and Chuquisaca and to concentrate at Challapata, close to the strategic center of Oruro.[20]

Rondeau's failings were compounded by Pezuela's efficiency. While Rondeau temporized, the Spanish commander was spurred on by the news (received on July 24, 1815) that the Spanish expeditionary army due to attack Buenos Aires had been diverted to Venezuela. This injected urgency into Pezuela's campaign because he knew that Buenos Aires could now redeploy forces into the interior and outnumber his forces. Indeed, Viceroy Abascal warned him that Buenos Aires could get an army of 10,000 men to Potosí in about three months, and that he therefore had to defeat Rondeau before it arrived.[21] Pezuela accordingly accelerated his preparations for a swift campaign against Rondeau's army as it began to advance northward towards him.[22]

Pezuela's forces were smaller than Rondeau's (which he estimated at about 5,500) and could not hold much more than the territory on which they stood. According to Pezuela, they had succeeded so far by modeling themselves on the Spanish army in the Peninsular War. By constant movement and occasional engagements, they had avoided being overcome by "the frightening cloud of insurrection which seemed about to break over their heads."[23] Now, however, he decided that a battle with Rondeau was his best strategy "because the swarm of local partisans that most afflict us would dissipate like smoke on seeing the ruin of the main enemy."[24]

To this end, in September–October, Pezuela set out his forces to intercept Rondeau's advance. His vanguard, led by Commander Pedro Antonio de Olañeta, inflicted the first blow by beating Rondeau's vanguard at Venta y Media on October 20, 1815, using only 600 men against nearly double their number and inflicting heavy losses in men and armaments. Encouraged by this victory, Pezuela took his main army on the offensive at the start of November, marching his men towards enemy positions in Chayanta with the intention of finishing off Rondeau's main army. After arduous marches through the mountains, short of supplies and transport, and vulnerable to harassment by hostile Indian peasants, he found Rondeau had taken up a well-defended position on the plain at Sipe Sipe. During three days of skirmishing and fighting, Pezuela succeeded in taking the heights of Wiluma, overlooking the battle field. On November 29, he decided to put his main army of about 4,000 men into action, using an oblique order of battle against an enemy that he counted at some 6,000 men plus 700 cavalry. Despite the imbalance, the battle was over in a couple of hours and ended in a royalist victory, thanks, in Pezuela's view, to the courage and fighting qualities of his army.[25] Pezuela soundly defeated Rondeau, inflicting losses of up to 1,000 men and causing rioplatense forces to abandon Upper Peru in disarray. Their expectations crushed, the remnants of the Army of the North fell back on secure territory in the Andean foothills, seeking shelter once again behind the defensive line of Güemes's gauchos.[26]

Most of the blame for defeat at the Battle of Wiluma fell on Rondeau himself. José María Paz, one of his officers at the time, blamed the general for failing to discipline the troops, tolerating corruption among officers, and offending civilians with heavy-handed policies. Indeed, Paz concluded, "the period of our campaigns in Upper Peru ... is one of the most sterile in glory and most fertile in disagreeable events."[27] Paz also believed that Rondeau had failed to take full advantage of the irregulars, who, grouped in the separate bands, were left to fight on their own account. Rondeau had absorbed some into his army, but they were too indisciplined to add much; Paz thought that he would have done better if he had recruited young men directly from the republiquetas and trained them as infantry.[28] While Paz did not fight at Wiluma, he believed that the royalists triumphed because they met "an army that was demoralized and beaten beforehand."[29]

The repercussions of defeat at Wiluma were felt in both political and military spheres. It weakened the revolutionary regime in Buenos Aires by deepening internal divisions and sharpening factionalism. In the north, Güemes became the *de facto* leader despite Rondeau's efforts to remove him from military command. In Buenos Aires, the consequences of military defeat were, as usual, echoed in political infighting within the governing elite. Rondeau's defeat also threatened to change the balance of military power throughout the Southern Cone for it reopened the option of a royalist counteroffensive into the lower provinces, leading to an assault on Buenos Aires. Indeed, during 1815, Viceroy Abascal became ever more eager to press forward onto the plains.

Royalist Upper Peru, 1815–20

Abascal's determination to launch an offensive against Buenos Aires was not shared by General Pezuela, however, and the royalist army remained in Upper Peru. The reason was plain. Although he had a victorious army of some 7,000 men, Pezuela was reluctant to move forward while rebel guerrillas still threatened his rearguard. He accordingly decided to deploy half the army in garrisoning Upper Peru, leaving insufficient manpower for an offensive into the lower provinces. Thus, Abascal had to shelve his strategic imperative once again while the Army of Peru remained in Upper Peru fighting a counterinsurgency.

When Pezuela became viceroy of Peru (1816–21), he attempted to revive Abascal's strategy for an offensive directed against Buenos Aires, but had no greater success. The new commander of the Army of Peru, General La Serna, was as unwilling to pursue an offensive strategy as Pezuela had been when he commanded the Army of Peru and for the same reason: the need to sustain the counterinsurgency in Upper Peru. Indeed, during the years that followed, Upper Peru never became the platform for attack on Buenos Aires that the viceroys wanted it to be. It was, rather, a region where the Army of Peru spent its energies in eradicating enclaves of insurgency.

Pezuela's failure to send an attacking army into the United Provinces of the Río de la Plata during his viceregency (1816–21) requires some explanation, as these were years when civil war among the independent provinces seemed to offer golden opportunities for a royalist counterattack against them. In fact, Pezuela was not responsible for the decision; it rested with General La Serna, who, after his arrival in the field in September 1816, preferred to concentrate his forces on the problem of insurgency within Upper Peru. La Serna occasionally moved large forces south to Jujuy, but these were brief mobilizations designed to probe enemy strength rather than attack it, to present a show of force rather than build an offensive. La Serna's main concern, reflected in reports from field commanders, was a war of attrition aimed at eradicating insurgency in both the mountainous areas where indigenous caudillos operated and in the border zones where gauchos threatened royalist forces.[30]

This was a classic counterinsurgency campaign organized by Spanish officers with some experience of guerrilla warfare acquired in the Peninsular War. They generally used units of dragoons and cavalry to patrol areas where enemy guerrillas operated, of a kind comparable to the 'flying detachments' used in Calleja's counterinsurgency in Mexico. They aimed to intercept enemy movements, eradicate their bases, eliminate their leaders, and seize weapons and livestock for use by the royalist army. It was a war of multiple minor actions, where the success of a single action was measured on a small scale: the killing or capture of a few dozen insurgents, the seizure of small numbers of muskets, sabers, and bayonets, the taking of horses and their equipment, as well as sheep, cattle, and llamas to feed the army.

Would the army have been better employed in launching a direct attack on Buenos Aires? All that can be said with any certainty is that La Serna's military strategy had important military consequences. First, his counterinsurgency in Upper Peru strengthened Spain's hold on a region that was an important source of economic and fiscal resources and a vital buffer zone for Peru. Second, by holding Upper Peru rather than invading Argentina, he discouraged Buenos Aires from undertaking any fresh offensive into the region. La Serna's presence at Tupiza and his success in suppressing insurgents in Upper Peru prevented Belgrano from returning to the offensive in the region, while Buenos Aires's wars with the federalists also drew its army away from the Upper Peruvian front. Thus, when La Serna moved south against Jujuy in March–April 1819 in response to news that Belgrano's army was on the move, he discovered that Belgrano was not deploying against him but marching his army southwards from Tucumán to Córboba to defend Buenos Aires against Artigas.[31] By 1819–20, Buenos Aires's Army of the North had evidently become incapable of forcing its way back into Upper Peru. Faced by a strong Spanish army and without the support of insurrection within Upper Peru, Belgrano did little more than rely on the guerrillas around Salta to hold the border region, while awaiting resolution of the civil war on the Littoral.

Stasis on the Upper Peruvian front did not, however, signal defeatism among rioplatense officers. While La Serna tightened the royalist grip on Upper Peru, some were contemplating the possibilities for attacking viceregal Peru on another front, so far unexploited. In their forefront was General José de San Martín, who, after giving up command of the northern Army at Tucumán, proposed an attack on Peru's southern flank in the royalist-held territory of Chile, followed by an attack by sea on the viceregal capital of Lima. After Buenos Aires's successive failures to occupy Upper Peru, this was a plan that, as we shall now see, was to expose the Spanish regime in Peru to a far greater threat than any previously posed by Buenos Aires.

Reorientation: San Martín's Strategy

San Martín's interest in the idea of a new front in Chile stemmed from his service as commander of the Army of the North in early 1814, when he became familiar with the formidable difficulties of invading Upper Peru. At the time, Chile was still under an independent government and seemed to offer better ground for a war against royalist Peru, if only as a means to divide Spanish forces. San Martín may also have seen an attack on Chile as part of a larger, more ambitious strategy, aimed at the royalist capital in Lima; indeed, when he requested the governorship of Cuyo, he was probably already thinking of Cuyo as the base for taking Chile and turning it into a platform for attacking Peru.

San Martín was not the first to conceive such a strategy. Sir Thomas Maitland had produced a plan for opening a Pacific front from the Río de la Plata in 1800, when the British government was contemplating attacks on Spanish America. Maitland's plan was to take Buenos Aires, send troops to Mendoza, and thence across the Andes into Chile, where they would combine for an invasion of Peru with other British forces, brought by sea. It is possible that San Martín knew of Maitland's ideas through his acquaintance with British officers during the Peninsular War or through his connections with English and Scottish Masonic lodges, and even possible that he was pondering a "continental strategy" before arriving in Buenos Aires. It is more likely, however, that the idea took firm shape while he was with the Army of the North. The concept of a Pacific campaign against Peru was already circulating among rioplatense officials and officers during 1813, and it is very likely that San Martín knew of them. These projects went unheeded at the time but were revived after the fall of Chile. During 1815, the Chilean political rivals Bernardo O'Higgins and José Miguel Carrera each pursued their separate plans for an invasion; San Martín continued meanwhile to build his army and, by expanding his forces, to reinforce his project for a continental strategy pivoted on taking Chile.[32]

Schemes for invading Chile were blocked by one barrier after another, however, and it took three years to change Buenos Aires's strategy. The first obstacle was Spain's overthrow of Chile's independent government in October 1814, for, once back under Spanish control, Chile changed from a potential platform for a patriot assault on Peru into a possible launching pad for a royalist attack on the Río de la Plata. Another obstacle was the situation within the Río de la Plata during 1815–16, when Buenos Aires was forced onto the defensive as never before. Its war in the Banda Oriental absorbed attention and resources, and the situation in

Upper Peru remained a matter of great concern after Rondeau's defeat at Wiluma. The leadership in Buenos Aires and the Congress of Tucumán continued to believe in sustaining the war for Upper Peru for the same reasons as before: to acquire its economic resources and to remove the royalist threat to the security of the United Provinces and ultimately Buenos Aires itself.

The ongoing war for Upper Peru did not, however, deflect San Martín from pursuing and implementing his own strategic vision. He supported Buenos Aires's strong central government on the grounds that war was still the first priority and required a unified government to mobilize men and resources from all regions. He also supported an ongoing campaign in Upper Peru because he recognized the need to hold down forces that might otherwise be redeployed for the defense of Chile. However, rather than focus solely on taking Upper Peru, San Martín continued to prepare for a much larger, more imaginative strategy; he aimed at an offensive into Chile and the Pacific, privately hoping that "we might have a Cromwell or a Robespierre to achieve it."[33]

What eventually made the expedition possible? One crucial factor was San Martín's readiness to go at it alone, building an army from the means immediately available to him in Cuyo. While the Río de la Plata foundered amid provincial infighting, San Martín set out "to create his own mini-state and his own authority, giving the revolution a new power base from which to launch his project." In this, he had the vital assistance of the people in that power base to supply men and materiel for war, turning their province of Cuyo into "the cornerstone of continental independence."[34]

With only about 43,000 people, Cuyo was a narrow base for a war economy. However, San Martín's authoritarian government and stringent demands were accepted by the municipal authorities and people of the region, especially those of the city of Mendoza, his capital. They mostly shared his commitment to the revolution, if only to prevent a Spanish invasion, which would cost them more. San Martín squeezed hard, extracting extraordinary contributions from taxation, voluntary and forced donations and loans, and sequestrations of property, including slaves. He made use of local skills and supplies to manufacture arms and ammunition, even forging church bells into gun barrels and bayonets. Regional provision of livestock also ensured supply of the large numbers of animals needed for an army to eat, fight, and move. His relentless demands required austerity but also delivered benefits. He provided some rudimentary medical services, promoted irrigation projects, and by his demands, encouraged local agriculture, trade, and artisanal industry. He provided for education and cultural patronage, too, all of which helped to strengthen the bonds between San Martín and the *mendocinos* and ensured their ongoing cooperation.[35]

Another critical element of San Martín's preparations was political. To secure the authority and support of his government, he had to persuade key figures that his plans were feasible. Gradually, the tide moved in his favor. Alvear's removal from the directorship in Buenos Aires and Rondeau's defeat in Upper Peru during 1815, followed by the declaration of independence at Tucumán and election of

Pueyrredón as supreme director in mid-1816, all helped to reshuffle the political pack and make room for new military thinking. But San Martín still had to press hard to get what he wanted, using all his influence, especially his friendship with Secretary for War Tomás Guido, to secure backing for the expedition to Chile. When the critical moment came, under Pueyrredón's directorship, San Martín's arguments hit their mark, and during months of intense lobbying, San Martín secured the supreme director's support not only for his expedition to take Chile but also for his greater goal of an offensive against Lima.[36] With Pueyrredón's backing, San Martín intensified his preparations and by January 1817 was ready to take his army into Chile and open a way into Peru.

The Army of the Andes

If San Martín's abilities as politician and administrator enabled him to build a political and material base for his expedition, his qualities as a soldier were essential for establishing the Army of the Andes and ensuring its operational success. His military talents had been nurtured by long professional experience. Unlike most of his contemporaries in the rioplatense forces, San Martín was not a self-taught soldier fighting on and for his own terrain. Most of his life had been spent in Spain, where in 22 years of service he had acquired considerable experience, including participation in campaigns at Oran and Roussillon during the 1790s and in the Peninsular War against Napoleon.[37] When he volunteered to serve the government of Buenos Aires in 1812, his military background and social status eased his way to early command; so, too, did his liberal political sentiments, his friendship with Carlos María de Alvear, and his connections to other members of the Logia Lautaro.

While San Martín brought experience and a trained military mind into the revolutionary army, these were coupled with a personal ability for creating effective forces and leading them into battle. Shortly after arriving in Buenos Aires, he had raised and trained a new contingent of troops—the Regiment of Mounted Grenadiers, based on the European model of mounted dragoons—and demonstrated his ability to deploy them in battle. His victory at San Lorenzo in 1813, his subsequent command of the defenses of Buenos Aires, and his political affinity to the capital's governing elite, all ensured his ascent to the highest ranks, and he was duly appointed to replace Belgrano in 1814, after the latter's defeats in Upper Peru. His time in Tucumán was spent in rebuilding the Army of the North and managing defense of the frontier with Upper Peru, an experience that was to serve him well in Mendoza, when he had to guard against Spanish invasion from Chile while also preparing his Army of the Andes for an attack on Chile.

The Army of the Andes was his own creation. Unlike Bolívar, San Martín did not have to build an army by imposing his authority on regional caudillos, but he set up from scratch a force shaped to his requirements and answerable to his command. His army was largely based in the militarization of the province of Cuyo, where he introduced conscription and which provided the bulk of his recruits, slave and free. The army grew rapidly. In late 1814, San Martín had only around 400 regular soldiers; by the end of 1815, he had added 700 slaves ("liberated" from Spanish owners) plus 100 artillerymen; by January 1816, he reported that he could field 1,400 soldiers, plus a large militia (of no use for battle, he noted, but valuable as auxiliaries and for giving the enemy the impression of large numbers).[38] On the eve of the invasion, the army was considerably larger, amounting to over 5,000 men. Of these, about 4,000 were soldiers, divided into nearly 3,000 infantry, 900 cavalry and artillery, plus over 1,200 militiamen. Several hundred others accompanied them to act as hospital attendants, artificers, and workmen to make mountain tracks passable.[39]

The army was made up of several constituents. The largest was composed of creole and mestizo volunteers and conscripts raised locally, together with several hundred men sent in detachments from other parts of Buenos Aires's army. Next came the slaves, the "libertos" especially freed from their owners in order to discharge military service. A final, much smaller contingent was made up of Chilean exiles who had been incorporated into San Martín's forces.

The small Chilean presence in the army reflected San Martín's determination to retain full control of his forces. When the Chileans defeated at Rancagua washed up in Mendoza in late 1814, they soon became unwelcome guests because their factionalism threatened San Martín's authority. José Miguel Carrera asserted that as the governor of Chile he recognized only the government of Buenos Aires and did not have to take orders from San Martín. Bernardo O'Higgins and his followers, on the other hand, blamed Carrera and his brothers for defeat at Rancagua and denounced them as traitors. Determined to defend his authority, San Martín insisted that Carrera's few hundred men be transferred to his command, and he expelled the Carreras from the province. He then moved many Chileans out, too, on the grounds that they were poor soldiers without adequate arms and thus simply not worth retaining.[40]

Later, the Chilean connection became more solid. Chileans played an essential role in San Martín's *guerra de zapa*, a clandestine war of espionage, propaganda, and guerrilla attacks. These were vital for providing information on enemy positions and political opinion in Chile, keeping patriot sentiment alive, and keeping the enemy off balance by harassing and stretching his forces.[41] Indeed, according to William Miller, the English officer who joined San Martín's army in 1818, the main guerrilla leader, Manuel Rodríguez, "with all the resources of his ready genius, and with a valour bordering upon rashness, occupied the attention of the royalists, and certainly contributed in great measure to pave the way to the subsequent successes of the army of the Andes."[42]

San Martín also benefited from the cooperation of Bernardo O'Higgins, who became his main Chilean political ally, and from the readiness of Chileans to join his army. In mid-1816, he acknowledged the Chileans as a distinctive group by placing them in a separate infantry battalion, and, in October 1816, he permitted the establishment of the *Legión Patriótica de Chile* (Chilean Patriotic Legion). These units were not, however, constituted as a "national" military force, fighting under its own flag. They were, rather, incorporated as fellow Americans fighting for the American cause, and their loyalty was to San Martín, not a "national" leader. A prominent role in the army was reserved for O'Higgins, who had emerged as the most eligible political leader for Chile, and when the invasion started, O'Higgins held high military command but not as a coopted nationalist general. His principal role was that of a president in waiting, a political ally who shared San Martín's ideas and his plans to attack Peru, and was thus earmarked for leadership in Chile.

The most distinctive and substantial part of the army was its large contingent of slaves who were released from bondage for military service. From the outset, San Martín was convinced that he needed slaves at the core of his army. At first he talked of 10,000 slaves; then he scaled it down to 4,000, and he eventually settled for fewer. Released slaves nonetheless became a major component of his army. This was not because San Martín was a social revolutionary; far from it. He did not raise slaves against their masters, as had happened under Artigas in the Banda Oriental, nor did he aim to abolish slavery. The slaves who entered his army were often still treated as slaves or, at best, regarded as of secondary social value, and he did not necessarily secure their freedom. In short, "they continued to be property, not citizens."[43] The conscription of slaves was essentially a pragmatic decision, arising from San Martín's desperate need for soldiers and conviction that slaves made the best infantrymen. He was, moreover, able to take advantage of the precedents and legal framework for recruiting slaves, with or without a promise of freedom, which had emerged in the Río de la Plata in previous years. Belgrano had employed freed slaves during the second Upper Peruvian war, and after his defeat, slave recruitment had expanded considerably to help rebuild the shattered army. These were unpopular measures among slave owners, and though the clamor of slave owners against arming slaves was partly quelled by focusing specifically on Spanish slave owners, the influx of slaves abated in 1816.[44] The recruitment laws remained in force, however, and San Martín exploited them when he could. In the end, he did not secure the numbers he wanted, but his army nonetheless had some 1,500 ex-slaves, or nearly 40% of its total, the largest component of slaves and blacks in any army mobilized by either side during these years.

A notable feature of the army was its relatively high degree of training, discipline, and organization. In the three years that he spent in raising men and resources, San Martín gradually created an unusually disciplined force, especially designed for the purpose of invading Chile and defeating its royalist army. Its effectiveness derived from instilling a sense of honor and purpose in its officers and imposing strict military discipline on soldiers. San Martín sought, as commanders on both sides usually did, to give religious sanction to the expedition; he designated Our Lady of Carmen as the army's "Generala" and presided over the blessing of its flags. When Miller joined the army, he was impressed by its good order and efficiency. He complimented the patriot artillery for its use of the European system, spoke of the cavalry as "comparable to the finest in Europe," and concluded that, in general, "the composition of the army of the Andes was very good . . . well armed, tolerably well disciplined, and very enthusiastic."[45]

War in Chile

The strategy for invading Chile had two basic goals: to get an army of at least 4,000 men across the Andes and to defeat royalist forces as quickly as possible. San Martín was confident that he could defeat royalist forces, as his intention was to go into battle with a larger and better-trained army; he therefore saw the first task as the more difficult, for he was well aware of the problems involved in moving large numbers of men and animals through the high altitude and dangerous terrain of the Andean passes.

To secure this goal entailed elaborate preparations. San Martín sent out scouts and spies to create detailed maps and plans for the campaign, to gather intelligence, and to spread misinformation about his intentions; he mounted guerrilla operations to weaken and divide enemy forces, and he collected and concentrated the large quantities of provisions and animals needed to sustain the army as it crossed the cordilleras. His attention to logistics was impressively thorough. Miller recorded that, at its departure, the Army of the Andes carried a varied supply of provisions for 5,200 men for about two weeks, including enough wine for an allowance of a daily bottle per man. It also hauled a field train of artillery and its ammunition, together with half a million musket cartridges, and marched with a military band. The army was accompanied by over 10,000 draught animals: 1,600 horses, over 7,000 saddle mules, and about 2,000 pack mules, plus about 700 oxen to provide meat en route.[46] The ratio of men to draught animals, with around two horses and mules per man, helped ensure that the fighting men arrived in Chile ready for an immediate campaign.

San Martín's military strategy aimed to deliver forces larger than those of the royalists at a point from which he could move rapidly on the capital. To prevent the enemy from concentrating against him and to secure some element of surprise, he spread false rumors and sent out small diversionary forces north to Coquimbo and south towards Talcahuano to lure the enemy away from his point of attack. He also divided his main force into two divisions for the Andean crossing. The first and smaller force was under Colonel Las Heras, who took the Uspallata route with the intention of distracting enemy attention from the main force. The main force, led by Brigadier General Soler in the van, Brigadier O'Higgins commanding the center, with Zapiola and San Martín in the reserve, aimed to cross the cordillera some 67 kilometers to the north, by the Los Patos road. These two forces were then to converge on the slopes of the sierra of Chacabuco in 18 days' time. Once there, San Martín planned to do battle immediately with the Spanish forces, which he expected to be waiting for him, and, having defeated them, he intended to march on Santiago.

The crossing of the cordillera produced losses, but San Martín's preparations paid off; the divisions of his army arrived more or less intact, and, remarkably, arrived at their rendezvous at the prearranged time. The Spanish forces that confronted him were fewer in number but held a reasonably strong defensive position. Aware of the patriot advance, Governor Marcó del Pont had sent Brigadier Maroto from Santiago with veterans from Spain's Talavera regiment to strengthen forces stationed on the heights of Chacabuco. Marcó del Pont held back some forces, however, as he was still unsure where the main attack would be. This hesitation reflected the larger defensive dilemma that faced the Spanish in their war with Buenos Aires. Viceroy Pezuela had long been aware of San Martín's presence in Mendoza and plans for an attack on Chile, but rather than send reinforcements to Chile, he continued to concentrate his main forces on Upper Peru. In so doing, Pezuela fell into the classic military trap of preparing for the next war as though it would be identical to the last—an error that became clear after San Martín had defeated the royalist army at Chacabuco. Governor Marcó compounded the error by stretching his forces too thinly. As a Spanish officer later pointed out, San Martín lured Marcó into "the grave error of trying to cover a line of many leagues in length, which consequently remained weak at all points."[47]

The Battle of Chacabuco (February 12, 1817) was a conventional military action, fought by European methods.[48] Maroto's forces took up a defensive position on the heights of Chacabuco and positioned his infantry and artillery so that they could throw back an enemy attack. San Martín's tactics were to send a large force under Soler to attack the enemy's left and envelop his rearguard, while O'Higgins attacked the enemy's front lines but held back from full engagement until Soler's forces were ready to join him. This flanking and turning movement was the classic tactic of professional armies of the age, frequently used by the attacking army in the battles of the Napoleonic wars. The aim was to disrupt the enemy's army, to break through its front line and thus divide it into isolated parts, which were difficult to defend, control, and organize for retreat.[49] In this instance, the tactic nearly failed to produce the result intended. Soler succeeded in his flanking attack and forced the enemy off the heights where they were positioned, but the plan was upset when O'Higgins launched a premature attack on the center and failed to break the royalists' main line. He was, however, saved by the intervention of three squadrons of mounted grenadiers—San Martín's favored soldiers—and then by the arrival of Soler. The enemy did not give up easily—around 600 were killed and many taken prisoner—but their army broke, departed the field, and fled back in the direction of Santiago. This defeat confounded the royalist governor, who, in an effort to save what was left of his forces, retreated to Valparaiso; there he was later captured, along with other leading officers, before he could escape by sea. Other soldiers went south to the royalist stronghold in Concepción, while some managed to escape to Lima.

The victory at Chacabuco owed much to San Martín's qualities as a general. If parallels with Hannibal or Napoleon are overstated, there is no doubt that San Martín's singular ability to assemble an effective army and take it into battle were the keys to its success.[50] All the years spent in building his army, training and disciplining his officers and soldiers, planning his campaign, and marshaling his resources had evidently not been wasted. While he may have chafed at the many delays he suffered, San Martín's meticulous preparations enabled him to march a substantial army across the Andes, merge its main components at a prearranged place and time, and go immediately into action.

The political sequel to Chacabuco also owed much to prior negotiations and planning. In Buenos Aires, San Martín had agreed with Pueyrredón and the Logia Lautaro to pass the political leadership of Chile to O'Higgins while he concentrated on military matters. This was partly to forestall Chilean suspicions that they had been taken over by rioplatenses, but it also showed the willingness of leaders to collaborate in an American cause, larger than that of their different countries. O'Higgins was, like San Martín, a member of the Lodge and one of that covert band of comrades (mostly military men) who were committed to the independence of South America as a whole.

Confident in O'Higgins, San Martín left him to manage government and mop up royalist resistance in Chile, while he turned to the second part of his plan, which was to send an army against the Viceroyalty of Peru. At first, San Martín saw Chacabuco as a decisive victory and was confident that, with support from Buenos Aires and the new Chilean government, he could move quickly on to the next phase of his strategy. Chacabuco was soon exposed as an incomplete victory, however, and San Martín was unable to proceed as he had intended. Now, he had to send Las Heras with 1,000 men against royalist resistance in the Chilean south, which had become the center for a new royalist offensive against the revolution.

The royalist revival was partly a consequence of Buenos Aires's failure to provide San Martín with the naval support he had wanted. Without armed vessels, he was unable to cut off the royalist movements by sea or combat the Spanish naval presence in the Pacific. Royalist troops were thus able to withdraw to Talcahuano, where General Ordoñez's 1,300 men resisted a patriot siege. The resurgence was, moreover, supported by Viceroy Pezuela's determination to reconquer Chile. In December 1817, Pezuela sent his son-in-law General Manuel Osorio from Lima to Talcahuano with 3,600 soldiers, where, combined with Ordoñez's men, they presented a serious threat to O'Higgins's regime. O'Higgins responded with the defiant gesture of declaring independence from Spain, but the royalists landed the first important military blow. General Osorio marched out from Talcahuano with nearly 5,000 men against the larger army of San Martín and O'Higgins and defeated it at Cancha Rayada on February 19, 1818. O'Higgins lost some hundreds of men as well as arms and animals and was himself wounded; nonetheless, substantial contingents of the patriot forces retreated in good order and were ready to fight again. While Osorio moved towards the capital, San Martín concentrated his forces to meet the royalist advance on the plain at Maipú, a short distance south of Santiago.

The engagement at Maipú (April 5, 1818) was crucial to both sides. Osorio and San Martín committed their main armies to the action and had little to fall back on in case of defeat. The armies were of similar size, at around 4,500 each, and included substantial numbers of veterans led by seasoned officers. The battle was fought according to conventional tactics. San Martín gave command of the infantry to General Balcarce while taking command of the cavalry and reserve himself. While the enemy deployed on some slopes facing him, the patriots took up a battle formation in three divisions. On the right, Las Heras led three infantry battalions and four squadrons of mounted grenadiers; on the left, Alvarado had three infantry battalions and some cavalry companies. The main artillery occupied a central position, while San Martín commanded a reserve of three battalions plus some artillery pieces. Using his artillery to bombard the enemy's front, he sent his right–hand division to turn the enemy's left flank with repeated charges from mounted grenadiers and infantry fire. This was successful in forcing the royalist right back from their lines, but did not end the battle, for the Spanish right had simultaneously attacked and almost overcame San Martín's left, until he stopped it by throwing in his reserve. The Spanish forces lost their cavalry and were gradually surrounded, fighting a fierce, five-hour battle to a bloody end. One witness recalled that the black soldiers in the patriot army took particularly heavy losses and, when their chance came, were keen to avenge themselves by shooting prisoners. General Osorio attempted an orderly retreat, but his forces were scattered, and he fled the field, later to escape by sea southwards to Talcahuano. In the battle and the pursuit that followed, the royalist forces lost up to 1,000 dead and about 2,000 prisoners; the patriots lost about 1,000 dead and wounded.[51]

San Martín reported that his victory stemmed from the oblique order of attack with which he had started the battle, moving against the enemy's right. However, when Las Heras wanted to emphasize the use of this order of battle in the official account, San Martín refused to explain what it meant, in case "they might complain . . . that I want to compare myself with Bonaparte or Epaminondas."[52] Perhaps he was right not to claim too much, for such a maneuver required a degree of discipline and training that was found in the Prussian armies of Frederick the Great, but few others.[53] Nonetheless, the fact that San Martín could attempt it shows that patriot armies were becoming much more effective than their predecessors. The royalist general José Canterac made precisely this point in a report he wrote in mid-1818 from his headquarters in Upper Peru. After commenting on San Martín's success in Chile, he observed that, while the insurgent troops did not equal those from Europe, neither their militias nor their troops of the line broke and fled as they had in earlier times, but had created systems or plans for making war that were adapted to their circumstances and that they followed efficiently and energetically. He concluded that the generals who commanded armies in the regions of Upper Peru and Chile should avoid underestimating their enemies and proceed with the caution dictated by military principles.[54]

At Maipú, San Martín eliminated the remainder of the royalist forces, which had been allowed to escape after Chacabuco, and thus removed a major threat to Chilean independence. The defeat of Spain's main army in Chile meant that royalist resistance was marginalized, and its remnants turned to guerrilla warfare in frontier areas. Around 900 men fought on in the province of Concepción until they were forced to retreat to the fortifications of Valdivia in early 1819. Royalist guerrillas also continued to operate in the interior under the leadership of Benavides, a plebeian soldier who led bands of deserters and Indians in defiance of repeated patriot attempts to eliminate them. Miller, who fought in this region, reported that Benavides fought for the Spaniards but hated them, while the Indians were keen to attack whites and "cared not on which side they fought, provided they were instrumental in the destruction of either, as they considered both parties their natural enemies."[55]

These guerrillas were a serious drain on Chile's scarce resources; Miller recalled that 2,000 men were needed to deal with them. However, without reinforcement from outside, they were incapable of mounting an assault on the main centers of power in Chile, and, when reinforcements did not materialize, they were gradually worn down. After 1818, Chile was never again attacked by a major royalist army, leaving San Martín and O'Higgins to concentrate on their plans to invade Peru.

Preparations for the Invasion of Peru

During 1818, San Martín fixed his sights on Lima. He issued a proclamation to the people of Peru announcing that he had been ordered by the independent states of Chile and the United Provinces of South America to enter into their territory "to defend the cause of liberty." He also proposed that Peru should join them in a union of three states in which a central congress of their representatives would create constitutions for each and establish "a perpetual alliance and federation." His proposal chimed with the suggestion Bolívar had made earlier that year to the government of the United Provinces that, once he had freed Venezuela, "we should hasten to establish an American pact which, raising from all our republics a single political body, would ensure that America be respected for its majesty and greatness."[56]

San Martín's vision of the liberation of Peru was clouded, however, by changes in the political climate in the United Provinces of South America, the state from which he derived his authority. The first was the collapse of support for his project in Buenos Aires, where the government became increasingly preoccupied with military threats close to home. San Martín made three journeys to Buenos Aires in 1818–19 in order to keep his strategy at the top of the political agenda, but these yielded nothing. On the contrary, the increasingly embattled directorate wanted San Martín to bring his troops back into the United Provinces to face threats from without and within.

The external threat was that of invasion from Spain. After Spain diverted its major military expedition from the River Plate to Venezuela in 1815, Buenos Aires was for some years relieved of a similar assault. However, from late 1818, its leaders received increasingly plausible reports that Spain was preparing a large army at Cádiz to send against the United Provinces. This news inevitably placed pressure on San Martín to bring his army back across the Andes for defense of the homeland, and by January 1819, he was convinced that Buenos Aires intended a radical change of strategy "not only to disavow the projected expedition but also to get rid of the Army of the Andes."[57] He tried to forestall this by appealing directly to the caudillos López and Artigas to desist from war with Buenos Aires and to deploy their forces against the anticipated invasion from Spain. He also secured support from O'Higgins, who objected to moving the Army back across the Andes on the grounds that this would expose Chile to a new invasion from Peru, and from his allies in the Lodge who feared that moving the Army might encourage Pezuela to renew his war from Upper Peru. San Martín argued, too, that naval action was the better way to confront the threat from Spain, and in July, he called on O'Higgins to send his navy around Cape Horn into the Atlantic to intercept the Spanish fleet.

In the end, the threat from Spain disappeared, as the army at Cádiz was afflicted by both yellow fever and political dissent in its ranks. In September 1819, agents of the Buenos Aires's government, who had infiltrated the lodges of Cádiz, sent news that the expedition was unlikely to take place, as officers in the expeditionary army were among those plotting to overthrow Ferdinand VII's government.[58]

The development of San Martín's continental strategy was, however, still hindered by the wars in the Littoral. In October 1819, he was repeatedly ordered to take his troops to the capital and to engage the federalist caudillos en route. San Martín was, however, determined to stay out of the civil war and to preserve his forces for the strategy of American liberation. His refusal to support Buenos Aires was echoed elsewhere, albeit for different reasons, and mutinies and rebellions in several areas kicked away the military props that had supported the directorate and congress. In February 1820, the praetorian regime of Buenos Aires was finally overthrown by the caudillos López and Ramírez at the Battle of Cepeda.[59] The United Provinces of South America were now disbanded, as was Artigas's Protectorate, and the Río de la Plata entered a long period of internal war and rivalry.

The defeat of Buenos Aires and the fragmentation of the Río de la Plata did not prevent San Martín from pushing ahead with the offensive against royalist Peru. His ability to do so stemmed largely from his partnership with O'Higgins, who, at the start of 1820, began active preparations for an amphibious landing on the coast of Peru. The fall of Buenos Aires was a turning point for both of them. San Martín now shifted his allegiance from the defunct Directorate of Buenos Aires to the government of Chile, presided by O'Higgins. In April 1820, he resigned from the command conferred by Buenos Aires and called on his officers to elect a successor as commander in chief of the Army of the Andes. They promptly confirmed the full authority he enjoyed, and in May, San Martín became commander in chief of the Army for the Liberation of Peru, a force of rioplatense and Chilean soldiers based on the Army of the Andes. Fully supported by O'Higgins, who unilaterally invested San Martín with a plenitude of political and military powers, San Martín now became an independent military chief committed to his own goals. Thus, at the very time that the centralist regime in Buenos Aires had collapsed and the provinces turned in on themselves, he set out to complete the mission that had so long eluded the revolutionaries of Buenos Aires—namely, a military invasion and political transformation of royalist Peru. Repudiating "the madness of federalism" as "signifying nothing but ruin and devastation," San Martín directed his military forces away from internal war into an external war against the imperial power.[60]

War in the Pacific

When San Martín began preparing his army for the campaign in Peru, he had one significant advantage: a naval force with an experienced commander. This derived from the crucial decision taken in 1817 to create a patriot navy for maritime operations in the Pacific. The importance of naval power was obvious enough. That Chile's first independent government had been overturned by a royalist army sent by sea from Lima was a lesson that did not pass unnoticed. Henceforth, the patriots aimed not only to guard against a repetition of that invasion but to turn the tables by launching their own invasion of Peru.

By 1817, it was clear that Spanish domination of the Pacific sea lanes was neither invincible nor inevitable. Spanish naval weakness had been exposed in 1815–16 when a small squadron from Buenos Aires (under William Brown, the victor of Montevideo) had seized Spanish shipping and attacked royalist ports; moreover, once Chile was in their hands, the patriot leaders had the means to finance the ships and sailors needed to launch a navy of their own.[61] By October 1818, O'Higgins had acquired a squadron of seven ships, together with the seamen and marines needed to make them effective as fighting ships. Most of the sailors and almost all the officers were British or North American, recruited by agents in England and the United States, though Chilean peasants were also quickly drafted for training at sea. Their first commander was a Chilean artillery officer, Colonel Manuel Blanco Encalada, until the famous British naval hero Lord Cochrane arrived to take command in November 1818.[62]

The first actions of the Chilean navy made important contributions to both the security of O'Higgins's Chile and the future of San Martín's continental strategy. In October 1818, Blanco sailed south to intercept the convoy of transports carrying Spanish regiments sent from Cádiz and succeeded in capturing most of the ships and many soldiers from the decimated ranks of those who had survived the voyage.[63] In January 1819, Cochrane began his campaign to destroy Spanish naval power and undermine Spanish commerce in the Pacific. He sought to seize Spanish shipping wherever he found it and in 1819 blockaded Callao on two occasions. Frustrated by the failure of an attack on Callao using the new (and flawed) Congreve rockets, Cochrane redeemed himself with a daring amphibious operation against the Spanish fortifications at Valdivia in February 1820, an operation that not only captured "the Gibraltar of South America" but also harvested large quantities of stores, arms, and munitions for use by his navy. His subsequent attack on Chiloé, the Spanish island stronghold in the south, was beaten off but succeeded in two important respects: it inflicted casualties on Spanish forces in one of their most secure bases and removed any possibility of a renewed royalist attack from the south.[64]

Nor was the importance of patriot naval operations limited to their direct military impact; they were equally important in undermining Spain's economic and financial strength by curtailing Peru's overseas trade, to the detriment of important economic activities and government finances. In this sense, the first Chilean navy imitated Britain's use of naval power in order to weaken the enemy's maritime commerce and thereby sap his economic strength, while also providing incentives for sailors by allowing captured ships and cargoes to be taken as private prizes.

If the development of the patriot navy was one reason why the balance of sea power in the Pacific passed from Spanish into patriot hands, the other was the debilitation of Spain's navy. Spain had suffered immense damage to its maritime and naval strength during the international wars that preceded the onset of imperial crisis in 1808, and the interregnum governments, fighting for survival in the Peninsula, lacked sufficient resources to rebuild Spain's armada. Ferdinand VII's feeble efforts to rebuild the navy by purchasing ships from Russia did nothing to arrest decline. Indeed, it was exacerbated by the capture of much of the Spanish fleet sent from Cádiz to Peru in 1818 with reinforcements for Pezuela. The viceroy later recalled that this "catastrophe" had cost him domination of the Pacific and forced him to alter all his plans.

The royalists' naval weakness not only hindered Peru's trade and deprived the viceregal government of vital revenues; it also removed an important defense against invasion. Pezuela knew that San Martín was preparing an expedition at Valparaiso during August 1820 but found the captains of his few ships so fearful of Cochrane that they refused to leave the shelter of Callao's guns. When he finally forced his ships to sea on September 10, it was too late. On the day they sailed, San Martín had already landed on the coast south of Lima; a day later, on September 11, 1820, he disembarked his main army at Pisco, the first base for his campaign of liberation.[65]

The Army for the Liberation of Peru that departed from Valparaiso on August 19, 1820, was the largest amphibious military force ever assembled by patriot generals anywhere in Spanish America. It consisted of some 4,400 men (including 300 officers), of whom about two-thirds were from the Army of the Andes and the remainder from the Chilean army. With them went 800 horses, 35 cannon, 15,000 muskets, and 2,000 replacement sabers, together with large amounts of supplies and munitions. They were transported in 16 merchant vessels escorted by 8 warships and 11 armed launches, with a total crew of over 2,000 men.[66]

This operation was one of the most extraordinary events of the Spanish American wars. It was the denouement of a strategic plan long contemplated by revolutionaries in the Río de la Plata and long delayed by the political upheavals and military reverses suffered by successive revolutionary regimes, and it showed how far revolutionary mobilization had progressed since 1810. In the short term, it demonstrated an ability to undertake a major logistical effort to concentrate men and supplies, backed by the huge expenditure to pay the navy and the merchant vessels gathered by a private contractor to serve as troop transports. The effort was made possible in the short term by O'Higgins's willingness to let Chile take on the financial burden, with the expectation that Buenos Aires would also provide substantial support. Seen in a longer perspective, it also shows how far the fighting capacity of Spanish American revolutionaries had developed since the interregnum. San Martín and O'Higgins were able, from 1818, to field regular armies and mount naval operations that ravaged Spanish commerce, undermined Spanish finances, and prevented the movement of royalist armies.

San Martín's progress was greatly facilitated by Spain's inability to respond adequately, due in great part to the damage done to Peru by Chilean independence. This had removed Peru's principal trading partner, Lima's main source of wheat, and one of the government's key sources of revenue. The damage grew worse in the years that followed as Viceroy Pezuela's desperate financial position forced him into fiscal expedients that weakened his regime politically. For, while Spain refused to allow free trade, Pezuela issued licenses for trade with foreigners, which brought in vital revenue but aroused strong opposition from Lima merchants. The Spanish officers grouped around General La Serna, commander of the Army of Peru, were another source of opposition. They became more critical of the viceroy following his defeats in Chile and thus more inclined to oppose his strategy for dealing with the threat from San Martín.[67] And, after Osorio had been defeated at Maipú, even Pezuela himself seemed to lose confidence in his prospects for defending Peru. He had shifted forces from the highlands to the coast, but his loss of naval dominance in the Pacific undermined coastal defenses. Nor was there much chance of recovery, given that the loss of trade through Lima cut off the revenues required to finance viceregal forces. At the start of 1820, Pezuela reported that his inability to raise sufficient money was the key problem: "the real difficulty in conserving these dominions," he told Madrid, "consisted in being able to find the necessary means to sustain its large land and sea forces."[68] Without them, he was lost, for he could no longer expect much help from Spain. On the contrary, Ferdinand VII's attempt to send an expedition against Buenos Aires had made matters much worse, as it had triggered another great crisis of authority at the center of the monarchy and, by undermining Spain's political stability, further loosened Spain's tenuous hold on its remaining possessions.

Notes

1. Cited by Street, *Artigas*, p. 373.
2. Ibid., pp. 243–58, 311–28.
3. Ibid., pp. 206–13.
4. Ibid., pp. 227–30.
5. The confederation was eventually composed of the Banda Oriental, Entre Ríos, Misiones, Corrientes, Santa Fe, and Córdoba.
6. Street, *Artigas*, pp. 279–90.
7. Ibid., pp. 295–31, for details of the Portuguese campaign and Artigas's response.
8. J.P. and W.P. Robertson, *Letters on Paraguay; Comprising an Account of a Four Years' Residence in that Republic under the Government of the Dictator Francia*, 3 vols. (London: John Murray, 1838–9), 2, pp. 241–2.
9. Ibid., 3, pp. 77–81.
10. Ibid., 3, pp. 101–6.
11. Ibid., 3, pp. 106–7.
12. Bowles to Croker, Buenos Aires, November 21, 1816, Graham and Humphreys, *The Navy and South America, 1807–1823*, pp. 172–3.
13. On Lecór and his policies, see Street, *Artigas*, pp. 330–3.
14. Cited by Lynch, *San Martín*, p. 58.
15. San Martín to Arenales, Tucumán, March 29, 1814: cited by Pasquali, *San Martín*, p. 183.
16. Joaquín de la Pezuela, *CDIP*, XXVI, pp. 295–6.

17. On the guerrilla campaigns in the regions of Santa Cruz de la Sierra and La Laguna, led by Arenales and Warnes, see Díaz Venteo, *Campañas militares del Virrey Abascal*, pp. 331–2.
18. CDIP: Pezuela, *Compendio*, pp. 300–7.
19. Roca, *Ni con Lima*, pp. 349–56.
20. For Pezuela's account of his regrouping of forces, see CDIP: Pezuela, *Compendio*, pp. 319–25.
21. CDIP: Pezuela, *Compendio*, pp. 330–1.
22. Díaz Venteo, *Campañas militares*, pp. 354–68, for an account of the offensive.
23. This campaign is covered in the second part of Pezuela's account of his campaigns, not previously published together with the first part. It is published in a new edition of the *Compendio*: Joaquín de la Pezuela, *Compendio de los sucesos ocurridos en el ejército del Perú y sus provincias*, ed. Pablo Ortemberg and Natalia Sobrevilla Perea (Santiago: Centro de Estudios Bicentenario, 2011), pp. 97–133.
24. Ibid., p. 100.
25. Ibid., pp. 105–24, for Pezuela's account of the campaign and what he called the battle of Wiluma (also Viluma).
26. For an account of the battle seen from the porteño side and for their position at Sipe Sipe, see Paz, *Memorias*, 1, pp. 273–5.
27. Paz, *Memorias*, pp. 219–21.
28. Ibid., p. 272.
29. Ibid., p. 274.
30. These activities are recorded in the summary of field reports compiled by Francisco Javier Mendizábal, an officer on La Serna's staff: Mendizábal, *Guerra de la América del Sur*, pp. 120–52.
31. Ibid., pp. 145–6.
32. Vera y Pintado called for joint operations with Chile and later joined San Martín in Mendoza as his judge advocate for war. Paillardelle suggested that forces from Río de la Plata and Chile combine at Valparaiso for an amphibious operation against Lima. The idea that San Martín was the sole author of the plan, supposedly shown by a letter to Rodríguez Peña of March 1814, is no longer taken seriously as the letter has never been found. On precedents and variants of the "continental plan" and San Martín's role in its genesis and implementation, see Pasquali, *San Martín*, pp. 194–9; and Lynch, *San Martín*, pp. 65–6.
33. San Martín to Guido, May 14, 1816: quoted by Pasquali, *San Martín*, p. 240.
34. Lynch, *San Martín*, p. 71.
35. Lynch, *San Martín*, pp. 75–8.
36. On the political context, see Pasquali, *San Martín*, pp. 240–4; and Lynch, *San Martín*, pp. 84–5.
37. On his life and career before arriving in Buenos Aires, see Pasquali, *San Martín*, pp. 27–55; and Lynch, *San Martín*, pp. 4–21.
38. Pasquali, *San Martín*, pp. 227–9.
39. These were the figures given in San Martín's army list and recorded by William Miller, the English soldier who travelled from Buenos Aires to join San Martín's army in Chile: see John Miller, ed., *Memoirs of General Miller in the Service of the Republic of Peru*, 2 vols. (London, 1829, New York: AMS Press, 1973), 1, pp. 105–6.
40. Ossa, "Armies, Politics and Revolution in Chile, 1780–1826," chap. 3.
41. Pasquali, *San Martín*, pp. 233–5; Juan Luis Ossa, "The Army of the Andes: Chilean and Rioplatense Politics in an Age of Military Organisation, 1814–1817," *JLAS*, forthcoming, 2014.

42. Miller, *Memoirs*, 1, p. 129.
43. Blanchard, *Under the Flags of Freedom*, p. 15.
44. Ibid., pp. 48–50.
45. Miller, *Memoirs*, 1, pp. 175–6.
46. Ibid., 1, pp. 105–6.
47. García Camba, *Memorias*, 1, p. 359.
48. For a detailed account of the battle, see Bartolome Mitre, *Historia de San Martín y de la emancipación subamericana* (Buenos Aires: Ed. Peuser, 1950), pp. 368–78; also Pasquali, *San Martín*, pp. 274–7.
49. Rory Muir, *Tactics and the Experience of Battle in the Age of Napoleon* (New Haven: Yale University Press, 1998), p. 239–40.
50. The characterization of San Martín as an American Hannibal or Napoleon is Mitre's: see Mitre, *Historia de San Martín*.
51. Mitre, *Historia de San Martín*, pp. 474–86; Lynch, *San Martín*, pp. 103–4; Pasquali, *San Martín*, pp. 307–9.
52. Quoted by Pasquali, *San Martín*, pp. 309. Epaminondas figures in military history for his success in preventing the Spartans from successfully using their technique for turning the enemy's flank: see Jones, *The Art of War in the Western World*, pp. 4–6. Bonaparte, famous for his flanking maneuvers, was the more likely comparison with San Martín.
53. The "oblique order of attack" was used by Frederick the Great's Prussian armies. It was basically a feinting and flanking maneuver in which an advance guard screened the main body of troops from the enemy while the main body moved across in columns to attack the enemy's flank. It was not Frederick's invention but the Prussian army was the only one that had sufficient precision of its infantry movements to carry it off in the field: see Rothenburg, *The Art of Warfare in the Age of Napoleon*, pp. 18–19.
54. José Canterac, Tupiza, June 30, 1818: in CDIP, Tomo V, 1, pp. 24–5.
55. Miller, *Memoirs*, 1, pp. 226–8.
56. Quotations from Pasquali, *San Martín*, p. 325.
57. San Martín to Guido, January 12, 1819: quoted by Lynch, *San Martín*, p. 108.
58. Pasquali, *San Martín*, pp. 331–4.
59. Ibid., pp. 338–45.
60. Proclama de San Martín, Valparaiso, July 22, 1820: quoted by Lynch, *San Martín*, p. 110.
61. On the origins of the Chilean navy, see Donald E. Worcester, *Sea Power and Chilean Independence* (Gainesville: University of Florida, 1962), pp. 11–23.
62. On Cochrane's background and recruitment, see Brian Vale, *Cochrane in the Pacific: Fortune and Freedom in Spanish America* (London: I.B. Tauris, 2008), pp. 26–45.
63. William Miller gives a vivid sketch of the Chilean navy when it took to sea in October 1818, carrying him as commander of the marines and of its operations in the south: Miller, *Memoirs*, 1, pp. 191–206.
64. Miller gives a firsthand account of the assaults on Valdivia and Chiloé (where he was badly wounded): Miller, *Memoirs*, 1, pp. 242–54, 261–6. Also Vale, *Cochrane*, pp. 65–73.
65. Marks, *Deconstructing Legitimacy*, pp. 206–9.
66. These are the figures given by Pasquali, *San Martín*, p. 351. Those in Mitre, *Historia de San Martín*, p. 666, are very close; Lynch gives slightly though not substantially different figures: Lynch, *San Martín*, p. 120.
67. On the implications of defeat at Maipú for Pezuela and royalist Peru, see Anna, *Fall of Royal Government in Peru*, pp. 133–45.
68. Ibid., p. 149.

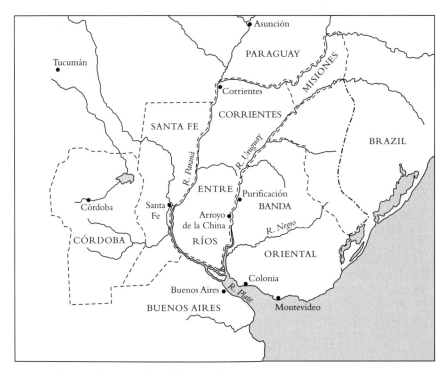

MAP 5. The Banda Oriental and Artigas's Protectorate

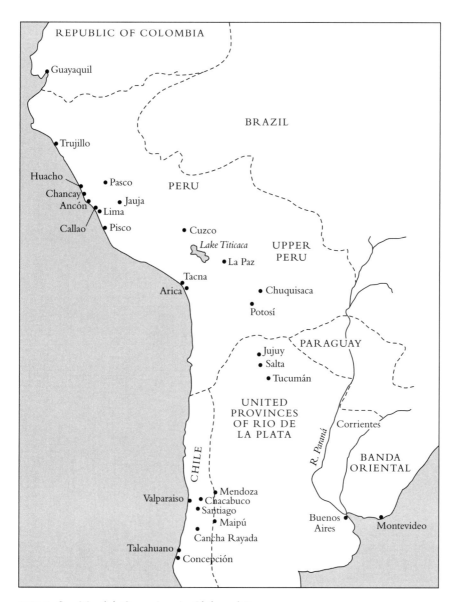

MAP 6. San Martín's Campaigns in Chile and Peru

13

DEFEAT AND RETREAT IN MEXICO AND PERU

The advances of Bolívar into New Granada and of San Martín into Chile transformed the struggle between Spain and its insurgent enemies. In the first place, their successes damaged Spain's strategic position in South America by providing the patriots with resources for revolutionary war against the remaining royalist territories in New Granada, Venezuela, and Peru. More significant, however, were the political repercussions of these military events in Spain, for the failures of Spain's armies in South America were a catalyst for crisis at the center of the monarchy.

The crisis began in January 1820, when a disaffected element in the Spanish army rebelled against the government, triggering a wider revolution against Fernandine absolutism and forcing a return to constitutional government. Spain's 1820 Revolution then spread to Spanish America. In Mexico, the return to constitutional government started a chain reaction among soldiers and civilians, which led within little more than a year to Mexican independence. In South America, the Spanish revolution changed the face of war, as Spain backed away from the military solution sought by Ferdinand VII and sought accommodation with its American opponents. This shift in relations between metropolis and colonies also impinged on the position of the international powers with interests in the Western Hemisphere. As Spain's ability to sustain its empire faltered, so governments in Britain, France, and the United States became less respectful of Spanish sovereignty and more inclined to accept, if only tacitly, that the insurgent governments might prefigure a future of independent states.

It took some years for the implications of Spain's political crisis of 1820 and its military crisis in South America to work themselves out, with variations shaped by local settings. However, for all their regional differences, political developments in Spanish America began to converge into a movement towards independence throughout Spain's continental territories during the five years that followed Spain's liberal revolution. All of Spanish America was touched by Spain's political convulsions, and, as in Spain's first crisis of 1808, the upheaval started in Spain enmeshed with American struggles for power. To trace the course of these struggles toward its conclusion, this chapter will examine the repercussions of the 1820 Revolution in the principal regions of the Spanish monarchy, starting with the revolt of the army and the reestablishment of constitutional monarchy in Spain itself.

The 1820 Revolution in Spain

Rebellion against Ferdinand VII's regime was triggered by revolt within the army, stirred by Rafael Riego among officers and soldiers of the expeditionary force that was waiting for embarkation from Cádiz to attack Buenos Aires. Launched on January 1, 1820, in the name of the 1812 Constitution, the revolt nearly aborted in Andalusia. However, in February and March, rebellion spread to other regiments and towns throughout Spain, drawing energy from civilians, who, across class lines, gave voice to their grievances against a regime that had lost their confidence. The 1820 Revolution was, then, more than a militarist putsch; it was a combination of military and civil protests designed to bring change to Ferdinand VII's regime without ejecting the king himself. Though not the first such protest to take place during the restoration, it stands apart because it brought down the existing regime and replaced it with another.

Among the several causes of the 1820 Revolution, most were linked to the inability of Ferdinand VII's regime to solve Spain's deep fiscal and economic crisis. His government presided over a bankrupt state and had failed to find any solution to its gravest problems.[1] Army discontent reflected the impoverishment and lack of credibility of the state, as it was mostly connected to the regime's central dilemma of paying for an army to recover America without the American revenues needed to do so. Grievances of one kind or another pervaded the army's ranks: officers resented the insecurity of their careers as the government cut back forces inherited from the Peninsular War; conscripts were badly paid and supplied, and neither officers nor men wanted to be shipped across the Atlantic to fight against Americans, whom they did not necessarily regard as enemies. Some officers were liberals, who actively sought to topple absolutism; others withheld support from the government, even if they did not act directly against it. Civilian liberals, who had been antagonized by the loss of the freedom in Spain under Ferdinand VII, also drove the rebellion forward, taking the army's reluctance to defend Ferdinand's regime as a cue to change it. But it was the army's refusal to support the government that was the crucial catalyst for political change. Indeed, it set the pattern for Spain's liberal revolutions in the nineteenth century, those *pronunciamientos* (declarations of rebellion) in which an army revolt was followed by provincial uprisings until political change was consecrated by a change of government in Madrid.[2]

The "constitutional triennium"—from the 1820 Revolution to Ferdinand VII's second restoration to absolute authority in 1823—affected the political life of the Spanish world in ways that were as disruptive and creative as those of the biennium 1808–10. It began with the return to power of the *doceañistas*, the moderate liberals from the 1812 Cortes who had been imprisoned, exiled, or marginalized under Ferdinand VII, and a widespread political mobilization in patriotic clubs that sought to promote the new regime and tailor it to their ends. The liberals' grip on authority was fragile, however, and soon undermined by divisions that tore Spain apart. While the Church rallied conservative opposition to reform, the *exaltados* (radical liberals) forced the moderates out, provincial rebellion undermined central authority, and, after the Royal Guard failed in an attempt at counterrevolution in 1822, France mounted an armed intervention, which reinstalled Ferdinand VII to the plenitude of power.[3] These extraordinary events in Spain were matched by events no less extraordinary in Spanish America, where the Spanish liberal revival accelerated political changes in both royalist and republican regions and where military officers also played a crucial role in shaping new directions in politics.

Spanish America felt the first effect of the 1820 Revolution in the political reorganization required to reinstate the constitution. Once again, the regions under Spanish control were unified in a constitutional monarchy, and those outside it were invited to join. The first liberal ministry ordered crown officials to disseminate news of the return to constitutional government and prepare for elections in areas under Spanish control while seeking to persuade insurgents to accept a peaceful solution via recognition of the 1812 constitution. To this end, they ordered a temporary armistice and prepared to send peace commissioners to discuss with Americans how they might reconcile themselves with the new order; they even allowed the possibility of recognizing rebel leaders as rulers of the areas they controlled if they were to accept Spanish sovereignty. While offering peace, liberal ministers also prepared for war. Military action was suspended but not permanently ruled out, largely because ministers recognized that the insurgents would see a renunciation of force as tacit recognition of their independence.[4]

Spanish hopes that a return to the constitution would resolve the American question were soon shown to be unrealistic. The governments of New Spain and Peru were all plunged into a crisis of legitimacy comparable to that of 1808–10 and became more politically divided than ever. At the same time, the insurgents in New Granada, Río de la Plata, and Chile saw no reason to abandon their demands for independence. On the contrary, San Martín continued his war against Peru, while Bolívar concentrated on destroying the remaining Spanish forces in Venezuela, New Granada, and Quito. Indeed, the most striking feature of the post-1820 period—the time when Spain was seeking to restore constitutional rule—was the emergence of military leaders and armies as key players in politics.

This militarization of politics was already quite pronounced before 1820. On the insurgent side, generals such as Bolívar and San Martín played leading roles in imposing political discipline on insurgent forces and creating new states. On the royalist side, mobilization for counterrevolutionary wars had induced a parallel process of militarization, as the officer corps who directed military affairs also became an active and powerful force in politics.

The Army and the Collapse of Spanish Mexico

Military intervention in Spain's government was mirrored, first, in the politics of the Viceroyalty of New Spain as it followed Spain's return to constitutional government. The restoration of the constitution in June–August 1820 was widely welcomed by Mexicans, but the policies and instability of Spain's new liberal regime soon encouraged important groups to rethink their positions. Some doubted the bona fides of the new regime, given that the Cortes focused primarily on Spain and did little to attend to American needs. Spain simply repeated the errors of the first constitutional period of 1810–14 by refusing to allow free trade, political autonomy, or equal electoral representation for all Americans. Dislike of the new regime was aggravated by liberal reforms, which attacked the corporate privileges of the Church and the army in Spain. Although these did not affect Mexico immediately, they alarmed the bishops and the officer corps and encouraged them to consider other political alternatives.

The most appealing alternative came from Colonel Agustín de Iturbide, the army officer who had defeated Morelos at Valladolid and forged a prominent career in the royalist counterinsurgency. Viceroy Apodaca had removed him in 1816 on suspicion of corruption and abuse of power but in 1820 reinstated him to command of the southern army. This position, at the head of an army established for the purpose of pursuing and eliminating the guerrilla chieftain Vicente Guerrero, gave Iturbide a chance to exercise political influence not only within but also beyond the army, and was the vehicle of his rebellion. In February 1821, Iturbide proclaimed the "Plan of Iguala"—published with Guerrero's assent—which proposed that New Spain become an independent monarchy. Ferdinand VII or one of his brothers was invited to become its constitutional king, and Mexico was to be governed by the Constitution of Cádiz until a Mexican Cortes produced its own charter.

Iturbide's plan was bold and shrewd. It aimed to build a political coalition around three guarantees for "Religion, Independence, Union," thereby attracting support by promising to satisfy the clergy, the Spaniards, and those who favored independence, without disturbing social order. It offered a peaceful, consensual political change, backed by the "Army of the Three Guarantees," made up of soldiers who switched allegiance from the existing army, together with Guerrero's few hundred insurgents. By the end of May 1821, Iturbide had become virtually unstoppable. Not only did Viceroy Apodaca have insufficient forces to attack Iturbide, but his decision to suspend key items of the Cádiz Constitution undermined the legitimacy of his government. By June and July, most royalist garrisons had capitulated to Iturbide; by August 1821, he had achieved such solid support that the incoming captain general of New Spain, Juan O'Donojú, unilaterally recognized Mexican independence. Although this was rejected by Spain, the viceregal regime collapsed, and in September 1821, Iturbide took over at the head of the new "Mexican Empire." This marked the end of Spanish rule in Mexico, for although some loyalists held out at Veracruz, Spain was incapable of supplying the means needed to defend this royalist enclave and lost the city in October 1821. A group of army diehards then retreated to the island fortress of San Juan de Ulúa in the harbor of Veracruz, where, to the frustration of the new government, they held out for several years. They were removed when the new state finally managed to build a naval flotilla capable of enforcing a blockade and starving the garrison into surrender in 1825.[5]

Historians have disputed whether this separation was driven by conservative elites who objected to Spanish liberal reforms or backed by a wider movement among Mexicans to regain the political freedoms introduced during the constitutionalist period of 1810–14.[6] What is clear is that the officer corps of the army, shaped by a decade of militarization and counterinsurgency aimed at defending Spanish rule, played an important role in its overthrow. This is not to say that the viceregal regime was overthrown solely by military means; it collapsed because it lost all political authority. However, the army contributed to this loss of authority by gradually removing its support from the viceroy, joining Iturbide's Trigarantine Army and supporting the unified leadership that Iturbide offered.

To explain the army's role in Mexican independence, it is essential to understand its transformation during the years of internal war, when the struggle against the insurgency increased both the scale of the military and the part that it played in government. In 1811–16, the Peninsular component of the army grew by about 10,000 soldiers as reinforcements arrived from Spain; by 1820, the Mexican provincial and urban militias reached unprecedented numbers, estimated at around 66,000 men. With this growth went a process of militarization that altered the balance of power between civil and military authorities. Shortly after the outbreak of internal war in 1810, army officers started to take powers that civil authorities had previously held and to replace civil with martial law. In 1813, Calleja's counterinsurgency carried the process of militarization much further. Facing an insurgency scattered over many regions, he decentralized the army and allowed his regional and local commanders to take precedence over civil authorities. Their powers were an essential means of sustaining forces in the field because without payments from central government, royalist officers met the needs of their troops by imposing exactions on people in the areas where they were stationed. And like the insurgent leaders, army officers often became involved in local trade and business for their own profit. They became, in short, a set of "autonomous military satrapies," whose commanders and officers grew accustomed to exercising considerable political as well as military power in their regions.[7]

The system was, however, threatened by government penury as the central authorities found it difficult to reduce the large forces accumulated during the counterinsurgency. Regional commanders were reluctant to demobilize men whom they feared might go over to the insurgents if removed from the government payroll, and they became increasingly skeptical about a government that appeared to have no solution to the army's impoverishment. The reinstatement of constitutional rule made matters worse by threatening to curtail military powers and further undercut army finances. In these circumstances, where officers feared that the army was slipping from their control, many were attracted to Iturbide's promise of an independent state that would confirm officers in their posts and guarantee the army's privileges.

The subsequent split in the army eased Iturbide's progress. While he rallied support from his base in the Bajío, Viceroy Apodaca concentrated his forces in Mexico City. This prevented Iturbide from seizing the capital, but left the government heavily dependent on a small group of Spanish soldiers who were confused and alarmed by defections from the army. Iturbide, on the other hand, lost nothing by his exclusion from the capital; he secured widening support from regional military commanders, both Spanish and American, and one by one the provincial garrisons went over to him without firing a shot. By July 1821, only Mexico City and Veracruz were left in royalist hands. In a last-ditch attempt to save the Spanish regime from Iturbide, two leading officers, Pascual Liñán and Francisco Novella, led a coup against Viceroy Apodaca. Novella subsequently took over as viceroy and affirmed his determination to defeat Iturbide by force. He had insufficient men to do so, however, and his coup did more harm than good to the royalist cause, undermining the legality of the Spanish government in Mexico without recovering support from royalist commanders in the provinces. Iturbide's forces outnumbered those of the royalist garrison in Mexico City, and Novella duly withdrew from the capital, then from Mexico, taking only the remnants—perhaps a couple of thousand men—of the once large royalist army with him. Having won over most of Spain's disaffected army of Mexico, Iturbide entered the capital on September 28, 1821, not with gunfire but to the sound of military bands and celebratory cannonades.

Mexico had thus moved towards independence by way of a pronunciamiento, which, like Riego's in Spain, originated within a section of the army, then spread to other parts of the army and to civilian allies in the provinces, and climaxed in a change of government at the center. The role of the army was crucial. After playing a vital part in defending royalist Mexico during the long and bloody war against the insurgents, it ended by overturning the royalist government it had previously preserved. While some officers and men remained loyal to the crown—notably in the city of Veracruz and the island fortress of San Juan de Ulúa—most did not. Indeed, there were more royalist commanders than insurgent leaders among the front ranks of those who supported Iturbide. Having built their careers and cultivated personal and business ties in Mexico, such men had stronger connections to Mexico than Spain, and a number decided to continue their careers in the Mexican army.[8] The experience of military participation in politics was, moreover, to have long-term effects on Mexico, nourishing a praetorian tradition that placed army officers squarely alongside civilians in the many political conspiracies and pronunciamientos that characterized the first half-century of the country's independence.[9]

San Martín and the Crisis of Royalist Peru

While royalist Mexico was undermined by the reverberations from the political upheaval that affected Spain in 1820, the Viceroyalty of Peru was exposed to its shockwaves at precisely the time that its government was threatened by San Martín's invasion from Chile. Viceroy Pezuela received the constitution on September 4 and implemented it on September 15, 1820, without great fanfare or public disturbance. However, the seemingly smooth internal transition from one form of government to another could not disguise the political upset caused by the liberal revolution in Spain, particularly as the return to constitutional government coincided with San Martín's landing at Pisco and orders from Spain to organize a cease-fire, pending full negotiations with the insurgents. On September 25, Viceroy Pezuela entered into a temporary truce with San Martín, and their delegates met at Miraflores (near Lima) to discuss terms.

The truce lasted only a couple of weeks: Pezuela rejected San Martín's demand for recognition of Peru's independence, and hostilities were resumed on October 7, 1820. Nevertheless, the conjuncture of political reorganization in the Spanish monarchy and military invasion in Peru fundamentally changed the context of Peruvian political life. On the one hand, the restoration of the constitution promised to alter the character of the Spanish state and revive liberal reform; on the other, San Martín's military presence made the case for Peruvian independence a much stronger prospect than it had ever previously been.

The decision between these alternatives did not come quickly. Although Cochrane pressed for a swift offensive by land and sea, San Martín prepared for a longer game. Indeed, for reasons that were partly political, partly military. When asked why he had not marched immediately on Lima, San Martín told the English naval officer Basil Hall that his aim was to release Peru from oppression and that this was best done by making "fresh allies in the hearts of the people." This political strategy, he noted, also had military benefits. The shift in opinion had allowed him to be "equally successful in augmenting and improving the liberating army; while that of the Spaniards has been wasted by want and desertion."[10] Indeed, knowing that he could not take Peru by force alone and conscious that war might provoke social and regional conflicts, San Martín aimed instead to use his military resources for political effect. His plan was to encircle Lima and force its surrender by blockade; then, using the capital as his base, to prize the rest of Peru from Spanish rule.[11]

The plan worked well initially, albeit not with the speed that Cochrane wanted. In late October 1820, San Martín divided his forces between the coast and the interior. He took the main part of his army north by sea to Ancón, then to the port of Huacho, where in late December, he set up headquarters some 70 miles from Lima. Meanwhile, General Alvarez de Arenales (the Spanish soldier who had fought for the patriots in Upper Peru) advanced into the Peruvian highlands with about 1,000 men. His orders were to raise rebellion among the communities of the central sierra and advance northwards parallel with the coast, along the Jauja valley, in order to isolate the capital from the interior.

This two-pronged advance had considerable impact. San Martín's move north of Lima cut off food supplies from neighboring agricultural regions and divided the capital from the cities of northern Peru, while Arenales took the towns of Huamanga, Huanta, Jauja, and Tarma in the central highlands and raised support for the patriot cause among peasant communities. He withdrew from Huamanga in early November to avoid a royalist force sent from the Army of Upper Peru against him, but on his retreat, he scored another important victory by defeating Brigadier O'Reilly's army at Cerro de Pasco. There, Arenales's division of around 1,000 men, supported by Indians recruited locally, overcame a force of similar size and made substantial gains.[12] They acquired the resources of an important mining town and took several hundred royalist prisoners (including Andrés de Santa Cruz, a creole royalist officer who changed sides and became an important asset to the patriots).[13]

Taken together, these first campaigns were an unalloyed success for the patriot cause. San Martín exposed the viceroy's difficulties in defending the coast and the capital without naval support, while Arenales's thrust into the highlands stimulated Peruvian rebellion. In both areas of operation, patriot commanders provided money and arms to local groups and established structures of command to link them to the patriot army. San Martín, for example, attached the guerrilla leader Francisco Vidal and sent him to join Arenales; Arenales deployed some of his officers to train the members of the insurgent bands known as *montoneras*. One notable example was José Félix Aldao, a friar from Mendoza, who did much to turn motley groups of montoneras into organized guerrilla groups, which he could politicize and militarize by training them in the disciplined use of arms.[14] Military activities also had repercussions beyond their areas, notably in the northern province of Trujillo. At the end of December 1820, the Marqués de Torre Tagle, recently appointed by Viceroy Pezuela as independent of Trujillo, changed sides and led the cabildo of Trujillo to declare independence, thereby dislodging northern Peru from Spanish control.

One reason why San Martín made such progress in the first months after his arrival in Peru was that the royalist military response was cautious and defensive. Viceroy Pezuela was strongly committed to holding Lima because of its political importance, its access to maritime commerce, and its naval station and fortifications at Callao. He aimed to defend the whole viceroyalty from the capital, using a system of "echelons," whereby troops were distributed among several strategic locations and required to provide each other with tactical support when necessary. Pezuela also established and took command of an Army of Lima in March 1820, ordered the transfer of troops from Upper Peru to reinforce it, and began training soldiers to repel invasion of the city.

The viceroy did not, however, oppose San Martín at Pisco or when he moved closer to Lima. Pezuela apparently contemplated attacking San Martín in December–January and concentrated an army of some 8,500 men at Aznapuquio, outside Lima, for that purpose. He did not advance, however, despite growing pressure from the army's general staff. He stated later that he had no reason to so, since San Martín did not present an immediate threat. Not only was the invading army small compared to the 23,000 royalist troops in Peru, but Pezuela also believed that it would suffer attrition from disease and desertion while the royalist army remained firm in its strongholds.[15]

Pezuela's inaction was heavily criticized in the army. General La Serna and other officers censured him for being too slow to attack San Martín, inadequately prepared, and too willing to seek a political settlement. They argued that although the viceroy had some 23,000 men at his disposal—plenty to overcome San Martín—he deployed his divisions too thinly to counter San Martín's operations or to support each other, while allowing them to run down to around 15,000 men in the closing months of 1820. Resources were, they believed, wasted in a static defense of Lima. Their preference was to unify the army in one large force that could be moved around the country, living off the land and attacking the enemy at will.[16]

Differences over strategy and tactics within the military high command might have counted for less had it not been for the viceroy's steady loss of authority after the reintroduction of the Cádiz Constitution and San Martín's arrival in Peru. In October 1820, he lost Guayaquil, the key naval and commercial port to the north of Peru, which declared its independence. In November–December, while San Martín was maneuvering to encircle Lima, he suffered further damaging reverses closer to home. Cochrane conducted a successful surprise attack on Callao harbor and captured Peru's best warship, the *Esmeralda*; San Martín cut Lima's communications with the interior; the Numancia Regiment, brought to Lima from New Granada, defected to the independents; the newly elected constitutional city council in Lima pressed for further negotiations with San Martín, and Torre Tagle declared the independence of Trujillo. Meanwhile, Pezuela refrained from taking any military action that might risk his army in battle. His patience was construed as defeatism and alienated his officers.[17] As a result, the viceroy was brought down, not by military action from San Martín and his forces, but in a coup launched by the army's leading army commanders on January 29, 1821.

Military Coup in Lima

The coup stemmed from a conspiracy among officers who were grouped at the army of Lima's encampment at Aznapuquio. There, leading officers sent an ultimatum to Pezuela informing him that he should resign his office in favor of General La Serna if he wished to avoid removal by force. Their jointly signed letter to the viceroy accused him of many faults, the foremost of which were the apathy and incompetence he had shown in defending Peru. Pezuela duly resigned, withdrew to his residence outside the city, and prepared to return to Spain. He was replaced by La Serna, the most senior army officer in Peru, who placed his comrades in charge of the army—José de Canterac as commander and Jerónimo Valdés as chief of staff—and proceeded to formulate a new strategy for the defense of Peru.[18]

The officers involved justified their coup on grounds both political and military. Above all, they accused Viceroy Pezuela of dereliction of duty and loss of public confidence; his inadequacies as head of government and military commander, they argued, were such that they feared he would lose Peru without a fight. They affirmed that La Serna had neither planned nor participated in the coup, that he was chosen for reasons of seniority, and that, rather than pursuing any personal ambition, had taken up the position required of him in time of crisis.[19] Viceroy Pezuela rejected these arguments on two major counts. First, he defended his record with detailed refutations of the charges made against him. He was particularly determined to show that his military strategy had been sound and that far from surrendering to San Martín, he was about to deploy the army at Lima against him. While defending his own behavior, Pezuela condemned that of his opponents. The coup was, he said, "a purely military insurrection," which started as a conspiracy of "four hotheads" in the army's high command, acting covertly for General La Serna. Their action was consistent with the arrogance consistently shown by La Serna and the officers who had joined him after serving in Spain and reflected their recurrent refusal to respect the viceroy's authority and military strategy. Pezuela argued that he had resigned only to prevent a civil war that would aid the enemy and did not concede any of the accusations made against him.[20]

The coup had an obvious political dimension, related to the 1820 Revolution in Spain. In Peru as in Mexico, the reversion to the constitutional system caused some prominent creoles to lose faith in Spain's ability to defend their interests. Thus, for example, the Lima city council recommended that the government come to terms with San Martín, knowing that he would demand independence, while the Marqués de Torre Tagle moved to anticipate Peruvian independence by withdrawing the province of Trujillo from Spanish rule. The return to constitutional rule may also have encouraged liberals within the army to oust the viceroy. In his private correspondence, Pezuela suggested that La Serna and other officers had a hidden political agenda, alleging that they were linked by freemasonry to liberals in the Cortes. It is, however, simplistic to see the coup as the consequence of an ideological breach between liberals and absolutists. Pezuela, who had been appointed by Ferdinand VII during the restoration, was a conservative but did nothing to oppose the return of the constitutional regime; La Serna, on the other hand, did not unquestionably obey the Spanish Cortes to his approval while he led the government of Peru.[21]

A more plausible interpretation of the coup is that it arose from the many differences that had separated the viceroy and leading officers since their arrival in 1816. La Serna and his staff officers had never shown much respect for Pezuela as a general; La Serna opposed his strategy in Upper Peru in 1816–17 and continued to be insubordinate thereafter. Indeed, by 1820, his request to be relieved of his command had been ratified in Spain, and he was in Lima awaiting transfer. Rather than leave La Serna to agitate against him, Pezuela had tried to win him over by promotion to lieutenant general and inclusion in the deliberations of the military staff. This was, however, to turn La Serna into a potential successor and even more determined opponent. He maneuvered himself into a position at the head of the junta of generals responsible for strategy, ensuring that his officers occupied prominent commands in Lima, and colluded with the viceroy's civilian enemies to undermine Pezuela's reputation. He then seized the chance to supplant Pezuela when the viceroy concentrated the army at Aznapuquio and before he was transferred away from Lima. Gathered together close to the capital, La Serna and his officers seized the reins of government and proceeded to impose their solutions to the problems of defending Peru.

This extraordinary behavior has parallels with the coup that overturned Mexico's Viceroy Apodaca a month later. In both capitals, the removal of the viceroy was carried out by royalist army officers who were responding to a crisis of Spain's authority. In Mexico, the army split between those who joined Iturbide and sought a solution in independent monarchy and those who remained loyal to Viceroy Apodaca, then Novella, in defense of Spanish rule. Iturbide finally won because resistance in the Spanish army dissolved when O'Donojú, the new commander sent from Spain to replace Novella, decided to accept Iturbide's terms in the hope that Mexico would thus retain some connection to Spain.

In viceregal Peru, the royalist army also played a central role in the political struggle over Spanish rule. It differed from Mexico, however, in that the challenge to the viceroy came not from within the royalist army but from a revolutionary general leading a foreign army. There were, nonetheless, some semblances. First, San Martín behaved in a manner akin to Iturbide: he set up a base for his army near the capital, sought to attract allies to his cause, and tried to cajole the viceroy and other authorities into negotiating a peaceful settlement, hinting at his readiness to turn Peru into an independent monarchy under a Bourbon prince. Second, the commanders of the Peruvian army launched a takeover of viceregal government, akin to Novella's, in order to preserve Peru as a Spanish colony. La Serna engineered a careful deployment of officers and troops to provide backing in Lima; high-ranking officers then drew up a document demanding that the viceroy resign in favor of the army's commander, General La Serna. Pezuela's removal was then publicly presented as voluntary resignation, and he was dispatched to Spain.

So, like Viceroy Apodaca's officers in Mexico, the Peruvian military mutineers did not call for a change of government. They publicly justified their conduct by reference to Pezuela's incompetence and lack of public support, and they claimed that La Serna had replaced him at the invitation of army officers concerned for the future of Peru. In short, La Serna and his colleagues did not claim their right to create a new government; they argued that they had simply removed the viceroy in order to preserve Peru for Spain. There were signs of civilian complicity in the coup, notably from among the Lima merchants who opposed Pezuela's free trade policy.[22] Nonetheless, its most striking characteristic was that officers in Peru's royal army became, like their counterparts in Mexico, principal actors in politics and heirs to the powers of royalist government.

The ascendancy of a military clique had important consequences, though they differed from those in Mexico. Whereas the division of Mexico's army led to independence, in Peru it triggered a major shift in royalist strategy, away from a political solution and into a prolongation of war. After taking power, La Serna had to permit the peace commissioner sent from Spain, Manuel de Abreu, to set up talks with San Martín in April–June 1821, but he frustrated Abreu's efforts to negotiate a peaceful solution. La Serna rejected San Martín's suggestion that they create a regency over which La Serna would preside and, with it, a commission that would travel to Spain to arrange the independence of Peru under a Spanish prince. Instead, he implemented his strategy for defending Peru from the interior and abandoned Lima. At the end of June, General Canterac left with half the army; La Serna then publicly proclaimed that he was completing the army's evacuation to avoid its complete loss from the ravages of an epidemic. Those soldiers who were too ill to move were transferred to the fortress at Callao together with arms and munitions, thus leaving the royalists with a toehold on the coast, which they hoped later to exploit. On July 6, La Serna finally headed out of Lima for the highland town of Huancayo, completing an orderly withdrawal, which offered a chance to rebuild the army and restart the war.[23] Shortly afterwards, on July 12, San Martín took possession of the capital. On July 28, he formally proclaimed Peruvian independence; on August 3, 1821, he took the title of "Protector of the State of Peru," thereby installing himself as the head of the independent government based in the capital.[24]

San Martín in Lima

Change of possession of the capital brought a change in the armed struggle for Peru, as both sides took up new positions. La Serna had pulled out of Lima for military rather than political reasons. The city's population did not threaten rebellion against him, but his army was at risk because, without naval support, he could not sustain its supply nor counter the threat of encirclement by land and sea. His tactical retreat allowed him to reposition his forces where they could be properly supplied and where he was able to rebuild his army, dominate large areas of the interior, and await the opportunity to turn back onto the offensive.

San Martín, on the other hand, did not significantly strengthen his military position by taking Lima. He had to occupy the capital because of its obvious symbolic importance, and he also believed that, while his navy allowed him to consolidate his hold on the Pacific coast, the city provided him with a platform from which to propagate independence throughout Peru. However, despite his talent for organizing armies, mounting offensive operations, and winning battles, San Martín did not seek out and destroy the royalist army. Instead, at a time when all the other countries of continental Spanish America had achieved de facto independence, Peru was caught in a military and political stalemate. There were some military initiatives in this period, but several years passed before the deadlock was broken. That moment awaited the intervention of an external army led by Bolívar, the liberator and president of the Republic of Colombia.

To explain this delay, historians have tended to criticize San Martín's decision to remain at Lima and his desire to rely on political rather than military means to promote independence.[25] An early expression of this view, probably reflecting opinion among San Martín's officers, comes from the memoirs of the English soldier William Miller. According to Miller, the Protector made a bad mistake by installing his army at Lima rather than enlarging his operations in the interior; had he done so, "the war would have been terminated in very few weeks; whereas, for want of timely energy, unhappy Peru continued to suffer, and her capital and provinces were alternately in the hands of the friends and foes to freedom."[26] Nor did San Martín take advantage of Arenales's 4,000-strong army in the interior to attack La Serna and Canterac's retreating forces. Instead, the royalists were allowed to take gradual possession of the southern Peruvian provinces, an "extraordinary oversight on the part of the patriots," which, said Miller, "compensated the royalists for the loss of Lima."[27]

The criticism that San Martín allowed the momentum of his military campaign to dissipate is plausible. In 1821, Arenales was in the highlands and had support from Peruvian montoneras and guerrilla bands. The montoneras were probably of limited military value, given their character. Drawn mostly from Indian communities, they were poorly armed, transitory groups, which occasionally attacked royalist targets, then went back to their farms. The guerrillas, on the other hand, had greater military potential. Although they were generally small groups—a few dozen at most—they were better organized and had greater continuity than the montoneras. They operated in a terrain they knew, and like guerrillas everywhere, their mode of war was the surprise attack and a commitment to plunder, which sometimes tipped into simply banditry.[28]

San Martín did not, however, exploit the potential for converting the guerrillas of central Peru into an organized network of espionage and armed resistance, nor did he launch a campaign in the interior. While he provided some support for the guerrillas and sought to turn them into auxiliaries under his command, he made no systematic attempt to create an irregular army in the interior. Instead, he recalled Arenales to Lima, and neglected operations in the interior for many months. San Martín stuck to this cautious approach even when Canterac returned to Lima in September 1821 in a bid to relieve royalist forces in the garrison at Callao. Canterac marched over 3,000 men on the road past Lima to Callao and entered the fortress unchallenged; when he left some days later, he again passed Lima without any intervention from the patriot army. San Martín's refusal to attack made sense in the short-term, since it avoided risking a major battle with seasoned troops and allowed San Martín to pressure the Callao forts into surrender shortly after Canterac's departure. However, according to Miller, San Martín was "greatly blamed" for failing to organize an aggressive pursuit of the retreating royalists and saw his authority diminish, even though "many of the chiefs appeared to be less than eager to prosecute hostilities than to indulge in the gayeties of Lima."[29]

Whoever was to blame, the patriots undoubtedly wasted military opportunities at this time. Miller observed that San Martín had more than 8,000 men in the vicinity of Lima at this time and stated that "half of this force, if properly led on, would have been sufficient to drive the last Spaniard beyond the Peruvian frontier." The patriots' military inertia was, in the Englishman's view, partly caused by lassitude among San Martín's officers, who preferred the pleasures of life in the capital to the rigors of military campaigning. But he also held San Martín responsible for failing to sustain army discipline. Instead of dispensing some exemplary punishments among recalcitrant officers, the Proctector allowed Lima to carry "the burden of an army kept unemployed, while an enemy . . . retained undisturbed possession of the interior."[30]

It would be wrong to see the decision to remain at Lima as simple negligence by San Martín and the army's high command. San Martín made a conscious political choice to stay in Lima rather than mount offensives inland because he believed that Peru was not ready for independence and could not be forced into it by military means. He told Basil Hall that Peru differed from other Spanish American countries because it had long been culturally and politically isolated, so that "the people were still not only very ignorant of their own rights, but required time and encouragement to learn how to think justly on the subject."[31] He believed, in short, that Peruvian independence could only be consolidated by "Peruvianising" the revolution. Given the size and diversity of Peru, this determination to pursue a policy of persuasion from the coast seems reasonable, particularly since he had a small army compared to the substantial royalist forces in Southern and Upper Peru.

Unfortunately for San Martín, Lima turned out to be more of a trap than a springboard. It is true that there were 3,504 signatories to the declaration of independence in July 1821, but given San Martín's intimidation of the electorate, this was scarcely a reliable commitment. Moreover, when San Martín took up the title of "Protector" (in conscious emulation of Oliver Cromwell), he created an authoritarian government that did not represent the *limeño* political class, still less that of Peru more generally. With chief ministers who were mostly outsiders, an army presence that disturbed the peace, and policies that imposed heavy fiscal burdens on the better-off and persecuted Spaniards, San Martín's Protectorate did little to win limeños over to the cause of independence.

If Lima was politically volatile, it was also an unsuitable platform for patriot warfare. As La Serna had discovered, the city lacked the economic resources needed to support a large army; it was also tenuously connected to important areas of Peru, and had fragile lines of communication with the interior. The government of the Protectorate was, then, just as prone to penury as the preceding viceregal regime and lurched from one financial crisis to another. Starved of specie from the interior and unable to attract much foreign trade, Lima's economy contracted, undermining government revenues, and leaving San Martín's government constantly on the edge of bankruptcy. Confiscations and forced contributions averted collapse, but such expedients were mere stopgaps for the chronic deficit of a government whose spending always outpaced its revenues. And with deficit came problems with the army. While arbitrary fiscal measures turned the citizens of Lima into San Martín's enemies, they did not provide sufficient funds to ensure the stability and loyalty of his army.

The army was further stressed by divisions between the Rioplatenses and Chileans who had formed the Army for the Liberation of Peru. While he was in Chile, O'Higgins had tried to foster cooperation between them by giving all the rioplatense officers the same rank in the Chilean army that they held in the Army for Peru's liberation, and this had helped to sustain a superficial harmony during the first stage of the campaign. However, relations deteriorated after the army took up position in Peru, as consciousness of regional differences deepened. Chilean officers were angered by discrimination against them in government posts and because they were regarded as simple-minded military men without administrative and political skills. At the same time, O'Higgins tried to ensure that Chilean officers retained their connection to Chile, so, while allowing them to swear allegiance to the Protector while serving in Peru, he wanted to choose their commanders and ensure that the Chilean force retained some autonomy.[32]

The Viceroy in Cuzco

The royalists were at this time rather more united, and, under the skilled leadership of professional soldiers, their cause flourished while San Martín's faded. After leaving Lima, Viceroy La Serna consolidated his position in the southern highlands and played his own waiting game. Rather than challenge San Martín, La Serna planned to sustain royalist government in the interior until Spain provided the naval support needed to fight back against the independent enclaves of the coast. By this strategy, La Serna not only reduced the territory he had to defend, but he also allowed himself to place his forces at strategic points in Southern and Upper Peru where they could be fed and supplied and from which they could provide mutual tactical support.

Under these arrangements, the royalist army grew larger and stronger. By 1822, it consisted of tactical groups distributed around several key points: at Cuzco, La Serna with 3,000 men; at Jauja, Canterac with 3,000; at Arequipa, Valdés with 7,500; and at Pisco, Carratala with 700.[33] In addition to these divisions, Olañeta commanded a force of several thousand men in Upper Peru, positioned to prevent invasion from the Río de la Plata or from San Martín's forces in Peru. The overall distribution of royalist forces met with several basic military and logistical requirements: each commander had sufficient forces to defend key regions; each had sufficient space to provide the supplies needed to support his forces, and each had sufficient proximity to another to allow for a concentration of forces when needed.

The efficacy of La Serna's strategy was demonstrated in March 1822, when San Martín sent a couple of battalions from Lima to recruit in the region of Ica. Led by Domingo Tristán and his deputy Agustín Gamarra, they were quickly overwhelmed by a royalist army. Counting on Tristán's inexperience, General Canterac force-marched around 2,000 men from Jauja to confront him. In early April, he surprised the patriots in an ambush at Mamacona and went on to take the city of Ica. Canterac told the viceroy that this was an action, which, though fought by armies of only 5 or 6,000, was among those "that decide the fate of an Empire." He claimed that "victory at Ica has decided the destiny of Peru" and assured that Peruvians, who were already mostly disillusioned with promises made by so-called liberators, would remain an integral part of the Spanish monarchy.[34]

If this claim was premature, there is no doubt that Tristán's defeat in the southern campaign was a disaster for the patriots. They lost at least half their army, together with large quantities of arms and money.[35] In consequence, "union was again restored in the royalist councils, while the patriots were distracted by dissensions, and weakened by insubordination."[36] La Serna no doubt found further encouragement in San Martín's abdication. In September 1822, the Protector handed over power to Peru's first independent congress, which chose a three-man junta as its executive. At the end of the year, San Martín sailed for Chile, en route to exile in Europe.

If Viceroy La Serna could congratulate himself on defeating San Martín, his situation was not without its problems. The economies of the regions he occupied had been badly disrupted by years of conflict in Upper Peru and did not easily support a continuing war effort. Indian communities resented the burdens of the head tax and military draft and occasionally mounted violent protests. Indeed, before San Martín's arrival, Indian resentments had already surfaced in the substantial Indian rebellion that took place in Aymaraes in 1818. This was crushed by force but Indian rebellion resurfaced shortly after San Martín's landing, when, in December 1820, major Indian uprisings occurred in the regions of Cangallo and Huancayo. They were once again crushed by military force—in this case, by a substantial contingent of royalist troops from Arequipa.[37]

Over the next few years, such peasant uprisings became rare, but popular resistance was never completely crushed. Guerrillas continued to spy on royalist troop movements and attack supply lines, and they even tried to drive a wedge between royal forces at Cuzco and Arequipa in the south and those at Huancayo in the center.[38] They were, however, more a nuisance than a significant threat to the royalists. San Martín could occasionally call on local caudillos for support but never succeeded in turning peasant rebels into consistent allies, bound to his regular forces, for they were concerned primarily with their own local interests and resisted being welded into an auxiliary army.[39]

The establishment of Cuzco as political capital for the viceregal regime was a clear sign of the continuity of Spanish government. The royalist press could represent the move to the ancient capital of Peru as a sign of strength and contrast it favorably with San Martín's entanglement in enfeebled Lima. The city also gave La Serna a firm base on which to establish an administrative system capable of sustaining Spanish authority and providing the revenues needed for both government and army. Funds were short, as always, and the usual emergency expedients came into play, with sequestrations of property and forced and voluntary loans. However, the Indian head tax provided a crucial source of income, together with other traditional fiscal sources, such as the sales tax and state monopolies, and, although these returns were unstable, the income of the Cuzco treasury nearly doubled in 1823. By ruthless pressure, La Serna secured money to support his armies, and in late 1822, he encouraged the Spanish government to believe that royalist Peru could hold out against the independents.[40] The question remained, however, whether royalist rule could survive new challenges from Peru's independent neighbors, a question that, as we shall now see, became increasingly urgent when Bolívar completed the liberation of Colombia.

Notes

1. Fontana, *La quiebra de la monarquía absoluta,* p. 353.
2. On the 1820 revolution and its aftermath, see Carr, *Spain,* pp. 124–46. On the role of the army, see: Christiansen, *The Origins of Military Power in Spain,* pp. 18–22. On the origins and consequences of the revolution in Spanish history and a critical commentary on the historiography on militarism and praetorianism in nineteenth-century Spain, see Roberto L. Blanco Valdés, "Paisanos y soldados en los orígenes de la España liberal," in *Las nuevas naciones: España y México, 1800–1850,* ed. Jaime E. Rodríguez O. (Madrid: Mapfre, 2008), pp. 273–92.
3. Esdaile, *Spain in the Liberal Age,* pp. 50–62.
4. Anna, *Spain and the Loss of America,* pp. 221–34; Costeloe, *Response to Revolution,* pp. 85–90.
5. On the restoration of the constitutional regime, Iturbide, and independence, see Anna, *The Fall of the Royal Government in Mexico City,* pp. 197–223. On events in Veracruz and San Juan, see Ortiz Escamilla, *El teatro de la guerra: Veracruz,* pp. 175–80, 234–49.
6. For the former, see Lynch, *The Spanish American Revolutions,* pp. 319–26. For the latter, see Anna, *The Fall of Royal Government in Mexico City,* pp. 191–209; Hamnett, *Revolución y contrarrevolución en México y el Perú,* pp. 304–22, 345–8; Rodríguez O., *The Independence of Spanish America,* pp. 205–9.
7. Archer, "Where Did All the Royalists Go?" pp. 29–43; and his "Politicization of the Army of New Spain during the War of Independence," pp. 27–37.
8. Christon I. Archer, "Beber del cáliz envenenado: la política, la tradición y el ejército mexicano, 1820–1848," in *Las nuevas naciones: España y México, 1800–1850,* ed. Jaime E. Rodríguez O. (Madrid: Mapfre, 2008), pp. 293–314.
9. On the role of the military in the practice of the pronunciamiento in Mexico, see Will Fowler, "El pronunciamiento mexicano del siglo XIX: Hacia una nueva tipología," *Estudios de Historia Moderna y Contemporánea de México* 38 (2009): pp. 5–34.
10. San Martín made these comments a year after his landing at Pisco. See Basil Hall, *Extracts from a Journal Written on the Coasts of Chile, Peru and Mexico in the Years 1820, 1821, 1822,* 2 vols. (Edinburgh: Constable and Co., 1824), 1, p. 216.
11. On San Martín's strategy while the Spaniards held Lima, see Lynch, *San Martín,* pp. 121–30.
12. Mendizábal, *Guerra de la América del Sur,* p. 163.
13. On Santa Cruz's extraordinary career from royalist to patriot military officer and from military commander to leading political figure in republican Peru, see Sobrevilla Perea, *The Caudillo of the Andes: Andrés de Santa Cruz.*
14. For these and other examples of early guerrilla mobilization, see Raul Rivera Serna, *Los guerrilleros del centro en la emancipación peruana* (Lima: P.L. Villanueva, 1958), pp. 31–41. Also Gustavo Vergara Arias, *Montoneras y guerrillas en la etapa de la emancipación del Perú, 1820–1825* (Lima: Editorial Salesiana, 1974), pp. 70–86.
15. A key source for Pezuela's military and political thinking in 1820–1 is the long, self-justificatory document he wrote in 1821, shortly after he had been removed from office. This was the *Manifiesto en que el Virrey del Perú Don Joaquín de la Pezuela refiere al hecho y circunstancias de su separación de mando* (Madrid: Imprenta de D. Leonardo Núñez de Vargas, 1821). Pezuela's "manifiesto" was the touchstone for a protracted polemic started by Gerónimo Valdés, a colonel in the royalist army in 1816 who served in the Spanish army in Peru (and became a general) prior to its defeat in 1824. Valdés wrote several accounts of the wars in Peru in which he aimed to show, inter alia, that Viceroy Pezuela's failure to fight San Martín was the error from which issued all the subsequent problems

of royalist Peru. The "manifiesto" was thus reprinted with Valdés's critique in 1827. It is included with several of Valdés's writings, compiled by his son the Conde de Torata in the collection of *Documentos para la historia de la guerra separatista en el Perú*. For the manifiesto, see the *Documentos*, vol. 2, apendice 2, pp. 221–302. For Pezuela's description and defense of his military strategy, see especially pp. 231–7, 245–52.

16. The army's critique of Pezuela's government was detailed by Jerónimo Valdés in his justification of the coup and repudiation of Pezuela's account: see his "Refutación al manifiesto," in Conde de Torata, *Documentos para la historia de la guerra separatista en el Perú*, 2, pp. 17–137. This critique was colored by Valdés's desire to vindicate himself and the group of officers, including La Serna, García Camba, and Canterac, who led the royalist forces, whose defeat in 1824 marked the end of Spanish rule in Peru. On the specific flaws of Pezuela's military strategy and the alternative recommended by his officers, see especially pp. 26–37, 53–70.

17. On the decline of Pezuela's authority during 1820 and the emergence of opposition within the army, see Anna, *Fall of the Royal Government in Peru*, pp. 163–70; and Marks, *Deconstructing Legitimacy: Viceroys, Merchants, and the Military in Late Colonial Peru*, pp. 280–301.

18. A careful reconstruction of the events, participants, and motives of the coup, using the documentation issuing from royalist polemics about the loss of Peru, is given by Marks, *Deconstructing Legitimacy*, pp. 303–15.

19. The arguments in favor of the coup are laid out at length in the writings of Jerónimo Valdés, one of its principal participants. For Valdés's presentation of the case against Pezuela, see his reply to Pezuela's manifesto, in "Refutación que hace el Mariscal del Campo Don Jerónimo Valdés del Manifiesto que el Teniente General Don Joaquín de la Pezuela imprimió en 1821," in Conde de Torata, *Documentos para la historia de la guerra separatista en el Perú*, 2, pp. 17–137.

20. Pezuela's refutation of the charges leveled against him and his explanation of the reasons why the coup took place are laid out in his "manifiesto": see Conde de Torata, *Documentos para la historia de la guerra separatista en el Perú*, vol. 2, apendice 2, pp. 226–31. The "four hotheads" are named as Brigadier José Canterac, Colonel Gerónimo Valdés, and commanders Andrés García Camba and Antonio Seoane: see pp. 226–7.

21. John R. Fisher, "The Royalist Regime in the Viceroyalty of Peru, 1820–1824," *JLAS* 32 (2000): pp. 55–84. On the coup, see pp. 65–8.

22. On the role of Lima merchants, see Marks, *Deconstructing Legitimacy*, pp. 315–24.

23. On the end of the peace talks and La Serna's withdrawal, see Anna, *Fall of Royal Government in Peru*, pp. 175–7.

24. For a vivid contemporary account of La Serna's withdrawal from Lima, stressing fears of social turmoil, see Hall, *Extracts*, pp. 220–30.

25. For a succinct summary of San Martín's strategy and the problems that arose from his decision to remain in Lima, see Anna, *Fall of Royal Government in Peru*, pp. 192–213. San Martín's recent biographers also regard his Lima-based strategy as flawed: see Pasquali, *San Martín*, p. 360–1; Lynch, *San Martín*, pp. 133–5.

26. Miller, 1, p. 365.

27. Ibid., p. 368.

28. On the distinction between montoneras and guerrillas, see Vergara Arias, *Montoneras*, pp. 30–3.

29. Miller, *Memoirs*, 1, pp. 379, 373.

30. Ibid., pp. 410–11.

31. Hall, *Extracts*, 1, p. 218.

32. Diego Barros Arana, *Historia jeneral de Chile* (Santiago: Rafael Jover, Editor, 1894), 13, pp. 508–10.

33. Mendizábal, *Guerra de la América del Sur*, p. 184.

34. Canterac to La Serna, April 17, 1822, in CDIP, XXII, vol. 2, p. 245.

35. For the royalist account, see Mendizábal, *Guerra de la América del Sur*, p. 181.

36. Miller, *Memoirs*, 1, p. 417.

37. Led by the area commander Brigadier Rocafort: see Mendizábal, *Guerra de la América del Sur*, p. 165.

38. On guerrilla activity in 1820–22, see Rivera Serna, *Los guerrilleros*, pp. 46–65; Vergara Arias, *Montoneros*, pp. 70–100.

39. Rivera Serna, *Los guerrilleros*, pp. 109–13; Lynch, *Caudillos in Spanish America, 1800–1850*, pp. 51–3.

40. Historians give varying accounts of La Serna's government at Cuzco, but concur in portraying it as a reasonably solid structure with sufficient resources to fight the independents: see Anna, *Fall of Royal Government in Peru*, pp. 211–13; Walker, *Smoldering Ashes*, pp. 109–15; and Fisher, "Royalist Regime," pp. 74–9.

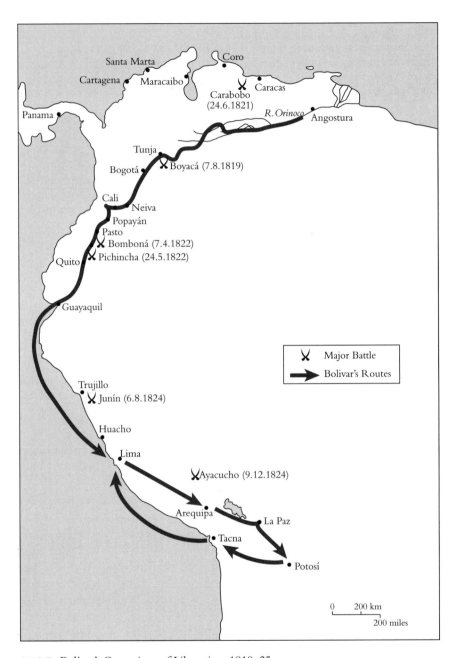

Santa Marta

Coro

Cartagena · Maracaibo

Caracas

Carabobo
(24.6.1821)

Panama ·

R. Orinoco

Angostura

Tunja

✗ Boyacá (7.8.1819)

Bogotá ·

Cali

Neiva

Popayán

Pasto

✗ Bombóná (7.4.1822)

Quito ✗ Pichincha (24.5.1822)

Guayaquil

| ✗ | Major Battle |
| ➤ | Bolívar's Routes |

Trujillo
·
✗ Junín (6.8.1824)

Huacho

Lima

✗ Ayacucho (9.12.1824)

Arequipa

La Paz

· Tacna

· Potosí

0   200 km

200 miles

MAP 7. Bolívar's Campaigns of Liberation, 1819–25

14

BOLÍVAR AND THE FALL OF ROYALIST PERU

Peru was, as we have seen, the single greatest bastion of Spanish rule in South America during the decade after 1810. Its viceroys had stifled rebellion within the viceroyalty and held back revolution in Upper Peru, Quito, and Chile. However, royalist Peru faced its greatest test after 1820, when political upheaval in Spain and armed incursions from neighboring territories generated fresh challenges. San Martín presented the first, inconclusive, challenge when he landed his expeditionary army at Pisco in 1820; the second, much more effective challenge originated when Bolívar entered the Peruvian theater of war in 1823. Indeed, Bolívar went on to become the nemesis of the Spanish Viceroy of Peru and, by 1825, was acclaimed as both the Liberator of Peru and the founder in Upper Peru of Bolivia, the state that bore his name.

The contribution that Bolívar made to the final destruction of Spanish rule in the two Perus and their transformation into independent republics was built on his extraordinary career as the Liberator and president of Colombia. In some ways, he resembled San Martín, the Liberator and Protector of Peru. In 1819, he had followed San Martín's example with a trans-Andean offensive aimed at opening a new front in a neighboring territory, then using that territory as a platform from which to extend his war of liberation against the main body of royalist forces. And like San Martín, Bolívar focused on creating a standing army that was well-trained and committed to the military life, ready to follow him in transregional campaigns and bound to the cause of American independence.

However, by the time that he entered Peru, his career differed in several important respects from those whom he later described as the "three Caesars" of America: Iturbide, O'Higgins, and San Martín. Iturbide had led Mexico to independence at the head of an ex-royalist army and created a conservative independent monarchy; O'Higgins had established a republic in Chile on the back of San Martín's Argentine army only to be forced out by rivals; San Martín had achieved partial independence in Peru but failed to install the independent monarchy he wanted and left an undefeated royalist army in control of a large part of the country. Bolívar, by contrast, had forged a movement towards independence that was driven by armies formed from the forces of several caudillos and shaped by an unusually broad strategic vision. He was, moreover, convinced that the cause of independence required the elimination of royalist power wherever it remained. It was this conviction that led Bolívar to move into the unfamiliar arena of Peruvian politics once he had defeated royalist armies in New Granada, Venezuela, and Quito in the campaigns of 1820–22.

Bolívar and the Creation of Colombia

Bolívar's emergence as a force for continental liberation was boosted by the effects of the Spanish Revolution of 1820. As his enemy General Morillo immediately recognized on hearing the first accounts of events in Spain, the 1820 Revolution was an augury of Spain's defeat in America. If the news about Spain were true, said Morillo, the crisis of 1808 would be replayed, with doubly destructive consequences for Spanish rule. Another political revolution in Spain, he believed, would not only encourage the insurgents but undermine the loyalty of his overstretched troops and hence his ability to hold Venezuela.[1]

Morillo's gloomy predictions were not immediately realized. In May, the proclamation of the Spanish constitution was preceded by a month-long armistice, which offered the royalists a respite from military pressures. This was counterbalanced, however, by the effects of Spain's liberal revolution on Morillo's ability to sustain his army. From June 1820, he had to cede his absolute authority to civilian officials, and as financial administration was again decentralized, he endured further deterioration in the conditions of his army.

The core of the army made up of Spanish expeditionary soldiers had already fallen to a third of its original size, and the army shrank still further as hundreds of Venezuelan soldiers deserted. While Morillo's enemies were bringing in foreigners to fight for them, the decay of the royalist army seemed unstoppable. Morillo thought this understandable; if Spain had shown itself reluctant to sacrifice its sons in American wars, there was no reason why Americans should be willing to do so.[2] Conspiracies, mutinies, and desertion were undermining the army; so too were the constitutional *ayuntamientos*, which told people that under the new system they no longer had to contribute recruits or money to the war and that even those already enlisted into the army could legally leave the ranks. Public opinion was, indeed, now definitely in favor of independence, and those who were reluctant to serve the king were ready to join his enemies.[3]

The constitutional regime also forced Morillo to change his relations with Bolívar and the insurgents. Instructed by Madrid to offer the insurgents a chance to accept the constitution, Morillo had to negotiate an armistice, which he did in late 1820. At meetings with Bolívar on November 26–27, he ratified two accords, one for a six-month truce on land and sea; the other for ensuring respect for the rules of war.⁴ In December, Morillo then handed over command to his deputy, Miguel de la Torre, of the royalist army of about 10,000 men.⁵

If the prospects for the defense of Venezuela looked poor in mid-1820, the chances of a royalist recovery in New Granada diminished even faster. Spain's return to constitutional government was largely to blame because of its divisive effects on the royal authorities and army. The royalist garrison of Cartagena split as soon as the constitution was proclaimed in early June 1820; some units demanded promulgation of the constitution; others opposed it, and the civil and military authorities soon saw the situation slip from their grasp. Governor Gabriel de Torres convoked meetings of an army council and the city council, and both advised the viceroy to accept the constitution. However, when Viceroy Sámano demurred, American troops turned against the Spanish soldiery, calling for the implementation of the constitution and seizing the chance to demand long delayed wages. In these circumstances, Sámano's position became untenable. He left Torres with military command in Cartagena, and the governor promptly used it to adopt the constitution, depose the viceroy, and take political as well as military command of the city and province.⁶

The overthrow of the viceroy weakened unity among the royalists when it was most needed. Divisions among officers undermined army discipline and facilitated desertion from the ranks, distracting royalist forces from the essential task of fighting the republican enemy. When Bolívar launched offensives against their remaining positions in New Granada, royalist forces soon lost ground. José María Córdova gradually pushed royalist forces out of Antioquia and took control of the lower Magdalena Valley. The campaigns conducted by Mariano Montilla on the coast, backed by Brion's flotilla, threatened royalist positions at Riohacha and Santa Marta, and, despite the mutiny of the Irish Legion at Riohacha, prepared the way for the siege of Cartagena in July 1820. In the south, General Manuel Valdés, who had brought patriot troops in from Venezuela, took Popayán.⁷ Thus, towards the end of 1820, the royalist military had been forced back onto defensive fronts at New Granada's geographical extremes—in the north, the fortified city of Cartagena stood virtually alone; in the south, royalist forces had a fragile grip on the region between Popayán and Pasto.

While Bolívar pursued war on these New Granadan fronts, his principal object in 1820–1 was to liberate Venezuela from Morillo's main forces. Their field positions were essentially those they had held for several years: Bolívar controlled the Orinoco basin and his army was mostly in the Llanos, either in the Apure region under Páez or further north under Cedeño and Zaraza. Republican forces on the coasts of Eastern Venezuela and at Margarita Island were smaller, but strategically important because they could be projected by sea and used to create diversionary attacks. Guayana also remained in republican hands and, though no longer the principal base for republican offensives, remained a key point for republican trade with the exterior. Morillo's army, on the other hand, was deployed defensively. He no longer had any plans to retake Guayana or make any substantial inroads into Eastern Venezuela but concentrated instead on defending the routes from New Granada into Venezuela in order to hold back invaders.

Both sides were largely American. Morillo's army had changed considerably since 1815: only about a third of the expeditionary army he brought from Spain remained; the rest were mainly Venezuelans, together with some neogranadinos. Many of these were no doubt committed to the royalist cause, their loyalty having been tempered in a war where desertion or surrender usually meant death at enemy hands. However, Morillo increasingly drew Madrid's attention to the fact that, as their living conditions worsened, his soldiers' loyalty was not unbreakable. And, while his army was becoming ever more fragile, Morillo was disadvantaged at sea. Although he had some support from Spanish naval vessels, the republican fleet (vigorously commanded by Luis Brion until his death in September 1821) allowed Bolívar to import arms and soldiers and move men along the coast with relatively little opposition.

How did Bolívar exploit royalist weaknesses and develop his campaign to retake Venezuela? His first reflex was to move onto the offensive as soon as possible, using the new resources acquired in New Granada. He faced two principal problems: to increase the size of his army in Venezuela and to find a means of concentrating it against the enemy. Neither was easy. To enlarge his forces in Venezuela, he used forced recruitment in New Granada, with a particular emphasis on the mobilization of slaves.

Bolívar's interest in slave recruitment was partly ideological—like San Martín, he wished for an end to slavery—but his primary concern was to fill his armies' ranks with suitable recruits. Levies of a thousand slaves from several provinces could make a dramatic difference to both the quantity and quality of his soldiers because, Bolívar believed, slaves made good soldiers. They were "robust and vigorous men; men accustomed to harshness and fatigue; men who embrace the cause and the career with enthusiasm; men who identify their interest with the public cause and for whom the price of death is little different from that of life."[8] Bolívar's emphasis on slaves is a reminder that, like San Martín, he could not rely on patriotic sentiment to furnish his army. During his campaigns, he had created a core of officers and men who were dedicated to war under their various caudillos, but they had to be constantly supplemented by larger cohorts, most of whom were forced recruits who were reluctant to fight and keen to desert.

Bolívar's ability to move quickly onto the offensive was hampered by the considerable logistical problems that stood in the way of concentrating forces and sustaining large forces. Troops, horses, and draught animals had to be fed in the weeks and months when preparations were being made to bring them to bear against the enemy. This involved various difficulties. Troops being gathered in encampments in the New Granadan provinces and neighboring Venezuelan Cordillera could not rely on local towns to provide indefinite supplies of food and shelter. When in the Llanos, troops brought in from the outside depended on disorganized culls of cattle and sometimes starved. Not only did troops go hungry, but they suffered from unsanitary conditions in military camps and from abrupt changes of environment. Men from the plains found it difficult to acclimatize to Andean altitudes; those from the Andes were, when sent to the Llanos, vulnerable to tropical diseases, such as malaria. The army was also constantly weakened by desertion, for, in addition to disliking removal from their local "patria" and preferring to fight on terrain they knew, recruits were often desperate to escape the harsh conditions of military service. Thus, an inflow of troops was needed simply to replace those who were removed by disease and desertion. No wonder that Bolívar likened the army to "a bottomless bag" that emptied as it was being refilled.[9]

Bolívar was, nonetheless, determined to end Spanish rule in Venezuela as soon as he could. He may initially have seen the November armistice as a genuine chance for peace, but he spent most of its six months preparing for war.[10] That included taking action that risked the truce with the royalists, notably in January 1821, when Urdaneta used his army to support a patriot rebellion in the port of Maracaibo. The change of sides in the city strengthened the patriots by giving them a position from which to intercept royalist movements to the south, and it was almost certainly a violation of the truce. However, though General La Torre protested strongly, he did not resume the war, perhaps because he was still hoping for reinforcements from Spain. Bolívar also wanted to sustain the truce, but only to prolong his preparations for war. Indeed, as the truce approached its end, Bolívar rejected the offer of an extension because, to avoid the constant difficulties of sustaining forces in the field, he wanted to move onto the offensive sooner rather than later. In May 1821, he accordingly embarked on his plan to bring all his main forces to bear against La Torre's army, uniting the leading generals under his command in a combined offensive.

Bolívar's planning shifted according to information on enemy positions, but his basic aim was to divide enemy forces while concentrating the main republican armies at a place where La Torre was vulnerable. The strategy unfolded in May–June 1821, beginning in early May with advances on all fronts. The first was a diversionary attack from Eastern Venezuela towards Caracas, using small forces led by Bermudez. Meanwhile, General Urdaneta moved south from Coro (which he had recently taken) and Páez north from the Apure, to meet with Bolívar at a prearranged point close to royalist positions in San Carlos.

The offensive proceeded as planned. Bermudez's attack on Caracas (which he took temporarily in mid-May) persuaded La Torre to abandon his intention to attack Bolívar; instead, he sent a division of his troops to defend the capital and fend off attacks from the east. La Torre then fell back towards Carabobo, a defensible position standing between forces advancing from the Llanos and royalist strongholds in the coastal Cordillera and its valleys. Bolívar countered by establishing his headquarters in the Llanos at San Carlos, where he awaited the armies led by Urdaneta and Páez before beginning his offensive in early June. He made Mariño his chief of staff and organized his army of about 10,000 men into three divisions led by Páez, Cedeño, and Plaza. General Páez's division had a couple of battalions of infantry (one was the British Legion) but was mostly cavalry; Cedeño had three infantry battalions and a cavalry regiment, and Plaza was also primarily infantry with a regiment of cavalry. The army was smaller than the 10,000 men Bolívar had wanted; the number of effectives was about 6,500 men, the residue of larger forces that had been drained by disease and desertion.

The decisive battle took place on June 24, 1821, at Carabobo, the place where La Torre chose to make a stand against the larger force that marched across the plain towards him. He built earthworks and artillery defenses to guard against entry from the south and guarded his flanks with skirmishers placed on the heights that overlooked the plain. However, Bolívar avoided a frontal attack on the main body of La Torre's army (of about 5,100 men); instead, he sent Páez to attack La Torre's right flank by way of a narrow defile overlooked by royalist infantry.

This tactic paid off. The republican infantry assault dislodged the royalists from the heights after heavy losses (of about 30%) among the attacking battalions, and Páez was able to push his cavalry through and attack the enemy's flank. When the outnumbered royalist cavalry was overcome, the infantry also gave ground. Many surrendered, others fled, and only La Torre's reserves and part of his cavalry were able to make a fighting retreat as they were pursued across the plains back towards Valencia. The carnage was considerable. The royalists lost around 3,000 men, of whom about a third were dead and wounded; those who evaded capture made their way to the fortified garrison of Puerto Cabello. The patriot losses are not known, but it seems that they were particularly heavy among the officers, including Cedeño and Plaza, two of Bolívar's three divisional commanders.[11]

The Battle of Carabobo greatly reduced the scale and scope of the war in Venezuela. La Torre retreated to Puerto Cabello and, with access to the sea and a couple of thousand soldiers under his command, continued to harass the patriots with raids along the coast. Morales, who had been La Torre's second at Carabobo and whose experience of war went back a decade, was also still at large. He fought on in the Llanos of Calabozo and the Aragua valleys before falling back to Puerto Cabello, then continued to campaign in the coastal region, where he won back the towns of Coro and Maracaibo. Bolívar lacked the artillery needed to bring down Puerto Cabello's fortifications and had to content himself with trying to blockade the port with inadequate naval forces. He also had to maintain large forces in Venezuela to counter the royalist presence, thereby imposing a further strain on an already devastated region. His generals succeeded, however, in preventing royalist forces from regrouping in the west around Coro and Maracaibo, and during the next two years, they wore down the remnants of Morillo's army. In August 1823, Morales was forced to surrender at Maracaibo; in October, La Torre surrendered Puerto Cabello and evacuated his forces to Puerto Rico.[12]

After Carabobo, Bolívar's first concern was to consolidate his Colombian Republic by taking royalist towns in the highlands of southern New Granada and Quito. At first, he saw this as part of a larger picture that included the independence of Peru. Rather than attempt a direct overland attack on Pasto and Quito, he proposed to send troops by sea to Guayaquil to assist San Martín in the liberation of Peru and thus to encircle and isolate Quito and its allies. He accordingly proposed collaboration to San Martín. On August 28, 1821, he told San Martín that his first thought after Carabobo was of San Martín, Peru, and its liberating army; at the same time, he wrote to Santander with orders to "Make me an army which may triumph at the foot of Chimborazo and at Cuzco and show the way to victory to the heroes of Maipú and the liberation of Peru." He quickly formulated an imaginative, trans-regional strategy in which the liberation of Colombia would intersect with that of Peru. Calling on San Martín and O'Higgins for military cooperation and Cochrane for naval support, he envisaged sending an army of 4,000 men from Venezuela to the Isthmus of Panama and another 4,000 from New Granada to Buenaventura. They would then converge on Guayaquil and take part in the liberation of Peru.[13]

To get the ball rolling, Bolívar left Venezuela to pursue the war in southern Colombia (stopping briefly at Cúcuta to accept the presidency of the Colombian Republic). His grandiose strategy for an offensive on Quito was, however, thwarted by lack of ships to convey troops from Panama to Guayaquil and fears of attack by recently arrived Spanish frigates in the Pacific. Bolívar consequently decided to take his army overland into Quito, by way of the royalist enclave at Pasto. Like other commanders before him, Bolívar found Pasto hard to crack. The *pastusos* held back his forces at Bomboná in April 1822 and cost him so many men that he was unable to move on towards Quito. The campaign for Quito was nonetheless won, thanks to José Antonio de Sucre's advance into the highlands from Guayaquil and his defeat at Pichincha of Spanish forces defending the city of Quito. The royalist government of General Aymerich folded following the battle of Pichincha, and, after Sucre accepted the surrender of the city in May 1822, Bolívar incorporated the region into the Republic of Colombia.

The capture of Quito not only completed Bolívar's tripartite Republic of Colombia, comprising Venezuela, New Granada, and Quito, but it was also to be an important step towards the liberation of Peru. For, although southern Colombia was not as yet completely secure—Pasto was to rebel again on two occasions—Bolívar now controlled the main territories of his imagined republic and could realistically contemplate armed intervention in the war for Peru. His intervention was, as we shall now see, to play a crucial role in overturning the royalist regime and establishing an independent Peru.

Bolívar and San Martín

After Bolívar took Quito, the only significant areas that remained under Spain's control were in the central and southern Andes, stretching into Upper Peru. There, royalist Peru had weathered the political storm of the Spanish Revolution of 1820, thanks largely to the strategy of Viceroy La Serna and the loyalty of his armies. La Serna's decision to move out of Lima and establish a new capital at Cuzco reduced royalist Peru to a smaller territory, partitioned from an independent coast, but left him in control of key towns and regions and an undefeated army of some 20,000 men.[14] By downsizing royalist Peru, La Serna had saved it. Flanked by armies at Huancayo in central Peru, around Arequipa in the south, and in various towns in Upper Peru, he was able to turn the highland regions into a defensive phalanx that protected Spanish rule.

By mid-1822, San Martín had made little headway against these royalist positions, and unable to overturn the royalist regime entrenched in the interior, he turned towards a new solution: military collaboration with the Liberator Simón Bolívar. He had good reason to do so, given that there was already a successful precedent. Just months earlier, San Martín had responded to Bolívar's appeal for military support in Quito by sending Andrés de Santa Cruz with 1,500 men to join Sucre in the war for the province.[15] Their success at the battle of Pichincha opened the way to plans for further collaboration, and after taking Quito, Bolívar informed San Martín that "the war in Colombia has now ended and its army is ready to march wherever it is needed, and particularly to the lands of our neighbors in the South."[16] San Martín was keen to discuss this offer of military aid, together with two other key issues: first, whether Guayaquil—a city with historic links to Lima—should be annexed to Peru or Colombia; and second, whether Bolívar would support San Martín's project to make independent Peru a constitutional monarchy. Thus, after an exchange of correspondence, San Martín decided to talk directly to Bolívar about the future of Peru and in July 1822, sailed to Guayaquil to meet him.

The exact content of their private meetings on July 26–27, 1822, is disputable, but the outcome was clear.[17] The issue of Guayaquil was put to one side as Bolívar had already taken control of the port; San Martín's idea for an independent monarchy in Peru was rejected. Finally, Bolívar's offer of military aid fell short of what San Martín considered necessary to finish the war in Peru. In these circumstances, San Martín decided to relinquish his project for an independent Peru and leave it in Bolívar's hands. Bolívar was in no hurry to intervene, however. He remained in the province of Quito for a year, setting up an administration, dealing with another rebellion in Pasto, and attending to the consolidation of the Republic of Colombia. He was nonetheless drawn into the Peruvian sphere in 1823, when he was invited to send troops and, before the year was out, to take command of the armies of independent Peru.

The invitation to Bolívar was, of course, a tribute to his extraordinary record of military and political success and a reflection of San Martín's declining prestige. Whereas San Martín achieved only partial independence in Peru against an undefeated royalist army, Bolívar had forged a movement towards independence that was driven by his own armies and took a very distinctive shape. Like San Martín, Bolívar had focused on creating a veteran army that was capable of transregional campaigns and bound to the cause of American independence. There was, however, an important difference in their strategies. After taking Lima in 1821, San Martín stopped short of attempting the military conquest of the whole of Peru. He believed that the army brought from Río de la Plata and Chile was too small to overcome royalist forces and decided the best way forward was to build up political support among Peruvians. Bolívar, on the other hand, approached the Peruvian question as a military leader who had forged New Granada, Venezuela, and Quito into the Republic of Colombia during years of unremitting war. His Colombian experience shaped his behavior in Peru. Rather than seek to win over

Peruvians, he sought to turn Peru into an independent republic at the point of a bayonet.

The Contraction of Independent Peru

Bolívar's intervention began soon after San Martín's departure from Peru, starting with the dispatch of Sucre and some 5,000 troops to Lima. This was not, however, soon enough to ward off military disaster. Before leaving, San Martín had made preparations for a grand offensive on three fronts, aimed at attacking the royalist forces in Southern, Central, and Upper Peru, and thus encircling La Serna at Cuzco. He chose General Rudecindo Alvarado to lead a southern campaign, taking 4,000 troops by sea to "Puertos Intermedios" (the ports between Lima and Arequipa), and thence to advance inland towards Upper Peru. Meanwhile, General Arenales was to conduct a campaign in Central Peru, advancing inland from Lima to Huancayo with another army of some 4,000 men in order to prevent the royalists from sending troops south against Alvarado. San Martín also tried to get Buenos Aires to reopen its front in the provinces of Upper Peru, with the promise that, when removed from royalist control, they should be annexed to the United Provinces.

None of these aims was realized. Buenos Aires showed no interest in participating in San Martín's war, and the pincer movement aimed against La Serna in Cuzco collapsed. In central Peru, the offensive led by Andrés de Santa Cruz against Huancayo foundered due to lack of resources, frustrating General Arenales's plan to take a strategic area of the central highlands. In the south, Alvarado's army fared even worse: after sailing over 600 miles to land at Arica, it was routed by Canterac in battles at Torata and Moquegua in January 1823.

The memoirs of Colonel Miller, who commanded a battalion in Alvarado's army when it landed at Arica, suggest that the crushing defeat of the independents' southern army resulted from poor military leadership and organization.[18] According to Miller, the patriots started with a strategic advantage and a good plan. The royalists had large forces, but because these were distributed around distant points and separated by mountainous terrain, they were vulnerable to concentrated attack on a single front.[19] The patriots, on the other hand, had greater mobility; their maritime dominance allowed them to transport troops by sea and establish bridgeheads at points that the enemy could not predict. Miller thought well of their troops too; most of those under his command were Quechua-speaking Indians, who had been trained according to Spanish army regulations, had high morale, and enjoyed good relations with their officers. However, if Miller believed in the soldiery, he had a poor opinion of their officers. He portrayed Alvarado as inexperienced, indecisive, and unable to inspire confidence in his officers; Miller himself was so dissatisfied with the general that he left the expedition to lead his men in an operation further south.

Alvarado's prevarications certainly seem to have been costly. After a successful voyage from Lima—it took just over a month to reach Arica—Alvarado landed with his army intact but then delayed on an unhealthy coast and allowed his opponents time to prepare their defenses. When he finally moved inland and engaged the enemy, he made tactical errors, which caused dissent among his officers and confusion among the soldiers, and opened the way to total defeat. The royalists, on the other hand, showed once again the quality of their officers and soldiers. Despite enmities and divisions between the royalist commanders, Miller admiringly recalled that "they all made every exertion to overcome the disadvantages of their position" in sharp contrast to the "apathy pervading every department of the government" on the patriot side.[20]

Alvarado's defeat was a huge setback for the independents in Lima. First, a major component of its forces disappeared due to large losses in men and armaments.[21] Defeat also caused panic among the civilians of Lima, a rift between congress and military commanders, and a coup that shifted power from civilians to the army. In February 1823, army officers led by Andrés de Santa Cruz forced the congress to replace the governing triumvirate with the Peruvian aristocrat José de la Riva Agüero. The new president rewarded the leading military plotters (all of whom had previously served in the royalist army) with commanding posts in the army: Santa Cruz became commander in chief; Colonel Agustín Gamarra was made chief of staff; and Colonel Ramón Herrera became minister of war.

With these changes came renewal of war against the royalists. Riva Agüero concentrated on improving Peru's navy and army and planned a new southern offensive. Meanwhile, at Riva Agüero's request, Bolívar agreed to send 6,000 troops to Lima under General Sucre, to reinforce the 5,000 men of the Peruvian army and the 2,000 Chileans and Argentines who had previously fought with San Martín.[22] In May 1823, Santa Cruz was sent south to open an ambitious new offensive against Upper Peru via the Intermedios ports, while Sucre remained in Lima with his Colombians.

The results of the second Intermedios campaign were, for the independents, no better than the first. No sooner had it started than the Lima government suffered a humiliating reversal when Canterac's army invaded Lima. As this drew royalist divisions away from the republican campaign in the south, Canterac's move went unopposed. Sucre withdrew his army from Lima, and Riva Agüero's government moved north to the city of Trujillo. Canterac spent a month in Lima (June 16–July 16, 1823) before returning inland to join in royalist efforts to deal with the threat posed by Santa Cruz's campaign in southern Peru.

Canterac's withdrawal from Lima offered the independents an opportunity to strengthen their political or military position. However, their ability to take it was impeded by political division and military failure. First, their government split in two: President Riva Agüero set up his government at Trujillo, and the Marqués de Torre Tagle established a rival in Lima. Then, to make matters worse, Santa Cruz's military campaign failed badly.[23]

Santa Cruz had started with high ambitions, telling Riva Agüero that his campaign was "the only way to save the country and make ourselves Peruvian."[24] But his aspiration to become the savior of independent Peru did not survive a couple of months of campaigning in the high Andes. He began well, taking his army of around 2,000 men across country into the highland basin of Lake Titicaca and defeating a royalist army of comparable size at Zepita (August 25, 1823). However, his poor military judgment soon reversed this promising advance. While Sucre placed himself at Arequipa in readiness for a concerted campaign against royalist Cuzco, Santa Cruz preferred to operate alone, probably because he wanted to claim all the credit for success. He pushed forward into Upper Peru towards Oruro in the hope that, by meeting up with his deputy, Agustín Gamarra, he could take control of Upper Peru. In the event, he allowed himself to be outmaneuvered by his opponents. Viceroy La Serna and General Olañeta concentrated royalist forces against him, and, to escape encirclement, he was forced into a hasty flight from Lake Titicaca back to the coast, losing most of his men and nearly all their arms in the process. Chilean reinforcements under General Pinto arrived at Arica soon afterwards, but too late to restart the campaign; by the end of the year, Pinto had withdrawn his men to Chile, and the hopes for a southern offensive were buried.

Santa Cruz's abortive campaign vanquished hopes for a victory against the viceroy and deepened divisions among Peruvian politicians and army officers. Torre Tagle wanted to break away from the Riva Agüero presidency, and both he and Riva Agüero became increasingly suspicious of Bolívar. Peru's armed forces were also bedeviled by divisions, as factionalism and indiscipline among officers worsened after San Martín's departure. Shortly after arriving in Lima, Sucre told Bolívar that he had decided to segregate his Colombian troops in order to avoid the contagion of indiscipline; he also warned that the attitude of Peruvian politicians toward soldiers from Colombia, Chile, and Río de la Plata was so hostile that Bolívar should think carefully before taking up a position of leadership in Peru.[25]

The royalist regime in Peru was, however, the rock on which the independents' armies broke. The resilience of the royalist army was remarkable, and the efficiency of its generals and loyalty of their men was the main reason why most of Peru remained under Spanish rule. The leading generals—La Serna, Canterac, Valdés, and Olañeta—were very experienced officers, seasoned by years of war in the Peninsula and/or in Upper Peru, and more expert than their rivals. La Serna's strategy for holding Peru by pulling back from Lima into the interior was well-chosen. With Canterac positioned at Huancayo to hold the strategic Jauja valley, La Serna at Cuzco, Olañeta in Upper Peru, and Valdés guarding the region inland from Arequipa, La Serna's strategy was designed to exploit the resources of the interior (including its silver mines) while restricting the independents' territory to a fringe along the Pacific coast. And, thanks to the ability of his generals to march and countermarch across the Peruvian highlands in support of each other, he was able to fend off patriot attempts to penetrate the interior.

So, by late 1823, the attempt by Peruvian leaders to secure independence using their own armies had run into the sand. Royalist propagandists at Cuzco crowed over the viceroy's successes and proclaimed their confidence in the survival of Spanish Peru. They had held the highlands of central, southern, and Upper Peru, leaving the Peruvian independents to quarrel among themselves on a diminishing margin of territory on the coast. Indeed, now that the Peruvians had failed to secure their own independence, they were to depend on Bolívar's forces to wrench Peru from the royalists' grip.

Bolívar's Liberation of Peru

When Bolívar took up residence in Lima in September–November 1823, the prospects of turning Peru into an independent country were more distant than at any time since San Martín had arrived with his army two years earlier. Indeed, independent Peru was falling apart. It had two presidents who were fiercely opposed to each other, and now that Bolívar had been given supreme power by the Lima congress, a dictator too. As Bolívar observed before leaving Guayaquil, it would be difficult to save Peru, where the "different administrations which have ruled it, the chiefs and soldiers of the country, and the auxiliary troops from Chile and Buenos Aires have almost never been in agreement."[26]

His first task, indeed, was to engage in civil war in order to defeat the Riva Agüero government in Trujillo. Having done so, he then concentrated on establishing control in the province of Trujillo and building up defenses against what he believed would be an inevitable Spanish offensive. As the territory under his command contracted, his demands on the Colombian government became ever greater. In December 1823, he called for 12,000 troops, arguing that it was better for Colombia to fight the royalists in Peru than allow them a victory that would open the way to an invasion of southern Colombia. None were forthcoming. Worse still, Bolívar did not have the means to pay and feed his existing forces; in January 1824, he was so desperate that he threatened to withdraw from Peru altogether unless the government provided vital subsidies.

His ability to exert influence was further diminished by illness, for, on attempting to return to Lima, Bolívar fell seriously ill at the Pacific port of Pativilca. While he remained there in January–February 1824, the existence of independent Peru was called into question. President Torre Tagle started negotiations with the Spaniards for a separate peace, and a key element of the army defected. On February 5, the garrison of Callao—which was composed mainly of rioplatense troops who had originally arrived with San Martín—handed the fortress over to the enemy with around 1,000 men. The Lima congress responded to this dramatic blow by formally investing Bolívar with full dictatorial powers on February 10. However, as this was shortly followed by the defection of President Torre Tagle, together with his vice president, minister of war, and more than 337 army officers and their forces, Bolívar decided that Lima was lost, and that his best chance was to fall back on the northern provinces around Trujillo.[27]

The war for Peru now entered a crucial phase. The royalist armies were in the ascendant and likely to concentrate in a major offensive against Bolívar. His response was to set up defenses in the three independent provinces of the north, with Trujillo at the core. General La Mar commanded Peruvian forces in these provinces, while Sucre and his Colombians occupied advance positions in the Cordillera, reaching south to Huánuco. Sucre was given freedom to choose his own strategy as commander in chief of the army, but Bolívar advised him to oppose an enemy offensive with a "scorched earth" retreat, removing supplies and recruits while falling back as slowly as possible through the mountain valleys towards Trujillo. Meanwhile, Bolívar concentrated on building up his forces while awaiting the reinforcements requested from the Colombian Congress.

This was not the first time that Bolívar had found himself facing larger and better-supplied forces, and he applied methods he had learned in the wars of Venezuela and New Granada. His field commanders were given three key goals: to instill discipline and improve morale among the troops, where possible by augmenting their supplies of muskets and lances; to recruit 5,000 men to ensure that 1–2,000 remained permanently in the ranks; and to collect and manufacture all the equipment needed by the army "without leaving a straw unused in the whole of the free territory."[28] He also ordered a ruthless harvest of money, materials, and supplies wherever available through the expropriation of property, seizure of silver plates from churches, and imposition of local taxes. While in Trujillo in March–April 1824, he mobilized people and soldiers to the point where "the city took on the appearance of an immense arsenal where no one was idle" and where "everything needed by the army was made, including a large quantity of uniforms, leather belts, arms and ammunition," as well as the shoes and nails needed for the army's horses.[29] He adopted a defense in stages, with forward positions in the fertile mountain valleys of the interior, where the troops could be well fed and acclimatized for campaigning at high altitude, while also preparing to fall back on Trujillo if necessary.

The moment for this potentially crucial encounter between Bolívar and the royalist army passed, however, for the expected Spanish offensive did not materialize. This was fortunate for the independents as their army was short of money and men. Bolívar's revenues covered only about half the costs of the army and the rest had to be forced from town councils, property owners, and the clergy. Military manpower was also inadequate. A contingent of about 900 reinforcements arrived from Colombia, together with 6–7,000 muskets and some other articles. Francis Burdett O'Connor, who had briefly served in Venezuela and New Granada, came with the first contingent from Panama and on joining the army in the Andes became Sucre's chief of staff and played a crucial part in the organization of Bolívar's campaign.[30] But this was far short of what Bolívar regarded as essential, and he called on the governments in Santiago de Chile and Buenos Aires to provide support. Appeals to the Chilean government for military aid (sent via Bernardo O'Higgins, who was in Trujillo) fell on deaf ears, however, while Buenos Aires was also too preoccupied with internal affairs to lend support.

Despite the silence of his allies, Bolívar continued with plans to fight the royalists, encouraged by the news he received late in April that General Pedro Antonio de Olañeta, commander of the royalist army in Upper Peru, had broken with the viceroy. In May, he wrote to Olañeta to embrace him as a fellow patriot, and though he was unsure what Olañeta's motives were, he understood that the split in the royalist army offered a golden opportunity. By early June, Bolívar was ready to move southwards against the enemy. He sent his forces through the Cordillera along three parallel routes, each separated by about a day's march, with a plan to converge at Huaraz at the start of July.

This concerted advance was difficult to achieve but proved successful. When Miller joined the army at Huaraz, he found that the army had completed the first steps of the campaign in good order and without losses, despite the difficulties of moving men and horses through the rugged terrain and freezing night-time temperatures of the high Andes. Those from tropical coastal cities and river plains were most vulnerable, especially to altitude sickness, but Bolívar had taken steps to ensure that his men could withstand the hardships of campaigning in the high Andes. He also paid particular attention to the welfare of the army's horses, so that they were ready for immediate action. From past experience, Bolívar understood the critical role the cavalry might play in battle, and in asking for men from Colombia, he had stressed the need to provide llanero horsemen from those who had fought in Venezuela and New Granada. According to Miller, Bolívar achieved his objective: "the patriot cavalry was composed of perhaps the best horsemen in the world . . . the *gauchos* of the Pampas, the *guasos* of Chile, and the *llaneros* of Colombia . . ."[31]

The army was organized in three divisions of infantry, two of which were Colombian troops led by Generals Jacinto Lara and José María Córboba, with a third made up of Peruvians under General La Mar. The cavalry was organized in three squadrons: Peruvians led by Miller, Colombians under Carvajal, and the horse grenadiers of Buenos Aires under the German officer Braun. Miller found the army in good order after arduous marches through the mountains, "tolerably well clothed and armed," and accompanied by a train of 300 hundred mules carrying a reserve depot of ammunition and emergency supplies, followed by 6,000 head of cattle to provide the beef that was the soldier's staple. Morale was good, no doubt helped by Bolívar's insistence that the troops were paid regularly once a week, if only at half-wages, in the presence of their regimental commanders.[32] Bolívar thus moved forward with some confidence during July 1824, a confidence reinforced by the appearance of unexpected divisions among the royalist forces.

Royalist Rifts

When Bolívar first entered Peru, the royalist army was a formidable enemy, composed of some 20,000 troops of whom 16,000 were on active service in important theaters. In 1823, Canterac had about 8,000 men at Huancayo; Valdés had around 3,000 men at Arequipa; Olañeta had 4,000 men in Upper Peru, and Viceroy La Serna had a reserve division of about a 1,000 at Cuzco. These armies were, as in Pezuela's day, composed largely of mestizos and Indians led by Peruvian and Spanish officers; they were thus more "Peruvian" in character than the largely Colombian army of the independents, which the royalists depicted as an intrusive foreign force.

In mid-1823, the royalists appeared to be on the brink of another successful campaign. Viceroy La Serna planned to combine Canterac's army with Valdés's forces from Arequipa in an offensive against Bolívar and Sucre in the north; meanwhile, General Olañeta's army was to redeploy from the center of Upper Peru to the Lake Titicaca area in order to guard against any southern movements by the independents. La Serna's intention was, in short, to attack the independents while they were still regrouping, using well-fed and well-rested forces against them.

The viceroy's plans were frustrated by the political reverberations within the royalist camp of another extraordinary political crisis in Spain. In April 1823, Spain's constitutional regime came under attack from an invading French army, and by October, French arms had cleared the way for Ferdinand VII's second restoration as an absolute monarch. With it came orders to remove all traces of the Spanish Constitution of 1812 throughout the Hispanic world. When news reached La Serna and his generals, they had no difficulty in accommodating to the new regime, even though they had previously accepted the constitutionalist government. But they could not preserve their unity, for General Olañeta had different ideas. Instead of obeying Viceroy La Serna's order to move north from Oruro to back up the royalist army, he went south, forcing leading officials from power and declaring himself independent of the viceroy of Peru.

Olañeta's motives blended the personal and the political. A Spaniard who was closely attached to Upper Peru by marriage and business, he resented the disparaging treatment he received from Spanish officers and disliked them for their association with the constitutional government in Spain.[33] Olañeta's intention was to secede from the Viceroyalty of Peru, not the Spanish monarchy, and he justified his actions in ultra-royalist terms. This, an Argentine newspaper noted at the time, smacked of the long-standing struggle in Spain between liberals and serviles, reincarnated in Upper Peru.[34] In February 1824, Olañeta proclaimed a new government in the name of Ferdinand VII, installing himself as supreme army commander, placing his relatives and friends in positions of power, and claiming the viceregency of Río de la Plata. Legitimizing himself as the king's most faithful servant, Olañeta seemed to see a future as an autonomous royalist caudillo, fighting under the banners of an absolutist Ferdinand VII.

Olañeta's extraordinary conduct frustrated the viceroy's military plans and did great damage to the royalist cause in Peru. Viceroy La Serna initially responded by negotiation, sending General Valdés to persuade Olañeta to return to his duties. Diplomacy failed, however, and La Serna was forced to move one part of his army against another. He ordered General Valdés to bring Olañeta to heel, starting a civil war between royalists that engaged two royalist armies at the moment when Bolívar was advancing towards the center of Peru. However, before this internal conflict could be resolved, Bolívar's advance forced the viceroy to recall Valdés to Peru in late August 1824.[35] By then, the secessionist war in Upper Peru had already done considerable damage to La Serna's military plans. For as soon as Bolívar became aware of the division among the Spaniards, he moved onto the offensive and went in search of Canterac's army.

At this point, the problems caused by divisions within the royalist army became increasingly obvious, First, Canterac failed to respond to Bolívar's advance. Miller found this "inexplicable," given that Canterac had a larger, well-appointed, and highly efficient army. He could only suggest that Canterac had underestimated the independents' army.[36] There might have been some truth in this: Canterac and other Spanish commanders in Peru had not yet fought against Bolívar and Sucre and thus might not have realized the extent of their military ability and experience.[37] However, it is equally likely that Canterac held back because the diversion of thousands of troops to deal with Olañeta deprived him of the reinforcements that he would have preferred to have.[38]

The Defeat of Royalist Peru

In these circumstances, Bolívar seized the initiative. Having advanced south from Huaraz in search of Canterac, he entered into operations against him in early August. After days of maneuvering, Bolívar succeeded in interposing his army between Canterac's cavalry and his base, and thus forced Canterac to engage on ground that he had not chosen. On August 6, the two armies met on the plain at Junín, at an altitude of 9,000 feet. They fought with lances and swords, without shots being fired. Bolívar's army showed the potency of its cavalry, vindicating his insistence on bringing llanero horsemen from Colombia and his constant insistence on the need to care for the army's horses. The contribution of the Venezuelan llaneros was crucial. Their adroit horsemanship, the long lances they used, and their battle tactic of simulating flight only to turn on the enemy in a coordinated movement, quickly overcame the royalist cavalry.[39] The battle was over in 45 minutes and put the royalist cavalry to flight, with the loss of a few hundred men and 300 horses.[40]

Junín was not a definitive battle. Canterac retreated to Cuzco with his remaining forces, merging them with those of La Serna and Valdés and spending the next few months in preparing for another campaign against the independents. It was, however, the first serious reversal the royalist army had experienced for several years and, together with Olañeta's rebellion in Upper Peru, made the military balance more equal. Viceroy La Serna responded by concentrating his forces at Cuzco, while Bolívar advanced southwards towards him. After Junín, the independent forces occupied Huamanga and then moved to establish a forward line along the west bank of the Apurimac River, from which to observe enemy movements around Cuzco (which lay to its east). Bolívar assumed that the royalists would not move onto a full-scale offensive at this time, as it was the rainy season; he accordingly moved to Lima to attend to affairs of government, to await reinforcements from Colombia, and to intimidate the royalists in the fortress of Callao. He left Sucre in command, with freedom to act as circumstances demanded, but with a reminder that the stakes were so high that he should engage in battle only if absolutely sure of victory.[41]

Sucre spent October and November in reconnoitering the region and by early December was ready to select a battlefield.[42] Viceroy La Serna had meanwhile concentrated his forces of over 9,000 troops and set out to swing south of Sucre's smaller army of fewer than 6,000 men with the intention of encircling him. After the royalists had made long and exhausting marches across more than a hundred miles of mountainous terrain—in what Miller called "a perfect steeple chase"[43]—they finally found Sucre camped on the plain of Ayacucho, near the city of Huamanga, at about 10,000 feet above sea level. On December 8, the royalists took up position on hills overlooking the plain and awaited Sucre's response. He remained on the plain, and on the morning of December 9, 1824, La Serna made ready to move down the slopes on the plain to engage Sucre's lines.

The armies that faced each other on the day of battle were of unequal size; the independents had about 6,000 men; the royalists were close to 9,000.[44] Details of their social and ethnic composition are scarce, but there is no doubt that the viceroy's army was more Peruvian than Bolívar's, which was mostly made up of Colombian veterans. Among the Peruvians, however, were many recent recruits who were reluctant to fight and ready to desert. The viceroy's battle plan was to take the offensive; he ordered General Gerónimo Valdés to engage Sucre's left flank with artillery and musket fire, while the main army took advantage of the diversion by moving into a full attack along the front. The royalist center could not, however, hold its position, possibly because it attacked before Valdés's division had time to fully engage Sucre's army from the left, or possibly because troops who had taken the field reluctantly were all too ready to give up. When the infantry broke ranks, the royalist cavalry arrived too late to save them and was itself badly mauled by the independents' horsemen. In the ensuing melee, La Serna was taken prisoner, and after a battle of only two hours, the viceroy and his generals capitulated.[45]

This was an extraordinary defeat, for, as General Valdés observed, the royalists had enjoyed three years of "glorious and uninterrupted triumph" against the independents' forces, and in 1823 were confident of expelling Bolívar's smaller forces from Peru. Victory was snatched from their grasp, according to Valdés, by the actions of Pedro Antonio de Olañeta, "a wicked man, betraying his King, country and companions in arms."[46] In explaining defeat (and seeking to refute the accusations of those who blamed the royalist high command for the loss of Peru), Valdés focused on two factors. First and most important was the division in the army caused by Olañeta's treachery and its effects on the viceroy's ability to overcome Bolívar's forces. He argued that the repercussions of Olañeta's secession were disastrous, for, instead of fighting the independents, royalist forces were turned against each other. This split in royalist ranks not only expended military energy that should have been directed against Bolívar, but it also demoralized the troops and caused an epidemic of desertion so bad that officers had to guard their men at night to prevent them from running off. Indeed, in seeking to explain the defeat, Valdés also accused the soldiers of the royal army at Ayacucho of cowardice. Despite the desperate efforts of a few Spanish officers to regroup a fleeing army, they ran, he said, because they preferred to surrender to Sucre than to Olañeta.[47]

Valdés's tirade was, of course, far from a full explanation of Spain's loss of Peru—by 1825, the Peruvian urban elites had mostly been converted to the cause of independence, despite their widespread dislike and distrust of the Venezuelan Bolívar and his Colombian army—but it is important for underlining the importance of the royalist military presence for sustaining Spanish rule there. While the Spanish army was intact, the viceroy could "offer His Majesty a peaceful Peru and a pleasing picture of bringing that benefit to the rest of South America."[48] Once the army was defeated, the viceregal regime, which depended so much on the military, could not survive. The battle of Ayacucho was thus the climax of the war for Peru, for, in breaking the back of the royalist army, it forced a complete surrender. The terms of the capitulation stated that all royalist forces in Peru would lay down their arms and return to Spain, while those who wished could join the Peruvian army at the same rank. The viceroy and his officers, together with around 700 men, left Peru and sailed back to Spain, where some went on to prominent political careers.[49]

A few recalcitrants refused to accept Bolívar's terms. The high-ranking officials of the viceroyalty tried to hold on: the judges of the audiencia at Cuzco remained in place and appointed General Pío Tristán, commander of the army at Arequipa, to replace La Serna as viceroy. Tristán soon gave up and surrendered in mid-January 1825; the audiencia also disappeared when Sucre and Bolívar occupied Cuzco. It was, however, to take more than the republican victory at Ayacucho to dissipate royalist sentiment and hopes. While General Olañeta still held command of an army in Upper Peru and Brigadier Rodil held the Callao fortress, some of the officers who had surrendered at Ayacucho decided to continue fighting. They took refuge in areas of the central highlands of Peru where towns had supported the royalist cause against Bolívar and in late 1825 joined in mobilizing the Indian peasantry of the province of Huanta behind an attempt to restore royalist government in Peru.[50] This was, however, a lost cause. By the time that the Huanta rebellion against the republic was fully underway, Bolívar and Sucre had defeated General Olañeta in Upper Peru and taken control of Spain's last important stronghold in Andean America.

From Upper Peru to Bolivia

Royalist rule in Upper Peru ended because, faced with the prospect of war against Bolívar's liberating army, its creole political and military elites decided to withdraw their support from Olañeta. At first, Bolívar hoped to take Upper Peru without a fight by converting Olañeta into an ally, as he was genuinely unsure of Olañeta's motives and aims. He therefore decided to go on treating him as though he were in sympathy with the independents' cause and sent Sucre to negotiate with him over the future of Upper Peru.[51] Olañeta refused Sucre's overtures, however. In January 1825, he issued a "no surrender" proclamation, swearing to fight for Spanish sovereignty in Upper Peru in the name of throne and altar, and it thus seemed likely that Bolívar's war of liberation in Central and Southern Peru would be followed by another for Upper Peru. In fact, Sucre's mission to complete Peruvian independence by liberating Upper Peru was to be more a political than a military matter. For when Sucre moved his army from Cuzco, Olañeta's forces began to disintegrate. In mid-January, the garrison at Cochabamba defected to Sucre; at the end of January, La Paz fell to the guerrilla leader Lanza, who emerged from his republiqueta at Ayopaya to cooperate with Sucre. In February, Sucre crossed the Desaguadero River and, on entering La Paz, issued his famous decree proclaiming the freedom of Upper Peru and announcing his decision to keep the peace while altoperuanos decided their own future.

Olañeta remained passive in Potosí, with forces of only around 1,300 men, while Sucre increased the size of his army to over 6,000 men. Conscious of his superiority, Sucre called on Olañeta to accept an end to war, while sending a large force led by the Irishman Francis Burdett O'Connor to capture him.[52] Olañeta had no option but to retreat from Potosí as Sucre approached. He was pursued and, with only a few hundred men on his side, trapped by one of his own ex-officers. Forced to fight, Olañeta was mortally wounded at Tumusla on April 1, 1825, close to the border with the provinces of the Río de la Plata, which the Spaniards had successfully defended for so long. The only remaining royalist unit, with about 500 men, surrendered a week later.[53]

Sucre's army had, then, taken Upper Peru with scarcely a shot fired. On April 9, 1825, the "Grand Marshal of Ayacucho," as he was now titled, issued a decree that announced "the absolute and final end of the war" in Peru. All that now remained of royalist Peru was the fortress of Callao, where the intransigent Brigadier Rodil held out until starvation forced surrender in January 1826. When Rodil and his soldiers departed from Peru, the republics of Peru and Bolivia were entering their first stages of construction and, in recognition of the extraordinary contribution he had made to their independence, Bolívar was to become president of both.

Notes

1. Morillo to Minister of War, Valencia, April 15, 1820: Rodríguez Villa, *El Teniente General Don Pablo Morillo,* 4, pp. 172–8.
2. Morillo to Minister of Ultramar, July 26, 1820: Ibid., pp. 204–9.
3. Morillo to Minister of War, August 28, 1820, and September 28: Ibid., pp. 220–7, 229–32.
4. A formal account of the negotiations is given in Pablo Morillo, *Memorias de Pablo Morillo* (Bogotá: Fundación Fica, 2010), pp. 185–223. For a contemporary description of the meeting between the two generals and their conduct towards each other, see O'Leary, *Bolívar and the War of Independence,* pp. 183–4.
5. Stoan, *Morillo,* pp. 222–32.
6. Earle, *Spain and the Independence of Colombia,* pp. 147–52.
7. On these campaigns, see Lecuna, *Crónica razonada,* 2, pp. 381–415.
8. On Bolívar's changing attitude towards slave recruitment, see Blanchard, *Under the Flags of Freedom,* pp. 72–8, quotation from p. 75.
9. Quoted by Lecuna, *Crónica razonada,* 3, p. 47.
10. My account of his campaign of 1821 draws on two main sources. First, the account of Daniel O'Leary, who participated in the campaign as one of Bolívar's officers: see O'Leary, *Memorias del General Daniel Florencio O'Leary,* 3, pp. 79–92 (or O'Leary, *Bolívar and the War of Independence,* pp. 185–96). Second, Vicente Lecuna's history of Bolívar's wars: see Lecuna, *Crónica razonada,* 3, pp. 1–56.
11. For descriptions of the battle of Carabobo, see O'Leary, *Memorias,* 3, pp. 81–88 (or O'Leary, *Bolívar and the War of Independence,* pp. 194–5); also Lecuna, *Crónica razonada,* 3, pp. 46–52.
12. Lecuna, *Crónica razonada,* 3, pp. 61–3, 234, 287, 382.

13. Ibid., 3, pp. 65–8.
14. Far to the south, the royalist garrison at Chiloe also held out (until January 1826) but was too small and distant to have any relevance to the larger struggle started by Bolívar in 1823.
15. Santa Cruz had been an officer in the Spanish army until captured by Arenales at Pasco in December 1820; he then joined Arenales's forces and subsequently fought with him in the central highlands of Peru. He arrived in Guayaquil in February 1822 with orders to join Sucre, and he fought under Sucre at the battle of Pichincha, which won Quito for Bolívar and the Colombian Republic: see Perea, *The Caudillo of the Andes: Andrés de Santa Cruz*, pp. 51–63.
16. Bolívar to San Martín, Quito, June 17, 1822: quoted by Lynch, *San Martín*, p. 186.
17. Lynch, *San Martín*, pp. 185–90. For an account incorporating discussion of the historical controversy about the content of the meetings, see Lecuna, *Crónica razonada*, 3, pp. 181–226.
18. Miller, *Memoirs*, 2, pp. 1–23.
19. Miller suggests that about 8,000 royalist troops came together against Alvarado, Canterac with about 5,000 men, and Valdés, 3,000. He thought that there ware another 3,000 men in Upper Peru: see Miller, *Memoirs,* 2, p. 6.
20. Miller, *Memoirs,* 2, pp. 7–8.
21. Mendizábal recorded that Canterac killed most of the enemy troops at Moquegua, as well as taking 1,000 prisoners from the survivors, plus some 3,000 muskets left on the field: Mendizábal, *Guerra de la América del Sur,* pp. 185–6.
22. Figures from Lecuna, *Crónica razonada*, 3, p. 267.
23. On Santa Cruz's campaign, seen mainly through the correspondence of Sucre and Bolívar and critical of Santa Cruz's military ineptitude, see Lecuna, *Crónica razonada*, 3, pp. 307–14. For an account that is less critical of Santa Cruz, presenting him as more unlucky than inept, see Sobrevilla Perea, *Caudillo of the Andes,* pp. 68–74.
24. Santa Cruz to Riva Agüero, June 22, 1823: quoted in Sobrevilla Perea, *Caudillo of the Andes,* p. 69.
25. Sucre to Bolívar, July 19, 1823: quoted by Lecuna, *Crónica razonada,* 3, pp. 299–300.
26. Bolívar to Secretario de Relaciones Exteriores de Colombia, August 3, 1823: quoted by Lecuna, *Crónica razonada,* 3, p. 300.
27. For a brief but graphic account of the growing political crisis in Lima during 1822–24, see Anna, *Fall of the Royal Government in Peru,* pp. 214–27; for greater detail, see Lecuna, *Crónica razonada,* 3, pp. 305–74.
28. Lecuna, *Crónica razonada,* 3, pp. 377–8.
29. O'Leary, *Memorias,* 2, pp. 246–7; O'Leary, *Bolívar and the War of Independence*, pp. 250–1.
30. O'Connor recorded his participation in Francisco Burdett O'Connor, *Independencia Americana. Recuerdos* (La Paz: González y Medina, 1915), pp. 80–159. On O'Connor's career, see James Dunkerley, *The Third Man: Francisco Burdett O'Connor and the Emancipation of the Americas* (London: Institute of Latin American Studies, 1999).
31. Miller, *Memoirs,* 2, p. 155.
32. Ibid., pp. 148–56, quotation p. 148. With his description of the army, Miller also provides a vivid account of the experience of moving through the mountain passes.
33. For an assessment of Olañeta by a serving royalist officer, see Mendízabal, *Guerra de la América del Sur,* pp. 190–1.
34. On Olañeta's motives, see Arnade, *The Emergence of the Republic of Bolivia,* pp. 117–27; Siles Salinas, *La independencia de Bolivia,* pp. 320–1.
35. Arnade, *Emergence of the Republic of Bolivia,* pp. 116–38.
36. Miller, *Memoirs*, 2, pp. 157–8.

37. General Jerónimo Valdés thought little of Bolívar: he told Canterac that "as a soldier he has done nothing apart from Quito . . . he has no reputation; the troops from Peru from the highest chief to the lowest soldier hate him deeply, and his troops are all untrained . . .": quoted by Lecuna, *Crónica razonada,* 3, p. 404–5.
38. Mendízabal, *Guerra de la América del Sur,* p. 194.
39. This was the tactic developed by Páez in the Venezuelan wars and known as "volver cara": it involved charging the enemy's cavalry, retreating, then unexpectedly turning back to the attack.
40. On Junín, see Miller, *Memoirs,* 2, pp. 158–65; O'Connor, *Recuerdos,* pp. 117–21; Lecuna, *Crónica razonada,* 3, pp. 413–19.
41. Lecuna, *Crónica razonada,* 3, pp. 444–5. For his full account of Sucre's campaign leading up to the battle of Ayacucho, see pp. 431–59.
42. Miller gives an account of Sucre's preparations and a vivid picture of his own adventures on reconnaissance patrols; see *Memoirs,* pp. 170–82. Sucre's chief of staff, Francis Burdett O'Connor, recalled that Sucre told him in early December to find a suitable place for battle.
43. Miller, *Memoirs,* 2, p. 189.
44. Lecuna, *Crónica razonada,* 3, pp. 459-60.
45. For a full account of the battle and a critical assessment of the descriptions given by both royalist and patriot participants, see Lecuna, *Crónica razonada,* 3, pp. 459–72. The best contemporary account in English is Miller's: see his *Memoirs,* 2, pp. 198–200. For another vivid account from a participant who took tea with Miller at the start of the battle, see O'Connor, *Recuerdos,* pp. 149–53.
46. Gerónimo Valdés, "Refutación: Traición de Olañeta," in *Documentos para la historia de la guerra separatista en el Perú,* ed. Conde de Torata, 2, pp. 61–104, quotation from p. 61.
47. Ibid., pp. 94–103.
48. Ibid., p. 61.
49. Natalia Sobrevilla Perea, "From Europe to the Andes and Back: Becoming 'Los Ayacuchos,'" *European History Quarterly* 41 (2011): pp. 472–88.
50. Méndez, *The Plebeian Republic: The Huanta Rebellion and the Making of the Peruvian State,* pp. 30–51.
51. Arnade, *Emergence of the Republic of Bolivia,* pp. 148–51.
52. O'Connor, *Recuerdos,* pp. 165–78 on his activities in Upper Peru.
53. Ibid., pp. 160–81.

CONCLUSION

Looking back on his experience of the war in Venezuela, the Spanish officer Rafael Sevilla recalled the royalists' retreat from their last stronghold, in the fortress at Puerto Cabello, in a few bitter words:

> Thus ended that war which Spanish titans had fought in a burning climate against the unfettered elements, against wretchedness and the greatest hardships, against the ferocity of a numerous and battle-hardened army, and, what is most terrible, against the constant treachery of Spain's bastard offspring, the degenerate Judases whose insatiable greed and ambition can always be bought by thirty pieces of silver . . .[1]

This was a soldier's sense of why Spain had lost the war for America, one shared with the Spanish officers who, three years later, were defeated on the battlefield at Ayacucho and starved out of the fortress of Callao. Seen from this perspective, the royalist army was not defeated by a worthy foe in a war fought to its end. It had instead been betrayed by enemies within its own camp, both the Spanish politicians who sought peace at all costs and the Spanish Americans who, as defeat came to seem inevitable, abandoned the royalist cause.

Of course, soldiers often refuse to accept that their defeat came from failure in the field, preferring to believe that they would have won if only they had been better supported by their governments and the peoples for whom they were fighting. In fact, the Spanish armies in which men like Sevilla and the *ayacuchos* served were soundly defeated by determined and able enemies. Indeed, as we have seen in the course of this book, Spain's defeat owed much to the tenacity of the Americans who fought against Spain's counterrevolutionary forces. In long and exhausting wars of attrition, they gradually wore down Spain's political will and military resources, and, as Spanish power and influence receded, their leaders were able to take advantage of the changes in the European balance of power brought about by the French wars. It was in this setting, post-1815, that the Spanish American wars that had started in 1810 entered their crucial phase. After defeats throughout the major theaters of war of the interregnum—in Venezuela, New Granada, Upper Peru, and Mexico—American dissidents fought their way back against a restored Spanish monarchy with renewed military mobilizations, reorganized armies, and new strategies. Their politics of the wars war gradually paid off: Spain was progressively weakened by its efforts to cope with the American question, and a decade after Ferdinand VII's return in 1814, Spanish American generals led their armies from local to regional campaigns and then to campaigns of continental liberation, finally overcoming Spain's last armies in their deepest redoubt, in Andean Peru.

The struggle between Spain and its Spanish American enemies had, as we have seen in the course of this work, started from an unexpected point and developed through different forms and phases. To recapitulate briefly, we have seen that the wars for independence did not have a clearly defined beginning, for they did not originate in a desire for independence that was firmly implanted or clearly announced at their outset. On the contrary, they emerged from the crisis of the Spanish monarchy in 1808–10, as it fractured under the pressures of international war. In Spain, Napoleon's invasion triggered internal war and political transformation; in Spanish America, this generated confusion and division, and by undermining existing authorities and triggering demands for autonomy, produced political contention that led to civil wars. Wars in Spanish America thus started as an offshoot of the larger international conflicts that carried international war into Spain's territory in 1808–13 and removed the old regime. Once started, Spanish America's wars took on a life of their own, moving from civil warfare between groups previously subject to the same sovereign authority, into wars of independence under leaders who rejected Spanish rule as that of a foreign power, wanted entirely separate states, and demanded international recognition as Spain's equals. The restoration of Ferdinand VII broke the momentum of this emerging movement for independence but could not eradicate it. With Spain wrecked by war and Britain becoming the leading power in the new balance of European power that followed Napoleon's defeat, American advocates of independence continued to fight an enfeebled metropolis and, as Spain grew progressively weaker, emerged as realistic competitors for international approval.

Fought in the name of the "people," Spanish America's wars took many different forms. Mexico was the only country where struggle against Spanish rule began with a mass rebellion among rural communities and provincial towns. In Caracas, Cartagena, Bogotá, Buenos Aires, and Santiago, the first moves towards independence were bloodless coups managed by urban elites and only turned into wars where competing cities had the military means to try to impose their authority on others, either to overturn the old regime or defend it. Thus, though the wars that stemmed from the crisis of 1810 were essentially civil wars over the same constitutional question—the location of sovereignty in the absence of the king—they were shaped by different social settings. In Mexico, war began with the mobilization of an irregular army based on the peasants and plebeians who joined Hidalgo's rebellion as he moved through the countryside. This was an inchoate force that mutated in size and shape, was unreliable in battle, and was quick to disperse in defeat. In South America, the urban elites that established provisional governments in 1810 used more conventional means. Rather than rebelling against a central authority, they took it over and sought to use the existing conventional forces and militias inherited from the old regime, supplemented by "patriotic" volunteers recruited from among the urban bourgeoisie, artisans, and laborers.

The new Spanish parliamentary regime inaugurated in 1810 was largely responsible for the initial shift from political into military conflict, from bloodless transfers of power into war. This was not because the Cortes was totally intransigent or blindly colonialist. On the contrary, its liberal reforms that brought elections, freedom of the press, and an end to the most oppressive institutions of the old regime (such as the Inquisition, Indian tribute, state monopolies), offered Americans considerable concessions. The Cortes insisted, however, that these had to be enjoyed within the body of what it regarded as the Spanish nation, without special treatment for the juntas or tolerance of American autonomy. It thus legitimated war against the Spanish American juntas and their successors, wars that were facilitated by the fact that in America the competing sides had the military means to fight each other.

The contenders for power often had military resources inherited from the Bourbon regime. Although Bourbon governments had been less successful in strengthening American forces than they had hoped, they left a system of Spanish regular forces, militias, and armories that provided the juntas and their successor governments with the bases on which to build the forces they needed to defend and extend their political revolutions. Royalist governments used military resources of a similar kind. In Mexico, the royalist authorities fought back against Hidalgo's improvised rebel "army" by using regular soldiers, militias, and volunteer companies to defend key cities, while Brigadier Calleja created a field army for the purpose of pursuing and destroying the rebel forces. In Peru, the existing military establishment of regular soldiers garrisoned in leading cities provided a core force for defending royal authority both within Peru and in its neighboring territories, while Viceroy Abascal created a new "Army of Peru" to fight back against the incursions of Buenos Aires's expeditionary army into Upper Peru. In New Granada, the royalists lost their major military resource when the main garrisons went over to the independents, but the governors of the royalist towns of Santa Marta and Popayán were able to supplement their small regular units with improvised militias.

The first phase of war did not begin with violence on a large scale. The plebeian rebels in Mexico acquired a reputation for murder and mayhem, and certainly attacked the people and property of those whom they saw as their enemies, especially the hated *gachupines*. However, such violence, though driven by anger and resentment against the wealthy was not evidence of a desire to annihilate class and ethnic enemies; it was often more akin to traditional disorders in which plebeians defended a moral economy by attacking agents of government. Indeed, contemporary sources leave the impression that most of the violence of Hidalgo's rebellion was caused by the counterinsurgent forces that overwhelmed the rebels in battle and hunted them down. The early wars in South America involved more structured forces, but several factors constrained the scale and spread of war. On one side, Spain was too preoccupied with fighting the French in the Peninsula to provide effective military support for its American governments; on the other side, the Spanish Americans elites tended to engage in "civic wars" between rival towns. The efforts of the autonomist cities to export revolution to their neighbors thus tended initially to be low-intensity affairs, involving small armies and producing indecisive outcomes. However, as the contending groups turned to popular mobilization, they became to unleash violence on a growing scale as, without the means for mediation and compromise, each sought complete victory over the other.[2]

This escalation of war slowed and paused around the time of Ferdinand's restoration. By 1815, attempts to implant enduring independent governments in Spanish America had failed or were on the brink of collapse in most regions; only Buenos Aires and its allied cities remained independent amidst the generalized return to royalist rule that coincided with the restoration. The royalist recuperation has several explanations. To Ferdinand VII and his ministers, it confirmed the belief that the breakaway movements of 1810–14 were the work of a few malcontents who had cynically exploited Spain's moment of weakness. Under the Cortes, the official view was that the majority of Spanish Americans did not want to break with Spain and that military means were sufficient to uproot rebellion. This was no doubt a simplistic and self-serving view, but it was no less important for that. True or not, the royalist representation of rebellion helped to shape and sustain the counterrevolutionary war effort. Under the constitutionalist regime, it legitimated loyalist resistance and by relentless repetition in official propaganda played a part in winning the battle for public opinion and international support against the rebels. It was also important because it shaped Ferdinand VII's position on the American question and informed the policies of his ministers when they attempted to rebuild Spain's authority after 1814.

Moreover, although it is impossible to accept such an obviously partisan view, it should not be dismissed completely. For the royalist revival undoubtedly owed something to the fact that a significant proportion of Americans retained a sense of loyalty to the Spanish monarchy, while those firmly committed to complete independence were relatively few. For the former, the break with the Regency in 1810 had been perfectly compatible with loyalty to Spain, since it seemed at the time the only means of avoiding domination by Napoleon. Among the creole minorities that created autonomous juntas, there were many individuals who took this view, retaining a belief in the rights of the captive king and the inviolability of ties with Spain. Only a much smaller minority aspired to complete separation and full independence, and, conscious of the political gap that separated them from the majority, this minority rarely stated their commitment to independence openly, especially at the start of the rebellion in 1810–11. The idea of independence was thus often concealed under cover of the "mask of Ferdinand" because it was unacceptable to many creoles and even less welcome among the peasants and plebeians who were called to fight for their "patria."

There were many reasons for Spanish Americans to retain their commitment to the Spanish monarchy. If it was sometimes just a flag of convenience for those who wished to break with Spain without alienating public sympathy, it also reflected the resilience of a political culture rooted in the past and anchored by religion.[3] The images, institutions, and practices of kingship were so deeply embedded in Hispanic political and cultural life that they dominated the political imagination and shaped thinking about the monarchy's crisis. Those who entered the political spaces opened by the *vacatio regis*—the lawyers, clerics, cabildo members, and other notables who took part in the debates held in cabildos and *juntas de gobierno* in 1808–10—invariably reflected the political practices and thinking of local elites under the old regime of composite monarchy that had been modified but not transformed by the Bourbons. Only a few were ready to embrace ideas from the American and French Revolutions; most interpreted their dilemma in terms of established Hispanic political thought. Thus, in debates about the locus of authority in the king's absence, they interpreted their position in terms of the neoscholastic vision of the sovereign who derived his right to power from a pact with the "people," and drew on concepts taken from Hispanic intellectual traditions, transmitted through the study of natural and canon law in American universities.[4]

The appeal to an Hispanic "ancient constitution" was one such invocation of Hispanic intellectual and political traditions.[5] At the same time, the cabildo was the primary forum for decision-making, again reflecting recourse to Spanish political traditions, in this case to political bodies that had probably been strengthened by Bourbon reform in the later eighteenth century.[6] In sum, the continuity of ideas and institutions of the old monarchy, particularly in Mexico and Peru, meant that a return to absolutist rule after 1814 was not a deep reversal, particularly if the restored monarchy was prepared to revert to a flexible form of government that allowed Americans a degree of autonomy.

However, while Ferdinand VII's restoration was justified by an appeal to the legitimacy and continuity of monarchy, the political and military upheavals of the interregnum had irrevocably altered the political landscape. In the first place, the political revolution promised by the *doceañistas,* the liberal deputies of the Cortes of Cádiz, had raised expectations that were difficult to satisfy. While Spanish parliamentarians tended to regard the Cádiz Constitution as the panacea for all ills, they stopped short of addressing the issue of equality between the provinces of Spain and those of the Americas. A Cortes dominated by Peninsular Spaniards placed strict limits on American political rights, as the Spanish majority refused to permit Americans to be represented in numbers proportionate to their populations. They also invariably took the view that Spain's interests should prevail and would not allow Americans to achieve reforms that ran counter to important Spanish institutional and economic interests.[7] This was particularly obvious in the key area of Spanish American commerce, where the Spanish merchant community was unprepared to make any serious concessions to American demands for trade outside the Spanish monopoly. Commercial interests in Spain, especially in Cádiz, ensured that the mercantilist system on which its American trade depended always prevailed over proposals for free trade.[8]

The failings of the Cortes and Constitution were, of course, even clearer in regions such as Venezuela, New Granada, and Río de la Plata, where independent governments had been established. There, outside Spanish rule, the limitations of Spain's constitutional regime and the *doceañista* reforms seemed more obvious than their benefits. Because the Cádiz Constitution did not provide Americans with representation proportionate to their populations, the Spanish constitutional regime was unlikely to change the minds of creoles who wanted greater autonomy, still less those who favored independence. This was made still more unlikely by the fact that the Cortes failed to establish a coherent policy for communicating with American rebels, repeatedly rejecting British offers to mediate and pursuing military repression rather than seeking negotiated solutions.

If the Cortes had contributed little to defeating American dissent, then why did the dissidents and their governments fail to break permanently from Spain before Ferdinand VII was restored? To royalists, the answer was deceptively clear: the American governments of 1810–14 lacked legitimacy and were therefore unable to build durable independent states. Some of Spain's leading opponents shared a similar view, albeit in modified form. Simón Bolívar, for example, attributed the downfall of independent governments in both Venezuela and New Granada to the fact that "the mass of the population is still ignorant of its rights and unmindful of its interests," while also blaming patriot politicians for their lack of vision and preparedness.[9] These men had, he argued, devoted attention to constitutional debates at times when they might have better engaged in ensuring the defeat of Spanish loyalist forces. Instead of concentrating on the common enemy, they had fought amongst themselves and, for all their protestations about freedom from tyranny, they had invariably imposed new and unwelcome burdens on their populations. In short, Spain's counterrevolution had succeeded because its American opponents had adopted political models that failed to create central command or generate the militarization needed to fight Spanish forces.

To support his arguments, Bolívar contrasted the forms of government and conduct of war in Venezuela and New Granada with those of the Río de la Plata. He noted that the "warlike state of the La Plata River provinces has purged the territory and led their victorious armies to Upper Peru, arousing Arequipa and worrying the royalists in Lima."[10] If this was an overstatement, it had an element of truth: Bolívar was right to suppose that the survival of the River Plate provinces as an independent state was related to the priority that Buenos Aires had given to organizing an army commanded from the center and sent to make war in enemy territory. Gradually, Buenos Aires became weaker when some of its provinces broke away and formed confederations of their own autonomous states; however, this proved less dangerous to independence than it had been in Venezuela and New Granada because the royalist Army of Peru was too far from Buenos Aires to take full advantage of the disunity.

Bolívar's catalogue of patriot political errors does not exhaust explanation of royalist revival in 1814–15. There was another vital ingredient of the counter-revolution that Bolívar was unwilling openly to admit, but that had been crucial to the outcomes of political struggle: namely, the strength of American loyalists and their willingness to fight for the royalist cause. Restoration of Spanish control was accomplished by years of counterrevolutionary warfare, and most of the credit for Spanish success must go to the officials and soldiers who persisted in fighting the rebels. Such success was all the more remarkable given the inability of Spain's constitutionalist regime to project force across the Atlantic. Not only were army reinforcements scarce, but Spanish naval power declined significantly during the interregnum. At sea as on land, Spain's American wars were mainly left to the royalist officials *in situ*, using local men and resources with little direction or help from Spain. Americans had fought Americans, and, although Bolívar was reluctant to admit it, the survival of the empire owed as much to loyalist military action as to patriot political error.

The loyalist position had often been precarious, given that civil and military authorities were poorly prepared for an internal war and neither side had any special advantage in the technology or logistics of warfare. In all the cases we have considered, opposing sides fought with similar weapons, forces, and firepower. When their armies met in battle, they tended to consist of men from similar backgrounds under officers who used conventional linear infantry formations, with support from cavalry and a few units of light artillery. They faced similar logistical difficulties, too. Shortages of money and supplies and difficulties in sustaining supply lines over long distances meant that they relied mainly on resources extracted, often by force, from the regions in which they operated. There was, however, one important difference. In the first phases of war, the royalists were more often led by men with military experience and, before the international arms trade got into full swing after the Napoleonic wars, they had better access to arms. Also important was the fact that they faced opponents who, though they claimed to be the legitimate heirs of the old order, were unable to command credibility as heirs of the king or take complete control of government institutions.

Another influence on the direction and outcome of the wars of the interregnum was the position taken by the leading international powers on the Spanish crisis. The international context differed notably from that of previous rebellions and wars of independence in the Americas, when foreign powers had intervened on the side of colonial rebels against their parent power. France and Spain played a famously important part in Britain's loss of its North American colonies, while the later interventions of Spain and Britain loosened France's hold on Haiti. By contrast, the leading powers abstained from direct military intervention during the early Spanish American wars. France hoped to dominate Spanish America by controlling Spain; Britain committed to defending the territorial integrity of the Spanish monarchy in order to secure the Spanish alliance against Napoleon. Thus, though the international context provided Spanish Americans with an opportunity to assert political independence, they had no powerful foreign allies to help them achieve that. Bolívar pointed this out to the editor of Jamaica's *Royal Gazette* in 1815, when he informed him that, during the previous five years, Spanish America's independent states had been "abandoned by the entire world." Unlike North America, "No foreign nation ever aided us with its wisdom and experience, defended us with its arms, or encouraged us with its resources." Instead, "every recourse, military and political, denied to us has been made abundantly available to our enemies." Indeed, "the very victories of the great and immortal Wellington have been, indirectly, fatal favors to us since the Spaniards, who are ignorant of the art of war, learned it from the heroic British army commanded by that illustrious soldier who, at one time, intended to help liberate South America."[11]

This was a plausible argument. Although Spaniards complained that British neutrality was duplicitous because Britain was always ready to support its merchants' commerce in Spanish America, even with Spain's enemies, on balance the British position was more helpful to imperialist Spaniards than dissident Spanish Americans. First, Britain's intervention in the Peninsular War played a crucial role in saving Spain as an independent state. Second, Britain's refusal to recognize the dissident Spanish American states or allow them to be supplied with arms weakened their stance against Spain. British determination to support Ferdinand VII's restoration, combined with the desire of European statesmen to rebuild the political structures torn down during the French wars, evidently favored the reconstruction of authoritarian monarchy in Spain and its empire after 1814. Indeed, the Anglo-Spanish agreement drawn up in July–August 1814 was particularly reassuring in this respect, since it provided guarantees that Britain would neither give nor permit external armed support for Spain's American enemies.[12] Ferdinand VII thus had the advantage of an international agreement that recognized Spain's right to assert authority in America by whatever means it chose, without fear of foreign intervention on the side of the American rebels. In practical terms, too, the King's policy options seemed wider than those of the Cortes, given that peace in the Peninsula left him with a large army (about 184,000 men) which, although it had not always distinguished itself in the war against France, was more experienced, combat-ready, and, above all, available for overseas deployment than any Spanish army had been since 1810.

The royalist revival did not endure, however, largely because the wars of the interregnum had brought about a politicization and militarization that reshaped politics, bringing in new men, new ideas, and armies attuned to political ends, as well as the routine use of violence as an instrument of politics. As royalists and patriots pursued their struggles for power, they increasingly turned to the populace for the military manpower needed to outdo the enemy and loosened the constraints of social discipline imposed under colonial rule. Leaders on both sides widened recruitment by reaching out to the free coloreds, Indians, and slaves who occupied the lowest ranks of society and, in so doing, they initiated an unprecedented militarization of political and social life. These trends were most obvious where social grievances and racial antagonisms were acute. In Mexico, Hidalgo's rebellion against Spanish government attracted widespread popular support because it intersected with rural distress, conflicts over land, the resentments of the *castas* against discrimination, debt, and taxes, and the desire of indigenous communities to defend their cultures against insult and encroachment. It continued after his death because rural strife provided a fertile recruiting ground for insurgent leaders of various kinds. It allowed men bent on the pursuit of personal power to recruit followers with the promise of plunder and exploit the cause of revolution for their own ends. It also enabled an idealist like José María Morelos to forge a network of support among local leaders and create an insurgent army capable of taking the field against royalist armies in the name of an independent government. The militarization caused by the insurgents was, of course, amplified by the counterrevolutionary militarization directed by Calleja, as he built armies to fight the insurgents and police the countryside.

Civil wars among the elite opened fractures along racial and social fault lines in South American countries too, as peasants, plebeians, and slaves were drawn into local struggles for power. Such popular mobilizations were rarely spontaneous phenomena. Slave participation seems at first sight to represent the most extreme form of social rebellion triggered by civil war in Spanish America, but it illustrates the ambiguities and complexities of subaltern mobilization. In the first place, it rarely arose from slave rebellion. There were some small rebellions among slaves on the Venezuelan coasts and in the mining regions of Colombia, but, without great plantations there were no slave insurrections of the kind that took place in revolutionary Haiti. Indeed, though slaves tried to escape servitude by joining the forces of one side or the other, most were drawn into war by royalist and independent generals who conscripted them by force and motivated them to fight with promises of freedom in return for a fixed period of military service. This practice seems to have been started by royalist officers who fought the first independent governments of Venezuela and New Granada and promised freedom in return for fighting the King's enemies. Creole revolutionaries were initially reluctant to follow this lead: as members of the class that owned slaves, they were averse to disrupting the social order and the laws of property for temporary military advantage. However, once started, the recruitment of slaves into armies could not be confined to the royalists. Military leaders such as Bolívar and San Martín recognized that, if they were to field regular armies capable of fighting in a European style, slaves were crucial sources of military manpower. They acquired slaves by appropriation and expropriation from their owners, starting first with Spanish owners, and incentivized slaves with promises of freedom in return for military service. Amidst populations that were often reluctant to commit to long periods of military service, the contribution of slaves to the armies of both sides was such that, Blanchard has suggested, the wars might not have followed the trajectory they did, nor lasted for so long without them.

Indian peasants were also drawn into wars started by others, sometimes for the royalists, sometimes for the independents. Indians often seemed to prefer the Spanish monarchy to its political rivals, possibly because their leaders saw good relations with the king as the best means to protect and conserve their communities and customs. This seems to have been the case in places throughout Andean America, from Pasto and Quito to Central and Southern Peru and parts of Upper Peru. However, loyalty to the King and religious piety did not necessarily bind Indians to the Spanish cause: as Eric Van Young has shown, in Mexico members of some Indian peasant communities used the imagery of crown and altar to legitimate their rebellion against royalist government and to kill Spaniards.

Plebeian participation of these kinds was never the mobilization of the "nation in arms," as there were no nations to fight for. When participants talked of their "patria," they invariably meant their local community, and in joining one side or the other, poor whites, free colored, blacks, and Indians tended to fight for their own interests. They drew on local traditions of community autonomy and self-defense, and sometimes sought the freedom outside the law that had existed in the colonial period in activities such as smuggling and local banditry. The promise of material reward, whether from plunder, or from the defense of existing land-holdings or seizure of land and property from enemies (which as in past rebellions could be justified by traditional ideas of moral economy), was doubtless a more important source of motivation than were royalist or republican political ideas. Plebeians and peasants tended to see the wars through the prism of their own local interests and disputes, set within close and localized horizons.

A particularly striking form of popular insurgency emerged among the pastoral communities of the South American plains, whose people became the exponents of guerrilla warfare of a particularly effective sort. This phenomenon appeared first in Venezuela, where the royalist caudillo Boves turned the llaneros of the plains into warriors for the crown. Then, after the Spanish reconquest of 1815, it stood at the heart of the republican revival in Venezuela when the llaneros of the Apure, Arauca, and Casanare regions turned the plains into republican territory. The role of pastoral communities also played an important part in revolutionary war in the Southern Cone. On the plains of Uruguay and the neighboring cattle countries of the Argentine littoral, gauchos, supplemented by Indians from the missions and led by Artigas and his allied caudillos, fought guerrilla wars against outsiders; in the ranching lands of the pampas around Salta, deep in the interior, Güeme's gauchos held the frontier against the royalist army of Peru. This was not just "politicized banditry" on lawless frontiers, as Michael Broers has it.[13] It was, rather, the mobilization of people who were ready to defend local autonomy against intruders and whose way of life as cattle-herders made them particularly effective in doing so.

Nor was this the only form of popular guerrilla war. Other kinds of guerrillas emerged in the Andean interiors of the continent. In the Cauca Valley, free blacks fought for the royalists, as did Indians from the communities of Pasto; in Central Peru, Indians and mestizos joined *montoneras* who fought on both sides, as well as plundering property for their own benefit; in Upper Peru, creole leaders recruited among the mestizo and Indian peasantry and created the *republiquetas* that acted as zones of refuge for opponents of the royalist regime and bases for guerrilla warfare against it. In all these regions, irregular and guerrilla wars played an important part in the wars of independence because, although they could not defeat Spanish governments and armies by their own efforts, they helped to keep the cause of independence alive by harassing royalist forces, absorbing royalist resources, and, in the case of Bolívar's llaneros, becoming the expert cavalry of a regular army.

The repercussions of militarization varied regionally but displayed some common features. First, it tended to intensify and prolong war by adding to the fighting capacity of armies on both sides. Second, it increased the political power of military leaders: independent generals and caudillos as well as royalist officers became key figures in government and, as Clément Thibaud has shown in the case of Bolívar's armies, military forces provided an institutional bedrock for the emergent republic, a "republic in arms" that anticipated the civilian republic. Third, the creation of armies to fight for and against the revolution greatly accentuated the tendency, already launched by the Bourbon military reforms, towards an Americanization of armed force. After 1810, both sides needed larger forces and hence widened the scope of their recruitment. While the royalist high command and leading officers were mostly Peninsular Spaniards, the rank and file was recruited from plebeians and peasants who were often drawn into the army via local networks led by creole and mestizo landowners or Indian community leaders: the royalist army created by Calleja and Flon in Mexico, and by Goyeneche in Peru are prime examples.

Alongside the regular armies, a new kind of force also emerged, composed of irregulars who fought under leaders of their choice, for goals that they decided. The most striking examples of such personal armies led by charismatic caudillos appeared in the South American plains, where the people of frontier communities were ready to fight for their own way of life, adapting for war the skills with horse, lance, and knife that they acquired in herding horses and cattle. In the Venezuelan llanos, Boves and Morales provide the outstanding example of an irregular army raised in the name of the King but outside formal royalist control, created by a combining personal followers with and forced drafts of men when numbers ran down. Páez did the same on the republican side, as did Artigas in the Banda Oriental and Güemes in Salta.

Thus, though not launched on a wave of popular rebellion, the outbreak of civil wars initiated the first widespread popular militarization of modern Spanish America. As the competing sides marshaled support, they turned to groups previously marginalized from politics for reasons of race and class, and created contacts among people who had been isolated from each other. Their leaders did so with incentives and promises of different kinds: material rewards; freedoms and civil rights under new governments; protection, privileges, and honors in return for loyalty to the King.

In the first phase of war, during Ferdinand's interregnum, this struggle moved in favor of the royalists. Of the proto-states that fought these wars, only the government of Buenos Aires outlived the restoration of Ferdinand VII; all the others were defeated in 1814–16, as from Mexico to Chile royalist governments recovered their hold on territories previously lost to insurgents. In Mexico, the defeat of Morelos fragmented rebel resistance and rendered it ineffective; in Venezuela, the republican army was defeated by an enemy that employed growing violence, aimed at annihilating their opponents and cowing the civilian population into submission; New Granada's confederated states slid to defeat amidst disunity, demoralization, and lack of popular support, as did independent Chile. There were some common causes of defeat: the first independents failed to establish states that were capable of sustaining prolonged warfare; they lacked the means to fully overcome their enemies; and they were unable to win international recognition and external allies during a period when the attention of the European powers was absorbed by war amongst themselves. But the defeat of the rebellions of the interregnum proved to be an interruption, not a destination. After Ferdinand VII was reinstated, the challenge to Spain was reignited in another cycle of warfare, started in the surviving nuclei of insurgency and carried onto a new and more violent plane as the independents fought to defend themselves against Spanish plans to extirpate all vestiges of their enemy.

This new phase of warfare began as a continuation of the previous wars, initially on a reduced scale and with a different character. After 1814, the main axes of war shifted away from cities and conventional armies. After the defeat of their urban governments, the independents of Mexico, Venezuela, and New Granada moved into the backlands and avoided confronting their enemies in pitched battles. So, too, did the caudillos of the Río de la Plata. Even the militarized government of Buenos Aires, with its penchant for building armies and seeking to project power over large regions, preferred for a few years to rely on irregular war: it depended on the republiquetas of Upper Peru and the gauchos of Salta to harass the royalist army and prevent its advance into the heartlands of the revolution. War was, however, to take on new characteristics. On the royalist side, the champions of a military solution wanted a final war to extirpate rebellion, using both conventional armies and counterinsurgent terror tactics as the means to bring about a lasting peace. This intransigent approach generated its opposite: the insurgents moved from defensive local warfare towards more total war, exemplified in widespread conscription for armies of liberation.

With the shift towards ruralized and irregular wars during the early years of the restoration, when the independents held out against royalist forces by guerrilla warfare, went the continuing development of a phenomenon which, as John Lynch has shown, became an increasingly prominent and formative feature of politics: the "caudillo" or local war leader who was instrumental in mobilizing popular support and taking it to war.[14] In Mexico, the mestizo curate Morelos was the most outstanding of the caudillos who emerged in regional rebellion and war, rising from a narrow local leadership to a position where he came close to establishing an independent Mexican state; however, when his attempts to build an army of liberation failed in 1814, leadership of the war against Spain splintered, devolving among chiefs who focused on local wars. The caudillos of Venezuela followed a similar path, fighting "little wars" separately until they were pulled together under Bolívar's overarching leadership. In the south, the local caudillos who commanded men from the pastoral communities of the plains were also for a time the crucial force in war, largely on the side of the independents against royalist armies: Artigas and his gauchos drove Spain out of the Banda Oriental; Güemes maneuvered his gauchos to stop Peru's royalist armies from invading Buenos Aires's territory.

The guerrilla wars that succeeded the conventional wars of the interregnum were not simply a form of retreat. By keeping war going, they punctured the Spanish colonial order at crucial points. They disrupted production and commerce, as well as the labor systems on which farms and mines depended; they undermined the networks that sustained law, administration, and tax collection, thus making it much more difficult to govern; and, last but not least, they sustained a series of armed enclaves in which Spain's opponents could cultivate their ambitions to create independent states and incubate the field armies needed to build them. The growth of these armies responded to the realization, clear to men such as Bolívar and San Martín, that they could not rely on the allegiance and obedience of the "people" in whose name they spoke: they had to have regular, disciplined, and permanent forces, for these were essential to overcome enemy armies, to take and hold new territory, and to advance the cause of independence from the countryside to the cities, and from one country to another.

The construction of such armies took the wars of independence into their final phase from about 1817. It began with San Martín's establishment of his Army of the Andes and his invasion of Chile, a feat that was followed, in 1818–19, by Bolívar's offensive against Morillo's forces in Venezuela and invasion of New Granada. The independents' expansion into occupied territories cleared the way, in turn, for the conclusive stage of the independence wars, in which the liberation armies established by San Martín and Bolívar converged on royalist Peru. Now, the independents had more experienced, more motivated, better organized armies at their disposal, in contrast to the localized and loosely assembled forces that they had mobilized during the interregnum and the guerrillas who had kept the cause alive during the early years of the restoration.

At the core of Bolívar's and San Martín's armies was a body of officers and men who not only became more effective in military terms; they also became increasingly identified with the cause of independence and made the army its political as well as military instrument. Such armies were not, however, the vehicles of nation-making and nationalism that historians find in the mass-conscripted armies of nineteenth-century Europe. The permanent forces at their core were small and fought as professional soldiers rather than patriotic conscripts. Conscription was, indeed, very unpopular during the wars and after. Bolívar's armies were continually drained by desertion, and conscripts often had to be treated more as prisoners than willing soldiers.[15] As Santander observed when trying to enlarge Bolívar's armies in 1821,

> our soldiers are not like those of Europe. In the latter there is enlightenment, they know the cause that they defend, and know the laws to which they are subject. With the former it is just the opposite; their ignorance is well known; it is regularly hidden from them for whom they fight; and however much they are instructed in the General Dispositions, very few succeed in understanding them.[16]

Santander referred to conscripts raised in New Granada rather than to the forces that Bolívar deployed in his post-1821 wars of continental liberation. These were men of a different kind, more akin to the regular soldiers of a standing army. But they were not primary material for nation-making either. Most were drawn from regiments and battalions created in Venezuela and New Granada, then transferred to Peru, where they were supplemented by the remnants of San Martín's forces from Chile and the River Plate, and by Peruvian officers who saw alliance with Bolívar as the means to overcome royalist armies that they had been unable to defeat. Bolívar's army for the liberation of Quito and Peru did not, then, represent a single nation, nor fight for national goals. It was essentially a personal army, held together by Bolívar's prestige and will, and dedicated to his goal of continental liberation from Spain.

If the armies created by San Martín and Bolívar did not embody nations, they undoubtedly played a critical role in establishing the independent states that became nation states during the century that followed. Above all, they kept up the military pressure on Spanish forces and, by allowing them no respite, thoroughly exposed Spain's problems of projecting power across the Atlantic. From 1817, elements in Spain's governing circles began to acknowledge that the military solution chosen by Ferdinand VII had no future. It was not only hugely expensive to sustain fighting forces in America, but it was increasingly obvious that Spain lacked the essential attribute of a maritime empire: a navy capable of maintaining reliable lines of communication and supply, and preventing the destruction of Spanish trade by the independents' privateers. Worse still, as the independents made ground from 1817 onwards, Spanish soldiers and officials sensed that they were losing the war of opinion and, with it, the cooperation of a population loyal to Spain or at least disposed to accept Spanish rule. Though royalist armies could continue fighting by using local recruits, local taxes, and local supplies, they were increasingly deprived of resources as the independents advanced and brought new territories under their control.

Thus, while at the start of Ferdinand VII's first restoration in 1814 the royalists fought to destroy republican enclaves, by its end in 1820 the positions had been reversed. Royalist forces were being displaced on every front and increasingly isolated both from each other and the populations they were supposed to defend. Spain's 1820 Revolution seemed to offer the last chance to salvage something, as Spanish politicians finally acknowledged the need for a negotiated solution. It was, however, too late to resurrect the empire by combining the threat of war with the promise of conciliation. In Mexico, military men believed that only by rejecting Spain could they now conserve what they had saved by war. In South America, peace talks demoralized Spanish officers while convincing the independents that a last round of war, one final push, would bring about a complete and uncompromised independence.

Spain was, then, drummed out of Spanish America by war. Ferdinand VII's search for an uncompromising victory against the independents succeeded only in provoking a revival of American hostility that gradually exhausted Spain's material resources and sapped its political support. Indeed, the main reason for Spain's loss of America was the ability of its American enemies to revive and sustain warfare after Ferdinand VII's restoration and the return of peace in Europe. The wars of the restoration drained Spain's prestige, credibility, and finances, as, from relatively small beginnings in 1816–17, American insurgents applied continuous pressure to the weaknesses caused by the wars of the interregnum. Spain was dragged into a series of counterinsurgency wars that its forces could fight but not win. Without victory, and with no signs of military or naval support from Spain, the King's forces lost motivation and morale. Thus, when Ferdinand VII was restored to the plenitude of his powers for the second time—this time on the back of the French army that came to his aid in 1823—most of Spanish America had already fallen from his grasp and the will to fight for what remained was vanishing. One army had already refused to leave Cádiz for America in 1820 and, as Spaniards refused to cross the Atlantic to fight and die for a discredited King, so Americans fell away from his cause and became reconciled to a new future in independent states.

The effects of war in making those states were to be worked out over many decades after the return of peace, but it was soon apparent that, while wars had cleared the ground for new states by demolishing Spanish rule, the war for independence had not created an architecture conducive to state formation. Unlike the wars of early modern Europe, Spanish America's wars did not produce "military revolutions" or their political corollaries. While they created some strong leaders, notably Simón Bolívar with his model for a centralized liberal republic, they had also generated countervailing forces. In settings where, during centuries of Spanish rule, the state had been weak and national identities undeveloped, war tended to dissipate and disperse authority, and to shift violence into the private realm rather than reinforcing power at the center.[17] Wars had swept away the old order; in their wake they left leaders and groups who had found in violence and militarism an efficient means to remake their societies, to exercise political command, and to impose their demands. This was a legacy that, despite idealistic efforts to create a republican political life on the basis of liberal constitutions, was to bedevil Spanish American politics throughout much of the ensuring century.

Notes

1. Rafael Sevilla, *Memorias de un official del ejercito español (Campañas contra Bolívar y los separatistas en América)* (Bogotá: Editorial Incunables, 1983), p.283.
2. For a thoughtful discussion of the roots of violence and its development into a primary instrument of politics during the Spanish American wars, see Adelman, "The Rites of Statehood: Violence and Sovereignty in Spanish America, 1789–1821," pp. 391–422.
3. On the sincerity of Mexican commitment to Ferdinand VII, see Marco Antonio Landavazo, "Fernando VII y la insurgencia mexicana: Entre la 'máscara' y el mito," in Marta Terán and José Antonio Serrano Ortega (eds.), *Las guerras de independencia en la América española* (Zamora, Michoacán: El Colegio de Michoacán et al., 2002), pp. 79–98.
4. Gutiérrez Ardila, *Un Reino Nuevo*, pp. 81–110.

5. José Carlos Chiaramonte, "The 'Ancient Constitution' after Independence (1808–1852)," *HAHR* 90, no. 3 (2010): pp. 455–88.

6. Calderón and Thibaud, *La Majestad de los Pueblos*, chap. 2.

7. On Spanish attitudes and policies during the Regency and constitutional periods, see: Anna, *Spain and the Loss of America,* pp. 63–114.

8. Costeloe, *Response to Revolution,* pp. 128–32.

9. Bolívar to Maxwell Hyslop, Kingston, May 19, 1815: in Lecuna and Bierck (eds.), *Selected Writings of Bolívar,* 1, p. 97.

10. Bolívar, "Reply of a South American to a Gentleman of this island," September 6, 1815: Lecuna and Bierck (eds.), *Selected Writings,* 1, p. 105.

11. Bolívar to Editor of the Royal Gazette, Kingston, Jamaica, September 28, 1815: Lecuna and Bierck (eds.), *Selected Writings,* 1, pp. 123–4.

12. Heredia, *Planes españoles,* pp.122–4.

13. Michael Broers, *Napoleon's Other War: Bandits, Rebels and their Pursuers in the Age of Revolutions* (Oxford: Peter Lang, 2010), p.131.

14. Lynch, *Caudillos in Spanish America,* chap. 2.

15. On Bolívar's army during Santander's government, see David Bushnell, *The Santander Regime in Gran Colombia* (Newark: University of Delaware, 1954), pp. 249–57.

16. Santander to Congress of Cúcuta, September, 1821: cited in ibid., p. 254.

17. Centeno, *Blood and Debt: War and the Nation State in Latin America,* chap. 3.

BIBLIOGRAPHY

Abbreviations

Archives and Document Collections

ACD: Archivo del Congreso de los Diputados, Madrid
AGI: Archivo General de Indias, Seville
AHNM: Archivo Histórico Nacional, Madrid
SHM: Archivo del Servicio Histórico Militar, Madrid
RAHM: Archivo de la Real Academia de Historia, Madrid
CDIP: *Colección documental de la independencia del Peru*. 30 vols. Lima: Comision Nacional del Sesquicentenario de la Independencia del Peru, 1971

Journals

BLAR: Bulletin of Latin American Research
HAHR: Hispanic American Historical Review
JLAS: Journal of Latin American Studies

Published Documents and Collections

Abascal y Sousa, José Fernando de. *Memoria de Gobierno*. Edited by Vicente Rodríguez Casado and José Antonio Calderón Quijano. 2 vols. Seville: Escuela de Estudios Hispanoamericanos, 1944.

Biblioteca de Mayo, 19 vols. Buenos Aires: Senado de la Nación, 1960–74.

Friede, Juan, ed., *La batalla de Boyacá, 7 de agosto de 1819, a través de los archivos españoles*. Bogotá: Banco de la República, 1969.

Graham, G.S., and R.A. Humphreys, eds. *The Navy and South America, 1807–1823: Correspondence of the Commanders-in-Chief on the South American Station*. London: Navy Records Society, 1962.

Grases, Pedro, and Manuel Pérez Vila, eds. *Las fuerzas armadas de Venezuela en el siglo XIX (Textos par su estudio), La Independencia*. 3 vols. Caracas: Presidencia de la República, 1963.

Hernández y Dávalos, J.E. *Historia de la Guerra de Independencia de México*. 2 vols. Mexico City: José M. Sandoval, 1878.

Lecuna, Vicente, and Harold A. Bierck, eds. *Selected Writings of Bolívar*. 2 vols. New York: The Colonial Press, 1951.

Lee López, Alberto, ed. *Los ejércitos del Rey, 1819*, 2 vols. Bogotá: Biblioteca de la Presidencia, 1989.

López González, Valentín, ed. *Documentos sobre el sitio de Cuautla*. Mexico City: Porrúa, 1992.

Memoria sobre la táctica de infantería dirigido al gobierno de S.M. por la comisión encargada de revisar el actual reglamento. Madrid: Imprenta de M. Rivadeneyra, 1856.

Molinari, Diego Luis. *La representación de los hacendados de Mariano Moreno*. Buenos Aires: Facultad de Ciencias Económicas, Universidad de Buenos Aires, 1939.

Pombo, Manuel Antonio, and José Joaquín Guerra. *Constituciones de Colombia*. 2 vols. Bogotá: Biblioteca Popular de la Cultura Colombiana, Ministerio de Educación, 1951.

Rodríguez Villa, Antonio. *El Teniente General Don Pablo Morillo, Primer Conde de Cartagena, Marqués de la Puerta (1778–1837)*. 4 vols. Madrid: Real Academia de Historia, 1908–1910.

Torata, Conde de, ed. *Documentos para la historia de la guerra separatista en el Perú*. Madrid: Imprenta de la viuda de M. Minuesa de los Rios, 1895.

Contemporary Works

Alamán, Lucas. *Historia de Méjico*. 4 vols. Mexico City: Editorial Jus, 1942.

Austria, José de. *Bosquejo de la Historia Militar de Venezuela*. 2 vols. Caracas: Academia Nacional de la Historia, 1960.

Bustamante, Carlos María. *Campañas del General D. Felix Maria Calleja, comandante en gefe del ejercito real de operaciones, llamado del Centro*. Mexico City: Imprenta del Aguila, 1828.

———. *Cuadro histórico de la revolución mexicana*. Mexico City: Comisión Nacional para la celebración del seisquicentenario, 1961.

Cajigal, Juan Manuel de. *Memorias del Mariscal de Campo Don Juan Manuel de Cajigal sobre la revolución de Venezuela*. Caracas: Archivo General de la Nación, 1960.

Coll y Prat, Narciso. *Memoriales sobre la independencia de Venezuela*. Caracas: Academia Nacional de la Historia, 1960.

Espinosa, José María. *Memorias de un abanderado*. Bogotá: Plaza & Janes, 1983.

Estrada, Alvaro Flórez. *Examen imparcial de las disensiones de América con España y de los medios de su recíproco interés*. London, 1811.

Flinter, George. *A History of the Revolution of Caracas, Comprising an Impartial Narrative of the Atrocities Committed by the Contending Parties*. London: T. and J. Allman, 1819.

Gage, Thomas. *Thomas Gage's Travels in the New World*. Edited by J. Eric S. Thompson. Norman: University of Oklahoma, 1958.

García Camba, Andrés. *Memorias del General García Camba para la historia de las armas españolas en el Perú, 1809–1821*. Madrid: Ed. América, Biblioteca Ayacucho, 1916.

Hall, Basil. *Extracts from a Journal Written on the Coasts of Chile, Peru and Mexico in the Years 1820, 1821, 1822*. 2 vols. Edinburgh: Constable and Co., 1824.

Heredia, J.F. *Memorias del Regente Heredia*. Madrid: Editorial América, Biblioteca de Ayacucho, 1916.

López, José Hilario. *Memorias*. 2 vols. Bogotá: Biblioteca Popular de Cultura Colombiana, 1942.

Mendizábal, Francisco Javier. *Guerra de la América del Sur, 1809–1824*. Buenos Aires: Academia Nacional de Historia, 1997.

Miller, John, ed. *Memoirs of General Miller in the Service of the Republic of Peru*. 2 vols. London: Longman, Rees, Orme, Brown, and Green, 1829. Facsimile of the first edition, New York: AMS Press, 1973.

Moreno, Mariano. *Plan revolucionario de operaciones*. Buenos Aires: Ed. Plus Ultra, 1993.

Morillo, Pablo. *Memorias de Pablo Morillo, Conde de Cartagena, Marqués de la Puerta*. Bogotá: Fundación Fica, 2010.

O'Connor, Francisco Burdett. *Independencia Americana. Recuerdos*. La Paz: González y Medina, 1915.

O'Leary, Daniel Florencio. *Bolívar and the War of Independence*. Translated and edited by Robert F. McNerney. Austin: University of Texas, 1970.

———. *Memorias del General Daniel Florencio O'Leary: Narración*. 3 vols. Caracas: Imprenta Nacional, 1952.

Paz, José María. *Memorias póstumas del General José Maria Paz*. 2 vols. La Plata: Imprenta La Discusión, 1892.

Pezuela, Joaquín de la. "Compendio de los sucesos ocurridos en el ejército del Perú y sus provincias desde que el General Pezuela tomó el mando de él," in *Colección de Documentos de la Independencia del Perú*, XXVI, vol. 1.

———. *Manifiesto en que el Virrey del Perú Don Joaquín de la Pezuela refiere al hecho y circunstancias de su separación de mando*. Madrid: Imprenta de D. Leonardo Núñez de Vargas, 1821.

Pezuela, Joaquín de la, Pablo Ortemberg, and Natalia Sobrevilla Perea, eds. *Joaquín de la Pezuela, Compendio de los sucesos ocurridos en el ejército del Perú y sus provincias*. Santiago: Centro de Estudios Bicentenario, 2011.

Restrepo, José Manuel. *Historia de la Revolución de la República de Colombia,* 6 vols., Bogotá: Bolsilibros Bedout, 1974.

Robertson, J.P., and W.P. Robertson. *Letters on Paraguay; Comprising an Account of a Four Years' Residence in that Republic under the Government of the Dictator Francia*. 3 vols. London: John Murray, 1838–9.

Santos Vargas, José. *Diario de un comandante de la independencia americana, 1814–1825*, ed. Gunnar Mendoza, Mexico: Fondo de la Cultura Económica, 1982.

Secondary Works

Adelman, Jeremy. "The Rites of Statehood: Violence and Sovereignty in Spanish America, 1789–1821," HAHR 90, no. 3, pp. 391–422.

———. *Sovereignty and Revolution in the Iberian Atlantic*. Princeton: Princeton University Press, 2006.

Aguilera Peña, Mario. *Los Comuneros: Guerra Social y Lucha Anticolonial*. Bogotá: Universidad Nacional, 1985.

Albi, Julio. *Banderas Olvidadas: El ejército realista en América*. Madrid: Ediciones de Cultura Hispánica, 1990.

———. *La defensa de las Indias (1764–1799)*. Madrid: Instituto de Cooperacion Iberoamericana, Ediciones Cultura Hispánica, 1987.

Alonso, José Ramón. *Historia Política del Ejército Español*. Madrid: Editora Nacional, 1974.

Andrien, Kenneth J., ed. *The Human Tradition in Colonial Latin America*. Wilmington, DE: Scholarly Resources, 2002.

Andújar Castillo, Francisco. *Los militares en la España del siglo XVIII: Un estudio social*. Granada: Universidad de Granada, 1991.

———. *El sonido del dinero: Monarquía, ejército y venalidad en la España del siglo XVIII*. Madrid: Marcial Pons, 2004.

Anna, Timothy E. *The Fall of the Royal Government in Mexico City*. Lincoln: University of Nebraska Press, 1978.

———. *The Fall of the Royal Government in Peru*. Lincoln: University of Nebraska, 1979.

———. *Spain and the Loss of America*. Lincoln: University of Nebraska Press, 1983.

Archer, Christon I. *The Army in Bourbon Mexico, 1760–1810.* Albuquerque: University of New Mexico Press, 1977.

———. "The Army of New Spain and the Wars of Independence, 1790–1812." *HAHR* 61, no. 4 (1981): pp. 705–14.

———. "Beber del cáliz envenenado: la política, la tradición y el ejército mexicano, 1820–1848." In *Las nuevas naciones: España y México, 1800–1850,* edited by Jaime Rodríguez O., pp. 293–314. Madrid: Mapfre, 2008.

———. " 'La Causa Buena': The Counterinsurgency Army of New Spain and the Ten Years' War." In *The Independence of Mexico and the Creation of the New Nation,* edited by Jaime Rodríguez O., pp. 85–108. Los Angeles: UCLA Latin American Center, 1989.

———. "The Cutting Edge: The Historical Relationship between Insurgency, Counterinsurgency and Terrorism during Mexican Independence, 1810–1821." In *Terrorism: Roots, Impact, Responses,* edited by Lawrence Howard, pp. 29–45. Westport, CT: Greenwood Press, 1992.

———. "Fighting for Small Worlds: Wars of the People during the Independence Ear in New Spain, 1810–1821," *Cuadernos de Historia Latinoamericana* 6 (pp. 63–92). Leiden: Asociación de Historiadores Latinoamericanistas Europeos, 1998.

———. "Insurrection-Reaction-Revolution-Fragmentation: Reconstructing the Choreography of Meltdown in New Spain during the Independence Era." *Mexican Studies / Estudios Mexicanos* 10 (1994): pp. 63–98.

———. "New Wars and Old: Félix Calleja and the Independence War of Mexico, 1810–16." In *Military Heretics. The Unorthodox in Policy and Strategy,* edited by B.J.C. McKerchar and A. Hamish Ion, pp. 33–56. Westport, CT: Greenwood Press, 1993.

———. "Politicization of the Army of New Spain during the War of Independence, 1810–21." In *The Origins of Mexican National Politics, 1808–1847,* edited by Jaime Rodríguez O., pp. 11–37. Wilmington, DE: Scholarly Resources, 1993.

———. "La revolución militar de México: Estrategía, tácticas y logísticas durante la Guerra de Independencia, 1810–1821." In *Interpretaciones de la Independencia de México,* edited by Jaime Rodríguez O. and Josefina Zoraida Vázquez, pp. 123–35. Mexico City: Nueva Imagen, 1997.

———. "The Royalist Army in New Spain: Civil-Military Relationships, 1810–1821." *JLAS* 13 (1981): pp. 68–9.

———. "Soldados en la escena continental: Los expedicionarios españoles y la guerra de la Nueva España, 1810–25." In *Fuerzas militares en Iberoamérica, siglos XVIII y XIX,* edited by Juan Ortiz Escamilla. Mexico City: Colegio de Mexico et al., 2005.

———, ed. *The Wars of Independence in Spanish America.* Wilmington, DE: Scholarly Resources, 2000.

———. "Where Did All the Royalists Go? New Light on the Military Collapse of New Spain, 1810–1822." In *The Mexican and Mexican Experience in the Nineteenth Century,* edited by Jaime Rodríguez O., pp. 24–43. Tempe, AZ: Bilingual Press, 1989.

Areces, Nidia R. *Estado y frontera en el Paraguay: Concepción durante el gobierno del Dr. Francia.* Asunción: Universidad Católica, 2007.

Arnade, Charles W. *The Emergence of the Republic of Bolivia.* Gainesville: University of Florida Press, 1957.

Artola, Miguel. *La España de Ferdinand VII.* Madrid: Espasa Calpe, 1999.

Bañon Martínez, Rafael and Thomas M. Barker, eds. *Armed Forces in Spain Past and Present.* Boulder, CO: Social Science Monographs, 1988.

Barros Arana, Diego. *Historia jeneral de Chile.* Santiago: Rafael Jover, Editor, 1894.

Bassi, Juan Carlos. "La expedición libertadora al Alto Perú." In *Historia de la Nación Argentina*, edited by Ricardo Levene, vol. 5, pt. 2, pp. 247–72. Buenos Aires: Academia Nacional de Historia, 1939.

Batista, Juan. *La estrategía española en América durante el siglo de las luces*. Madrid: Mapfre, 1992, pp. 116–30.

Belgrano, Mario. *Rivadavia y sus gestiones diplomáticas con España (1815–1820)*. Buenos Aires: Editorial Huarpes, 1945.

Bell Lemus, Gustavo. *Cartagena de Indias: de la Colonia a la República*. Bogotá: Fundación Guberek, 1991.

Beverina, Juan. *El Virreinato del Río de la Plata. Su organización militar*. Buenos Aires: Círculo Militar, 1935.

Bidondo, Emilio A. *La expedición de auxilio a las provincias interiores (1810–1812)*. Buenos Aires: Círculo Militar, 1987.

———. *La guerra de la independencia en el Alto Peru*. Buenos Aires, Círculo militar, 1979.

Black, Jeremy, and Philip Woodbine, eds. *The British Navy and the Use of Naval Power in the Eighteenth Century*. Leicester: Leicester University Press, 1988.

Blanchard, Peter. *Under the Flags of Freedom: Slave Soldiers and the Wars of Independence in Spanish South America*. Pittsburgh, PA: University of Pittsburgh: 2008.

Blanco Valdés, Roberto L. "Paisanos y soldados en los orígenes de la España liberal." In *Las nuevas naciones: España y México, 1800–1850*, edited by Jaime Rodríguez O., pp. 273–92. Madrid: Mapfre, 2008.

Blaufarb, Rafe. *Bonapartists in the Borderlands: French Exiles and Refugees on the Gulf Coast, 1815–1835*. Tuscaloosa: University of Alabama, 2005.

Blossom, Thomas. *Antonio Nariño. Hero of Colombian Independence*. Tucson: Arizona University Press, 1967.

Bobbit, Philip. *The Shield of Achilles: War, Peace and the Course of History*. London: Penguin Books, 2003.

Borreguero Beltrán, Cristina. "Antiguos y nuevos modelos de reclutamiento en el ejército borbónico del siglo XVIII." In *Por la fuerza de las armas: Ejército e independencias en Hispanoamérica*, edited by Juan Marchena Fernández and Manuel Chust, pp. 63–82. Castelló de la Plana: Universidad Jaume I, 2007.

Brading, David A. *The First America: The Spanish Monarchy, Creole Patriots and the Liberal State, 1492–1867*. Cambridge: Cambridge University Press, 1991.

Breña, Roberto. *El primer liberalismo español y los procesos de emancipación de América, 1808–1824*. Mexico City: El Colegio de México, 2006.

Broers, Michael. *Napoleon's Other War: Bandits, Rebels and their Pursuers in the Age of Revolutions*. Oxford: Peter Lang, 2010.

Broseta, Salvador, and Carmen Corona, Manuel Chust, et al., *Las ciudades y la guerra, 1750–1898*. Castelló: Universitat Jaume I, 2002.

Brown, Matthew. *Adventuring through Spanish Colonies: Simón Bolívar, Foreign Mercenaries and the Birth of New Nations*. Liverpool: Liverpool University Press, 2006.

———. "Inca, Sailor, Soldier, King: Gregor MacGregor and the Early Nineteenth-Century Caribbean." *BLAR* 24, no. 1 (2005): pp. 44–71.

Bruijn, Jaap R. "States and their Navies from the Late Sixteenth to the End of the Eighteenth Centuries." In *War and Competition between States*, edited by Philippe Contamine. Oxford: Clarendon Press, 2000.

Brumwell, Stephen. *Redcoats: The British Soldier and War in the Americas, 1755–63*. Cambridge: Cambridge University Press, 2002.

Cahill, David. "New Viceroyalty, New Nation, New Empire: A Transnational Imaginary for Peruvian Independence." *HAHR* 91, no. 2 (2011): pp. 203–35.

Cahill, David, and Scarlett O'Phelan Godoy. "Forging Their Own History: Indian Insurgency in the Southern Peruvian Sierra, 1815." *BLAR* 11 (1992): pp. 127–40.

Caillet-Bois, Ricardo. "La revolución en el Virreinato." In *Historia de la Nación Argentina*, edited by Ricardo Levene, vol. 5, pt. 2, pp. 93–240. Buenos Aires: Academia Nacional de Historia, 1939.

Calderón, María Teresa, and Clément Thibaud. *La Majestad de los Pueblos en la Nueva Granada y Venezuela, 1780–1832*. Bogotá: Taurus, 2010.

———. *Las Revoluciones en el Mundo Atlántico*. Bogotá: Taurus, 2006.

Calvo Stevenson, Haroldo, and Adolfo Meisel, eds. *Cartagena y la independencia*. Cartagena: Banco de la República, 2011.

Campbell, Leon G. "The Army of Peru and the Túpac Amaru Revolt, 1780–1783." *HAHR* 56, no. 1 (1976): pp. 31–57.

———. "After the Fall: The Reformation of the Army of Peru, 1784–1816." *Ibero-Amerikanisches Archiv* 3 (1977): pp. 1–28.

———. *The Military and Society in Colonial Peru, 1750–1810*. Philadelphia: American Philosophical Society, 1978.

Carr, Raymond. *Spain, 1808–1939*. Oxford: Clarendon Press, 1966.

Carrera Damas, German. *Boves: Aspectos socio-económicos de su acción histórica*. Caracas: Ministerio de Educación, 1968.

Centeno, Miguel A. *Blood and Debt: War and the Nation State in Latin America*. University Park: Pennsylvania State University Press, 2002.

Cervera Pery, José. *La marina española en la emancipación de Hispanoámerica*. Madrid: Mapfre, 1992.

Chasteen, John Charles. *Americanos: Latin America's Struggle for Independence*. Oxford: Oxford University Press, 2008.

Christiansen, E. *The Origins of Military Power in Spain, 1800–1854*. Oxford: Oxford University Press, 1967.

Chust Calero, Manuel. *La cuestión nacional americana en los Cortes de Cádiz*. Valencia: Fundación Instituto de Historia Social, 1999.

———, ed. *1808: La eclosión juntera en el mundo hispano*. Mexico City: Fondo de Cultura Económica, 2007.

Collier, Simon. *Ideas and Politics of Chilean Independence, 1808–1833*. Cambridge: Cambridge University Press, 1967.

Colmenares, German, Zamira Díaz de Zuluaga, José Escorcia, and Francisco Zuluaga. *La independencia: Ensayos de historia social*. Bogotá; Instituto de Cultura Colombiana, 1986.

Contamine, Philippe, ed. *War and Competition Between States*. Oxford: Clarendon Press, 2000.

Cook, Warren L. *Flood Tide of Empire: Spain and the Pacific Northwest, 1543–1819*. New Haven: Yale University Press, 1973.

Cornejo Bouroncle, Jorge. *Pumacahua: La revolución del Cuzco de 1814*. Cuzco: Editorial H.G. Rozas, 1956.

Costeloe, Michael. *Response to Revolution: Imperial Spain and the Spanish American Revolutions, 1810–1840*. Cambridge: Cambridge University Press, 1986.

Deas, Malcolm. "Some Reflections on Miranda as Soldier." In *Francisco de Miranda: Exile and Enlightenment*, edited by John Maher, pp. 77–87. London: Institute for the Study of the Americas, 2006.

Demélas, Marie-Danielle. *La invención política: Bolivia, Ecuador, Perú en el siglo XIX*. Lima: IFEA, 2003.

Díaz Venteo, Fernando. *Las campañas militares del Virrey Abascal*. Seville: Escuela de Estudios Hispanoamericanos, 1948.

Dominguez, Jorge. *Insurrection or Loyalty: The Breakdown of the Spanish American Empire*. Cambridge, MA: Harvard University Press, 1980.

Ducey, Michael T. *A Nation of Villages: Riot and Rebellion in the Mexican Huasteca, 1750–1850*. Tucson: University of Arizona Press, 2004.

———. "Village, Nation, and Constitution: Insurgent Politics in Papantla, Veracruz, 1810–1821." *HAHR* 79, no. 3 (1999): pp. 463–93.

Duffy, Michael. "World-Wide War and British Expansion, 1793–1815." In *The Oxford History of the British Empire*, edited by P.J. Marshall. Vol. 2. Oxford: Oxford University Press, 1998.

Dunkerley, James. *The Third Man: Francisco Burdett O'Connor and the Emancipation of the Americas*. London: Institute of Latin American Studies, 1999.

Earle, Rebecca A. *Spain and the Independence of Colombia 1810–1825*. Exeter: University of Exeter, 2000.

Eissa-Barroso, Francisco A. "'Of Experience, Zeal and Selflessness': Military Officers as Viceroys in Early Eighteenth Century Spanish America." *The Americas* 68, no. 3 (2012): pp. 317–45.

———. "The Illusion of Disloyalty: Rumours, Distrust and Antagonism, and the Charges Brought against the Viceroy of New Spain in the Autumn of 1808." *Hispanic Research Journal* 11, no. 1 (2010): pp. 25–36.

———. "Politics, Political Culture and Policy Making: the Reform of Viceregal Rule in the Spanish World under Philip V (1700–1746)." PhD diss., University of Warwick, 2010.

Elliott, J.H. *Imperial Spain*. Harmondsworth, UK: Penguin Books, 1970.

Esdaile, Charles J. *The Peninsular War: A New History*. London: Allen Lane/Penguin Books, 2002.

———. *Spain in the Liberal Age: From Constitution to Civil War, 1808–1939*. Oxford: Blackwell, 2000.

Farriss, Nancy M. *Crown and Clergy in Colonial Mexico, 1759–1821*. London: Athlone Press, 1968.

Fisher, David Hackett. *Washington's Crossing*. Oxford: Oxford University Press, 2004.

Fisher, John R. *Bourbon Peru, 1750–1824*. Liverpool: Liverpool University Press, 2003.

———. *Commercial Relations between Spain and Spanish America, 1778–1796*. Liverpool: University of Liverpool, 1985.

———. "Royalism, Regionalism and Rebellion in Colonial Peru, 1808–1815." *HAHR* 59, no. 2 (1979): pp. 232–57.

———. *Trade, War and Revolution: Exports from Spain to Spanish America, 1797–1820*. Liverpool: Institute of Latin American Studies, 1992.

Fisher, J.R., Allan J. Kuethe, and Anthony McFarlane. *Reform and Insurrection in Bourbon New Granada and Peru*. Baton Rouge: University of Louisiana, 1990.

Fisher, L.E. *The Last Inca Revolt, 1780–1783*. Norman: University of Oklahoma, 1966.

Floyd, Troy S. *The Anglo-Spanish Struggle for Mosquitia*. Albuquerque: University of New Mexico, 1967.

Fontana, Josep. *La quiebra de la monarquía absoluta, 1814–20*. Barcelona: Ariel, 1987.

Fowler, Hill. "El pronunciamiento mexicano del siglo XIX: Hacia una nueva tipología." *Estudios de Historia Moderna y Contemporánea de México* 38 (2009): pp. 5–34.

Fradkin, Raul, and Jorge Gelman, eds. *Desafíos al orden: Política y sociedades rurales durante la Revolución de Independencia*. Rosario: Prohistoria, 2008.

Frega, Ana. "La junta de Montevideo de 1808." In *1808: La eclosión juntera en el mundo hispano*, edited by Manuel Chust, pp. 251–263. Mexico City: Fondo de Cultura Económica, 2007.

Friede, Juan. *La otra verdad: la independencia vista por los españoles*. Bogotá: Tercer Mundo, 1972.

Gallo, Klaus. *Great Britain and Argentina: From Invasion to Recognition, 1806–26*. Basingstoke, UK: Palgrave, 2001.

García-Baquero González, Antonio. *Comercio colonial y guerras revolucionarias*. Seville: Escuela de Estudios Hispanoamericanos, 1972.

Garrett, David T. *Shadow of Empire: The Indian Nobility of Cusco, 1750–1825*. Cambridge: Cambridge University Press, 2005.

Garrido, Margarita. *Reclamos y representaciones: Variaciones sobre la política en el Nuevo Reino de Granada, 1770–1815*. Bogotá: Banco de la República, 1993.

Gates, David. *The Spanish Ulcer: A History of the Peninsular War*. London: Allen and Unwin, 1986.

Geggus, David. "Slavery, War and Revolution in the Greater Caribbean, 1789–1815." In *A Turbulent Time: The French Revolution and the Greater Caribbean*, edited by David Barry Gaspar and David Patrick Geggus. Bloomington: Indiana University Press, 1997.

Gilmore, Robert L. "The Imperial Crisis, Rebellion and the Viceroy: Nueva Granada in 1809." *HAHR* 40, no. 1 (1960): pp. 2–24.

Glover, Michael. *The Peninsular War, 1807–1814: A Concise Military History*. London: Penguin Books, 2001.

Goldman, Noemi. "Crisis del sistema institucional en el Río de la Plata." In *1808: La eclosión juntera en el mundo hispano*, edited by Manuel Chust, pp. 230–3. Mexico City: Fondo de Cultura Económica, 2007.

Golte, Jurgen. *Repartos y rebeliones: Túpac Amaru y las contradicciones de la economía colonial*. Lima: Instituto de Estudios Peruanos, 1986.

Gómez Pérez, Maria del Carmen. *El sistema defensivo americano: siglo XVIII*. Madrid: Mapfre, 1992.

González, Marcela. *Las milicias, orígen y organización durante la colonia*. Córdoba, Argentina: Centro de Estudios Históricos, 1995.

Gortari Rabiela, Hira de. "La minería durante la guerra de independencia y los primeros años del México independiente." In *The Independence of Mexico and the Creation of the New Nation*, edited by Jaime Rodríguez O., pp. 129–49. Los Angeles: University of California, 1989.

Guardino, Peter F. *Peasants, Politics, and the Formation of Mexico's National State: Guerrero, 1800–1857*. Stanford, CA: Stanford University Press, 1996.

Guedea, Virginia. "Los indios voluntarios de Fernando VII." In *Estudios de Historia Moderna y Contemporánea de México*. 10. México: Universidad Nacional Autónoma de México, Instituto de Investigaciones Históricas, 1986, pp. 11–83.

———. *La insurgencia en el departamento del norte: Los Llanos de Apan y la Sierra de Puebla 1810–1816*. Mexico City: Universidad Nacional Autónoma de México, 1996.

Guerra, François-Xavier. "Lógicas y ritmos de las revoluciones hispánicas." In *Revoluciones hispánicas: Independencias americanas y liberalismo español*, edited by François-Xavier Guerra. Madrid: Editorial Complutense, 1995. pp. 13–46.

———. *Modernidad e independencias*. Madrid: Mapfre, 1992.

Gutiérrez Ardila, Daniel. *Un Reino Nuevo. Geografía política, pactismo y diplomacia durante el interregno en Nueva Granada (1808–1816)*. Bogotá: Universidad Externado de Colombia, 2010.

Gutiérrez Ramos, Jairo. *Los indios de Pasto contra la República (1809–1824)*. Bogotá: Instituto Colombiano de Antropología e Historia, 2007.

Gúzman Pérez, Moisés. "Los métodos de represión realista en la revolución de independencia de México, 1810–1821." In *Las guerras de independencia en la América española*, edited by Marta Terán and José Antonio Serrano Ortega, pp. 323–35. Zamora, Michoacán: El Colegio de Michoacán et al., 2002.

Habron, John D. *Trafalgar and the Spanish Navy*. London: Conway Maritime Press, 1988.

Haigh, Robert M. "The Creation and Control of a Caudillo." *HAHR* 44, no. 4 (1964): pp. 481–90.

Halperin-Donghi, Tulio. *The Aftermath of Revolution in Latin America.* New York: Harper and Row, 1973.

———. *Politics, Economics and Society in Argentina in the Revolutionary Period.* Cambridge: Cambridge University Press, 1975.

Hamill, Hugh M. "Caudillismo and Independence: A Symbiosis?" In *The Independence of Mexico and the Creation of the New Nation*, edited by Jaime Rodríguez O., pp. 171–4. Los Angeles: UCLA Latin American Center, 1989.

———. "Early Psychological Warfare in the Hidalgo Revolt." *HAHR* 41 (1961): pp. 206–35.

———. *The Hidalgo Revolt: Prelude to Mexican Independence.* Gainesville: University of Florida Press, 1966.

———. "Royalist Counterinsurgency in the Mexican War for Independence: The Lessons of 1811." *HAHR* 53 (1973): pp. 470–89.

———. "Royalist Propaganda and 'La Porción Humilde del Pueblo' during Mexican Independence." *The Americas* 36 (1980): pp. 437–8.

———. "'Vencer o morir por la Patria!' La invasión de España y algunas consecuencias para México, 1808–1810." In *Interpretaciones de la Independencia de México*, edited by Josefina Zoraida Vásquez and Jaime E. Rodríguez O. Mexico City: Editorial Patria, 1997.

Hamnett, Brian R. "The Appropriation of Mexican Church Wealth by the Spanish Bourbon Government. The Consolidación de Vales Reales, 1805–1808." *JLAS* 1 (1969): pp. 85–113.

———. "Mexico's Royalist Coalition in the Response to Revolution, 1808–1821." *JLAS* 12 (1980): pp. 57–62.

———. *La política española en una época revolucionaria, 1790–1820.* Mexico City: Fondo de Cultura Económica, 1985.

———. "Popular Insurrection and Royalist Reaction: Colombian Regions, 1810–1823." In *Reform and Insurrection in Bourbon New Granada and Peru*, edited by J.R. Fisher, Allan J. Kuethe, and Anthony McFarlane, pp. 292–326. Baton Rouge: University of Louisiana, 1990.

———. *Revolución y contrarrevolución en México y el Perú: Liberalismo, realeza y separatismo, 1800–1824.* Mexico City: Fondo de Cultura Económica, 1978.

———. *Roots of Insurgency: Mexican Regions, 1750–1824.* Cambridge: Cambridge University Press, 1986.

Hassig, Ross. *Aztec Warfare: Imperial Expansion and Political Control.* Norman, Oklahoma, University of Oklahoma Press, 1988.

Helg, Aline. *Liberty and Equality in Caribbean Colombia, 1770–1835.* Chapel Hill: University of North Carolina Press, 2004.

Heredia, Edmundo A. *Planes españoles para reconquistar Hispanoamerica, 1810–1833.* Buenos Aires: Universidad de Buenos Aires, 1974.

Herreros de Tejada, Luis. *El Teniente General D. José Manuel de Goyeneche, Primer Conde de Guaqui.* Barcelona: Oliva de Vilanova Impresor, 1923.

Hoffman, Paul E. *The Spanish Crown and the Defence of the Caribbean, 1535–1585.* Baton Rouge: Louisiana University Press, 1980.

Howard, Lawrence, ed. *Terrorism: Roots, Impact, Responses.* Westport, CN: Greenwood, 1992,

Humphreys, R.A. *Liberation in South America, 1806–1827: The Career of James Paroissien.* London: Athlone Press, 1952.

Ibarra, Antonio. "Crímenes y castigos políticos en la Nueva España borbónica: Patrones de obediencia y disidencia política, 1809–1816." In *Las guerras de independencia en la América española*, edited by Marta Terán and José Antonio Serrano Ortega, pp. 255–72. Zamora, Michoacán: El Colegio de Michoacán et al., 2002.

Izard, Miguel. *El miedo a la revolución: La lucha por la libertad en Venezuela, 1777–1830.* Madrid: Ed. Tecnos, 1979.

Jaksic, Iván. *Andrés Bello: Scholarship and Nation-Building in Nineteenth-Century Latin America.* Cambridge: Cambridge University Press, 2001.

Jiménez Molinares, Gabriel. *Los martires de Cartagena de 1816.* 2 vols. Cartagena: Imprenta Departmental, 1948–50.

Johnson, Lyman L. "Juan Barbarín: The 1795 French Conspiracy in Buenos Aires." In *The Human Tradition in Colonial Latin America*, edited by Kenneth J. Andrien, pp. 259–77. Wilmington, DE: Scholarly Resources, 2002.

———. "The Military as a Catalyst of Change in Late Colonial Buenos Aires." In *Revolution and Restoration: The Rearrangement of Power in Argentina, 1776–1860*, edited by Mark D. Szuchman and Jonathan D. Brown, pp. 36–7. Lincoln: University of Nebraska, 1994.

———. *Workshop of Revolution: Plebeian Buenos Aires and the Atlantic World, 1776–1810.* Durham: Duke University, 2011.

Jones, Archer. *The Art of War in the Western World.* Urbana: University of Illinois Press, 1987.

Kamen, Henry. *Philip V of Spain: The King Who Reigned Twice.* New Haven: Yale University Press, 2001, pp. 8–9, 62–4, 81–4, 108–9.

———. *The War of the Spanish Succession in Spain, 1700–1715.* Bloomington: University of Indiana, 1969.

Kaufmann, William W. *British Policy and the Independence of Latin America, 1804–1828.* New Haven: Yale University Press, 1951.

King, James F. "The Colored Castes and American Representation in the Cortes of Cádiz." *HAHR* 33 (1953): pp. 33–64.

———. "El comisionado regio don Antonio Ignacio de Cortabarría y la primera república de Venezuela." *Boletín de la Academia Nacional de la Historia*, 37, no. 146 (1954): pp. 125–78.

König, Hans-Joachim. *En el camino hacia la nación: Nacionalismo en el proceso de formación del estado y de la Nueva Granada, 1750–1856.* Bogotá: Banco de la República, 1994.

Kuethe, Allan J. *Cuba, 1753–1815.* Knoxville: University of Tennessee, 1986.

———. "Decisiones estratégicas y finanzas militares del siglo XVIII." In *Por la fuerza de las armas: Ejército e independencias en Hispanoamérica*, edited by Juan Marchena and Manuel Chust, pp. 84–6. Castelló de la Plana: Universidad Jaume I, 2007.

———. "The Development of the Cuban Military as a Sociopolitical Elite, 1763–83." *HAHR* 61, no. 4 (1981): pp. 695–704.

———. *Military Reform and Society in New Granada, 1773–1808.* Gainesville: University of Florida, 1978.

LaFaye, Jacques. *Quetzalcóatl and Guadalupe: The Formation of Mexican National Consciousness, 1531–1813.* Translated by Benjamin Keen. Chicago: Chicago University Press, 1976.

Lasso, Marixa. *Myths of Harmony: Race and Republicanism during the Age of Revolution, Colombia, 1795–1831.* Pittsburgh, PA: University of Pittsburgh, 2007.

Leach, Douglas E. *Arms for Empire: A Military History of the British Colonies in North America, 1607–1763.* New York: Macmillan, 1973.

Lecuna, Vicente. *Crónica razonada de las guerras de Bolívar.* 3 vols. Caracas: Presidencia de la República, 1983.

Lenman, Bruce P. *England's Colonial Wars, 1550–1688: Conflicts, Empire and National Identity.* London: Pearson, 2001.

Leon, Leonardo. "La corona española y las guerras intestinas entre los indígenas de Araucania, Patagonia y las Pampas, 1760–1806." *Nueva Historia: Revista de Historia de Chile* 5 (1982): pp. 31–67.

Levene, Ricardo, ed. "La formación del Triunvirato." In *Historia de la Nación Argentina*, edited by Ricardo Levene, vol. 5, pt. 2, pp. 539–83. Buenos Aires: Academia Nacional de Historia, 1939.

————. *Historia de la Nación Argentina*, 10 vols. Buenos Aires: Academia Nacional de Historia, 1936–50.

Lewin, Boleslao. *La rebelión de Túpac Amaru y los orígenes de la independencia de Hispanoamérica.* Buenos Aires: Librería Hachette, 1957.

Lewis, William F. "Simón Bolívar and Xavier Mina: A Rendezvous in Haiti." *Journal of Inter-American Studies* 11, no. 3 (1969): pp. 458–65.

Liss, Peggy. *Atlantic Empires: The Network of Trade and Revolution, 1713–1826.* Baltimore: Johns Hopkins University, 1983.

Loza, Emilio. "La campaña de la Banda Oriental (1810–1813)." In *Historia de la Nación Argentina*, edited by Ricardo Levene, vol. 5, pt. 2, pp. 837–8. Buenos Aires: Academia Nacional de Historia, 1939.

————. "Yatasto, Tucumán y Salta." In *Historia de la Nación Argentina*, edited by Ricardo Levene, vol. 5, pt. 2, pp. 782–4. Buenos Aires: Academia Nacional de Historia, 1939.

Lynch, John. *Bourbon Spain*. Oxford: Blackwell, 1989.

————. "British Policy and Spanish America, 1763–1808." *Journal of Latin American Studies* 1 (1969): pp. 1–30.

————. *Caudillos in Spanish America, 1800–1850*. Oxford: Clarendon Press, 1992.

————. *San Martín: Argentine Soldier, American Hero*. New Haven: Yale University Press, 2009.

————. *Simón Bolívar: A Life*. New Haven: Yale University Press, 2006.

————. *The Spanish American Revolutions, 1808–1826*. London: Wiedenfield & Nicolson, 1973.

————, ed. *Andres Bello: The London Years*. Richmond: Richmond Publishing, 1982.

————, ed. *Latin American Revolutions, 1808–1826*. Norman: University of Oklahoma, 1994.

Lynn, John A., ed. *Battle: A History of Combat and Culture*. Boulder, CO: Westview Press, 2003.

Maher, John, ed. *Francisco de Miranda: Exile and Enlightenment*. London: Institute for the Study of the Americas, 2006.

————. *Oficiales y soldados en el ejército de América*. Sevilla: Escuela de Estudios Hispanoamericanos, 1983.

Marchena Fernández, Juan. *Ejército y milicias en el mundo colonial americano*. Madrid: Editorial Mapfre, 1992.

————. "The Social World of the Military in Peru and New Granada." in *Reform and Insurrection in Bourbon New Granada and Peru*, edited by J.R. Fisher, Allan J. Kuethe, and Anthony McFarlane. Baton Rouge: University of Louisiana, 1990.

————, and Manuel Chust, eds. *Por la fuerza de las armas: Ejército e independencias en Hispanoamérica*. Castelló de la Plana: Universidad Jaume I, 2007.

Marco Dorta, Enrique. "Cartagena de Indias: riquezas ganaderas y problemas." In *Tercer Congreso Hispanoamericano de Historia*. Cartagena: Talleres Mogollón, 1962, pp. 335–52.

Marichal, Carlos. *The Bankruptcy of Empire: Mexican Silver and the Wars between Spain, Britain and France, 1760–1810*. Cambridge: Cambridge University Press, 2007.

Marks, Patricia. *Deconstructing Legitimacy: Viceroys, Merchants, and the Military in Late Colonial Peru*. University Park: Pennsylvania University Press, 2007.

Marshall, P.J., ed. *The Oxford History of the British Empire*. Vol. 2. Oxford: Oxford University Press, 1998.

Martínez Garnica, Armando. *El legado de la Patria Boba*. Bucaramanga: Universidad Industrial de Santander, 1998.

Masur, Gerhard. *Simon Bolívar*. Albuquerque: University of New Mexico, 1969.

McAlister, Lyle N. *The Fuero Militar in New Spain, 1764–1800*. Gainesville: Florida University Press, 1957.

————. "The Reorganization of the Army of New Spain, 1763–1766." *HAHR* 33, no. 1 (1953): pp. 1–32.

McFarlane, Anthony. "The American Revolution and the Spanish Monarchy." In *Europe's American Revolution*, edited by Simon P. Newman, pp. 26–50. London: Palgrave Mac-Millan, 2006.

———. *The British in the Americas, 1480–1815*. London: Longman, 1994.

———. "La caída de la monarquía española y la independencia hispanoamericana," in *Las independencias hispanoamericanas. Interpretaciones dos años después,* edited by Marco Palacios, pp. 31–60. Bogotá: Norma, 2010.

———. "Civil Disorders and Popular Protests in Late Colonial New Granada." *HAHR* 64, no. 1 (1984): pp. 17–54.

———. "Los ejércitos coloniales y la crisis del imperio español, 1808–1810." *Historia Mexicana* 58, no. 1 (2008): pp. 229–85.

———. *Colombia before Independence: Economy, Society and Politics under Bourbon Rule*. Cambridge: Cambridge University Press, 1993.

———. "Guerras e independencias en las Americas." In *Las Revoluciones en el Mundo Atlántico,* edited by María Teresa Calderón and Clément Thibaud, pp. 178–80. Bogotá: Taurus, 2006.

———. "Identity, Enlightenment and Political Dissent in Late Colonial Spanish America." *Transactions of the Royal Historical Society,* Sixth Series, 8, 1998, pp. 309–35.

———. "The Rebellion of the Barrios: Urban Insurrection in Bourbon Quito." *HAHR* 69, no. 2 (1989): pp. 283–330.

———. "Rebellions in Late Colonial Spanish America: A Comparative Perspective." *Bulletin of Latin American Research* 14 (1995): pp. 313–39.

———. "'La revolución de las Sabanas': Rebelión popular y contrarrevolución en el Estado de Cartagena, 1812." In *Cartagena y la independencia,* edited by Haroldo Calvo Stevenson and Adolfo Meisel, pp. 215–47. Cartagena: Banco de la República, 2011.

McKerchar, B.J.C. and A. Hamish Ion, eds. *Military Heretics. The Unorthodox in Policy and Strategy.* Westport, CT: Greenwood Press, 1993.

McKinley, Michael. *Pre-Revolutionary Caracas: Politics, Economy and Society, 1777–1811.* Cambridge: Cambridge University Press, 1985.

Méndez, Cecilia. *The Plebeian Republic: The Huanta Rebellion and the Making of the Peruvian State, 1820–1850*. Durham: Duke University Press, 2005.

Mercado, Jorge. *Campaña de invasion del Teniente General Don Pablo Morillo, 1815–1816.* Bogotá: Ejército de Colombia, Estado Mayor General, 1919.

Merino Navarro, José P. *La Armada Española en el Siglo XVIII.* Madrid: Fundación Universitaria Española, 1981, pp. 34–89.

Miller, Gary. "Status and Loyalty of Regular Army Officers in Late Colonial Venezuela." *HAHR* 66, no. 4 (1986): pp. 667–96.

Miranda Arrieta, Eduardo. "Los Bravo del Sur: Relato de una familia insurgente, 1810–1821." In *Las ciudades y la guerra, 1750–1898,* edited by Salvador Broseta, Carmen Corona, Manuel Chust, et al., pp. 47–59. Castelló: Universitat Jaume I, 2002.

Mitre, Bartolome. *Historia de San Martín y de la emancipación subamericana.* Buenos Aires: Ed. Peuser, 1950.

Molas Ribalta, Pere. "The Early Bourbons and the Military." In *Armed Forces in Spain Past and Present,* edited by Rafael Bañon Martínez and Thomas M. Barker, pp. 51–80. Boulder, CO: Social Science Monographs, 1988.

Moliner Prada, Antonio. "De la Juntas a la Regencia. La difícil articulación del poder en la España de 1808." *Historia Mexicana* 58, no. 1 (2008): pp. 143–64.

———. "El movimiento juntero en la España de 1808." In *1808: La eclosión juntera en el mundo hispano,* edited by Manuel Chust. Mexico City: Fondo de Cultura Económica, 2007.

Morillo, Stephen, and Michael T. Parkovic. *What is Military History?* Cambridge: Polity Press, 2006.

Muir, Rory. *Tactics and the Experience of Battle in the Age of Napoleon.* New Haven: Yale University Press, 1998.

Múnera, Alfonso. *El fracaso de la nación: Región, clase y raza en el Caribe colombiano, (1717–1810).* Bogotá: Banco de la República/El Ancora, 1998.

Newman Simon P., ed. *Europe's American Revolution.* London: Palgrave MacMillan, 2006.

O'Phelan Godoy, Scarlett. *Rebellions and Revolts in Eighteenth Century Peru and Upper Peru.* Cologne: Bohlau Verlag, 1985.

Ornstein, Leopoldo R. "La expedición libertadora al Paraguay." In *Historia de la Nación Argentina,* edited by Ricardo Levene, vol. 5, pt. 2, pp. 273–304. Buenos Aires: Academia Nacional de Historia, 1939.

Ortiz Escamilla, Juan. *Guerra y gobierno: Los pueblos y la independencia de Mexico.* Seville: Universidad de Sevilla et al., 1997.

———. *El teatro de la guerra: Veracruz, 1750–1825.* Castelló de la Plana: Universitat Jaume I, 2008.

———, ed. *Fuerzas militares en Iberoamérica, siglos XVIII y XIX.* Mexico: Colegio de Mexico et al., 2005.

Ossa, Juan Luis. "Armies, Politics and Revolution in Chile, 1780–1826." D.Phil. diss., Oxford University, 2011.

———. "The Army of the Andes: Chilean and Rioplatense Politics in an Age of Military Organisation, 1814–17." *JLAS,* forthcoming, 2014.

Ozanam, Didier. "La politica exterior de España en tiempo de Felipe V y Fernando VII." In *Historia de España,* edited by R. Menéndez Pidal. Vol. 29. Madrid: Espasa Calpe, 1985.

Palacios, Marco, ed. *Las independencias hispanoamericanas. Interpretaciones dos años después.* Bogotá: Norma, 2010.

Pan-Montojo, Juan. "La construcción del nuevo Estado y la fiscalidad: España, 1808–1845." In *Las nuevas naciones: España y México, 1800–1850,* edited by Jaime E. Rodríguez O., pp. 169–90. Madrid: Mapfre, 2008.

Paquette, Gabriel B. "The Dissolution of the Spanish Atlantic Monarchy," *The Historical Journal* 52, no. 1 (2009): pp. 175–212.

———. *Enlightenment, Governance and Reform in Spain and its Empire, 1759–1808.* Basingstoke: Palgrave MacMillan, 2008.

Pares, Richard. *War and Trade in the West Indies, 1739–1763.* London: Cass, 1963.

Parra-Pérez, Carraciolo. *Historia de la Primera República de Venezuela.* 2 vols. Caracas: Academia Nacional de Historia, 1959.

Pasquali, Patricia. *San Martín: La fuerza de la misión y la soledad de la gloria.* Buenos Aires: Emecé, 2004.

Paz, Gustavo. "'El orden es el desorden.' Guerra y movilización campesina en la campaña de Jujuy, 1815–1821." In *Desafíos al orden: Política y sociedades rurales durante la Revolución de Independencia,* edited by Raul Fradkin and Jorge Gelman. Rosario: Prohistoria, 2008.

Pearce, Adrian J. *British Trade with Spanish America, 1763–1808.* Liverpool: Liverpool University Press, 2007.

Perez Gilhou, Dardo. *La opinion pública española y las Cortes de Cádiz frente a la emancipación hispanoamericana, 1810–1814.* Buenos Aires: Academia Nacional de Historia, 1982.

Pérez-Maillaína Bueno, Pablo Emilio. *Política naval española en el Atlántico, 1700–1715.* Seville: Escuela de Estudios Hispanoamericanos, 1982.

Perez Tenreiro, Tomás. *José Tomás Boves, Primera Lanza del Rey.* Caracas: Ministerio de Defensa, 1969.

Phelan, John L. *The People and the King: The Comunero Revolution in Colombia, 1781.* Madison: University of Wisconsin, 1978.

Portillo Valdés, José M. *Crisis atlántica: Autonomía e independencia en la crisis de la monarquía española*. Madrid: Marcial Pons, 2006.

Quintero, Inés. "La Junta de Caracas." In *1808: La eclosión juntera en el mundo hispano*, edited by Manuel Chust. Mexico City: Fondo de Cultura Económica, 2007, pp. 334–55.

Racine, Karen. *Francisco de Miranda. A Transatlantic Life in the Age of Revolution*. Wilmington, DE: Scholarly Resources, 2003.

Rausch, Jane M. *A Tropical Plains Frontier: The Llanos of Colombia, 1531–1831*. Albuquerque: University of New Mexico, 1984.

Redondo Díaz, Fernando. "El Ejército." In *Historial General de España y América*. Vol. 10, pt. 2. Madrid: Editorial Rialp, 1984.

Resnick, Enoch F. "The Council of State and Spanish America, 1814–20." PhD diss., The American University, 1970.

Restrepo Canal, Carlos, ed. *Nariño periodista*. Bogotá: Academia Colombiana de Historia, 1960.

Restrepo Mejía, Isabela. "La soberanía del 'pueblo' durante al época de la Independencia, 1810–1815." *Historia Crítica* 29 (2005): pp. 101–23.

Riaño, Camilo. *Historia Militar. La independencia (1810–1815): Historia Extensa de Colombia*. Vol. 18, part 1. Bogotá: Lerner, 1971.

Rieu-Millan, Marie Laure. *Los diputados americanos en las Cortes de Cádiz*. Madrid: CSIC, 1990.

Rivera Serna, Raul. *Los guerrilleros del centro en la emancipación peruana*. Lima: P.L. Villanueva, 1958.

Robertson, William Spence. "La política inglesa en la América española." In *Historia de la Nación Argentina*, edited by Ricardo Levene. 3rd ed. Buenos Aires: Academia Nacional de Historia, 1939, vol. 5, pt. 1.

Robson, Martin. *Britain, Portugal and South America in the Napoleonic Wars*. London: I.B. Tauris, 2011.

Roca, José Luis. *Ni con Lima, ni con Buenos Aires*. La Paz: Plural Editores, 2007.

———. *1809: La revolución en la Audiencia de Charcas en Chuquisaca y en La Paz*. La Paz: Plural, 1998.

Rodríguez O., Jaime E. *The Independence of Spanish America*. Cambridge: Cambridge University Press, 1998.

———. *The Origins of Mexican National Politics, 1808–1847*. Wilmington, DE: Scholarly Resources, 1993.

———. *La revolución política durante la época de la independencia: El Reino de Quito 1808–1822*. Quito: Universidad Andina Simón Bolívar-Corporación Editora Nacional, 2006.

———, ed. *The Independence of Mexico and the Creation of the New Nation*. Los Angeles: University of California Press, 1989.

———, ed. *Las nuevas naciones: España y México, 1800–1850*. Madrid: Mapfre, 2008.

Rodríguez, Mario. *"William Burke" and Francisco De Miranda: The Word and the Deed in Spanish America's Emancipation*. Lanham, MD: University Press of America, 1994.

Rothenberg, Gunther E. *The Art of Warfare in the Age of Napoleon*. Bloomington: Indiana University Press, 1978.

Rubio, Julián María. *La Infanta Carlota Joaquina y la política de España en América (1808–1812)*. Madrid: Biblioteca de Historia Hispano-Americana, 1920.

Rydjord, John. *Foreign Interest in the Independence of New Spain*. New York: Octagon Books, 1972.

Saether, Steinar A. *Identidades e independencia en Santa Marta y Riohacha, 1750–1850*. Bogotá: Instituto Colombiano de Antropología e Historia, 2005.

Sala i Vila, Nuria. *Y se armó el tole tole: Tributo indígena y movimientos sociales en el Virreinato del Perú, 1784–1814*. Huamanga: IER José María Arguedas, 1996.

Scheina, Robert L. *Latin America's Wars: The Age of the Caudillo, 1791–1899.* 2 vols. Dulles, VA: Brassey's Inc., 2003.

Schmitt, Karl M. "The Clergy and Mexican Independence." *HAHR* 34 (1954): pp. 289–312.

Semprún, Jorge, and Alfonso Bullón. *El ejército realista en la independencia americana.* Madrid: Mapfre, 1992.

Serulnikov, Serge. *Subverting Colonial Authority: Challenges to Spanish Rule in the Eighteenth-century Southern Andes.* Durham: Duke University Press, 2003.

Siles Salinas, Jorge. *La independencia de Bolivia.* Madrid: Mapfre, 1992.

Skocpol, Theda. *States and Social Revolutions: A Comparative Analysis of France, Russia, and China.* Cambridge: Cambridge University Press, 1979.

Slatta, Richard, and Jane Lucas de Grummond. *Simón Bolívar's Quest for Glory.* Texas: A & M University, 2003.

Sobrevilla Perea, Natalia. *The Caudillo of the Andes: Andrés de Santa Cruz.* New York: Cambridge University Press, 2011.

———. "From Europe to the Andes and Back: Becoming 'Los Ayacuchos.'" *European History Quarterly* 41 (2011): pp. 472–88.

Sourdis de De La Vega, Adelaida. *Cartagena de Indias durante la Primera República, 1810–1815.* Bogotá: Banco de la República, 1988.

Stavig, Ward. *The World of Túpac Amaru: Conflict, Community and Identity in Colonial Peru.* Lincoln: University of Nebraska Press, 1999.

Stein, Stanley J., and Barbara H. Stein. *Apogee of Empire: Spain and New Spain in the Age of Carlos III. 1750–1789.* Baltimore: Johns Hopkins University Press, 2003.

———. *Edge of Crisis: War and Trade in the Spanish Atlantic, 1789–1808.* Baltimore: Johns Hopkins University Press, 2009.

———. *Silver, Trade and War: Spain and America in the Making of Early Modern Europe.* Baltimore: Johns Hopkins University Press, 2000.

Stoan, Stephen K. *Pablo Morillo and Venezuela, 1815–1820.* Columbus: Ohio State University, 1974.

Street, John. *Artigas and the Emancipation of Uruguay.* Cambridge: Cambridge University Press, 1959.

———. *Gran Bretaña y la independencia del Río de la Plata.* Buenos Aires: Paidos, 1967.

Szuchman, Mark D., and Jonathan D. Brown, eds. *Revolution and Restoration: The Rearrangement of Power in Argentina, 1776–1860.* Lincoln: University of Nebraska, 1994.

Taylor, William. *Drinking, Homicide and Rebellion in Late Colonial Mexican Villages.* Stanford: Stanford University Press, 1979.

———. *Magistrates of the Sacred: Priests and Parishioners in Eighteenth-Century Mexico.* Stanford, CA: Stanford University Press, 1996.

TePaske, John Jay. "The Financial Disintegration of the Royal Government of Mexico during the Epoch of Independence." In *The Independence of Mexico and the Creation of the New Nation,* edited by Jaime Rodríguez O., pp. 63–83. Los Angeles: University of California, 1989.

Terán, Marta, and José Antonio Serrano Ortega, eds. *Las guerras de independencia en la América española.* Zamora, Michoacán: El Colegio de Michoacán et al., 2002.

Ternavasio, Marcela. *Gobernar la Revolución: Poderes en disputa en el Río de la Plata, 1810–1816.* Buenos Aires: Siglo XXI, 2007.

Thibaud, Clément. *Repúblicas en armas: Los ejércitos bolivarianos en la guerra de Independencia en Colombia y Venezuela.* Bogotá: Planeta, 2003.

Thomson, Sinclair. *We Alone Will Rule: Native Andean Politics in the Age of Insurgency.* Madison: University of Wisconsin, 2002.

Timmons, William H. *Morelos of Mexico. Priest, Soldier, Statesman.* El Paso: Texas Western Press, 1963.

Torre, Ernesto de la. *La independencia de México*. Madrid: Mapfre, 1992.

Tutino, John. *From Insurrection to Revolution in Mexico: Social Bases of Agrarian Violence 1750–1940*. Princeton, NJ: Princeton UP, 1989.

Uribe Urán, Victor M. *Honorable Lives: Lawyers, Family and Politics in Colombia, 1780–1850*. Pittsburgh, PA: University of Pittsburgh, 2000.

Vale, Brian. *Cochrane in the Pacific: Fortune and Freedom in Spanish America*. London: I.B. Tauris, 2008.

Valencia Llano, Alonso. *Marginados y 'Sepultados en los Montes': Orígenes de la insurgencia social en el valle del río Cauca, 1810–1830*. Cali: Universidad del Valle, 2008.

Valle de Siles, Maria Eugenia del. *Historia de la rebelión de Túpac Catari, 1781–2*. La Paz: Ed. Don Bosco, 1990.

Van Young, Eric. "Islands in the Storm: Quiet Cities and Violent Countrysides in the Mexican Independence Era." *Past and Present*, no. 118 (1988): pp. 120–56.

———. *The Other Rebellion: Popular Violence, Ideology, and the Mexican Struggle for Independence, 1810–1821*. Stanford, CA: Stanford University Press, 2001.

———. "Quetzalcoatl, King Ferdinand and Ignacio Allende go to the Seashore, or Messianism and Mystical Kingship in Mexico, 1800–1821." In *The Independence of Mexico and the Creation of the New Nation*, edited by Jaime E. Rodríguez O., pp. 109–27. Los Angeles: University of California, 1989.

Vázquez, Josefina Zoraida, and Jaime Edmundo Rodríguez O., eds. *Interpretaciones de la Independencia de México*. Mexico City: Nueva Imagen, 1997.

Vergara Arias, Gustavo. *Montoneras y guerrillas en la etapa de la emancipación del Perú, 1820–1825*. Lima: Editorial Salesiana, 1974.

Vergara y Velasco, F.J. *1818: Guerra de independencia*. 2nd ed. Bogotá, Editorial Kelly, 1960.

Vinson III, Ben. *Bearing Arms for His Majesty: The Free Colored Militia in Colonial Mexico*. Stanford, CA: Stanford University Press, 2001.

Voelz, Peter M. *Slave and Soldier: The Military Impact of Blacks in the Colonial Americas*. New York: Garland Press, 1993.

Waddell, D.A.G. "British Relations with Venezuela, New Granada and Gran Colombia, 1810–1829." In *Andrés Bello: The London Years*, edited by John Lynch, pp. 26–7. Richmond: Richmond Publishing, 1982.

Walker, Charles. *Smoldering Ashes: Cuzco and the Creation of Republican Peru, 1780–1840*. Durham: Duke University Press, 1999.

Warren, Harris G. "Xavier Mina's Invasion of Mexico." *HAHR* 23, no. 1 (1943): pp. 52–76.

Weber, David J. *Bárbaros: Spaniards and their Savages in the Age of Enlightenment*. New Haven: Yale University Press, 2005.

———. *The Spanish Frontier in North America*. New Haven: Yale University Press, 1992, pp. 133–45.

Williams, John H. *The Rise and Fall of the Paraguayan Republic, 1810–1870*. Austin: University of Texas Press, 1979.

Woodbine, Philip. "Ideas of Naval Power and the Conflict with Spain, 1737–1742." In *The British Navy and the Use of Naval Power in the Eighteenth Century*, edited by Jeremy Black and Philip Woodbine. Leicester: Leicester University Press, 1988.

Woodward, Margaret. "The Spanish Army and the Loss of America," *HAHR* 48 (1968): pp. 589–90.

Worcester, Donald E. *Sea Power and Chilean Independence*. Gainesville: University of Florida, 1962.

Zapatero, Juan Manuel. *La Guerra del Caribe en el siglo XVIII*. San Juan, Puerto Rico: Instituto de Cultura Puertorriqueña, 1964, pp. 7–8.

Zuluaga, Francisco. "Clientilismo y guerrillas en el Valle del Patia, 1536–1811." In *La independencia: Ensayos de historia social*, German Colmenares, Zamira Díaz de Zuluaga, José Escorcia, and Francisco Zuluaga, pp. 111–36. Bogotá; Instituto de Cultura Colombiana, 1986.

————. "La independencia en la gobernación de Popayán." In *Historia del Gran Cauca*. Cali: Universidad del Valle, 1996.

INDEX

The annotation of an italicized "f" indicates a reference to a figure on the specified page.
The annotation of an italicized "t" indicates a reference to a table on the specified page.